White Robes
and Burning Crosses

ALSO BY MICHAEL NEWTON
AND FROM McFARLAND

---

*Hate Crime in America, 1968–2013: A Chronology
of Offenses, Legislation and Related Events* (2014)

*The Texarkana Moonlight Murders:
The Unsolved Case of the 1946 Phantom Killer* (2013)

The FBI Encyclopedia (2003; paperback 2012)

The Mafia at Apalachin, 1957 (2012)

*Chronology of Organized Crime Worldwide,
6000 B.C.E. to 2010* (2011)

The Ku Klux Klan in Mississippi: A History (2010)

Mr. Mob: The Life and Crimes of Moe Dalitz (2009)

*The Ku Klux Klan: History, Organization, Language,
Influence and Activities of America's Most Notorious
Secret Society* (2007; paperback 2014)

*The FBI and the KKK:
A Critical History* (2005; paperback 2009)

*Encyclopedia of Cryptozoology: A Global Guide to
Hidden Animals and Their Pursuers* (2005)

White Robes and Burning Crosses

A History of the
Ku Klux Klan from 1866

MICHAEL NEWTON

McFarland & Company, Inc., Publishers
Jefferson, North Carolina

LIBRARY OF CONGRESS CATALOGUING-IN-PUBLICATION DATA

Newton, Michael, 1951–
White robes and burning crosses : a history of the Ku Klux Klan
from 1866 / Michael Newton.
p.   cm.
Includes bibliographical references and index.

ISBN 978-0-7864-7774-6 (softcover : acid free paper) ∞
ISBN 978-1-4766-1719-0 (ebook)

1. Ku Klux Klan (1915–)—History.   2. Ku Klux Klan (19th century)
3. Domestic terrorism—United States—History.   4. Racism—
United States—History.   5. United States—Race relations.   I. Title.
HS2330.K63N499 2014   322.4'20973—dc23   2014023632

BRITISH LIBRARY CATALOGUING DATA ARE AVAILABLE

On the cover: Klansmen march in Virginia, circa 1920s (Library of Congress)

Printed in the United States of America

*McFarland & Company, Inc., Publishers
Box 611, Jefferson, North Carolina 28640
www.mcfarlandpub.com*

For Stetson Kennedy
(1916–2011)

Table of Contents

Preface

The Ku Klux Klan was 95 years old when I "discovered" it in 1961. The vehicle of my enlightenment was a Hollywood film, *The FBI Story,* which presented that agency's history in a series of fictionalized, sometimes fabricated, vignettes. Nothing about the Klan's brief moment on the screen was factual, as I soon learned, and yet it captured my imagination. Fiery crosses, nightriders in pointed hoods and flowing robes, a secret society—as the film's narrator proclaimed—"so powerful it didn't have to be secret."

I set out to learn more, collecting every book and article about the Klan that I could find. As luck would have it, Klansmen frequently made headlines for the next eight years. They staged impressive riots in at least five states, killed dozens of victims and assaulted countless others, bombed and burned scores of churches, schools, and homes, even conspired to kill Chicago's mayor. Congress investigated and pronounced the Klan a dying order, yet it lived on through the next three decades, greeting the twenty-first century with fresh acts of mayhem.

I was in my twenties when I learned that my paternal grandfather had been a Klansman, in the days before his family left Oklahoma in 1927. My father recalled a night when "the boys" arrived in a flatbed truck, asking John Newton if he planned to join them for the evening. My grandfather declined on that occasion, but I have no doubt that there were other nights when he did not.

The Klan is a recurring nightmare in America, our country's—and the world's—oldest surviving terrorist organization. Its story follows, told without embellishment. In this case facts are biased, and the truth is bad enough.

Introduction:
"Good Ole Rebels"

In February 1956, well-fueled with bourbon, Mississippi Nobel laureate William Faulkner discussed the South's impending racial crisis with a reporter for the London *Sunday Times*. After agreeing that the National Association for the Advancement of Colored People (NAACP) was a "necessary organization," and confirming that "the Negroes are right—make sure you've got that—they're right," Faulkner said, "The South is armed for revolt. These people will accept another Civil War knowing they're going to lose." Faulkner was ready for the battle to begin. "If I have to choose between the United States government and Mississippi," he said, "then I'll choose Mississippi.... As long as there's a middle road I'll be on it. But if it came to fighting I'd fight for Mississippi against the United States even if it meant going out into the streets and shooting Negroes."[1]

Later, Faulkner offered an apology of sorts, writing that his comments had been "statements which no sober man would make nor, it seems to me, any sane man believe."[2]

In that, he was mistaken.

A half-century after publication of Faulkner's comments, Arkansas state representative Loy Mauch earned a reputation for his letters to Little Rock's *Democrat-Gazette*. His published comments include a reference to the Confederate flag as "a symbol of Christian liberty vs. the new world order," characterization of the Civil War's Union victors as "Wehrmacht leaders," and the question: "If slavery was so God-awful, why didn't Jesus or Paul condemn it, why was it in the Constitution and why wasn't there a war before 1861?"[3]

Faulkner's inebriated ranting and the sober thoughts of Mauch would strike a chord with the founders of America's oldest surviving terrorist organization. As they believed in 1866, with certain minor deviations, their descendants in the Ku Klux Klan believe today. Those founders risked their lives in defense of slavery, and in the decade after their defeat fought on to maintain white supremacy. Their marching anthem says it all.

I'm a good ole Rebel
And that's just what I am.
And for this Yankee nation I do not give a damn.
I hate the starry banner
That's stained with Southern blood.
I hate the pizen Yankees
And fit em all I could.

I followed ole Marse Robert
For four years nearabout;
Got wounded at Manassass
And starved at Point Lookout.
I cotched the rheumatism
From fightin' in the snow,
But I kilt a chance of Yankees
And I'd like to kill some mo'.

3

Three hundred thousand Yankees
Lie still in Southern dust.
We got three hundred thousand
Afore they conquered us.
They died of Southern fever
And Southern steel and shot;
And I wisht we'd got three million
Instead of what we got.

I hates the Yankee nation
And the uniform of blue;
I hates the Constitution
Of this "Great Republic" too.
I hates the Freedmen's Bureau
With all its mess and fuss.
And the lyin' thievin' Yankees
I hates em wuss and wuss.

I can't take up my musket,
And fight 'em any mo';
But I ain't gonna love em
And that is sartin sho'.
I don't want no pardon
For what I done or am;
And I won't be reconstructed,
And I do not give a damn.[4]

Six generations later, members of the Ku Klux Klan still are not "reconstructed." They have inflicted misery and death on countless victims nationwide over 150 years, and since the early 1920s have expanded into distant corners of the globe. This is their story, told as it occurred, without hyperbole. The facts are grim enough.

CHAPTER 1

"This Is a White Man's Country" (1866–1873)

"Gone with the wind." It was a fair description of Southern society in April 1865. The Confederacy had fielded 1,082,119 fighting men, losing 258,000. Most of the war's 10,000 military clashes had occurred on Southern soil, leaving half of the region's livestock dead and $10 billion in property destroyed.[1] Worse yet, to white sensibilities, was the liberation of 3,521,110 slaves held by 385,000 masters.[2] The world they knew was upside-down.

What was the prostrate South to do?

A "Circle of Brothers"

For some, the time had come to celebrate survival. In Pulaski, Tennessee, six young veterans "hungering and thirsting for amusement" gathered to form a "hilarious social club." Their number included ex–Captains James Crowe, John Lester and John Kennedy, with former enlisted men Calvin Jones, Frank McCord and Richard Reed. Today a plaque commemorates their gathering.[3]

> Ku Klux Klan
> Organized In This,
> The Law Office of
> Judge Thomas M. Jones
> December 24th, 1865[4]

Although we may accept the place of their first gathering, the date is almost certainly apocryphal. Most historians place the Klan's creation in late May or early June of 1866, supported by published recollections of two founders, the timing of the Klan's first-anniversary parade in Pulaski, and Klan documents published long after the fact.[5] Stories of Klan activity before the Civil War clearly confuse the KKK with antebellum slave patrols that helped inspire the order formed in 1866.[6]

The new group's name was not a strange selection. All six founders of the Klan were college-educated men, familiar with the Kuklos Adelphon fraternity—"Old Kappa Alpha," the "Circle of Brothers"—founded at the University of North Carolina in 1812. *Kuklos* is Greek for "circle," and they simply added "clan," spelled with a "k" for uniformity. Kuklos Adelphon was heavily influenced by Masonic ritual, and Pulaski harbored eight Masonic lodges. Klan founder James Crowe subsequently served as Masonic Grand Master for Tennessee.[7]

Kuklos Adelphon was not the Klan's sole inspiration. Its founders were also familiar with the stridently nativist "Know-Nothing" movement, embodied in the American Party. Fond of violence, the American Party had called its local units "clans"—including one that dominated Pulaski politics by 1854.[8]

Ku Klux "hilarity" consisted of tormenting former slaves with nightly visits in the guise of ghosts, decked out in bizarre costumes, playing ghoulish "jokes." A shrouded Klansman might remove his head (molded from papier-mâché) or shake hands, leaving his skeletal arm in a startled freedman's grasp. Others begged for water, then downed a full bucket with aid of a funnel and rubber bag under their robes. Such pranks were popular with many prewar slave patrols, and Tennessee's patrol law had required all men of military age to take their turn.[9]

When ghostly hoaxes failed to cow "darkies," the slave patrols were not averse to whipping, branding, even killing slaves whom they deemed insubordinate. Klansmen did not mimic the patrols in that respect, at first. Their focus was on drunken fun at the expense of their perceived inferiors.

But that would quickly change.

With Malice Toward Some

On March 4, 1865, President Abraham Lincoln closed his second inaugural address with a plea for good will, if and when the South was defeated. "With malice toward none; with charity for all; with firmness in the right, as God gives us to see the right," he said, "let us strive on to finish the work we are in; to bind up the nation's wounds ... to do all which may achieve and cherish a just and lasting peace among ourselves and with all nations."[10] One month later, General Robert E. Lee surrendered his army to Ulysses Grant. Sporadic fighting continued into June, but for all practical purposes, the Civil War was over.

Lincoln had proposed a lenient plan for readmission of the rebel states, offering pardon, with few exceptions, to

Klan costumes in Reconstruction were highly individualized (North Carolina Department of Cultural Resources).

any ex–Confederate who swore allegiance to the Union and the Constitution. Any state was eligible to rejoin the Union once 10 percent of its white electorate took that oath and abolished slavery. Leaders of the Republican Party—so-called "Radicals"—rejected that plan, prescribing more punitive measures, but Lincoln's veto left them frustrated. Five days after Lee's surrender, an assassin's bullet placed Vice President Andrew Johnson in the White House. A Tennessee Democrat hand-picked to balance the ticket in 1864, Johnson proceeded with Lincoln's plan, pardoning 7,000 rebels by 1866 and returning all property except slaves to rebels who endorsed the Thirteenth Amendment.[11]

The South reacted badly. State legislators passed a series of "Black Codes" aimed at returning freedmen to virtual slavery, imposing mandatory employment on blacks of all ages, prescribing prison or whipping for "crimes" including vagrancy, "malicious mischief," "insulting" whites, "misspending what they earn," even smoking in public. Abolitionist Daniel Goodloe deemed it "little short of madness" for Southern lawmakers to believe "the triumphant North ... would tolerate this new slave code," but Dixie legislators forged ahead.[12]

And there was worse to come, as Southern whites resorted to terrorism from force of habit. In May 1866, a Memphis riot left 46 blacks and two whites dead, 75 persons injured, five black women raped, and 102 black homes, schools and churches burned. Two months later, New Orleans erupted, with whites killing 38 blacks and wounding 46. General Augustus Chetlain reported one freedman murdered per day around Jackson, Mississippi, while Heggie's Scouts, a vigilante group whose members later joined the Klan, slaughtered 116 blacks in a single massacre, dumping their corpses into the Tallahatchie River. Even in Kentucky, loyal to the wartime Union, terrorists raided Lebanon's black district, razing homes and crops, driving its occupants away.[13]

Republicans responded furiously. Failing in their effort to impeach President Johnson, they passed a series of Reconstruction Acts over Johnson's vetoes. The first, in March 1867, placed 10 Southern states under military control. Later amendments imposed a strict loyalty oath on ex–Confederates who wished to vote, granted the franchise to male freedmen, and demanded ratification of the Fourteenth Amendment, granting blacks full citizenship. Tennessee was exempt from those provisions, having elected a Unionist governor in 1865, followed by ratification of the Fourteenth Amendment in July 1866.[14]

The Ku Klux Klan had expanded from its cradle in Pulaski since spring 1866, with local "dens" throughout Tennessee and scattered outposts in neighboring states. The Klan's founders had chosen cryptic titles for themselves: McCord was the "Grand Cyclops" (president); Kennedy served as "Grand Magi" (vice president); Crowe became "Grand Turk" (master of ceremonies); Reed was "Lictor" (sergeant-at-arms); Jones and Lester were "Night Hawks" (guards of the den). Each new den replicated Pulaski's slate of officers, while common members were designated "ghouls."[15]

No guiding purpose had been laid down for the Klan as yet, Crowe insisting that the order was "purely social and for our amusement," its aim simply to "have fun, make mischief, and play pranks on the public."[16] Nonetheless, some dens had turned to vigilantism by October 1866, when reports of "numerous revolting outrages" spread from Pulaski through neighboring counties.[17] With passage of the Reconstruction Acts, the Circle of Brothers would adopt a very different role.

In April 1867 McCord summoned officers from all known dens to a meeting in Nashville. Convening at the Maxwell House Hotel, they reorganized the Klan on paramil-

Artist's representation of a KKK raid during Reconstruction (Library of Congress).

itary lines, to resist the evils of "Radical Reconstruction" and keep former slaves "in their place." General Lee reportedly sent a letter endorsing the new "protective order" but declining to lead it, saying that his support must remain invisible. The meeting's goal was "to bind the isolated Dens together; to secure unity of purpose and concert of action; to hedge the members up by such limitations and regulations as are best adapted to restrain them within proper limits; to distribute the authority among prudent men at local centers and exact from them a close supervision of those under their charge."[18]

To that end, a prescript (constitution) was prepared by ex–General George Gordon, a Pulaski lawyer and early Klan recruit. Taking his cue from Lee, Gordon divided the Klan's "Invisible Empire" into realms (states) led by Grand Dragons, dominions (congressional districts) led by Grand Titans, provinces (counties) led by Grand Giants, and local dens led by Grand Cyclopses. Overseeing all would be a Grand Wizard, assisted by 10 Genii and other subordinates. Elected officers suspected of malfeasance would be tried by a Grand Council of Yahoos, while errant ghouls faced trial before a Grand Council of Centaurs.[19] The "character and object of the order," overlooked in 1867 but inserted when the prescript was revised in 1868, seemed praiseworthy when taken at face value.

> This is an institution of Chivalry, Humanity, Mercy, and Patriotism; embodying in its genius and its principles all that is chivalric in conduct, noble in sentiment, generous in manhood, and patriotic in purpose; its peculiar objects being,

First: To protect the weak, the innocent, and the defenceless [*sic*], from the indignities, wrongs, and outrages of the lawless, the violent, and the brutal; to relieve the injured and oppressed; to succor the suffering and unfortunate, and especially the widows and orphans of Confederate soldiers.

Second: To protect and defend the Constitution of the United States, and all laws passed in conformity thereto, and to protect the States and the people there of from all invasion from any source whatever.

Third: To aid and assist in the execution of all constitutional laws, and to protect the people from unlawful seizure, and from trial except by their peers in conformity to the laws of the land.[20]

The catch lay in definitions. As seen by Klansmen, the "injured and oppressed" were Southern whites, "suffering" in a world where blacks were citizens; the "lawless, violent and brutal" were Northern soldiers and anyone else who supported Congressional Reconstruction. "Constitutional laws" were those supporting white supremacy; all others were, by definition, illegitimate. "Invasion" of the South was carried out by Union troops and "carpetbaggers" from the North, aided by native Southern "scalawags" who had opposed secession and now supported black suffrage. As for protecting "the weak, the innocent, and the defenseless," by the time George Gordon (or whoever) penned those words in 1868, the Klan was killing, torturing and terrorizing citizens throughout the old Confederacy and at least two border states.

In their futile quest for discipline, the Nashville delegates chose military heroes of the South to serve as Ku Klux officers whenever possible. The 1867 prescript appointed a Grand Scribe—later identified as Lieutenant Colonel Minor Meriwether of Tennessee—to conduct Klan correspondence, write out orders as required, and collect membership lists from local dens, then contrarily ordered that "[t]he origin, designs, mysteries and ritual of this [Klan] shall never be written, but the same shall be communicated orally."[21] Official records are thus nonexistent, but published recollections of survivors from the Reconstruction era have identified some of the order's grand dragons.

In Tennessee, George Gordon assumed the mantle, later serving in Congress from 1907 to 1911.[22] Alabama boasted three dragons: Brigadier General James Holt Clanton, murdered in September 1871, was succeeded by Major General (and future six-term U.S. Senator) John Morgan, then by General Edmund Pettus of Selma (also a U.S. senator from 1897 to 1907).[23] Multiple sources name Brigadier General Albert Pike as the grand dragon of Arkansas, one also calling him the Klan's "chief judicial officer," but spokesmen for the Scottish Rite Masonic lodge—which Pike served as Sovereign Grand Commander of the Southern Jurisdiction from 1859 to 1891—reject that assertion.[24] Another source identifies Arkansas's grand dragon as Augustus Garland, future governor, U.S. senator, and attorney general under President Grover Cleveland.[25] Colonel James George served as Mississippi's grand dragon and defended Klan terrorists in court, before his election to the U.S. Senate in 1880.[26] Most accounts agree that Georgia's grand dragon was General John Brown Gordon (no relation to Tennessee's George Gordon).[27] Colonel Zebulon Vance, future governor and U.S. senator for North Carolina, was the Tarheel State's grand dragon.[28] In South Carolina, Major General Wade Hampton III (later governor and U.S. senator) stands identified as the Klan's highest-ranking state officer.[29] In Texas the post was filled by Colonel Roger Mills, a prewar state legislator, later serving in the U.S. House of Representatives (1873–92) and Senate (1892–99).[30] No grand dragons were identified in Florida, Louisiana or Virginia.

One question remained: who would rule the Invisible Empire as Grand Wizard? Once Lee declined the post, Klansmen agreed that there was only one man for the job.

Enter the Wizard

Nathan Bedford Forrest was born in 1821. His father died in 1838, leaving Nathan to provide for his widowed mother and 11 siblings. In 1841 he entered the mercantile trade with an uncle, Jonathan Forrest, in Hernando, Mississippi. Four years later, Jonathan was slain in a quarrel with the three Matlock brothers and Nathan retaliated, killing two with a pistol and wounding the third with a knife.[31]

His fighting reputation, coupled with a head for business, allowed Forrest to prosper despite his near-illiteracy. By 1852 he was a planter and slave trader, later boasting that he had imported 400 slaves and that "only six percent died." "They were very fond of grasshoppers and bugs," he recalled, "but I taught them to eat cooked meat, and they were as good niggers as I ever had." His slave market in Memphis collapsed in January 1860, killing eight Africans, but Forrest rebounded quickly. By the outbreak of the Civil War he was one of the South's richest men.[32]

Although exempt from military service as a wealthy planter, Forrest joined the Confederate army as a private in July 1861, soon found himself promoted to lieutenant colonel on the basis of his wealth, and within three months of his enlistment took command of a regiment known thereafter as Forrest's Cavalry Corps. What Forrest lacked in military training or experience, he made up in audacity, marksmanship, and skill as a horseman. Recruits were lured by his advertisements for men "with good horse and gun," invited to join "if you want a heap of fun and to kill some Yankees." After bloody engagements at Fort Donelson, Shiloh, Murfreesboro and Vicksburg, Forrest—by then a brigadier general—earned a reputation as "the only Confederate cavalryman of whom [Union General Ulysses] Grant stood in much dread." Forrest also could be grossly insubordinate, arguing profanely with his superiors and threatening them on occasion. Nonetheless, his reputation as a winner kept him out of the stockade and in command of his hard-charging troops.[33]

Forrest's most notorious wartime action was the capture of Fort Pillow, Tennessee, on April 12, 1864. Half of the fort's 600 defenders were black troops, condemned to enslavement or execution by order of Confederate President Jefferson Davis on Christmas Eve 1862.[34] While southern historians would later claim that Forrest "begged" the garrison to surrender, Union survivors of the battle described Forrest's men advancing with cries of "No quarter!" In fact, the fort surrendered after initial resistance and a bloodbath ensued, with two-thirds of the captured blacks summarily executed. In a dispatch to headquarters, Forrest wrote: "The river was dyed with the blood of the slaughtered for 200 yards. The approximate loss was upward of 500 killed, but few of the officers escaping. My loss was about 20 killed. It is hoped that these facts will demonstrate to the Northern people that negro soldiers cannot cope with Southerners."[35] Historian Richard Fuchs concluded, "The affair at Fort Pillow was simply an orgy of death, a mass lynching to satisfy the basest of conduct—intentional murder—for the vilest of reasons—racism and personal enmity."[36]

Back in civilian life at war's end, Forrest returned to cotton planting, then found work as a railroad promoter, eventually rising to head the Memphis, Okolona & Selma Railroad.

Violence still followed him, typified by an incident in April 1866, where Forrest killed one of his field hands with an axe. The black man, Forrest said, had first insulted him, then tried to stab him after Forrest restrained the sharecropper from beating his wife.[37]

Mystery surrounds the date when Forrest joined the Ku Klux Klan. Years after the fact, he would deny belonging to the order even as he claimed intimate knowledge of its membership and activities. Klan founder James Crowe claimed that Forrest was inducted during autumn 1866, at Nashville's Maxwell House, with the oath administered by Captain John Morton, Jr., one of Forrest's wartime subordinates. Other accounts suggest that George Gordon introduced Forrest to the Klan, prompting Forrest to say, "That's a good thing; that's a damned good thing. We can use it to keep the niggers in their place."[38]

In any case, denials notwithstanding, Forrest was the original Klan's first and only grand wizard. While not responsible for founding every Ku Klux den across the South, and clearly hopeless at controlling them once they were organized, Forrest visited various towns where dens sprang up during 1867 and 1868. His travels on railroad business provided a perfect cover for proselytizing new members and granting charters to units in various states.[39]

Building an Empire

Between June 1867 and March 1868 Klan chapters spread throughout the late Confederacy and beyond. Its farthest northern outpost was allegedly in Watertown, New York, where 10 young dandies posed for a photo as members of KKK "Division 289," but no further record exists of a New York Klan during Reconstruction.[40] Officially, the Klan's prescript of 1868 declared that "The territory embraced within the jurisdiction of this Order shall be coterminous with the States of Maryland, Virginia, North Carolina, South Carolina, Georgia, Florida, Alabama, Mississippi, Louisiana, Texas, Arkansas, Missouri, Kentucky, and Tennessee; all combined constituting the Empire."[41]

Maryland, Missouri and Kentucky, although slave states prior to 1865, had not seceded from the Union and were thus spared from Reconstruction. Historian Wyn Wade refers in passing to Ku Klux dens in southern Maryland's tidewater district, also some Klan activity in southeastern West Virginia, but he offers no further details and no evidence of their existence surfaced during research for this volume.[42] Kentucky and Missouri, by contrast, both had active Klans. Bluegrass Klansmen shared the white Confederacy's hatred of "radical" Republicans, though blacks were barred from voting in the state until 1872. Nonetheless, Kentucky was wracked by violence, with 117 lynchings reported during Reconstruction.[43] Missouri, scene of bloody conflict for five years preceding the Civil War, remained in a chaotic state for years afterward, with Klansmen persecuting freedmen and Republicans. A sideline for the Klan in both Kentucky and Missouri was defense of moonshine stills, resisting efforts by both state and local governments to tax homemade liquor.[44] Author Susan Davis, writing in 1924, identified Missouri's grand dragon as William Clark Kennerly, formerly a captain under Confederate General Sterling Price. Davis heard that account directly from Kennerly, who owed his middle name to uncle William Clark, explorer of the Far West with Meriwether Lewis in 1803–06, later governor of Missouri and Superintendent of Indian Affairs.[45]

Klan dens were widely organized and armed for battle by early 1868. Virginia was the

Photograph of supposed New York Klansmen in 1870 (Library of Congress).

least successful realm, although its ghouls engaged in sporadic nightriding and mailed threats to Republican leaders in Congress during April of that year.[46] Klan founder James Crowe told Susan Davis that a "Grand Monk" of the Klan—Colonel Sumner Cunningham—infiltrated Washington to investigate a "spurious Ku Klux Klan ... in which were many of the radical Senators and Congressmen," but details of that episode (if it occurred) are lost to history.[47]

Elsewhere, most Klan activity in 1868 occurred in conjunction with the year's presidential election. Grand Wizard Forrest and South Carolina's Wade Hampton attended the Democratic National Convention in New York City, where Forrest reportedly faced down a bully clamoring to meet the "damned butcher" of Fort Pillow.[48] The delegates nominated former New York governor Horatio Seymour as their presidential candidate, with a friend of Forrest, ex-congressman Francis Blair, Jr., of Missouri, as his running mate.[49] Together, they campaigned under the slogan "Our Ticket, Our Motto: This Is a White Man's Country; Let White Men Rule."[50] On the campaign trail, Blair railed against Republican support for "a semi-barbarous race of blacks who are worshipers of fetishes and polygamists," whom he feared would "subject white women to their unbridled lust." Some Democrats blamed Blair for their ticket's ultimate defeat, calling his tirades "stupid and indefensible."[51]

Klansmen shared Blair's apprehension and did their best to give his ticket a majority in Dixie. Their tactics, predictably, were violent. In Louisiana alone, white terrorists killed at least 1,081 freedmen between April and November 1868; another tally lists the total as

1,884.[52] Texas was nearly as bad: the state's military commander, General J. J. Reynolds, reported that thanks to the Klan and similar groups, "civil law east of the Trinity river is almost a dead letter." A writer for the Cincinnati *Commercial* agreed, observing that "You cannot pick up a paper without reading of murders, assassinations and robbery.... And yet not the fourth part of the truth has been told; not one act in 10 is reported."[53]

Violence on a slightly smaller scale was seen in every Southern state. In Maury County, Tennessee, Klansmen seized 400 guns from black homes during February 1868, killing several persons in the process and flogging many more, including one man who received 900 lashes.[54] In Abbeville County, South Car-

TIS BUT A CHANGE OF BANNERS.

A Northern cartoon from the 1868 presidential election (Library of Congress).

olina, terrorists executed two state legislators and barred 80 percent of the county's black voters from casting ballots on election day.[55] Threats were more common than murders in North Carolina, so far, but Klansmen in Columbus, Georgia, assassinated one of the state's leading Republicans, George Ashburn, at his home in March. By October 1868 the state's tally included 31 murders, 43 nonfatal shootings, five stabbings, 55 beatings, and eight whippings of 200 to 500 lashes per victim.[56] Violence in Alabama ranged from individual murders to mob assaults on Republican gatherings, prompting Republican Daniel Price to say, "This state of things cannot long continue. Either we must have protection, or leave."[57] In Mississippi, after Klansmen whipped white "carpetbagger" Allen Huggins, friends sent his shredded, blood-soaked shirt to Washington, where Massachusetts representative Benjamin Butler displayed it in Congress as a symbol of southern barbarity—an inflammatory tactic henceforth known as "waving the bloody shirt."[58]

In Arkansas—officially readmitted to the Union in June 1868, under Republican Governor Powell Clayton—Klan violence assumed the aspect of another civil war in miniature. Freedmen were warned against voting and murdered if they persisted, while Klansmen tried to force the registration of disfranchised Confederate veterans. Governor Clayton began recruiting mostly-black militiamen in August, but refused pleas for assistance from voter registrars around the state until registration stalled completely in 12 Klan-ridden counties. Klansmen were often better armed than the militia and intent on keeping that advantage.

Georgia Klansmen assassinate George Ashburn in 1868 (Library of Congress).

When Clayton bought 4,000 rifles from New York, the Democratic *Memphis Avalanche* announced their arrival in time for Klansmen to hijack the shipment on October 15. Terrorism persisted to election day in November, but Clayton waited another day before declaring martial law in 10 counties, later extended to 14. Led by Adjutant General Keyes Danforth, Clayton's militia captured 60 Klansmen at Center Point on November 12. More skirmishes ensued, Klansmen inevitably on the losing end, and many fled to Tennessee. Arkansas legislators passed a law banning the Klan on March 12, 1869, and organized violence had ceased by the time Clayton lifted martial law nine days later.[59]

Despite their best efforts, Klansmen failed to elect Seymour and Blair. The Democratic ticket carried only eight of 34 states where ballots were cast, trailing Grant and running mate Schuyler Colfax by 306,592 votes out of 5,720,250.[60]

Ten weeks before the election, on August 28, Grand Wizard Forrest granted an interview to a correspondent from the Cincinnati *Commercial*. Questioned concerning the Klan, he denied membership but expressed "sympathy," then went on to present a surprising amount of detail for a supposed outsider. Klan membership, he claimed, exceeded 40,000 in Tennessee and totaled some 550,000 throughout the South. The Klan, he said, was "a protective, political, military organization ... giving its support, of course, to the [D]emocratic party."[61]

Concerning Governor William Brownlow's efforts to raise a militia in Tennessee, Forrest predicted an apocalypse.

> If they attempt to carry out Governor Brownlow's proclamation by shooting down Ku Klux—for he calls all southern men Ku Klux—if they go to hunting down and shooting these men, there will be war, and a bloodier one than we have ever witnessed. I have told these radicals here what they might expect in such an event. I have no powder to burn killing negroes. I intend to kill the radicals. I have told them this and more. There is not a radical leader in this town but is a marked man; and if a trouble should break out, not one of them would be left alive.[62]

We may never know if Forrest's estimate of total Klan membership was accurate or wildly inflated, but one thing is clear: the Klan had no shortage of allies.

Armies of the Night

Throughout its history, the Klan has operated in disguise—not only physically, but through "front" groups contrived to mask its true identity. Those groups often bear patriotic-sounding names or hark back to the Klan's beginnings as a social club, but their behavior ultimately lays their purpose bare.

Dixie was overrun with vigilante bands during Reconstruction. Some, like Heggie's Scouts in Mississippi, organized before the Klan turned militant and later merged with it as Ku Klux dens proliferated.[63] Others, like the Young Men's Democratic Club in Florida, sometimes dispensed with masks, but otherwise "differed in no important respect from the Klan" and served as a "probable screen for" Ku Klux operations.[64]

A larger, more clearly independent group was the Knights of the White Camellia (KWC), founded at Franklin, Louisiana, in May 1867, later expanding into Alabama, Arkansas and Texas. Its oath informed initiates that the order's "main and fundamental object is the MAINTENANCE OF THE SUPREMACY OF THE WHITE RACE in this Republic." A Tennessee newspaper report from 1869 claims that the KWC had 38,000 members in Texas alone, and while historian Stanley Horn acknowledges that figure as a probable exaggeration, he notes that the order "was in fact immensely popular in that section." When Arkansas lawmakers banned the Klan in 1869, their statute named "The Knights of the White Camellia ... more generally known as the Ku-Klux," and while the two groups certainly cooperated on occasion, probably with overlapping membership, they maintained distinct and separate hierarchies. Louisiana's KWC apparently disbanded in the summer of 1869, with some chapters surviving as Caucasian Clubs, while others rallied as a new '76 Association.[65]

In Texas, Klansmen and KWC members had to compete with a third organization, the Knights of the Rising Sun (KRS), founded in September 1868 under Grand Commander William Saufley, who doubled as chairman of Marion County's Democratic Party. Soon afterward, on October 4, KRS members lynched white Republican George Smith and two black prisoners held in custody on charges of assault—namely, wounding two terrorists who tried to murder them. Saufley left the state to avoid prosecution, while authorities jailed 35 others. Two turned state's evidence, implicating their defense attorney as a member of the lynch mob, whereupon he fled to Canada. Seven of 24 defendants tried in 1869 were convicted, three for murder and the rest on reduced charges (pardoned soon after by President

Grant). With the case closed, Saufley returned to Marion County and lapsed into obscurity.[66]

North Carolina hosted two Klan-allied groups, the Constitutional Union Guard—which called its local chapters "klans"—and the White Brotherhood, both active during 1868–70. In addition to murder and other crimes, the CUG also rescued five of its members from jail at Kingston in January 1869. Leaders of both groups voted to disband in July 1870, releasing an unprecedented statement that read: "Unless the crimes which have been committed by this organization can be put a stop to and the organization itself entirely broken up, civil liberty and personal safety are at an end in this county [Alamance] and everything else will soon be at the mercy of an organized mob."[67]

In Tennessee, meanwhile, Klansmen collaborated with—or posed as—members of an organization called the Order of Pale Faces. Deliberate confusion surrounds this group, allegedly founded at Columbia sometime in 1869. General Forrest admitted membership in the order, while denying that he was a Klansman, then admitted that the Pale Faces were "something similar" to the Klan, "only it was a different order." He also skewed the Pale Face timeline by contending that he joined in Memphis, sometime during 1867. One Tennessee terrorist killed in a skirmish with freedmen, John Bicknell, was identified as a member of both the KKK and Pale Faces. Officially, the latter order called its local chapters "camps." Its newspaper, *The Pale Face,* began publication from Nashville in December 1869.[68]

Other groups collaborating with the Klan or mimicking its tactics during Reconstruction were the Red Caps, Red Jackets and Yellow Jackets of Tennessee; the Native Sons of the South, Society of the White Rose, Knights of the Black Cross and the Robertson Family in Mississippi; Alabama's Knights of the White Carnation; South Carolina's Red Strings and Heroes of America; and Louisiana's Seymour Knights. Throughout the late Confederacy, Democratic Clubs and Rifle Clubs also committed wholesale acts of terrorism, frequently without disguises.[69]

"Entirely Abolished and Destroyed"

Despite his bold talk of slaughtering Tennessee "radicals" in August 1868, Grand Wizard Forrest balked at waging all-out war against Governor Brownlow's militia. New laws passed in September punished Klan membership with five years in prison and a $500 fine, while permitting Brownlow to discount election results in any county where he felt voters had been disfranchised. On February 20, 1869, Brownlow declared martial law in nine counties, then left office for the U.S. Senate five days later, leaving successor Dewitt Senter to deal with the fallout. Senter vowed to hound the Klan out of existence, then disbanded the militia in May 1869, while announcing his support for restoring suffrage to Confederate veterans.[70]

Meanwhile, on January 25, 1869, Wizard Forrest issued a long-winded General Order No. 1, stating that "Whereas, the Order of the K.K.K. is in some localities being perverted from its original honorable and patriotic purposes ... and is becoming injurious instead of subservient to the public peace and public safety for which it was intended.... It is therefore ordered and decreed that the masks and costumes of this Order be entirely abolished and destroyed. And every Grand Cyclops shall assemble the men of his Den and require them to destroy in his presence every article of his mask and costume and at the same time shall destroy his own."[71] Was that, in fact, disbandment of the Klan? Hardly. Forrest's decree went on to say: "*This is not to be understood to dissolve the Order of the Ku Klux Klan, but it is hereby held more firmly together and more faithfully to each other in any emergency that may come.*" (Original italics.) Moving on, Forrest wrote that "All demonstrations are positively prohibited until they are ordered by a Grand Titan or higher authority," concluding that "[t]he profoundest quiet and deepest secrecy concerning everything that relates to the Order shall, at all times, be maintained."[72]

In short, the Klan was not disbanding, merely going deeper underground.

Questions persist as to when—or if—the Klan's various realms received Forrest's order. Historian Allen Trelease reports that the order faded in Virginia during summer 1868 and "virtually disappeared" by that year's end from Arkansas, Louisiana and Texas.[73] In Tennessee, by contrast, violence continued, with local dens ignoring commands for restraint from Grand Dragon Brown until late in 1871.[74] Klan leaders in northern Alabama tried to enforce Forrest's order, but their efforts proved fruitless as terrorism escalated statewide.[75] Likewise, in Mississippi, incidents of violence proliferated from 1869 onward, climaxing with guerrilla warfare against black schools in 1871 and a Klan-led riot at Meridian in March of that year, claiming some three dozen lives.[76] Georgia was equally chaotic, with Klansmen raiding well into 1871, counting state senator Joseph Adkins as their most prominent murder victim.[77] Florida's Jackson County, with at least 100 murders logged through 1871, was as deadly as any in Dixie.[78]

Klansmen in the Carolinas ignored Forrest's order completely, to the point that Republicans in North Carolina considered forming their own "vast vigilance committee ... designed expressly to Kuklux the K.K.K." Following the Klan lynching of mulatto town commissioner Wyatt Outlaw in February 1870, and the assassination of state senator John Stephens three months later, Governor William Holden imposed martial law over Caswell and Alamance Counties, hiring former Union guerrilla leader George Kirk to lead 300 volunteers against the Klan. Kirk arrested nearly 100 suspects, including ex-congressman John Kerr, Jr., and Caswell County sheriff Jesse Griffith, but a federal judge ordered their release and none ever stood trial. Holden disbanded the militia in September and lifted martial law in November, whereupon Democratic legislators impeached and removed him from office. With Holden gone, nightriding continued statewide until new arrests quelled the bloodshed in February 1872.[79]

South Carolina was worse

A warning to "carpetbaggers," posted by Alabama Klansmen in 1869 (Library of Congress).

yet, with nocturnal raids involving masked bands of 500 men. In York County alone, authorities estimated that 1,800 of the district's 2,300 white males were Klansmen, judged responsible for 11 murders and 600 assaults between November 1870 and September 1871. Statewide, Klansmen rode, whipped, raped and murdered at will, despite the best efforts of outnumbered militiamen fielded by Governor Robert Scott. In Laurensville, a Klan-led riot killed at least a dozen Republicans, most of them black, in October 1870. Terrorists counted two state legislators among the victims they murdered at an estimated rate of one per day during Reconstuction.[80]

Congress: Round One

On December 5, 1870, President Grant delivered a special message to Congress, declaring that the "free exercise of franchise has by violence and intimidation been denied to citizens in several of the states lately in rebellion." Indiana senator Oliver Morton responded with a resolution calling on Grant to provide information on any "disloyal or evil-designed organizations" at large in Dixie. Grant's reply, delivered on January 13, 1871, listed nearly 5,000 incidents of violence across the South.[81]

On April 7, 1871, the House of Representatives passed the Enforcement Act of 1871, commonly known as the Ku Klux Klan Act. The Senate followed suit on April 14, and President Grant signed the act into law on April 20.[82] The statute imposed fines of $500 to $5,000, plus prison terms ranging from six months to six years, on any persons who conspired to "go in disguise upon the public highway or upon the premises of another for the purpose, either directly or indirectly, of depriving any person or any class of persons of the equal protection of the laws, or of equal privileges or immunities under the laws, or for the purpose of preventing or hindering the constituted authorities of any State from giving or securing to all persons within such State the equal protection of the laws."[83]

Moments after passing the Ku Klux Act on April 7, Congress also voted to create a Joint Select Committee to Inquire into the Condition of Affairs in the Late Insurrectionary States. That panel included seven senators and 14 representatives, with 13 Republican members and eight Democrats. At its first meeting, on April 20, the panel's majority chose Pennsylvania senator John Scott as chairman. From that day forward, the committee's partisan division determined the course of its investigation and the contents of its final report. As aptly described by Stanley Horn, "The Republican members diligently sought to establish ... that the Ku Klux Klan was a political organization, composed exclusively of Democrats, and designed primarily for the persecution of Republicans, black and white, and especially for the intimidation of negro [sic] voters. The Democrats, on the other hand, worked just as hard to sustain the theory that the Ku Klux had no political purposes whatever, that they did not concern themselves with the politics of their victims, but were organized and operated as a widespread vigilance committee for the preservation of law and order."[84]

Between June 1871 and February 1872 the committee held numerous hearings, interviewing scores of witnesses in Washington and seven Southern states. One subcommittee toured the Carolinas, Florida and Georgia, while another heard testimony in Tennessee, Alabama and Mississippi.[85] Witnesses ranged from Ku Klux victims, black and white, to military officers, politicians, and suspected Klansmen. Among Southern Democrats such as

Alabama's Edmund Pettus, denials notwithstanding, they were often one and the same. Without question, the star performer was Grand Wizard Forrest, testifying in Washington on June 27, 1871.[86]

While pledged to tell the truth and nothing but, Forrest proved evasive at best, flatly dishonest at worst. Questioned concerning his August 1868 interview, in which he recited Klan membership numbers and claimed to know the order's leader, Forrest claimed that "the whole statement is wrong." He "had information" on the Klan "from others," but could not recall their names, except for an elusive "gentleman by the name of Saunders." He had seen a copy of the Ku Klux constitution, mailed to him anonymously, but had burned it. Forrest denied membership in the Knights of the White Camellia but admitted joining the Pale Faces, granting that "some call them Ku-Klux." In fact, he claimed, "I was trying to keep it down as much as possible."[87] Then followed a revealing exchange.

Q: Did you want to suppress this organization?
A: Yes, sir. I did suppress it.
Q: How?
A: Had it broken up and disbanded. I talked with different people that I believed were connected with it, and urged its disbandment. I wrote a great many letters to people, and counseled them to abstain from all violence, and to be quiet and behave themselves, and let these things take their course.
Q: Did you get any answers to your letters?
A: To some of them I did.
Q: What did you do with them?
A: Perhaps I have some of those, but most of the letters I burned up, for I did not want to get them into trouble.[88]

As he left the hearing room, asked by a reporter how the session had gone, Forrest winked and replied, "I lied like a gentleman."[89]

The committee adjourned on February 19, 1872, authorizing publication of its 13-volume report, more than 7,000 pages in all.[90] Forrest, by then, was back in Tennessee, embroiled in conflict with his former followers over his latest project, seeking to import 1,000 Chinese workers as replacements for the blacks Klansmen had driven out of Dixie.[91] Now it remained for Washington to halt the reign of terror that Forrest had been unable to end.

Cracking Down

Sweeping arrests under the Ku Klux Act began in 1871, with federal and state prosecutions proceeding over the next two years. In South Carolina, where Klansmen rode most openly, President Grant declared martial law over nine counties on October 12, 1871.[92] Arrests and indictments followed swiftly: 1,849 in South Carolina, where Grand Dragon Wade Hampton billed each affected county $2,000 to hire "eminent counsel from the North"; 1,180 in North Carolina; 930 in Mississippi; and smaller numbers in four other states. There was a world of difference, though, between charging Klansmen and convicting them. Courts in Tennessee and Florida convicted one raider apiece. Mississippi saw 262 convicted, including 28 who pled guilty to murder, but their sentences were all suspended in exchange for promises to quit the Klan. Fifty-seven Klansmen were convicted in South

Carolina's York County, while 161 others were spared the ordeal of trial. None of the 160 indicted in Alabama and Georgia ever went to court. By late 1872, 65 Klansmen were in federal prison, with several times that number held in state lockups, but pardons and parole freed nearly all of them by 1875.[93]

Against the paltry punishment dished out to Klansmen, how many victims suffered their abuse in Reconstruction? No final tally of whippings and other non-lethal attacks is possible, but historian David Chalmers's estimate of "close to a thousand" blacks and Republicans slain is clearly too conservative.[94] Louisiana terrorists killed nearly twice that number

in 1868 alone, while congressional investigators identified 109 murder victims from Alabama, 74 from Georgia, 58 from Mississippi (excluding the Meridian riot), and 40 from Tennessee. No tabulation was attempted for the Carolinas, but we know that Palmetto State Klansmen killed 35 victims in the first six months of 1871. Investigators passed over Texas, Arkansas, and Kentucky, with minimum tallies of racist murders standing at 977, 90, and 86, respectively.[95]

Most Klansmen were well satisfied with their performance during Reconstruction, but a few had second thoughts. Consider Benjamin Harvey Hill of Georgia, a Know-Nothing Party supporter from the 1850s, ex–Confederate senator, associate of Grand Dragon John Gordon in the Southern Life Insurance Company, future U.S. representative (1875–77) and senator (1877–82). Before voters sent him to Washington, Hill told a reporter, "The Ku Klux business ... is the greatest blunder our people ever committed."[96]

But it was not over yet.

Captured Klansmen in their uniforms, ca. 1871–73 (Library of Congress).

CHAPTER 2

Never Sound Retreat
(1873–1914)

President Grant won re-election easily in November 1872. Democrats, bereft of candidates, could do no better than Horace Greeley, publisher of the *New York Tribune,* already nominated by the breakaway Liberal Republican Party in a bid to challenge Grant on charges of corruption. On election day, Greeley trailed Grant by 763,474 votes, then died before electoral votes were tabulated, revealing 286 for Grant against 66 for the loser.[1] Already beset by multiple scandals, with more on the way, Grant was increasingly distracted from the plight of freedmen and Republicans below the Mason-Dixon Line.

Colonizing Fiji (1872–74)

Grant was still campaigning for reelection when the Klan's first foreign chapter surfaced in faraway Fiji, an archipelago of some 332 islands located in Melanesia, 1,300 miles northeast of New Zealand's North Island. The Fiji Klan's founders were Europeans, whose number had increased from 40 to 2,000 during America's Civil War. News of the Klan had traveled far by 1872, and was distorted in transit. For whites in Levuka, then capital of Fiji, it seemed the perfect vehicle for opposition to King Cakobau, a native Fijian who spurned the so-called benefits of white supremacy.[2]

No details survive of the Klan's operations in Fiji. Its leaders, apparently, were drawn from the "right sort" of European settlers—planters and businessmen—while its ranks were filled with the dregs of distant empires who had transformed Levuka into a frontier "hellhole." Cakobau tried to unite rival chiefs for mutual defense, but charges of corruption plagued his government and violence spread from Levuka to the hinterlands. Britain had closed its consulate in Fiji five years earlier, but returned in 1874—"reluctantly," its leaders claimed— to bring order out of chaos. Sir Hercules Robinson arrived in September, signed a "Deed of Cession" with Cakobau on October 10, making Fiji a British colony, and then took office as interim governor. By the time his successor reached Fiji in June 1875, Robinson had suppressed the Klan in true British style.[3]

Redeeming Dixie (1873–75)

The first blow to newly established black civil rights in the South came unexpectedly from Washington, specifically from the Supreme Court. In 1869, after a series of cholera outbreaks caused by indiscriminate dumping of offal from butcher shops in New Orleans, Louisiana's legislature had chartered a firm to run a "grand slaughterhouse" in that city, effectively monopolizing production of meat at a central location. Various butchers filed suit against the monopoly, claiming that it violated the Fourteenth Amendment's ban on "any law which shall abridge the privileges or immunities of citizens of the United States." Deciding that issue by a five-to-four vote in April 1873, the Supreme Court held that the amendment protected only federal civil rights, not "civil rights heretofore belonging exclusively to the states."[4] Without addressing racial matters, the court had laid the groundwork for a revolution in the South.

Louisiana was the first state to react, disputing the election of Republican Governor William Kellogg. Unable to depose the governor directly, Sheriff Christopher Nash led white terrorists, including 45 Klansmen, to seize the Grant Parish courthouse in Colfax on April 13, 1873—Easter Sunday—slaughtering black militiamen and freedmen who tried to defend it. A report submitted to Congress in 1875 listed 81 victims by name, further stating that 15 to 20 corpses were thrown into the Red River and another 18 secretly buried, for a total of "at least 105" victims. (A state historical marker, erected in 1950, refers to 150 murdered blacks and three whites killed in "the Colfax riot" which "marked the end of carpetbag misrule in the South." Other sources place the death toll at 280.)[5] Three gunmen were eventually convicted on federal conspiracy charges, but the Supreme Court overturned those verdicts in 1876, ruling that the Fourteenth Amendment "prohibits a State from depriving any person of life, liberty, or property, without due process of law; but this adds nothing to the rights of one citizen as against another."[6]

Sheriff Nash went on to found the White League in March 1874, recruiting former Klansmen and Knights of the White Camellia as defenders of "hereditary civilization and Christianity menaced by a stupid Africanization."[7] Pledged to "the extermination of the carpetbag element," the White League operated without masks and was recognized as "the military arm of the Democratic Party."[8] The League struck first at Coushatta, in August 1874, assassinating six white Republican officials and 20 freedmen.[9] A month later, on September 14, 5,000 White Leaguers staged a *coup d'état* against Governor Kellogg, routing 3,500 police and state militia to seize City Hall, leaving 27 dead and 105 wounded. Federal troops restored Kellogg in office by September 19, but the "Battle of Liberty Place" effectively doomed Reconstruction in Louisiana.[10]

In Kentucky, on September 8, 1874, the Louisville *Courier-Journal* published a report from U.S. Marshal Willis Russell, stating that "more than 100 men have been killed, wounded, or driven away from that portion of Owen and Henry Counties lying on the Kentucky River by the Kuklux in the last three years." A federal grand jury indicted several Klansmen, then dismissed all charges against them in October 1874, when every prosecution witness disappeared. That same month, Klansmen murdered a teenage black girl and whipped several field hands, going on to burn a black church in Todd County on February 16, 1875. Governor Preston Leslie offered a $9,000 reward for capture of the girl's killers, while sheriffs "scoured the country, captured arms, implements, masks and disguises." Four Klansmen finally faced trial in November 1875, one receiving a five-year sentence and another three years. A third defendant, convicted of trying to kill Marshal Russell, escaped prison time on grounds that he had been injured while pursuing the lawman. Even then, raiding in parts of Kentucky continued through December 1875.[11]

Matters were little better in Florida, despite Stanley Horn's assurance that "as the need for their services diminished, the Ku Klux faded out of existence."[12] Jonathan Gibbs, a black Presbyterian minister from Pennsylvania, endured Klan threats during his tenure as Florida's secretary of state (1868–72) and as superintendent of public instruction (1873–74), while doubling as a lieutenant colonel in the state militia. His sudden death in Tallahassee, on August 14, 1874, was officially ascribed to apoplexy, but close friends insisted that he was poisoned by Klansmen. A year later, Columbia County Klansmen murdered Dr. Elisha Johnson, a white Republican state legislator, near his home in Lake City.[13]

While Florida's terrorists stalked individual targets, Mississippi's favored wholesale murder in their campaign to "redeem" the Magnolia State. President Grant offered the Klan carte blanche in January 1874, telling the *New York Herald*, "I am tired of this nonsense.... I don't want any quarrel about Mississippi State matters referred to me. This nursing of monstrosities has nearly exhausted the party. I am done with them, and they will have to take care of themselves."[14] Mississippi Democrats responded with a "straight-out policy" of terrorism, bluntly dubbed the "Shotgun Plan," wherein masked Klansmen joined forces with "irregular militia companies" clad in "the red-shirt badge of southern manhood" to terrorize Republicans and freedmen. On December 7, 1874, rioters in Vicksburg killed at least 50 blacks—some reports claim 300 slain—and drove black sheriff Peter Crosby into exile. It required a plea from the state legislature for President Grant to send troops in support of Crosby on January 5, 1875. On March 11, the *Meridian Mercury* declared, "The negroes are our enemies.... [W]e must accept them as our enemies and beat them as enemies."[15]

Heeding that advice, Democrats staged riotous demonstrations statewide. Sheriff Crosby was shot in Vicksburg by his own white deputy in June, and the city suffered another deadly riot on July 4, followed by an outbreak at Water Valley days later. In August, thugs from Alabama visited Macon to join in the murder of two white Republicans and 13 blacks gunned down in church. September brought mass murders of freedmen in Yazoo City and Clinton. When Governor Adelbert Ames requested aid from Washington, President Grant refused, writing that "the whole public are tired of these annual autumnal outbreaks in the South." Terrorism flourished in the absence of federal troops, including raids by recognized Klansmen in their traditional garb throughout Jefferson and Yalobusha Counties. On election day, Democrats carried the state by a margin of 50,000 votes, compared to a Republican majority of 30,000 two years earlier. Five counties with large black majorities polled 12, seven, four, two, and zero votes from freedmen, respectively.[16]

Despite his weariness of dealing with Dixie, Grant made a final gesture toward protection of freedmen in March 1875, when he signed a Civil Rights Act theoretically ensuring equal treatment of African Americans in public accommodations, public transportation, and selection for jury service. Dixie's white "redeemers" ignored the new law and were rewarded eight years later, when an eight-to-one vote by the Supreme Court found its ban on discrimination by private parties unconstitutional.[17]

Fighting Illini (1872–75)

August 1875 brought reports of Klan activity in Franklin County, Illinois, but the trouble had begun in April 1872, when elderly Isaac Vancil received a warning to leave the county or die. He ignored the threat until April 22, when a mob in full regalia raided his home and hanged him. Authorities charged 18 men with murder, but all were acquitted. By summer 1874, Klan units had spread into Saline and Williamson Counties, threatening and sometimes whipping "those whom they thought out of the line of domestic duty, and even in financial affairs."[18]

On October 23, 1874, nightriders visited the Franklin County home of Henry Carter, warning him to leave within 40 days. Gunfire erupted, leaving several Klansmen wounded and 22 bullets lodged in Carter's house. Soon afterward, a gang of armed men gathered at a local church by daylight, issuing another warning to the Carters. Instead of leaving, Henry Carter sent their names to Governor John Beveridge, whose investigation ended the terror campaign.[19]

Headquartered in a Franklin County village called "Sneak Out," Klansmen kept a low profile until August 1875, when they targeted retired Union army captain John Hogan. Hogan procured 100 muskets from Governor Beveridge to arm a local company, and joined Sheriff James Mason to lay an ambush. When 14 Klansmen came calling on August 17, Hogan's forces opened fire, wounding all but one. Most escaped, leaving their bloodied robes behind, but John Duckworth turned state's evidence and named his fellow raiders, leading to their arrest. One of seven held for trial was Aaron Neal, "reputed grand master of the Franklin County Ku-Klux, or Golden Ring." Again, the Klansmen were acquitted, but the scrutiny dissolved their order.[20] It would rise again in Williamson County, with even greater violence, a half century later.

Compromise with Terror (1876–77)

By January 1876, U.S. troops had been withdrawn from all but three of the former Confederate states. Occupation continued in Florida, Louisiana and South Carolina, but President Grant—already determined not to seek a third term—would evacuate the Sunshine State before leaving office.[21] Elsewhere, Red Shirts and "former" Klansmen prepared to seize control by force.

With Grant out of the running, Republicans chose Rutherford Hayes of Ohio as their presidential candidate, with running mate William Wheeler from New York. Democrats nominated New York Governor William Tilden, running in tandem with Indiana Governor Thomas Hendricks. According to the Democratic platform: "Reform is necessary to rebuild and establish in the hearts of the whole people the Union 11 years ago happily rescued from the danger of the secession of States, but now to be saved from a corrupt centralism which, after inflicting upon 10 States the rapacity of carpet-bag tyrannies, has honeycombed the offices of the Federal Government itself with incapacity, waste and fraud; infected States and municipalities with the contagion of misrule, and locked fast the prosperity of an industrious people in the paralysis of hard times. Reform is necessary to establish a sound currency, restore the public credit and maintain the national honor."[22]

In the South, that "reform" still demanded violence. Mississippi was typical, with Kemper County terrorists firing a cannon at the home of ex-sheriff William Chisolm after he announced his candidacy for Congress. (Chisolm and two of his daughters died at a mob's hands the following year.) In Hernando, "DeSoto Blues" shot black Republicans, while Red

Shirts in Yalobusha County marched with banners reading "White man's country, white man's rule" and "We are going to control or die." In Washington County, a signed "Ku Klux" warning ordered freedmen to flee within 24 hours. Klan defense attorney Edward Walthall led the mob that drove black voters from Grenada on election day.[23]

South Carolina witnessed the year's worst mayhem, with Grand Dragon and Red Shirt champion Wade Hampton campaigning for governor. The bloodshed began on July 8, in Hamburg, where terrorists disarmed black militiamen, then executed five, leaving three more wounded.[24] Freedmen defended themselves more successfully at Charleston, on September 6, but South Carolina's "redeemers" continued to press their offensive. Two weeks later, at Ellenton, Red Shirts killed at least 39 black Republicans, while losing two of their own. In that clash, future U.S. senator Benjamin "Pitchfork Ben" Tillman led the group that captured and murdered state legislator Simon Coker.[25] Black Republicans turned the tables on Hampton's Red Shirts at Cainhoy, killing six and wounding 16 on October 16, but it was too little and too late.[26] Statewide, historians report at least 150 freedmen murdered in the weeks preceding election day. Violence continued at the polls on November 7, and while Republicans claimed a 3,145-vote lead over Hampton in the state's gubernatorial race, Democrats insisted that they held a 1,134-vote majority. With dual governors and legislatures clamoring for power, Georgia Senator John Gordon introduced a resolution in Congress, proposing federal proclamation of his fellow grand dragon as the victor. South Carolina's Supreme Court settled the issue by endorsing Hampton on March 7, 1877.[27]

Meanwhile, on the national stage, presidential balloting proved equally contentious. Tilden polled 4,284,020 popular votes against 4,036,572 for Hayes, but Hayes held a one-vote lead in the Electoral College, with results from Florida, Louisiana and South Carolina disputed. Both candidates seemed content to let Congress decide the election, but in fact, frantic negotiations proceeded, climaxed by a closed-door meeting at Washington's Wormsley Hotel. Chief among Democratic negotiators at that gathering was Klan senator John Gordon of Georgia, who offered Tilden's surrender in return for a promise that Hayes would end "Radical" Reconstruction.[28] Thus was achieved the "Compromise of 1877," better known to defenders of black civil rights in Dixie as "The Great Betrayal."[29]

Senator Gordon's role in that bargain was suspicious enough, but Klan historian Susan Davis paints a more detailed picture of Ku Klux involvement, based on interviews with self-described participants. As she describes the event:

> On March 4, 1877, President R. B. Hayes was inaugurated, and he requested Governor Wade Hampton and Governor [Daniel] Chamberlain [Hampton's Republican rival in South Carolina] to come to Washington, after General John B. Gordon and Captain John C. Lester, representing the Grand Wizard who was at that time ill, delivered General Nathan B. Forrest's message to President R. B. Hayes that, "The Ku Klux Klan requested him to devise some policy by which the Military would be withdrawn from the South, and the people left in peace with the negroes as employer and employee, with separate schools, no social or political equality, and if this was not done they would insist on the negroes being colonized or deported as was Lincoln's intention and which had been the policy of the whole country regarding all free negroes since the foundation of our government....
>
> President Hayes is said to have been greatly impressed with the earnestness of these Southern gentlemen, and not wishing to further harass and worry them into greater retaliation, he issued an order to the Secretary of War, to remove the troops from the State House of South Carolina, and at noon, on April the 10th, 1877, the order went into effect.[30]

Fact or fantasy? The "whole country" had never agreed on any program of deporting free blacks as Davis claimed, nor was school segregation formalized under President Hayes, but Chamberlain did surrender South Carolina's governorship to Hampton on April 11, 1877. Hayes ordered withdrawal of troops from the state on April 20, and they departed four days later.[31] For all intents and purposes, the South had been "redeemed" for white supremacy.

Jim Crow, Disfranchisement and Mob Rule

If Southern whites could no longer enslave African Americans, they were determined at least to separate them from white society at every level, from cradle to grave. And once again, the Supreme Court collaborated in that effort. In the 1877 case of *Hall v. DeCuir,* the court held that states could not prohibit segregation aboard common carriers.[32] Thirteen years later, in *Louisville, New Orleans and Texas Railway Company v. Mississippi*, the court went further, ruling that states could require segregated seating on public conveyances.[33] Finally, in *Plessy v. Ferguson* (1896), the court established a doctrine of "separate but equal" facilities for different races that would govern civil rights for over half a century.[34]

Thus encouraged by Washington, the ex–Confederate states set about segregating railroads, street cars, restaurants, theaters, public parks and residential neighborhoods, hospitals and cemeteries—anything and anyplace, in fact, where persons from two or more races might conceivably meet. In Birmingham, Alabama, long described as America's "most segregated city," black and white witnesses swore their oaths of truthfulness on separate court bibles. Nor was the South alone in codifying racism, as 26 states above the Mason-Dixon Line passed various segregation statutes. Eighteen northern states banned interracial marriage; Oklahoma segregated hearses and showers for miners; Nevada barred Asians, blacks and Indians from public schools; Connecticut separated members of its state militia by race; California forbade public employment for Chinese immigrants; New Mexico mandated separate classrooms for black and white students within public schools.[35] Collectively, such laws were known as "Jim Crow" statutes, a name derived from a song-and-dance caricature of blacks performed by white actor Thomas Rice in the 1830s.[36]

Successful segregation of minorities required their disfranchisement in future elections. The Constitution's Fifteenth Amendment flatly states that "The right of citizens of the United States to vote shall not be denied or abridged by the United States or by any State on account of race, color, or previous condition of servitude," but since that prohibition barred the road to white supremacy, racists began to seek a path around it. Five years after the amendment's ratification, the Supreme Court ruled, in *Minor v. Happersett*, that nothing in the Constitution granted women voting rights.[37] In *Williams v. Mississippi* (1898), the court found no discrimination in a state's requirement for poll taxes and literacy tests, as long as they applied to all voters.[38] (In fact, a "grandfather clause" exempted many illiterate whites, while egregious discrimination in the manner of literacy testing effectively barred nearly all blacks from voting.) Five years later, in *James v. Bowman*, the court held that federal laws punishing private or official interference with the right to vote were unconstitutional.[39] By 1902, every former Confederate state had banned blacks from voting in Democratic Party primaries—which, in fact, determined the winners of subsequent general elections in the one-party South.[40]

Lynching enforced white supremacy after Reconstruction, ca. 1920s (Library of Congress).

Where new laws failed to secure white supremacy, racists fell back on terrorism, flaunted in the form of lynchings and race riots. Lynching—the extralegal killing of persons accused of some crime or violation of social mores—has occurred throughout recorded history, and was a common tactic of the Reconstruction-era Klan. No consistent log of American lynchings existed prior to 1882, when Alabama's Tuskegee Institute began compiling statistics. That tabulation lists 3,705 victims killed by lynch mobs through 1910, including 2,503 blacks and 1,202 whites.[41] A tabulation by the NAACP lists 2,716 lynchings between 1889 and 1910, with 2,087 of the victims African Americans.[42] Other sources cite higher numbers, while modern scholars note frequent omission of Chinese, East Indian, Hispanic, and Native American victims from published tallies.[43] Pitchfork Ben Tillman, speaking on the Senate floor in 1900, told his colleagues and the world at large, "We of the South have never recognized the right of the negro to govern white men, and we never will. We have never believed him to be the equal of the white man, and we will not submit to his gratifying his lust on our wives and daughters without lynching him."[44]

Rape and murder were the common charges lodged against lynching victims, but mobs also rallied to execute blacks for arson, theft, miscegenation, poisoning livestock, "insulting" or "frightening" white women, "inflammatory" language, "disputing a white man's word," testifying against white offenders, and defending themselves against white assailants. One in 20 black victims were lynched with no specified charges against them.[45]

When mob slaughter of individuals failed to cow African Americans, white rioters stormed black communities en masse. At Danville, Virginia, in November 1883, racists attacked a black political rally, killing seven persons and preventing most of the city's 1,300 registered black voters from casting ballots on election day.[46] White longshoremen in New Orleans executed six black strikebreakers in March 1895.[47] A lawsuit filed against a white man sparked the courthouse massacre of 23 blacks in Carrollton, Mississippi, on March 17, 1896.[48] Inflamed by the election of a biracial city council, whites in Wilmington, North Carolina, staged a *coup d'état* in November 1898, slaying at least six victims (some reports claim 100 dead) and driving another 2,100 from the city.[49] Even relatively cosmopolitan Atlanta was not spared: in September 1906, rumors of rape brought 10,000 white men into the streets, killing an estimated 25 to 40 blacks against two losses on their side.[50]

Such terrorism was a daily fact of life for African Americans, and random mobs were not the only perpetrators. If the KKK was theoretically retired, its heirs still donned their masks and rode by night, whipping and killing in the same old style.

White Caps (1888–1906)

Vigilantism did not begin in the United States with Reconstruction, nor was it restricted to the South. A historical survey, excluding the Southern terrorists of Reconstruction, lists 326 vigilante groups active in 32 states between 1767 and 1901, claiming at least 734 lives.[51] Amidst that carnage rose the White Cap movement, cited by Professor Richard Brown as "an important link between the first and second Ku Klux Klans."[52]

White Caps first surfaced in Indiana during 1888, then spread to at least a dozen other states by the early 1890s. Conceived as "a sort of spontaneous movement for the moral regulation of the poor whites and ne'er-do-wells of the rural American countryside," they donned hoods to whip "loose women" and the "drunken, shiftless, and wife-beating whites" who would, a generation later, rate attention from the 1920s Klan. At the same time, however, some White Caps were clearly racist, targeting blacks and Hispanics.[53] Mississippi's White Caps added anti–Semitism to the volatile mix with attacks on Jewish merchants and rants against "Wall Street gold bugs."[54] In Georgia, White Caps deviated from their law-and-order theme, staging 42 percent of all recorded raids against informers who reported outlaw whiskey stills. Conversely, a group of masked riders specifically labeled as "Ku Klux" raided suspected brothels in Dalton, Georgia, killing one black man who tried to defend his white mistress.[55]

The NAACP's lynching tally lists 15 persons executed by White Caps in 10 states, between 1891 and 1904. Nine of those victims were white, the rest African American. No motive was cited in eight cases, including the Tennessee lynching of a white married couple in March 1897. Two victims were slain for giving evidence against White Caps, one for killing a nightrider, one for wife-beating, and two simply for being black.[56] Aside from two lynchings, White Caps in Sevier County, Tennessee, were credited with seven other murders between 1892 and 1897.[57] Nationwide, historian William Holmes reports 239 episodes of "whitecapping"—mostly nonlethal—between 1897 and 1900.[58] Georgia jurors acquitted White Caps charged with murder, while 309 indicted raiders pled guilty on various charges in Mississippi, their number including a sheriff, a state legislator, and several local officials.[59] The movement was officially extinct by 1906, but its tradition of masked vigilantism, inherited from the Klan, survived with little damage.

The A.P.A. (1887–1914)

While White Caps upheld the original Klan's nightriding tradition, another precursor of the 20th-century order sprang up in the North, operating in broad daylight. Founded by Iowa attorney Henry Bowers in March 1887, the American Protective Association set its sights on Roman Catholics, campaigning to drive them from public life—including politics and schools—on grounds of their supposed "dual loyalties" to Rome and the United States.[60] The A.P.A.'s membership oath said it all:

> I do most solemnly promise and swear that I will always, to the utmost of my ability, labor, plead and wage a continuous warfare against ignorance and fanaticism; that I will use my utmost power to strike the shackles and chains of blind obedience to the Roman Catholic church from the hampered and bound consciences of a priest-ridden and church-oppressed people; that I will never allow any one, a member of the Roman Catholic church, to become a member of this order, I knowing him to be such; that I will use my influence to promote the interest of all Protestants everywhere in the world that I may be; that I will not employ a Roman Catholic in any capacity if I can procure the services of a Protestant.
>
> I furthermore promise and swear that I will not aid in building or maintaining, by my resources, any Roman Catholic church or institution of their sect or creed whatsoever, but will do all in my power to retard and break down the power of the Pope, in this country or any other; that I will not enter into any controversy with a Roman Catholic upon the subject of this order, nor will I enter into any agreement with a Roman Catholic to strike or create a disturbance whereby the Catholic employees may undermine and substitute their Protestant co-workers; that in all grievances I will seek only Protestants and counsel with them to the exclusion of all Roman Catholics, and will not make known to them anything of any nature matured at such conferences.
>
> I furthermore promise and swear that I will not countenance the nomination, in any caucus or convention, of a Roman Catholic for any office in the gift of the American people, and that I will not vote for, or counsel others to vote for, any Roman Catholic, but will vote only for a Protestant, so far as may lie in my power. Should there be two Roman Catholics on opposite tickets, I will erase the name on the ticket I vote; that I will at all times endeavor to place the political positions of this government in the hands of Protestants, to the entire exclusion of the Roman Catholic church, of the members thereof, and the mandate of the Pope.
>
> To all of which I do most solemnly promise and swear, so help me God. Amen.[61]

By 1896, claiming 2.5 million members nationwide, the A.P.A. dominated local politics in Omaha; Kansas City; Toledo; Rockford, Illinois; Duluth, Minnesota; Saginaw, Michigan; and Louisville, Kentucky, while boasting strong outposts in Detroit, St. Louis, and Denver. At least 20 members of the Fifty-fourth Congress (1895–97) were A.P.A. members, and Kentucky governor William Bradley openly courted the group's support. Unlike the Reconstruction Klan—but very much like its successor—the A.P.A. drew members from both major political parties. Perhaps ironically, aside from Tennessee and Kentucky, it made little headway in the South, where White Caps held the line against perceived foreign incursions.[62]

The A.P.A. would wither over time, lasting longest in Ohio—where it helped defeat incumbent governor James Cox and U.S. Senate hopeful Timothy Hogan in 1914[63]—but the modern Klan would resurrect its nativist propaganda, including recycled tales of "escaped nuns" fleeing the sexual horrors of convent-brothels. While the A.P.A. abstained from violence, its paranoia fertilized the soil that northern Klan recruiters would till to great profit in the 1920s.

Populism Fails (1891–1908)

An antidote of sorts to White Capping and nativism was the People's (or Populist) Party, founded by leaders of the Southern Farmers' Alliance and the Knights of Labor in July 1892.[64] Active on both sides of the Mason-Dixon Line, the party practiced fusion politics, collaborating with Democrats in the Midwest and Southwest, allied with Republicans in Dixie.[65] Hard-line southern Democrats resisted Populism's call for racial parity, as voiced by Georgia's Thomas Watson in October 1892, when he declared, "To the emasculated individual who cries 'Negro supremacy!' there is little to be said. His cowardice shows him to be a degeneration from the race which has never yet feared any other race. Existing under such conditions as they now do in this country, there is no earthly chance for Negro domination, unless we are ready to admit that the colored man is our superior in will power, courage, and intellect."[66]

Two years later, a Populist-Republican coalition swept state and local offices in North Carolina, rolling on to elect Republican Daniel Russell as governor in 1896.[67] "Great Commoner" William Jennings Bryan made history that year, securing presidential nominations from the Democratic, Populist, and Silver Parties, but he still trailed winner William McKinley by 609,687 votes in November.[68] Bryan would try for the White House twice more as a mainstream Democrat, leaving Tom Watson to carry the Populist banner in 1904 and 1908. Watson's 117,183 popular votes in 1904 more than doubled Populist candidate Wharton Barker's tally from 1900, but they were still restricted to Georgia. Four years later, Watson polled a mere 28,862 and abandoned the dying movement, shifting his focus to become Georgia's political kingmaker. By then, he was a dedicated white supremacist, advocating black disfranchisement.[69]

Meanwhile, North Carolina Populists lost their grip on the Tarheel State through a *coup d'état* in November 1898. Two days after voters in Wilmington chose a white fusionist mayor and a biracial city council, 1,500 Democratic insurrectionists led by Alfred Waddell toppled the government at gunpoint, killing many African Americans and driving some 2,000 from the city. Two years later, the terrorists backed Democratic gubernatorial candidate Charles Aycock. On the night before that election, Waddell told supporters, "You are Anglo-Saxons. You are armed and prepared and you will do your duty.... Go to the polls tomorrow, and if you find the negro out voting, tell him to leave the polls and if he refuses, kill him, shoot him down in his tracks. We shall win tomorrow if we have to do it with guns." As expected, Aycock carried the state by a landslide.[70]

Next door, in South Carolina, voters advanced the career of Ben Tillman, fully cognizant of his Reconstruction membership in a Red Shirt "rifle club" (which he called "Ku Klux") and the equally violent Sweetwater Sabre Club. In 1892 Tillman ran for governor and won, billing himself as the "Champion of White Men's Rule and Woman's Virtue," with a pledge that he would "willingly lead a mob in lynching a Negro who had committed an assault upon a white woman." African Americans, in his view, "must remain subordinate or be exterminated."[71] In 1900, five years after his election to the U.S. Senate, Tillman proudly said, "We have done our level best [to prevent blacks from voting] ... we have scratched our heads to find out how we could eliminate the last one of them. We stuffed ballot boxes. We shot them. We are not ashamed of it."[72] A year later, after President Theodore Roosevelt invited Booker T. Washington to the White House, Tillman railed, "The action of President

Roosevelt in entertaining that nigger will necessitate our killing a thousand niggers in the South before they learn their place again."[73]

So was the South "redeemed" once more from any vestige of equality.

Kentucky Klan Wars (1893–1904)

While various historians date the first Klan's demise anywhere from 1872 to 1877, Kentucky Klansmen, operating as such, remained active into the early 20th century. A *New York Times* article from November 1872 listed four murders, plus scores of floggings and other crimes in Shelby County, committed by masked nightriders persecuting white Republicans and freedmen.[74] Lynchings also continued apace, with 110 recorded over the next two decades.[75] Then, in 1893, increased competition for jobs between whites, blacks, and Italian immigrants prompted a public resurrection of the Klan.[76]

The order surfaced first in eastern Kentucky's Pike and Letcher Counties, led by the Reynolds brothers—John, Morgan and Noah—with Judge S. E. Baker, Benjamin Johnson, and Abraham Potter, expanding in successive years to Harlan, Knott, Perry and Breathitt Counties.[77] Its first reported action came in 1894, against Allen Hall's family, escalating into full-scale guerrilla warfare between Klan and anti–Klan forces by 1896. Historian Benjamin Luntz names feudists Edward Callahan and Judge James Hargis as leaders of the Klan in "Bloody Breathitt" County, battling forces led by Captain William Strong until they ambushed Strong and murdered him in May 1897. Over the next six months, Klansmen burned several homes and at least one church in a tri-county area, whipping multiple victims and driving voters from the polls. Klan opponent William Wright thus lost a judgeship and was charged with false arrest, after he jailed John Reynolds and others for "ku-kluxing" would-be voters.[78]

Wright beat that charge and continued his opposition, wounding Noah Reynolds with birdshot in July 1899, during a Ku Klux raid that left Wright's barn and mill in ashes. Other homes were also torched, with occupants of both sexes flogged by firelight. In November 1899, Wright led a force that cornered Klan terrorists in Boone County, killing two horses and capturing several raiders. After Klansmen raped victim Mary Sexton, in December 1899, William Wright—now deputized—pursued them with a bloodhound, but John Reynolds shot the dog from ambush. One month later, on January 30, 1900, it was Wright's turn, murdered by two Klansmen who were subsequently tried, convicted and hanged. Less than an hour after Wright's assassination, Governor William Goebel was shot from ambush in Frankfort, dying three days later despite the best efforts of 18 physicians.[79]

Arrests and nightriding continued through 1900, climaxed with the November raid that killed Jemima Hall and her son in Letcher County. Authorities arrested Klansman Elijah Fleming, who turned state's evidence, implicating Noah Reynolds in January 1901. William Wright's son, William Jr., joined uncle "Bad John" Wright in arresting four Klansmen by March, when Noah Reynolds challenged Bad John to a showdown. The ensuing battle, at Yonts Hill on April 10, left William Jr. dead, with John Reynolds and several others wounded. Judge W. H. Blair cabled Governor John Beckham for troops on April 12, and another pitched battle was fought three days later, at Whitesburg. On April 17, Klansmen burned J. H. Frazier's store in Whitesburg, next-door to the Letcher County courthouse, as a warning to Klan opponents. John Reynolds surrendered in July 1901, to face trial for the slaying of William Wright, Jr., and received a 15-year sentence for manslaughter. A year later, brother Noah and Klansman George Cook were convicted of murder in the same case, drawing life prison terms.[80]

And still, the Blue Grass Klan refused to die. In March 1901, Lexington's *Morning Democrat* reported Klansmen firing into Pike County homes. During the same month, Paducha's nightriders renamed themselves White Caps. Letcher County jurors acquitted Jemima Hall's killers in autumn 1903, whereupon sporadic raiding resumed. A summary published in September 1905 listed 75 flogging victims in Letcher County—two-thirds of them women—and "perhaps 20" murders committed by Klansmen in the last six months of 1901. The last reported Ku Klux whipping, of two women, occurred in Letcher County during January 1904. Around the same time, Noah Reynolds sued a Klan opponent, Dr. T. A. Cook, claiming that Cook had impregnated Noah's sister.[81]

Rewriting History

While Kentucky's Klan wars were in progress, an academic trend began that would revise the history of Reconstruction, casting Klansmen as saviors of the South. That movement's dean was William Dunning, for whom the "Dunning School" of history is named. New Jersey born in 1857, Dunning earned his various degrees at New York's Columbia University between 1881 and 1885, and remained as a professor there from 1886 until his death in 1922. Beginning with his Ph.D. dissertation, *The Constitution of the United States in Civil War and Reconstruction: 1860–1867*, continuing through *Essays on the Civil War and Reconstruction and Related Topics* (1898) and *Reconstruction, Political and Economic: 1865–1877* (1907), Dunning argued that allowing freedmen to participate in politics was "a serious mistake," propelling southern whites toward violence and institution of Jim Crow.[82]

To Dunning, the Klan was a necessary evil—if, indeed, it was evil at all. Dunning wrote: "Between 1868 and 1870 ... there developed that widespread series of disorders with which the name Ku Klux is associated. While these were at their height the Republican party was ousted from control in five of the old rebel states.... The inference was at once drawn that the whites of the South were pursuing a deliberate policy of overthrowing the negro party [*sic*] by violence. No attention was paid to the claim that the manifest inefficiency and viciousness of the Republican governments afforded a partial, if not wholly adequate explanation of their overthrow. Not even the relative quiet and order that followed the triumph of the whites in these states were recognized as justifying the new régime."[83]

Dunning's disciples took his creed to heart and passed it on. Ellis Oberholtzer opined that Yankees could not understand the South because they "had never seen a nigger except Fred[erick] Douglass." Freedmen, he wrote, were "as credulous as children, which in intellect they in many ways resembled." John Burgess, a colleague of Dunning's at Columbia, wrote that "a black skin means membership in a race of men which has never of itself succeeded in subjecting passion to reason." James Rhodes agreed, claiming that "what the whole country has only learned through years of costly and bitter experience was known to this leader of scientific thought before we ventured on the policy of trying to make negroes [*sic*] intelligent by legislative acts."[84] As late as 1947, Ellis Coulter deemed the involvement of freedmen in government a "diabolical" scheme, "to be remembered, shuddered at, and execrated."[85]

The Klan could be forgiven—even praised—for resisting that state of affairs. Claude Bowers, in *The Tragic Era* (1929), granted that some Klansmen were "deservedly convicted," but naively blamed most of the order's crimes on "youths of little education who had joined the Klan for a lark without any real feeling of hostility to the blacks.[86] Future president Woodrow Wilson, in his epic *History of the American People*, waxed hagiographic in praising "the real *Ku Klux Klan,* an 'Invisible Empire of the South,' bound together in loose organization to protect the southern country from some of the ugliest hazards of a time of revolution." (Original italics.) Its members, he wrote, were "men half outlawed, denied the suffrage, without hope of justice in the courts, who meant to take this means to make their will felt." Later excesses were the fault of "[r]eckless men not of their order, malicious fellows of the baser sort who did not feel the compulsions of honor and who had private grudges to satisfy, imitated their disguises and borrowed their methods."[87]

While historians spun facts to suit their bias, pseudo-scientists did likewise in the field of eugenics. Charles Carroll's *"The Negro a Beast" or "In the Image of God"* (1900) cited scripture to prove that only whites bore the likeness of their Creator, while miscegenation led to atheism and belief in evolution.[88] William Calhoun's *The Caucasian and the Negro in the United States* (1902) may be fairly judged from its subtitle: *They Must Separate. If Not, Then Extermination.*[89] In *The Color Line: A Brief on Behalf of the Unborn* (1905), William Smith argued that "[c]ompared with the vital matter of pure Blood, all other matters ... sink into insignificance."[90] Dr. Robert Shufeldt, of the U.S. Army's medical corps, railed against libidinous "black beasts" in *The Negro: A Menace to American Civilization* (1907), declaring that "[i]t is the presence of the negro among us that is responsible for lynch-law, and not the taste of our people for such brutal horrors."[91]

Fueled by such venom, mob violence was inevitable. In New Orleans, a deadly shootout between white police and black gunman Robert Charles sparked a four-day race riot in July 1900.[92] Rumors of rape brought 10,000 whites to the streets of Atlanta in September 1906, killing at least 25 African Americans (some reports claim 40).[93] Two years later, in August 1908, blacks defended their homes against white rioters in Springfield, Illinois, killing five terrorists and losing two of their own before National Guardsmen intervened.[94]

"The Fiery Cross of Old Scotland's Hills"

Into that atmosphere of sound and fury strode Southern prodigy Thomas Dixon, Jr., son of a slave-owning Baptist minister who joined North Carolina's

Thomas Dixon, a novelist whose works rekindled public interest in the KKK (Library of Congress).

Klan when his firstborn was four years old. So did Dixon's uncle, Leroy McAfee, rising to the rank of grand titan. As a child, after he witnessed the Klan lynching of a black rape suspect, Dixon's mother told him, "The Klan are our people—they're guarding us from harm." It was a message he would long remember and repeat to others as historical fact.[95]

Dixon loathed the family farm but proved himself a star student, graduating from Shelby Academy in only two years, then earning a master's degree from Wake Forest University in four. Moving on to Johns Hopkins University, he befriended classmate Woodrow Wilson, then left academia to pursue a stage career in New York. Failing there, in large part due to his skeletal frame—150 pounds, at six foot three—Dixon returned to North Carolina, earning a degree from Greensboro Law School in 1885. Rather than practice law, however, he turned to politics, winning a seat in the state legislature before he attained voting age. Bored with that, in turn, he tried religion and was ordained as a Baptist minister in October 1886. Promotion to pulpits in Boston and Manhattan followed, but the church eventually paled as all things did for Dixon. In 1899 he resigned to pursue secular speaking tours full-time.[96]

Finally, in 1902, Dixon found his true métier as an author of florid "romantic" novels. His early works—a trilogy including *The Leopard's Spots* (1902), *The Clansman* (1905), and *The Traitor* (1907)—have been aptly described as "racist sermons in the guise of fiction."[97] Dixon populated his works with flaxen-haired damsels who choose suicide over defilement by bestial black rapists, and heroic Klansmen who avenge them in the name of justice. Those novels became best-sellers, popularizing the Klan beyond any dry work of the Dunning School, and they added a twist that the next Klan would adopt through ignorance of history. Dixon's fictional Klansmen came from hearty Scottish stock, and signaled one another with "the Fiery Cross of old Scotland's hills"—a symbol unknown to the Klan before 1905, and never used in fact until 1915.[98]

"Progressive" Racism

While Dixon made his literary mark, ex-classmate Woodrow Wilson advanced his own career. A Virginia native who practiced law in Georgia before earning his Ph.D. from Johns Hopkins in 1886, Wilson taught at Bryn Mawr College, Wesleyan College, and finally at Princeton University, where he was deemed "enormously successful as a lecturer and productive as a scholar."[99] His writings clearly approached "the race question from a Southern point of view," but he went further still. As Princeton's president, from 1902 to 1910, Wilson actively discouraged black applicants in the guise of upholding "social peace."[100]

In 1912, campaigning for the White House against fellow Progressive Theodore Roosevelt, Wilson deemed it prudent to mute his racism. Three weeks before election day, he declined an invitation to speak before the National Colored Democratic League of New York City, but penned a letter to League spokesman Alexander Walters, bishop of the African Zion Church, which read in part: "The colored people of the U.S. have made extraordinary progress towards self-support and usefulness, and ought to be encouraged in every possible and proper way. My sympathy with them is of long standing and I want to assure you that should I become President of the United States they may count on me for absolute fair dealing of everything by which I could assist in advancing the interest of their race in the

U.S."[101] Black voters trusted him, deserting the party of Lincoln to vote Democratic, then received a rude surprise.

Barely a month after his inauguration, at a cabinet meeting on April 11, 1913, Wilson endorsed Postmaster General Albert Burleson's plan to segregate the Railway Mail Service, relegating white and black workers to different cars. Jim Crow soon spread to Post Office Department headquarters in Washington, with black employees banished to the dead letter office or forced to work behind screens, beyond view of white customers. When the NAACP protested, Wilson replied that segregation was "in the interest of the Negroes. We are rendering them more safe in their possession of the office and less likely to be discriminated against."[102] Monroe Trotter, founder of the *Boston Guardian,* led a black delegation to Wilson's office in 1914, only to be chastised by the president and ejected from the White House.[103] Three years later, as America joined the First World War, Wilson relegated black soldiers to noncombatant service units, at least in part from fear of "giving them training with guns, which they might use to defend themselves from racist attacks once the war was over." At the Paris Peace Conference of 1919, Wilson opposed measures advancing black equality in the United States.[104]

The Dreamer

The modern Klan owes its existence to William Joseph Simmons, the ninth of 10 children born to Dr. Calvin Simmons and wife Lavonia (Davis) Simmons, on a farm near Harpersville, Alabama, on May 6, 1880.[105] Calvin, a Georgia native, later tried his hand at running a mill, but floods drowned that business in April 1886 and he returned to medicine until his death, six days after William's thirteenth birthday.[106] That loss forced young William to abandon his own hopes of being a doctor, and despite later claims to the contrary, no record exists of him studying medicine at Johns Hopkins University.[107]

From childhood, William Simmons was indoctrinated in the glory of the Ku Klux Klan. He later told an interviewer, "My father was an officer of the old Klan in Alabama back in the 60s. I was always fascinated by Klan stories.... My old Negro mammy, Aunt Viney, and her husband, used to tell us children about how the old Reconstruction Klansmen used to frighten the darkies." Inspired by those tales, he experienced a mystic vision of the Klan reborn: "On horseback in their white robes they rode across the wall in front of me. As the picture faded out, I got down on my knees and swore that I would found a fraternal organization that would be a memorial to the Ku Klux Klan."[108]

Reports differ widely as to when and where Simmons was graced with that epiphany. Some say it came to him as a teenager, stricken with fever on the family farm; others date it from 1900, with Simmons either reading a book on the Klan or drunk and staring at the moon.[109] In any case, the rigors of real life postponed his plan to resurrect the Klan.

America declared war on Spain in April 1898, prompting Simmons to desert the farm and join the 1st Alabama Volunteer Infantry, shipping out for Cuba in August. The unit spent 30 days in camp and apparently saw no action; one historian notes that even in bivouac "the volunteers showed that they were having some difficulty taking their duties seriously."[110] Despite a biographer's claim that Simmons "advanced more rapidly in military knowledge than the other men of his company," he remained a common private when the unit mustered out in October 1898.[111]

Back in civilian life, Simmons studied briefly at Birmingham–Southern College, then dropped out to become a circuit-riding preacher for the Methodist Episcopal Church, South, which had split from its parent body in 1844, in support of slavery.[112] At six foot two, with red hair and a gold-rimmed pince-nez, dressed in a frock coat and striped trousers, he cut a dashing figure in small-town pulpits, lecturing on such alliterative topics as "Red Heads, Dead Heads, and No Heads," "Women, Weddings, and Wives," and the "Kinship or Kourtship and Kissing." He rarely earned more than $300 per year from the church, but dreamed of assignment to a major urban congregation at the sect's general conference in May 1912. Instead, he was suspended for a year on grounds of "inefficiency and moral impairment."[113]

Stung by that rejection, Simmons tried his hand at selling ladies' garters, but was soon dismissed—again, for inefficiency.[114] One source claims he spent the remainder of 1912 teaching Southern history at Lanier University, in Atlanta, but in fact that school did not exist until 1917.[115] By then, Simmons had found his true calling in the world of fraternalism. An inveterate joiner, Simmons claimed memberships in the Masons, Knights Templar, Knights of Pythias, Odd Fellows and at least eight other lodges, peddling memberships in some or all of them. The Woodmen of the World, founded in 1890, proved the most rewarding. Simmons rose to the rank of "colonel" within it, commanding five "regiments," and in 1914 advanced to serve as district manager, earning $10,000 per year at his post at headquarters.[116]

Simmons never lost his fascination with the Klan, but he had no time to pursue it until early 1915, when a careless driver ran him down in Atlanta. Convalescing for three months, he read newspaper reviews of an epic film based on Thomas Dixon's pro–Klan novels and, thus inspired, began revising the first Klan's 1867 prescript. Leaving some of the ancient verbiage intact, Simmons expanded it and added personal touches, including a vocabulary full of words beginning with the letters "kl." "It was rather difficult, sometimes," he said, "to make the two letters fit in, but I did it somehow." The end result, he claimed, "is vastly different from anything in the whole universe of fraternal ritualism. It is altogether original, weird, mystical, and of a high class…. It unfolds a spiritual philosophy that has to do with the very fundamentals of life and living, here and hereafter."[117] He called it *The Kloran*.

Now, all he had to do was sell it to the public.

CHAPTER 3

Rebirth of an Empire
(1915–1921)

Launching the new Klan proved more difficult than Simmons had imagined. First, he hoped it would be one of Georgia's "locker clubs," created after statewide prohibition arrived in 1908, with a loophole permitting gentlemen to stash "any kind or quantity" of liquor in lockers at private clubs. Atlanta boasted locker clubs called the Beavers, Buffaloes and Panthers, but when Simmons approached City Clerk Walter Taylor with a plan to found the Klan as a drinking fraternity, Taylor dismissed the notion on account of the Ku Klux label. "They all want to be animals," he advised Simmons.[1] And, in fact, temperance zealots in Atlanta had their sights fixed on the locker clubs already, banning them by law in November 1915.[2]

Some other impetus was clearly needed to jump-start the Klan, and Simmons found it where the movement had begun, where it would thrive thereafter: in the realm of racial and religious hatred, with a boost from failed Populist Thomas Watson.

"Lynch Law Is a Good Sign"

In the years since his last presidential campaign, Watson had undergone complete reversal of his former views on white supremacy, adding a virulent strain of nativism borrowed from the old Know-Nothing movement and the A.P.A. Through twin publications—*The Weekly Jeffersonian* and *Watson's Magazine,* both premiering in 1910—Watson warned his fellow paranoids about the dangers of the Catholic Church. He damned the confessional as a "sink of perdition" where "the priest finds out what girls and married women he can seduce. Having discovered the trail, he wouldn't be human if he didn't take advantage of the opportunity."[3]

Nor were the victims blameless. "No man," he wrote, "can imagine a woman who could maintain her self-respect after being compelled to act as a sewer pipe for a bachelor priest's accumulation of garbage."[4] Black priests were worst of all. "*Heaven's above!*" Watson raved. "*Think of a negro priest taking the vow of chastity and then being turned loose among women.... It is a thing to make one shudder.*"[5]

Blacks in general were now anathema to Watson, his prior views notwithstanding. Presidential candidate Woodrow Wilson had not only "kow-towed to the Roman hierarchy," in

Watson's view, but was also *"ravenously fond of the negro."* Wilson's greatest sin? In March 1911 he "SENT BOOKER WASHINGTON A MESSAGE OF CONDOLENCE AND CONFIDENCE WHEN THAT COON WAS CAUGHT AT A WHITE WOMAN'S BEDROOM DOOR AND DESERVEDLY BEATEN FOR IT."[6] Regarding "the negro" in general, Watson wrote, "In the South, we have to lynch him occasionally, and flog him, now and then, to keep him from blaspheming the Almighty, by his conduct, on account of his smell and his color. This country has nothing to fear from its rural communities. *Lynch law is a good sign: it shows that a sense of justice yet lives among the people.*"[7]

In 1911 Watson joined military hero Nelson Miles to found the Guardians of Liberty, a group recruiting "American Americans" dedicated to restricting immigration and opposing political "interference from foreign ecclesiastical authority."[8] Active until the outbreak of World War I, the Guardians attacked Catholicism in vitriolic terms, while insisting that "[i]t is not a question of religion. It is a question of using religion as a cloak to carry on treasonable work against the fundamental principles of the United States Government."[9]

Forgetting no one in his litany of hate, Watson also branded Jews as "moral cripples" with "an utter contempt for law and a ravenous appetite for the forbidden fruit—a lustful eagerness enhanced by the racial novelty of the girls of the uncircumcised."[10] Objective readers may suspect that Watson's ravings said more about his own psychosexual quirks than those of his targets, but his broadsides found an eager audience during America's so-called "Progressive" era.

And in 1913, Watson found a classic *cause célèbre.*

On April 26 of that year, 13-year-old Mary Phagan collected her last paycheck from Atlanta's National Pencil Company, where she worked for 12 cents per hour. Superintendent Leo Frank gave her the money, and was the last person to admit seeing Mary alive. That night, the plant's black watchman, Newt Lee, found her strangled body in the basement and summoned police, who recovered two notes from the crime scene. One read: "he said he wood love me land down play like the night witch did it but that long tall black negro did boy his slef." The other read: "mam that negro hire down here did this i went to make water and he push me down that hole a long tall negro black that hoo it wase long sleam tall negro i write while play with me." Newt Lee admitted to being the "night witch," but officers charged Frank with Phagan's murder, igniting a firestorm in Georgia.[11]

A Jewish native of Texas, whose family moved to New York soon after his birth, Leo Frank made a perfect scapegoat for Tom Watson's racist tirades—more attractive, in fact, than Newt Lee, who also spent the next few months in jail. Disgruntled ex-employees branded Frank a womanizer who harassed female workers with indecent proposals—the very epitome of Watson's depraved "moral cripple." In May 1913, Jim Conley, the factory's black janitor, told a grand jury that Frank had dictated the two "murder notes" while Conley wrote them out. His ever-changing stories climaxed with a claim that he—Conley—helped Frank hide Phagan's corpse in the factory's basement. Jurors convicted Frank, resulting in a death sentence, but Governor John Slaton wavered in the face of 100,000 letters and telegrams pleading for clemency, commuting Frank's sentence to life imprisonment in May 1915.[12]

Tom Watson waxed apoplectic over Slaton's betrayal. Under the headline "RISE! PEOPLE OF GEORGIA," he wrote:

"Knights of Mary Phagan" pose with the Leo Frank corpse, August 16, 1915 (Library of Congress).

Our grand old Empire State HAS BEEN RAPED!

We have been violated, AND WE ARE ASHAMED!

The great Seal of State has gone, LIKE A THIEF IN THE NIGHT, to do for an unscrupulous law firm, a deed of darkness which dared not bask in the light of the sun....

We have been betrayed! The breath of some leprous monster has passed over us, and we feel like crying out, in horror and despair, "Unclean! UNCLEAN!"[13]

To Frank's Jewish lawyers, funded by the fledgling Anti-Defamation League (ADL) of B'nai B'rith, Watson offered a warning: "You have blown the breath of life into the monster of Race Hatred: AND THIS FRANKENSTEIN, whom you created at such enormous expense, WILL HUNT YOU DOWN!"[14]

The Frankenstein in question would not be the Ku Klux Klan—at least, not yet. On the night of August 16, 1915, a band of armed men kidnapped Frank from the state prison at Milledgeville, drove him to Marietta—Mary Phagan's hometown—and hanged him there, posing for photographs with his dangling corpse.[15] Northern outrage at Frank's lynching prompted Tom Watson to fire back in kind. "The North can rail itself hoarse, if it chooses to do so. We've already stood as much vilification and abuse as we intend to put up with; and we will meet the 'Leo Frank League' with a Gentile League, *if they provoke us much further.*" In fact, he prophesied, "another Ku Klux Klan may be organized to restore HOME RULE."[16]

On October 16, 1915, Frank's killers—now calling themselves the Knights of Mary Phagan—climbed Stone Mountain, 18 miles outside Atlanta, and, in homage to Thomas Dixon's fictional Klansmen, burned a huge cross "visible throughout the city." Ten days later, William Simmons and 33 others, including members of the lynch mob, sought a state charter for the Knights of the Ku Klux Klan Inc. Simmons listed himself as imperial wizard, describing the Klan as a "purely benevolent and eleemosynary" fraternal order. On Thanksgiving night, November 25, he rode to the peak of Stone Mountain with 15 charter members, in a rented bus, and lit the second fiery cross in U.S. history. The Klan's charter came through on December 4, and Simmons got his next great boost from far-off Hollywood.[17]

"Writing History with Lightning"

Director David Wark Griffith, a Kentucky native and son of a Confederate colonel turned state legislator, bought dramatic rights to Thomas Dixon's trilogy of racist novels in 1913 and set about producing America's first epic motion picture. The film cost $110,000 ($2.56 million today), filled 12 reels, and clocked in at 190 minutes. The final product premiered in Los Angeles as *The Clansman*, but was retitled *The Birth of a Nation* before it reached Manhattan. Griffith's groundbreaking techniques—including panoramic long shots, iris effects, and night scenes—failed to mask the racist tone of Dixon's prose, prompting NAACP complaints that Griffith had used "every resource of a magnificent new art to picture Negroes in the worst possible light." Riots erupted at screenings in Boston, Philadelphia, and other major cities; some municipalities—Chicago, Denver, Minneapolis, St. Louis, and others—banned the film entirely.[18]

Clearly, the movie needed help.

On January 27, 1915, Dixon wrote to Woodrow Wilson in Washington, asking him to personally witness "the birth of a new art—the launching of the mightiest engine for mould-ing public opinion in the history of the world." Wilson was qualified to judge it, Dixon wrote, "not as the Chief Magistrate of the Republic but as a former scholar and student of history and sociology."[19] Dixon and Griffith joined Wilson for a White House screening on February 18, and after the closing credits, Wilson allegedly said, "It's like writing history with lightning, and my only regret is that it is all so terribly true."[20]

The next day, seeking further endorsement, Dixon approached Chief Justice Edward White with an offer to view the film. White refused, until Dixon mentioned the KKK, then asked, "You tell the true story of the Klan?"

"Yes," Dixon replied, "for the first time."

"I was a member of the Klan, sir," White confided. "Through many a dark night, I walked my sentinel's beat through the ugliest streets of New Orleans with a rifle on my shoul-der. You've told the true story of that uprising of outraged manhood?"

"In a way I'm sure you'll approve," Dixon said.

"I'll be there!" White vowed.[21]

And so he was, with "scores of high officials" from Congress and the State Department, flanked by numerous reporters.[22] White emerged to praise the film, but later backpedaled in the face of public criticism, angrily denying "rumors" that he had endorsed it.[23] President Wilson, likewise, soon thought better of his praise for Griffith's work. He would deny the "lightning" quote—today attributed by some historians to Dixon himself—while presidential aide Joseph Tumulty told journalists, "The President was entirely unaware of the nature of the play before it was presented and at no time has expressed his approbation of it." Wilson finally went further still, writing that he disapproved of Griffith's "unfortunate production."[24]

Belated second thoughts accomplished nothing. *The Birth of a Nation* earned $10 mil-lion during its initial run, inflated to $50 million by 1939, when *Gone with the Wind* finally broke its record as Hollywood's highest-grossing film.[25] Violence followed the film across country. Southern audiences peppered movie screens with gunfire at the first appearance of the film's black rapist (played by a white actor in blackface), and one white viewer in Lafayette, Indiana, left the theater to kill the first black teenager he saw. It all thrilled Dixon to his very core. "The real purpose of my film," he proudly declared, "was to revolutionize Northern audiences that would transform every man into a Southern partisan for life."[26]

The movie's Atlanta premiere, on December 6, made a perfect launching platform for the reborn Klan. Simmons plastered the city with recruiting posters, bought newspaper ads—"A Classy Order of the Highest Class ... No 'Rough Necks,' 'Rowdies,' nor 'Yellow Streaks' Admitted"—and circulated photos of Klansmen featuring black models masked and robed.[27] Now, all he had to do was sit back and wait for the cash to roll in.

Or, so he thought.

Lean Years

At first, it seemed that Simmons might be vindicated in his dream. Ninety-two recruits joined the Klan within two weeks of its coming-out party, while Simmons hired a local firm to make robes on the cheap, for sale at a substantial profit.[28] The order soon expanded into Alabama, claiming more than 1,000 members by early 1917, but there it stalled. "There were

William Simmons (in skull mask) leads an early Klan meeting, ca. 1915–1922 (Library of Congress).

times," Simmons later admitted, "during those five early years, before the public knew of the Klan, when I walked the streets with my shoes worn through because I had no money." One observer noted that imperial headquarters "had less strength in Atlanta than the B'nai B'rith."[29]

War raged in Europe for nearly three years before the United States joined in, on April 6, 1917. Simmons knew a good thing when he saw it, hoping to profit from a surge of rampant paranoia on the home front. His model was the American Protective League, a vigilante organization founded by Chicago advertising executive A. M. Briggs, who won a federal endorsement for his group to serve as "a volunteer unpaid auxiliary of the Department of Justice." Claiming 250,000 members in 600 cities, the APL joined local police and agents from the Bureau of Investigation (later called the FBI), in mass arrests of "slackers" and harassment of "radical" labor unions, chiefly the Industrial Workers of the World (IWW).[30]

It was exciting, but Simmons hit a roadblock when the APL declined affiliation with his Klan. He consoled himself by joining forces with the smaller Citizens' Protective League. Klansmen shadowed suspected spies and saboteurs, marched with patriotic signs, and arranged the disappearance of selected labor organizers in Alabama.[31] In Birmingham, its raids on local hoodlums impressed police chief T. J. Shirley so much that he joined the order and urged his counterpart in Nashville, Tennessee, to form a klavern.[32]

The war prompted a change in Klan recruiting. As Simmons explained, "I issued a decree during the war submerging membership in the Klan. Our secret service work made this imperative. I ordered members to keep their membership in the Klan a secret from everybody, except each other. I told them not to admit publicly that they belonged to the Klan. Membership in the Klan was *always* a secret thereafter."[33] Perhaps *too* secret, in fact. Despite Atlanta's best efforts, by war's end, total membership remained "well under 2,000."[34]

The wizard needed help, and he found it close to home.

Bonanza

In 1919, while Simmons struggled to expand the Klan, Atlanta residents Edward Young Clarke and Mary Elizabeth Tyler founded the Southern Publicity Association, promoting clients that included the Salvation Army, YMCA, Anti-Saloon League, Armenian Relief Fund, and the Theodore Roosevelt Memorial Association. The latter group sued Clarke for embezzling $5,000, and there were other indications that he might not personify the Klan's ideal of Christian fundamentalist morality. Although a married man, he was arrested once with Tyler—both inebriated, nearly nude—when police stormed an Atlanta brothel.[35] Simmons chose to ignore such peccadilloes, focused with single-minded zeal on the promotion of his brainchild.

Clarke met Simmons in 1920, after Clarke's son-in-law joined the Klan. At the time, Clarke said, Simmons "couldn't pay his rent. The receipts were not sufficient to take care of his personal needs.... After we had investigated it from every angle, we decided to go into it with Colonel Simmons and give it the impetus that it could best get from publicity." It helped that Clarke's brother was managing editor of the *Atlanta Constitution.*[36]

Seduced by visions of wealth, Simmons named Clarke and Tyler to head a new Klan "Propagation Department," granting them 80 percent of all revenue received. The partners divided America into nine "domains," each administered by "grand goblins" based in Atlanta, Boston, Chicago, Houston, Los Angeles, New York City, St. Louis, and Washington, D.C. Beneath the goblins, each state was supervised by a "king kleagle." Lesser kleagles (recruiters) peddled Klan memberships at 10 dollars per head (the "klecktoken"). From each klecktoken, kleagles kept four dollars, king kleagles banked one dollar, grand goblins kept 50 cents, and $4.50 went to Atlanta. Clarke and Tyler claimed $2.50 for themselves, depositing the remainder for Simmons in the Klan's imperial treasury. By September 1921, Klan membership had leaped from an estimated 3,000 to 100,000, earning more than $1.5 million ($19.5 million today), including sale of robes, literature, and other paraphernalia. Simmons personally made $170,000 in "commissions" for doing next to nothing.[37]

Salesmanship alone was not enough to boost the Klan, however. Throughout the First World War and the "Red Scare" that followed, white Protestant Americans were obsessed with race and revolution. Between 1900 and 1920, some 14.5 million immigrants from Southern and Eastern Europe, nearly all Catholics or Jews, had flocked to the United States, prompting President Wilson to warn that "any man who carries a hyphen about with him carries a dagger that he is ready to plunge into the vitals of this Republic whenever he gets ready." Psychologist William McDougall proposed that Washington create a Bureau of Eugenics, to keep the white race pure. Boston attorney Prescott Hall diagnosed a "lust for equality" and the "fatuous belief in universal suffrage" as symptoms of mental illness. Communist revolution in Russia and thousands of post-war strikes in America raised the specter of global Bolshevik domination. Migration of 750,000 African Americans, lured from Dixie to wartime industrial jobs in the North, sparked a new wave of lynchings and white riots spanning the county from Knoxville, Tennessee, to Chicago, Omaha, and Washington. Wartime prohibition of liquor became permanent in January 1920, under the Constitution's Eighteenth Amendment, with legal sanctions imposed by the Volstead Act.[38]

Clearly, there was much for the Klan's self-proclaimed "100-percent Americans" to do in the postwar era. If they went about it in a heavy-handed way—as when Tulsa's "Knights of Liberty" flogged, then tarred and feathered 17 alleged IWW members in November 1917[39]—what of it?

Imperial Headquarters would soon discover there was no such thing as bad publicity.

Exposed

Northern newspapers were divided in their coverage of Klan affairs. The *New York Herald* was mostly complimentary, describing Simmons as "a powerful man, something over 40 years of age, smooth-shaven, clear-eyed, deep-voiced, more than six feet tall. When he grasps your hand you feel that he has to hold himself back to keep from crushing it."[40] Joseph Pulitzer's competing *New York World* was less enamored of the KKK.

Beginning on September 6, 1921, the *World* published a three-week series of caustic exposés on the Klan, syndicated to 15 other major papers ranging from Boston to Seattle, Milwaukee and Minneapolis to New Orleans and Galveston, Texas. The first article—headlined "Ku Klux Klan Wars on Catholics, Jews; Reap Rich Returns"—focused on Klan recruiting methods and mounting profits, crediting the order with five times its actual current membership.[41] On September 7, ex-kleagle Henry Fry of Tennessee condemned the Klan as "un–American, conceived in avarice, sired by ignorance, and damned in greed."[42] The next day's story detailed Klan attempts to infiltrate the U.S. military via New York City's Army and Navy Club, where kleagles received applications "through a semi-secret mailbox."[43] Further articles charged Simmons with plagiarizing verse from 19th-century New York poet Josiah Gilbert Holland in *The Kloran,* mimicking Christian baptism in Klan initiation rituals, and scuttling Klan secrecy when he copyrighted *The Kloran,* thereby making copies publicly accessible through the Library of Congress.[44] Potential recruits were fired up, said the *World,* with "bitter anti–Catholic propaganda," including a fraudulent Knights of Columbus oath, wherein members allegedly vowed to "make and wage relentless war, openly and secretly, against all heretics, Protestants and Masons."[45]

Rounding the home stretch on September 18, *World* reporters turned a spotlight on Ku Klux violence, describing Klansmen as vigilantes who "substitute terrorism for law, kidnap, beat, tar and feather victims, then turn them loose on other communities." Some targets were not so lucky, including four Texas murder victims listed on September 19, among objects of 152 outrages also including 41 floggings and 27 tar-and-feather parties. According to the *World,* "Ku Kluxism as conceived, incorporated, propagated, and practiced has become a menace to the peace and security of every section of the United States." Congress had crushed the original order, *World* reporters recalled, but now they declared that "federal, state, [and] city officials are giving protection to Klan."[46]

Klan headquarters threatened a libel suit against the *World* on September 9, 1921, seeking

$10 million in damages, but finally took no action.[47] Meanwhile, following the *World*'s sixteenth installment on September 21, congressmen Thomas Ryan of New York and Peter Tague of Massachusetts introduced a resolution to investigate the Klan. Edward Clarke feared exposure of his past, tendering his resignation as imperial kleagle, which Simmons declined to accept. In fact, the *World* series had boosted Klan recruiting, forcing Clarke to hire three secretaries to cope with his correspondence. Many would-be Klansmen joined the order using facsimile membership applications clipped from newspapers. On September 30, Simmons spent $2,000 on telegrams, urging every member of Congress to vote for the proposed investigation.[48] He wrote:

> From our knowledge of the Klan, its membership and activities, we know that the investigation will officially reveal that the Klan was founded only on the principles of democracy, does not countenance religious or racial prejudice, and seeks only to bind together men for mutual service, and is inspired by love of justice, respect for the law, and a deep faith in the glorious future of the American people.[49]

Congress: Round Two

The House of Representatives left the matter to its Committee on Rules, which opened preliminary hearings on October 11, 1921. *World* editor Rowland Thomas led off as the committee's first witness, summarizing details of Klan violence collected by his staff. "Florida and Texas seemed to be the hotheads," Thomas testified. "Other cases were reported from Georgia, from Alabama, and, as I remember it, from Mississippi, from Oklahoma, and, I think, one case from Missouri." In Georgia, a merchant abducted by Klansmen in March 1921, on a charge of passing bad checks, had fatally stabbed one kidnapper and wounded two others, subsequently winning acquittal on a manslaughter charge. At trial, prosecutors were aided by "Capt. W. S. Coburn, who was publicly known and acknowledged in Atlanta at that time as the supreme attorney of the Ku-Klux Klan."[50]

Next on the witness stand was Anderson Wright, until recently New York's king kleagle and national commander of the Klan's ephemeral air force, the Knights of the Air. While discussing Klan finances, Wright was asked if Mary Tyler ranked "over the imperial wizard." His response was telling: "Not officially, no, sir; but unofficially, yes. It is an absolute fact—there is no question about it—that Mrs. Tyler and Mr. Clarke own the Klan and control the Klan in every way. All documents are issued by Clarke, possibly signed by Col. Simmons or possibly signed by his secretary ... using his signature at Mr. Clarke's direction." Tyler was "the directing genius," presently living with Clarke on an estate outside Atlanta. Wizard Simmons was "absolutely sincere" but had "simply been led astray" by his high-pressure promoters. Wright's orders from Clarke had boiled down to "simply starting in and giving the Jews the dickens in New York."[51]

Why had Wright resigned and blown a whistle on the Klan? "My idea," he testified, "was not to expose so much race hatred, which would drive lots of people into the Klan. In other words, there are enough narrow-minded people who would be glad enough to join an order against the Jews, Catholics, foreign born, and Negroes; but if you can show a man where he was simply taken in and made a goat of in order to get money out of him by selling all these mystic contrivances and show him how his money went and the men it was making wealthy and the woman who was behind the whole thing and show him where the man at the head of the order was not receiving any money or the imperial treasury was not receiving any money, I figured the Klansmen should know that and would he glad to know that, whether they had done any violence or anything else.... [W]hen you can show them where their money goes and what a fool he is made and the character of the people getting it, then I think the Klansmen of the country will realize and wake up to what they have gone into."[52]

Wright was followed by O. B. Williamson, a postal inspector who had investigated the Klan for violations of federal law. He found none, but noted that the Klan had recently purchased Lanier University, a Baptist college in Atlanta, for $22,474.32.[53]

William Burns, chief of the Bureau of Investigation, advised the committee that a federal probe of the Klan had been launched and was "going right along," with no results available.[54] His statement is intriguing, but ultimately useless. No reports of any such investigation presently remain in FBI files, and published accounts universally agree that the Bureau took no interest in the Klan until September 1922, following a double murder in Louisiana.[55] Considering Burn's background as a Red-hunting strikebreaker, and his dismissal from the Bureau for corruption in 1924, it is likely that he simply lied to Congress in an effort to appear efficient.[56]

Next up was William Trotter of Boston, spokesman for the National Equal Rights League of Colored Americans, who described the Klan as "a private, unofficial organization which interferes with the actions and activities and personal liberty of persons and citizens, most of whom are outside of its own membership, millions of them being ineligible to membership because of the rightful unchanging conditions of race and religion." Its tactics included "a method of coercion, through the agencies of terror and of corporal punishment."[57] The Rev. S. E. J. Watson testified that Alexander Johnson, a black bellboy in Texas, had been "whipped almost to the point of death," then branded with the letters "KKK" on his forehead for being "friendly" with white hotel guests. Another victim, white Episcopal archdeacon Philip Irwin, had been tarred and feathered in Miami for leading a black congregation.[58] The Rev. N. A. N. Shaw, president of the Boston-based Equal Rights League, quoted a statement from New England grand goblin A. J. Pardon that Klansmen planned to "annihilate Negroes as American citizens."[59]

First to speak on the Klan's behalf was Atlanta attorney Paul Etheridge, doubling as imperial klonsel (legal counsel) and a member of Fulton County's Board of Commissioners. He denied that Mary Tyler played any role in directing Klan affairs, and described Edward Clarke's suburban estate as "a very modest cottage" standing on "something like 20 acres of as poor land as we have in Fulton County. It is out in the woods, so to speak."[60]

Wizard Simmons would be the committee's star witness, but before he appeared, Georgia congressman W. D. Upshaw provided a testimonial to the Klan leader's "sterling character." Upshaw said, "I can not know what all Col. Simmons has been doing behind closed doors, but I do know that, as a sturdy and inspiring personality, as a heroic veteran of the Spanish-American War, as an honored Knight Templar and member of something like a dozen other honored and well-known fraternities, as a consecrated churchman, and a God-fearing citizen, he is as incapable of an unworthy, unpatriotic motive, word or deed as the chairman of this committee, the Speaker of the House of Representatives, or the President of the United States."[61]

Simmons began his testimony with a plea of illness. "I may not look sick," he granted.

"My sickness is not expressed in looks. I belong to the Irish race, and I believe if I was dead, I would be a handsome corpse. I have suffered with an attack of tonsillitis combined with laryngitis, which developed into bronchitis with threatened pneumonia. So it looks like I have had all the 'itises.'... I will state to you frankly that at any time, under the strain of talking, I am liable to have a coughing spell that may result in a vomiting spell, which has been with me now for over 10 days."[62]

That said, Simmons recounted his history and credentials, detailed his youthful vision of the Klan reborn, and its eventual foundation in 1915 "for the purpose of memorializing the great heroes of our national history, inculcating and teaching practical fraternity among men, to teach and encourage a fervent, practical patriotism toward our country, and to destroy from the hearts of men the Mason and Dixon line and build thereupon a great American solidarity and a distinctive national conscience which our country sorely stands in need of." Despite traitors in the ranks who looted the Klan's treasury, Simmons remained "true to the dictates of unsullied honor" and "steered the infant organization through dangerous channels and finally succeeded in making good in the payment of all debts and starting the institution about a year ago upon a nationwide expansion."[63]

Reports of Klan profiteering were false, Simmons declared. His home had indeed been purchased by Klansmen, "not by the Klan, but by voluntary subscriptions of 25 cents and 50 cents and a dollar." As for violence, "If the Knights of the Ku Klux Klan has been a lawless organization, as has been charged, it would not have shown the remarkable growth it has, for in the Klan is as fine a body of representative citizens as there is in the United States.... These men would not stand for lawlessness."[64]

Lanier University, Simmons averred, "does not teach nor even touch the Knights of the Ku Klux Klan; I mean, in its teaching. The only two courses that are compulsory, in addition to the standard collegiate curriculum, is a course in the fundamentals of our civilization, which are the tenets of the Christian religion, using the Holy Bible as a basic textbook. The other course is teaching and inculcating the fundamentals of pure Americanism and the development of correct American citizenship." Neither the school's instructors nor trustees, he said, were Klansmen.[65]

Edward Clarke and Mrs. Tyler, likewise, were above reproach in Simmons's view. "When the Klan as a fraternal order could not be hurt by being attacked, a personal character attack was made against Mr. Clarke and Mrs. Tyler, but no statements made in these attacks have been proven. The Klan is at present conducting a searching investigation of these character attacks, and when all facts are in our possession the Klan will officially issue a statement regarding them and give the exact truth."[66] (No such statement was forthcoming.) Simmons clearly erred in saying that "[t]he life, character, and record of every official of the Klan has been searched by those attacking us, but nothing has been found against any of us that would stand the field test of court proof or of proof before this committee," and he lied outright in claiming that Mobile's klavern had lost its charter "due to a very silly, uncalled-for, and ridiculous thing that occurred, prompted by one man who was a member of the Klan" placing the order's name on a petition to clean up the town.[67] In fact, Mobile's Klan was going strong, claiming 2,500 members in 1921.[68]

In a second day of testimony, Simmons extolled the Klan's charitable acts, compared witness Anderson Wright to "Judas Iscariot," and read at length from *The Kloran,* until Chairman Philip Campbell admonished him to summarize for brevity's sake. The subject then returned to Klan finances and membership—95,000 by Simmons's estimate—and the Klan's exclusion of blacks and Jews. Simmons compared it to other exclusive fraternities and claimed the right to discriminate as long as the Klan preached "pro–Americanism." Any innocent missteps, he said, were due to the fact that "this organization is in the act of being born. You cannot compare the actual working of this organization like you can these old fraternal orders that have been here for a hundred years."[69]

Regarding Klan finances, Simmons maintained that since November 1920 he had not done "any detailed work on account of my sickness and sickness in my home, except to answer correspondence addressed to me personally and to have general supervision of the work." Violence by the original Klan was "a matter of history," but Simmons had "never heard of an instance, in my studies, where any innocent man was ever terrorized or anything perpetrated against an innocent person." He denied any knowledge of recent Klan mayhem, but suggested that incidents may have been staged by impostors in "counterfeit" costumes. He would investigate no further, unless "these allegations can be definitely established in a court having jurisdiction."[70]

Simmons concluded with high drama, telling the committee:

> I have come here, as I shall stand before my God on the day of judgment, in justice to your committee, to get the truth as I know it, and I have tried to speak the truth as I knew it in all the statements I have made…. [I]f this organization is unworthy to live let me know it, please, and I shall destroy it. If it is worthy to live, then we as an organization should be accorded our rights as we accord rights to all other organizations, of all races, to live and teach their doctrines to their members, and to go their way in peace and in justice to all mankind…. I want to say to my persecutors and the persecutors of this organization in all honesty and sincerity, no matter to what creed or race you may belong in your persecutions, … that you do not know what you are doing. You are ignorant of the principles as were those who were ignorant of the character and work of the Christ. I can not better express myself than by saying to you who are persecutors of the Klan and myself, "Father, forgive you, for you know not what you do," and "Father, forgive them, for they know not what they do."[71]

And with that, he collapsed in a faint.

Congress ultimately passed no judgment on the Klan, but Simmons was pleased with the hearing's outcome. "Congress gave us the best advertising we ever got," he later declared. "Congress made us."[72]

CHAPTER 4

Glory Days
(1922–1929)

How successful was the Klan's recruiting drive from 1920 to 1922? The lowest estimate of peak national strength, at 2,028,000, is almost certainly conservative, though it claims to include "all male and female persons initiated into the Klan between 1915 and 1944."[1] The highest, at 8,904,887 for 1925 alone, seems both inflated and impossibly precise.[2] Most estimates place peak membership, in 1924 and 1925, between four million and five million. That meant cash for kleagles in the field, for their grand dragons, and for reigning leaders in Atlanta. None spared any effort when it came to boosting numbers and the bottom line.

A Palace Coup

Vast wealth, by 1920s standards, amplified the greed of individuals atop the Ku Klux pyramid. Everyone craved a larger slice of the expanding pie. In November 1921 four of the Klan's top Northern goblins met in Washington, D.C., to discuss the high-handed tactics of Edward Clarke and Mary Tyler. All agreed that the pair should be fired, and Wizard Simmons seemed to agree, but in fact did nothing. Z. R. Upchurch, one of Clarke's top aides, resigned in disgust and went public, claiming that Clarke fed Wizard Simmons liquor while looting the treasury and defrauding various charities linked to the Klan, leaving the order "practically bankrupt."[3] Tyler soon resigned on her own initiative, citing her daughter's illness and "need of rest." In June 1922 Simmons began a six-month vacation from his imperial duties, leaving Clarke as de facto wizard *pro tempore*.[4]

Enter Hiram Wesley Evans, a Texas dentist, who led the Dallas klavern, served briefly as grand titan of Province No. 2, then moved to Atlanta as imperial kligrapp (national secretary), drawing a yearly salary of $7,500 ($104,000 today) plus a share of all fees collected from the 13 realms already chartered. On Clarke's behalf, Evans traveled widely, soon befriending Indiana's up-and-coming Ku Klux powerhouse, David Curtis Stephenson. With Fred Savage, a New York strikebreaker lately appointed to lead the Klan's Department of Investigation, Evans and Stephenson hatched a plot to seize the Klan's reins for themselves. With Simmons absent at Clarke's urging, spurred by Evans, the wheels began to turn.[5]

A national "klonvocation," marking the Klan's seventh anniversary, was scheduled for Thanksgiving 1922. Simmons opened the proceedings with a tearful prayer and a chorus of "Onward Christian Soldiers" that seemed to ensure his pro forma reelection as imperial wizard the following day, but the conspirators had other plans. Arriving at Simmons's home before dawn, Savage and Stephenson warned their chief of a crisis in the making. When the vote was called that morning, dissident Klansmen planned to rise and attack Simmons from the convention floor, defaming his reputation. Savage urged him not to worry, saying, "The first man who insults your name will be killed by a sharpshooter right on the spot as he speaks. There'll be enough of us with firearms to take care of the whole convention, if necessary." Aghast at the thought of a massacre, Simmons bowed to his visitors' suggestion that he endorse Hiram Evans as the Klan's next wizard, while accepting the ceremonial office of emperor, complete with a throne room for greeting visitors. So went the morning's vote, and Simmons was immediately "kicked upstairs," soon stripped of all powers by a revised constitution.[6] Clarke, despite a public resignation from Klan affairs in October 1922, emerged from the coup an imperial giant.[7]

Despite his initial, reluctant support for Evans, Simmons refused to surrender the Klan quietly. In early 1923 he embarked on a national speaking tour, seeking support for a bid to reclaim his brainchild. Evans blocked him with injunctions in some cities, while Stephenson relied on dirty tricks, hiring a sloppy drunk to impersonate Simmons at other stops. On April 2, with Evans out of town, Simmons obtained a temporary injunction barring his rival from headquarters. Another court reversed that ruling six days later, but the legal wrangling dragged on until a three-man commission was formed to run Klan affairs, led by the marshal of Atlanta's municipal court. That panel finally rubber-stamped a settlement drawn up by an "imperial kloncilium" whose 15 members included five Simmons partisans, five Evans men, and five knights chosen at large. The decision went to Evans, commending his "fearless and generous" conduct throughout the dispute. Simmons traded his Klan copyrights for a lifelong stipend of $1,000 per month.[8]

But the battle was not over yet. Feeling cheated by the settlement, Simmons resumed his attacks on Evans, facing a libel suit in return. On November 5, 1923, Philip Fox—editor of the Klan's *Night Hawk* newsletter—shot William Coburn, a lawyer for the "insurgent faction," in his Atlanta office. Convicted of murder despite an insanity plea, Fox received a life sentence on December 21.[9] Evans denied any hand in the slaying, but it hardly mattered. Simmons surrendered, later saying, "This murder was too much for me. I didn't want to fight men who could kill that way."[10]

Edward Clarke fought on, writing to President Calvin Coolidge on December 27 that Evans and company meant to use the Klan as "a cheap political machine." On January 11, 1924, grand dragons loyal to Evans gathered in Washington, voting banishment for Simmons and Clarke.[11] Clarke's ouster seemed pointless, since he had severed all "official" links to the Klan 15 months earlier, but he remained a stubborn obstacle at headquarters until March 1924, when he pled guilty to a violation of the Mann Act—interstate transportation of women for "immoral purposes"—and paid a $5,000 fine.[12] Simmons finally folded, accepting a one-time payment of $145,000 which spelled, as reporters explained, "the complete elimination of Colonel Simmons's connection with the Klan."[13]

It was a new day in the Invisible Empire. Time to look forward.

Expanding Frontiers

The Kloran restricted Klan membership to "picked" adult men, specifically "native born American citizens who believe in the tenets of the Christian religion and owe no allegiance of any degree or nature to any foreign Government, nation, political institution, sect, people, or person."[14] Exclusion of women and minors was typical of most fraternities, but entrepreneurs Clarke and Tyler had quickly recognized that stricture as an obstacle to maximum earnings. Why accept klecktokens only from men, when women and children comprised more than half of the country's white population? Women could also vote, since 1920, which increased the Klan's political potential if those votes were properly controlled.

In 1922 Klan publications such as the *Fiery Cross* and *Fellowship Forum* published letters complaining of the order's ban on female members. The same year saw a Grand League of Protestant Women founded in Texas to merge social work with "white supremacy, protection of womanhood, [and] defense of the flag." A similar group, led by reputed Klansman E. F. Keith, was the White American Protestants, whose members pledged never to employ or vote for immigrants or non–Protestants. Yet another group founded in 1922, Ladies of the Invisible Empire (nicknamed "Loties"), was, despite its title, unconnected to the Klan. Other competing groups included the Dixie Protestant Women's Political League, Hooded Ladies of the Mystic Den, Ladies of the Cu Clux Clan, Ladies of the Golden Den, Ladies of the Golden Mask, Ladies of the Invisible Eye (counting Elizabeth Tyler as a member), Order of American Women, Puritan Daughters of America, Queens of the Golden Mask (led by David Stephenson), and Women's Krusaders.[15]

Before official recognition from Atlanta, would-be Klanswomen became embroiled in the Evans-Simmons feud. In March 1923 Simmons founded Kamelia, absorbing the White American Protestants en masse. Evans fired back in June, creating the rival Women of the Ku Klux Klan and obtaining a court order that dissolved all competing sororities. Simmons filed his own lawsuit against the WKKK, seeking disbandment of any auxiliary using the Klan's name, but saw his petition dismissed as part of the February 1924 settlement with Evans. That ruling also disbanded Kamelia, leaving Simmons adrift in obscurity and alcohol until his death, in May 1945.[16]

Recruiting for the WKKK proceeded swiftly. By November 1923 chapters existed in 36 states, claiming 250,000 members age 16 and older. The group held national klonvocations in 1923, 1926 and 1928, used by outside observers to chart its waxing and waning membership. While some knights feared that female suffrage and Klan membership would promote "masculine boldness and restless independence," others accepted Klanswomen as part of the norm. Imperial headquarters focused on payoffs and power.[17]

Once women were admitted to the order, why not children? In 1923 headquarters launched the Junior Ku Klux Klan for boys age 12 to 17, boasting chapters in 15 states by 1924. A parallel order for girls, the Tri-K Klub, emerged at the same time. Each group had its own klavern meetings, but leadership—and control of the cash—rested firmly in adult hands. In New Jersey, for example, Major Kleagle Leah Bell, wife of the Garden State's grand dragon, supervised the Tri-K girls.[18] Another auxiliary, the Ku Klux Kiddies, welcomed children of both sexes between the ages of three and 12.[19] The Texas realm played to all ages through the order's emphasis on family in 1924, with establishment of a "Kool Koast Kamp" near Rockport, on the Gulf of Mexico, featuring "Moonlight sailing parties, day light yachting.

Women of the KKK join in a Klan parade, ca. 1923–1925 (Library of Congress).

Watermelon parties, boating excursions to strange islands, covered with historical relics of the deep.... Swimming and bathing on sandy shallow beaches for babes or in the BLUE DEEP SERF [*sic*] for grown ups."[20]

Where else might kleagles find members and money? One obvious target was the mass of naturalized U.S. citizens who met the order's other prerequisites as white, Protestant Christians. At least two groups existed to accommodate such recruits. The Royal Riders of the Red Robe, led by a "grand ragon"—*dragon* minus the "d"—was active nationwide by November 1922, with chapters from Seattle to New Jersey.[21] Another, the American Krusaders, published its ritual from "supreme headquarters" in Little Rock, Arkansas, in 1924.[22] Both groups pointedly excluded immigrants from Greece, Italy and the Balkans, regardless of their religion.[23]

Jews and Roman Catholics would never qualify for knighthood in the Klan, regardless of their views on race or politics, but halting efforts were made to recruit a "colored division" of "Protestant Negroes" in Indiana and elsewhere. While promised "all the rights of membership," black Klansmen would be strictly segregated, dressed in red robes with blue masks and white capes, never rallying in public with white knights or handling any Klan funds. No evidence exists of any takers for the scheme.[24]

Alien Knights

Unlike the first Klan's 1868 prescript, *The Kloran* set no geographical boundaries upon the invisible empire, aside from its requirement that members must be native-born U.S. citizens. Once that bulwark was breached, with formation of auxiliaries for naturalized Americans, the order saw its way clear to expand worldwide. Canada was a natural target, and

Montreal produced the Klan's first Canadian newspaper advertisement on October 1, 1921. British Columbia was next, with an ad in the *Cranbrook Courier* on November 17, 1922. Kleagles reached Ontario in September 1923, and Saskatchewan in November 1926. They played primarily to anger against "unassimilable" immigrants and Catholic "subversion" of public schools, but they were flexible. As Hoosier kleagle Pat Emory later explained, "We fed the people 'antis.' Whatever we found that they could be taught to hate and fear, we fed them."[25]

As in the States, that recipe proved successful. By 1928 there were at least 100 klaverns in Saskatchewan, claiming 40,000 members, though outsiders placed the true number closer to 25,000. Moose Jaw hosted the Canadian Klan's largest rally—some 7,000 knights—on June 7, 1927. In February of that year, Vancouver Klansmen passed a resolution demanding "complete prohibition of Asiatic immigration into Canada, repatriation of all Asiatics at present domiciled in this country, and expropriation of their property ... with fair recompense." From the Maritime Provinces, kleagle C. L. Fowler, wrote, "As I see the situation we shall have no trouble at all along the border land. The entire territory from Nova Scotia which is richly and predominantly Protestant and all along via Quebec, Montreal, Ottawa and Toronto should be fine territory and should make it possible for us to gather in large numbers at once." As for New Brunswick, he added, "the men up there are wild for the organization."[26]

Typically, Klan expansion soon led to intimidation, violence, and scandal. In 1922 Klan threats preceded fires at Catholic churches; a Catholic rest home in Oka, Québec; and at Manitoba's Université de Saint-Boniface, claiming 10 lives on November 25, 1922. A "strange man" was seen lurking on campus in the latter case, but Manitoba's provincial fire commissioner blamed the tragedy on careless student smoking.[27] Klansmen have also been named as suspects in the unsolved Kettle Valley Railway bombing of October 29, 1924, near Farron, British Columbia. The blast killed eight persons, including exiled Russian Peter "Lordly" Verigin, quasi-deity of the Doukhobor ("spirit wrestlers") religious sect. Conspiracy theorists speculate that American knights may have killed Verigin to prevent his followers from moving to Oregon.[28]

Greed also helped to discredit Canada's Klan. In June 1927 kleagles Pat Emmons, Lewis Scott, and son Harold Scott absconded with most of the Saskatchewan realm's treasury. Police caught Emmons in Florida with $20,000, while the Scotts escaped to Australia with $500,000. Emmons alone returned for trial, and was acquitted upon demonstrating that Toronto headquarters had granted him carte blanche in handling provincial funds. Strangely, the trial boosted recruiting in Saskatchewan, where membership peaked in 1928, including no less then eight mayors, 11 village clerks, seven reeves, 12 secretary-treasurers, and 37 councilors.[29]

Postwar Germany, seething under harsh terms of the Treaty of Versailles, also offered fertile soil for right-wing radicals who blamed the nation's plight on Jews and traitors. The Rev. Otto Strohschein, a naturalized U.S. citizen from Germany, returned home in February 1921 with his son, Gotthard, and native-born Klansman Donald Gray. Together, they founded the German Order of the Fiery Cross, planting three klaverns in Berlin, claiming more than 1,000 members nationwide before the Strohscheins left in 1925, to proselytize in Silesia. With their departure, Richard Brant assumed command of the order, titling himself "Wotan" and penning an oath that read, in part: "If I should betray the aims of this order,

I will take upon myself the most frightful martyrdom. All my bones shall be broken, my eyes shall be gouged out, my body drawn, quartered, and thrown to the vultures." In September 1926 Jewish residents of Cologne received letters saying, "Hebrew, we warn you for the first time that when you see the fiery cross, think of your hour of death." Klansmen joined in pogroms and street fighting until 1933, when Adolf Hitler assumed power as Germany's chancellor. *Der Führer* tolerated no competition for the hearts and minds of "Aryan" anti–Semites, and the German Order of the Fiery Cross was soon extinct.[30]

In November 1924, Klan fliers appeared in Czechoslovakia. As reported by the *New York Times,* the Czech Klan was "being formed on the American plan and is against Germans, Jews, Clericals and Communists."[31] July 1928 brought news of Klan chapters in Lithuania, wearing traditional robes and burning crosses "with the avowed purpose of undermining the work of the Catholic Church."[32]

Farther afield, black-robed knights kidnapped José Campos, editor of Mexico City's *Excelsior* newspaper, in August 1923, after the paper ran articles denouncing the Klan and denying its existence in Mexico.[33] One day later, from Australia, came reports that "nearly 1,000" Klansmen had organized in Auckland, New Zealand, "to combat Asiatic labor and traders."[34] Nothing more was heard of Klans Down Under or in Mexico, until Australia's order was revived six decades later.

Onward Christian Soldiers

Racism was a facet of the modern Klan, as with its Reconstruction ancestor, but modern knights concerned themselves as much with the morality of neighbors—often white—as with their attitudes on race or politics. As expressed in Ku Klux publications, "We magnify the Bible—as the basis of our Constitution, the foundation of our government, the source of our laws, the sheet-anchor of our liberties, the most practical guide to right living, and the source of all true wisdom.... We honor the Christ as the Klansman's *Only Criterion of Character*.... We believe that the highest expression of life is in service and in sacrifice for that which is right; that selfishness can have no place in a true Klansman's life and character; but that he must be moved by unselfish motives, such as characterized our Lord the Christ and moved Him to the highest service and the supreme sacrifice for that which was right."[35] The gross hypocrisy behind those words would take time to sink in.

In many towns, the Klan's first public outing was a visit to some local church. Masked knights would interrupt a Sunday service, marching in formation to the pulpit, where their leader would hand money to the minister, then either silently retreat or fill a pew reserved for them by prearrangement with the pastor. Nationwide, an estimated 40,000 preachers joined the Klan, often serving as a klavern's first exalted cyclops. Others—including 26 of the Klan's 39 "klokards" (national lecturers)—became itinerant Ku Klux evangelists. In Colorado, North Dakota, Pennsylvania and Texas, fundamentalist preachers ruled as the states' grand dragons.[36] Nor were the ministers who chose a klannish path all backwoods snake-handlers. In fact, they included some of the decade's most prominent spokesmen for God.

One such was Robert Shuler, Sr., nicknamed "Fighting Bob" by his admirers for his tendency to rail at Jews and Catholics, police and politicians. Born in a Tennessee log cabin and ordained in the Methodist Episcopal Church, South, Shuler preached across Dixie before settling in Los Angeles and founding America's first "megachurch," Trinity Methodist. He was also one of the country's first radio preachers, until revocation of his broadcasting license in 1931. A year later, he ran for the U.S. Senate as a Prohibition Party candidate, collecting more than half a million votes.[37] No proof exists that Shuler personally joined the Klan, but we may logically infer it from his fervent endorsements. In 1921, after a notorious vigilante raid that left one Klan constable dead, Shuler praised the fallen officer as "every inch an American hero." Touring California during 1922, Shuler proclaimed that he would "rather die than to have the Klan disbanded under the existing condition." To Shuler, "the solemn march of the American men of the Ku Klux Klan is as sweet music as my ears have ever heard." In fact, he could not understand why "any 100 percent American should not join the Ku Klux Klan." Six hundred knights in full regalia used Trinity Methodist for a seminar on the "KKK and Citizenship" in July 1924. Atlanta, in return, praised Shuler as "a fair-minded man with real American blood in [his] veins."[38]

Billy Sunday was another favorite with Klansmen. A mediocre professional baseball player in the 1880s, Sunday abandoned sports for a fundamentalist pulpit in 1890, working his way up from YMCA lectures to fame as an evangelist on the Midwestern "kerosene circuit," so called because most small towns lacked electricity. Sunday preached "masculine" Christianity, with emphasis on banning alcohol, a stance that leads historians to credit him in part for Prohibition's passage in 1919. As with Bob Shuler, no documentary evidence exists linking Sunday to the Klan, but biographer William McLoughlin grants that "it seems undeniable that there was a high correlation between Sunday's supporters in the 1920s and the members of the Klan." Sunday welcomed masked Klansmen—and their cash—to his revivals in at least four states, beginning with a $50 donation delivered in Richmond, Indiana, in May 1922. Similar incidents occurred in Tennessee (April 1923), West Virginia (July 1923), and Louisiana (March 1924). Sunday praised Klansmen for "assisting" police on vice raids, and when asked if he preached Ku Klux sermons, replied in the affirmative, saying, "For when an American service is preached the Klan endorses it."[39]

Yet another prominent friend of the Klan was Robert "Bob" Jones, Sr., founder of a Southern preaching dynasty and of ultraconservative Bob Jones University. The son of a Confederate veteran, raised in poverty on an Alabama farm, Shuler staged his first revival at age 12, claiming 60 converts. Licensed as a Methodist circuit preacher at 15, by the 1920s Jones ranked second only to Billy Sunday as a renowned traveling evangelist. Like Sunday, Jones accepted Klan donations at his services. He also endorsed known Klansmen for public office, notably Alabama governor Bibb Graves, whom Jones considered a comrade. Another "close personal friend," William Simmons, invited Jones to join the Klan, but Jones allegedly declined. Nonetheless, in 1928 Jones collaborated with Klansmen opposing presidential candidate Al Smith, a Catholic, on grounds that Smith might be manipulated from the Vatican.[40] Nearly half a century later, Bob Jones, Jr., marked the passing of Pope Paul VI by branding the pontiff an "archpriest of Satan, a deceiver, and he has, like Judas, gone to his own place."[41] Bob Sr. was also a lifelong segregationist, an attitude mirrored by his heirs and university, which barred black students until 1971 and forbade interracial dating until the 21st century.[42]

The nearest thing to a true Klan church was Alma White's Pillar of Fire congregation in Zarephath, New Jersey. Branded "holy rollers" for their religious frenzies, White's flock displayed a mix of feminism, racism, anti–Semitism, anti–Catholicism, and opposition to immigration. In 1922 White told a Brooklyn audience, "The Klansmen stand for the supremacy of the white race, which is perfectly legitimate and in accordance with the teachings of the Holy Writ, and anything that has been decreed by the Almighty should not work a hardship on the colored race.... It is within the rights of civilization for the white race to hold the supremacy; and no injustice to the colored man to stay in the environment where he was placed by the Creator."[43] In 1923 the Klan bought White's Alma College, leaving her in charge as president, openly pleased that Klan membership would "sweep through the intellectual student classes as through the masses of the people."[44] Two years later, she published *The Ku Klux Klan in Prophecy*, declaring, "The unrepentant Hebrew is everywhere among us today as the strong ally of Roman Catholicism.... The Jews in New York City openly boast that they have the money and Rome the power, and that if they decide to rule the city and state, it is their prerogative."[45] In *Heroes of the Fiery Cross* (1928), White wrote, "The Jews are as unrelenting now as they were 2,000 years ago."[46]

White's congregation nearly suffered martyrdom for its Klan ties in May 1923, when 1,000 furious opponents surrounded their church, pelting it with stones until police arrived.[47] Two decades later, White reprinted her various pro–Klan essays in a three-volume work titled *Guardians of Liberty,* albeit with some revisions. "My people are not members of the Klan," she wrote, "but we agree with some of the things that they stand for to assert our American right of free speech. We have always stood for 100 percent Americanism and so does the Klan, so naturally we agree there." And one page later: "We have no connection with the Klan organization. We endorse them in the principles for which they stand. However there is no room in our hearts for racial prejudice."[48] Still, she could not resist defending slavery, writing, "The slaveholder, in many instances, was as much to be pitied as the slaves. He, too, was a victim of the system.... Where the slaves were well treated they were happy and contented.... But some radicals could never see this side of the question."[49] Only in 1997 would White's heirs publicly repent of prior associations with the Klan.[50]

Religious affiliation did not exempt some Protestant pastors from the Klan's hostile attention. On June 30, 1924, Klansmen kidnapped the Rev. Oren Van Loon of Berkeley, California's Community Church, after he preached a sermon against cross-burnings. Van Loon surfaced 11 days later, in Battle Creek, Michigan, delirious and raving, his back branded with the letters "KKK."[51] Speculation also links the Klan to a still-unsolved murder of Episcopal minister Edward Hall and his lover, Eleanor Mills, shot in New Brunswick, New Jersey, in September 1922. Prosecutors indicted Hall's widow and her brothers but failed to convict them. Decades

Bishop Alma White, a staunch supporter of the 1920s Klan (Library of Congress).

later, author William Kunstler theorized that Klansmen killed the couple as punishment for their adultery.[52]

A strange twist on Protestant fundamentalism came from "Christian Identity," an off-shoot of 19th-century British Israelism, which holds that Western Europeans are the direct lineal descendants of the "Ten Lost Tribes" of Israel. As interpreted by Oregon clergyman Reuben Sawyer, active in the Klan from 1921 through 1924, that marked Jews as servants of Satan and the progenitors of godless Communism. Over time, that view evolved into a "two-seedline" theory, wherein Adam fathered Abel, whose descendants included Noah, Abraham, David, and Jesus. Brother Cain, however, was the spawn of Satan, who seduced Eve in a serpent's form. The heirs to that sin include Ham, Ahab, and Judas Iscariot.[53] Blacks, as theorized by author Charles Carroll in 1900, were not human at all, but rather soulless pre–Adamite beasts somehow ignored in scripture.[54] By 1946, Klansman and Identity minister Wesley Swift would claim that blacks were not of Earth at all, but had been "brought in from other planets in the Milky Way" by Lucifer.[55]

Ku Klux "Justice"

The Klan's combination of racism, religious bigotry, and ultra-moralism led inevitably to the kind of vigilante action that distinguished its progenitor. Some states were spared the violence, but most experienced fiery cross warnings to "undesirable" elements, often followed by floggings, tar-and-feather raids, mutilation, arson, and murder. Targets included Catholics and Jews, nonwhites caught straying from "their place," and "radicals" who risked their lives to organize workers. Frequently, though, Klan victims were white Gentile Protestants, whose actual or rumored behavior offended some klavern's notion of fundamentalist morality.

No definitive tally of Klan crimes exists. The *New York World*'s 12-month list, published in September 1921, included two murders, one attempted lynching, 39 whippings (with two victims also branded), 20 tar-and-feather raids (nine victims also flogged), one castration, one strong-arm robbery, and one church arson. Most of those crimes occurred in Texas, where one Klansman also lost his life in a botched kidnapping.[56]

Exposure of those incidents, as we have seen, drew members to the order rather than repelling them, and there was more to come. In Farmville, Virginia, the Klan announced its 1921 arrival with placards warning "Gamblers, Bootleggers, High-Speeders, Thieves, Crooks, Houses of Ill Fame and Proprietors" to depart.[57] Arkansas knights hanged a suspected arsonist and joined police for vice raids, killing one man in Smackover and jailing dozens more.[58] Klansmen stalked hostile attorney Leroy Percy in Greenville, Mississippi, but botched a plot to abduct him.[59] Prosecutors in Duplin County, North Carolina, credited the Klan with 25 of their 27 convictions for 1923.[60] Colorado's grand dragon personally threatened a young playboy with castration if he failed to wed his pregnant girlfriend.[61] Similar tales emerged from most states where the Klan organized—which was all 48, in the Twenties—but some stood out for the frequency and severity of their mayhem.

Texas, ground zero for much of the Klan's early violence, maintained that reputation through the 1920s with more than 500 whippings and other attacks reported.[62] In neighboring Oklahoma, Governor Jack Walton declared martial law to suppress epidemic nightriding, but overstepped his bounds by trying to strong-arm state legislators and was removed

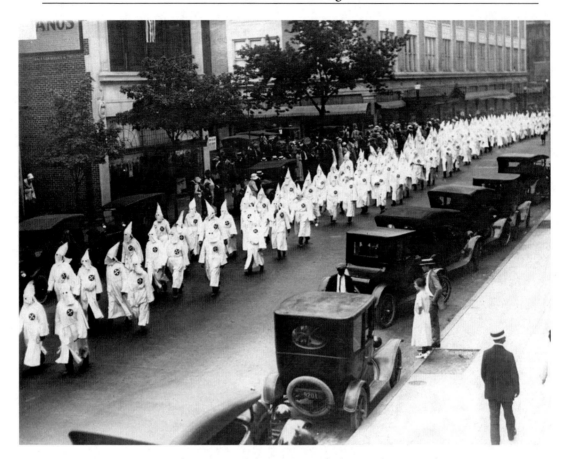

1920s Klansmen march in Virginia (Library of Congress).

from office by impeachment.[63] Things were nearly as bad in Georgia, home to imperial head-quarters, where prominent knights included the governor, attorney general, and chief justice of the state's supreme court.[64] Alabama, with its government and law enforcement agencies thoroughly infested, witnessed scores—perhaps hundreds—of floggings, often encouraged by officers such as Birmingham police chief T. J. Shirley, while knights in high office feigned blindness.[65]

The real surprise for most Americans was not Klan violence in Dixie, but rather its eruptions in the North and West. Pennsylvania's knights indulged in flogging, tortured two black men to death, shot up a black Boy Scout camp, and were suspected in the still-unsolved disappearance of a three-year-old Pittsburgh girl abducted from her home.[66] Arizona Klans-men whipped at least three victims and branded a high school principal with acid.[67] The masked invasion of a black family's home in Lewiston, Idaho, prompted a shoot-to-kill order against nightriders.[68] Klansmen flogged the mayor of Liberty, Kansas, when he refused to let them meet at City Hall.[69] In Buffalo, New York, members killed a private detective who infiltrated the order, losing one of their own in the shootout.[70]

Chicago spawned a host of violent gangs during Prohibition, but "Bloody Williamson" County, downstate, also saw its share of action as Klansman Glenn Young led his knights to war against bootleggers. Young was a rogue, fired by the Treasury Department's Prohibition

Unit after four months of service, when supervisors "found him to be of a belligerent nature, prone to make threats of violence ... and apparently convinced that he is a law within himself." That sounded good to Klan leaders in Herrin, who invited Young to close the county's roadhouses and raid the homes of Catholics who made small quantities of wine for personal consumption. In the process, Young beat up a restaurateur and was charged with assault, winning acquittal when he led his knights to court armed with pistols and a machine gun. Anti-Klan forces armed for battle, killing one knight on February 8, 1924. Members of the liquor-trading Shelton gang soon joined the fray, bringing National Guardsmen to Herrin after Young declared himself acting police chief. In May gunmen ambushed Young's car, wounding him and blinding his wife. Klansmen retaliated, killing one of the suspected shooters. Twenty-odd persons died before the Klan expelled Young in September—for "ostentatious display of firearms and braggadocio," coupled with "inordinate craving for personal publicity"—but only death would stop him. In January 1925 he shot it out with an anti–Klan deputy sheriff. Both men died in the exchange of fire, along with two bystanders.[71]

California kleagles recruited many law enforcement officers in their attempt to purge the Golden State of sin. Departments of all sizes were infested, from Los Angeles and San Francisco to Bakersfield and tiny Taft, where officers supervised flogging parties at the local ballpark.[72] Klan kops made their most impressive headlines in Inglewood, an L.A. suburb, for a liquor raid in April 1922. They tried to snatch bootlegger Fidel Elduayen, but were interrupted by a city marshal who demanded their surrender. When the gunsmoke cleared, Constable Medford Mosher lay dead in his robe; his son and another Klansman were wounded. A grand jury indicted King Kleagle Gus Price and 42 other knights, including another patrolman. Jurors acquitted them all, and when federal agents jailed Elduayen for bootlegging, the charges were later dismissed.[73]

Masked Politics

In September 1924 Hiram Evans told a Kansas City klonvokation, "The Klan is not in politics, neither is it a political party." Eighteen months later, in Dallas, he contradicted himself, saying, "The policies of the Klan have been changed, and it is now completely out of politics. It is not interested in the candidacy of any many or woman."[74]

Neither statement was true.

From its foundation in 1915 the modern Klan had recruited and supported politicians in Georgia and Alabama, expanding its scope as new klaverns and realms were chartered. Southern knights were Democrats, like their forefathers, while Klansmen in the North and West backed whichever party seemed more receptive and willing to help them advance their agenda. The order tried its hand at politics in every state, with sharply mixed results.

Georgia governor Clifford Walker (1923–27) was a Klansman, as were countless lesser officeholders, from the state legislature to small town mayors, sheriffs, and judges. Klan letters survive from the Twenties, addressed to "brother" Richard Russell, Sr., chief justice of Georgia's Supreme Court. No proof exists pro or con for Senator Tom Watson, who had clamored for a Klan revival in 1915, but he did turn up to shake hands with William Simmons during the House Rules Committee's investigation in October 1921.[75]

In Alabama, Bibb Graves used his position as exalted cyclops of Montgomery's klavern to win election as governor in 1926, returning for a second term in 1934. Senators "Cotton Tom" Heflin and Hugo Black were both Klansmen when elected, though Black went through the motions of resigning (while accepting a lifelong "passport" to the Invisible Empire). Black's predecessor, Oscar Underwood, had bucked the Klan in 1924 and thus became a one-term senator. In Birmingham, most officeholders were Klansmen, including Sheriff T. J. Shirley and nearly all his deputies.[76]

Political historian Arnold Rice deemed the Klan's influence in Mississippi "negligible," yet Episcopal bishop Duncan Gray, Sr., recalled that "every man running for state office in 1923 was a Klan member, with two exceptions."[77] One avowed member, Theodore Bilbo, won his second term as governor in 1927, advancing to the U.S. Senate in 1935. As late as August 1946 he admitted membership in Bilbo Klan No. 40, a klavern named in his honor.[78]

Texas Klansmen dominated the municipal governments of Dallas, Fort Worth, and Wichita Falls in the 1920s, and ran member Felix Robertson for governor in 1924. He lost the Democratic primary to Miriam "Ma" Ferguson, wife of disgraced ex-governor James Ferguson, running on a platform that included passage of a state anti-mask law. Elected as the country's first female governor, Ferguson kept that promise, but the law was later ruled unconstitutional. Recurring scandals dogged the Ferguson administration—including gubernatorial pardons for 100 convicts per month—and state attorney general Daniel Moody defeated Ferguson's bid for reelection in 1926, despite Ma's claim that he was the Klan's candidate, sworn to pardon knights whom he had convicted while serving as district attorney of Williamson County. The Texas Klan's most controversial candidate was Earle Mayfield, elected to the U.S. Senate in 1922. Defeated rival George Peddy demanded an investigation of the "rigged" election and senators obliged, spending two years on a fruitless search for evidence of wrongdoing before Mayfield took his seat in 1925. Mayfield's bid for reelection failed three years later.[79]

Klansmen swept Colorado's elections in 1924, victorious knights including Governor Clarence Morley, Secretary of State Carl Milliken, U.S. Senator Rice Means, and Denver mayor Benjamin Stapleton. The Klan won a majority of the legislature's lower house and carried municipal offices statewide, except for the Republican stronghold of Colorado Springs. Controversy surrounding Grand Dragon John Locke spoiled that triumph, however, and the order failed to win a single office in 1926.[80]

In Oregon, Klansmen endorsed gubernatorial candidate Walter Pierce in 1922 and carried him to victory. Portland mayor George Baker was a member, as was Kaspar K. Kubli, speaker of the State House of Representatives. Kubli, beloved by Klansmen for his monogram and bigotry, sponsored a bill banning parochial schools in November 1922, despite opposition from Catholics and Seventh-Day Adventists. The bill passed, and Governor Pierce signed it into law, but challenges continued until June 1925, when the Supreme Court ruled it unconstitutional. Other bills penned by Kubli—striking Columbus Day from the state's holiday calendar, banning sacramental wine and taxing Catholic church property while leaving Protestant churches exempt—never made it off the drawing board. He did succeed with the Alien Property Act of 1923, barring Japanese nationals from owning land, and a follow-up excluding foreigners from ownership of any hospitality business.[81]

Nationwide, other prominent Klan officeholders included Indiana governor Edward Jackson, Indianapolis mayor John Duvall, Los Angeles mayor John Porter—and, perhaps, President Warren Harding. Atlanta Klansman Alton Young, on his deathbed in the late

1940s, claimed that he had joined William Simmons and three other members of an "imperial induction team" who initiated Harding in the Green Room of the White House, shortly after his inauguration. Afterward, Harding allegedly gave the knights special War Department license plates, exempting their cars from traffic citations.[82] When Harding died in August 1923, ostensibly from apoplexy, Klansmen blamed his death on Catholic assassins and staged a 50-car mourning motorcade in Tampa, Florida.[83] For years afterward, knights reportedly stood guard at Harding's tomb in Marion Ohio. Half a century later, Imperial Wizard James Venable claimed to have photos of Harding's Klan funeral ceremony, but he never produced them.[84] Scholars have searched in vain for any proof that Harding ever joined the order.

Presidential politics held center stage in 1924, and the Klan became a critical issue at June's Democratic National Convention in New York City. Ku Klux delegates arrived at Madison Square Garden supporting Georgia native William Gibbs McAdoo, Jr., secretary of the treasury under Woodrow Wilson, and dead set against the nomination of New York governor Alfred Smith, a "wet" Catholic linked to Tammany Hall. McAdoo led on the first ballot, with 431.5 votes to Smith's 241, but 17 other hopefuls kept either candidate from claiming the required majority. So it went through 98 more ballots until, on the hundredth, McAdoo slipped to third place, behind Smith and dark horse John Davis, ex-ambassador to Britain. Three more ballots gave the nomination to Davis, with Nebraska governor Charles Bryan as his running mate.[85]

Next it was time to draft the party's platform, and no issue inspired more acrimony than a plank intended to denounce the Klan by name. Debate raged among the convention's

THE END

A Klan cartoon celebrates the order's victory over Al Smith and "Romanism" at the 1924 Democratic National Convention (Library of Congress).

14,000 delegates, climaxed when the anti–Klan plank failed by the closest possible margin: 543³⁄₂₀ to 542⁷⁄₂₀—four-fifths of one vote. Republicans were cagier, taking their cue from President "Silent Cal" Coolidge and ignoring their own party's Klan infestation. In November, Davis trailed Coolidge by a margin of 7.3 million votes.[86]

Klansmen felt triumphant at year's end. They claimed credit for blocking Al Smith's nomination—thereby saving the country from "Rome, Rum, and Ruin"—and for a new Immigration Act passed by Congress in May. Whatever their actual input, the new law had klannish terms, preserving "the ideal of American homogeneity" by virtually excluding Asians and tightening quotas on immigration from Southern and Eastern Europe.[87] What better way for knights to celebrate than by storming the nation's capital?

Marching on Washington

Despite his protestations, Hiram Evans craved political influence, from the smallest towns to Washington, D.C. A year before his false claim that "the Klan is not in politics," he moved imperial headquarters to a suite of offices on Massachusetts Avenue, leaving a second-string team in Atlanta to field inquiries.[88] After the 1924 elections, Evans laid plans for a spectacular event that would electrify the nation and the world: a march through Washington in full regalia, showing off the power of the Ku Klux Klan.

On August 8, 1925, an estimated 50,000 Klansmen and -women trooped down Pennsylvania Avenue with flags and banners, bands and bagpipes, choirs and characters dressed as early American heroes, some knights offering stiff-armed salutes borrowed from Benito Mussolini's Italian Fascists. President Coolidge, invited to review the parade, embarked on a month-long vacation instead, leaving armed marines to guard the U.S. Treasury until the knights packed up and left for home.[89] Overall, it was a grand event, unrivaled for size until 1963, and as such, deserved to be repeated. Why not make the march an annual event?

And so it was—for one more year.

The knights returned to Washington on September 13, 1926, many in new uniforms, this time with two floats. One celebrated the "Little Red Schoolhouse," while the other carried "Miss 100-percent America," holding an open Bible. Despite those flourishes, however, there was no disguising the Klan's shrunken ranks. Membership was on the wane nationwide, reflected in slender columns of fours where Klansmen had marched 16 to 20 abreast one year earlier. Observers pegged their numbers at approximately half the last turnout. The demonstration was embarrassing and would not be repeated.[90]

As to *why* the mighty Klan was fading, that was best explained by looking to the hinterlands where members rallied, ranted, flogged, and killed.

Mer Rouge

On October 2, 1922, Louisiana governor John Parker addressed a letter to President Harding, which read in part:

> Due to the activities of an organized body reputed to be the Ku Klux Klan ... not only have the laws been violated, but men taken out, beaten and whipped. Two men have been brutally

murdered without trial or charges.... [M]y information tonight is that six more citizens have been ordered to leave their homes (in Morehouse Parish) under penalty of death. These conditions are beyond the control of the Governor of this State ... [as] a number of law officers and others charged with the enforcement of law in this State are publicly recognized as members of this Ku Klux Klan.[91]

The murder victims in question were two white cousins, Filmore Daniel and Thomas Richard, who had criticized the Klan despite repeated warnings to desist. Their defiance irked Dr. Bunnie McKoin, ex-mayor of Mer Rouge and exalted cyclops of the local klavern. Kidnapped by Klansmen on August 24, 1922, the men were whipped and otherwise tortured, Daniel castrated by someone "skilled in the use of a surgical knife," before both were dropped into Lake Lafourche. Federal agents were scouring the parish, undercover, when a dynamite blast in the lake brought two nude, headless corpses to the surface. Dr. McKoin, acquitted in a previous homicide case from August 1916, fled to Baltimore but was arrested there and returned for trial on murder charges, slandering Daniel and Richard as "bootleggers, gunmen, and men who kept negro [*sic*] concubines."[92]

Jurors acquitted McKoin and his Klan codefendants, leaving the case officially unsolved, but FBI historians rank it as a triumph of sorts, writing that—

> On a more personal note, [the Bureau] found that "Imperial Kleagle" Clarke had lined his pockets with $8 of each $10 initiation fee he had secured ... and that he was also netting tidy profits from his new-member sales of the Klan's bed-sheet regalia. It also found that he was using his wealth to lead a high life, including taking on a mistress ... and it found he was crossing state lines with her.
>
> Now this last was an interesting point. "How about the Mann Act?" some enterprising Bureau lawyer suggested. "That's a federal law we can use in this case." Accordingly, Clarke was arrested the next trip he made with his mistress over a state line, leading to his guilty plea in federal court.
>
> It was just the beginning of the Bureau's fight to bring these early day domestic terrorists to justice.[93]

The first and last, as we shall see, for over two decades, since FBI agents would not pursue the Klan again until the latter 1940s. A worse deception is manipulation of the dates surrounding Clarke's arrest. He was, in fact, convicted on Mann Act charges in March 1924, 17 months after agents began their Louisiana investigation, but he was *arrested* on those charges in February 1921, 17 months *before* the Daniel-Richard murders. Defense attorneys had delayed his trial for three years with various legal maneuvers.[94] The FBI investigation in Mer Rouge accomplished nothing.

"What Is the Matter with Us?

Florida seethed with vigilante mayhem in the postwar decade. Between March 1919 and November 1929, lynch mobs claimed 50 identified victims, all but three of them black (with one of the whites a Latino).[95] While other Southern states led Florida in the number of lynchings reported, demographics made a difference: Mississippi, Georgia, Louisiana and Alabama boasted higher body counts, yet members of Florida's relatively sparse black population were 12 times more likely to be slain by mobs than African Americans in any other state.[96]

Klansmen, as usual, were in the thick of it.

One of their great fears was black suffrage. Daytona's knights threatened civil rights activist Mary McLeod Bethune in August 1920, but her armed neighbors repelled them. Two months later, blacks were beaten at the polls in Orange County, one left permanently paralyzed. Ocoee, a small all-black town, was wiped off map after black men resisted white efforts to stop them from voting. Officially, the death toll stood at eight, but other estimates range from 35 to 56—the latter supplied by one of the lynchers, who boasted of killing 17 victims himself. Ocoee's survivors fled for their lives, leaving the site deserted.[97]

A year late, in December 1921, Key West Klansmen belatedly noticed saloon owner Manuel Cabeza, owner of a waterfront speakeasy. Illegal liquor sales were serious enough, but Cabeza also kept a mulatto mistress believed to practice voodoo. Knights kidnapped Cabeza on December 23, beating him viciously, leaving him with ruptured kidneys and a coat of hot tar on his flesh, but he rebounded with a vengeance, killing Exalted Cyclops Walter Decker before police and U.S. marines captured him. On Christmas morning, Sheriff Roland Curry dismissed the military guards and sent his deputies home, allowing Klansmen to hang Cabeza and riddle him with bullets. Curry and several of the lynchers died in freak accidents soon afterward, allegedly victims of curses cast by Cabeza's grieving lover.[98]

Next came pogroms at Perry and Rosewood. Inflamed by a white teacher's murder in December 1922, Perry residents immediately lynched the black suspect, then welcomed thousands of reinforcements from Georgia and South Carolina to raze the town's ghetto, burning a church, school, Masonic lodge and an amusement hall, along with many homes. On New Year's Eve, Gainesville hosted a Klan parade that drew "the largest crowd in the history of the city," robed knights bearing banners that proclaimed their goal: "First and Always Protect White Womanhood."[99]

On January 1, 1923, they got their chance. In Sumner, Fannie Taylor spun a tale of rape by an unidentified black man. Sheriff Robert Walker pinned the crime—perhaps a hoax—on Jesse Hunter, a black convict missing from a road gang. Klansmen and allied vigilantes focused their wrath on Rosewood, another all-black town near Sumner, and proceeded to destroy it in a week-long orgy of bloodshed. Once again, official figures minimize the death toll, claiming eight victims, while other published reports mention "nearly 20" and "close to a hundred" dead.[100] That atrocity appalled even the editor of Gainesville's *Daily Sun,* a proud Klansman who praised the order in his newspaper. After Rosewood and the local lynching of a black man charged with stealing a cow, he wrote, "What is the matter with us? Will the blood lust created by the World War never subside? Shall we go on until anarchy reigns supreme and government is dethroned?"[101]

That was a fair question in Gainesville, where both Mayor George Waldo and police chief Lewis Fennell (Waldo's father-in-law) were Klansmen, openly supportive of vigilantism. One local target, Father John Conoley of St. Patrick's Church, angered knights by admitting Protestant university students to his amateur dramatic company, thereby placing them within "the pernicious clutch of Catholicism." In February 1924 three robed Klansmen snatched Conoley from St. Patrick's, beat and castrated him, then left him near death on the steps of a church in Palatka. Conoley survived, naming two of his attackers as Waldo and Fennell, but neither faced prosecution.[102]

A home in flames in Rosewood, Florida, January 1923 (Library of Congress).

The Old Man

No Klansman of the 1920s held more personal power than Indiana grand dragon David Stephenson, dubbed "The Old Man" of Hoosier politics at age 33. A key participant in the coup that deposed William Simmons, Stephenson got his reward when successor Hiram Evans named him to command a subempire of 23 states, ranging from the Mississippi Valley to the Atlantic Coast. With an estimated 250,000 knights in Indiana alone, and his Queens of the Golden Mask operating as a "poison society" of gossips, Stephenson sat atop a political empire, dreaming of a U.S. Senate seat or even higher office. More than 100,000 attended his inauguration as grand dragon in Kokomo, on July 4, 1923, where Stephenson kept them waiting—with Hiram Evans—before swooping in by air. Climbing from the small plane, "Steve" told his cheering audience, "My worthy subjects, citizens of the Invisible Empire, Klansmen all, greetings. It grieves me to be late. The President of the United States kept me unduly long counseling on matters of state. Only my plea that this is the time and the place of my coronation obtained for me surcease from his prayers for guidance."[103]

Behind that hoopla lay a savvy sense for politics and a penchant for corruption. As the master of a mighty voting bloc, Stephenson picked the winners of elections from Indiana's highest office, Governor Edward Jackson, to congressmen, state legislators, and municipal officials. Each vowed in writing to obey their benefactor, notes preserved by Stephenson with rosters of bribes in a fabled "little black box," implicitly archived to scuttle careers if his minions ever dared to think for themselves.[104] The pledge from Indianapolis mayor John Duvall was typical.

> In return for the political support of D. C. Stephenson, in the event I am elected mayor of Indianapolis, Ind., I promise not to appoint any person as member of the board of public works without they first have the indorsement [*sic*] of D. C. Stephenson....
> I also agree and promise to appoint Claude Worley as chief of police and Earl Klinck as captain. Signed by me, this 12th day of Feb., 1925.[105]

Stephenson's growing power worried Evans in Atlanta, and a Klan investigation of The Old Man prompted his banishment for being "disrespectful to virtuous womanhood." Evans installed Walter Bossert as grand dragon, while Stephenson declared himself chief of a separate Indiana Klan, branding Evans "an ignorant, uneducated, uncouth individual who picks his nose at the table and eats his peas with his knife."[106] When bombers destroyed his yacht at

David Curtis Stephenson, "The Old Man" of Indiana's 1920s Klan, ca. 1921–1925 (Library of Congress).

its berth on Lake Erie, Stephenson blamed "yellow-livered Southerners who hate everything that is pure throughout the state of Indiana."[107]

Purity, however, seldom crossed The Old Man's mind. A hedonist at heart—once shouting at a drunken orgy, "I am the counterpart of Napoleon, the master mind of all the world! Drink her down!"—Stephenson caroused extensively with Captain Klinck and Earl Gentry, his personal bodyguards, assaulting several women in a series of near-rapes.[108] By early 1925 he was obsessed with Madge Oberholtzer, manager of the Indiana Young People's Reading Circle, a special section of the Department of Public Instruction. Stephenson ingratiated himself with Madge by killing an appropriations bill meant to wipe out her job, and they began dating. On March 27 he invited her to his mansion, ostensibly to discuss a job offer, then plied her with liquor and hustled her aboard a train bound for Chicago. In their sleeper car, with Klinck and Gentry standing guard, Stephenson raped Oberholtzer and savagely gnawed her from face to ankles. Afterward, when she warned that the law would punish him, he replied, "I am the law in Indiana."[109]

At a stop in Hammond, Stephenson let Madge got to a pharmacy for painkillers. She bought mercuric chloride instead and drank a lethal dose. Stephenson's cronies drove her home, where she died on April 14, after giving a detailed recitation of her ordeal. An attending physician described her wounds as resembling those of a victim "chewed by a cannibal."[110] Prosecutors charged Stephenson, Klinck and Gentry with kidnapping and murder. Jurors convicted The Old Man in November 1925, while acquitting his codefendants. Sentenced to life imprisonment, Stephenson called in political favors but found no one willing to help him. In July 1927 he released the contents of his "little black box," sending Governor Jackson to trial. (A hung jury released him.) Paroled in March 1950, Stephenson skipped to Minneapolis and received another 10-year sentence. Released again in 1956, he was jailed in

Missouri five years later, for attempting to molest a teenage girl. The Old Man died at last in Tennessee, in June 1966.[111]

While some loyalists maintained that Stephenson was "framed" for Oberholtzer's murder, his downfall shattered Indiana's Klan and spread shockwaves throughout the Invisible Empire, undermining faith in the order's dedication to morality and the sanctity of female virtue. More than any crime against blacks, Jews, or Catholics, it coupled with repeated exposures of Klan embezzlement to paint the order as a cancer on American society.

Death by Mail

Another headline-grabbing murder rocked the Klan in 1926, this time in Minnesota. Asa Bartlett was the top knight in Blue Lake Township, a World War veteran and blacksmith with political aspirations. His primary rival, resort owner August Krubaech, defeated Ku Klux candidate Jennie Norlin in a 1925 campaign to become the township's supervisor, and Bartlett—himself a town constable—plotted revenge. As he later explained, "I could not stand to have Krubaech running the township."[112]

On May 27, 1926, a package arrived by mail at Krubaech's Three Lakes Tavern, in the midst of preparations for his daughter's wedding the next day. When Krubaech opened the parcel, its contents exploded, killing him, his daughter, and her fiancé, William Franke. Police traced the bomb to Bartlett and he confessed in custody, saying, "I am certainly sorry about killing Jeanette and Franke. I did not think about the wedding when I sent the bomb." Remorse did not spare him from conviction or a life prison term. By the time of his parole, in 1963, he was largely forgotten.[113]

Exit the Dragon

One of the odder episodes in Ku Klux history began in Mississippi's Coahoma County, on October 15, 1925, when thieves killed clerk Grover Nicholas at a store owned by planter J. T. Traynham. A posse led by bloodhounds arrested six black suspects, spending the next three weeks grilling them via "the third degree with rope and the water cure." One died under torture and four more confessed, leaving suspect Lindsey Coleman alone to plead his innocence in court.[114]

Amazingly, when Coleman faced trial in Clarksdale, he came represented by septuagenarian Grand Dragon T. S. Ward. Fireworks began on day one, when Traynham accused Ward of "seeking to force him to give false testimony." As described in the *Clarksdale Register,* "Col. Ward asked the witness if he thought he was that kind of man and Mr. Traynham ... replied that any man who would come from south Mississippi to defend a negro [*sic*] who had killed a white man, might be guilty of most any offense." The drama ended with a shock, as jurors returned from deliberating to pronounce Coleman innocent.[115]

This was Mississippi, though, and matters could not rest at that. As Ward escorted Coleman from the courtroom, Traynham accosted them and a scuffle ensued, during which other whites kidnapped Coleman and fled in two cars, dumping his bullet-riddled body on Desoto Avenue. Governor Henry Whitefield called the lynching a "horrible crime," and

Ward went further, charging Sheriff S.W. Glass with complicity in the murder. A December grand jury charged Traynham and three others with Coleman's murder, while Glass and three deputies faced charges of criminal malfeasance. Glass pled guilty in January 1926 and paid a $500 fine, while retaining his office. Jurors acquitted one accused lyncher, and charges against the rest were dismissed. Grand Dragon Ward resigned his post in March 1926. Hiram Evans installed successor Fred Wankan in April, with a vow to "drop out the undesirable material from the mass mobilization days."[116]

"Klarion Kall for a Krusade"

On August 2, 1927, President Coolidge announced that he would not seek reelection the following year. He gave no reason, but his wife was quoted as remarking, "Papa says there's going to be a depression." Republicans gathered in June 1928 to nominate Secretary of Commerce Herbert Hoover, a self-made millionaire so publicly devoid of emotion that his party had to run advertisements headlined "That Man Hoover—He's Human."[117] Democrats convened in Houston 10 days later, considering a list of 20 candidates including Mississippi's Theodore Bilbo and New York governor Al Smith. Dan Moody's Texas delegation opposed Smith's stand against Prohibition, but this time Smith was unstoppable. Despite the ardent prayers of temperance groups camped outside Sam Houston Hall, Smith won nomination with 849⅔ votes.[118]

Hiram Evans had promised more Klan delegates in Houston than New York, four years earlier, but he could not deliver.[119] Ku Klux ranks had thinned dramatically since 1924, shrinking to "no more than several hundred thousand" nationwide.[120] Nonetheless, Evans issued a "Klarion Kall for a Krusade" against Smith, and his knights eagerly complied.[121] In July, knights in Wahouma, Alabama, lynched Smith in effigy, while grand dragons in Georgia and North Carolina appealed to their klaverns for money to battle the Tammany candidate. Tarheel dragon Amos Duncan wrote to Klansmen, "I am immediately putting five more whirlwind speakers on tour in this State, using them seven days per week until November 6th. I am having prepared literally tons of powerful campaign literature which you Klansmen must distribute during the final phases of this crusade to every voter in North Carolina."[122]

The Klan's "powerful" literature attacked Smith on four fronts: his Catholicism; his "alienism" (the son of Irish immigrants); his "wet" stance on Prohibition; and his longtime Tammany ties. In September 1928 the Mississippi realm's *Official Monthly Bulletin* warned knights that if Smith was elected president, he would "no doubt fill every key position in the Republic with Roman Catholics ... [and] no doubt leave the Army and Navy in the hands of Rome." From New Jersey, Alma White cautioned that under Smith, "Free speech, free press, free public schools ... would soon be things of the past." The Klan's *Fellowship Forum*, published in Washington, D.C., declared that "Mr. Smith represents a body of voters who do not believe in ... American principles and traditions; who wish another and a different set of ideas to become dominant in this nation."[123] Some Klan-affiliated ministers assured their congregations that a vote for Smith was a one-way ticket to Hell. The school board in Daytona Beach, Florida, sent notes home in every child's lunch pail that read: "We must prevent the election of Alfred E. Smith to the presidency. If he is chosen president, you will not be allowed to read or have a bible."[124] Some propaganda sheets aspired to poetry, like this one from New York.

> When Catholics rule the United States
> And the Jew grows a Christian nose on his face
> When Pope Pius is head of the Ku Klux Klan
> In the land of Uncle Sam
> Then Al Smith will be our president
> And the country not worth a damn.[125]

Smith sought the high road, saying, "Let the people of this country decide this election upon the great and real issues of the campaign and upon nothing else," but his patience had limits.[126] After his campaign train passed a trackside burning cross in Indiana, Smith fumed, "So far as I am concerned, I would sooner go down to ignominious defeat than to be elected to any office in this country if to accomplish it I had to have the support of any group with such perverted ideas of Americanism."[127]

Election day brought that defeat, as Hoover polled 21,428,584 votes to 15,015,863 cast for Smith; in the Electoral College, he swept the field with 444 votes to Smith's 87.[128] Klansmen took credit for "saving" America, and their agitation no doubt helped exacerbate dissatisfaction with Smith, but membership in most realms still continued to decline, due chiefly to the way Klansmen themselves behaved.

"Filthy Hands"

While the great campaign of 1928 was under way, legal problems distracted Hiram Evans from the fray. Pennsylvania had been an uneasy realm since August 1923, when a riotous parade through Carnegie left one knight dead, two others wounded by gunfire, and bystanders scooping up "hundreds of discarded revolvers."[129] Another riot at Lilly, near Altoona, claimed three lives in April 1924 and left 20 persons injured.[130] Those clashes with violent Catholic opponents enhanced Klan recruiting, but internal disputes soon threatened the realm.

Leadership, as always, was the problem. By 1925 Philadelphia Klansmen simmered under the thumb of kleagle Paul Winter, named by Hiram Evans as Atlanta's point man in the Keystone State. Winter formed a black-robed Triple-S Super Secret Society to intimidate dissident knights, then pressed his luck by having an affair with the wife of the elite unit's leader, but when Klansmen brought him up on charges, interference from Atlanta spared Winter from punishment. In retaliation, Winter disbanded Philadelphia's rebellious Warren G. Harding klavern. Frustrated knights next turned their wrath upon Grand Dragon Sam Rich, charging him with inefficiency, embezzlement, and inconsistent discipline. Evans stalled, but finally agreed to try Rich before a Klan tribunal. Meanwhile, he installed a temporary dragon, whom Pennsylvania knights accused of "defiling the state office by immoral relations with his stenographer." Next, Evans promised Keystone Klansmen they could choose their own new leader—but the meeting convened for that purpose saw the Rev. Herbert Shaw rammed down their throats in a typical power play.[131]

The stage was set for open revolt. In 1926 dissident knights attended the third biennial klonvocation in Washington, airing their complaints about Shaw to Evans directly. In

Complaints against Grand Dragon Sam Rich (in dark robe) sparked a grass roots rebellion among Pennsylvania Klansmen in the late 1920s (Library of Congress).

response, Evans banished spokesman John Strayer—a state legislator, minister of the United Brethren Church, and exalted cyclops of Westmoreland's klavern—then disbanded chapters in Coraopolis, Duquesne, Homestead, Jeanette, Latrobe, Manor, New Kensington and Vandegrift, when they protested Strayer's removal. When the banished units refused to shut down, Evans filed a federal lawsuit, seeking $100,000 in damages for unauthorized use of the Klan's name and regalia.[132]

If Evans thought he could intimidate his former knights, he was mistaken. They countersued, demanding that Atlanta's version of the Klan be banned from Pennsylvania after headquarters accounted for some $15 million looted from the Keystone realm's coffers. At trial, in April 1928, Judge W. H. S. Thomson dismissed the counter-suit, ruling it a state matter beyond his jurisdiction. Defense attorney and Klansman Van Barrickman then fell back on the "clean hands doctrine," which requires petitioners for action by a court to be above reproach.[133] In his opening statement, he said:

> This is an organization which threatens to overthrow the government. If ever a congressional investigation was needed, it is in the matter of the Klan. Take this man Evans.... He boasts that he can make presidents, that he controls congressmen and governors. He boasts that congressmen and governors have to sign on the dotted line before he will stand back of their elections.

This man has reduced the state of Indiana to the condition of a Medieval barony. I went to Oklahoma and found that this secret despicable organization had worked itself into the legislature and that when the governor refused them what they wanted, they overturned him. This Imperial Wizard Evans has used all of our money for riot, murder and arson, such as the Dark Ages and the French Revolution never heard of. We want them to do with our money what we were told would be done with it. We want the schools and hospitals established. But our money has not been used for that. Instead, it has been used to create race riots and for other purposes never dreamed of by us.[134]

To support those charges, Barrickman produced a series of eyewitnesses to Klan offenses. One described a grand dragon masquerading as a Catholic priest in June 1926, to infiltrate the 28th International Eucharistic Congress in Chicago. Another charged that Klan evangelists received 50 dollars per night for diatribes vowing to gun down Catholics "like the dog in the streets." Evans himself had predicted a religious pogrom in Detroit, wherein Woodward Avenue would "run knee deep with Catholic blood."[135]

Nor did Klan action stop at threats. J. F. Ramsey, an ex-member of Dayton, Ohio's "Night Riders," described the group's purpose as "horse-whipping, tar and feathering, barn-burning, bombing—a regular reign of terror." Acting under penalty of death for disobedience, the unit had received orders to murder several men, including one slain at Bellaire. In another case, a black man had been burned alive near Dayton. Night Riders had tried to burn one Dayton church, and on another raid bombed their own klavern, hurling a brick through the window, bearing a note that implicated Catholics. Ramsey began to describe Evans sending a carload of Klansmen to Mexico, with orders to "stir up trouble," but Judge Thomson cut him off.[136]

Clarence Ludlow, a Dallas Klansman during 1920–21, described his personal acquaintance with Evans before the dentist moved to Atlanta. As exalted cyclops, Evans had presided over "kangaroo courts" where men were sentenced to flogging or death. He personally directed one victim's torture—whipping and a coat of hot tar afterward—"with a big grin on his face." Ludlow had also seen "seven or eight" men doused with kerosene and burned to death. One victim, a white man from Terrell, was incinerated before an audience of 300 to 400 Klansmen in full regalia. Harry MacNeel, former exalted cyclops of Kittanning, Pennsylvania, described a cross-burning at St. Mary's Church, meant to "throw the fear of God into the Catholic people." Later, during the dispute with Atlanta, Evans loyalists had raided his home, stealing money and documents.[137]

Concerning riots, ex-knight Roy Barclay described a melee at Niles, Ohio, in November 1924, where Klansmen clashed with members of an opposition group, Knights of the Flaming Circle. Both orders scheduled marches for the same day, some Klansmen manning machine guns while others, deputized as sheriff's officers, roamed around town, insulting and assaulting foreigners. Governor Harry Davis refused the mayor's request for troops, then relented after an 18-hour battle left 12 men wounded, imposing martial law over the city for 10 days.[138] James Miller, ex-cyclops of Scottdale, Pennsylvania, recalled that in September 1923 Grand Dragon Rich "told us that if one Klansman fell we should go over the top and not leave a Catholic alive in Scottdale or Alverton."[139]

Blanket denials from Evans notwithstanding, Judge Thomson reached the only possible conclusion, ruling that the parent Klan had come to court with "filthy hands" and was, in fact, "directly responsible for the breaking down of the fundamental principles upon which our Government is founded."[140] Evans appealed that decision, but the Third Circuit Court of Appeals upheld Thomson's verdict in August 1929.[141]

By then, Klan membership had dwindled further, men and money slipping through the battered wizard's hands. The order's strength was waning, and Calvin Coolidge's prediction would prove accurate. A depression *was* coming, and nothing would ever be the same.

CHAPTER 5

Depression and Decline
(1930–1944)

Klansmen suffered as much from the Great Depression as anyone else—more, in some cases, since many were farmers, sharecroppers, or laborers in industries facing ruin. They sought explanations and settled for scapegoats. In the Klan's case, targets included "Jewish bankers," blacks competing for "white" jobs, "radical" labor unions, and President Franklin Delano Roosevelt's New Deal. The order's response was predictably angry, disorganized, and often violent.

Ebb Tide

Two years before FDR humiliated incumbent Herbert Hoover with a Democratic landslide, in September 1930, Hollywood released a 90-minute cut of *The Birth of a Nation*, with a musical soundtrack and a six-minute prologue, wherein D. W. Griffith and actor Walter Huston discussed the Klan's role in 19th-century Dixie. Kleagles haunted screenings of the film, distributing membership applications but winning few converts. As the Memphis *Commercial Appeal* observed, "Not many persons have $10 to throw away on an oversized nightshirt."[1]

That year found even Klansmen in high places facing painful challenges. Alabama senator Tom Heflin had bolted Democratic ranks to support Herbert Hoover against Al Smith in 1928, accusing Smith and the Catholic Church of conspiring to overthrow the U.S. government. Huge crowds cheered Heflin's inflammatory speeches in Birmingham and Montgomery, but the state's major newspapers flayed him, and Democratic leaders barred Heflin from the 1930 ballot. Undaunted, Heflin campaigned independently, in tandem with Ku Klux gubernatorial candidate Hugh Locke on the so-called "Heflox" ticket. On election day, orthodox Democrat John Bankhead II defeated Heflin by a margin of 50,000 votes, while Locke lost by 59,000 to Klan opponent Benjamin Miller.[2]

Predictions of a "new day" in Alabama, or the South at large, were premature, however. While Heflin fought for his political life, the American Communist Party (CPUSA) opened its southern regional office in Birmingham, agitating workers and preaching interracial collaboration against management, provoking furious reactions from Klansmen and their patrons among the state's industrial "Big Mules." In March 1931, the Scottsboro case saw nine black youths accused of raping two white girls aboard a freight train. The suspects avoided lynching, but faced near-certain execution from the Cotton State's judicial system.

The "Scottsboro boys" in custody in 1930 (Library of Congress).

Klansmen rallied to the cause, their rage intensified when lawyers from the CPUSA's International Labor Defense team stepped forward to represent the accused. ILD headquarters received a telegram from the Klan, reading: "You Negroes are invited to Alabama. We want your scalp[s] along with the nine we already have." Elsewhere in the state, Klansmen whipped a Birmingham mail carrier, threatened black Illinois congressman Oscar DePriest for condemning lynching, terrorized African Americans in Pickens County, and led a riot that left six Sumter County residents dead on July 4, 1931. State authorities intervened in the latter case but, predictably, convicted and imprisoned only black offenders.[3]

"Communism Will Not Be Tolerated"

Klansmen had been alert to Bolshevik invasion of their realms since 1917, imagining Red hands at work in strikes, race riots, bootlegging, and any baby-steps toward racial parity.

The establishment of CPUSA outposts in Dixie ratified their conspiracy theories. Atlanta's knights, already inflamed by Communist "propaganda and reading material," rallied to defend the white murderer of Dennis Hubert, a Morehouse College theology student who allegedly insulted two drunk women on a public street. White jurors acquitted the triggerman, and while the *Kourier* pretended to regret Hubert's death, it noted that whenever Red-inspired blacks demanded "social rights" in Dixie, "extreme measures might be necessary."[4]

Klansmen everywhere were vigilant to Communist incursions, but Birmingham became ground zero in their struggle. The city—later known as "Bombingham" for the frequency of local dynamite explosions—logged its first blast during a milk pricing war in July 1931, while another bombing shattered the home of an Italian-born CPUSA member. Klansmen disrupted a Communist rally in 1932 by dropping leaflets from a nearby building, onto the crowd. They read: "Negroes of Birmingham, the Ku Klux Klan is watching you. Tell the Communists to get out of town. They mean only trouble for you, for Alabama is a good place for good Negroes, and a bad place for Negroes who believe in racial equality. Report Communist activities to the Ku Klux Klan, Box 651, Birmingham."[5]

NEGROES BEWARE

DO NOT ATTEND COMMUNIST MEETINGS

Paid organizers for the communists are only trying to get negroes in trouble. Alabama is a good place for good negroes to live in, but it is a bad place for negroes who believe in SOCIAL EQUALITY.

The Ku Klux Klan Is Watching You.
TAKE HEED

Tell the communist leaders to leave. Report all communist meetings to the
Ku Klux Klan
Post Office Box 651, Birmingham, Alabama.

A Klan flier warning African Americans against association with Communists in Birmingham, Alabama, in 1932 (Library of Congress).

Race, inevitably, was the key to Ku Klux opposition against Communism. Birmingham kligrapp John Murphy told congressional investigators, "Our organization [is] interested in the [Communist] proposition purely from the fact ... that they [are] teaching social equality." Writing in the *Kourier,* wizard Hiram Evans warned Birmingham's blacks to avoid "breathing hot communistic airs" if they wished to remain safe and sound. "The negroes," he wrote, "are led to believe that the communists practice racial and social equality." Reds "dangle before the ignorant, lustful and brutish negroes ... a tempting bait ... that negro men should take white women and live with them, declaring this is their God-given right under a Communist regime." To forestall that nightmare, Klansmen lit crosses and burned CPUSA organizer Tom Johnson in effigy, disrupted party meetings, kidnapped and beat party members, sometimes fatally.[6]

Nor was anti–Semitism absent from the Klan's war on Communism. Black communists were led, the Klan explained, by "Russian Jews of the low intelligence type," and one such— Rabbi Benjamin Goldstein, a supporter of the Scottsboro defense team—was driven by vigilantes from his post at Montgomery's Temple Beth-or. The taint of Jewish conspiracy stretched from New York to California, where the *Kourier* deemed movie production "the most putrid and evil smelling business in the United States.... The White Slave business is respectable ... compared to the ... oceans of filth ladled out by the greasy hawk nosed merchants of Hollywood.... The Jews, parasites, filchers, usurers always, have found ... an ideal vehicle for the coining of the dirtiest kind of dollars and the pleasurable debauchery of the morals of the young.... American youth is being crucified by the Jews through their movies as surely as they martyred Christ 2,000 years ago.... Hollywood certainly needs a Hitler!"[7]

"Communism will not be tolerated," a Klan flyer cautioned, its message driven home by anti–Red mayhem in Huntsville, Mobile, Montgomery and Tuscaloosa. When CPUSA presidential candidate William Foster announced plans to visit Alabama in 1932, he also got a warning from the Klan. "Your presence in Birmingham is not wanted," it read, adding "Send nigger Ford"—a reference to Foster's black running mate, Alabama native James Ford.[8]

"Beware of the 8th of November!"

Despite his open support for Al Smith's two presidential campaigns, Klansmen initially seemed eager to vote for Franklin Roosevelt in 1932. Granted, the alternatives were grim: Smith himself, or Texan John Nance Garner IV, who had fought the Klan in Congress since 1929. Although a liberal, Roosevelt was also a frequent visitor to Warm Springs, Georgia, where his largesse endeared him to locals. Klansmen flocked to join Roosevelt Southern Clubs, chaired from Atlanta by Imperial Klonsel Paul Etheridge, but a falling out occurred when headquarters realized that money raised by the clubs was meant for Democratic coffers, rather than the Klan's.[9]

Suddenly, wizard Evans "discovered" that James Farley, FDR's campaign manager, was a Roman Catholic who actively recruited black voters on both sides of the Mason-Dixon Line. Days before November's election, the *Kourier* warned its readers: "Don't be fooled. Farley is ROOSEVELT; Tammany Hall, Catholic controlled, is ROOSEVELT.... EVERY PROMINENT ROMAN CATHOLIC YOU CAN FIND IS FOR ROOSEVELT.... The Underworld is a unit for Roosevelt. The gangsters of Chicago, St. Louis ... and New York are for Roosevelt.... Roosevelt, their subservient tool, will turn our country over to Tammany and thus we will have CATHOLIC CONTROL OF AMERICAN GOVERNMENT AND LIFE, if he is elected.... BEWARE OF THE 8TH OF NOVEMBER!"[10]

Klan support for Herbert Hoover was too little and too late. Roosevelt crushed Hoover at the polls, carrying 42 states and winning 472 electoral votes to Hoover's 59.[11] With Garner as vice president, the Klan expected little sympathy from FDR's administration, and matters went from bad to worse in March, when Roosevelt named Farley as postmaster general and chose a Jew, Harold Ickes, as secretary of the interior. New York Republican William Woodin seemed a fair choice for secretary of the treasury, but he lasted less than a year, replaced in January 1934 by another Jew, Henry Morgenthau, Jr.[12] Even before that switch occurred, Klansmen agreed that Roosevelt's New Deal reeked of Socialism, if not outright Communism directed from Moscow.

From Atlanta, Hiram Evans declared a "crusade" against the New Deal. In July 1934 he wrote, "Public-spirited people, Klansmen and non-members alike, realize that this nation is in great danger. Because of its record of heroic achievement, the Klan has been called upon by them to mobilize and co-ordinate those who are interested in preserving our Constitutional Government set up by our forefathers."[13] Speakers at a Virginia rally complained that Roosevelt had "honeycombed Washington with Communists." In Pennsylvania, Klan orators denounced revolutionary "brain trusters." In Westchester County, New York, a kleagle praised Adolf Hitler while railing against the "communism of FDR and the Jews." "The Klan is needed now," he said, "particularly in this section of the country, so that we can give back to the American people the fundamental rights conveyed by the Constitution. Communism must be stamped out. The New Deal has become communistic and I feel certain that the American public will rise in protest and soundly defeat President Roosevelt at the next general election."[14]

That prediction proved wildly inaccurate, as FDR rolled on to win reelection three times, nor did the Klan's crusade inflate the order's thinning ranks. Republicans welcomed most New Deal opponents to their Roosevelt-bashing fold, but generally stood at arm's length from the Klan and affiliated radicals, such as Gerald L. K. Smith. Repentant New Dealer Huey Long briefly offered hope for a third party rebellion against the New Deal, but he wanted no part of the Klan. After Evans condemned Long's "dictatorial" behavior in Louisiana, promising to tour the state in support of Long's Senate rival in 1934, the Kingfish replied, "You tell that tooth-puller that he is a goddamn lying sonofabitch! I know him personally. This isn't second-hand information and it isn't confidential! Quote me as saying that the imperial bastard will never set foot in Louisiana, and that when I call him a sonofabitch, I am not using profanity but am referring to the circumstances of his birth!" More ominously, Long warned that if Evans *did* visit the Pelican State, he would leave "with his toes turned up." Evans canceled his trip, advising reporters, "You don't get in an open contest with a polecat."[15]

"We Shall Fight Horror with Horror!"

For most Southern Klansmen, fighting the New Deal meant fighting labor unions. This posed a conflict of interest, as noted by author Gerald Dunne, since "90 percent of Birmingham's union members were also involved with the Klan." Klansmen still harbored their enmity toward "Big Mule" John Bankhead II, dating from the 1920s, while campaigning for government health insurance and for public control of the Muscle Shoals dam project.[16] When race entered the equation, however—as it always did in Dixie—knights of the Invisible Empire voted and acted against their own best interests. White employers held them captive with reminders that "you may not be making a lot, but at least you're making more than the niggers."[17]

One group guaranteed to ignite Ku Klux fury was the CPUSA's International Labor Defense. Klansmen joined police in Atlanta and Birmingham to raid and ransack ILD offices, smashing furniture and looting files. In Lakeland, Florida, ILD organizer Frank Norman was lured from home in April 1934, by Klansmen posing as sheriff's deputies, and disappeared forever.[18] Another target of Ku Klux wrath, the Southern Tenant Farmers' Union (STFU), harbored many ex–Klansmen in its racially integrated ranks.[19] Prior membership in the order would not spare them, however, when current Klansmen joined police and growers to beat and murder STFU members, burn their church meeting halls, and riddle their homes with gunfire.[20]

While that was going on in Arkansas and Mississippi, Florida Klansmen focused on the Modern Democrats, a tiny pro-union Socialist group in Tampa. On November 30, 1935, police arrested six party leaders, detained them briefly, then released three—Eugene Poulnot, Dr. Samuel Rogers, and Joseph Shoemaker—to a waiting gang of Klansmen. Driven to a rural wooded area, the three were stripped, severely beaten, tarred and feathered, then warned to leave Tampa or face further punishment. Poulnot and Rogers survived their injuries, but Shoemaker died 10 days later, in hideous pain. Newspapers united to condemn the floggers. Tallahassee's *Democrat* deemed the crime "so revolting that no civilized community or state can permit it to go unpunished." The *Miami Herald* branded the Tampa mob "as venomous as a mad dog, and its leaders should be dealt with just as dispassionately as we would a rabid animal." The *Tampa Tribune* editorialized that "No crime in the history of Hillsborough County has brought so great a clamor for punishment of the guilty."[21]

Identifying those responsible was relatively easy; bringing them to book proved more difficult. Police chief R. T. Tittsworth initially denied that any lawmen were involved in the abductions, then resigned "in order to devote all his time to the Shoemaker case." A grand jury indicted 11 defendants, including six policemen, and while Grand Dragon George Garcia admitted knowing two of the suspects, he claimed ignorance of their status as Klansmen. "The Tampa klavern," Garcia said, "could not take such an unusual action as a flogging without consulting me." The case dragged on until autumn 1937, when jurors acquitted the defendants of all charges.[22]

Another Klan adversary was the Committee of Industrial Organizations (CIO), born in November 1935 from a rift within the older American Federation of Labor (AFL), renamed three years later as the Congress of Industrial Organizations. Deemed "radical" by comparison with the AFL, chiefly because it welcomed African American members and (until 1948) also admitted Communists, the CIO was a natural target for the Klan and its newly affiliated White League.[23] Wizard Evans warned his followers, "The CIO is infested with Communists. The Klan will not sit idly by and allow the CIO to destroy our social order, nor shall the CIO flout law and promote social disorder without swift punishment. We shall fight horror with horror!" In Alabama, Georgia, and Tennessee, that meant whippings and cross-burnings, accompanied by the first upsurge in Klan membership since 1929.[24] In South Carolina, where *The Fiery Cross* cautioned Klansmen that the "CIO wants whites and blacks on the same level," robed knights packed a meeting of the Greenville city council to intimidate protesters from the National Textile Workers Union.[25] Nor were anti–CIO reprisals confined to the South. When rubber workers struck a Goodyear plant in Akron, Ohio, Klansmen lit a cross outside the factory.[26]

Losing Ground Abroad

Klan offshoots clung to life in several foreign countries during the Depression, but their days were numbered. At Oakville, Ontario, 75 masked Klansmen visited the home of Ira Johnson and Isabel Jones, protesting the presence of an interracial couple in their midst. While a cross blazed in her yard, Jones was ordered from the house and "reunited" with her parents at the local Salvation Army shelter. Oakville's police chief arrived with the raid in progress, but declined to make arrests, voicing sympathy with the Klan's goal and "orderly" conduct. On March 3, the *Globe* newspaper editorialized: "The work the nocturnal visitors did in Oakville in separating a white girl from a colored man may be commendable in itself and prove a benefit, but it is certain that the methods are wrong." Provincial authorities later charged four of the raiders with "being disguised by night," a wrist-slap that encouraged the offenders to return and burn Johnson's home. No arson charges resulted, but the Klan suffered embarrassment upon discovering that Johnson was, in fact, a white man. Thereafter, membership and influence in Canada declined.[27]

The Klan got a late start in England, founded in 1935 as White Knights of Britain, also called the Hooded Men. It shared headquarters with a proto–Nazi group, the Nordic League, and most of its members switched from robes to paramilitary garb when the White Knights dissolved in 1937. Other League allies—or front groups—included the Militant Christian Patriots and the Liberty Restoration League. The Nordic League survived for another two years, but came under increasing scrutiny after Germany's *Kristallnacht* pogroms of November 1938. Its public statements were extreme enough to make Oswald Mosley, head of the British Union of Fascists, keep the group at arm's length, but the BUF absorbed most of the League's remaining members after war broke out with Germany in 1939. The Klan, as such, had disappeared.[28]

Meanwhile, in Scotland, Kormack's Kaledonian Klan bore the Ku Klux standard from 1935 to 1939, when global war drained its ranks and cast fascism into disrepute throughout the United Kingdom. Founder and "Khieftain" John Cormack of Edinburgh was a member of the Rome-hating Orange Order, Protestant Action, and the Masonic Grand Lodge of Scotland. Humiliated by their thrashing at the hands of Catholic Vigilance Association members in August 1935, Protestant Action members sought to cover their tracks (and faces) by defecting into Cormack's newborn Klan. Members rallied weekly at Edinburgh's Kaledonian Klub and pumped iron in their own gymnasium. Local newspapers noticed the Klan in January 1938, with feature articles in the *Scottish Daily Express* and *Sunday Post*—the latter, curiously, featuring a photo of a Klansman dressed in women's auxiliary garb from America. "Hoods are worn at the meetings," the *Sunday Post* advised, "so that possible traitors among the members do not know who has been assigned to carry out a certain job." Some 5,000 spectators turned out for the Kaledonian Klan's first public appearance, but it quickly went downhill from there, its members regularly losing brawls with groups of Catholics. Some modern racists dismiss the Scottish Klan as being "firmly part of the Jew-loving, Lowland Scots, Orange, loyalist tradition," oddly crediting its inspiration to one Matthew Perkins, a black member of the Protestant Reformers' Church in Liverpool, England.[29]

The Black Legion

Southern raids and rallies were overshadowed briefly, in the mid–1930s, by startling news from the Midwest. There, in Ohio, a group of ex–Klansmen formed the Black Legion, trading their white robes for black ones, with masks topped by headgear resembling old-fashioned pirates' hats, complete with the skull and crossbones emblem of a Jolly Roger flag. Led by Virgil Effinger, an electrician and former Klansman from Lima, the Black Legion developed its greatest strength in Michigan, recruiting Detroit policemen alongside past and present Klansmen. Before the bitter end, observers credited the Legion with "tens of thousands of members" across the Wolverine State.[30]

Critics branded Effinger a "dour and humorless fanatic," which made him perfect for his role as head Black Legionnaire. Inevitably, his group followed its white-robed parent into vigilante violence, targeting "uppity" blacks, labor unions, and leftist political groups. Some attacks were directed by Heinrich Pickert, a secret Legion member who doubled as Detroit's police commissioner. One victim may have been the Rev. Earl Little, an African American crushed beneath a Lansing streetcar in 1931. Police logged the death as an accident, but Little's son Malcolm grew up believing his father was murdered by the Black Legion. Decades later, Malcolm Little joined the Nation of Islam, replaced his surname with an "X," and became America's preeminent spokesman for black nationalism.[31]

If there were doubts about the Legion's role in Little's death, none existed in the case of victim Charley Poole. Lowell Rushing, Poole's brother-in-law, belonged to a Legion front called the Wolverine Republican Club, and told his fellow Legionnaires that Poole abused his wife (Rushing's sister). Fired by Klan-style moralism, "Colonel" Harvey Davis directed his men to dispose of Poole, an act accomplished with five point-blank gunshots on May 12, 1936. By May 22, Davis was in custody, newspapers trumpeting "a fantastic tale of terrorism ... straight from the heart of the Deep South of Carpetbag days." Becky Poole denied any mistreatment by her husband, and displayed the infant allegedly miscarried after one of Charley's mythical beatings. From jail, Legion assassin Dayton Dean described a second murder—of black victim Silas Coleman, shot in May 1935 so Davis could see "how it felt to shoot a Negro"—and added a long list of floggings, fire-bombings, and attempted murders. Would-be victims who survived included a Highland Park newspaper publisher who ran for office against a Legion member, and the mayor of Ecorse, condemned for hiring African Americans. Dean himself had molested a 14-year-old girl, escaping prosecution after Legionnaires threatened to kill the victim's mother if she pressed charges.[32]

Dean pled guilty on two murder counts in June 1936, receiving a life prison term, then testified against a dozen other Legionnaires, all but one of whom were convicted in the Poole and Coleman cases. Meanwhile, Oakland County circuit judge George Hartrick launched a personal investigation of the Legion, revealing that its members included "scores" of policemen in Pontiac and Royal Oak—one of them Royal Oak's chief of police—plus 86 other officials, including the county prosecutor and a state legislator. Following the Detroit trials, Wayne County prosecutor Duncan McCrea confessed to "accidentally" signing a Black Legion membership card. Other "black knights" testified that McCrea had, in fact, been initiated to the order and attended secret meetings. Farther afield, investigators linked the Black Legion to four other slayings in Pontiac, Michigan, and Cleveland, Ohio. Floggings in Kentucky were reportedly conducted by "Black Legs" who mimicked the Legion's regalia.[33]

The Legion's final death knell came from Hollywood, where Warner Brothers released *Black Legion* in January 1937. Humphrey Bogart starred as Frank Taylor, a factory worker lured into racism, alcoholism and murder by Legion cohorts, raging, "We ain't afraid o' nuttin' or nobody!" Imprisoned for killing an immigrant coworker, Bogart finished the film behind prison bars, but Klansmen missed the message. Soon after the movie's release, imperial headquarters sued Warner Brothers for using copyrighted Klan insignia on the black robes of their celluloid villains.[34]

Hollywood's take (1937) on the real-life Black Legion (author's collection).

"A Good Exit"

The Klan suffered its own embarrassments while the Black Legionnaires faced judgment in Detroit. The trouble began on August 12, 1937, when President Roosevelt nominated Alabama Senator Hugo Black to replace retiring Supreme Court Justice Willis Van Devanter. FDR wanted a "thumping, evangelical New Dealer," and Black fit the bill, but his past was problematical. For the first time since 1853, instead of confirming him automatically, the Senate referred his nomination to its Judiciary Committee. The chief objection raised by certain colleagues, journalists, and many grass-roots citizens, was Black's affiliation with the 1920s Klan.[35]

Black was forthcoming, more or less. "I did join the Klan," he admitted. "I later resigned. I never rejoined.... Before becoming a Senator I dropped the Klan. I have had nothing to do with it since that time. I abandoned it. I completely discontinued any association with the organization. I have never resumed it and never expect to do so."[36] On paper, it appeared that Black had joined the Klan in September 1923 and resigned two years later, with blessings from Atlanta, to pursue his Senate race. In parting, he had received a lifetime "imperial passport" from Hiram Evans, a document which Black declared was "unsolicited and had no meaning."[37] Critics noted Black's 1921 defense of the Rev. Edwin Stephenson, a Birmingham

Klansman, on charges of killing the Catholic priest who married Stephenson's daughter to her Puerto Rican fiancé.[38] Black won acquittal for his client in that case, every lawyer's goal, but also faced later accusations of anti–Catholicism. Biographer Howard Ball writes that Black "sympathized with the [Klan's] economic, nativist, and anti–Catholic beliefs," while author Roger Newman says Black delivered anti–Catholic speeches to Klan rallies across Alabama during his 1926 Senate campaign, a year after "abandoning" the order.[39]

Regardless of when and how he left the Klan, Black proved unstoppable in Senate confirmation hearings, assuming his Supreme Court seat on August 18, 1937. Klansmen were not pleased, remembering Black's support for presidential candidate Al Smith in 1928, and their mood would have been worse if they were psychic. Over the next four decades, before retiring in September 1971, Justice Black would vote for desegregation of public schools in 1954 and press for the court to demand "immediate desegregation" 15 years later.[40]

Black's departure from the Senate left a vacancy, which Governor Bibb Graves filled with his wife. Dixie Graves thus briefly became Alabama's first female senator and the first married woman to serve in the Senate.[41] Charges of nepotism worried her husband less, that year, than questions from the *New York Times* concerning his Klan membership. Graves admitted joining the order and attending a klorero in September 1926, where he received "some kind of badge," but claimed that he had left the Klan prior to his first gubernatorial inauguration in January 1927, simply "dropping out" in lieu of formal resignation.[42] Critics questioned that story, noting Graves's sponsorship of an August 1927 "muzzling bill" in the state legislature, designed to stop newspapers from reporting on Klan violence. Graves *had* ordered a special investigation of floggings statewide, but then refused to let his attorney general—another Klansman, Charles McCall—see the final report. A police raid on Montgomery's klavern revealed a letter from Grand Dragon James Esdale to Exalted Cyclops Ira Thompson, promising support from Governor Graves "which has been so nobly lent in the past."[43] Graves certainly left the Klan before his second term as governor began, in 1937, and a year later, he welcomed 1,200 delegates to the founding session of the Southern Conference on Human Welfare, one-fifth of whom were African Americans.[44]

Farther west, in California, William McAdoo hit a Klan roadblock in his 1938 campaign for reelection to the U.S. Senate. No taint of klannishness was raised in 1932, during McAdoo's first senatorial campaign, but six years later, Republican contender Sheridan Downey produced a dog-eared, gold-engraved certificate from Hiram Evans, identifying McAdoo as "a citizen of the Invisible Empire" and entreating all members to grant him "the fervent fellowship of Klansmen." McAdoo branded the document a forgery, declaring that accusations of Klan membership were "utterly and wantonly false," a sentiment echoed by Evans from Atlanta. Nonetheless, McAdoo resigned from the Senate on November 9, 1938, ceding his seat to Downey.[45]

California's Klan survived the 1930s, and its San Diego klavern enjoyed substantial growth under leaders Wayne Kenaston, Sr., and Richard Floyd. Members harassed Mexican Americans and patrolled the border for illegal immigrants, while dominating the local Elks lodge. Floyd also formed the American-Mexican Republican League in July 1934, feeding Klan coffers with dues from Mexican merchants, ostensibly collected to "promote business" with America. Some refugees from Mexico's Cristero War mistook Klan symbolism for a welcome sign and tried to join, but kleagles quickly disabused them. In the latter 1930s, Klansmen fraternized with local Silver Shirts until federal agents cracked down on the home-

KKK Imperial Headquarters (1921–1939), purchased by the Catholic Church in 1939 (Library of Congress).

grown fascists for killing a Marine Corps infiltrator. Through the next war and beyond, Klan spokesmen such as Wayne Kenaston held the Golden State's color line against blacks and Hispanics.[46]

While newspapers branded Klan membership a political kiss of death, the order suffered declining finances. Evans had sold imperial headquarters in 1928, and the property passed through several hands prior to January 1939, when Bishop Gerald O'Hara purchased it for the Savannah-Atlanta Catholic Diocese. Twisting the knife, O'Hara invited Evans to the dedication ceremony, and Evans agreed, posing for photos with his hosts and calling the ceremony "one of the most beautiful services I ever saw."[47] Klansmen were not amused. A *Kourier* editorial blared, "Protestants! Why did the Catholics buy our old national headquarters and turn it into a Catholic church? Did they want that particular property because of its fitness for a church or just to show you up?"[48]

Six months later, Evans retired as Imperial Wizard, ceding his throne to former Indiana veterinarian James Colescott. A Klansman since 1923, Colescott had served under Hoosier Grand Dragon David Stephenson, and was drafted to work at imperial headquarters in 1936. Speaking to *Atlanta Constitution* editor Ralph McGill, Evans said, "You were hard on me, but not for publication, I will tell you, I was not a fool. I wanted out." Of the Catholic ceremony that subjected him to ridicule, Evans said, "This was a good exit."[49]

Even in retirement, though, Evans could not escape the Klan. In May 1940, Georgia attorney general Ellis Arnall charged the ex-wizard and a former state highway purchasing agent with illegally fixing asphalt prices. Evans pled no contest in January 1941 and paid a $15,000 fine. Two months later, Arnall filed a civil action against Evans under the Sherman Anti-Trust Act, seeking treble damages in the amount of $384,901.39.[50] Evans subsequently sank into obscurity and died in Atlanta in September 1966.[51]

"Mopping Up Cesspools"

Imperial Wizard Colescott had his work cut out for him. Despite some flurries of publicity and violence, the Klan was in decline as he assumed control. Its membership was evaporating, some bleeding into rival racist groups such as William Dudley Pelley's Silver Shirt Legion, Donald Shea's National Gentile League, Joe McWilliams's Christian Mobilizers, and the Knights of the White Camellia, led by ex–Klansman George Deatherage.[52]

In the face of so much competition, often clad in spiffy paramilitary uniforms that mimicked Adolf Hitler's stormtroopers, Colescott seemingly had little to offer. "I am against floggings, lynchings and intimidations," he told the *Atlanta Constitution* in July 1939. "Anyone who flogs, lynches or intimidates ought to be in the penitentiary."[53] How, then, would he proceed with his expressed goal of "mopping up the cesspools of Communism in the United States"?[54] No easy answer was apparent, but Colescott did offer new Klansmen a break, shaving four dollars off the traditional 10-dollar initiation fee, while cutting the price of robes from $6.50 to $3.50. As membership increased, he vowed, "The fiery cross will again blaze on the hilltops of America."[55]

While Colescott publicly condemned violence, he could not control Klansmen who practiced it. South Carolina's knights joined police to suppress registration of black voters, flogged victims of both races, and twice raided a National Youth Administration camp at Fountain Inn, beating and robbing African American youths, leaving signs that read: "Niggers, Your Place is in the Cotton Patch."[56] In Alabama, Klansmen and White Legionnaires continued their beatings of actual and suspected Communists, once again enjoying the collaboration of police.[57] But it was in Atlanta, Colescott's own backyard, where mayhem proved most embarrassing to the new wizard. Whippings by East Point Klavern members left three victims dead, including black barber Ike Gaston and a young white couple, Benton Ford and Sarah Rawls, who offended Klan morality by parking in lover's lane. A grand jury investigation revealed 50 floggings during 1939–40 and identified the ringleaders as Deputy Sheriffs W. W. Scarborough, Edwin Burdette, and Herb Eidson. Scarborough, who doubled as East Point's exalted cyclops, admitted fielding floggers "whenever someone wasn't doin' like he ought to do." Eight Klansmen were convicted and imprisoned, then pardoned by sympathetic Governor Eugene Talmadge. Colescott's response was feeble at best, instructing his knights to remove the masks from their hoods.[58]

West Virginia's realm had enjoyed political success in the 1920s, then faded from headlines after Al Smith's presidential nomination, but its spirit lingered in small towns like Crab Orchard, where young butcher Robert Byrd joined the order in 1942, recruiting 150 friends to form a new klavern. Grand Dragon Joel Baskin came from Virginia to celebrate the unit's launch, telling Byrd, "You have a talent for leadership, Bob. The country needs young men like you in the leadership of the nation." As Byrd later recalled, "Suddenly lights flashed in my mind! Someone important had recognized my abilities! I was only 23 or 24 years old, and the thought of a political career had never really hit me. But strike me that night, it did." Four years would pass before Byrd tossed his hat into the ring, as a candidate for the state legislature with his sights set on Congress, but in the meantime he doubled as kleagle and exalted cyclops of his klavern. Long after the fact, in a self-serving autobiography, Byrd would claim his Klan engaged in no public demonstrations, other than a funeral ceremony for one member killed in a pistol duel, and that he left the Klan after a year or so, but published correspondence trace his role as organizer well into the postwar years.[59]

"The Spark That Fired Hitler"

While traditional violence was embarrassing in the short run, it also drew new members from the disaffected, brutal fringe of white society. The Klan's worst problem, under Wizard Colescott, was its public fraternization with Nazis. The first Ku Klux link to Germany's fascists came in early 1925, when Leipzig's *Hammer Magazine* editorialized:

> May these American reports tend to encourage many German minds; may they be valuable as evidence that the Nordic people in all parts of the world are arousing themselves, and consider themselves on a holy mission: to be a guardian of the spirit of truth and the highest human ideals. If the Klan fulfills its task, it will necessarily reach out its hand over the borderlands with a similar endeavor, to a realization of mutual aims. Then as the cunning enemy of people is united internationally, we will also need a world-wide confederacy of the Nordic races in order to shatter the bonds in which the Jewish offender has smitten all honorable nations.
>
> Thus, then, we greet the gallant men of the Ku Klux Klan with our warmest sympathies and cherish the hope to find such cordial expressions of feeling with them in the accomplishment of our mutual aims, as are necessary to victory over the powerful enemy.[60]

Upon seizing power in 1933, Adolf Hitler instantly suppressed Germany's Klan—the German Order of Fiery Crosses—but American Klansmen happily forgave him. In March 1934, the *Kourier* took credit for Hitler's triumph, saying:

> While the Ku Klux Klan has been waging its valiant fight to save America for Americans, we wonder if it has not done a more effective job (or so it seems at the moment) of keeping Germany safe for Germans.... The spark that fired Hitler and other German nationalists to build a new Germany may easily have been ignited by the example of the American Ku Klux Klan.... Frankly, we are not so concerned with German problems as we are with the affairs of our own country, and it is indeed high time that those of true American stock follow the banner of the Ku Klux Klan to preserve our own ship of state with the same zeal that patriots of foreign nations display in following the Klan's example.[61]

A Klansman in Miami put it more succinctly: "When Hitler has killed all the Jews in Europe, he's going to help us drive all the Jews on Miami Beach into the sea!"[62]

Collaboration between Nazis and the Klan began soon after Hitler's ascension to the German chancellorship. George Deatherage, a 1920s Klansman who led a revived Knights of the White Camellia, claimed Hitler had learned anti–Semitism from the Klan; he also switched from cross-burnings to fiery swastikas, intended, as he said, to strike "terror and fear into the hearts of many."[63] Nazi activist Leslie Fry (née Louise Chandor) offered Hiram Evans $75,000 for control of the Klan in 1939, then fled to Europe the following year, ducking subpoenas from Congress.[64] Edward James Smythe, an active Klansmen and head of the

August Klapprott addresses a joint Bund-Klan rally in New Jersey, 1940 (Library of Congress).

Protestant War Veterans Association, swapped his hood and robe for paramilitary khaki when addressing rallies of the German-American Bund.[65]

It was the Bund, in fact, which finally exposed the Klan's Nazi alliance. Launched in 1934, as the Friends of New Germany, the Bund adopted its better-known name in March 1936. Its members were ethnic Germans, many of whom—with their leader, immigrant Nazi Fritz Julius Kuhn—were employed as strike-breaking thugs at Henry Ford's automobile factories.[66] While many Southern Klansmen looked askance at brownshirts, their brethren in the North proved more accommodating. In August 1940 Edward Smythe orchestrated a joint rally of Klansmen and Bundists at the Bund's Camp Nordland, near Andover, New Jersey. Camp Director and Deputy *Bundesführer* August Klapprott told the audience, "When Arthur Bell, your Grand Dragon, and Mr. Smythe asked us about using Camp Nordland for this patriotic meeting, we decided to let them have it because of the common bond between us. The principles of the Bund and the Klan are the same."[67]

Those were fighting words to many Americans, as the country edged toward involvement in World War II. Complaints swamped Congress, demanding that the House Committee on Un-American Activities investigate Klan ties to the Bund. Committee chairman Martin Dies, Jr., a die-hard Texas segregationist, was more interested in chasing Communists, but politicians often heed a squeaky wheel. Slowly, by fits and starts, the inquiry began.

Congress: Round Three

Dies had actually learned of Klan ties with the Bund four months prior to the Camp Nordland rally. In April 1940, while investigating William Pelley's Silver Shirts and allied groups, the committee, uncovered letters seized from Pelley's North Carolina headquarters in 1934, written by Captain Samuel Rubley of the Michigan National Guard. Rubley told Pelley he was training members of the Klan in horsemanship and gunnery, and offered similar instruction to the Silver Shirts. Dies issued subpoenas for Rubley and several Michigan knights, but no further news of the investigation was forthcoming.[68]

Two years later, in April 1942, the Southern Workers' Defense League challenged Dies and company to mount a full-scale Klan investigation, focused on the order's anti–Semitism, its attacks on unions, and stockpiling of arms by Klan auxiliaries called "Faithful Fifties."[69] In fact, Dies had announced a probe of the Klan three months earlier, on January 26, and while Congress funded the investigation, it quickly died on the vine.[70] Colescott faced the committee, received a soft scolding for the order's anti–Catholicism, and was urged to guide his knights "back to the original objectives of the Klan." Committee member Joe Starnes of Alabama deemed the Klan "just as American as the Baptist or Methodist Church, as the Lions Club or the Rotary Circle."[71] Soon afterward, when Dies addressed an Elk's lodge in Atlanta, reporters spotted Colescott in the audience.[72]

The rally at Camp Nordland did have repercussions in New Jersey. Colescott dismissed Bell as grand dragon, and the Garden State realm lost members.[73] In 1943, when Bishop Alma White republished her pro–Klan screeds from the 1920s, she selectively deleted the worst racist, nativist, and anti–Semitic passages.[74]

Klansmen had nothing to fear from the Dies Committee, but another branch of the federal government proved more dangerous.

Death and Taxes

Klan finances had been shady from the start, perhaps deliberately so during the great membership boom of the 1920s. Local officers made headlines by absconding with their klaverns' treasuries from time to time, and no one seemed to know exactly how much money was received by Imperial Headquarters.

No one, that is, except the Bureau of Internal Revenue.

In April 1944 Colescott received a bill for $685,305, including taxes, penalties and interest from the Klan's glory days under Hiram Evans.[75] As he described the scene, "I was sitting there in my office in the Imperial Palace in Atlanta one day, just as pretty as you please, when the Revenuers knocked on my door and said they had come to collect three-quarters of a million dollars the government had just figured out the Klan owed on profits earned during the 1920s! We had to sell all our assets and hand over the proceeds to the government and go out of business."[76] On April 23, a klonvokation in Atlanta "repealed all decrees, vacated all offices, voided all charters, and relieved every Klansman of any obligation whatever."[77] To the press, Colescott declared, "The Klan is dead. The whole thing is washed up."[78]

Or, was it?

When his temper cooled, Colescott—en route to retirement in Florida—told reporters,

"This does not mean that the Klan is dead. We have simply released local chapters from all obligations, financial and otherwise, to the imperial headquarters. I am still the imperial wizard. The other officials still retain their titles, although of course the functions of us all are suspended. We have authority to meet and reincarnate at any time."[79]

When might that occur?

"About that," Colescott said, "you can't tell. The Klan has always come out, and come out on top, when it was needed. Lots of people tell us that it is needed now more than any time in history."[80]

For the moment, however, journalists were more concerned with former Klansmen, and specifically with Senator Harry Truman of Missouri. Tapped by FDR as his fourth vice president in 1944, Truman endured the usual media scrutiny, including his rise to prominence through Kansas City's corrupt Pendergast machine, and his application for Klan membership in 1922. Truman admitted joining the Klan for political benefit, but claimed that he demanded a refund of his klecktoken after attending his first meeting, where a kleagle railed against Catholics. Henceforth, Truman declared, "If I had shown up at a meeting, the Klan would have pulled me apart."[81]

Perhaps, but if Truman drew the line at persecuting Catholics, his attitude toward other minorities, revealed in his posthumously published private letters, was distinctly klannish. He referred to New York City as "kike town," dismissed Slavs as "Bohunks," branded Italians "Dagos," and labeled Mexico as "Greaserdom."[82] A decade before signing up with the Klan, Truman wrote to his fiancée, "I think one man is just as good as another so long as he's honest and decent and not a nigger or a Chinaman. Uncle Will says that the Lord made a white man from dust, a nigger from mud, then He threw up what was left and it came down a Chinaman. He does hate Chinese and Japs. So do I. It is race prejudice, I guess. But I am strongly of the opinion Negroes ought to be in Africa, yellow men in Asia and white men in Europe and America." Later, as a senator, he described one White House banquet as "nigger picnic day," served by "an army of coons."[83]

Nor did Truman's attitude change much after FDR's death propelled him into the Oval Office. After a meeting with Henry Morgenthau in July 1947, discussing refugees in Palestine, Truman wrote in his diary: "The Jews, I find are very, very selfish. They care not how many Estonians, Latvians, Finns, Poles, Yugoslavs or Greeks get murdered or mistreated as [displaced persons] as long as the Jews get special treatment. Yet when they have power, physical, financial or political neither Hitler nor Stalin has anything on them for cruelty or mistreatment to the under dog."[84]

Truman's flirtation with the Klan would not stop FDR from winning reelection to a fourth term in 1944, but other politicians suffered by association with the Invisible Empire. Robert Lyons, a millionaire attorney, chain-store lobbyist, and member of the Republican National Committee from Indiana, resigned his seat on that august body in June 1944, when he was exposed as an active 1920s Klansman. Four months later, Hal Styles, Democratic nominee to the House of Representatives from California's Fifteenth Congressional District, found himself unmasked as a former Kluxer. Styles admitted joining the Klan in 1926, but had resigned in 1930, penning a series of newspaper exposés lambasting the order.[85] All in vain, as it turned out: on election day, Styles trailed his Republican opponent by a margin of 26,605 votes.[86]

CHAPTER 6

Fire in the Ashes
(1945–1953)

Knights who had weathered the Depression were in no mood to disband in April 1944. On May 21, Georgia's former grand dragon, Atlanta obstetrician Samuel Green, announced creation of a new order, the Association of Georgia Klans (AGK).[1] Three days later, in Virginia, Joel Baskin chartered a new front group for his dwindling realm, a short-lived American Shore Patrol, ostensibly concerned with fighting illegal immigration.[2] On September 7, Sunshine State officials granted a charter to the Knights of the Ku Klux Klan of Florida, led by A. F. Gulliam, H. F. McCormack, and A. B. Taylor.[3] Other Klans would sprout and flourish in the postwar years, defying Hiram Evans's warning that "you can't start a fire in wet ashes," but Dr. Green's AGK emerged as the era's dominant Klan.[4]

Rebuilding an Empire

Green announced his Klan's revival on October 13, 1945, with a cross-burning ceremony atop Stone Mountain.[5] Klansman James Reagan Venable, owner of the mountain and soon-to-be mayor of nearby Stone Mountain Village, had granted the Klan a perpetual easement in October 1923, with full rights to hold meetings any time.[6] Reporters billed Green's rally as the first cross-burning since Pearl Harbor, but in fact it was not even the first of 1945. Three had been lit in Knoxville on March 18; five around Birmingham on March 28; and two in August near Flemington, New Jersey, visible for 60 miles. Days after the Stone Mountain rally, Miami Klansmen burned five crosses at the homes of African American families.[7]

Despite its name and lack of a national charter, the AGK was not confined to Georgia. The order soon expanded, planting klaverns in Alabama, Florida, the Carolinas, and Tennessee, making Dr. Green the predominant Klan leader of the latter 1940s.[8] "All factions," Green declared, "had to unite to win the war" against Communism, embodied in "radical" labor unions, proposed anti-lynching legislation, integration of America's armed forces, and President Truman's call for a permanent Fair Employment Practices Commission.[9] Virginia kleagle Robert Byrd particularly feared removal of the military color line, writing to Mississippi senator (and Klansman) Theodore Bilbo in December 1945: "I shall never fight in the armed forces with a negro by my side. Rather I should die a thousand times, and see Old Glory trampled in the dirt never to rise again, than to see this beloved land of ours become degraded by race mongrels, a throwback to the blackest specimen from the wilds." In 1946, while campaigning for a seat in his state's House of Delegates, Byrd wrote to Dr. Green: "The Klan is needed today as never before, and I am anxious to see its rebirth here in West Virginia and in every state in the nation."[10]

Despite such enthusiasm, the Klan faced opposition on all sides. Green sought to revive the order's Georgia charter in March 1946, paying dues from 1943 forward, but he was blocked by hostile state officials and the federal tax lien that put James Colescott out of business.[11] California's attorney general revoked the Klan's charter on May 21, 1946, declaring that the order "taught racial hatred through violence and intimidation." Two months later, a New York court dissolved that state's charter, leaving anyone who tried to launch a new Klan subject to jail time and a $10,000 fine. Other legal bars to Klan activity were raised in Kentucky, New Jersey, and Wisconsin.[12]

Things looked better in Georgia, despite official opposition. Klansmen had escaped prosecution for the murder of a black Atlanta cab driver, Porter Turner, in August 1945, and Green had initiated 227 new recruits before an audience of 2,000 atop Stone Mountain, on May 9, 1946, declaring, "We are revived."[13] Best of all, longtime friend Eugene Talmadge was seeking his third term as governor, stumping the state with a series of racist speeches that prompted one audience to burn a black church in Soperton. Proud of his record for pardoning floggers, Talmadge nonetheless proclaimed himself "the only candidate in Georgia who isn't a Klansman." Still, when Atlanta policeman and active knight Samuel Roper approached Talmadge, seeking his advice for discouraging black voters, Talmadge grabbed a notepad and scrawled one word: "Pistols."[14]

Talmadge won the Democratic primary, and thus the office, since Republicans offered no candidate, but a liver ailment killed him in December, before his inauguration. Three weeks later, state legislators chose Herman Talmadge as his father's successor, contested by incumbent Ellis Arnall and lieutenant governor-elect Melvin Thompson. In March 1947, Georgia's Supreme Court declared Thompson victorious in the "three governors controversy," but Herman Talmadge would return in 1948, backed by the AGK.[15]

While Georgians tried to choose a governor, Klan expansion continued nationwide. Crosses blazed in Flint, Michigan, opposing a black political candidate, and around Los Angeles, including one planted at a Jewish fraternity house at the University of Southern California. Indiana king kleagle Harold Overton announced that his office was processing 121,000 new applications. Opposition came swiftly from the American Legion, the Jewish War Veterans, the South Carolina Baptist Convention, and various Presbyterian synods. In May 1946, Attorney General Tom Clark reported that FBI agents were investigating Klan resurgences in Georgia, Florida, Mississippi, Tennessee, New York, Michigan, and California. No results of that inquiry were published—if it ever occurred—but in December 1947 Clark added Green's AGK to an ever-growing federal list of "subversive" organizations.[16]

"Have You Got Three Dollars?"

Also added to that roster was America's first postwar neo–Nazi group, the Atlanta-based Columbian Workers Movement, better known as the Columbians Inc. Borrowing its uniforms and lightning-bolt insignia from Adolf Hitler's Third Reich, the group was founded in August 1946 by rabid anti–Semites Homer Loomis, Jr., and Emory Burke, a disciple of George Deatherage who attended the joint Klan-Bund rally at Camp Nordland in 1940.[17] Recruits pronounced an oath that read:

> I believe America today is a battlefield upon which two forces are contending for mastery; those two forces are the authentic American spirit and the anti–American, anti-western spirit of invasion and materialism.
>
> I believe the question which most clearly marks the line of battle between these two opposing, world shaking forces, is the subject of race.
>
> I believe the idea of Race Purity is born of the authentic American spirit, and those who champion this holy idea count among their fellow fighters the spirit of our great dead.
>
> I believe the idea of Racial Amalgamation is spawned by that anti–American, anti-western, alien spirit and that those who carry the banner of this idea are in mortal conflict with the whole depths of the American soul.
>
> I believe the time has come for every man to step forward and enlist to fight in the struggle either on the side of the American Spirit or on the side of the alien Asiatic spirit.
>
> I take my stand to fight in the ranks of those who believe in the holy American ideals of RACE, NATION and FAITH.[18]

Recruitment was much simpler. Application blanks asked only: "Do you hate niggers? Do you hate Jews? Have you got three dollars?"[19] Appealing to "those of our brothers and sisters that many of the politicians call 'poor white trash,'" the Columbians recruited at least 500 members in Atlanta and planted tiny outposts in Philadelphia, Indianapolis, New York City and Gary, Indiana. Financial supporters included George Deatherage, Gerald L. K. Smith, and young Klansman Jesse Benjamin Stoner, an AGK kleagle in Chattanooga. While Dr. Green shunned the group, Columbians talked tough, planning to control Atlanta within six months, Georgia by 1948, and the United States by 1956.[20]

Those ambitious plans soon unraveled. The Anti-Defamation League and the Non-Sectarian Anti-Nazi League planted informers within the Columbians' ranks, including one Stetson Kennedy, a Floridian who also joined the AGK as "John Perkins," reporting back on the activities of both groups. Kennedy was present when J. B. Stoner addressed Dr. Green's Atlanta klavern, raving, "We ought to get all Jews out of our country, and I don't mean send them to some other country! I'll never be satisfied as long as there are Jews here or anywhere. I think we ought to kill all Jews just to save their unborn generations from having to go to Hell!" Kennedy pegged Stoner as "stark raving crazy," and Dr. Green agreed, banishing Stoner from the AGK after his hysterical performance."[21]

Meanwhile, the Columbians were busy defending Atlanta's residential color line, climaxed on October 31, 1946, with the bombing of an black couple's home. Investigation of that crime exposed a Columbians "lynch list" including the names of Mayor William Hatsfield, *Atlanta Constitution* editor Ralph McGill, and Assistant Attorney General Dan Duke, who dubbed Columbians "the juvenile delinquents of the Klan." Author Steven Weinburger suggests that police applied themselves industriously to the Columbians' case, not to protect local blacks, but because the group drew members from the AGK, which many officers had joined. (FBI director J. Edgar Hoover, conversely, dismissed the group as "just a front for the KKK.") The net result was prosecution on multiple charges, sending Burke and Loomis to prison. By the time state authorities revoked the Columbians' charter in June 1947, die-hard members had moved on to Columbus, Georgia, joining longtime Klansman Evall "Parson Jack" Johnston as members of his new Christian Crusaders League.[22] J. B. Stoner, cut

Stetson Kennedy infiltrated the Klan and Columbians in 1946 (National Archives).

adrift from both groups, rebounded with formation of the Stoner Anti-Jewish Party, late in 1946.[23]

"Bombingham" and Beyond

The AGK reluctantly surrendered its own Georgia charter in June 1947, but unlike the Columbians, it was not prepared to disband. If anything, Green's Klan appeared to be rejuvenated by announcement of the CIO's "Operation Dixie" campaign, launched in 1946 to unionize labor in twelve Southern states. As in the past, labor organizers faced a coalition of Klansmen, police (often Kluxers themselves), and political puppets of the South's ruling class. Violence was routine, with Alabama governor James "Big Jim" Folsom candidly admitting that Ku Klux raids were "directed from tall buildings."[24] Stetson Kennedy, appointed as the CIO's southeastern editorial director, opined, "In a very real sense, the conflict between progress and reaction on the Southern front is the struggle of the CIO vs. the KKK, for these two organizations spearhead the opposing forces: democracy versus white supremacy."[25]

Dr. Green agreed, declaring, "No CIO or AFL carpetbagging organizers or any other damned Yankees are going to come into the South and tell Southerners how to run either their businesses or their niggers." Green spoke vaguely of a Klan alliance with Georgia's taxi drivers, hinting, "The time may soon come when we might need every cab in Atlanta to do some quick work."[26] Additionally, he could count on policemen like John "Trigger" Nash, honored at a klavern meeting on November 1, 1948, for killing his thirteenth black man "in the line of duty." As recorded by Stetson Kennedy, Nash rose to applause "and said he hoped he wouldn't have all the honor of killing the niggers in the South and he hoped the people would do something about it themselves."[27]

Something was being done in Birmingham, where a federal court banned racial zoning on July 31, 1947. Eighteen days later, Klansmen bombed a home purchased by blacks in a formerly all-white neighborhood. By 1949, so many blasts had echoed through the "Magic City" that residents dubbed its bitterly disputed Smithfield district "Dynamite Hill." Others referred to Birmingham as "Bombingham." Most—if not all—of those blasts were later laid at the door of Robert "Dynamite Bob" Chambliss, a Klansman since 1924, whose criminal record dated from October 1935. He and his fellow terrorists were sheltered from arrest by Eugene "Bull" Connor, who controlled both the police and fire departments as Birmingham's commissioner of public safety. Under Connor, police not only ignored crimes committed by Klansmen, but actively collaborated in them, sometimes delivering bombs in their city patrol cars.[28]

No definitive tally of Birmingham bombings exists—at least nine are confirmed between August 1947 and May 1951, while most reports claim "about 50" blasts between 1947 and 1965—but the conviction count remained at zero while terrorists elsewhere emulated Alabama's example.[29] Klansmen in Nashville burned a fifteen-foot cross at the site of a proposed black housing project in April 1949, then returned to bomb it in January 1950. By July 1952, homes purchased by blacks were bombed, burned, or stoned in Warren, Ohio; New York City; Richmond, Virginia; Atlanta; Dallas; Los Angeles; and Chicago.[30] Prosecutors indicted AGK grand klaliff (vice president) Charles Klein for the Atlanta bombing on July 27, 1951, but jurors deadlocked at his trial in January 1952, despite Klein's confession that he and two other Klansmen bombed the house "to teach them niggers on East Avenue a lesson."[31]

"Bolshevik Klans" and Dixiecrats

Dr. Green's AGK certainly committed its share of violent crimes, but competitors were also active in the field. Green dubbed them "Bolshevik Klans, which pulled out because they couldn't run things themselves," led by men whose goal was "to make a potful of money."[32] Their number included:

The *Federated Knights of the Ku Klux Klan*, also called the Federated Ku Klux Klans Inc., founded in Birmingham by Georgia native William Hugh Morris on June 21, 1946.

Other high-ranking members included a physician, Dr. E. P. Pruitt, and real estate developer Robert Gullege.[33]

The *Original Southern Klans Inc.*, launched on June 30, 1948, by Alton Pate of Columbus, Georgia, with aid from "Parson Jack" Johnston and attorney Fred New. While immensely irritating to Dr. Green, the OSK was short-lived, disbanding in February 1949.[34]

The *Southern Knights of the Ku Klux Klan*, founded by Grand Dragon William Hendrix of Tallahassee in March 1949. The ink was barely dry on its first run of hate literature when Hendrix renamed it the Southern and Northern Knights, dreaming of vast expansion under his rule as "National Adjutant."[35]

The *Federated Klans of Alabama*, founded in Birmingham by Dr. E. P. Pruitt, in July 1949, after William Morris and his Federated Knights ran afoul of the law on flogging charges.[36]

None of the pretenders rivaled Green's Klan in size or geographic range, but all would make their presence known through public demonstrations, cross-burnings, whippings, bombings, and other crimes. Even old Klansmen could still rate headlines, as when paroled killer Philip Fox surfaced in Texas, serving as an aide to gubernatorial candidate Beauford Jester in August 1946. Rival Homer Rainey trumpeted Fox's record in an effort to derail Jester, but in vain.[37] Jester won the election but suffered a fatal heart attack in July 1949, the only Texas governor to die in office.[38]

Politics was all the rage for Klansmen in 1948, in Georgia and nationwide. Herman Talmadge returned as promised, challenging Governor Melvin Thompson, who had pressed Green's Klan to surrender its charter. Thompson's legal pursuit of the AGK had foundered in November 1947, when Attorney General Eugene Cook reported that files on the Klan, allegedly naming "prominent individuals," had been stolen from his office.[39] Talmadge, by contrast, had attended Green's birthday party in November 1946, declaring that the Klan, "through its power and influence was of tremendous assistance in electing my father. My father and I were among the first to point out the dangers of Negro voting, particularly since they are easily controlled by a shrewder race. I believe in the Ku Klux Klan, and will fight for it and white supremacy with the last drop of my blood."[40] Green returned the compliment in 1948, calling Talmadge "the only hope for white supremacy in Georgia," touting his election as the Klan's top priority. It would be a "hot year," Green promised, with "something doing almost every night."[41]

In practice, that meant terrorizing Georgia's registered black voters with masked parades and motorcades, cross-burnings, threatening letters, and placement on doorsteps of miniature coffins labeled "KKK". Where intimidation failed to keep blacks at home on primary day, mayhem followed. Klansmen beat D. V. Carter in Montgomery County, for recruiting black voters, and when Isaiah Nixon—one of those he registered—cast his ballot on September 8, white brothers Jim and Johnny Johnson shot Nixon the same day, with his wife and six children watching. Prosecutors filed murder charges, but an all-white jury acquitted Johnny Johnson on November 8, while his brother's case was dismissed.[42] Talmadge, meanwhile, swept a field of four candidates, securing 97.5 percent of the mostly-white vote and a two-year term as governor.[43]

Dr. Green was among the first to congratulate Talmadge on his landslide, afterward declaring, "At last the Klan has a friend in the governor's chair. We're sitting on top of the world and nothing can stop us. Herman has assured me of his cooperation at all times, and

Georgia Klansmen led by Dr. Green campaign for Herman Talmadge in 1948 (Library of Congress).

has promised to go all the way down the road to protect the Klan. If you ever need anything from him, be sure to make it known that you are a friend of Sam Green's." As a gesture of appreciation, Talmadge named Green's second-in-command, Atlanta policeman Sam Roper, to lead the Georgia Bureau of Investigation (GBI). Statewide, NAACP membership soon plummeted from 11,000 to 3,000, while Klan membership leapt to an estimated 100,000.[44]

A second black man who dared to vote in Georgia that year, Robert Mallard of Toombs County, paid the ultimate price on November 20, 1948. While driving home from a school function with his wife, son, and two other children, Mallard was ambushed by a group of white men, wearing Klan robes and hoods but unmasked, who shot him in his car. Sheriff R. E. Gray, also Klansman, pretended to investigate, initially casting suspicion on Mallard's wife. Later, he grudgingly admitted that the killers wore "some white stuff," but labeled Mallard "a bad Negro ... hated by all who knew him." Governor Talmadge ordered a GBI investigation on November 24, and Sam Roper dispatched Lieutenant W. E. McDuffie—who arrested Mrs. Mallard at her husband's funeral, telling reporters, "I think the Ku Klux Klan has been wrongfully accused in this case." Sheriff Gray gave Dr. Green an official statement exonerating the AGK, and GBI Sergeant J. W. Robertson voiced his "belief" that "the KKK had no part in killing this mean Negro." Meanwhile, Klan kop "Trigger" Nash addressed

Atlanta's klavern, telling his hooded brethren Governor Talmadge had ordered GBI agents "not to believe everything the niggers tell them" about Mallard's slaying.[45]

Police soon dropped their specious murder charge against Mrs. Mallard, and five white suspects surrendered on December 4, accompanied by attorney T. Ross Sharpe, a reputed Klansman. Mrs. Mallard identified one suspect—William Howell—as a member of the gang that shot her husband, but Sheriff Gray refused to file charges. At a special grand jury hearing, Mrs. Mallard repeated her identification of Howell, and identified a car owned by suspect Roderick Clifton as part of the fatal roadblock. Both defendants were indicted, while the others were discharged. At Howell's trial, on January 11, 1949, Mrs. Mallard broke down on the witness stand while, *Time* magazine reported, "A lot of people in the audience couldn't help laughing." Defense attorneys blamed "outsiders" and a home-grown "enemy"—Ralph McGill at the *Atlanta Constitution*—for persecuting their innocent clients, and called two jury members to testify as character witnesses for the accused. (Both declared their disbelief of Mrs. Mallard's testimony.) Spectators cheered Howell's same-day acquittal, and prosecutors dismissed all charges against Clifton.[46]

Georgia was not the only state to witness voter intimidation in 1948. In Florida, black half-brothers Harry Moody and J. T. Smith registered 150 African Americans in Gadsden County, despite persistent threats and drive-by shootings. Klansmen bombed one brother's home, crippling one of his children, and ultimately drove both from the county. Mississippi's *Jackson Daily News* printed the names of black voting activists, warning African Americans that voting might produce "unhealthy and unhappy results." In Louisiana, Klansmen mailed threats that blacks who voted would be put "out of business," and that whites were "figuring on raising Hell" for any who cast ballots.[47]

That violence was tacitly encouraged by leaders of the "Dixiecrat" movement, a group of southern racists who abandoned the mainstream Democratic Party at its national convention in 1948. Bull Connor led the Alabama delegation's walkout on July 13, and four days later welcomed delegates to Birmingham for the foundation of the States' Rights Party. Among those present were Gerald L. K. Smith, J. B. Stoner, Oklahoma anti–Semite William "Alfalfa Bill" Murray (author of *The Negroes' Place in Call of Race*), and 1920s Klansman Horace Wilkinson—who told reporters, "I'm against Truman for the same reason I was against Al Smith. He thinks too damn much of the niggers." Keynote speaker Frank Dixon, nephew of racist author Thomas Dixon, drew criticism from the *Anniston Star* for sounding as if he were "addressing the Ku Klux Klan convocation." The assemblage took only one ballot to nominate South Carolina governor Strom Thurmond—another friend of Dr. Green—as its presidential candidate, with Mississippi governor Fielding Wright as his running mate.[48]

Ten days after the Dixiecrat defection, Democrats suffered another loss when their party's left wing broke away to create the Progressive Party, nominating ex-vice president Henry Wallace. Progressives in Dixie faced harassment from police and Klansmen alike, if there was any difference, and Birmingham set the standard. When the city's all-black Sixteenth Street Baptist Church offered to host a rally of the Southern Negro Youth Conference, Bull Connor warned the pastor of a "risk of damage to church property," declaring that God—using Klansmen as his agents—would "strike the church down." On election day, Harry Truman surprised his critics by polling 24.1 million votes to 21.9 million for Republican rival Thomas Dewey. Thurmond carried five southern states, with 1.6 million votes, while Wallace did nearly as well, logging 1.15 million.[49] The South had not risen again, but it was far from defeated.

Dixie Burning

Despite their national defeat, or because of it, Klansmen rode into violent action across four states in 1949. William Morris probably inflated his claim that 30,000 knights swore allegiance to his Federated Klans, but Dr. Green boasted authentically of active klaverns in each of Georgia's 159 counties. Even the defunct Columbians were stirring in Atlanta, disguised as the "American Bilbo Club."[50] In Chattanooga, Klansmen staged a series of raids and floggings, forcing Dr. Green to revoke their klavern's charter.[51]

Matters were more serious in Florida, where admitted ex–Klansman Fuller Warren won election as governor in 1948. Despite courting support from the all-black Progressive Voter's League, Warren was a staunch segregationist who recruited "former" Klansmen for the state police and named John Matthews, a "bed-fellow of the Ku Klux Klan," to serve on the state supreme court.[52] In July 1949, after teenager Norma Padgett claimed four blacks had raped her near Groveland, Klansmen ran amok for three days, burning shops and homes, riddling others with gunfire. Sheriff Willis McCall, a friend of the Klan who escorted Ku Klux motorcades through Lake County, observed the violence without interfering until National Guardsmen arrived with bayonets and tear gas. Hooded parades through neighboring counties scattered leaflets stamped with AGK logos.[53]

Closer to home, in Georgia's Dade County, black resident Mamie Clay came under harassment when she refused a white stranger's offer to buy her rural home. Sheriff John Lynch and his deputies joined a Klan campaign to make her life miserable, finally leading a raid to break up a "wild party" on April 2, 1949. They arrested seven visitors and delivered them to a waiting mob of masked Klansmen who drove their captives to a wooded area, flogged each in turn, then warned them to "go home and not breathe a word to anyone about this."[54] A federal grand jury convened in early August and questioned 70 witnesses, including Dr. Green, who claimed the floggers were merely "disguised as Ku Klux Klansmen."[55] (Nonetheless, he had already stripped the local klavern of its charter.[56]) The panel listened, then indicted Lynch, three deputies, and eight Klansmen on charges of violating the 1871 Ku Klux Act.[57] Jurors at their first trial failed to reach a verdict, in December 1949, but a second panel convicted Lynch and Deputy William Hartline in March 1950, acquitting the rest.[58] Lynch and Hartline each received the maximum one-year prison term, with a $1,000 fine.[59]

It was in Alabama, however, where Klansmen under William Morris conducted the postwar era's most sustained reign of terror. Aside from Birmingham's bombings, members of the Federated Klans attacked unionized workers and, in June 1948, raided a Girl Scout camp in Jefferson County, harassing its interracial group of counselors. The raid's leader told his captive audience, "White women have no business living in a Negro camp. We don't like it and the people around here don't like it. We mean to see that our orders are carried out." While local newspapers criticized the raid, Morris penned his own justification, declaring that "first three and later two white women were living within the confines of said camp on equal basis with Negro women, eating at the same table with and at the same time that the

Negro women ate. Using the same toilet facilities with and at the same time the Negro women did. Visiting the white merchants of the locality to make purchases and telephone calls arm in arm with Negro women, calling them by their first names and in turn being called by their first names; and in other ways and physical embraces and contacts becoming the said Negro women's social equals."[60]

No indictments resulted, despite formation of a short-lived anti–Klan group called Citizens Against Mobism, and Klansmen took that lapse as an invitation to further aggression. Kidnappings and floggings ensued, with many of the victims being white, selected for their deviation from Klan "morality." One such victim was Mrs. Hugh McDanal, dragged from her home with three guests for punishment on charges of selling whiskey, renting rooms to unmarried couples, and "dancing nude on her front porch." Mrs. McDanal fought back, ripping off one Klansman's mask and recognizing Coleman "Brownie" Lollar, formerly a "special deputy" of Jefferson County's sheriff until his attendance at Klan rallies in full uniform got him fired.[61] A local grand jury indicted Lollar, his brother, and fifteen other Klansmen on felony charges, while demanding that Morris produce his membership list. He refused, then claimed the roll was stolen, and spent 67 days in jail before recreating a partial list "from memory." At Brownie Lollar's trial, defense attorneys produced a photo of Mrs. McDanal unclothed at her home, and jurors earned thunderous applause by acquitting the ex-deputy. Charges against his codefendants were dismissed.[62] Likewise, no indictments were filed in Birmingham's ongoing series of bombings through 1949–50, including five attacks on homes of black ministers, one whose house was bombed three times.[63]

Despite the failure of police and prosecutors to perform their duties, times were gradually changing. State legislators, fearing federal intervention, introduced a law to ban wearing of masks in public. Dr. E. P. Pruitt, now leading his own splinter Klan, solicited Governor James Folsom's friendship, telling him, "Your enemies are my enemies. My friends are your friends." Pruitt also ordered his knights to unmask voluntarily, while Morris stood firm on tradition.[64] Lawmakers passed the anti-mask law overwhelmingly, imposing a one-year jail term and $500 fine for donning masks aside from Halloween, Mardi Gras and similar occasions. Governor Folsom signed the bill into law on June 28, 1949.[65]

Death of a Dragon

Two weeks after his grand jury testimony in Dade County, on August 18, 1949, Dr. Green collapsed from a fatal heart attack at his home in Atlanta. Sam Roper succeeded Green as grand dragon of the AGK on August 27, already facing trouble. On August 24, Internal Revenue agents had slapped the Klan with a tax bill for $9,322.40, spanning the years 1946–48. Roper paid under protest, then was hit with another lien, demanding $8,382.72.[66]

Rival Klans continued to proliferate, with a new Knights of the Ku Klux Klan of America founded in Montgomery on August 8, 1949, by 50 delegates from splinter Klans in Alabama, Arkansas, Louisiana, Mississippi, Missouri, and Tennessee. "Imperial Emperor" Lycurgus Spinks—an aging self-ordained minister and "sexologist," who sometimes billed himself as the reincarnation of George Washington—ran the show, claiming to speak for every Klansmen in the country, whether or not they acknowledged his leadership.[67] "There's a million of them now," Spinks claimed, "and in five years there'll be five million. If you ain't one of them, you won't know who they are and you won't know where they are. You'll just know they are there, and there ain't no power on earth can stop them."[68] That kind of braggadocio won Spinks a spot on radio's *Meet the Press* program, on September 9, where his unintentionally hilarious performance heaped ridicule on the Klan. Among other gems, he claimed Jesus Christ was a Klansman, dodged questions concerning an embezzlement charge in South Carolina, and generally made a fool of himself. Asked if a cross should be burned or borne, Spinks said, "Both," then added, "How you going to *borne* a cross. Who ever heard of such a fool thing?"[69]

While the Spinks sideshow dragged on, Sam Roper sought a new alliance of his own. In November 1949 he announced "a working agreement" between the AGK and Hugh Morris's Federated Klans that would "eventually lead to consolidation."[70] In fact, that merger never occurred. The next big news—and scandal—of the Invisible Empire was already brewing in the Carolinas.

"A Special Thermometer in Hell"

Thomas Lemuel Hamilton was born in Aiken, South Carolina, in 1907, the son of a grocer who died in 1910. Saturated from birth with tales of the gallant Confederacy, Hamilton followed is father's trade with the A&P grocery chain and joined the Klan in 1926, the same year Aiken witnessed a triple lynching. A reporter for the *New York World* called Hamilton's hometown "a sore spot in South Carolina" and the Klan's greatest stronghold within the Palmetto State, noting that "[a]lmost every petty official in Aiken has at least one dead Negro to his credit, and there is an acquittal of murder in almost every case." The Klan was equally strong in nearby Augusta, Georgia, where A&P transferred Hamilton in 1930, coinciding with a new klavern's foundation by Dr. Green. There, Hamilton met his bride-to-be, a teacher and Klanswoman who shared his passion for "100-percent Americanism."[71]

By 1940 Hamilton had his own grocery store in Augusta's Frog Hollow section, ironically serving a largely black clientele, and was rising through the ranks of the local Baptist Church and Masonic lodge. He remained loyal to the Klan after the national order's dissolution in 1944, and helped Dr. Green launch the AGK two years later. Despite condemnation from the Augusta Citizens Union, Hamilton's klavern gained strength through 1948, expanding to pursue what he called "contract work in the two Carolinas." According to one report, Green chartered Thomas L. Hamilton Klavern No. 42 in Langley, South Carolina, in April 1949. At Green's death, four months later, the *Augusta Chronicle* reported that an unnamed "Augustan prominent in local Ku Klux Klan circles is understood to be in line for the position of Grand Dragon of the Association of Georgia Klans."[72]

That job went, instead, to Sam Roper, who told a very different story of Hamilton's Carolina recruiting efforts in November 1949. According to Roper, he had named Hamilton as South Carolina's grand dragon on September 2, followed swiftly by Hamilton's defection to form an Association of Carolina Klans. "As soon as he became acquainted with all the klaverns," Roper said, "Hamilton attempted to pull them out of the Association of Georgia Klans. I believe the majority of the Carolina klaverns will remain loyal to the parent organization."[73]

Thomas Hamilton (in dark robe and glasses) led the early 1950s Association of Carolina Klans (Library of Congress).

He was mistaken. By year's end, Hamilton had sold his Augusta grocery and moved to Leesville, South Carolina, while Roper sent loyalist Tommy Panther to proselytize for the AGK. Panther vowed to "organize a unit of Klan in every incorporated city and town in North Carolina and Virginia," but fell far short of that goal. Operating in tandem with—but without approval from—Billy Graham's evangelical crusade, Hamilton recruited hundreds, perhaps thousands, of knights in the Carolinas. By spring of 1950 his Klan's greatest strength was concentrated in the border region of Columbus County, North Carolina, and Horry County, South Carolina. In July, Tabor City's police chief volunteered to lead a Klan parade through town, noting that "he had several places in mind he would like the parade to pass, all of which were in the city limits and would not take much time." Horace Carter, editor of the *Tabor City Tribune*, described a procession complete with wailing sirens and blank pistol shots, while Klansmen "monopolized the streets" and "created a general confusion."[74]

Five weeks later, on August 26, another parade sparked violence in Myrtle Beach, South Carolina. The target was Charlie's Place, a black nightclub named for owner Charlie Fitzgerald, rumored to accept white patrons. On their first pass, Klansmen brandished guns and clubs, shouting, "Look out nigger, we're coming!" They returned two hours later, firing 300 shots into Charlie's Place, wounding Fitzgerald's sister and two other victims, then kidnapped Fitzgerald, whipped him, and cropped his ears with a knife. Miraculously, the only fatality was a Klansman—Conway policeman James Johnson, shot by persons unknown while wearing a hood and robe over his uniform.[75]

In the wake of that raid, Horry County Sheriff Ernest Sasser jailed Hamilton and several other knights, delivering documents seized from Hamilton's home to the FBI. A preliminary hearing on September 30 found probable cause to hold the suspects for trial, but a grand jury convened on October 5 refused to indict them. Hamilton emerged from custody triumphant and staged a rally on Armistice Day, inviting spectators to "come and hear the Klan side of the Myrtle Beach affair." Eight thousand turned out, treated to a recorded message from Florida Klansman Bill Hendrix, who "leveled most of his charges against the Jews on the grounds that they were Communists and seeking to destroy the United States." Hamilton followed that theme in his hour-long speech, adding the CIO and NAACP for good measure. Charlie's Place, meanwhile, was "touched on only lightly as the Grand Dragon proceeded to blast everything from churches, schools, newspapers and the United Nations to the President of the United States."[76]

North Carolina suffered the next violence, as Whiteville's Kolumbus Kounty Klavern unleashed a reign of nightriding terror led by policeman William Farrell. Early targets included Bessie Page, a white woman, and her reputed black lover Will Fowler, as well as Fowler's wife, said to be "going with" a white man. One Klansman later testified that Hamilton commanded, "Don't beat them until we get better organized. I'll give the orders." He gave them on January 18, 1951, at a meeting with Bill Hendrix in attendance, instructing his knights to "Give 'em a good whipping or you'll have to do it again." While Hamilton and Hendrix moved on to a public rally near Aiken, Klansmen struck the Flowers home, whipping both victims. Bessie Page, who lived nearby, witnessed the furor and escaped unharmed. The same night, raiders flogged two white disabled war veterans, prompting Sheriff Sasser to jail seven raiders. Hamilton responded by branding Sasser as "corrupt and ineffective."[77]

Hamilton's next rally, at Tabor City, saw him jailed "for having an illegal red light in the form of a cross on the front of his auto," but not before he exhorted Klansmen to defend the color line. "Do you want some burr-headed nigra to come up on your porch and ask for your daughter's hand in marriage?" he challenged. "If your preacher is telling you that, then he needs a special thermometer in hell to burn him with."[78]

It was all downhill from there, for Hamilton and his Klan. In June, a federal grand jury indicted Hamilton for violating postal laws by mailing a "libelous, scurrilous and defamatory" attack on ex-senator Wilton Hall to members of the state legislature. Convicted on October 30, Hamilton paid a $1,000 fine in lieu of prison time. Meanwhile, at least 10 floggings were reported from October 1951 through January 1952, most staged by Fair Bluff's klavern, led by policeman and two-time murder suspect Early Brooks. Eight of the targets were white, whipped for various "moral" infractions. More important, from the FBI's viewpoint, was the fact that two victims—Ben Grainger and Dorothy Martin—had been snatched in North Carolina, then driven across the state line for their beatings. While Hamilton disbanded the Fair Bluff klavern for "un–Klannish" behavior in January 1952, G-men prepared sweeping raids that jailed nearly 100 Klansmen. Brooks received a five-year prison term in May, and Hamilton was charged that same month with conspiracy in the Flowers floggings. Leading rallies to the very eve of his trial, he pled guilty on July 22 and received a four-year sentence. While incarcerated, he repudiated the Klan and apologized to his victims, emerging from prison in February 1954 to become a full-time Baptist preacher.[79]

Brushfire Battles

While Birmingham's floggers awaited their day in court, Alvin Horn of Talladega began recruiting Alabama members for the AGK. Recently banished from the Federated Klans "for the rest of his miserable life," Horn was suspected of participating in a raid that killed white victim Charlie Hurst of Pell City on February 22, leaving Hurst's son wounded. The raiders, all unmasked, were named as Charlie Carlisle, Jr., Roy Heath, Claude Luker, and Albert Wilson. Heath committed suicide on February 26, after telling Horn "he had been on a ride with some of the boys and a man got killed." Police also charged Horn, E. L. Hudson, and Jessie Wilson (Albert's father), but Carlisle was the only Klansman finally convicted, drawing a five-year sentence in June 1950. The other cases collapsed when prosecutors dismissed Horn's charges in October 1952.[80]

As Horn pursued his Klan career, a future friend of the order entered Alabama politics. Rear Admiral John Crommelin, Jr., enjoyed a distinguished naval career until 1950, when his paranoia and rampant anti–Semitism forced his separation from the service. Returning to his native Alabama, he tried his hand at farming, then cast his hat into the ring as the "white man's candidate" opposing incumbent Senator Lister Hill. Hill's Jewish ancestry and opposition to the 1920s Klan became an issue in the race, with Crommelin branding Jews as the mortal enemies of "white Christian Alabamians," and while those sentiments earned him 38,477 votes, he was swamped by Hill's tally of 125,534.[81]

Florida was even more unsettled in those years than Alabama, as Harry Moore's Progressive Voters' League campaigned against lynching and sought to expand the black franchise. Bill Hendrix responded with an ever-changing cast of Klans, disbanding his Southern Knights in May 1949 to become Florida's grand dragon for the Georgia-based Original Southern Klans. By August, he deserted that group to create the Northern and Southern Knights, serving as "national adjutant" under an anonymous "Permanent Emperor Samuel II." After Stetson Kennedy identified that mysterious figure as Edgar Waybright, head of Duval County's Democratic Executive Committee, Hendrix announced "Samuel's" replacement by an imperial wizard known only as "No. 4-006800." In January 1950, Hendrix trumpeted the merger of his Klan with those led by Tom Hamilton and William Morris, joined in a war against "hate groups" including the NAACP, the Anti-Defamation League, and the Council of Churches of Christ in America.[82]

By early 1951, Florida's Klans had lapsed back into terrorism, beating and shooting a black Orlando janitor suspected of molesting girls in February, returning to murder his brother-in-law a month later. Florida's sluggish legislature banned public masking and unauthorized cross-burning in April, but the violence continued. A seven-month bombing campaign struck synagogues and Hebrew schools, integrated housing projects and a Catholic church, then climaxed on Christmas Day with a blast at Harry Moore's home, killing him and his wife on their 25th wedding anniversary. Governor Warren assigned former Klansman Jefferson Elliott to investigate Moore's murder, while FBI agents conducted a parallel probe, identifying most of Orange County's law enforcement officers as Klansmen. No arrests resulted, but Orlando Klansman Joseph Cox shot himself after his second FBI interview, and two other suspects died from natural causes during 1952. A federal grand jury indicted 10 Kluxers for perjury, but Klan attorney Edgar Waybright persuaded a friendly judge to dismiss the charges in January 1954. Successive announcements of renewed investigations in 1978, 1982, and 1991 revived interest in the Moore slayings, but produced no solutions.[83]

Bill Hendrix dodged the Moore investigation, announcing his gubernatorial candidacy in June 1951, then ran afoul of federal agents in February 1952, for mailing postcards that attacked Governor Warren and journalist Drew Pearson in terms "too libelous to appear in the public record." Fined $700, with a one-year prison term suspended, Hendrix told reporters, "It looks like I'm out of the mailing business." In July 1952 he created an ephemeral American Confederate Army, pledged to battle "if the Supreme Court ever outlaws racial segregation."[84] That winter, he announced plans to revive Virginia's Klan, but Dominion State legislators responded with new legislation mimicking Florida's ban on masks and cross-burning.[85]

A Waning Light

Across the country, Klans were in decline by 1953. Only ex-member Robert Byrd, on his way to Congress in January, could boast of success—and he was forced to fabricate a redacted version of his Klan membership, falsely claiming that he only belonged to the order from "mid–1942 to early 1943." He had joined, Byrd claimed, "because it offered excitement and because it was strongly opposed to communism." "After about a year," he continued, "I became disinterested, quit paying my dues, and dropped my membership in the organization. During the nine years that have followed, I have never been interested in the Klan." Conveniently forgotten were his role as kleagle and his 1946 correspondence with Dr. Green, urging Klan expansion in West Virginia.[86]

In 1952, J. B. Stoner renamed his neo–Nazi clique the Christian Anti-Jewish Party, moving from Tennessee to Georgia, where he studied nights to earn a degree from Atlanta Law School. In Atlanta, he renewed acquaintance with Klansman James Venable and struck up a friendship with classmate Edward Fields, a 20-year-old ex–Columbians member enamored of all things Hitlerian. Specifically, he admired Stoner's plan to "out–Hitler Hitler"—whom Stoner called a "moderate"—and his vow "to make being Jewish a crime, punishable by death." They briefly parted ways in 1953, Stoner remaining in Georgia to earn his degree, while Fields moved on to the Palmer School of Chiropractic in Davenport, Iowa, but they would reunite before the decade's end to battle integration and the vast Jewish conspiracy.[87]

Meanwhile, the Klans were struggling. C. L. Parker replaced Bill Hendrix as head of the Northern and Southern Knights in June 1953, renaming it the United Klan. In October he opened membership to blacks who supported segregation, but none accepted the offer.[88] Between those events, in July 1953, a defector from the Hendrix camp—private detective William Griffin, a Klansman since 1918—founded his own Association of Florida Ku Klux Klan in Tampa.[89] In Atlanta, meanwhile, Eldon Lee Edwards took time off from his job as a paint sprayer at General Motors' Fisher Body plant to launch the U.S. Klans of Georgia in September 1953, collecting remnants of Sam Roper's moribund AGK.[90] He would be ready eight months later, when nation's highest court breathed new life into the flagging Invisible Empire.

CHAPTER 7

Beyond "Black Monday"
(1954–1960)

Florida's Bill Hendrix had not experienced a psychic revelation in July 1952, when he warned of coming federal attacks on segregation. Storm clouds had been gathering since 1951, with lawsuits filed by the NAACP against segregated schools in Delaware, Kansas, South Carolina, Virginia, and Washington, D.C. Those petitions reached the Supreme Court in December 1952, consolidated under the collective title of *Oliver Brown, et al. v. Board of Education of Topeka, et al.* On May 17, 1954, a unanimous court overturned *Plessy v. Ferguson*, ruling that "in the field of public education the doctrine of 'separate but equal' has no place. Separate educational facilities are inherently unequal."[1] That ruling was a shot heard round the Jim Crow world, the opening gun of a 14-year guerrilla war against the tide of change.

"You Are Obligated to Defy It"

The *Brown* ruling affected schools in 20 states. Some instantly complied, some petulantly dragged their feet, while former members of the late Confederacy braced themselves for all-out resistance. In Mississippi, Senator James Eastland told his white constituents, "You are not required to obey any court which passes out such a ruling. In fact, you are obligated to defy it."[2] Another son of the Magnolia State, congressman John Bell Williams, dubbed the day of the court's decision "Black Monday"—soon purloined as the title of a racist tract by Judge Tom Brady, warning members of the race "Homo Caucasius" against acquiring the "mark of the beast" through race-mixing.[3] For Eastland and Brady, integrated classrooms were a short step from integrated bedrooms and the ultimate Communist goal of "mongrelization."

White resistance in Dixie formed along parallel lines. "Respectable" racists flocked to join Citizens' Councils, a loosely knit network of groups launched by Mississippian Robert "Tut" Patterson in July 1954, claiming 60,000 members by 1955.[4] Leadership in Mississippi soon passed to William James Simmons, no relation to the century's first imperial wizard.[5] In Georgia, the movement was led by Roy Harris, former campaign manager for governors Eugene and Herman Talmadge.[6] Council members bristled when critics labeled their group the White Citizens' Council, retorting—but never proving—that their ranks included black members. Nonetheless, the Councils practiced crude intimidation. Boycotts, mass firing of black employees, and public naming of blacks who registered to vote, soon gave way to lethal violence. Black minister George Lee ignored Council warnings to cease his voter registration work in Belzoni, Mississippi, and died in a drive-by shooting on May 7, 1955. The local sheriff first claimed buckshot pellets found in Lee's head were "fillings from his teeth," then blamed the slaying on "some jealous nigger."[7] Gus Courts, another Belzoni activist, survived a shooting with critical wounds six months later. The sheriff's considered opinion: "Some nigger had it in for him, that's all."[8] In years to come, Council members would be prominent on juries that acquitted homicidal Klansmen.

Still, despite their similar goals, shared anti–Semitism, and occasional overlapping membership—Edward Fields served briefly as a Council leader in Kentucky[9]—the Councils tried to distinguish themselves from the Klan. They met openly and unmasked, as author Charles Payne notes, "pursuing the agenda of the Klan with the demeanor of the Rotary Club."[10] Mississippi newsman Hodding Carter II dubbed Councils "the uptown Klan," while Alabama journalist Grover Hall declared, "The manicured Kluxism of these White Citizens' Councils is rash, indecent, and vicious."[11] Author George Thayer distinguished the two groups by saying, "If the mark of a Klansman is cracking skulls, then the mark of a member of the Citizens' Councils is twisting arms."[12] Within a decade, as the Councils proved themselves incapable of blocking integration, their influence would fade, Council members would stage joint demonstrations with Klansmen, and investigators would describe some Council chapters as "fronts" for Klan klaverns.[13]

Empires Revived

Predictably, the *Brown* decision—and *Brown II,* in May 1955, ordering school integration to proceed "with all deliberate speed"—sparked a flurry of Klan recruiting and demonstrations in Jim Crow states. Front-runner Eldon Edwards received a Georgia charter for his U.S. Klans on October 25, 1955, soon claiming units in at least nine states.[14] A Stone Mountain rally in September 1956 drew 3,000 Klansmen, while overall membership peaked around 50,000 in the late 1950s.[15] Grand dragons included H. L. Jones in Georgia, A. C. Hightower in Arkansas, Edgar Taylor in Louisiana, William Griffin in Florida, Thurman Miller in North Carolina, James Bickley in South Carolina, and Horace Miller in Texas. Alabama had dueling dragons, Alvin Horn and Robert Marvin Shelton vying for power, alternately favored by Edwards over time.[16] In Virginia, virtually untapped territory, Klansmen still managed an August 1955 cross-burning at the Richmond home of school desegregation activist Oliver Hill.[17]

South Carolina's knights preferred burning homes and churches, specifically those occupied or served by the Rev. Joseph DeLaine, a leader in one of the *Brown* school cases. In September 1955 they torched his home in Summerton and stoned another residence, then burned his Lake City church on October 6. Four days later, after mailing bomb threats, Klansmen returned to fire on DeLaine's house. He fought back, then fled the state after prosecutors charged him with assault.[18] In September 1956 Clarendon County Klansmen shot up an NAACP leader's home and burned his uncle's church.[19]

Some veteran Klansmen sought alternative vehicles for protest after *Brown.* In Georgia, Parson Jack Johnston launched the Christian Civic League of America and published the

weekly *Georgia Tribune*, featuring photos of interracial couples and declaring, "It has long been known that it is Communism's plan to mongrelize the races." A typical headline warned of African Americans: "They Not Only Spread Red Propaganda but Gonnorhea."[20] Bill Hendrix founded the Tallahassee-based White Brotherhood in autumn 1954, replacing his defunct American Confederate Army, but he could not forsake the Klan.[21] In August 1956 he penned an open letter to United Press, announcing that "the imperial council of the Ku Klux Klan" had "demanded" nationwide revival of the order, starting with a rally scheduled in Lakeland.[22]

"Keep 'Bama White"

Alabama became Dixie's first civil rights battleground of the postwar era in 1955, when police jailed three black women for refusing to vacate "white" seats on city buses. Claudette Colvin was the first arrested, in March, followed by Mary Louise Smith in October, but the black community did not begin its bus boycott until NAACP member Rosa Parks was jailed on December 1. By December 5, 30,000 African Americans had abandoned municipal bus lines. The Montgomery Improvement Association (MIA), led by young ministers Ralph Abernathy and Martin Luther King, Jr., had taken a historic stride toward freedom that would culminate in victory a year later.[23]

But first, they had to deal with white police, Citizens' Councils, and the Ku Klux Klan.

Alvin Horn was busily recruiting members for the U.S. Klans, but he soon faced competition from younger activist Asa Earl Carter—"Ace" to his friends and enemies alike. Born in 1925, in Oxford, Alabama, Carter was voted most likely to become a "famous movie star" by his senior high school class, but World War II intervened. He joined the navy, then spent a year studying journalism at the University of Colorado, courtesy of the G.I. Bill. He worked for several Alabama radio stations before settling on Birmingham's WILD, in 1953. After *Brown,* Carter joined the Alabama Citizen's Council and his broadcasts—sponsored by the American State's Rights Association—veered sharply into racism and anti–Semitism. The NAACP, he declared, had "infiltrated" and corrupted Southern youth with "immoral" rock and roll music. Syndicated over more than 20 stations by 1955, Carter finally lost his job when WILD's owners took note of his rants against Jews.[24]

Defecting from the Alabama Citizen's Council after his dismissal, Carter founded a rival North Alabama Citizen's Council, explicitly appealing to "rednecks" left out by their button-down "betters." In fact, the NACC was a launching pad for Carter's best-known vehicle, the Original Ku Klux Klan of the Confederacy, sometimes donning paramilitary garb, expanding from Birmingham to poach from Alvin Horn's realm. Various accounts date the creation of Carter's Klan from October 1955 to November 1956, but his Citizen's Council included Klansmen from day one—Robert Chambliss among them—and their violent escapades date from early February 1956.[25]

In January of that year, African American coed Autherine Lucy won a three-year court battle for admission to the all-white University of Alabama in Tuscaloosa. Formally enrolled

Opposite: **Eldon Edwards, imperial wizard of the U.S. Klans from 1953 to 1960 (Florida State Archives).**

on February 1, she was denied a dormitory room but managed to attend her first classes on February 3. That night and the following evening, 2,000 racists ran amok on campus, vandalizing property, hurling rocks and eggs, chanting, "Keep 'Bama white!" Only four arrests were made, including Chambliss, but no trials resulted. Instead, university trustees suspended Lucy "for her own safety." When black attorney Arthur Shores—a frequent Klan target—publicly accused administrators of conspiring with the mob, Lucy was expelled on February 28. A court overturned her suspension one day later, but let the expulsion stand, leaving 'Bama lily-white for the next seven years. Chambliss and three others jailed during the riot sued Lucy and the NAACP, seeking $4 million as compensation for their brief detention.[26]

Flushed with triumph from the Tuscaloosa melee, Ace Carter planned a coup targeting blacks and their "jungle music." He aimed to field 150 men, to kidnap singer Nat "King" Cole during a concert at Birmingham's Municipal Auditorium, but only seven made the show on April 10, 1956. While Cole sang for an all-white audience, six Klansmen leaped onstage and tackled him, one breaking a policeman's nose before he was clubbed and subdued with the others. Officers arrested Carter's men, seizing a carload of rifles, blackjacks, and brass knuckles at the scene. They questioned Carter briefly, but his Klansmen stood alone in court for trial, four receiving six-month sentences and $100 fines on April 18.[27]

While his foot soldiers faced trial and prison, Carter turned to politics. Excommunicated from Citizens' Council ranks for his anti–Semitism in March 1956, by April he had found an ally in John Crommelin, supporting and counseling Crommelin in his second bid to unseat incumbent senator Lister Hill. Voters rejected Crommelin on May 3, casting 247,519 ballots for Hill, against 115,440 for the ex-admiral, but the losing campaign was important to Carter for another reason. It introduced him to his next and most notorious comrade-in-arms.[28]

Outside Agitator

Frederick John Kasper, Jr., was a New Jersey native, born in 1929, educated at Columbia University. There, while living in Greenwich Village and dating young women of various races, he became obsessed with poet Ezra Pound, a British subject living in America who suffered a mental breakdown in 1945, while jailed for serving as a fascist agent, spending the next 12 years in mental institutions. Kasper corresponded with Pound, calling him "Master" and "Granpaw," aping his literary style while poring over *Mein Kampf* and other Nazi tomes. In 1953 he picketed the White House, carrying a placard reading "Burn All Reds" to celebrate the execution of Julius and Ethel Rosenberg.[29]

In March 1956, after a failed bid to secure Pound's release, Kasper turned his attention to Dixie and school integration. He founded the Seaboard White Citizens' Council with Florida carpenter Fred Hockett, plagiarized extensively from Pound in its racist publications, fell under suspicion of cross-burning in Charlottesville, Virginia, was jailed there for distributing hate literature, and campaigned with Ace Carter in John Crommelin's failed Alabama senate campaign.[30] By August 1956, working in tandem, Kasper and Carter set their sights on the seething racial cauldron of Clinton, Tennessee.

Clinton High School had been marked for integration since the *Brown* decision, its delaying tactics scotched in January 1956 by a federal court order to desegregate in August.

Twelve black students registered without incident on August 20, but Kasper and Carter arrived to stage mass rallies the weekend before classes opened. By August 29 tension had escalated to the point that a federal injunction barred Kasper and company from further interference. Undeterred, Kasper addressed a mob of 1,500 the same day, prompting imposition of a one-year prison sentence for contempt. Carter filled the void, whipping Clinton's white populace into a frenzy on Labor Day weekend, unleashing them to smash windows, overturn cars, and hurl dynamite charges into a black neighborhood. Governor Frank Clement crushed the rebellion with National Guardsmen and tanks, but violence continued. Drive-by terrorists fired on black homes, tossing more bombs, and Kasper returned in November to organize a Junior White Citizens Council for teens. Federal judge Robert Taylor slapped Kasper with a new contempt charge, held in abeyance pending appeal. Bobby Cain became Clinton High's first black graduate in May 1957, but it was a Pyrrhic victory. Bombers demolished the school on October 5, 1958.[31]

By then, Kasper had suffered a series of setbacks. His appearance at Florida Klan rallies

Admirers greet John Kasper (center, in suit) before a Tennessee court hearing, ca. 1956–1958 (Library of Congress).

prompted state legislators to investigate his background, eliciting admissions that he had dated black women as recently as 1955.[32] Expelled from the Seaboard White Citizens' Council, Kasper also found himself estranged from Ace Carter, who warned Kasper that "we didn't want him back in Alabama."[33] He returned to Tennessee instead, replicating Clinton's mob scenes in Nashville on September 8, 1957, telling a white mob, "Blood will run in the streets if nigra children go to school with whites! When they fool with the white race, they're fooling with the strongest race in the world, the most bloodthirsty race in the world."[34] The next morning, 19 black students reported for classes, braving stones and spittle from white thugs. That night, three dynamite blasts virtually destroyed Nashville's new Hattie Cotton School. On September 10 police arrested Kasper and 30-odd others, including seven local Klansmen.[35] One of the knights told officers that he and Kasper had concealed explosives in an abandoned house on the night of September 8, but a search revealed nothing.[36] The bombing went unpunished, but Kasper was convicted of inciting a riot, jailed when he refused to pay the $200 fine. Friends bailed him out, but U.S. marshals were waiting. His appeal of the Clinton contempt citation had failed, and Kasper headed off to prison. November 1958 brought more bad news, with conviction on the Nashville riot charges and another six-month sentence. By the time Kasper emerged from custody, in August 1959, even Ezra Pound had forsaken him.[37] His two-man welcoming committee consisted of Klansman Bill Hendrix and ex–Columbian George Bright, now a member of J. B. Stoner's latest neo–Nazi enterprise.[38]

White Terror

While Kasper's saga played out, blacks in Montgomery, Alabama, won their boycott against segregated buses. A federal court ruled segregated seating illegal in June 1956, supported by the Supreme Court on December 17. That ruling took effect three days later, and Ku Klux terror swiftly followed. A sniper fired into the Rev. King's home on December 23, and five Klansmen attacked a black girl at a bus stop on Christmas Eve. Two days later, shots fired at a bus left Rosa Jordan wounded in both legs.[39] In Birmingham, a six-year bombing lull was broken on December 25, when dynamite knocked activist the Rev. Fred Shuttlesworth's home off its foundation.[40]

On January 10, 1957, Bob Chambliss drove a carload of dynamite from Birmingham to Montgomery.[41] That night, Klansmen bombed four African American churches and two homes, one of them Ralph Abernathy's. A seventh bomb, found on the Rev. King's porch, failed to explode.[42] On January 23, Montgomery's knights kidnapped black Winn-Dixie trucker Willie Edwards, Jr., suspected of "harassing" white women, and beat him to force a confession. They had the wrong man, but it made no difference. At gunpoint, Edwards leaped 125 feet from a highway bridge, into the Alabama River. Police found his corpse three months later, stating that decomposition made determining a cause of death impossible.[43]

On the same night Willie Edwards died, Ace Carter faced a contentious gathering in Birmingham. Klansman J. P. Tillery accused him of embezzlement and dictatorial behavior, insults that prompted Carter to pull a pistol, wounding Tillery and another critic. Police charged Carter with attempted murder, but prosecutors dropped the case.[44] With Klan membership rising, mayhem continued across Alabama. Bombers struck two homes and a taxi

The Rev. Fred Shuttlesworth outside his Montgomery, Alabama, home, bombed by Klansmen in December 1956 (National Archives).

stand in Montgomery on the night of January 27–28, a Mobile home in March, a Birmingham minister's home on April 10, a church and union leader's home in Bessemer on April 28.[45]

Carter sought to shield his knights from prosecution in 1957 by seeking to become Birmingham's commissioner of public safety. One of his campaign promises involved removal of all records by black performers from jukeboxes.[46] Despite his strong racist credentials, he could not defeat ex-commissioner Bull Connor, storming the polls to reclaim his job after a 1953 sex scandal had driven him from office. Two other contenders also challenged incumbent Robert Lindbergh, and while Lindbergh won the primary by a small margin, Connor rebounded to carry the runoff election by 103 votes.[47] Once again, the Klan had a friend in office.

Mike Wallace Meets the Wizard

Eldon Edwards scored a coup of sorts for his U.S. Klans, accepting newsman Mike Wallace's invitation to a live interview on television's ABC network, on May 5, 1957. Appearing in full regalia but unmasked, Edwards did his best for the cause, perhaps relying on the adage that there is no such thing as bad publicity. Interspersed with commercials from Philip Morris—"probably the best natural smoke you ever tasted"—Edwards maintained his composure through most of the grilling, against heavy odds.[48]

Straight-faced, Edwards denied Wallace's assertion that most southerners viewed the Klan as "kind of a comic opera," dismissing derogatory articles from the *New York Times* as "propaganda sheet material." He hedged on reports that his Klan claimed 50,000 members—"No one has that information but me. I do not divulge it."—then called the stated figure "a gross understatement." He denied any link to bloodshed, saying, "This organization does not go in for violence in no respect." Wallace replied by quoting Alvin Horn, telling *Look* magazine that "Negroes who try to force their way into our white schools, are not looking for an education. They're looking for a funeral." Edwards first replied, "I didn't hear him say that," then attacked the authors, saying, "I don't believe anything that one of those birds said on it."[49]

When Wallace pressed Edwards for proof that the Klan was "denied freedom of the press," Edwards clarified, "It is a controlled press. You well understand that." Controlled by whom? "We won't go into that at this time," Edwards said. Why not? "Well ... the Anti-Defamation League." The *Atlanta Constitution* was a prime example, "owned by Cox in Ohio and ... financed and supported by the business of Atlanta. And then it's edited and published by the NAACP." Which, in turn, was "a foreign inspired organization from start to finish," well known for its "communistic leanings."

In the wizard's mind, it boiled down to one central point: "Mongolization [*sic*] means destruction. It means the destruction of the white race. It means the destruction of the nigger race." If Klansmen had received "black" transfusions during World War II, Edwards worried that "it could show up in the offspring." Given a choice, Edwards preferred to "continue to help the nigger, support the nigger, give him his education, pay his schools, pay his teachers," on a segregated basis.[50]

Edwards denied Klan involvement in politics, but claimed that "we have a good government in Georgia." Rebuttals from "good governor" Marvin Griffin proved less disturbing than a statement from Herman Talmadge's office, declaring, "The Senator doesn't want to have anything to do with Eldon Edwards. He's a very objectionable character and we don't want to be associated with him in any way." Bemused, Edward answered honestly that "Klannish minded people sent Herman Talmadge to the office he holds."[51]

In closing, Wallace asked about klaverns north of the Mason-Dixon Line. Was their a Klan in New York? "Yes," Edwards replied. "I'm looking for a Grand Dragon, how about you? You would make a pretty good one." Instead of answering, Wallace thanked Edwards for appearing. The wizard—doubtless knowing that like-minded souls would hear his voice and screen out Wallace's—deemed it "a pleasure to be here."[52]

"Fighting for Our Way of Life"

Alvin Horn's remark about funerals seemed prophetic in Alabama, where terrorist raids occurred on a near-nightly basis. In Montgomery, when a Klansman dropped his wallet next to a bomb that fizzled on the Rev. King's porch, police bestirred themselves to arrest four knights in early 1957.[53]

Suspects Raymond Britt, Jr., and Sonny Livingston, Jr., signed confessions in custody, while Henry Alexander and James York kept mum. Bombing occupied dwellings carried a death penalty, but the Klansmen had nothing to fear. Defended by John Hill, a cousin of Alabama's senior senator, Britt and Livingston smirked while their counsel grilled the Rev. King on rumors that he once proposed marriage to a white woman. Jurors ignored their confessions and acquitted the pair, after which prosecutors dismissed charges filed against Alexander and York.[54]

Alabama Klansmen rightly saw that outcome as a victory, unleashing further terror against African Americans. They whipped four blacks at Evergreen on August 8, and six more at Maplesville the following night. Governor Folsom ordered state police to investigate those crimes, but no arrests resulted. South Carolina authorities proved less tolerant: after Klansmen beat Claude Cruell at Greenville, in July, six knights were arrested. Exalted Cyclops Andrew Rochester received a six-year sentence in January 1958, while codefendant Wade Howard got two years.[55]

The worst was yet to come. On September 2, 1957, six members of Ace Carter's Klan abducted Edward "Judge" Aaron, a mildly retarded black handyman, from the Birmingham suburb of Zion City, driving him to their dirt-floored "lair" outside Clarkesville. Their aim was to discourage local integration efforts led by the Rev. Fred Shuttlesworth, and to prove Klansman Bart Floyd worthy of promotion to the rank of "captain." Supervised by Exalted Cyclops Joe Pritchett, the knights beat Aaron and interrogated him about his nonexistent civil rights activities. Finally, Floyd castrated Aaron with a razor blade and doused the wound with turpentine to make him scream. Left beside a rural highway, Aaron nearly bled to death before a passing driver called police to rescue him.[56]

Enraged, Governor Folsom dispatched state police to find the "castrationists." By September 8, all six were in custody and two—John Griffin and William Miller, Carter's "captain of intelligence"—had turned state's evidence against the rest. Initially complacent, the defendants soon realized their predicament. By selecting an innocent victim—"a good nigger" in local parlance—they had outraged members of the white community who normally supported, or at least ignored, Klan violence. Tried separately for mayhem, the remaining knights—Pritchett, Bart Floyd, Grover McCullough, and Jesse Mabry (one of Nat Cole's 1956 attackers)—were swiftly convicted and sentenced to 20-year terms. For their cooperation with the state, Griffin and Miller got probation.[57]

Two weeks after Aaron's ordeal, the Klan went after the Rev. Shuttlesworth himself. On September 17, Shuttlesworth and his wife took their daughters to enroll at all-white Phillips High School. Ace Carter and 20-odd followers waited, armed with clubs, chains, and other weapons. They mobbed Shuttlesworth, and a TV crew caught Klansman Bobby Cherry pounding the minister's head with brass knuckles. Someone stabbed Shuttlesworth's wife in the hip, and daughter Ruby suffered a broken ankle when Klansmen slammed a car door on her leg. Police appeared belatedly, the Shuttlesworths survived, and Carter was briefly detained for questioning. No criminal charges were filed.[58]

Klansmen had failed to kill their enemy, but they did not surrender. On November 1 they bombed a black family's home in Bessemer. Explosives rocked five more houses on Birmingham's "Dynamite Hill" in December.[59]

Little Rock

While Alabama's knights fought in the streets and courts, national attention shifted to Arkansas in September 1957. Faced with a federal desegregation order, Governor Orval Faubus announced on September 2 that he would mobilize National Guardsmen to prevent "disorder" at Central High School. That was music to the ears of Little Rock's Capital Citizens' Council, whose followers joined in riotous mob scenes at Central High until September 25, when President Dwight Eisenhower dispatched U.S. troops to escort nine black students inside.[60] Soldiers remained on call through May, then Little Rock's leaders closed city schools for the 1958–59 school year, leaving students and parents adrift.[61] As classes prepared to resume, fully integrated, in August 1959, the terrorists were waiting.

Trouble started early. A. C. Hightower chartered the Arkansas realm of the U.S. Klans on June 5, 1959. Four days later, after Secretary of State C. G. Hall criticized the Klan's revival, arsonists set fire to his porch. Hightower resigned on August 2, after quarreling with Klansmen who advocated violence, but his knights pressed on without him. On August 25, police arrested two Klansmen for bombing a newly integrated school. Two days later, a pair of white women detonated tear gas grenades at a school board meeting. On September 7, bombs destroyed the school board's office, wrecked property owned by the mayor, and damaged the fire chief's car—punishment, presumably, for using high-pressure hoses against white rioters on August 12. By September 11 police had arrested five members of the Capital

Arkansas governor Orval Faubus commuted the prison sentences of convicted Klan bombers in 1957 (Library of Congress).

Citizens' Council. J. B. Sims pled guilty on September 18, receiving a five-year sentence. Jurors convicted Jesse Perry on October 28 (three years) and Council leader E. A. Lauderdale, Sr., on December 31 (three years). Grady Sims pled guilty in October 1960 and was sentenced to five years. Testimony at Lauderdale's trial proved the bombings were planned at a Klan meeting.[62]

Convictions were a setback, but appeals delayed Lauderdale's imprisonment until February 1961. Barely six months later, Faubus pardoned Lauderdale and two codefendants, personally refunding their $500 fines. Only one bomber, who had confessed his crime, remained in custody. Meanwhile, in July 1960, FBI agents caught three Klansmen planting a bomb at Little Rock's all-black Philander Smith College. The team's leader, Emmett Miller, was both a kleagle and president of the Crittenden County Citizens' Council. Federal prosecutors filed conspiracy charges, but FBI headquarters scuttled the case in May 1961, refusing to identify its source of information on the plot. None of the would-be bombers ever went to trial.[63]

Divisible Empire

Soon after claiming status as the country's largest Klan, the U.S. Klans began to suffer discord and defections. Elmo Barnard—a Mobile, Alabama, gunsmith with one black teenager's death to his credit—was first to desert, founding the Gulf Ku Klux Klan in autumn 1956. He decried terrorism, but said "a little violence" might be required to halt integration.[64] Grand Dragon James "Catfish" Cole bailed out next, founding his own North Carolina Knights before year's end.[65] In early 1957, Eldon Edwards banished Horace Miller for misappropriating funds and failing to establish any Texas klaverns. Miller, a tubercular invalid, retaliated by founding the Aryan Knights, a Klan without formal members, whose newsletters circled the globe from Texas to Mexico, South America, Britain and Europe, the Middle East, Australia, and South Africa. In May 1958, an associate of Sherman—Franz Heinz, self-styled Grand Dragon of Chile—faced trial with several other Klansmen on charges of terrorizing Jews in Santiago.[66] In October 1957, after a series of Tennessee bombings, Edwards also banished most of Chattanooga Klavern #1, whose members regrouped as the Dixie Klans, led by brothers Jack and Harry Brown, later expanding into Georgia and Alabama.[67]

Alabama remained the most troublesome realm for Edwards. Alvin Horn, appointed grand dragon in 1956, had established more than 100 klaverns by early 1957, when his wife committed suicide. Seeking a new mother for his six children, Horn wooed and impregnated 15-year-old Barbara Richardson, described in press reports as "a pretty girl with peculiar eyes, one brown and the other blue." They eloped to Georgia in May, adding five years to Barbara's age on their wedding license. Her parents filed criminal charges and sought annulment of the marriage, then surrendered when Barbara revealed her pregnancy. Edwards announced Horn's resignation on June 11, citing "unfair and unjust publicity." Georgia authorities considered prosecuting Horn for perjury, then dropped the case. Horn's replacement, Robert Shelton of Tuscaloosa, stepped in to relieve the Klan's "turmoil and ridicule."[68]

Aside from rebels in his own ranks, Edwards also faced competition from outside rivals. The Association of South Carolina Klans, founded in 1955, defied state anti-mask laws and let Grand Kludd D. R. Hooker do most of its talking, feuding with at least five other splinter groups statewide. Next door, brothers Arthur and Joseph Bryant launched the North Carolina Knights, then were jailed for possession of dynamite; Arthur and Klansman Clarence Wyatt also paid fines for mailing slanderous letters. A 1956 contender, James Swenson's Original Knights of Louisiana, soon splintered and lapsed into dormancy, awaiting vigorous revival in the early 1960s. In Florida, where J. C. Kirkland, Sr., had replaced Bill Griffin as grand dragon of the U.S. Klans, four rival factions vied for members. By 1958, Catfish Cole had to contend with Lester Caldwell's National Christian Knights, based in Charlotte. The same year saw Walter Bailey's Mississippi Knights established, with headquarters in Gulfport. Klan veteran Hugh Morris—already a police informer—revived his Federated Klans in 1959, planting outposts in Georgia.[69]

Bad Medicine

James Cole was the first U.S. Klans defector to make serious headlines. Born in 1924, a veteran of World War II, Cole had founded Southern Bible College with wife Carolyn in 1953, at Marion, South Carolina. He later toured the Carolinas as a tent evangelist and was ordained by the Wayside Baptist Church, juggling a Sunday "Free Will Hour" on radio with his duties as grand dragon. His rallies drew thousands of spectators, often followed by motorcades hazing black neighborhoods, sometimes with police escorts.[70] Violence began in December 1956, with the burning of a black family's home in Kershaw. Klansmen bungled the bombing of a Charlottesville school in February 1957, but succeeded with another in Greensboro, nine months later.[71] Between those efforts, Cole's knights picketed a Charlotte theater screening *Island in the Sun*, a film depicting interracial romance, and welcomed John Kasper to Mecklenburg, where he railed against school integration and denounced visiting evangelist Billy Graham as a "nigger-lover."[72]

In Monroe, Klansmen paid particular attention to Dr. Albert Perry, a black physician suspected of funding the local NAACP. After multiple death threats, chapter president Robert Williams organized a Black Armed Guard composed of military veterans, to watch Perry's home. The rationale was simple, later expressed in his book *Negroes with Guns* (1962): "Racists consider themselves superior beings and are not willing to exchange their superior lives for our inferior ones. They are most vicious and violent when they can practice violence with impunity." On October 5, 1957, after Cole led a rally near Monroe, Klansmen roared off toward Dr. Perry's house and found the Black Armed Guard waiting. A flurry of gunfire routed Cole's knights, and Monroe's city council banned Klan motorcades the following day.[73]

Embarrassed by that skirmish, Cole's Klansmen tried to dynamite a Charlotte synagogue on November 11, but their bomb was another dud. On New Year's Day, also in Charlotte, they managed to blow up the marquee of an integrated drive-in theater.[74] Still they got no significant attention, so Cole cast about for new targets and settled on Robeson County's Lumbee Indian tribe.

Since 1913 the Lumbees had lived peacefully under Robeson's system of triracial segregation, separating whites, blacks, and Native Americans.[75] They were passive and appeared to be an easy target for Cole, who branded them a "mongrel" race. "There's about 30,000 half-breeds in Robeson County," he said, "and we are going to have a cross burning and scare them up." Two crosses blazed at Lumberton on July 12, 1957, followed by another in St. Pauls the following night, at the home of a Lumbee woman said to be dating a white man. Local police warned Cole against riling the tribe, but he forged ahead, announcing a rally near Maxton on January 18, with 5,000 Klansmen expected to remind Lumbees of "their place."[76]

On the appointed night, barely 50 Klansmen made the trip to Maxton, where they found themselves outnumbered 10-to-one by Lumbees armed with guns and clubs. In lieu of burning a cross, Cole's men raised a light bulb on a pole, quickly extinguished by a gunshot from the crowd. In the ensuing melee, four Klansmen were slightly wounded while the others fled, leaving behind their robes, banner, unlit cross, and public address system. Cole escaped on foot through a swamp but was later arrested, charged with inciting a riot, and sentenced to prison. Lumbee leaders posed for *Life* magazine's cameras, swaddled in Cole's captured banner. Tribe members still celebrate the "Battle of Hayes Pond" as an annual holiday.[77]

Cole's humiliation did not completely crush North Carolina's Klan. On February 9, 1958, Gastonia police found an unexploded bomb outside a synagogue. Six days later, officers in Charlotte caught National Christian Knights imperial wizard Lester Caldwell and five Klansmen planting a bomb at a newly integrated school. Three of those captured were sentenced to prison on March 20, while five others paid fines for illegal cross burning. On July 7, bombers struck the Durham home of a white minister active in the local Human Relations Committee. Three months later, in Greensboro, a judge fined two Kluxers for damaging property owned by NAACP members. Meanwhile, the Chessmen—a group of U.S. Klans defectors who donned black shirts and masks to harass Richfield merchants with black employees—escaped prosecution.[78]

Mutual Friends

Nineteen fifty-eight was an election year in Alabama. With Governor Folsom barred by law from seeking another term, 14 candidates entered the Democratic gubernatorial primary. John Crommelin was one of them, aided by future American Nazi Party leaders George Lincoln Rockwell and Matthias Koehl, Jr., but the clear front-runner was Attorney General John Patterson.[79]

Patterson had entered politics by accident. Born in 1921, he joined the army a year before Pearl Harbor, retiring as a major in 1945. He studied law in Tuscaloosa, then was called back for another tour of duty during the Korean War. In his absence, Patterson's father clashed with underworld elements in Phenix City. Outraged by their crimes, Albert Patterson ran for attorney general in 1954 and won the Democratic primary, then was murdered before taking office, leaving son John to take his place. Hitting the campaign trail, Patterson claimed that "outside agitators"—gangsters and the NAACP—had joined forces to oppose him. In the post–*Brown* climate, he was easily elected.[80]

As attorney general, Patterson's main bêtes noire were racketeers and integrationists. Of the two, he spent more time attacking blacks, and in 1956 filed a successful lawsuit to ban the NAACP from Alabama as a "foreign" corporation.[81] Klansmen remembered that in 1958, but Patterson took no chances. On March 19 he sent out letters on official stationery, addressed to members of the U.S. Klans, which read:

Dear Mr. *****

A mutual friend, Mr. R. M. (Bob) Shelton, of ours in Tuscaloosa has suggested that I write you and ask for your support in the coming Governor's race.

I hope you will see fit to support my candidacy and I would like to meet you when I am next in *****.

With warm personal regards, I am

Sincerely your friend,
John Patterson
Attorney General[82]

The Montgomery *Advertiser* obtained one of Patterson's letters and published it, deleting the recipient's name and hometown. Patterson raged in response, "This is amazing. I am not a member of the Ku Klux Klan. I have never been a member. I don't know anyone named Shelton."[83] The first two statements were probably true. As for the third, Klansmen were pleased to wink and cast their votes for Patterson. They also harassed his opponents, ripping down posters and assaulting at least one rival campaign worker, tattooing his forehead with a staple gun.[84]

Patterson's chief rival was George Corley Wallace, Jr., a protégé of James Folsom and a circuit judge who had defied U.S. Civil Rights Commission requests for voter registration records.[85] Even so, he saw that Patterson had clinched the racist vote and took a different approach, appealing for black support and touring the state with a bed on a truck, lifting the covers at each stop to ask, "Hey John, where are you? You down there under the sheets with the Ku Klux Klan?" Robert Shelton's campaign was more practical. "We delivered votes," he said. "When John Patterson ran for governor we decided one Sunday night to put one of his streamers on every other telephone pole in the state of Alabama. By Monday morning it was done. What other organization could do that?"[86]

On primary day, Patterson led the field with 196,859 votes to 162,435 for Wallace. John Crommelin placed eleventh, with 2,245.[87] Wallace learned his lesson, telling friends, "No other son of a bitch will ever out-nigger me again."[88] As for Shelton, an employee of the B.F. Goodrich plant in Tuscaloosa, he landed a million-dollar order in 1959, to put new tires on state vehicles.[89]

A sideshow to the main event in 1958 involved Ace Carter. Having dissolved his Klan soon after charges from the January 1957 shooting were dismissed, Carter ran for lieutenant governor in the Democratic primary. Unlike Patterson, however, his Klan appeal failed to sway voters. Ace ran fifth in a field of five candidates.[90]

Thunderbolts

While Alabamians concerned themselves with mainstream racial politics, leaders of the ultra-right prepared to form a party of their own. On February 1, 1958, they met in Louisville, Kentucky—lately home to Edward Fields—in an "Ultimatum Conference of Loyal Americans." Chaired by Fields, the gathering heard speeches from John Crommelin, Catfish Cole, and Millard Grubbs, chairman of Kentucky's Citizens' Council. A spat between Crommelin and Grubbs prompted some attendees to walk out, but most remained, including delegates from Alabama, Iowa, Michigan, Tennessee, Texas, and the Carolinas.[91]

Seven months later, on August 30–31, many of the same players returned to Louisville's Liberty Hall, convening to found the National States Rights Party (NSRP). Participants from 18 states included Crommelin and Fields; J. B. Stoner; John Kasper, lately paroled; George Rockwell, still a year away from founding the American Nazi Party; Klansmen Cole and Bill Hendrix; John W. Hamilton, an associate of Gerald L. K. Smith and chief of the National Citizens Protective Association; Joe Beauharnais, ex-leader of Chicago's defunct

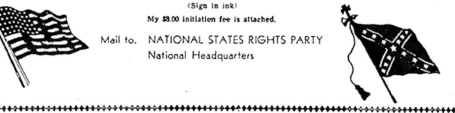

JOIN NSRP TODAY

BENEFITS AND PRIVILEGES LISTED HERE

The NSRP is by far the largest White Racist political party in America. Both Democratic and Republican Parties have betrayed the White People of America. The NSRP is the last hope of the White-man to save our White Christian Civilization.

Compare our Party Platform with that of the left-wing Democratic and Republican Parties. Only within our ranks can you find the full answer to the grave problems facing America.

MEMBERSHIP BENEFITS:

1) All Members receive "The Thunderbolt" newspaper automatically.

2) The right to attend Members only meetings and vote on Party policy and election of officers.

3) Legal protection: NSRP furnishes legal aid to any member per-secuted in the line of authorized Party duty, anywhere in America. We are the only right-wing organization to offer such a plan. If you are an ACTIVE PATRIOT you can not afford to be without this protection.

4) The deep personal satisfaction of knowing that you are a part of the largest right-wing political party in America, forging a sword of steel that will cut away the chains that shackle the White-man in America.

5) Any married man who joins may also receive a FREE membership card for his wife. She will receive the same benefits and privileges as her husband. (No additional cost.) Be sure and give your wife's full name.

RUSH YOUR MEMBERSHIP IN TODAY!

NATIONAL STATES RIGHTS PARTY

To: Ned Dupes, National Chairman
Berniece Settle, National Secretary
Dr. Edward R. Fields, National Director

Local Chapter
Headquarters

Application for Membership

As a loyal White Christian American, I hereby apply for membership in the National States Rights Party. Upon my word of honor, I pledge my loyalty to this Party and its great principles and will never betray it. I believe in Christianity, the White Race and its Preservation throughout the world, Only White Christian Immigration, the Complete Separation of the Races to Preserve White Civilization, a Free White America, America First and American Patriotism.

I am against Jewish communism, monopoly, race-mixing and internationalism.

I believe that I can best serve my Race and Nation by becoming an active member of this great Party.

Signature_____ Date_____ Phone_____

Street_____ City_____ State_____

County_____ Date of Birth_____ Occupation_____

(Sign in ink)

My $3.00 initiation fee is attached.

Mail to. NATIONAL STATES RIGHTS PARTY
National Headquarters

A recruiting poster for the National States Rights Party, ca. **1958–1964** (author's collection).

White Circle League; Allen Mann, publisher of *The Revere*; and onetime Columbian Emory Burke. The delegates chose Tennessean Arthur Cole as their national chairman, Edna Cowan of Indiana as vice chairman, and longtime anti–Semite Ned Dupes (also from Tennessee) as secretary. Looking forward to the 1960 elections, they drafted Crommelin as their presidential candidate and nominated Millard Grubbs as Kentucky's next governor.[92]

The cast of characters aside, little had changed from 1946, when the Columbians first organized. NSRP members favored Hitlerian uniforms, marched beneath a banner emblazoned with the SS lightning bolt, and published a newspaper titled *The Thunderbolt*. Their constitution was, perhaps, a bit more eloquent. Its preamble read, in part:

> We of the National States Rights Party believe in the Christian heritage of our people, the White Race and the Nation which the Whiteman created out of the wilderness of this continent....
> We believe in the principles laid down by our forefathers in the United States Constitution and the Bill of Rights contained therein....
> We will not allow the blood of our people to be polluted with that of black, yellow, or mongrel peoples....
> All that is patriotic, good, clean, and decent springs forth from the foundations of our White folk....
> We dedicate ourselves to the task of saving America and the White Race and the preservation of the pure blood of our forefathers, so that all future generations which come after us will be born as White children with a creative intelligence that will strengthen our civilized influence over the world for the good of all mankind.[93]

Soon after its formation, the NSRP augmented its membership by absorbing four other fringe groups. Those included Cole's North Carolina Knights; the Chicago-based Realpolitical Institute, founded by Maynard Nelsen in 1954 and sporting its own thunderbolt banner, with officers including Fields and Matt Koehl; the United White Party, founded at Knoxville in 1957 by Fields, Koehl, Kasper, Emory Burke, Dan Kurtz, Wallace Allen, and Ned Dupes; and the National White American Party, led by former Christian Anti-Jewish Party member Robert Bowling.[94] Within two months of its creation, the NSRP would find itself accused of dynamiting synagogues.

Bombs Away

The *Brown* decisions sparked a bombing war in Dixie and beyond. No definitive tally of blasts and attempted bombings exists, though one vague media report claimed 195 bombing and arson attacks in the last seven months of 1954 alone.[95] Only five racist bombings made national headlines that year: three in Virginia, with one each in California and Kentucky.[96] None were reported in 1955, but action resumed the following year, with 71 explosions or attempted bombings from the old Confederacy and two in Delaware, between February 1956 and April 1958.[97] Anti-Semitism flavored the attacks, as bombers struck at synagogues in Birmingham, Miami, Nashville, Jacksonville, Florida, and Charlotte, North Carolina.[98]

On May 3, 1958, police from 20-odd Southern cities met in Jacksonville to create the Southern Conference on Bombing as a clearinghouse for information leading to conviction of Dixie's new terrorists. Hoover's FBI declined to participate, pleading lack of jurisdiction, but ex-agent Milton Ellerin, lately employed by the ADL, distributed a list of anti–Semites likely to engage in bombing. The list included Alabama Klansmen Bob Chambliss and Bart Floyd, Florida's Bill Hendrix, currently raiding U.S. Klans ranks on behalf of his newly-founded Knights of the White Camellia—and Bull Connor, attending the conference from Birmingham. Ellerin apologized for that "clerical error," and Connor joined the vote appropriating $55,700 to reward informants. Tips were received, but none panned out. The SCB became an exercise in futility.[99]

Reporting the conference on May 6, the *Birmingham News* missed its point entirely, running a headline that asked, "Are Reds Behind Bombings?" Two days later, Klansman William Morris approached Bull Connor, naming J. B. Stoner as the man responsible for recent synagogue bombings in Birmingham and Jacksonville. With Connor's police and local FBI boss Clarence Kelley, Morris hatched a plan to trap Stoner red-handed, offering him $2,000 to bomb Fred Shuttlesworth's Bethel Baptist Church. Stoner visited Birmingham on June 14, using a car on loan from Morris to case the church, and returned on June 21 to meet his sponsors, two "steelworkers" who, in fact, were police Captain G. L. Pattie and Sergeant Tom Cook. Connor and Kelley eavesdropped on that meeting, as Stoner agreed to a discounted rate for the bombing. On June 29, Stoner and cohort Robert Bowling rode a bus from Atlanta to Birmingham. Later that night, custodians at Bethel Baptist found a hissing bomb outside the church and moved it in time to avoid any serious damage.[100]

Bull Connor panicked, knowing that his men had, in effect, commissioned "Bombingham's" latest attack. To cover his tracks, he secured a statement from Morris, naming Stoner as the bomber, and requested FBI aid on July 16, lamenting that his force could not shadow Stoner full-time. J. Edgar Hoover demurred, sending a memo to Kelley on July 24, ordering him "to hold contacts with Connor to a minimum because of his unsavory reputation." No arrests resulted, and the Bethel Baptist bombing went officially unsolved until 1977.[101]

Meanwhile, on July 17, 1958, black residents of "Dynamite Hill" caught Klansmen Ellis Lee, Cranford Neal and Herbert Wilcutt planting more bombs in their neighborhood. They beat those three before police arrived, while wheelman Bob Chambliss escaped. The *Birmingham News* shrugged off those "harmless explosions," complaining that blacks who "probably" set the charges had "ganged up" on innocent white men. The knights confessed in custody, and jurors convicted Wilcutt on December 9, first sentencing him to 10 years, then recommending probation. He was freed, with charges against his cohorts dismissed.[102]

On October 12, 1958, 50 sticks of dynamite shattered Atlanta's oldest synagogue, the Hebrew Benevolent Congregation. A phone call from "General Gordon of the Confederate Underground" claimed credit for the bombing. On October 13 NSRP member Kenneth Griffin approached Atlanta police, admitting that he planned the attack with fellow party members Wallace Allen, Billy Branham, George Bright, and Leslie Rogers (an FBI informant). On October 17 all five were indicted on capital charges of bombing an occupied dwelling. Bright faced trial alone in December, defended by U.S. Klans imperial klonsel James Venable— who, in turn, called Eldon Edwards, klabee (secretary) John Felmet, and Exalted Cyclops Arthur Cole to denounce key prosecution witness Leslie Rogers as a man of "bad reputation" who could not be trusted under oath. Jurors deadlocked on December 19, and Bright switched lawyers before his retrial—where jurors accepted an alibi furnished by an inmate of Milledgeville State Hospital, testifying during a supposed "lucid interval." The panel acquitted Bright on January 24, 1959, and charges against his codefendants were dismissed.[103]

Atlanta's Hebrew Benevolent Congregation, bombed by neo–Nazis in October 1958 (Library of Congress).

Bombings continued in the South over the next decade. The sole fatality on record prior to 1963 was victim Mattie Green, killed when bombers destroyed her home in Ringgold, Georgia, on May 16, 1960. Governor Ernest Vandiver offered a $500 reward for information leading to the bombers' arrest, but no charges resulted. FBI analysts determined that the bomb was made from ammonium nitrate fertilizer detonated with blasting caps, a method favored by the Dixie Klans in prior Catoosa County bombings. Informants fingered suspect

Lester Wares, protected by sheriff and fellow Klansman J. D. Stewart, but they produced no evidence to prove the case. Alternate theories suggest that Klansmen bombed Green's home by mistake, hoping to kill a black neighbor who quarreled with whites, or else chose the house for its location on the borderline between black and white neighborhoods.[104]

Lynch Law

Confusion surrounds the Klan's role in late–1950s Mississippi, but four sources refute claims that the state harbored no klaverns prior to 1963. Author William McCord reports that the Klan was "revamped" in Carthage after *Brown,* while Maryanne Vollers describes Louisiana's Original Knights recruiting Mississippi members in 1955. Pascagoula newsman Ira Harkey also reported Klan activity during the same period. Reed Massengill, related to one of the Mississippi Klan's most notorious members, confirms existence of a statewide KKK "death list" during the mid–1950s.[105]

And there was violent death aplenty for blacks in those years. Kidnappers murdered 14-year-old Emmett Till in August 1955, for "wolf whistling" at a white woman. White jurors acquitted suspects Roy Bryant and J. W. Milam, after which they sold their confession to *Look* magazine for $4,000.[106] In December 1955, while driving a car owned by Milam, Elmer Kimball killed black victim Clinton Melton after an argument at a gas station. Several white witnesses described the shooting as unprovoked murder, but jurors chose to ignore them. Prior to Kimball's trial, while researching her husband's death, Beulah Melton was run off a road near Glendora and drowned in a bayou.[107] An unidentified white gunman shot Charles Brown in June 1957, for "visiting a white man's sister." Ten months later, L. D. Clark shot Edward Smith at his victim's home, but grand jurors declined to indict. In October 1959 a motorist found Booker Mixon nude and dying near Marks, seemingly dragged behind a car. Police also did their share of the killing, with six confirmed victims during 1956–59.[108]

After Emmett Till, Mississippi's most renowned victim of the 1950s was Mack Charles Parker, accused of raping a white woman near Poplarville in April 1959. The NAACP had logged no lynchings in eight years, but old habits die hard. On April 22 a Hattiesburg Klansman met with vengeance-minded residents of Pearl River County to plan Parker's murder. According to FBI files, the conspirators included self-ordained minister James Lee, his son, and J. P. Walker, a former county deputy seeking election as sheriff. The gang seized Parker on April 25, conniving with his jailers, shot him, and dumped him in a river where he washed downstream to Bogalusa, Louisiana. FBI agents identified the lynchers, but a grand jury refused to charge them, preferring to grill Parker's alleged victim about "letting that nigger fuck you." Amidst widespread outrage—and with no apparent sense of irony—a North Carolina Klansman condemned Parker's slaying, telling reporters, "The Ku Klux Klan does not advocate violence. Mob action is ugly." J. P. Walker lost his race in 1959, but was elected on his next attempt, in 1963. During his four-year term as sheriff, Klansmen staged frequent parades through Poplarville.[109]

Another disappointed Klansman in December 1959 was Addison Thompson, campaigning to become Louisiana's governor. He lost that race—the first of many—placing eighth in a field of 10 candidates, with 4,200 votes out of 840,855 ballots cast.[110]

Gathering Storm

On February 2, 1960, four African American college students sat down at a whites-only Woolworth lunch counter in Greensboro, North Carolina, refusing to leave until they were served. By February 5, the "sit-in" protest and repeated bomb threats forced the store to close. Within a month, the new "direct action" civil rights movement had spread throughout Dixie—and, inadvertently, provided new impetus to the Ku Klux Klan.[111]

On February 27–28, Klansmen from seven states met at Atlanta's Henry Grady Hotel, creating a collaborative "National Klan Committee" representing various factions opposed to the U.S. Klans. On the night of March 26, members of the new group lit more than 1,000 crosses from Alabama and Georgia, through Florida and the Carolinas.[112] Violence swiftly followed: arson and bombings in Alabama, Arkansas, Georgia and Tennessee; a chain-flogging in Texas; white riots in Alabama and Mississippi. In the midst of chaos, Robert Shelton bolted from the U.S. Klans to lead his own Alabama Knights; Charles Maddox also defected, reviving the Association of Georgia Klans; and other Georgia Klansmen chose H. H. Jones as imperial wizard of their new Knights of the KKK. On February 21, police in Vienna, Austria, raided a klavern affiliated with Horace Miller's Aryan Knights.[113]

On August 1, 1960, a heart attack killed Eldon Edwards in Atlanta. His successor, Georgia grand dragon Robert "Wild Bill" Davidson—nicknamed for the leather fringed jacket he favored—announced plans to pursue an "activist" program, including use of buckshot "to keep the black race down."[114] Robert Shelton struck a more moderate pose for the moment, telling reporters, "I don't get myself connected with any fanatical movement" such as the NSRP or American Nazi Party.[115] In Florida, most of Davidson's realm soon defected to form a new, short-lived United Ku Klux Klan.[116]

Those events coincided with sit-ins at various Jacksonville restaurants, beginning on August 13. Ten days later, members of the Florida Klan met to plan a suitable response. Encouraged by the overt racism of Jacksonville's mayor and police chief, plus dedication of the city's newest school to Nathan Bedford Forrest, local knights and komrades from Georgia agreed to rally on August 27, leaving their Klan I.D. at home. Local department stores sold so many ax handles and baseball bats that morning, that reporters dubbed the ensuing riot "Ax-Handle Saturday." One black motorist died in the melee, shot by police, while some two dozen knights and 60-odd blacks were arrested. Mayor Haydon Burns blamed outside agitators, while his police chief told reporters, "All the fellows we arrested were local boys."[117] In either case, the riot was a preview of events to come.

"Heaven Help Your Soul"

The presidential race of 1960 threatened a replay of 1928, with Massachusetts liberal and Catholic John Kennedy opposing Vice President Richard Nixon, a Quaker conservative. Before either nominee was chosen, though, the NSRP convened in Dayton, Ohio, on May 19–20. Delegates demoted early draft choice John Crommelin to second place on the party's ticket, behind Arkansas Governor Faubus. Faubus declined the dubious honor, but the party ignored his wishes.[118]

West Virginia's Democratic primary, held on May 10, witnessed the most concentrated outpouring of anti–Catholicism in three decades. Ex-Klansman Robert Byrd, now a freshman U.S. senator, teamed with Texas hopeful Lyndon Johnson to derail Kennedy's campaign, while JFK strategists revived tales of Byrd's career as a kleagle.[119] Klansmen received warnings that a vote for Kennedy equaled "a vote against your God, and Savior, and your church.... Heaven help you if you vote away your religious liberty." John Kasper hit the campaign trail, vowing that if Kennedy triumphed, he would be "impeached before the sun rises."[120] Singer Frank Sinatra and his gangland cronies tipped the balance, disbursing an estimated $50,000 in bribes, while rival Hubert Humphrey complained, "I can't afford to run around this state with a little black bag·and a checkbook." One brand of dirty politics trumped the other, sweeping JFK to victory by a margin of 61 to 39 percent.[121]

By July, Kennedy's nomination was a foregone conclusion, yet the religious issue refused to die. In September, Kennedy felt obliged to tell the Greater Houston Ministerial Association, "I am not the Catholic candidate for president. I am the Democratic Party's candidate for president who also happens to be a Catholic. I do not speak for my Church on public matters, and the Church does not speak for me."[122]

Unimpressed, Florida grand dragon William Griffin announced his support for Nixon. That endorsement rebounded against Republicans on October 13, in a televised campaign debate. Asked about a statement from congressman Adam Clayton Powell that "all bigots will vote for Nixon and all right-thinking Christians and Jews will vote for Kennedy rather than be found in the ranks of the Klan-minded," JFK replied, "Well, Mr. Griffin, I believe, who is the head of the Klan, who lives in Tampa, Florida, indicated in a statement, I think, two or three weeks ago that he was not going to vote for me, and that he was going to vote for Mr. Nixon." Having sunk the shaft, he added, "I do not suggest in any way, nor have I ever, that that indicates that Mr. Nixon has the slightest sympathy, involvement, or in any way imply any inferences in regard to the Ku Klux Klan. That's absurd." Nixon awkwardly agreed, "I obviously repudiate the Klan; I repudiate anybody who uses the religious issue; I will not tolerate it, I have ordered all of my people to have nothing to do with it and I say, say to this great audience, whoever may be listening, remember, if you believe in America, if you want America to set the right example to the world, that we cannot have religious or racial prejudice. We cannot have it in our hearts. But we certainly cannot have it in a presidential campaign."[123]

From Tampa, Griffin fired back, "I don't give a damn what Nixon said. I'm still voting for him."[124] If Kennedy needed more help securing black votes, he found it on October 19, when Atlanta police jailed Martin Luther King during a sit-in. King refused to post bond, amid rumors of lynching and draconian prison terms. Kennedy placed a two-minute sympathy call to King's wife, later terming her "a friend of mine," although they never met. King was released the next day, as news of the call spread among African Americans nationwide. The brief call's impact is impossible to quantify, but King's father endorsed JFK, and Democrats carried black districts by wide margins in November.[125]

Historians still debate the outcome of 1960's election, including allegations of voter fraud on both sides, but Kennedy emerged victorious. The NSRP slate polled 214,195 votes, while John Crommelin—hedging his bets with another Alabama senate race—received 51,571 votes against 335,722 cast for incumbent John Sparkman.[126]

By decade's end, estimates of national Klan membership ranged from 35,000 to 50,000, with the U.S. Klans claiming 40 percent to 50 percent of the total.[127] In December 1960, the

Rev. Roy Davis of Texas founded Louisiana's Original Knights of the Ku Klux Klan, serving as figurehead imperial wizard while John Swenson ran the organization as grand dragon and national kleagle.[128] Klansmen, organized in every Southern state, stood armed and ready to confront what President-elect Kennedy called a "New Frontier." Others, in retrospect, would dub it America's Second Reconstruction.

CHAPTER 8

The Second Reconstruction
(1961–1969)

The new decade began with tumult in the Klan's Georgia stronghold, on January 6, 1961, when federal judge William Bootle ordered desegregation of the state university in Athens. Black students Charlayne Hunter and Hamilton Holmes registered on January 9, and violence followed two days later. Klansmen joined 2,000 students and outsiders in a full-scale riot, resulting in 16 arrests. Half of those jailed were Klansmen, including U.S. Klans grand dragon Calvin Craig. None faced trial, but the university suspended Holmes and Hunter "for their personal safety." Judge Bootle ordered their readmission on January 13, and they remained to graduate in 1963.[1]

Shockwaves from the campus melee split the U.S. Klans. On February 18, Imperial Wizard Davidson and Grand Dragon Craig bolted from the organization, assuming identical titles in a newly minted Invisible Empire, United Klans, Knights of the Ku Klux Klan of America. Earl George ascended to leadership of the U.S. Klans, while whole klaverns defected to join the new order. Davidson's opposition to violence, including Craig's involvement in the Athens riot, prompted his resignation on April 1, leaving Craig in charge. Headquarters remained in Atlanta, with membership confined to Georgia.[2]

Freedom Riding

Dissolution of the U.S. Klans came on the eve of Dixie's next great racial test, though the seeds of conflict had been planted decades earlier. In June 1946 the Supreme Court had banned segregated seating on interstate buses.[3] Southern states ignored that ruling, and Washington took no steps to enforce it. Likewise, racists paid little attention when the court ordered desegregation of interstate bus terminals in 1960.[4] It remained for the Congress of Racial Equality (CORE) to test both rulings with a series of integrated "freedom rides" through the heart of Dixie.

The protesters left Washington on May 4, 1961, bound for New Orleans on two buses chartered from Greyhound and Trailways. Police arrested CORE field secretary Joseph Perkins in Charlotte, North Carolina, on May 8. Violence followed on May 9, when Klansmen led by Elwin Wilson assaulted John Lewis at the Greyhound depot in Rock Hill, South Carolina. Two other riders were jailed for eight hours in Winnsboro.[5]

Then came Alabama.

In Birmingham, forewarned by FBI headquarters that freedom riders would arrive on May 14, Bull Connor hatched a plan with mayoral candidate Arthur Hanes, Sr. Hanes—an attorney, retired FBI agent, and sometime CIA collaborator—was also an ardent segregationist, formerly a featured speaker for Ace Carter's Citizens' Council. FBI informers also named him as a closet member of the Klan, though Hanes denied it till his dying day. Their plan was simple, spelled out to Klansmen by Detective W. W. "Red" Self and Sgt. Tom Cook during four April meetings.[6] As Cook explained:

> I don't give a damn if you beat them, bomb them, murder or kill them. I don't give a shit. There will be absolutely no arrests. You can assure every Klansman in the country that no one will be arrested. We don't ever want to see another nigger ride off the bus into Birmingham again. I want it to be something they remember as long as they live. Now, when you get the signal from Red to get the hell out of there, leave then. We've only got about two, three minutes at the most and you'll be swarmed with officers.[7]

On May 11, Grand Titan Hubert Page relayed instructions direct from Connor to Eastview Klavern 13: "By God, if you're going to do this thing, do it right!" Freedom riders should be beaten until they "looked like a bulldog got a hold of them," then stripped naked in the bus depot, allowing police to jail them for indecent exposure. Informant Gary Rowe warned his FBI handlers, who did nothing.[8]

The first mayhem on Sunday occurred in Anniston, northeast of Birmingham, where William Chapel and Ace Carter alumnus Kenneth Adams led 50 knights to mob the freedom riders' Greyhound, hammering its windows and flanks with bats, pipes, and chains, slashing its tires to make them go flat a few miles out of town. Police "escorted" the bus, trailed from Anniston by Klansmen, until it stalled outside Bynum. Unknown to all concerned, a pair of Alabama Highway Patrol officers had boarded the bus in Atlanta, under orders from Governor Patterson to secretly record any "inflammatory" comments from the demonstrators. Now, as a Klansman hurled his Molotov cocktail into the bus, officer Eli Cowling drove the rioters back at gunpoint and held the mob at bay until state reinforcements arrived.[9]

The Trailways bus reached Anniston next, its integrated passengers including retired Michigan State University professor Walter Bergman, and Bob Zellner—a son and grandson of Alabama Klansmen, whose sympathy for persecuted blacks got him briefly suspended from Montgomery's Huntington College, then drove him headlong into the civil rights movement.[10] Instead of torching that bus, Klansmen rushed aboard, battered its passengers, then directed the driver to Birmingham, where Shelton's mob waited with reinforcements from the NSRP, including J. B. Stoner and Edward Fields. Craving publicity, Fields had phoned CBS News reporter Howard K. Smith that morning, alerting him to some impending "action" at the Greyhound depot.[11]

In fact, news of the Greyhound's destruction diverted Klansmen at the last moment, but they reached the Trailways station in time to stage their riot. As Smith reported, they "grabbed the passengers into alleys and corridors, pounding them with pipes, with key rings and with fists…. Police did not appear until around 10 minutes later, when the hoodlums had got into waiting cars and moved down the street … where I watched them discussing their achievements…. That took place under Police Commissioner Connor's window."[12]

Connor's explanation for the lapse was simple. Police Chief Jamie Moore was attending a relative's funeral in Albertville, while most of his officers were home for Mother's Day.

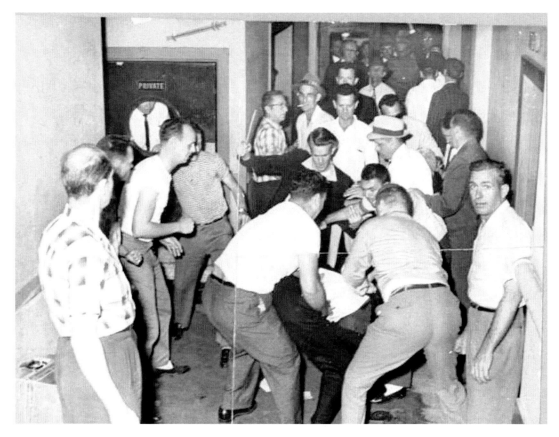

Klansmen beat freedom riders at Birmingham's Trailways bus terminal, May 14, 1961. FBI informer Gary Rowe is second from right in the foreground, back toward the camera (National Archives).

After the melee, Red Self congratulated Shelton's Klansmen, telling them, "Y'all did a good job. Now why don't you go on home and get a good night's sleep." Some were too keyed up to rest, however—Gary Rowe among them—and they set off prowling Birmingham for more blacks to abuse. They found some on Tenth Avenue, but their intended victims fought back, one slashing Rowe's throat with a knife. A Klan-friendly doctor saved his life and left him a scar to commemorate the battle. He was also caught on film beating the demonstrators, embarrassing his FBI sponsors no end.[13]

Patched up and ready for the road on May 15, freedom riders were stalled when Governor Patterson announced withdrawal of Highway Patrol escorts. "The people of the state are so enraged," he said, "that I cannot guarantee protection for this bunch of rabble-rousers." If troopers missed the point, Patterson vowed to fire any officers who helped the FBI investigate racial assaults. With Birmingham's depot besieged by Klansmen, the protesters flew out instead, their plane delayed by a bomb threat.[14]

The first freedom bus reached Montgomery on May 20, rolling into another mob scene. Police Commissioner Lester Sullivan watched the riot from his car, telling reporters, "We have no intention of standing guard for a bunch of troublemakers coming into our city." When federal observer John Siegenthaler was clubbed unconscious, journalists asked Sullivan why no ambulance had been summoned. The commissioner's reply: "He has not requested one."[15]

On May 21, as another raging mob besieged the Rev. King and 1,500 African Americans inside a local church, Washington ran out of patience. Faced with a threat of military intervention, Governor Patterson declared martial law in Montgomery and mobilized National Guardsmen to escort the captive parishioners home.[16] On June 2 the Justice Department sought a permanent injunction against the U.S. Klans, Shelton's Alabama Knights, and the Federated Klans, forbidding any further interference with the freedom rides. Lester Sullivan was also named, for "deliberately failing" to protect Klan victims. James Venable joined attorneys opposing that action, but in vain. Judge Frank Johnson, Jr., granted the injunction, adding a temporary order that forbade more freedom rides on Alabama soil.[17]

That verdict was relatively painless and enhanced Ku Klux recruiting drives, but several Klansmen still faced stiffer penalties. FBI agents charged nine Anniston knights with attacking the Greyhound on May 14. In January 1962, Judge Hobart Grooms sentenced five to probation, while one—Robert Couch—received a prison term concurrent with his sentence in an unrelated burglary. Charges were dismissed against two others, while Kenneth Adams was acquitted. A juror in that case was jailed for perjury in denying Klan membership.[18]

Though banned in Alabama, freedom rides continued elsewhere, finally reaching Monroe, North Carolina, on August 27. Klansmen rallied to attack protesters at the county courthouse, where riders were jailed and beaten in custody. Still craving action, knights raced off to Monroe's New Town ghetto, where Robert Williams stood ready with his Black Armed Guard. Shots were exchanged, and a white couple—Mr. and Mrs. Bruce Stegall—drove into the crossfire. Black witnesses later said the Stegalls had driven through New Town on August 26, flaunting a banner that read "Open Season on Coons." This time, they were mobbed, but Williams rushed to help them, escorting the pair into his nearby home and holding the mob at bay.[19] For his trouble, he was charged with kidnapping and fled the state, spending the rest of the decade in Cuba. Williams returned to face trial in 1969, but prosecutors stalled the case for six more years, finally dismissing all charges in January 1976.[20]

Soon after Judge Johnson issued his injunction, Alvin Horn suffered another personal tragedy. Fire swept his Ashland home on June 20, 1961, killing his 19-year-old wife and their two small children, while Horn was working in Wilsonville.[21] Horn would remain as grand dragon of the U.S. Klans, but his dim star was fading, along with the organization he served.

United Klans

On July 8, 1961, Klansmen from seven states convened in Indian Springs, Georgia, to forge a new alliance. Most represented Robert Shelton's Alabama Knights and the Invisible Empire, United Klans, led by Calvin Craig. They merged to form the United Klans of America (UKA), and moved headquarters from Atlanta to Shelton's home base in Tuscaloosa. Shelton served as imperial wizard of what would be the decade's strongest Klan, while Craig retained his post as Georgia's grand dragon. Robert Echols Scoggin—a Klansman since 1953, lately South Carolina's grand dragon of the U.S. Klans—left the Georgia meeting to lead Shelton's knights in the Palmetto State.[22] Other realms would be colonized over time.

The UKA's first challenge occurred in Albany, Georgia, where African Americans began protesting segregation in autumn 1961. By December, the Rev. King had arrived with members of his Southern Christian Leadership Conference (SCLC).[23] Police Chief Laurie Pritchett refused to help the movement by beating protesters, and while Calvin Craig struck a similar posture, urging his knights to "be nonviolent, just like the niggers," some Klansmen still craved action. They burned four churches in September 1962 and fired on half a dozen homes before meeting their match in Dallas.[24] When they stormed Kate Philpot's house on September 5, her daughter shot two Klansmen and put the rest to flight. Dead on the lawn was Leroy Parks, a candidate for county representative; shot through an arm was Gene Ables, a Dallas city clerk. Sheriff Jerome Clay jailed Ables and five others for attempted murder and violating Georgia's anti-mask law. Jurors convicted the six on October 19.[25] FBI agents arrested another Klansman for assaulting them at the scene of a church burning, but a federal grand jury refused to indict him.[26]

The Rev. King counted Albany as a failure, but local activists disagreed. "Things moved on," said Charles Sherrod of the Student Nonviolent Coordinating Committee (SNCC). "We never missed a beat." King, meanwhile, learned from his perceived mistakes, planning ahead for a campaign in Birmingham—where he would find the UKA prepared.[27]

"Another War Between the States"

Louisiana and Mississippi were braced for conflict by 1962. The Pelican State's Original Knights had grown since 1960 and become more militant. On February 18 Shreveport Klansmen bombed the home of dentist C. O. Simpkins, vice president of the state's NAACP and an SCLC board member.[28] On April 24 they dynamited a black Masonic lodge. Two days later, arsonists torched Dr. Simpkins's summer home in Bossier City. On September 1 they lit 15 crosses throughout northern Louisiana, including one at the state capitol. Catholic schools in New Orleans integrated one week later, prompting terrorists to fire on one and threaten several others. Police finally captured two knights on September 19, for the minor offense of illegal cross-burning in Marksville.[29] February 1963 saw four more jailed for painting "KKK" on 30 buildings around Bossier City.[30]

Tension in Mississippi set a standard for the South. Ross Barnett—once John Kasper's legal counsel, dubbed by *Time* magazine "as bitter a racist as inhabits the nation"—was elected governor in 1959 and stood four-square for white supremacy, although he also said he'd never met "a single Negro who has been discriminated against," claiming that most in Mississippi received "better treatment than whites."[31] It came as no surprise that he ignored white terrorism and denied the Klan's existence in his state. He missed incursions by Louisiana's Original Knights in 1960–61, and was oblivious when whites mobbed freedom riders in McComb, during November and December 1961.[32] By September 1962, when a federal court ordered James Meredith's admission to the state university, no Mississippi classroom had been integrated. Barnett and Lieutenant Governor Paul Johnson drew contempt citations for their refusal to register Meredith, leaving his installation to the hated "federals."[33]

Klansmen and their allies rallied to the cause. Robert Shelton predicted "another War Between the States" if Meredith entered the university. Edward Fields wired Barnett from Birmingham, promising NSRP warriors would "place our lives and fortunes at the disposal of your supreme authority as the governor of the sovereign state of Mississippi." (Only seven actually showed, including John Crommelin, the Bowling brothers, and future Klansman

Jerry Dutton.) Anniston's Klan sent a similar cable, saying hundreds of knights were on "stand-by alert." Calvin Craig claimed access to "a volunteer force of several thousand men," while Eastview Klavern 13 ordered members to mobilize for battle on September 29. That same night, 3,000 racists rallied in Shreveport, planning a 210-car procession to the Oxford campus. Melvin Bruce, an American Nazi Party member in Georgia, hit the road after wiring Barnett his pledge of service as "a combat infantryman." Even the "respectable" Citizens' Council was ready to fight, pledging 20,000 combatants from Louisiana and 1,500 from Florida.[34]

No one knows how many Klansmen actually reached the university. FBI memos placed 600 Alabama knights in Jackson and confirmed a 12-car caravan en route from Pritchard, Alabama, while Oxford attorney William Goodman saw many "scary people who had come to town to watch the show, armed with hunting rifles, shotguns, hatchets, and bricks." Oxford's airport traffic controllers denied Robert Shelton permission to land, but highway patrolmen cheerfully welcomed cars with license plates from Alabama, Arkansas, Florida, Georgia, Louisiana and Texas. Greenwood resident Byron De La Beckwith was stopped with a truckload of weapons and told to go home, but many more passed through without interference. At least one charter bus reached campus with 50 armed men aboard, loudspeakers blaring the UKA anthem "Cajun Ku Klux Klan."[35]

The result was bloody chaos, a nine-hour riot described by historian William Doyle as "the beginning of a Ku Klux Klan rebellion." With state police sidelined and cheering the rioters, snipers wounded 30 U.S. marshals, while another 136 suffered injuries from flying objects. A local resident, Ray Gunther, died from stray gunfire, and French reporter Paul Guihard was executed with a point-blank pistol shot behind a women's dormitory. Ballistics tests exonerated marshals in both slayings, which remain officially unsolved. Of 300 rioters arrested, a grand jury indicted only four: Melvin Bruce and three Alabama Klansmen. J. B. Stoner defended Bruce, while a member of Ross Barnett's law firm handled the rest. Jurors acquitted all four, leaving Barnett to blame the riot on "trigger-happy" marshals he accused of "instability and unwarranted brutality against unarmed youths."[36]

Mississippi's Klan prospered from the Ole Miss riot. Author James Silver claims that Walter Bailey disbanded his Mississippi Knights in 1962, but congressional investigators found the group still marginally active five years later. Meanwhile, on October 2, nightriders firebombed a black physician's clinic in Biloxi and the office of another who doubled as Gulfport's NAACP leader. One night later, raiders burned the Columbus home of another NAACP officer and lit a cross outside the Greenville residence of critic Hodding Carter II. On October 4 drive-by gunmen fired into the homes of Leake County blacks who had signed school integration petitions. Pascagoula sheriff Ira Grimsley led a gang of rioters to Oxford on September 30, then returned to form the Jackson County Citizens Emergency Unit, a Klanlike vigilante group that schemed in vain to snatch James Meredith from campus and to murder local newsman Ira Harkey. Years later, FBI reports confirmed that Meredith's admission to the university increased Klan membership statewide.[37]

"Segregation Forever!"

Alabama's constitution barred John Patterson from succeeding himself as governor in 1962, thus opening the field for other racists. Front-runner George Wallace remembered his vow to "out-nigger" all rivals, and to that end hired Ace Carter as his speechwriter. Wallace was also "on the most intimate terms" with Robert Shelton by 1962, and employed as his personal pilot ex-highway patrolman Albert Lingo, known statewide for being "hell on niggers." While Wallace courted Klansmen in private, Lingo attended their rallies, appearing on stage to be introduced as "a good friend of ours." Eastview Klavern 13 received $7,500 from Wallace headquarters, purchasing a panel truck to distribute campaign leaflets and copies of *The Thunderbolt.*[38]

In May's Democratic primary, Wallace faced seven contenders, including ex-governor Folsom, incumbent lieutenant governor Albert Boutwell, and Bull Connor. He swept the field, with Folsom running third and Connor fifth, while Boutwell— a Birmingham "moderate"— received only 862 votes out of 637,273 ballots cast. In June's runoff, Wallace defeated Tuscaloosa attorney Ryan DeGraffenried, Sr., by a margin of 71,608 votes. With no Republican contenders, victory was his.[39]

George Wallace allied himself with the Klan in 1962's gubernatorial election and thereafter (Florida State Archives).

The election was a double loss for Bull Connor, as Birmingham voters discarded their city commission in favor of a new mayor-council system. He ran for mayor, losing to Albert Boutwell, then joined Arthur Hanes in a futile lawsuit to block the changeover, clinging to office while the case dragged on. Meanwhile, on December 14, bombers struck Bethel Baptist Church, injuring two children. Connor told reporters the bombers "ought to be hung when they're caught," then reverted to type, saying, "We know the Negroes did it."[40]

On January 14, 1963, in an inauguration speech penned by Ace Carter, Wallace told supporters, "In the name of the greatest people that have ever trod this earth, I draw a line in the dust and toss the gauntlet before the feet of tyranny. And I say, Segregation now! Segregation tomorrow! Segregation forever!" That speech drew its punch line directly from 1920s Klan propaganda, and Wallace wasted no time rewarding his hooded allies. Robert

Shelton became a "consultant" with a state highway construction firm at $4,000 per year ($29,000 today). Al Lingo took charge of the Highway Patrol, renaming its officers "state troopers," decorating their cars and uniforms with Confederate flags. Wallace created an Alabama Legislative Commission to Preserve the Peace, hiring Ralph Roton—a high school dropout and head of the UKA's Klan Bureau of Investigation—as chief investigator of the civil rights movement. State schoolbook contracts went to the American Southern Publishing Company, producer of the UKA's *Fiery Cross* newsletter. Finally, Wallace's new parole board reviewed the sentences of Edward Aaron's mutilators, overturning prior decisions that each must serve at least one-third of his 20-year term. All were released between February 1964 and January 1965.[41]

A sideshow to 1962's main event was John Crommelin's latest campaign for the U.S. Senate. Railing against the Jews as usual, he ran third in a field of three, but Klansmen were encouraged by his tally of 56,822 votes.[42]

"American" Spelled Backwards

Even as Alabama's UKA secured friends in high places, the Klan suffered upheavals in Georgia. Earl George remained as wizard of the U.S. Klans until October 26, 1963, when College Park's klavern banished him on charges of embezzlement, replacing George with Exalted Cyclops H. J. Jones. Undaunted, George and his loyalists created a new Improved Order of U.S. Klans, incorporated on November 7.[43]

Between those events, on November 1, James Venable resigned as the UKA's imperial klonsel to launch his own faction, the National Knights. Officers included former Federated Knights founder William Morris and Herbert "Wally" Butterworth, a former UKA public relations man. Before joining the Klan, Butterworth had been a singer, radio announcer, and naval seaman. In 1962, with Venable, he formed the Defensive Legion of Registered Americans, which spawned an anti–Semitic Christian Voters and Buyers League dedicated to boycotting kosher food.[44] Over time, the National Knights formed a coalition of Klans rejected by Shelton's UKA, including the Association of Arkansas Klans, AGK, Association of South Carolina Klans, Dixie Klans, Original Knights, U.S. Klans, and the United Florida Klan, with Venable reigning as Imperial Wizard.[45]

While Klans split up and coalesced, in October 1961, Georgia's secretary of state issued a charter to Nacirema Inc.—a group whose name spelled "American" backwards. Journalist George McMillan broke the story two years later, describing Nacirema as a gang of black-robed defectors from various Klans and the NSRP, most sporting criminal records and/or physical deformities, who gathered to study the fine points of bomb-making.[46] In 1965 congressional investigators identified Nacirema's founders as UKA members Tom Gentry, C. J. Newborn, and R. H. Wynn, all from Mapleton, Georgia. In the month of its creation, Nacirema members met for a demolitions course on a farm near Macon, with Robert Shelton and Calvin Craig in attendance. Instructors for that seminar were UKA members William Anderson and William Crowe.[47] No identified Nacirema members were ever charged with any criminal activity, but in a South rocked by escalating explosions, the implications are clear. A similar group, called the Underground, trained South Carolina UKA members in marksmanship and demolitions.[48]

"Project X"

America's "most segregated" city, was a natural target for civil rights protests in 1963. In addition to its thriving klaverns, Edward Fields had moved NSRP headquarters to Birmingham in 1960, launching an Adolf Eichmann Trial Facts Committee to defend Hitler's architect of genocide.[49] Bombings continued apace, with three African American churches blasted in January 1962, and a fourth in December.[50]

Into that maelstrom stepped William Lewis Moore, a white postman from Baltimore. Diagnosed with paranoid schizophrenia in 1953 and treated with electroshock therapy, Moore published a memoir, *The Mind in Chains*, describing that experience in 1954. He drifted through various jobs before settling on the postal service, using his spare time to organize support groups for mental patients, marching against war and in favor of integration. Moore was outraged by Alabama's treatment of the freedom riders, unaware that an uncle-in-law, Klansman Charles Cagle, was one of the rioters. In November 1962, Moore began planning a one-man pilgrimage through Dixie.[51]

The idea was simple on paper. Moore would walk from Chattanooga to Jackson, Mississippi, living from a shopping cart, wearing a sandwich sign bearing integrationist messages. Planning ahead, he wrote to aunt-in-law Helen Cagle, hoping to arrange a Birmingham stopover in transit. She replied: "Our home will be closed to you on a trip of this nature. I'm sure I can't see how you can expect us to welcome you down here with the motive you have in mind." She signed off "with love and a prayer to God that He will deliver you from this thing that has taken possession of you."[52]

Moore arrived in Chattanooga on April 21, 1963, and pushed on from there, logging encounters with whites who jeered him and questioned his motives. April 22 found Moore in Fort Payne, Alabama, where a UKA klavern led by George Killian operated as the Wills Valley Hunting Club. The next afternoon, outside Colbran, he was stopped in turn by Killian, then Killian's cousin and Floyd Simpson, the klavern's "klokan" (investigator). All questioned Moore, and Gaddis Killian predicted Moore's death. Simpson told Moore, "Now I know who you are." At 9:00 p.m. a motorist found Moore sprawled on the roadside near Keener, shot twice with a .22-caliber rifle. Charles and Helen Cagle drove from Birmingham to identify the corpse.[53]

On April 25, Sheriff Dewey Colvard detained Simpson and Gaddis Killian on "open" charges. Three days later, FBI analysts matched the death bullets to Simpson's rifle. Colvard charged him with murder, but released Killian when he complained of claustrophobia. Simpson posted bond on April 28, pending grand jury action. That panel met on September 12 and declined to indict him. George Killian defended his klokan, claiming that "a stranger" followed Moore and killed him, after somehow obtaining Simpson's rifle.[54] The crime remains officially unsolved.

In Birmingham, meanwhile, the Rev. King had launched "Project X," a frontal assault on segregation citywide. They filled the streets and jails with demonstrators, many of them children, while Bull Connor retaliated with clubs, attack dogs, and fire hoses. Connor sent Detective Maurice House with a warning to the UKA: "We want to keep our friendship with the Klan, but if you try to help us you will be arrested." Robert Shelton got the message, but his Eastview mavericks met with Edward Fields and J. B. Stoner, charting a militant response. Their vehicle was a new action squad, dubbed the "Cahaba River Boys." On March

24 bombers struck a black family's home, wounding two occupants. Gary Rowe tipped his FBI handlers to Klan involvement, while Connor's police blamed unidentified blacks and called the bombing "non-racial." The UKA formed a new front group, United Americans for Conservative Government (UACG), enlisting members of the Citizens' Council and John Birch Society with Klansmen and NSRP Nazis. On April 14 Cahaba Klansman Tommy Blanton vandalized a Catholic neighbor's car, then accidentally shot a fellow knight, costing him a kidney.[55]

On May 10 a Senior Citizens' Committee agreed to limited desegregation of Birmingham's public facilities. Connor denounced the surrender, demanding a boycott of all integrated establishments. On May 11 Klansmen from six states rallied midway between Birmingham and Bessemer. Robert Shelton addressed the crowd, reading a list of merchants who had voted for appeasement, most of whom were "Jews or foreigners." He praised Bull Connor, adding that Klansmen were "willing to give their lives if necessary to preserve segregation in Alabama."[56]

They started that night, detonating two bombs at the home and parsonage of the Rev. A. D. King, then striking SCLC headquarters at the A. G. Gaston Motel. African Americans reacted violently, stoning police cars and torching several shops before Al Lingo arrived with 250 troopers and an "irregular posse" from Selma, led by Sheriff James Clark. Gary Rowe blamed Black Muslims for the bombings, but black witness Roosevelt Tatum told FBI agents that a uniformed policeman had planted the bomb at A. D. King's home. He remembered the patrol car's number—22—whose driver could be easily identified. Rather than investigate, agents charged Tatum with filing a false report; at trial, Tatum received a one-year prison term. On May 15 Arthur Hanes addressed a UACG audience, raging against Birmingham's "Congolese mob" and calling Martin Luther King a "witch doctor." Hanes vowed that he would not negotiate. "They haven't got a thing that we want," he said. "We have what they want." Eight days later, the state supreme court endorsed Birmingham's new city government, leaving Bull Connor unemployed, while Hanes retreated into private practice.[57]

The Schoolhouse Door

Birmingham would simmer for the next two years, erupting periodically, but June 1963 confronted George Wallace with a more pressing challenge. On May 16 a federal court ordered admission of two black applicants to the state university in Tuscaloosa, where Robert Shelton warned that integration would "touch off the bloodiest rioting ever seen in the United States." His men would "match the violence" of U.S. troops or marshals, and if local officers failed to enforce segregation, "the Klan will enforce it."[58]

Wallace, loath to share the spotlight with a hooded mob, had other plans. On June 5 Al Lingo warned Klansmen to avoid the campus or face arrest. Ace Carter passed the same warning to Ed Fields at NSRP headquarters, while Bull Connor urged Tuscaloosa's Citizens' Council to "let Governor Wallace and law enforcement handle the problem." Predictably, Eastview's knights ignored the message. On June 8, three days before the scheduled showdown, Gary Rowe and five others set off for Tuscaloosa in two cars loaded with guns, swords, bayonets and bludgeons. State troopers stopped them outside town, seizing the weapons but sharing a bottle of confiscated liquor. "Jesus Christ," one said, "we sure hate to bust you when you came down here to help us keep the goddamn niggers away from the school." In fact, no charges were filed. The Klansmen missed a rally where Calvin Craig praised Wallace as "the greatest man in Alabama," but they met a judge who ordered their weapons returned, saying, "I want to thank you men. You're outstanding American citizens. I wish we had 10,000 more like you guys."[59]

Wallace's moment in the schoolhouse door was anticlimactic. He read a statement written by Ace Carter, then stepped aside to admit the new students. Calm prevailed until November 16, when a bomb exploded near the dormitory housing black coed Vivian Malone. Three more detonated over the next five days, before police charged five National Guardsmen with setting the charges.[60]

"Ticket to the Eternal"

On the night 'Bama was integrated, President Kennedy delivered an impassioned address to the nation. "One hundred years of delay have passed since President Lincoln freed the slaves," he declared, "yet their heirs, their grandsons, are not fully free." Announcing plans for a new Civil Rights Act, he added, "We have a right to expect that the Negro community will be responsible, will uphold the law, but they have a right to expect that the law will be fair, that the Constitution will be color blind."[61]

One who celebrated that declaration was Mississippi NAACP leader Medgar Evers. On June 12 a sniper's bullet killed him at his Jackson home. Police found a rifle nearby and traced it to Greenwood resident Byron De La Beckwith, a Citizens' Council member who described himself as "rabid on the subject of segregation." Beckwith had threatened Hodding Carter III for his editorials condemning violence, and warned the National Rifle Association that "for the next 15 years we here in Mississippi are going to have to do a lot of shooting to protect our wives, children and ourselves from bad niggers." One such was Evers. Beckwith had told friends, "He's got to go."[62]

Beckwith's arrest rallied racist support. The Citizens' Council launched a White Citizens Legal Defense Fund to pay his attorneys, including a member of Ross Barnett's law firm and a past president of Greenwood's Council. Judge O. H. Barnett, the governor's cousin, shielded Beckwith from psychiatric evaluation, deeming it "evidence by compulsion." Jurors deadlocked seven-to-five for acquittal at Beckwith's first trial, in February 1964. At his retrial in April, after Ross Barnett appeared in court to shake Beckwith's hand, a second hung jury voted eight-to-four for acquittal. Beckwith rode home with a police escort, packing a carbine on loan from Hinds County's sheriff, and soon found work as an auxiliary policeman, patrolling Greenwood's ghetto.[63]

At some point, Beckwith also joined the Klan. Two weeks after shooting Evers, he told a jailer "that we definitely needed a Ku Klux Klan at this time, that it could do a lot of good." In September 1963, still jailed, he penned a letter saying he had been invited to join the Klan. After his second trial, Beckwith's wife said he was out every night, "running with hoodlums and everything, but he would say, well, they had a cause."[64]

Evers was not Mississippi's first victim of Klan-type violence in 1963. Sylvester Maxwell was slain and mutilated in January, near a white home in Canton. A month later, arsonists burned four Greenwood buildings but missed the SNCC office, their primary target. That same month, a drive-by shooting wounded three civil rights workers. Greenwood's SNCC center burned in March, when gunmen also blasted the home of a black applicant to Ole Miss and fled in a car resembling Beckwith's. In May, when a firebomb damaged Medgar Evers's carport, police dismissed it as "a prank."[65]

FBI files claim Louisiana's Original Knights invaded Mississippi in March 1963. Douglas Byrd served as grand dragon until December, when he and Natchez Klansman Edward McDaniel were banished for embezzlement. The state's strongest faction, the Mississippi White Knights (MWK), formally organized in February 1964, with Laurel resident Samuel Holloway Bowers, Jr., elected as imperial wizard. By 1965 observers credited the MWK with 6,000 to 10,000 members statewide.[66] They were some of the country's most militant Klansmen—and the only knights operating under explicit orders to commit violent crimes. On March 1, 1964, Bowers distributed an "executive lecture" saying, "As MILITANTS, we are disposed to the use of physical force against our enemies."[67] Bowers graded "projects" on a scale from one to four: cross-burning, whipping, arson or bombing, and "elimination," granting himself sole authority to order the most extreme mayhem. In May 1964 the *Klan Ledger* warned civil rights workers, "Take heed, atheists and mongrels, we will not travel your path to a Leninist Hell, but we will buy YOU a ticket to the Eternal if you insist."[68]

Bloody Sunday

Violence continued in Birmingham, where a firebomb razed a black church on August 10, 1963.[69] Klansmen tear-gassed newly integrated stores on August 14 and bombed Arthur Shores's home six days later.[70] Robert Shelton, flying north to observe the Rev. King's historic March on Washington, nearly died when his plane crashed in South Carolina.[71] Governor Wallace, through Al Lingo, arranged for NSRP members to riot on September 3, when Birmingham schools admitted their first black students. Bombers hit the Shores home again on September 4, sparking another riot. Two days later, Wallace addressed a UACG fundraiser in Birmingham.[72]

Then tragedy struck.

On September 15 a bomb shattered the Sixteenth Street Baptist Church, killing young victims Addie Mae Collins, Denise McNair, Carole Robertson, and Cynthia Wesley. The blast injured 22 others, including Sara Jean Collins, Addie's younger sister, who lost an eye. Subsequent riots claimed two more lives, both African American—one youth shot by police, another slain by two white teens after a visit to NSRP headquarters.[73]

The Sunday massacre panicked Governor Wallace and Robert Shelton. On September 22 Cahaba Klansmen joined UACG President Bill Morgan for a "kiss of death" meeting, vowing to kill anyone who leaked Klan involvement in the bombing. Three days later, with J. B. Stoner and George Bright in town, another bomb detonated in one of Birmingham's ghettoes. As policemen scoured the scene, a second bomb exploded, this one loaded with shrapnel designed to kill. On September 29 Al Lingo met with Shelton, other Klansmen, and ex-mayor Art Hanes to prepare a surprise for the FBI. Police then arrested Charles Cagle, Bob Chambliss, and John Hall on misdemeanor charges of illegally possessing dynamite. A judge convicted them on October 9, fining each $100 and imposing six-month jail terms, then freed them on bond pending appeal. Wallace boasted that "We certainly beat the

Kennedy crowd to the punch," but it was all for show. An appellate court reversed the trio's convictions in June 1964, with all charges dismissed.[74]

"Klanville, USA"

As Alabama and Mississippi seethed with violence, the UKA worked more quietly in the Carolinas, steadily gaining ground. Robert Scoggin expanded the Palmetto State realm to 20 klaverns by early 1964, increasing to 55 by 1966.[75] He publicly warned against violence, and his knights generally listened, although bombers struck the home of a black coed scheduled to enter the state university in August 1963.[76]

North Carolina was the UKA's great success story. Arthur Leonard served as the state's first grand dragon, replaced in late 1963 by James Robertson Jones, a second-generation Klansman and former grand nighthawk of the U.S. Klans. By 1965 the realm claimed more active members than any other state—at least 12,000, distributed among 192 klaverns—and

United Klans officers in 1964. Left to right (standing) North Carolina grand dragon James Jones, grand klabee (secretary) Fred Wilson, and South Carolina grand dragon Robert Scoggin (House Committee on Un-American Activities).

earned the label "Klanville, USA."[77] North Carolina suffered less mayhem than neighboring states, but it was not immune. In July 1963 terrorists stormed Camp Summerland, an integrated retreat near Rosman, stabbing one man, riddling the camp's bus with bullets, burning the gymnasium, then pouring gasoline into the lake and setting it ablaze. A year later, police jailed two UKA members for trying to burn an African American church in Elm City. August 1964 witnessed a cross-burning on the governor's lawn, in Raleigh.[78]

Killing Camelot

On November 22, 1963, sniper fire killed President Kennedy in Dallas. Samuel Bowers "danced around" in glee on hearing the news and "went into happy, crazy acting."[79] Charles Maddox, Georgia grand dragon of the National Knights, told a cheering audience, "We need to do a lot to stop these national politicians. A boy down in Texas did a lot already, remember?"[80] But did Klansmen play a greater role than that of simple cheerleaders in Kennedy's assassination?

From October 18 to 20, 1963, racists from around the country met in Indiana, to found the far-right Constitution Party. Delegates included James Venable, Jack Brown from Tennessee's Dixie Knights, Joseph Milteer of the NSRP, William Potter Gale of the Christian Defense League, Curtis Dall from the Liberty Lobby, and Kenneth Goff from Soldiers of the Cross.[81] On November 9, police recorded a conversation between Milteer and informant/Klansman Willie Somersett, in which Milteer predicted Kennedy's murder during an upcoming visit to Miami. Milteer named Jack Brown as one "likely to get" JFK, saying Kennedy would be shot "from an office building with a high-powered rifle," adding that police "will pick somebody up within hours afterwards ... just to throw the public off." Secret Service agents canceled the Miami stop and sent Kennedy on to Dallas, where Milteer's scenario played out.[82]

Coincidence?

Klan links to the assassination continued in Dallas, where police lieutenant George Butler supervised the bungled jailhouse transfer of alleged sniper Lee Harvey Oswald on November 24, ending with Oswald's murder by gangster Jack Ruby. Butler had received a 30-day suspension from the department in August 1941, for beating a black youth in custody. Five years later, according to author Seth Kantor, Butler had risen to become "the key man in the department contacted by the Chicago mob when they chose to move into Dallas." One of those mobsters was killer Jack Ruby. Butler was also an active Klansman. In 1962 he asked Midlothian journalist Penn Jones to help him print Klan literature, remarking that half of all Dallas policemen were Kluxers.[83]

As the Warren Commission prepared to investigate Kennedy's murder, it issued subpoenas to potential witnesses. One bore the name of Royson Everett Frankhouser, Jr., a Pennsylvania Klansman also affiliated with the NSRP, American Nazi Party, and the paramilitary Minutemen. Born in 1939, he was the son of an alcoholic ex-convict who hated Jews and Catholics, sometimes shouting, "Heil Hitler," as his wife claimed, "just to annoy the neighbors." Frankhouser's parents divorced in 1950, leaving him in a state children's home. Upon release, he dropped out of ninth grade and began collecting Nazi memorabilia, joined the army at 18, and received a psychiatric discharge in 1957. By 1958 he was a member of the

U.S. Klans, logging the first of 142 arrests for kicking a policeman during an Atlanta demonstration. Frankhouser, whose mendacity rivaled Baron Münchhausen's, claimed personal acquaintance with Michael and Ruth Paine, Texas friends of Lee Harvey Oswald, saying they recruited him for "leftist paramilitary activity." He also claimed that FBI headquarters quashed his Warren Commission subpoena on "national security grounds." Two agents allegedly called at his home, one day after a bungled attempt on Frankhouser's life, warning him, "If you release information on the Paines or the Commission, you'll be in deep trouble with the FBI."[84]

Fact or fantasy?

When New Orleans district attorney Jim Garrison began investigating JFK's murder in 1966, Frankhouser offered to furnish letters, allegedly containing proof of a conspiracy, which he had given to the FBI in 1964. Bureau memos refer to the "Payne letters" [*sic*], branding Frankhouser "a liar [and] a braggart, [who] often makes impressive statements he never carries out."[85] Another Klansman embroiled in Garrison's case was Jules Kimbel, a crony of assassination suspects David Ferrie and Clay Shaw, who in summer 1963 shared a New Orleans mail drop with Ferrie, Oswald, and alleged Oswald impersonator Kerry Thornley. Three weeks after Ferrie's mysterious death, in March 1967, Kimbel claimed he visited Ferrie's apartment with UKA grand klaliff Jack Helm, removing a briefcase filled with documents.[86] Another Klan-connected witness was Thomas Beckham, a Ferrie associate subpoenaed from Nebraska in December 1967. Arriving for his grand jury testimony, Beckham was accompanied by Klan wizard Addison Thompson.[87]

Freedom Summer

Months before James Meredith's admission to Ole Miss, leaders of CORE, the NAACP, SCLC and SNCC forged an umbrella group, the Council of Federated Organizations (COFO), to coordinate Southern civil rights campaigns. COFO scouts in Mississippi came under attack in summer 1962, but persevered to plan a statewide "freedom summer" drive for 1964.[88] Awaiting them were Mississippi's White Knights, led by Imperial Wizard Bowers and Grand Dragon Julius Harper, formerly Copiah County's sheriff.[89] Bowers, a New Orleans native born in 1924, hailed from aristocratic stock: maternal grandfather Eaton Bowers served four terms in Congress, once declaring that his state had solved its racial problem through "absolute denial of social intercourse and with every restriction on [black] participation in political affairs and government that is permissible under the Federal Constitution."[90] Samuel joined the Original Knights in 1955, around the time of his arrest for liquor violations, and sometimes donned Nazi garb, shouting, "Sieg heil!" before a mirror. By 1964 he owned Laurel's Sambo Amusement Company, selling vending machines and living on the premises with his male partner, prompting rumors of homosexuality.[91]

The MWK and an affiliated group, Americans for Preservation of the White Race (APWR)—called a Klan "shell organization" in FBI memos—forged a united front with Mississippi police against the summer's "invaders."[92] Bloodshed began in February 1964, with the murders of Louis Allen, witness to the 1961 slaying of black activist Herbert Lee by a state legislator, and Clifton Walker, ambushed outside Woodville while driving home from work. Highway patrolman R. W. Palmertree, named as a Klansman in FBI files, investigated Walker's slaying, but neglected to check Walker's car for fingerprints. Klan suspects were identified, but no arrests resulted.[93]

Bullwhip floggings accompanied murder. One Adams County deputy reported 17 whippings in January and February 1964, with 16 black victims and one white. In Franklin County, Klansmen demolished Leon Russell's home with a hand grenade. In April 1964 six men in black hoods waylaid black farmhand Richard Butler in Adams County. He escaped, despite three bullet wounds, and three suspects were jailed, including MWK exalted cyclops Edward Fuller.[94] No further record of their case survives today. On May 2 Klansmen snatched suspected COFO members Henry Dee and Charles Moore from Meadville, driving them into the Homochitto National Forest, where they were beaten and grilled about civil rights activity. Still alive, both teenagers were dropped into the Ole River near Tallulah, Louisiana, their bodies weighted with an engine block and sections of railroad track.[95]

The latter case inspired short-lived hopes for justice, after Dee's and Moore's corpses surfaced in July. Police arrested Klansmen Charles Edwards and James Seale, both of whom confessed to kidnapping and beating the victims, later recanting with claims of coercion. In January 1965 District Attorney Lenox Forman dismissed their statements "in the interest of justice and in order to fully develop the facts in this case." Neither went to trial.[96]

Authorities found Dee and Moore while searching for three other Klan victims. COFO volunteer Michael Schwerner arrived in Meridian in January 1964. Soon dubbed "Goatee" and "Jew Boy" by Klansmen, he joined local CORE member James Chaney to canvass surrounding counties. The pair visited Longdale's Mount Zion Church on May 25, then departed for a training session in Ohio. On June 16 masked Klansmen beat Mount Zion's parishioners and burned the church. By the time Schwerner and Chaney returned on June 20, with white volunteer Andrew Goodman, Sam Bowers had ordered "Goatee's" elimination.[97]

Schwerner, Chaney and Goodman returned to Longdale on June 23, then were arrested by Neshoba County deputy Cecil Price, a Klansman whose superior—Sheriff Lawrence Rainey, Sr.—was also an MWK member and slayer of two prior black victims. In Rainey's absence, Price detained the trio until Klansmen led by kleagle/minister Edgar Killen gathered nearby, then released them with orders to leave the county. Before they could do so, he stopped them again and delivered them to the mob. All three were shot, then buried on a farm owned by Klansman Olen Burrage. The disappearance of three victims—two of them white Northerners—galvanized public outrage. President Lyndon Johnson called Mississippi senator James Eastland, who branded the vanishing act "a publicity stunt," claiming "there's no organized white men in that area." "Preacher" Killen, meanwhile, boasted that he met with Eastland "very, very often." When Schwerner's burned-out car was found, President Johnson ordered a reluctant J. Edgar Hoover to "control and prosecute terroristic activity" by the Klan and APWR.[98]

Hoover authorized expenditure of $30,000 to recover the victims, while Robert Shelton arrived to conduct his own "investigation." George Wallace soon followed, joining Governor Paul Johnson for a rally in Jackson, launching Wallace's first presidential campaign. In his

Opposite, top: Searchers with the burned-out car driven by James Chaney, Andrew Goodman, and Michael Schwerner, June 1964. *Bottom:* Burial site of Chaney, Goodman and Schwerner on a Klansman's farm (**National Archives**).

speech, Wallace cited "a report by Col. Al Lingo ... that three persons resembling the group had been seen in Alabama" on June 23. Johnson told the audience, "Governor Wallace and I are the only two people who know where they are, and we're not telling."[99]

Directed by a paid informer, FBI agents unearthed the corpses on August 4. They charged Price and eight other Klansmen with conspiracy. Two members of the murder gang confessed in custody, then recanted. Hopes for a state trial evaporated after Governor Johnson assigned the case to Judge O. H. Barnett—a cousin of ex-governor Ross Barnett, dubbed "a Klansman judge" by Hoover, who was also "distantly related to some of the defendants." U.S. Commissioner Esther Carter dismissed federal conspiracy charges on December 10, branding a triggerman's confession as "hearsay."[100]

Silver Dollars

While the Neshoba case made international headlines, a new Klan faction organized in Mississippi and Louisiana, enlisting members of the MWK, UKA and Original Knights who thought their respective Klan's were "too soft." Recruits included James Seale, his brother and father, Earcel Boyd, Sr., and Raleigh Glover. Members identified themselves with silver dollars minted in the year of their birth, and called their squad the Silver Dollar Group (SDG). They emulated Georgia's Nacirema Inc. by staging demolition seminars, and practiced incessantly with firearms, including submachine guns. A new refinement was the use of "freeze balls," globs of ice fired through windows from slingshots, which melt to obliterate evidence. SDG members also pledged to kill any Klansmen caught cooperating with authorities.[101]

A favored SDG hangout was the Shamrock Motel in Vidalia, Louisiana. Huddled in the motel's café, Klansmen plotted their raids and found their first victim: Joseph "Jo-Ed" Edwards, the Shamrock's black porter. On July 12 Edwards left work as usual and disappeared forever. Police found his bloodstained car abandoned beside the Ferriday-Vidalia Highway, but never recovered his body. Decades later, retired FBI agent Billy Bob Williams told reporters that Edwards was "skinned alive" by Klansmen, then shot repeatedly and dropped into the Mississippi River, his body wrapped in chains. Earcel Boyd's son believes the SDG killed Edwards because he "saw too much" at the motel. A cousin of Edwards says he was threatened for dating white women. A third version claims that Edwards "grabbed" a white female guest at the Shamrock, kissing her "against her will." A friend of the supposed victim, probation officer James Goss, filed a police complaint for that alleged assault. Later, Goss blamed two sheriff's deputies—Frank DeLaughter and Bill Ogden—for abducting Edwards. The FBI considered them suspects but filed no charges. Reports of a "Klan torture chamber" found in an abandoned house remain unconfirmed.[102]

On the day Edwards vanished, Klansmen burned two black churches in Adams County.[103] No definitive tally of mayhem exists for Mississippi's freedom summer, but by August, COFO spokesmen listed three murders, four persons wounded in 35 shootings, 52 "serious" beatings, 65 buildings bombed or burned (including 30 churches), seven bombings bungled with no damage, and 10 cars destroyed or damaged.[104] At least in terms of homicides, that count was certainly conservative.

Some of Mississippi's violence followed the advent of UKA recruiters, luring members from the MWK. Kleagles arrived in autumn 1963, persuading Edward McDaniel of Natchez to quit the MWK and serve as the UKA's grand dragon. White Knights countered by accusing McDaniel of stealing Klan funds.[105] One UKA cell in particular—McComb's "Pike County Wolf Pack"—was especially violent, suspected in 23 bombings, six arsons, one shooting, one flogging, and four other assaults.[106] First, however, national attention shifted farther east, to Florida.

"A Segregated Super-Bomb"

America's oldest city planned to celebrate its quadricentennial in 1965, and publicity surrounding that event offered civil rights activists a golden opportunity to crack Florida's strongest bastion of segregation. Klansmen aplenty occupied St. Augustine and nearby Jacksonville, their ranks augmented by Holsted "Hoss" Manucy's Ancient City Gun Club (ACGC). Manucy, a hog farmer and convicted bootlegger, denied any ties to the Klan, but boasted that his favorite pastimes were "raisin' pigs and shootin' niggers." Manucy cited his Catholicism as proof he was not a Klansman, but J. B. Stoner acknowledged "some overlap" between the Klan and ACGC.[107] More tellingly, congressional investigators named Manucy's club as a front for Klavern 519 of the United Florida Klan.[108]

Trouble started early in St. Augustine. On September 18, 1963, Klan evangelist Charles "Connie" Lynch addressed a hooded audience outside town, praising Birmingham's recent church bombers. "If there's four less niggers tonight," he railed, "we're all better off!" Next, Lynch attacked local dentist Robert Hayling, head of St. Augustine's NAACP chapter. "He's got no right to live at all," Lynch said, "let alone walk up and down your streets and breathe the white man's free air. He ought to wake up tomorrow morning with a bullet between his eyes. If you were half the men you claim to be, you'd kill him before sunup."[109] Moments later, lookouts caught Hayling and three black companions spying on the rally. Dragged forward and beaten severely, they were at the point of being burned alive when Sheriff Lawrence Davis arrived to arrest them on charges of "assaulting" the Klansmen. Local jurors convicted all four.[110]

Violence escalated from there, claiming its first life on October 25, when ACGC member William Kinard suffered fatal gunshots during an armed motorcade through St. Augustine's ghetto. Nineteen sixty-four began with multiple arson attacks on black homes, while observers from the U.S. Civil Rights Commission dubbed St. Augustine "a segregated super-bomb ... [with a] ... short fuse." Martin Luther King's SCLC launched demonstrations in March, producing mass arrests and escalating brutality. Connie Lynch returned with J. B. Stoner, both collaborating with rival grand dragons Don Cothran of the UKA and Eugene Fallaw of the United Florida Klan. King arrived in May, narrowly avoiding death when terrorists shot up his rented cottage. May also witnessed the city's first riots, Klansmen mobbing and beating black marchers while police stood by watching and laughing.[111]

Sheriff Davis responded to the crisis by building outdoor "bullpens" for black prisoners and deputizing ACGC members, decisions that prompted federal judge Bryan Simpson to ban interference with peaceful protests. Klansmen twice set fire to the Rev. King's headquarters, and mob assaults continued through June, both in downtown St. Augustine and at nearby beaches. After a riot on June 25, Connie Lynch told Klansmen, "I'm inspired. I'm really thrilled." One month later he was jailed, with Stoner and two others, for illegal cross-burning, but no prosecution resulted. One target of protests, the Monson Motor Lodge, was firebombed after integrating its café. August brought another federal injunction, barring Manucy and the ACGC from intimidating blacks, while a state legislative committee condemned outsider J. B. Stoner for his "key role" in fomenting bloodshed.[112]

Jacksonville, meanwhile, suffered its own spate of violence. Judge Simpson had ordered admission of black first-grader Donald Godfrey to an all-white school in September 1963. Klansman William Rosecrans bombed Godfrey's home in February 1964, then fled to St. Augustine, where Hoss Manucy and Sheriff Davis hid him from FBI agents. Soon afterward, unknown persons dynamited the strike-bound Florida East Coast Railway during a visit by President Johnson, and a reward was offered for arrest of the bombers. Manucy, greedy and confused, betrayed Rosecrans to authorities, and while Rosecrans was absolved of the railroad bombing, he proved talkative on other matters. He named five accomplices in the Godfrey blast, including Bart Griffin, Eugene Fallaw's replacement as grand dragon of the United Florida Klan. Stoner defended the five at trial, and jurors acquitted one, deadlocking on the others, while a guilty plea from Rosecrans sent him to federal prison. At the second trial of Griffin and company, UKA imperial klonsel Matthew Murphy assisted Stoner, securing acquittal for all four defendants. A UKA plot to murder Rosecrans, using three Klansmen later charged with killing a civil rights worker in Alabama, fizzled on the drawing board.[113]

COINTELPRO

Though initially reluctant to attack the Klan, J. Edgar Hoover bowed to pressure from President Johnson, inaugurating a "counterintelligence program"—COINTELPRO, for short—against white hate groups on September 2, 1964. Previous operations had targeted the Communist Party (1956) and Socialist Workers Party (1961) for harassment tactics including illegal wiretaps and bugging, theft of mail, anonymous slander, and use of *agents provocateur* to incite criminal violence.[114] Hoover's first memo of the new campaign told bureau field offices:

> The purpose of this program is to expose, disrupt and otherwise neutralize the activities of the various klans and hate organizations, their leadership and adherents. The devious maneuvers and duplicity of these groups must be exposed to public scrutiny through cooperation of reliable news media, both locally and at the Seat of Government. In every instance, consideration should be given to disrupting the organized activity of these groups and no opportunity should be missed to capitalize upon organizational and personal conflicts in their leadership.[115]

To that end, agents hired informers, burgled Klan offices, tapped Klan phones, tried to brand loyal knights as turncoats, circulated cartoons accusing Klan leaders of theft and drunkenness, vandalized Klan property, met threats with "muscle," and funded splinter Klans to drain members from larger factions. Alabama informant Gary Rowe claimed that his bureau handlers ordered him to sleep with Klan wives, to disrupt marriages. Also targeted for special treatment were the NSRP and American Nazi Party. Klan leaders used polygraphs to screen members, banished suspected informers—and, in at least one case, murdered a Klansman accused of snitching.[116]

While COINTELPRO's tactics ranged from childish pranks to felonies, it initially had little impact. Bombings and arson attacks continued, with targets including two stores owned by Natchez mayor John Nosser, deemed a "moderate" on integration. Police were also implicated, as when patrolmen stopped three suspected bombers outside Natchez, discovering that they were former sheriff William Ferrell and two of his ex-deputies. McComb's "Pike County Wolf Pack" detonated nine bombs in September alone, while Sheriff A. A. Andrews dismissed the blasts as "plants set by COFO people." Armed with statements from informers, FBI agents arrested nine UKA knights between September 30 and October 7, seizing weapons and explosives at their homes. Georgia dragon Calvin Craig solicited donations for their defense fund, calling the bombers "victims of circumstances," but he need not have worried. At trial, despite unanimous guilty pleas, Judge W. H. Watkins suspended their prison terms on grounds that they were "unduly provoked, ill-advised, and so forth."[117]

Cartoon mailed to Klansmen by FBI agents as part of their COINTELPRO disruption campaign (National Archives).

"Kill Me a Nigger"

Georgia witnessed its own share of violence, much of it caused by UKA Klavern 244 in Athens. Member Joseph Sims was jailed for assaulting black protesters in March 1964, and June brought drive-by shootings at a black housing project, wounding two victims. On July 11, while patrolling rural roads, Sims, Cecil Meyers, and James Lackey saw a car with three black occupants, bearing license plates from Washington, D.C. Sims branded them "some of President Johnson's boys" and announced, "I'm gonna kill me a nigger." They overtook the car, fired shotguns at close range, and fled, later telling Klansman Hebert Guest, "We shot one but don't know if we killed him or not."[118]

They had. Lieutenant Colonel Lemuel Penn, returning from Army Reserve training at Fort Benning, died instantly from wounds to his neck and jaw; his companions, Lt. Col. John Howard and Major Charles Brown, escaped injury. FBI agents arrested Guest, Lackey, Meyers and Sims on August 6, for violating Penn's civil rights. Local prosecutors charged them with murder the following day, and formally indicted them on August 25. By then, Lackey had confessed to authorities, admitting that he drove the murder car, naming Meyers and Sims as the shooters. Guest, he said, had furnished one of the shotguns. Guest also signed a statement, saying Sims and Meyers admitted the killing in his presence.[119]

Conviction should have been simple, but this was Georgia in the Sixties. Calvin Craig and other leaders of the UKA's realm met on August 18, to plan a defense for their brethren. Afterward, Robert Shelton sent a fund-raising letter to every klavern in Dixie, collecting $3,000 for legal fees. Lackey and Guest recanted their statements, Lackey claiming coercion, while Guest said he had "blacked out" during questioning. Meyers and Sims faced trial in September. In his summation to the all-white jury, lawyer John Darsey shifted the focus from murder to "states rights," railing against Washington's "carpetbagging administration of justice," claiming "they loosed a horde of federal agents in our midst" with orders to "bring us white meat." "Never let it be said," he roared, "that a Madison County jury converted an electric chair into a sacrificial altar on which the pure flesh of a member of the human race was sacrificed to the savage, revengeful appetite of a raging mob." Jurors acquitted Meyers and Sims on September 4, while charges against Guest and Lackey were dismissed.[120]

Despite their acquittal, Penn's killers had embarrassed the UKA. Both were banished, but soon found a home in the National Knights, whose wizard, James Venable, told reporters, "You'll never be able to convict a white man that kills a nigger what encroaches on the white race of the South."[121] They soon resurfaced as members of the Black Shirts, a militant unit led by kleagles Earl Holcomb and Colbert McGriff. In October 1965 Crawfordsville police arrested Meyers, Sims, and five other Klansmen on charges of forcing a black motorist off the road and threatening his life. Officers seized 15 guns and several wooden clubs decorated with swastikas.[122]

Nor were federal authorities done with Penn's killers. Despite legal setbacks, they brought Guest, Lackey, Meyers, Sims, and two other Klansmen to trial in June 1966, charged with conspiring to violate Penn's civil rights. Jurors convicted Meyers and Sims, resulting in 10-year prison terms, but acquitted the rest. Sims received an additional 10-year state sentence after he pled guilty to shooting his wife.[123]

Between trials, in April 1965, leaders of the National Knights met to found a new Knights of the KKK, ostensibly led by William Morris, with James Venable serving as treasurer and legal counsel. In fact, investigators found that the group was created "to avoid possible legal problems confronting an incorporated Klan," specifically Ohio's 1964 revocation of the National Knights' charter. The front group absorbed former Buckeye State klaverns and proceeded with new recruitment.[124]

Presidential Politics

Passage of the 1964 Civil Rights Act galvanized racists in that election year. Neo-Nazis were first off the mark, as the NSRP convened in Louisville, Kentucky, on March 2. Regaled by UKA imperial klonsel Matt Murphy, the delegates nominated John Kasper for president, with J. B. Stoner as his running mate.[125]

Alabama's George Wallace held more appeal for traditional Klansmen, and he had his sights set on the White House. "If I ran outside the South and got 10 percent," he told reporters, "it would be a victory. It would shake their eyeteeth in Washington."[126] In fact, he did better than that, winning one-third of all votes in Wisconsin's Democratic primary, claiming 30 percent of Indiana's primary votes one month later, and scoring 47 percent of Maryland's primary ballots. After that strong showing, he declared, "If it hadn't been for the nigger bloc vote, we'd have won it all."[127]

Those impressive showings failed to stop President Johnson's nomination in August, and many Klansmen followed Robert Shelton's lead in shifting to the Republican Party. Senator Barry Goldwater had voted against the new Civil Rights Act, and bigots cheered his statement that "extremism in defense of liberty is no vice." Robert Creel, Shelton's Alabama grand dragon, declared that his constituents hated "niggerism, Catholicism, Judaism, and all the other isms of the whole world," then added, "I like Goldwater. He needs our help." Creel missed the fact that Goldwater was Jewish, while his running mate was Catholic. Goldwater formally repudiated Klan support, but at a September speech in South Carolina, he shared the stage with Grand Dragon Scoggin.[128]

The end result disappointed Klansmen. Johnson's landslide buried Goldwater, with 486 electoral votes to 52, the latter coming from Alabama, Georgia, Louisiana, Mississippi, South Carolina, and Goldwater's native Arizona. The NSRP fared even worse, polling a mere 6,957 votes from Arkansas and Kentucky.[129] Calvin Craig came closest to success, winning 40 percent of the vote in his bid for a state senate seat in Georgia.[130] NSRP defector Jerry Dutton, lately fronting the tiny American States Rights Party, likewise lost his race for Alabama's legislature.[131]

"Niggers Ain't Gonna Rule This Town"

Klan violence in Louisiana escalated during the winter of 1963–64, with shootings, cross-burnings, and arson attacks. Six thousand racists attended an Original Knights rally near Rayville, in November 1963, but quarrels over income from that gathering sowed seeds of dissent in the ranks, prompting James Swenson's banishment in December.[132] Klansman Addison Thompson entered that year's Democratic gubernatorial primary, running tenth in a field of 11 candidates, with 3,343 votes.[133]

In February 1964 Klansmen went gunning for James White, Sr., in Concordia, wrongly convinced that he was a Black Muslim. White traded shots with the raiders, ventilating the getaway car and wounding Tommy Lee Jones, who sought treatment on the sly from a Klan-allied physician.[134] By spring, as city officials in Bogalusa made grudging concessions to integration, kleagles flocked into Washington Parish, finding recruits at the Crown-Zellerbach paper plant. Mayor Jesse Cutrer permitted Klansmen to rally masked, in defiance of state law, and a local radio station broadcast their rants as a "public service." Klansman Howard Lee, a licensed firearms dealer, purchased 651 guns between May and August 1964, selling many to other knights while illegally failing to record the sales. In July, Klansmen whipped Clarence O'Berry, a white man accused of drinking and neglecting his family. Five months later, knights Charles Christmas and Saxon Farmer launched a new front group, the Anti-Communist Christian Association (ACC). Bogalusa city attorney Robert Restor belonged to that group, and to the Original Knights.[135]

The Silver Dollar Group claimed its second known victim in Ferriday, Louisiana, in December 1964. Frank Morris—best friend of Klan nemesis James White, Sr.—ran a shoe repair shop serving an integrated clientele, and considered Klansman Earcel Boyd a friend. Nonetheless, rumors circulated that Morris was flirting with white female customers. Four women who allegedly responded to his overtures were named in Klan flyers, scattered in local driveways. More animosity stemmed from a quarrel between Morris and deputy sheriff Frank DeLaughter, after Morris refused to repair DeLaughter's boots for free. DeLaughter boasted of beating Morris, but worse lay in store.[136]

Early on December 10, Klansmen smashed the windows of Morris's shop, where he also resided. Waking to the sound, Morris saw three men, one brandishing a shotgun while another poured gasoline into the shop. When he tried to flee, the gunman snarled, "Get back in there, nigger!" Flames consumed the shop, Morris escaping as the Klansmen fled, with burns from head to toe. FBI agents questioned Morris before he died on December 14, but his answers were vague. At one point, he described the arsonists as "two white friends," but would not speak their names. James White's children believe his silence was a favor to their father. One said, "Daddy believed Frank knew who did him in, but Frank didn't want Daddy to get involved. He probably knew Daddy would go after the people who did it."[137]

Mississippi grand dragon Edward McDaniel, doubling as an FBI informant by 1966, named Morris's probable killers as Klansmen E. D. Morace, Tommy Lee Jones, Thore Torgersen, and James Scarborough, all SDG members and employees of the International Paper Company in Natchez. Other reports name the killers as Bill Frasier, Leonard Spencer, and O. C. "Coonie" Poissot, with Frank DeLaughter cast as the ringleader. Earcel Boyd's children claim he "spent a lot of time and effort trying to find Mr. Frank's killers," without success, but an alternate version claims Boyd identified two of the arsonists, ordering them to leave town. The crime remains officially unsolved.[138]

An early target of the Bogalusa Klan was Ralph Blumberg, owner since 1961 of local radio station WBOX. In January 1965 he and other civic leaders invited former Arkansas congressman Brooks Hays, a political moderate, to speak in Bogalusa. Klansmen branded Hays "a traitor to the South," saying those who had invited him were bent on forcing Bogalusans into "hiring more [blacks] in your businesses, serving and eating with them in your cafes and allowing your children to sit by filthy, runny-nosed, ragged, ugly little niggers in your public schools." The same pamphlet warned, "Being a secret organization, we have Klan members in every conceivable business in this area. We will know the names of all who are invited to the Brooks Hays meeting and we will know who did and did not attend.... Those who do attend ... will be tagged as integrationists and will be delt [*sic*] with accordingly." Klansmen celebrated cancellation of Hays's speech by firing shots into Blumberg's station, smashing windows at his home, and boycotting his advertisers, closing WBOX within a month.[139]

CORE activists Steve Miller and William Yates arrived on February 1, 1965, meeting with Robert Hicks of the Bogalusa Civic and Voters League (BCVL). That night, police chief Claxton Knight called on Hicks with a deputy. As Hicks recalled, "They said the Klan was going to come to our house if we didn't turn the two civil rights workers over to them to be escorted out of town." Mindful of recent events in Mississippi, Hicks refused and summoned armed friends to guard his home.[140] During a second visit, two days later, Miller and Yates were pursued by police and beaten by Klansmen. That violence prompted blacks to organize the Deacons for Defense and Justice, armed and trained to resist Klan aggression.[141]

Attacks continued nonetheless. On February 15 Klansmen assaulted blacks seeking service at a Bogalusa gas station and an integrated group of café diners.[142] One week later, armed Deacons guarded Miller, Yates, and other CORE members when Klansmen chased them from Bogalusa to Covington, hitting speeds of 110 miles per hour. Chief Knight, determined that "niggers ain't gonna rule this town," ignored Klan violence while harassing civil rights workers at every opportunity, enlisting Klansmen as vigilante aides. On March 29 Klansmen tear-gassed a BCVL meeting. Over the next two months, in New Orleans, raiders firebombed two churches, a store, and several homes occupied by civil rights workers. During the same period, Carrollton suffered six arsons, Ferriday logged five bombings, and a grenade damaged a shop in Lafayette.[143]

CORE named Louisiana as its primary target for 1965, staging seminars for black would-be voters, and Klansmen responded predictably. Around Bogalusa that spring, assaults and drive-by shootings were routine. FBI agents investigated a firebombing on April 17, but made no arrests.[144] At a May 7 rally, Judge John Rarick shared the stage with Original Knights grand wizard Saxon Farmer and UKA grand dragon Jack Helm, denouncing Governor John McKeithen and other "outsiders" for meddling in Bogalusa's affairs. Nine days later, as BCVL leaders negotiated a truce with Bogalusa's mayor, Klansmen ringed City Hall and circulated pamphlets titled "Who Bought Jesse Cutrer?" The leaflet included a list of city and state officials whom, it said, should be "tarred and feathered." On May 19 Klansmen mobbed black picnickers at Cassidy Park, beating them with guns, belts, and brass knuckles. Street fighting resumed on May 23, and police reluctantly jailed two whites for trying to burn a church scheduled to host CORE founder James Farmer, Jr. Mayor Cutrer responded by banning further marches.[145]

Sheriff Dorman Crowe tried to placate CORE by hiring two black deputies, Oneal Moore and David "Creed" Rogers, to patrol African American neighborhoods. Days after their recruitment, on June 2, 1965, several white men in a pickup truck ambushed the officers, riddling their cruiser with rifle and shotgun fire. Moore died instantly, while Rogers was badly wounded. He described the murder truck, down to a Confederate flag decal on its front bumper, and a manhunt began. Hours later, Mississippi police found the truck and arrested its driver, Bogalusa Klansman and NSRP member Ernest McElveen. Officers found pistols in the truck, but no other weapons. McElveen never faced trial, but Robert Crowe—his father's successor as sheriff—remains convinced of his guilt, saying, "The KKK killed that officer, that's definite."[146]

Klansmen, sometimes disguised as police, continued their raids after Moore's slaying. J. B. Stoner and Connie Lynch arrived to lead marches in protest against CORE's processions. At one such rally, Stoner told cheering racists, "The nigger is not a human being. He is somewhere between the white man and the ape. We don't believe in getting along with our enemy, and the nigger is our enemy." On July 8, after Klansmen mobbed black marchers, Deacons member Henry Austin shot and killed assailant Henry Crowe. Two days later, the BCVL obtained a federal injunction ordering police to protect black protesters, but it did not good. On August 12 Klansmen bombed a Baton Rouge motel housing civil rights workers.[147]

On December 1, 1965, the Justice Department filed suit against the Original Knights, the ACCA, and various knights, seeking "an injunction to protect Negro citizens in Washington Parish" from further attacks. Their motion opened with the words "This is an action by the Nation against a klan," quoting orders for the Klan's "wrecking crew" and citing 10 specific incidents of violence since January. A three-judge panel granted the injunction, while exempting three specific Klansmen from its terms.[148]

"Open Season"

In November 1964 leaders of the Dallas County Voters League convinced Martin Luther King to stage his next campaign in Selma, Alabama, birthplace of Bull Connor and the state's first Citizens' Council. NSRP member James Robinson assaulted King at a downtown hotel on January 15, 1965, and demonstrations began three days later, prompting mass arrests that jailed 2,400 protesters by February 5.[149]

Selma had no klavern in 1965, but it did have Klansmen. They gathered at the Silver Moon Café, volunteered for Sheriff James Clark's "special posse," and fraternized with Al Lingo's state troopers. Knights from Birmingham made frequent visits to the latest battleground.[150] Statewide, membership peaked around 30,000 in 1965, one klavern meeting at Montgomery's Little Kitchen, six blocks from the state capitol.[151] Robert Shelton, though distracted by multiple libel suits filed against the *Tuscaloosa News,* kept a close eye on the protests.[152] So did Governor Wallace and Attorney General Richmond Flowers, a thorn in Wallace's side who insisted on investigating Klan terrorism. Elected in 1962, Flowers had authored a bill to restrict dynamite sales, but Wallace cronies killed it in committee.[153]

After a January 22 court ruling facilitated black registration in Selma, protests spread to surrounding counties. At Marion, on February 18, troopers darkened streets before attacking marchers, shooting one, Jimmy Lee Jackson, in the stomach. Jackson died eight days later, his death prompting calls for a protest march from Selma to Montgomery.[154] Governor Wallace banned that demonstration on March 6, but organizers proceeded the following day, met by Sheriff Clark's posse and Al Lingo's troopers on a bridge named for Reconstruction Klansman Edmund Pettus. The officers attacked with tear gas, clubs and bullwhips, sending 56 protesters to the hospital.[155]

News of "Bloody Sunday" shocked the nation, bringing volunteers to Selma from across the country. One was the Rev. James Reeb, a Unitarian minister from Boston, who arrived in Selma with colleagues on March 9. That evening, they passed the Silver Moon Café, attracting notice from its Ku Klux clientele. Three Klansmen armed with clubs attacked the ministers, one of them fracturing Reeb's skull. Transported first to a black infirmary, then to Birmingham, Reeb died without regaining consciousness on March 11.[156]

Police arrested four men for Reeb's murder—Elmer Cook, R. B. Kelly, Namon Hoggle, and William Hoggle—but an April grand jury declined to indict Kelly. Acquittal of the others was a foregone conclusion. While Klan pilots littered Selma with leaflets from above, soliciting donations for the trio's defense, prosecutor Blanchard McLeod—branded an "adamant segregationist" in FBI memos—warned reporters, "I don't have a very strong case." Informant Gary Rowe identified the suspects as UKA members, and Klan spokesmen defended them accordingly. Robert Shelton told reporters Reeb "had been dying of cancer before he ever came to Alabama," echoed by claims from Robert Creel that Reeb's corpse was cremated because it was "rotten with cancer and syphilis." At trial in December, when McLeod asked veniremen whether prejudice would sway their verdict, nine of 12 refused to answer. Sheriff Clark visited jurors during their deliberations, followed by speedy acquittal of the accused.[157]

Meanwhile, Judge Frank Johnson authorized the march from Selma to Montgomery on March 17. It began four days later, with the Rev. King leading 8,000 demonstrators, escorted by 2,000 National Guardsmen and federal marshals. That day, March 21, frustrated Klansmen planted bombs at a Catholic church and three other sites in Birmingham; none exploded, and police defused two more on March 22. One suspect questioned by the FBI was klokan Floyd Simpson. According to Bureau memos, "Simpson stated he had no information concerning these bombs ... and if he would have information, he is doubtful he would advise the FBI."[158]

The march to Montgomery climaxed on March 25, with the Rev. King addressing a crowd of 25,000 at the state capitol, while Governor Wallace watched from behind closed blinds. That night, Detroit volunteer Viola Liuzzo was among those driving marchers back to Selma. On her second trip through "Bloody Lowndes" County, with passenger Leroy Moton, four Klansmen overtook Liuzzo's car and killed her with a volley of gunfire. Moton, uninjured, told police that a second car stopped moments later, one of its occupants peering into Liuzzo's car with a flashlight, then sped off behind the killers.[159]

Gary Rowe, inside the murder car, identified the other "wrecking crew" members as William Eaton, Eugene Thomas, and Collie Wilkins. FBI agents arrested the trio on March 26, seizing a pistol at Wilkins's home that matched bullets retrieved from Liuzzo's body. On April 6 a federal grand jury indicted the Klansmen for conspiracy. A local grand jury filed murder charges on April 22. By then, FBI spokesmen were smearing Liuzzo's character, falsely claiming that her arms bore needle marks. J. Edgar Hoover shared that lie with President Johnson, adding that Liuzzo "was sitting very, very close to the Negro in the car. It had the appearance of a necking party."[160]

Imperial Klonsel Matt Murphy echoed those claims when Collie Wilkins faced trial for murder with Robert Shelton in attendance. Gary Rowe testified for the state, reviled by Murphy as a traitor for breaking the Klan's oath of secrecy. Jurors, including eight Citizens' Council members, deadlocked on May 7, 10 voting to convict Wilkins of manslaughter, two holding out for acquittal. Murphy died in a car crash on August 20, replaced by Arthur Hanes at Wilkins's retrial, where a new jury acquitted him on October 22. In the wake of that verdict, Klan cars sprouted bumper stickers reading "Open Season." Wilkins and his codefendants embarked on a publicity tour, signing autographs at UKA rallies.[161]

Robert Shelton (foreground) with attorney Matt Murphy at the murder trial of Collie Wilkins, in May 1965 (National Archives).

More blood spilled between those trials. On July 15, shortly after Connie Lynch addressed an NSRP rally in Anniston, drive-by gunmen shot black laborer Willie Brewster, Sr.; he died three days later. A $20,000 reward led FBI agents to suspects Hubert Strange, Clarence Blevins, and Johnny DeFries. J. B. Stoner defended the accused, but lost the first case with a surprise manslaughter conviction for Strange, on December 2. Another jury acquitted DeFries in February 1966, and charges against Blevins were dismissed. Agents investigating Brewster's murder also charged Klansman and NSRP member Kenneth Adams with caching explosives stolen from Fort McClellan, but jurors acquitted him in January 1966.[162]

President Johnson signed a new Voting

Rights Act on August 6, but the struggle continued in Alabama. Lowndes County was among the worst Klan-ridden districts, though, like Selma, it had no klavern of its own. Prominent among the local knights was Thomas Coleman, son of a former sheriff, who carried his own "special deputy" badge. Early in 1965 he confronted Attorney General Flowers at Hayneville's courthouse, saying, "If you don't get off this Klan investigation, we'll get you off." On August 20, in Hayneville, Coleman shot two civil rights workers, the Rev. Richard Morrisroe and seminarian Jonathan Daniels, killing Daniels. Moments later, he phoned Al Lingo in Montgomery, saying, "I just shot two preachers. You'd better get down here." Lingo brought a Klan bail bondsman and began his own "investigation" of the case, excluding both Flowers and FBI agents.[163]

Coleman's trial was a virtual replay of the Wilkins charade. Charged with murder and attempted murder, Coleman seemed amused when his name appeared on a list of prospective jurors. Judge Thomas Thagard removed Flowers from the case and refused to postpone the trial while victim Morrisroe recovered. With Robert Shelton and Viola Liuzzo's killers in the gallery, defense witnesses claimed Daniels and Morrisroe threatened Coleman with a knife and gun, neither ever found, thereby compelling him to fire in self-defense. A jury of Coleman's friends—one winked at him as they retired to deliberate—acquitted him on September 30.[164]

Federal prosecutors picked up where the state left off in Viola Liuzzo's case, indicting Eaton, Thomas and Wilkins for conspiracy on November 5, 1965. Jurors convicted them on December 3, resulting in 10-year prison terms. While free on appeal, Eaton died from a heart attack in March 1966, and Thomas was acquitted of murder six months later. Governor Wallace told reporters, "We've got good law enforcement in Alabama. Of course, if I did what I'd like to do I'd pick up something and smash one of these federal judges in the head and then burn the courthouse down. But I'm too genteel."[165]

Northern Klans

While mayhem in Dixie made headlines, two Klans expanded northward. In the mid–1960s, Robert Shelton's UKA established klaverns in Ohio, Pennsylvania, Delaware, Maryland, New York and Michigan; members also rallied in New Jersey, without a formal charter. James Venable's National Knights competed in Ohio, with klaverns in Columbus, Cincinnati, and Oregonia. Volatile members, including a self-proclaimed "grand empress," imported dynamite and debated assassinations, but stopped short of action.[166]

New Jersey and New York, active realms in the 1920s, fared poorly 40 years later. Both states drew their leadership from members of the American Nazi Party: king kleagles Frank Rotella, Jr., in the Garden State and Daniel Burros in New York. Shelton appointed both in 1965, with mixed results. Rotella, a Catholic, established no klaverns before he resigned in 1966, citing other "personal commitments." Burros was marginally more successful, rising to grand dragon with two klaverns in Manhattan by October 1965, when the *New York Times* revealed his Jewish ancestry. On Halloween, he killed himself at the home of Pennsylvania grand dragon Roy Frankhouser. Both New York klaverns folded under his successor, William Hoff.[167]

Frankhouser was the UKA's northern star. Named as grand dragon in 1965, he lost an eye that same year in one of the many brawls that led Klansmen to call him "Riot Roy." Frankhouser spread himself thin, combining Klan membership with active roles in the NSRP, American Nazi Party, Minutemen, and other racist groups, sometimes claiming association with the Mafia. He also encouraged neo–Nazis to join the UKA's Delaware realm, prompting Grand Dragon Ralph Pryor to resign in January 1966, leaving five small klaverns leaderless. Maryland's realm, led by Vernon Naimaster, fractured in March 1966 with defection of knights loyal to Xavier Edwards. Fearing UKA violence, Edwards formed his own short-lived Maryland Knights but accomplished nothing.[168]

UKA kleagles planted three klaverns in Michigan, with 200 members, but the realm failed to rate a grand dragon.[169] One of Detroit's active knights was Jim Burwell, a mechanic and part-time bus driver who ferried thousands of black children to church and on field trips. He also loaned cash to Detroit's Black Panther Party. Only at his death, in 1990, was his secret life revealed.[170]

Congress: Round Four

Five days after Viola Liuzzo's murder in Alabama, the House Committee on Un-American Activities voted to investigate the Invisible Empire.[171] Four of the committee's nine members were Southern segregationists, including chairman Edwin Willis of Louisiana, and the rest were staunch conservatives. Scourging the Klan in public, they hoped, might make their own "respectable" racism seem more palatable.

Committee investigators fanned out nationwide, meeting Klansmen and police officers, collecting documents and news clippings. Between October 1965 and February 1966 the panel questioned 187 witnesses. Most Klansmen pled the Fifth Amendment, some refusing even to admit their names, while the committee documented incidents of violence and published evidence of financial chicanery that was a staple of the modern Klan. Robert Shelton used a UKA front—the Alabama Rescue Service—as a personal bank account, joined by his wife, who forged checks under the name "James Hendrix." Various Klan officials had been banished from one faction or another as suspected embezzlers; others boasted psychiatric records and police rap sheets ranging from public drunkenness to crimes of violence.[172] J. B. Stoner, one of the last witnesses called, infuriated Edwin Willis with a *Thunderbolt* article claiming the committee's chairman was "half ape."[173]

The committee's final report, published in December 1967, identified 18 active Klans, with a combined membership of "approximately" 16,810; 15,075 belonged to the UKA, with the remainder scattered far and wide.[174] Some historians regard those figures as conservative, perhaps an effort to minimize Klan influence in Dixie.

The panel proposed legislation to curb Klan activity, but the bills died in committee. Its last resort, in February 1966, was a resolution citing Robert Shelton and six other UKA leaders for contempt of Congress, based on their refusal to provide Klan documents under subpoena.[175] The seven were formally indicted on March 3, and four of them—Shelton, Calvin Craig, James Jones, and Robert Scoggin—pled guilty on November 18, 1966, while charges filed against the others were dismissed.[176] Craig ultimately paid a fine, while Shelton and his Carolina dragons received one-year prison terms in March 1969.[177]

Death in the Delta

Mississippi's mayhem continued unabated during 1965–66, despite congressional investigation and the FBI's COINTELPRO campaign. On August 8, 1965, Klansman and part-time constable Jasper Burchfield killed John Queen, an elderly black paraplegic, in Fayette. A coroner's jury required only minutes to rule the shooting self-defense.[178] Eight days later, officers in Franklin County found Klansman Earl Hodges apparently beaten to death, though another coroner's panel deemed his death accidental. Evidence collected by the FBI and Congress suggest Hodges was murdered over a dispute with the homicidal Seale family, prompting him to quit the MWK. Questioned about his death in 1966, all three Seale brothers pled the Fifth Amendment.[179]

Eleven days after Hodges died, the Silver Dollar Group attempted its third murder. Target George Metcalfe served as president of the Natchez NAACP, infuriating his Klan coworkers at Armstrong Tire and Rubber. On August 27, 1965, a bomb wired to his car's ignition shattered Metcalfe's legs, leaving him near death. He took months to recover, thereafter carpooling to work with NAACP treasurer Wharlest Jackson. FBI informer "Coonie" Poissot reported Raleigh Glover's boasts that he had put the bomb in Metcalfe's vehicle, while Klansman Kenneth Head admitted serving as Glover's lookout. Prosecutors filed no charges.[180]

On October 30, 1965, a UKA rally in Natchez drew 3,700 Klansmen and spectators.[181] Ten days later, Solicitor General Thurgood Marshall appeared before the Supreme Court, defending the federal government's authority to charge 18 Klansmen with conspiracy in the murders of Neshoba County victims Chaney, Goodman and Schwerner. The court approved those indictments in March 1966, by which time the White Knights had claimed their next victim.[182]

Vernon Dahmer was light-skinned enough to pass for white, but his integrity demanded that he face life in Mississippi as an African American. He prospered in Forrest County's Kelly Settlement, operating a grocery store, sawmill, planing mill, and a 200-acre farm, while serving as president of the county's NAACP chapter. His chief offense, in 1965–66, was helping poor blacks pay the poll tax required of registered voters. On the night of January 10, 1966, Klansmen struck Dahmer's home and nearby store, firebombing both and trading shots with Dahmer while his family escaped. Burned over 40 percent of his body, Dahmer died the following day.[183]

The crime scene offered evidence aplenty: a discarded pistol, cartridges, a Halloween mask—and a car owned by Howard Giles, exalted cyclops of MWK Klavern No. 2, shot up by nervous knights in the heat of battle. FBI informers reported a boast from Sam Bowers that "[t]he Laurel group scored a big one and the men involved were better than the Philadelphia group. The technical end was not as good as the Philadelphia job, but these men won't talk." In fact, they did. By March, raiders Lawrence Byrd and Cecil Sessum had confessed, prompting arrests of Bowers and 13 others. A federal grand jury indicted the 14 in June 1966, while attention shifted to other parts of the Magnolia State.[184]

As agents were rounding up White Knights, defector Dale Walton declared himself grand dragon of a new Klan faction, the Tupelo-based Knights of the Green Forest. The group auditioned by protesting Senator Robert Kennedy's visit to Oxford in March, then tackled the Beatles in August, after singer John Lennon declared his group "more popular

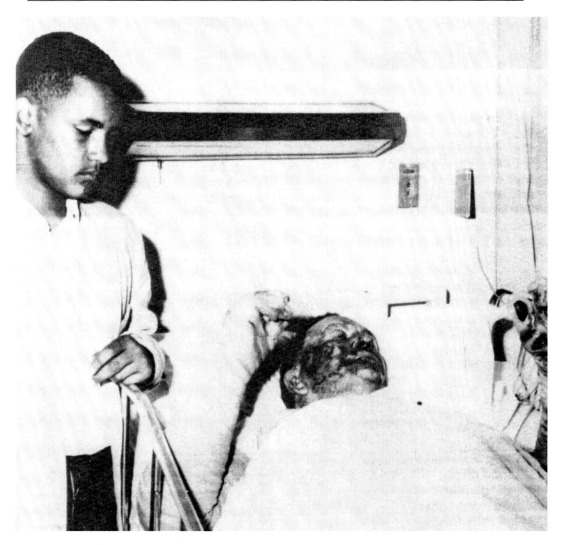

Vernon Dahmer on his deathbed, observed by one of his sons, after Klansmen burned his home in January 1966 (Southern Poverty Law Center).

than Jesus Christ."[185] Walton's sudden religious zeal seemed ironic, since he had previously been convicted on 68 counts of selling groceries on Sunday, in violation of Tupelo's "blue" law.[186]

With statewide violence on the rise, James Meredith announced a one-man "march against fear" in June 1966. He planned to walk 220 miles, from Memphis to Jackson, but his protest ended on its second day, June 6, when Tennessee resident Aubrey Norvell shot him from ambush. Meredith survived three shotgun blasts, and Norvell was captured at the scene. Authors David Chalmers and Christine Gibson name Norvell as a Klansman.[187]

Martin Luther King picked up the march where Meredith fell, prompting another Klan plot against him. The conspirators belonged to a group formed in May, known to its handful of members as the Cottonmouth Moccasin Gang. Founder Claude Fuller planned to kill a black man picked at random, hoping King would visit the death scene and thus make himself a clear target. With cohorts Ernest Avants and James Jones, Fuller chose elderly sharecropper Ben White, soliciting his help to find a lost dog on June 10. They drove him to the Homochitto National Forest, where Fuller shot White 16 times with a carbine, before Avants blasted his head with a shotgun. They tossed White's body from a bridge and torched Jones's bloodstained car, both found by police on June 12. Jones confessed in custody, and prosecutors charged the Klansmen with murder. Jurors deadlocked at Jones's trial in December 1966, and the state later dropped all charges.[188]

Meanwhile, King's march wound its way across Mississippi, reaching Philadelphia on the second anniversary of Neshoba's triple murder. Addressing a courthouse audience, King said, "I believe in my heart that the murderers are somewhere around me right now." Deputy Price, at his elbow, growled, "You're damn right they are. They're standing behind you right now." That night, Klansmen drove through Philadelphia's ghetto, firing into homes. Blacks returned fire, wounding one knight in the neck. Louisiana's Deacons for Defense rallied in Jackson for the march's climax, on June 26, forestalling further bloodshed, but June claimed one more victim. While driving through Franklin County, Klansman James Seale struck and killed Bailey Odell, an elderly black man who stepped in front of his truck.[189]

Grenada, home of a thriving UKA klavern, was another hotbed of violence, including the attempted murder of two FBI agents in July. Police caught the shooters, but jurors freed them in August. Mass arrests of SCLC demonstrators produced street fighting, climaxed on September 12 when whites armed with axe handles, pipes and chains barred black students from John Rundle High School and Lizzie Horn Elementary, sending three victims to the hospital. Federal prosecutors charged Grenada's mayor, city council, police chief and sheriff with "willful failure and refusal" to protect black children, but white jurors acquitted all concerned. Governor Johnson had reluctantly supported integration of the city's schools, prompting APWR members to petition for his impeachment, but state legislators declined to oblige.[190]

Brushfire Wars

Violence continued on both sides of the Mason-Dixon Line through 1965 and 1966. In Virginia, UKA grand dragon Marshall Kornegay escaped conviction for contempt of Congress, supervising some 2,000 knights statewide. After bombers demolished Richmond's Second Bethel Baptist Church on October 5, 1965, Kornegay branded the blast a "dastardly crime," offered a futile $200 reward for capture of the terrorists, and vowed that Klansmen would rebuild the church with "our own workmanship and our materials." Governor Mills Godwin denounced the Klan in December, and while Kornegay responded with several rallies, his realm was on the wane.[191]

Americus, Georgia, witnessed black protests in July 1966, prompting a parade by 700 Klansmen in August. Crawfordsville simmered through October, with Calvin Craig jailed for twisting a demonstrator's arm, while seven of James Venable's knights faced charges of terrorizing black motorists. Whites mobbed SCLC marchers in Lincolnton and pursued them on the highway, causing a car crash. After fire razed two black churches in Jones and Twiggs Counties, prosecutors charged a white Florida physician with arson.[192]

North Carolina suffered discord while James Jones awaited orders to report to prison.

August 1965 had seen brawling between Klansmen and black demonstrators in Plymouth, with 13 knights jailed on weapons charges, and 12 more were held after a spate of bombings in Charlotte, that November.[193] Catfish Cole returned from exile in Virginia, hoping to revive the Klan in Greensboro, but a fatal car crash canceled his comeback.[194]

Jones branded dissident UKA member Joseph Bryant a "provocateur" and banished him in September 1966 for "conspiring against the prosperity of the order." A week later, Bryant launched the North Carolina Knights at a rally where defectors nailed their UKA membership cards to a cross and burned them. Imperial Kleagle George Dorsett was next to depart, in summer 1967, leading his own Confederate Knights. The FBI bankrolled both splinter groups as part of COINTELPRO. A memo from the Charlotte office told headquarters, "[Our] attempt to split the UKA in North Carolina and diminish its power was successful."[195]

In Maryland, violence exceeded that witnessed in some parts of Dixie. Connie Lynch led NSRP rallies in Baltimore during July 1966, branding Mayor Theodore McKeldin a "superpompous jackassie nigger-lover," telling his audience of 1,000, "To hell with the niggers, and those who don't like it, they can get the hell out of here!" White youths rampaged through Baltimore's ghetto on July 28, and a grand jury indicted Lynch the next day, with four other party leaders, on charges of riot and conspiracy. Despite the best efforts of a black attorney furnished by the American Civil Liberties Union, Lynch and two cohorts received two-year prison terms.[196]

While Lynch appealed his conviction, five would-be Klansmen sought to earn their robes by torching St. Mark's Methodist Church in Laurel, Maryland's ghetto. They bought gasoline from a service station owned by Klan leader Xavier Edwards, but the cinder-block building refused to ignite, whereupon they turned to a nearby black family's home. There, the tenants drove them off, and armed neighbors patrolled the streets until police captured the raiders, sending two to prison for 10 years. Edwards escaped indictment in that case.[197]

On April 1, 1965, Birmingham Klansmen bombed a black accountant's home; police found two other bombs at the homes of Mayor Boutwell and a city council member. Investigators linked Collie Wilkins and other Klansmen to a series of bombings and shootings at Bessemer's strikebound W. S. Dickey Clay Manufacturing Company, between February and August 1965. On February 19, 1966, Sheriff Mel Bailey discovered a "bomb factory" in the woods outside Birmingham. The stash included cases of dynamite, blasting caps, and timers "identical" to those that failed in April 1965. No arrests resulted.[198]

Louisiana's Klans vacillated between farce and ferocity in the mid–1960s. Addison Thompson entered the New Orleans Democratic mayoral primary again, in 1965, running third behind incumbent Victor Schiro, with 2,121 votes.[199] General Lewis Hershey, head of the Selective Service System, fired Grand Dragon Jack Helm from his local draft board in 1966, saying, "No grand lizard, whatever that is, is needed."[200] On a more serious note, Concordia Parish Klansmen clashed with occasional supporter Carlos Marcello, boss of Louisiana's Mafia, over illegal gambling dens and brothels: crosses blazed at a club in Monterey, another in Morville closed after threats from the Klan, and a third in Tallulah burned to the ground.[201] In Bogalusa, Klansmen fired on Robert Hicks's home in December 1965, and jurors acquitted white defendant John Copling, Jr., in the July 1966 assassination of civil rights activist Clarence Triggs.[202]

Hoods in the Ring

Southern elections allowed Klansmen to flex their political muscles in 1966. Grand dragons in Alabama, Mississippi, North Carolina and Tennessee promised "Klan candidates" seeking office "from the courthouse up," but few materialized outside North Carolina, where the *Charlotte Observer* identified 28 members campaigning in four counties. Most lost their races, but voters chose ex-cyclops James Davis as Rowan County's registrar of deeds and elected a Klansman to Franklin County's board of education. John Stirewalt played coy, denying "active" Klan membership with a wink and a nod. He defeated Rowan County's "unbeatable" incumbent sheriff and held office until 1986.[203]

Alabama's gubernatorial race was the year's headline attraction. Barred from succeeding himself, George Wallace ran wife Lurleen as his stand-in, parroting speeches penned by Ace Carter.[204] Mrs. Wallace swept the Democratic primary, nearly tripling the votes cast for Richmond Flowers, leaving ex-governors John Patterson and James Folsom in the dust.[205] John Crommelin fared worse in his latest Senate race, running third in a field of four behind incumbent John Sparkman.[206]

In Georgia, restaurateur Lester Maddox had sought public office since 1957, failing twice in bids to become Atlanta's mayor, beaten in the 1962 lieutenant governor's race. In 1964 he drove black diners from his establishment with an axe handle, earning a federal contempt citation and the Klan's eternal admiration. While not a member, Maddox welcomed Klan support in the 1966 gubernatorial race, sharing the stage with George Wallace and Calvin Craig at a July rally where blacks were beaten in the audience. In September's Democratic primary Maddox trailed ex-governor Ellis Arnall by 135,808 votes, then rebounded in a runoff two weeks later, winning by 70,051 and crowing that despite having "no money, no politicians, no television, no newspapers, no Martin Luther King, no Lyndon Johnson, we made it!"[207]

Calvin Craig, meanwhile, lost his bid to join Fulton County's Democratic Executive Committee, but came within 272 votes of election.[208]

Robert Shelton visited Arkansas in August 1966, telling a Star City audience that the Klan was "getting in a position in Arkansas where it can use its power and influence to help elect a governor. We've done it in Alabama." With six-term incumbent Orval Faubus stepping down, the UKA and Citizens' Council backed segregationist James "Justice Jim" Johnson, sweeping him to victory in the July Democratic primary and September's runoff. Democrats were stunned when Winthrop Rockefeller claimed 306,324 votes in November, to 257,203 for Johnson, becoming the state's first Republican governor since Reconstruction.[209]

In Louisiana, John Rarick declared his candidacy for Congress in May 1966, branding 12-term incumbent James Morrison an "LBJ rubber stamp" and a tool of "the black-power voting bloc." Morrison named Rarick as a Klansman, prompting a libel suit and Rarick's promise to quit the race if the FBI "can produce evidence that I am now or ever have been a member of the KKK." (Bureau headquarters ignored the challenge, but memos released in 1973 name Rarick as exalted cyclops of a klavern in St. Francisville.) Still, Rarick refused to shun Klan votes, unless Morrison rejected ballots from CORE and the NAACP. In that case, he vowed, "I would not only repudiate the Klan vote but would tell them to go to Chicago and help with law enforcement." Klansmen laughed all the way to the polls, electing Rarick to the first of four terms.[210]

Unholy War

In February 1967 NAACP activist Wharlest Jackson received a promotion at Armstrong Tire & Rubber in Natchez, Mississippi. The new position, formerly "white," increased his pay by 17 cents per hour. On February 27, leaving work, a bomb exploded in his pickup truck, killing Jackson instantly. FBI informants named Silver Dollar Group member Raleigh Glover as a prime suspect. Another, James Seale, refused to speak with agents and lost his latest job as a result. The crime remains officially unsolved.[211]

Jackson's death presaged another Ku Klux reign of terror in Mississippi. Klansmen burned a black church in Grenada on March 4, bombed Liberty's Head Start office nine days later, dynamited the home of a white dean at Tougaloo College on October 6, blasted the parsonage of Laurel's St. Paul's Church on November 15, and bombed a Jackson rabbi's home four days later. In 1968 they bombed a Jackson realtor's office on March 7, wounded Hattiesburg civil rights activist Kaley Duckworth with a car bomb on May 15, and hit Meridian's Temple Beth Israel on May 28.[212]

Most of those attacks were executed by an odd trio of terrorists. One, Joe Daniel "Danny Joe" Hawkins, was a second-generation Klansman addicted in violence, arrested 13 times between 1963 and 1980. Another, Thomas Albert Tarrants III, had flirted with the Klan and NSRP from adolescence, earning suspension from his Mobile, Alabama, high school over racial incidents in 1963. June 1964 saw him jailed with an NSRP member, for possession of a sawed-off shotgun. His probation on that charge expired on December 20, 1967; one day later, police caught Tarrants with Samuel Bowers, riding in a stolen car with a submachine gun on the backseat. After robbing several Mississippi supermarkets, he penned a note that read: "Please be advised that since March 28, 1968, I Thomas A. Tarrants have been underground and operating guerrilla warfare."[213]

The team's most surprising member was Kathryn Ainsworth, a Jackson fifth-grade teacher born in 1941. Raised by a Hungarian immigrant mother, Ainsworth was immersed in the anti–Semitic teachings of Wesley Swift and Gerald L. K. Smith, though she concealed her simmering hatred from coworkers. By 1966 she held membership in the APWR and three different Klans. Her nocturnal raids with Tarrants were, apparently, kept secret even from her husband when they wed in August 1967.[214]

Some Meridian Jews advocated fighting fire with fire, killing Danny Joe Hawkins and his father, but cooler heads prevailed, collecting a reward for capture of the terrorists dead or alive. They found an ally in police chief Roy Gunn, who issued "shoot to kill" orders after Klansmen burned five Meridian churches in as many weeks. Sergeant Lester Joyner organized a "blackshirt squad" of officers to harass local Klansmen, detonating small explosive charges on their lawns by night, yearning for a chance to act more forcefully.[215]

While bombs rocked Mississippi, Byron De La Beckwith announced his candidacy for lieutenant governor, billing himself as "a straight-shooter." Statewide, observers listed "slightly over 100 candidates" seeking office with Klan support in 32 counties. Murderers Deavours Nix, Cecil Price and James Seale ran for sheriff in their respective counties, while Grand Dragon Julius Harper sought a seat in the state legislature. In the gubernatorial contest, honky-tonk singer Jimmy Swann hired Tupelo Klansman Dale Walton as his campaign manager; Ross Barnett addressed APWR rallies, but replied "What Klan?" when asked about the front group's true masters; and ex-congressman John Bell Williams carried the day on a campaign slogan of "White Mississippi, Awake!"[216]

In the midst of that campaign, 18 White Knights faced trial on federal conspiracy charges in the Neshoba triple-murder case. Presiding judge Harold Cox was an outspoken racist, but even he flared at Klan arrogance when defendants Cecil Price and Alton Roberts threatened to bomb his courthouse. Jurors returned a compromise verdict on October 20, 1967, convicting Price, Roberts, Sam Bowers and four others, acquitting 11, and failing to reach verdicts on three more. Ringleader Edgar Killen escaped conviction when one holdout juror said she "could never convict a preacher." Bowers and Roberts received the maximum 10-year sentence; Price and Billy Posey got six years apiece; and the other convicted defendants drew three-year terms.[217]

"The Shots Kept Coming"

Klansman Addison Thompson hosted J. B. Stoner at a New Orleans NSRP rally in February 1967, but the real Louisiana action centered on Bogalusa.[218] BCVL president Albert Young led a march from Bogalusa to Franklinton on July 23, then organized another to the state capital for August 10. Governor McKeithen furnished 1,500 National Guardsmen to protect the demonstrators as they marched through pouring rain. Klansmen rallied in Baton Rouge when black marchers arrived on August 19, burning crosses and a Viet Cong flag. SNCC militant Hubert "Rap" Brown scheduled an appearance, then reneged, while Governor McKeithen told reporters, "Most of the stuff out of Bogalusa is hot air."[219]

John Rarick challenged McKeithen in November's Democratic primary, running on the strength of his June resolution asking Congress to renounce the Fourteenth Amendment, but he suffered a stinging defeat, polling 179,846 votes to McKeithen's 836,304. Even so, he beat Addison Thompson, running fifth among five candidates with 5,102 votes. During the campaign, Rarick survived a supposed assassination attempt, when drive-by gunmen strafed him in a New Orleans parking lot. "The shots kept coming," he told reporters. "You don't count when you're looking down a gun barrel."[220]

Confronting Terror

Mississippi state authorities belatedly addressed the Klan's long reign of terror in January 1968, charging 11 White Knights with murder and arson in the Dahmer case. Klan attorney Travis Buckley received a 10-year sentence in February, for kidnapping and threatening a prosecution witness. Defendant Billy Pitts pled guilty in March and turned state's evidence against his fellow Klansmen, naming seven other members of the raiding party. Jurors convicted Cecil Sessum on March 15, but results varied as separate trials continued. Henry De Boxtel's jury deadlocked on March 21, while later juries convicted two more Klansmen of murder and one of arson. Sam Bowers faced trial three times between May 1968 and January 1969, emerging with hung juries each time. In federal court, conspiracy charges went nowhere: jurors acquitted three defendants and reached no verdict on seven others, while an 11th Klansman saw his charges dismissed on grounds of poor health.[221]

In the midst of those trials, Klan bombings continued across Mississippi. FBI agents got their break in June 1968, when Klansmen Alton and Raymond Roberts agreed to sell out their nightriding comrades for $30,000. Police were waiting when Thomas Tarrants and Kathryn Ainsworth approached ADL leader Meyer Davidson's home on the night of June 29. A chaotic shootout ensued, killing Ainsworth, leaving Tarrants, a policeman, and a bystander wounded. At trial, Tarrants received a 30-year sentence, with five years added for a prison break in 1969.[222] It was the last hurrah of the White Knights, but not the end of Mississippi's Klan.

Dream Slayers

On April 4, 1968, a sniper killed Dr. Martin Luther King in Memphis, Tennessee. FBI agents cheered the news in Atlanta, then focused their manhunt on James Earl Ray, a thief who had escaped from Missouri's state prison 12 months earlier. Although charged with conspiracy to legitimize federal pursuit, Ray—like Lee Oswald before him—was touted by the Bureau as a "lone nut" assassin.

And yet....

Conspiracy evidence surrounded King's murder. One incident involved a citizens band radio broadcast in Memphis on April 4, misdirecting police in their search for the presumed gunman's white Ford Mustang. Police blamed that "prank" on an unidentified teenager, but years later, Kathryn Ainsworth's mother claimed her daughter and Thomas Tarrants perpetrated the hoax, to facilitate the assassin's escape.[223]

In Miami, meanwhile, informant Willie Somersett warned authorities of a plot to kill King the day *before* King died. His suspect, once again, was NSRP member Joseph Milteer.[224] On April 22 a waitress in Laurel, Mississippi, told agents Klansman Deavours Nix had "gotten a call on King" two days before the murder, delivered a rifle to fellow knights the same day, and received a telephone report of the slaying on April 4, before it made national news. Investigators "found no corroboration" for her story.[225]

Police in London captured James Ray on June 8, 1968. He chose Klan lawyer Arthur Hanes as his defense counsel, later discarding him in favor of celebrity attorney Percy Foreman, who negotiated a guilty plea to save Ray from the electric chair. Throughout those proceedings, Ray proclaimed himself the "patsy" of conspirators, a theme initially endorsed by Alabama author William Bradford Huie. Writing for *Look* magazine, Huie claimed to have evidence of a plot to kill King "for effect" during the 1968 presidential campaign. "In this plot," he wrote, "Dr. King was the secondary, not the primary target. The primary target was the Unites States of America." Five months later, Huie changed his tune, saying Ray killed King to gain "criminal status." Still, he conceded, "I believe that one or two other men may have had foreknowledge of this murder, and that makes it a little conspiracy." Following his guilty plea, Ray fired Percy Foreman and hired J. B. Stoner to file his appeals.[226]

Another Klan link to King's slaying, only revealed in 1990, was Jules Kimbel of New Orleans. Previously tied to JFK's assassination, imprisoned for an unrelated murder in the 1970s, Kimbel claimed to be "Raoul," a shadowy figure whom Ray described as directing and funding his movements between July 1967 and April 1968. Investigative reporters documented Kimbel's presence in Montreal, Québec, when Ray claimed he met "Raoul" there, and witnesses saw Ray drinking with a man who matched Kimbel's description. Kimbel's ex-girlfriend confirms seeing Kimbel with Ray at a Canadian "CIA training camp." Ray also visited New Orleans, allegedly to meet "Raoul," in December 1967.[227]

Other evidence suggesting Klan involvement in King's death includes a $100,000 bounty on King's life, offered by the MWK in 1967; a California meeting to discuss King's murder, attended by Joseph Milteer, Connie Lynch and William Gale (who officiated at Kathryn Ainsworth's memorial service); and testimony from UKA member George Wilson that his Klan paid Arthur Hanes $10,000 to defend Ray under the pretense of representing other Klansmen, a claim denied by Hanes.[228]

"Last Chance for the White Vote!"

In December 1967 Chicago police arrested six of their own for plotting to kill Mayor Richard Daley and other officials, placing the blame on black militants. One of those accused, grand kleagle William Plogger, admitted Klan membership since 1953. Three Klansmen resigned from the force, with three more dismissed, but none faced prosecution. From Atlanta, James Venable claimed 50 knights within the department, but no more surfaced.[229]

That incident was a sideshow to Chicago's main event in 1968, hosting the Democratic National Convention. Beleaguered president Lyndon Johnson refused a second term in March, leaving Vice President Hubert Humphrey to contend with a slate of anti-war rivals. George Wallace, meanwhile, launched his second presidential campaign at the head of a new third party.

His vehicle, the American Independent Party (AIP), was founded in July 1967, in Bakersfield, California. Wallace got the party's tardy presidential nod on September 13, 1968, aided by John Crommelin's creation of a Youth for Wallace movement based in Washington, D.C.[230] He lost Ace Carter in the process, disgruntled by a toning-down of racist rhetoric in campaign speeches, but Wallace maintained his ties to the UKA, welcoming votes from Klansmen and "anyone who supported my campaign." When a photographer caught Wallace shaking hands with Robert Shelton at a fundraiser, thugs seized his camera. Klansman Gerald Copeland led Alabama's AIP chapter; Xavier Edwards wired his "100 percent support" to Wallace from Maryland; and J. B. Stoner proclaimed, "Our slogan is the same as in 1964: Governor George C. Wallace—Last Chance for the White Vote!"[231]

Wallace lost in November, but his final tally of 9,901,118 votes remains the best third-party score in American history.[232] In 1969 the AIP renamed itself the American Party, while Crommelin's Youth for Wallace morphed into the National Youth Alliance, led by longtime anti–Semite Willis Carto. Carto quit the group in 1970, leaving former American Nazi Party member William Pierce in charge of a rechristened National Alliance.[233]

In Louisiana, John Rarick retained his congressional seat in 1968, while lambasting the late Dr. King as a "Communist errand-boy."[234] Klansman Dale Reusch fared worse, losing his first campaign for the sheriff's office in Medina County, Ohio.[235] Robert Shelton placed fifth in his bid to become Tuscaloosa's police commissioner.[236]

Hard Times

The UKA suffered repeated shocks as the Sixties ended. First came Calvin Craig's resignation, announced in April 1968, with Craig's plea for "black men and white men [to] stand shoulder to shoulder in a united America."[237] Robert Shelton entered prison on February 15, 1969, followed in March by James Jones and Robert Scoggin. Both named temporary successors, but Scoggin's public criticism of the UKA hierarchy resulted in his banishment on April 20.[238] The only cause for celebration was the downfall of a longtime enemy: Alabama jurors convicted Richmond Flowers in February 1969, on federal charges of attempting to extort money from firms seeking state contracts. Flowers served 16 months of an eight-year sentence and was pardoned by President Jimmy Carter in 1978.[239]

Elsewhere in the Invisible Empire, Addison Thompson challenged incumbent New Orleans mayor Maurice Landrieu in 1969, polling 1,248 votes.[240] A July 4th UKA rally at Swan Quarter, North Carolina, left three persons wounded by gunfire. Fourteen Klansmen and seven blacks pled guilty to reduced charges on July 19, paying fines and receiving suspended jail terms, while four other knights faced felony counts.[241] By September, acting grand dragon Joseph Bryant was in full revolt against UKA headquarters, accusing Shelton's stand-in wizard, Melvin Sexton, of looting Klan coffers.[242] Sexton banished Bryant and his followers, along with Virginia dragon Marshall Kornegay. Ten klaverns followed Bryant into his new North Carolina Knights, while FBI agents gloated that the split had "materially damaged" the UKA. Edward Fields branded Bryant an "FBI pimp" and *provocateur.*[243]

Mississippi offered the decade's last gasp of Klan terror in September 1969, when Klansmen planned to kill Charles Evers, newly elected black mayor of Fayette. Authorities caught Dale Walton and two other Tupelo Klansmen with a small arsenal of weapons, including a submachine gun, as they staked out Evers's office. Federal firearms charges joined Walton's rap sheet, lately including an indictment for obstructing justice in the Dahmer murder case. At trial, after feigned displays of insanity, Walton received probation with an order for psychiatric treatment.[244]

CHAPTER 9

"Growing and Improving All the Time" (1970–1982)

Predictions of the Klan's demise in 1969 were premature, as they had been in 1869. Two years after his conversion to the cause of racial harmony, including a brief stint on Atlanta's Model Cities program, Calvin Craig reverted to type and founded a secretive group called the Christian Americans Patriotic Society.[1] Mississippi's Klan was quiet when 26 school districts integrated for the first time, in April 1970, but the NSRP launched a statewide recruiting drive, supported by Byron De La Beckwith.[2] Multiple murderer James Seale made headlines in November, when he survived a plane crash that killed five other persons, including Klan victim Frank Morris's final attending physician.[3] In Louisiana, American Nazi Party member Jim Lindsay maintained his small Knights of the KKK, while UKA defector Jack Helm found common cause with the Minutemen, building a paramilitary training camp decorated with Nazi regalia in St. Bernard Parish.[4] Pennsylvania's Roy Frankhouser ran a similar Minutemen camp, raided by federal agents in September 1970, after bombers hit a synagogue in Reading.[5]

Carolina Chaos

In the Carolinas, FBI harassment and internal squabbling left both realms disorganized. Robert Scoggin, banished from the UKA, still had enough loyal followers to found the Invisible Empire Knights in June 1970, but they soon ran afoul of the law.[6] That September, a clash between IEK members and UKA rivals near Sumter left one Klansman dead, while Scoggin and nine of his knights were detained on suspicion of conspiracy and accessory after the fact to murder.[7] Those charges were later dismissed, and the Palmetto Klans endured.[8]

In North Carolina, Robert Shelton and James Jones shared the stage at a UKA klonvocation in June 1970, held at Salisbury's Catawba College, but COINTELPRO agents were at work behind the scenes, sowing seeds of dissension and canceling hotel reservations.[9]

One month later, the FBI fomented a rift in the National Socialist White People's Party

(NSWPP), publicizing leader Frank Collin's Jewish ancestry.[10] Collin moved on to found the National Socialist Party of America (NSPA), enlisting future stars of the North Carolina Klan such as Virgil Griffin.[11] In August, bombers struck a newly integrated school in Edgecomb County.[12]

Eyes of Texas

The Texas Klan, largely ignored during the 1960s, enjoyed a renaissance of sorts in the new decade, under UKA grand dragon Frank Converse. The order's first target was KPFT radio in Houston, part of the liberal California-based Pacifica Radio network. KPFT began broadcasting on March 1, 1970, and was bombed on May 12, shutting it down for five months.[13] Other targets of bombs, gunfire and arrows included *Space City!*, a local alternative newspaper, the Socialist Workers Party, a "hippie" restaurant, a motorcycle shop, and an architect's office. Houston policemen posed for photographs in uniform, masked by Klan hoods, and joined in harassing nonconformists. KPFT resumed broadcasting on October 1, demonstrating its commitment to free speech by giving Converse his own weekly program, but poor ratings prompted a second bombing on October 6.[14]

On October 29 Houston police detained two Klansmen, Louis Beam, Jr., and Jimmy Dale Hutto, found driving past another Houston radio station with their lights off, after the station received a bomb threat. Both wore paramilitary garb, while their car contained several rifles, a bottle of gasoline and a walkie-talkie.[15] No charges resulted, and Beam—a Vietnam veteran who joined the UKA in 1968—went on to later Ku Klux stardom.[16] Hutto was less fortunate: betrayed by an FBI informer, he was arrested with two other Klansmen in January 1971, en route to California, where he planned to bomb two more Pacifica stations.[17] Houston's grand jury indicted Hutto, Beam, and two other knights in June 1971, while Frank Converse announced plans to run for sheriff.[18] Only Hutto faced trial, in federal court, with two codefendants testifying against him. In October 1971 he received a 66-month sentence, with a stipulation that he only serve one year in prison.[19] State charges evaporated amidst claims that Hutto himself was an FBI *agent provocateur*.[20]

Soon after those dismissals, journalist Rob Laytner launched his own investigation of the Texas Klan, securing unparalleled cooperation from within the order. He interviewed Klansmen, including police officers, who detailed their war against "Communism" as they understood it. Louis Beam, hailed by fellow knights as an "American super patriot," identified himself as a member of the UKA's Klan Bureau of Investigation, pegging the order's national membership "well over 100,000." In the wake of Laytner's series, he reports, "Almost every Klansman I photographed who gave his permission to be identified lost everything he owned. His business or home was burned out. He was fined or sent to jail by the FBI." In retaliation, Laytner says, "The three Texas newspapers I was syndicated in were warned to never run my stories again or risk police tickets on all their cars and trucks and no cooperation on stories. I lost the papers and didn't go into Texas again for many years."[21]

By 1974 the Texas Klan had fallen on hard times. In Houston, Fred Hofheinz replaced mayor Louie Welch, a staunch George Wallace supporter, and purged the police department of Klansmen. FBI agents helped statewide, with polygraph tests resulting in dismissal or early retirement of some 200 Klan kops.[22]

"New South" Politics

Cancer claimed the life of Lurleen Wallace in 1968, leaving Lieutenant Governor Albert Brewer to complete her term. George Wallace returned with a vengeance in 1970's gubernatorial campaign, facing Brewer and five other rivals—Ace Carter among them—in the Democratic primary. In a particularly rough campaign, Wallace called Brewer "sissy britches," promised not to mount another presidential race if elected, and aired blatantly racist television ads. One asked viewers, "Do you want the black block electing your governor?" Another showed a white girl surrounded by seven black youths, with the caption "Wake up! Blacks vow to take over Alabama."[23]

Brewer won the first round, by a margin of 11,703 votes, while Carter ran third with 1.51 percent of ballots cast. In the runoff, mandated by Brewer's failure to achieve a clear majority, Wallace rebounded to carry the day by a margin of 33,881 votes.[24] He would begin his second term in January 1971, already planning his third presidential race. At Wallace's inauguration, blind to irony, Ace Carter led a group of pickets bearing signs reading "Wallace is a bigot" and "Free our white children."[25]

Georgia also elected a new governor in 1970. Lester Maddox, compelled to step down, consoled himself with a successful bid to become lieutenant governor. J. B. Stoner joined a list of seven contenders for the governor's mansion, running fourth with 17,663 votes in the primary that chose state senator Jimmy Carter to succeed Maddox. While billing himself as the "candidate of love," Stoner described African Americans as descendants of apes, branded Jews "vipers of hell," and labeled Adolf Hitler as "too moderate."[26] In Louisiana's congressional primary, John Rarick won renomination against liberal Democrat Jesse Bankston by a vote of 57,835 to 40,450.[27]

New Horizons

Klansmen struggled to stay relevant in North Carolina during the early 1970s, losing ground and members to more visibly militant groups such as Wilmington's Rights of White People.[28] In February 1971 arsonists torched the Chapel Hill office of lawyer Julius Chambers, involved in a school desegregation case.[29] Three months later, after Oxford's grand jury failed to indict a Klansman for killing a black man, bombers demolished the gunman's store.[30] Rebellious North Carolina Knights replaced founder Joseph Bryant with grand dragon Harold Murray.[31] FBI agents suspected Virgil Griffin of bombing Bryant's klavern at Cherry Hill, in October 1971, but they filed no charges.[32]

By 1971 Addison Thompson's Klan had dwindled to a handful of knights mixed with Minutemen, stockpiling arms and explosives.[33] In January 1972 he led a two-man demonstration, with imperial kludd Rene LaCoste, to celebrate Robert E. Lee's birthday. As they marched around Lee Circle, black passers-by slugged Thompson with a brick.[34] John Rarick remained in fine form, defending a Louisiana army captain who refused to shake hands with a black superior officer. When Michigan congressman Clarence Diggs rose in a hearing on home rule for the District of Columbia, branding Rarick "the leading racist in this Congress," Rarick fired back, calling the nation's capital a "sinkhole, rat infested ... the laughing stock of the free and Communist world."[35]

Maryland Klansmen under Tony LaRicci made headlines in June 1971, with a rally in Rising Sun that drew leftist pickets, but it was Michigan's UKA realm, led by Robert Miles, that set the standard for militancy above the Mason-Dixon Line.[36] On April 13, 1971, Willow Run's school board met to consider ways of honoring Martin Luther King. After the meeting, hooded knights kidnapped the high school principal at gunpoint, leaving him tarred and feathered.[37] On August 30 nightriders visited Pontiac, bombing 10 buses scheduled for use in school integration. FBI agents arrested Miles and five komrades a week later. They waived a jury trial and were convicted in May 1973. Miles received a nine-year sentence, serving six before he was released.[38] In his absence, Detroit Klansman Jim Burwell founded Michigan Convicts Aid, calling himself "a victim of discrimination" by insurance companies that hiked his rates for busing black children around Motor City.[39]

Mississippi Klansmen found an old rival on the gubernatorial ballot in 1971. Bill Waller, two-time prosecutor of Byron De La Beckwith, returned to challenge Lieutenant Governor Charles Sullivan for the state's top office, distracted by five other contenders. Sullivan won the primary, but votes distributed among the bottom five hopefuls forced a runoff, wherein Waller won the day. In November's general election, Waller easily defeated Sullivan and Charles Evers, both running as independents.[40]

Omens of the Klan's worst nightmare passed unnoticed in 1971, when Alabama lawyers Joe Levin and Morris Dees, Jr., founded the Southern Poverty Law Center (SPLC) to assist indigent clients. Dees had campaigned for George Wallace in 1958 and defended a Klansmen charged with beating freedom riders in 1961, but his conscience had rebelled at accommodating racists. Another decade would elapse before inauguration of the SPLC's Klanwatch project, monitoring hate groups nationwide and filing civil litigation to suppress them, but the groundwork had been laid.[41]

Meanwhile, Klansmen tried to keep their empire afloat. William Chaney, an ex-sheriff's deputy and UKA grand dragon for Indiana, held a press conference in February 1972, claiming dramatic membership growth. Over the next year, Klansmen burned six crosses in Elkhart alone, at schools, homes, and other sites.[42] Another February headline announced Dale Walton's murder indictment in Mississippi, but no conviction resulted.[43] Virgil Griffin led North Carolina Knights in a "white power march" through Monroe in June 1972, with Charles White's American White Nationalist Party, emerging as the tiny Klan's grand dragon three months later.[44] Roy Frankhouser marched alone down Manhattan's Fifth Avenue in black stormtrooper garb, protesting a city ban on Nazi uniforms, then offered his services to the FBI as an informer. Rejected there, he signed on with the Bureau of Alcohol, Tobacco and Firearms (ATF) in September 1972, roaming from New York to Toronto, taping conversations with his fellow racists.[45] Also in September, *New Solidarity* magazine warned against far-right infiltration of the "New Left," naming Michigan grand dragon Robert Miles as an enemy to watch.[46]

Last Hurrah

In 1972 George Wallace forgot his promise to Alabama voters, launching another presidential campaign. Endorsed by Lester Maddox and various Klan leaders, he shunned the AIP this time and returned to the Democratic primary trail, one of 15 contenders. Wallace

Virgil Griffin (in dark robe, center) leads a "white power" march in North Carolina, ca. 1982 (National Archives).

swept Florida's primary in March, claiming 42 percent of the vote, then nearly lost his life in Maryland, on May 15, from an assassin's bullets. He would survive, but there would be no more White House campaigns.[47]

In Georgia, J. B. Stoner's senatorial race met opposition from TV censors, but he sued and won an order from the Federal Communications Commission permitting ads that warned, "The main reason why the niggers want integration is because niggers want our white women." Running fifth in the Democratic primary, he still claimed more than 40,000 votes, prompting Edward Fields to crow that the NSRP had "held to our open and clear-cut message of White Racism and Anti-Jewism."[48] Ohio Klansman Dale Reusch lost his second bid to become county sheriff, while John Rarick was elected to his fourth and final term in Congress from Louisiana.[49]

Strange Days

Pennsylvania's Klan rebounded with a vengeance in 1973. Roy Frankhouser severed his ATF ties in February, while thieves stole 960 pounds of dynamite from mines around Reading. On August 28 five "professional" bombs rocked Reading's Jewish Community Center. On October 13, two more exploded in minority neighborhoods, killing one man and sparking retaliatory arson. Charles Sims, an imprisoned UKA bus-bomber, told federal agents Frankhouser had shipped 240 pounds of dynamite from Reading to Michigan between January and July 1973. On October 29 a beating in federal prison left Sims with brain damage.[50]

Indiana Klansman Railton Loy advertised for members in *The Elkhart Truth,* in February 1973, then found himself jailed in May, for making false statements to a firearms dealer and possession of a firearm as a convicted felon. In April three Elkhart knights tried to bomb a black woman's apartment in Monroe, but botched the job and wound up in prison.[51]

Byron De La Beckwith ran afoul of the law once more in September 1973. FBI informants told the Bureau that Beckwith planned to kill A. I. Botnick, an ADL leader in New Orleans, and agents mounted surveillance, watching on September 26 as Beckwith received a bomb from MWK member L. E. Matthews. Early next morning, Louisiana officers stopped Beckwith's car, discovering a time bomb, a .50-caliber machine gun, sundry other weapons, and a map bearing directions to Botnick's home. Beckwith denied any knowledge of the bomb, but jurors convicted him on weapons charges in May 1975. Sentenced to five years, Beckwith stalled incarceration with appeals for two years, granting him time to tour the country, gracing a Pennsylvania Klan rally in early 1977.[52]

Louisiana's Klan moved on without Beckwith, celebrating murderer James Seale's appointment as a policeman in Vidalia.[53] Addison Thompson lost another bid to become mayor of New Orleans, while Shreveport police jailed two dozen Klansmen for parading masked in August 1973, then dropped the charges.[54]

Carolina Klansmen flailed without purpose through 1973. By May, when leader Leroy Gibson was convicted of bombing a home and bookstore in Wilmington, the Rights of White People had dwindled to a single chapter. Gibson boasted of uniting Klansmen, Minutemen and Nazis, but support from the NSRP did not spare him from prison.[55] Only seven knights gathered to picket Edonton's X-rated theater in August, and James Jones resigned from the UKA two months later, to work as a factory night watchman.[56] In South Carolina, Robert Scoggin left his Invisible Empire Knights near year's end, to tend his dying wife, but he would resurface in Klan affairs before long.[57]

After his gubernatorial loss in 1970, Ace Carter left Alabama for Texas, renaming himself "Forrest Carter" in honor of the Klan's first grand wizard. Shedding family along with his name, referring to his sons as "nephews," Carter tried his hand at writing and produced a surprise bestseller, *Gone to Texas,* in 1973. Sequels would follow—and a film, *The Outlaw Josey Wales*—after he moved again, this time to Florida. His anti-hero clearly spoke for Carter in the novels, when he said, "What ye and me cares about has been butchered ... raped. It's been done by them lyin', double-tongued snakes that run guv-mints. Guv-mints lie ... promise ... back-stab ... eat in youre [*sic*] lodge and rape youre women and kill when ye sleep on their promises."[58]

Christian Identity maintained its grip on racist minds in 1973, despite a bitter rift between spokesmen-brothers Dan and Duane Gayman. A court battle left Duane in charge of Missouri's Church of Israel, while Dan formed a new Church of Our Christian Heritage, with Klansman Thomas Robb on the board of directors. By year's end, Dan's church was allied with the Rev. Dewey Tucker's Louisiana-based National Emancipation of Our White Seed, whose members included Byron De La Beckwith.[59]

Klansmen Abroad

In 1972 Louis Beam told Houston reporter Ron Laytner, "The new Klan has gone international. We have a unit in Australia. We have one in Italy and we have one in England.

In Canada we have just recently opened up a brand new Klan. Up in Calgary, Alberta, our new Klan almost overnight has become a tremendous influence on the people. It has achieved more success than I had any idea it would."[60] The boast was not entirely hollow, though, as usual, Beam tended to exaggerate.

Alberta's Klan was led by Tearlach Mac a'Phearsoin, a gay herbalist and minister of the National Spirit Church, who claimed worldwide ownership of all existing copyrights to the Knights of the Ku Klux Klan, while denying any taint of racism and saying it welcomed members "from all religious and racial backgrounds." Mac a'Phearsoin joined the Calgary Gun Club in 1973, and was fined $2,000 when a friend suffered fatal wounds while showing him how to unload a pistol.[61] As Mac a'Phearsoin's star faded, James McQuirter and German immigrant Wolfgang Droege sought to revive the order, aided by American Klansmen. McQuirter faced indictment for distributing hate literature in 1978, but the Canadian Knights hung on, claiming 2,500 members a year later, when it opened a Toronto office.[62]

J. B. Stoner and Edward Fields visited Britain several times in the mid–1970s, reporting "thundering cheers from the throng" as they addressed meetings of the racist National Front, best known for street riots in 1977.[63] Three years later, reporter Robert Douglas from London's *Sunday People* visited Robert Scoggin in South Carolina, recording his thoughts on submachine guns—"You'll get more niggers using these"—and his claims of planting klaverns from England (under Grand Dragon John Fisher) to Australia and New Zealand. "We need organizers in England," he said. "Come to America for a Klan initiation to prepare yourselves." In a burst of enthusiasm, Scoggin initiated Douglas on the spot. Douglas repaid him by stealing Scoggin's gavel.[64]

Rumblings

Stateside, racists strove to unite in 1974–75. Minutemen leader Robert DePugh, lately paroled from federal prison, announced creation of a new Patriots InterOrganizational Communications Center in September 1974, with Robert Shelton as a featured speaker at its inaugural meeting.[65] Ten months later, DePugh's Patriots Leadership Conference in Kansas city drew members of the UKA, Knights of the KKK, NSWPP, American White Nationalist Party, Liberty Lobby, American Party, Posse Comitatus, John Birch Society, and National Rifle Association. The NRA soon found itself competing with a National Alliance to Keep and Bear Arms, boasting board members DePugh and Shelton.[66]

Roy Frankhouser was up to his old tricks in 1974, arrested by ATF agents in February for smuggling dynamite to Michigan Klansmen. His lawyer claimed Roy was a "top secret" government asset, but Frankhouser languished in jail until June 1975 before raising $50,000 bail. Before trial, prosecutors lost witness Charles Sims to a prison lobotomy, two more were murdered, and a fourth was convicted of burglary. Frankhouser pled guilty to reduced charges in September 1975 and escaped with five years probation in lieu of jail time.[67] Already suspicious of Frankhouser's cloak-and-dagger activity, UKA leaders banished him in May 1977.[68]

Virgil Griffin's North Carolina Knights harbored an infiltrator of its own, Edward Dawson, earlier convicted in a 1967 shooting incident. Reporting to the FBI by 1975, he fingered Griffin and others for dynamite possession, but no charges resulted. While generally striking a nonviolent posture, Griffin offered a foretaste of things to come in 1975, when he joined in demonstrations with Frank Braswell's NSWPP.[69]

West Virginia witnessed unexpected Klan activity in 1974, after Kanawha County's school board voted to ban books by Malcolm X, George Orwell, and other "subversive" authors. Opponents of censorship rallied in protest, while a committee of "concerned citizens" threatened to pull their children from class if the books remained. Nightriders dynamited an elementary school on October 9, firebombed another school days later, and left a defective bomb at the school board office. Dale Reusch led Klansmen to Charleston in January 1975, while sneak squads lit crosses by night. Censorship champion Marvin Horan attended Reusch's rally, holding an umbrella for the wizard when it rained, but his campaign collapsed in April, when Horan received a three-year sentence for his role in the bombings.[70]

Violence also publicized the Louisiana Klan, in October 1974, after black teenager Gary Tyler allegedly shot and killed Timothy Weber, a white 13-year-old, outside newly integrated Destrehan High School in St. Charles. Controversy surrounded the crime—committed with a pistol stolen from the sheriff's firing range, later "lost" in custody—but it offered a spotlight for young David Duke, grand dragon of Jim Lindsay's Knights of the KKK. Duke launched "patrols" in St. Charles, where two of his knights were jailed for carrying stolen firearms, but prosecutors dismissed those charges.[71]

Klansmen and their friends fared poorly in politics during 1974. Dale Reusch lost his gubernatorial bid in Ohio's Democratic primary, claiming only 33 votes of 1,010,853 cast.[72] Louisiana voters denied John Rarick a fifth congressional term, preferring challenger Jeffrey LaCaze.[73] J. B. Stoner made the most impressive showing in his campaign to become Georgia's lieutenant governor, logging 73,000 votes to claim 10 percent of the total.[74]

That same year, future Klan star Frazier Glenn Miller, Jr., borrowed a copy of *The Thunderbolt* from his father and attended his first NSRP meeting in North Carolina. Early acquaintances included Charles Parker, who would join in the massacre of anti–Klan protesters five years later. An active-duty soldier at Fort Bragg, Miller writes that from his first day in the party he "became obsessed, totally, completely, and unashamedly" in the cause of white supremacy.[75]

Dale Reusch (front) with Marvin Horan at a Kanawha County textbook protest rally in January 1979 (author's collection).

A New Wave

On June 12, 1975, gunshots killed Klan leader Jim Lindsay at his real estate office in Metairie, Louisiana. Police charged his estranged wife with the murder, but jurors acquitted her, leaving the crime unsolved. David Duke assumed command, formally incorporating the Knights of the KKK in August 1975, naming himself as national director and wife Chloe as secretary. The order, in Duke's words, was "organized to bring peace, harmony and prosperity to these United States of America and her people, and to advance the cause of Fraternity [*sic*], education and charity of all Americans."[76]

As usual, reality was rather different. Duke's mentor, Lindsay, had admired Adolf Hitler and belonged to the American Nazi Party.[77] His protégé—Duke claimed Lindsay "was almost like a dad to me"—was cut from the same cloth.[78] Oklahoma born in 1950, Duke claims he joined the Klan at 17, a year before enrolling at Louisiana

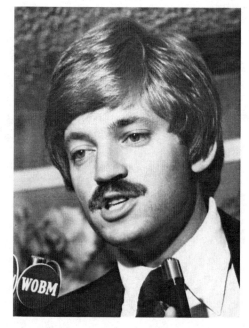

Early photo of Klan leader David Duke, before cosmetic alterations (Southern Poverty Law Center).

State University in Baton Rouge. There, he organized a White Youth Alliance, affiliated with the NSWPP, and donned Nazi regalia to peddle copies of George Rockwell's *White Power* on campus. When radical lawyer William Kunstler visited LSU, Duke protested in brownshirt and swastika armband, bearing a placard that read "Kunstler is a Communist Jew" and "Gas the Chicago 7."[79]

Summer 1971 found Duke in Laos, visiting his father. He later claimed the trip was a CIA "tour of duty," dropping supplies to anti–Communist guerrillas, but in fact he spent the season teaching English to Laotian military officers—and was dismissed after drawing a Molotov cocktail on the blackboard. Back at LSU, he resumed leadership of the White Youth Alliance, married member Chloe Hardin in 1972, and graduated in 1974. Their first child, Erika Lindsay, was named for Duke's martyred mentor.[80] Duke met Chloe in jail, when they were arrested with two others for stealing money from George Wallace's presidential campaign. A second charge accused Duke of making Molotov cocktails. Neither case went to trial.[81]

As national director of what soon became the country's largest Klan, Duke tried to overhaul the order's public image. He admitted women to full membership, recruited teenagers—including future imperial wizard Johnny Lee Clary[82]—and preferred suits to robes, never appearing in a hood. Cross-burnings became "illuminations" in Dukespeak, as he embarked on a whirlwind tour of TV and radio talk shows, college campuses, and surprise appearances at any site where racial tension flared from coast to coast. Despite his efforts to launder the Klan's reputation, Duke continued his infatuation with Fascism, selling various pro–Nazi books from his Metairie headquarters, flirting with Holocaust denial, and hiring John Crommelin to edit the Klan's monthly *Crusader* tabloid.[83] On the side, while pursuing countless women in his travels, he published two books under pseudonyms. *African Atto,* by "Mohammed X," was a martial arts manual for black militants, allegedly sold to help the Klan track agitators. *Finders-Keepers,* by "Dorothy Vanderbilt," was a dating-and-sex manual designed to aid women in "finding and keeping the man you want."[84]

Expansion of Duke's Klan was aided by a slate of grand dragons—or "state directors"—who soon made headlines in their own right. Louis Beam left the UKA for Duke's Knights in 1976, graduated from the University of Houston in 1977, led the Klan's paramilitary Texas Emergency Reserve, and recruited soldiers from Fort Hood to guard Klan rallies in full uniform.[85] Alabama dragon Don Black launched his racist career as a teenage volunteer with J. B. Stoner's 1970 gubernatorial campaign, but was shot at NSRP headquarters by Jerry Ray (brother of James Earl Ray), allegedly while stealing Stoner's mailing list for the rival NSWPP. In Duke, Black found "someone that really, fully understood the Jewish involvement" in civil rights turmoil.[86]

Louisiana headquarters was frequently without its leader as Duke traveled far and wide. In his absence, management of the realm fell to James Warner, a Pennsylvania native and founding member of the American Nazi Party, later associate editor of *The Thunderbolt,* who founded California's New Christian Crusade Church and Sons of Liberty publishing house in 1971. By 1976 he was Louisiana's grand dragon, launching a militant Christian Defense League in 1977. Warner's eventual replacement, Jerald Dutton, was a fourth-generation Klansman, information director of the National White Americans Party, and former youth director for the NSRP.[87]

Florida's Klan faced violent opposition under Grand Dragon Jack Gregory. In November 1977 arsonists struck the Palm Harbor home of Don Kersey, who leased acreage for the Klan's state headquarters, and drive-by gunmen fired on Gregory's home in March 1978. Still he persevered, holding rallies at the Palm Harbor site and vowing "war" on those who opposed him.[88]

Arkansas witnessed similar turbulence under Grand Dragon Randy Howard, arrested for brawling with anti–Klan protesters in Little Rock, then turning up in full regalia at a barbecue hosted by state legislator Clayton Little.[89] Largely overlooked, a lowly chaplain at the time, was future luminary Thomas Robb, a Michigan native raised on the gospel of Gerald Smith and other anti–Semites, "awakened to the myth of the Holocaust" at 13 and publishing his own racist newsletter at 19. Robb had passed through the John Birch Society on his way to the Invisible Empire, supporting himself as a Shaklee salesman. In 1979 he called an "emergency" meeting, drawing Klansmen from four states, haranguing them about the "secret Jewish tax" on kosher products—and a scheme to "keep money in the White Power movement" by purchasing Shaklee products from Robb.[90] Daughter Rachel, born in 1968 and later second in command of Robb's order, received her first Klan robe before she could walk and was "knighted" by Duke. By age 12 she was phoning Congress, urging defeat of the Equal Rights Amendment as a way to curb lesbianism.[91]

In California, NSWPP member Thomas Metzger joined the Knights in 1975, soon rising to lead the realm. An Indiana native and John Birch Society alumnus, employed as a TV repairman in Fallbrook, he organized a short-lived White Brotherhood before finding the Klan. As grand dragon he pioneered a "Klan Border Watch" against illegal immigration that drew international headlines, recruited teenage racists for a White Students Union, planted a klavern at Camp Pendleton, led marches that often sparked violence, and doubled as a minister of James Warner's New Christian Crusade Church, preaching that Jews are literal children of Satan.[92]

David Lane led Duke's Colorado realm. Yet another John Birch Society defector, son of a brutal alcoholic migrant worker, Lane later claimed that his father forced his mother into prostitution for "booze money" while terrorizing the family with vicious beatings. Placed in foster care at six, in 1944, Lane already idolized Nazi stormtroopers. As an adult, he tried his hand at real estate but lost his license for refusing to accept black clients. Lane moved on to an insurance agency, using the office photocopier to mass-produce his pamphlet *The Death of the White Race*. "Each morning I would run off 500–1000 copies," Lane wrote, distributing them on his lunch hour. In his free time, Lane and Klansman Fred Wilkins squabbled on-air with abrasive Denver radio host Alan Berg, whom Lane would later plot to kill.[93]

Such leaders breathed new life into the Klan. According to the ADL, Duke's Knights had 1,000 members by early 1978, doubling that by November 1979. Nationwide, his high profile helped other Klans as well, inflating membership from 6,500 in 1975 to 10,500 by 1979. More alarming, to Klan-watchers, was the proliferation of "nonmenber supporters," leaping from 30,000 in 1978 to 75,000 the following year. Most observers credited Duke with leading the Klan renaissance.[94]

But there were hiccups along the way. In September 1976 police arrested Duke and James Warner for inciting a riot at the Klan's International Patriotic Conference in Metairie. Jurors convicted them in May 1977, but an appellate court reversed that verdict. Convicted a second time in August 1979, Duke paid a $500 fine and received a sentence of one year's probation.[95] Politics began distracting Duke, first in a 1975 race for the Louisiana state senate, where he received 11,079 votes, and again for the same office in 1979, declining to 9,897 ballots. Another distraction was women. In October 1977, Tom Metzger complained that Duke seemed more concerned with chasing "tail" than "wetbacks" during the Klan Border Watch.[96]

Despite such lapses, Duke displayed a genius for capitalizing on racial tension. In 1974, when a federal court ordered busing to integrate Boston's public schools, Duke went north to defend "white rights" and confront angry foes, briefly dropping his mask of moderation as he told cheering racists, "The federal government is taking money out of your pockets to finance the production of thousands of little black bastards. The real issue isn't education. The real issue is niggers!"[97]

In April 1975 Duke led the Klan's largest rally in a decade, drawing 2,700 supporters to Walker, Louisiana. Ironically, that triumph sowed the seeds of schism, as rally organizer Elbert "Bill" Wilkinson accused Duke of absconding with the proceeds. A navy veteran, electric contractor and minor real estate mogul, Wilkinson left Duke's Klan in August 1975, to lead his own Invisible Empire Knights (IEK).[98] Within a year he would emerge as Duke's primary competition, an old-fashioned Klansman who eschewed moderation and cheered acts of violence. Jerry Dutton also left the Knights, in November 1976, to join the IEK and publish a scathing pamphlet, *The Truth About David Duke*.[99]

Restless Knights

While Duke hogged headlines, other Klans remained active. Calvin Craig announced a Georgia Klan revival in 1975, but nothing seemed to come of it.[100] Tony LaRicci's Maryland

Bill Wilkinson (center, in suit) was already an FBI informer when he left Duke's Klan to lead his own faction in 1975. Photograph ca. 1975–76 (Southern Poverty Law Center).

Knights rallied at Gamber that May, lighting a 100-foot cross and burning mimeographed "communist flags."[101] In September, William Chaney's Indiana UKA members gathered at an abandoned drag strip in Elkhart County.[102] Next door, in Illinois, UKA members Dennis Milam and Andrew Jackson vied for control of Kankakee, while Robert Shelton stripped Wilbur Foreman of his post as imperial representative, driving him into the arms of Robert Scoggin's Invisible Empire Knights (unrelated to Bill Wilkinson's group). Other klaverns rose and fell, scourged by internal dissent.[103]

Nineteen seventy-five was a hard year for dragons. James Venable banished North Carolina's Joe Grady for admitting Catholics to the order and attending meetings with rival Robert Scoggin. Grady then joined sometime Venable ally William Morris in a revived Federated Knights, before founding his own White Knights of Liberty in 1979. Meanwhile, in October 1975, four other National Knights dragons—including Ohio's Dale Reusch—accused Venable of senility and financial mismanagement, prompting their mass expulsion.[104] Two months later, a Senate committee investigating COINTELPRO's crimes exposed George Dorsett as a longtime FBI informer. Virgil Griffin convened a kourt to banish Dorsett in January 1976, ironically naming informer Edward Dawson as Dorsett's prosecutor.[105]

Senate revelations of FBI and CIA abuses spawned a new congressional investigation.

In September 1976 the House of Representatives established a select committee to investigate the murders of President Kennedy and Martin Luther King, continuing through 1978. Its final report found "a likelihood" that both assassinations resulted from conspiracies, yet failed on many fronts to track the known conspirators who had spent years planning Dr. King's murder. The committee ultimately ruled out plots by the Klansmen, the Minutemen, and J. B. Stoner, selectively accepting the denials of prime suspects, fuming over the silence of reluctant witnesses, and relying on incomplete FBI records to finger James Earl Ray as the lone gunman, perhaps supported by his brothers in pursuit of a hypothetical bounty on King, offered by two deceased Missouri businessmen.[106]

Klansmen saw nothing to celebrate in 1976's presidential race. Republican incumbent Gerald Ford was a tainted Yankee, handpicked in 1974 to ensure Richard Nixon's pardon for Watergate crimes, while Democratic front-runner Jimmy Carter was an outspoken Georgia liberal. John Rarick sought the AIP's nomination but lost out to Lester Maddox. In November, Maddox ran second among 10 minor candidates, polling 170,531 votes, while the splinter American Party robbed him of another 160,773, cast for Tennessee farmer Thomas Anderson.[107] Dale Reusch, lost in the shuffle, launched an independent bid for the vice presidency but only qualified for one primary ballot, in West Virginia. He won that contest with 103,861 votes, but was excluded from the party's national convention.[108]

FBI informer Gary Rowe testified before a Senate committee investigating federal intelligence abuses on December 2, 1975. He was in the WITSEC and his hood was universally described as a "disguise" by every major news source (National Archives).

Politics aside, Klansmen and their allies had mixed fortunes in 1976. Attorney General Edward Levi officially closed FBI investigations of the NSRP in April, concluding that it posed no threat to America.[109] Tired of the party's inaction, Glenn Miller, shifted allegiance to Harold Covington's Raleigh-based National Socialist Party of American (NSPA), seeking more militant action.[110] On May 11, 1976, William Chaney firebombed an Indianapolis advertising company. Federal jurors convicted him on October 19, but Chaney remained free on appeal until May 1979, when he received a five-year prison term. Between conviction and incarceration, in June 1977, Chaney founded a new Confederation of Independent Orders, serving as imperial wizard while Robert Scoggin was proclaimed honorary "imperial emperor." Grand dragons included Raymond Doerfler (Pennsylvania), Ed Reynolds (New Jersey), Tony LaRicci (Maryland), and New York prison guard Earl Schoonmaker. The group claimed 3,000 members in 1978, but collapsed with Chaney's imprisonment.[111]

While Chaney bungled his bombing, a federal grand jury indicted Klansman Jules Kimbel and Louisiana advertising executive James Leslie for interstate transportation of a stolen bulldozer. Three months later, on July 8, 1976, a gunman murdered Leslie in Baton Rouge. Prime suspect Russell Griffith died identically, from shotgun blasts, on October 15. Those crimes went unsolved until June 1981, when defendant Steve Simoneaux pled guilty to conspiracy in Griffith's death, naming brothers Jules and Clayton Kimble (who spells his surname differently) as the men responsible. A new grand jury indicted the brothers, alleging that they killed Leslie to curry favor with Shreveport Commissioner of Public Safety George D'Artois, previously indicted on testimony from Leslie. Both were convicted and sentenced to life in prison.[112]

Soon after Leslie's murder, UKA grand dragon Willis Kidd requested permission to lead a rally at the Rivergate Convention Center in New Orleans. City fathers demanded a $100,000 bond, forcing Kidd to downsize his expectations. Four months later, federal authorities blocked his move to rally at a public school, citing the Klan's exclusion of minorities. In August 1977, when Kidd complained of FBI harassment at another rally in New Orleans, only 14 knights gathered to hear him.[113]

Samuel Bowers left prison in 1976 and returned to Laurel, Mississippi, teaching Sunday school. Rumors of a "hard core" White Knights revival circulated, but no violence ensued. Thomas Tarrants, also freed that year, attended the University of Mississippi, then received a Master of Divinity degree from Eastern Mennonite Seminary, publishing a memoir, *The Conversion of a Klansman*, in 1978.[114]

Schisms continued in North Carolina. FBI informer Edward Dawson took command of the Confederate Knights in January 1976 and never called another meeting.[115] He subsequently joined William Chaney's Confederation of Independent Orders and was elected to national office.[116] Virgil Griffin attended Robert Scoggin's Conference of Eastern Dragons in autumn 1976, with Bill Wilkinson, Tony LaRicci, Dan Smithers of Texas, Wilbur Foreman of Illinois, Albert McCorkel of Missouri, Raymond Doerfler of Pennsylvania, Arkansas NSRP member Neumann Britton, and the Rev. Dewey Tucker.[117] By March 1977 the ADL estimated total Klan membership in North Carolina at 500 knights.[118]

"Forrest" Carter enjoyed new success in 1976, with publication of his fraudulent autobiography, *The Education of Little Tree*. Posing as the Cherokee Nation's "Storyteller in Council," he garnered rave reviews and won the American Booksellers Book of the Year award, published *The Vengeance Trail of Josey Wales,* and reaped more profits from Hollywood's release of *The Outlaw Josey Wales*. Interviewed by Barbara Walters on the *Today* show, he was recognized by former colleagues but ducked questions about the Klan, insisting that Ace Carter was in fact his "no good" brother. Carter followed up in 1978 with *Watch for Me on the Mountain*, a fictional biography of Geronimo. In June 1979, driving west with a new Josey Wales script, Carter stopped in Texas to visit his estranged son. A drunken brawl ensued, and Carter suffered fatal injuries.[119]

Robert DePugh and Robert Shelton staged a three-day conference of far-right groups in Kansas City, in May 1977, but their goal of unity eluded them.[120] One month earlier, California Klansmen fired into the homes of Hispanic families around San Diego, landing exalted cyclops Orville Watkins and two others in prison that November. Additional charges included plotting to kill a Jewish leader in Los Angeles.[121]

Hunting Humans

In 1976, Alabama Klansman and NSRP member Joseph Paul Franklin launched a one-man crime wave. Born James Clayton Vaughn in 1950, raised in an abusive racist family, Franklin legally changed his name at age 26, choosing "Joseph Paul" in honor of Third Reich propaganda minister Paul Joseph Goebbels and "Franklin" from 18th-century America's Benjamin Franklin. That September, in Atlanta, he followed an interracial couple down an alley and sprayed them with Chemical Mace. Thus began a pattern of stalking blacks, Jews, and mixed-race couples—"MRCs" in Franklin's terms—from coast to coast, claiming at least 21 lives.[122]

The spree began with bombings, in July 1977, at the home of a Jewish lobbyist in Rockville, Maryland, and a synagogue in Chattanooga, four days later. Next, he drove to Madison, Wisconsin, stalking a judge whom Franklin deemed too lenient in sentencing black rapists. On August 7, en route to the judge's office, Franklin fumed over the slow pace of a black driver in front of him. Drawing a stolen pistol, he killed the driver, Alphonse Manning, and his white girlfriend, Toni Schwenn. On October 8, in Richmond Heights, Missouri, he fired on worshipers outside a synagogue, killing Gerald Gordon and wounding two others.[123]

February 1978 found Franklin in Atlanta, where he shot another "MRC," killing Johnny Brookshire and paralyzing Joy Williams. Before leaving town, he read about the obscenity trial of porn king Larry Flynt in Lawrenceville, Georgia, and decided on a detour. Franklin nursed a hatred of Flynt over photos of interracial sex published in *Hustler* magazine. On March 6 he ambushed Flynt and lawyer Gene Reeves near Lawrenceville's courthouse, wounding both men and leaving Flynt a paraplegic. On July 29, in Chattanooga, Franklin shot another interracial couple, killing Bryant Tatum and wounding Nancy Hilton.[124]

Financed by bank holdups, Franklin moved on. In Jackson, Mississippi, on March 25, 1979, he killed Johnnie Noyes, Jr., a black medical student at Jackson State University. On July 12, in Doraville, Georgia, he murdered black restaurant manager Harold McInver for having "close contact with white women." In Falls Church, Virginia, on August 18, Franklin killed another black man, Raymond Taylor, at a fast-food restaurant. On October 21, in Oklahoma City, he murdered interracial lovers Jesse Taylor and Marian Bresette. On December 5, he shot and killed teenage prostitute Mercedes Masters, after she admitted dating black "johns."[125]

Franklin's rampage continued in 1980, with the January 8 sniper slaying of black diner Lawrence Reese at a restaurant in Indianapolis. Eight days later, still in Indianapolis, Franklin shot black victim Leo Watkins through a store window. On May 2 he shot hitchhiking student Rebecca Bergstrom in Monroe County, Wisconsin. Frustrated in his efforts to kill black leader Jesse Jackson, Franklin shot Urban League president Vernon Jordan instead, on May 29, after seeing him with a white woman in Fort Wayne, Indiana. On June 8, in Cincinnati, he murdered black cousins Dante Brown and Darrell Lane. One week later, he killed interracial lovers Arthur Smothers and Kathleen Mikula in Johnstown, Pennsylvania. On June

25 he shot white hitchhikers Vicki Durian and Nancy Santomero in Pocahontas County, West Virginia, after they admitted dating black men. In Salt Lake City, on August 20, Franklin killed black victims Ted Fields and David Martin.[126]

Police in Florence, Kentucky, arrested Franklin on September 25, 1980. He escaped and fled to Florida, where a nurse recognized his tattoos from police bulletins, resulting in his second capture on October 28. In custody, Franklin confessed 21 homicides and sundry other crimes, prompting a myriad of state and federal trials. He pled guilty in some cases and faced juries in others, accumulating four life prison terms and others totaling 70 years. In February 1997 a Missouri judge sentenced Franklin to death for Gerald Gordon's murder. He died by lethal injection in November 2013.[127]

Officially, Franklin remains the most prolific killer Klansman of all time. In 1989 neo-Nazi leader William Pierce published a novel, *Hunter,* depicting what one "exceptional individual" might do to cleanse a nation overrun by blacks and ruled by Jews. Pierce dedicated his work "to Joseph Paul Franklin, the Lone Hunter, who saw his duty as a White man and did what a responsible son of his race must do, to the best of his ability and without regard for the personal consequences."[128]

Justice Deferred

Alabama had a new attorney general in the 1970s. William Baxley was a law student in Tuscaloosa when Klansmen bombed Birmingham's Sixteenth Street Baptist Church, and the memory never left him. Upon taking office in 1971, he reopened that case and the still-solved slaying of Willie Edwards in Montgomery. Edward Fields—now grand dragon of his own New Order Knights—wrote to Baxley from Georgia, branding him "an honorary nigger" and implying threats of death. Responding on official stationery, Baxley wrote: "Dear 'Dr.' Fields: My response to your letter of February 19, 1976, is—kiss my ass."[129]

That same month, state troopers arrested Klansmen Henry Alexander, Sonny Livingston, and James York for the Edwards slaying, based on statements furnished by komrade Raymond Britt under a grant of immunity. Baxley charged the three with murder, despite reported FBI "begging" for Alexander's exemption as a Bureau informer, but Judge Frank Embry quashed the indictments, ruling that "[m]erely forcing a person to jump from a bridge does not naturally and probably lead to the death of such a person."[130]

Frustrated in Montgomery, Baxley turned to Bombingham. He fought another uphill battle with the FBI, which stubbornly refused to share its files until Baxley led parents of the murdered girls to Washington. The breakthrough came, and Baxley charged Robert Chambliss with four counts of murder in September 1977. A separate indictment charged J. B. Stoner with bombing Fred Shuttlesworth's church in 1958. While Stoner fought extradition from Georgia, Grand Dragon Don Black led marches supporting Chambliss. A Birmingham jury convicted Dynamite Bob of one murder—Carole Robertson's—on November 18, 1977. Chambliss received a life sentence and died in prison, still claiming innocence, in October 1985.[131]

Baxley's victory did not suppress Alabama's Klan, and voters punished him for it in 1978's Democratic gubernatorial primary, switching parties to support Guy Hunt and making him the state's first Republican governor since Reconstruction.[132] That September, Lowndes

County's grand jury indicted Gary Rowe for Viola Liuzzo's murder, alleging collaboration with the FBI, but federal attorneys won dismissal of the charge based on Rowe's grant of immunity from 1965.[133] Liuzzo's family sued the Justice Department for negligence in 1979, but Judge Charles Joiner dismissed the case in May and the family's appeal was rejected.[134]

In spring of 1979 a federal grand jury indicted 20 UKA members for shooting up the homes of NAACP members in Talladega County. One prosecution witness suffered a fatal beating in June, the day before his scheduled testimony, but police dismissed the "strange coincidence" as unrelated to the trial. Even without him, three knights pled guilty, while jurors convicted 10 more and dispatched them to prison.[135]

Alabama Klansmen reaped more headlines from the case of Tommy Lee Hinds, a mentally retarded black man unable to sign his own name at age 26, jailed in May 1978 on charges of raping three white women since February. Five thousand persons attended a Klan rally following Hines's arrest; 9,000 gathered for another on Labor Day. His defenders sought a change of venue in September, and marched in protest when it was denied. Jurors convicted Hines on one count, resulting in a 30-year sentence, and more protests ensued.[136] Klansmen responded as usual, claiming credit for the abduction and whipping of a black minister from Georgia who spoke against Hines's conviction at the Cullman courthouse.[137] On May 26, 1979, members of Bill Wilkinson's IEK mobbed black marchers in Decatur, leaving two wounded by gunfire and others beaten. FBI agents investigated the riot, but claimed to find no federal violations.[138] In June, Wilkinson returned with Alabama grand chaplain Bill Riccio, who vowed that "the day a black ape lays his black paw on a little white girl, the Ku Klux Klan will move in and trim that paw back."[139] In August, 176 Klansmen staged a "motorcade march" from Selma to Montgomery, pausing in Lowndes County to spit on the site of Viola Liuzzo's murder, then found themselves jailed in the capital for lack of parade permits.[140]

In November 1980 the SPLC sued Wilkinson's knights on behalf of Bernice Brown, a marcher shot by Klansmen in May 1979. After nine years of litigation, in November 1989, six defendants agreed to pay $10,500 in compensation, quit the Klan for 10 years, and attend a two-hour course on race relations taught by the SCLC. Roger Handley, defiant to the end, told reporters, "I will sit through that course, but I will leave with the same opinion I walk in there with." More tellingly, the SPLC's investigation unearthed evidence that convinced FBI agents to reopen their Decatur inquiry, pressing charges that sent nine knights to prison.[141]

Ballots and Bullets

Politics preoccupied selected Klansmen in 1978. J. B. Stoner sought Georgia's gubernatorial nomination, scheming to abort his extradition on bombing charges, but ran third among six candidates with 37,654 votes out of 695,911 ballots cast.[142] Dale Reusch did better in Ohio's Democratic gubernatorial primary, polling 88,134 votes, but lost out to rival Richard Celeste by 403,390 ballots.[143]

Locked in competition, David Duke and Bill Wilkinson each sought to dominate headlines by visiting England in March 1978. Both were deported, but not before Duke played hide-and-seek with police, posing for a photograph on London Bridge in full regalia. Before departing, Duke claimed meetings with "over 2,000 people in private homes, halls, meeting rooms in pubs, and universities," resulting in formation of several klaverns.[144]

In April 1978 two California knights picked up hitchhiker Juan Mendez-Ruiz, a legal immigrant from Mexico, and stole his passport before delivering him to Border Patrol officers as a "wetback." That stunt sent Klansman Carl Shipton, Jr., to federal prison for a year. Three months later, jurors convicted three of Tony LaRicci's Maryland Knights for plotting to bomb a synagogue and the home of black congressman Parren Mitchell. Gerald Allen and Robert White received eight-year sentences, while Robert Glover got five years suspended and three years' probation.[145]

Mississippi was the Klan's next battleground, with action centering on Tupelo. Trouble began in 1976, when a judge fined two policemen $250 for beating a black prisoner. Incensed by that paltry wrist-slap, blacks across northern Mississippi launched a United League to protest police and Klan brutality. By 1978 the league was boycotting white merchants in Okolona and threatening to take "a life for a life" in Byhalia, where murders of black men averaged one per week. (The killings ceased after that threat.) A demonstration by 400 African Americans in Tupelo, in March 1978, began a cycle of marches that drew Bill Wilkinson's Klansmen like moths to a flame.[146] In May state police seized a flamethrower, machine gun, and hand grenades from Klansmen in Tupelo.[147] By June, FBI agents were investigating Klan threats against journalists and the arrest of a reporter covering a Tupelo Klan rally, but no prosecutions resulted.[148]

Wilkinson's knights failed to halt racial progress in Mississippi, but the IEK gained members as a result, both in the Magnolia State and neighboring Alabama, where new klaverns in 11 towns claimed 1,000 recruits.[149]

Greenkil

Racism seethed in North Carolina during the late 1970s. Harold Covington led NSPA meetings, including joint rallies with local Klan groups and the NSRP. Glenn Miller recalls two that led to brawling, in Rocky Mount and Raleigh. The latter incident found Miller baiting Jews at a bar near North Carolina State University, telling patrons, "Next to the Eskimos and the niggers, the Jews are the ugliest people on Earth. How odd of God to choose the rats." Convicted of attempting to incite a riot, Miller paid a $100 fine.[150]

Matters were more serious elsewhere. On July 8, as Klansmen screened *The Birth of a Nation* at China Grove's community center, members of the Communist Workers Party (CWP) burned a Confederate flag outside. Police averted bloodshed, but the knights vowed revenge. CWP members mounted armed guards in the black community, while Sheriff John Stirewalt—a 1960s Klansman—sought to remain aloof.[151] Sniping remained verbal until November 3, when CWP leaders staged a "Death to the Klan" march in Greensboro. Klansmen and NSPA members turned out in force, disrupting the march with their own motorcade. When protesters swung at the cars with their placards, the knights and Nazis responded with gunfire, killing five marchers and wounding 11 more.[152]

Four separate camera crews filmed the shooting, aiding in solution of the massacre police had failed to prevent. Oddly, while footage showed 40 gunmen involved in the slaughter, only 14 were arrested, with six held for trial in 1980.[153] Virgil Griffin, not indicted, claimed his knights had simply fired into the air, attempting to disperse attackers. Asked how so many victims fell from harmless warning shots, he replied, "Maybe God guided the bullets."[154] Glenn Miller, likewise at liberty, remarked, "I was more proud to have been in Greensboro for 88 seconds in 1979 than 20 years in the U.S. Army. It was the only armed victory over communism in this country."[155] Testimony at the murder trial revealed that FBI informer Edward Dawson had obtained a map of the CWP's parade route from local police, delivering it to the Klan. Another informer—Bernard Butkovich, hired by the ATF—had encouraged NSPA members to stockpile firearms. Klansmen claimed they had been furnished photos of the slain CWP marchers days before the shooting. An all-white jury acquitted the defendants on November 17, 1980.[156]

In the wake of that surprise verdict, FBI agents continued their investigation of the massacre, code-named "Greenkil." In December 1980 U.S. Attorney H. M. Michaux announced plans to file federal civil rights charges against 10 of the Greensboro gunmen. A federal grand jury convened in February 1982, finally indicting nine defendants—Griffin and Dawson included—on conspiracy charges.[157] Another all-white jury acquitted the nine on April 15, 1984. Emerging from court, Griffin told reporters, "Man, I think I died and went to heaven."[158]

Operation Infiltration

From the 1920s onward, Klansmen have proselytized military personnel and tried to infiltrate units with access to weapons and explosives. In November 1976 a brawl between white and black marines exposed a klavern of David Duke's Knights at Camp Pendleton, California. Base commander Major General Carl Hoffman initially denied a Klan presence on base, then announced that its members had been transferred "because their views are not compatible with good race relations." Eight black marines accused of beating suspected Klansmen were freed from the brig in April 1977.[159]

More units of Duke's Klan surfaced on two army bases—Fort Carson, Colorado, and Fort Hood, Texas—in 1979, with no denials issued. Fort Hood's knights wore their military uniforms in June, while guarding Duke and Grand Dragon Louis Beam at a rally in Euless, and also appeared with Duke at a Labor Day rally in New Orleans. Fort Carson's klavern, led by Sergeants Kenneth O'Dell and Josef Stewart, met with fellow knights in Colorado Springs. Meanwhile, at Arizona's Yuma Proving Grounds, a lone soldier was disciplined for printing Klan literature on the base copy machine.[160]

Nor was the U.S. Navy immune. Between June and September 1979, members of the IEK led by Bill Wilkinson—himself a navy veteran—staged incidents on three separate ships. Racial fighting occurred on the supply ship *Concord,* based at Norfolk, Virginia; three robed knights confronted black shipmates aboard the aircraft carrier *Independence,* docked in Greece; and another carrier, the *America,* reported a shipboard cross-burning. Under prodding from the ADL, Admiral Thomas Hayward ordered fleet commanders to prohibit racist activities when they "create a clear danger to the loyalty, discipline or morale or military personnel, or materially interfere with the accomplishment of the military mission." Several *Concord* knights were transferred, and those from the *America* were remanded for court-martial. Four more in Norfolk were also convicted of attending a Klan rally declared off-limits by their commander.[161]

Shock Waves

Military recruitment suggested Klan expansion nationwide, and the ADL confirmed it, estimating 10,000 Klansmen at large in 1979, up from 6,500 in 1975 and 8,000 in 1978. The leap in nonmember supporters was even more dramatic: an estimated 100,000 in 1979, up from 40,000 the previous year. David Duke recruited adolescents, aided by Klansman and NSPA member Karl Hand, with Bill Wilkinson quick to follow suit. Alabama grand dragon Roger Handley welcomed 30 youngsters to the IEK's summer camp in 1979, by which time 13 cities in seven states boasted Klan Youth Corps chapters.[162]

It was not all growth and progress for the Klans, however. Rampant anti–Semitism led to ugly incidents in New Jersey, where Klansmen hanged a rabbi in effigy and vandalized a synagogue, and in Denver, where robed knights picketed a meeting of the Colorado Zionist Federation with placards reading "Zionism=Communism."[163] In May 1979 three members of Duke's Lakeside, California, klavern were convicted of killing Michael Henson, suspected of tipping police to Klan drug sales.[164] Further embarrassment arose in Oklahoma, when Grand Dragon Johnny Clary signed on for a public debate with the state's NAACP leader.

Clary was one of Duke's younger recruits, enlisted at age 14, three years after he witnessed his father's suicide. Raised in a violent, hard-drinking family, he found new purpose after watching Duke on a TV talk show and wrote to Klan headquarters. A kleagle appeared at his home, signed him up, and Clary—already large for his age—joined the Knights as a security officer, quickly rising through the ranks to become a kleagle, then Oklahoma's top Klansman at age 21. He jumped at the chance to debate the Rev. Wade Watts, a friend of Martin Luther King who had marched from Selma to Montgomery in 1965, but the confrontation went badly for Clary. Watts defused his racial epithets with prayers and platitudes, leaving the dragon tongue-tied. Soon afterward, Klansmen torched Watt's church in McAlester. When Clary called to gloat, Watts shamed him with a prayer—"Dear Lord, please, forgive Johnny for being so stupid"—and an invitation to dinner.[165]

David Duke, meanwhile, was easing away from his Klan. He ran for a Louisiana senate seat in 1979, finishing second in a three-person race with 9,897 votes, shifting his sights toward higher political office.[166] That cost money, and it had to come from somewhere. Florida grand dragon Jack Gregory told the *Clearwater Sun,* "David Duke is nothing but a con artist. Our members were pouring in money to the organization, and we never saw any of it. When I asked Duke where our money was going, I was thrown out of the Klan. Yeah, he tells everyone that he doesn't make anything from the Klan—that he's doing it for the cause. But that's the biggest lie there is."[167]

Other leaders of the Knights were equally dissatisfied. Tom Metzger managed Duke's 1979 campaign, concluding that "what he advocated on the surface was not what he practiced in private." Metzger defected that year, founding his own California Knights. The final straw, said Metzger, was a "big surprise" Duke sprang on Klansmen at a rally in Metairie. The curtain rose on stage, revealing Duke clad only in gym shorts, lifting weights to display his physique. "We couldn't believe the egotism," Metzger said. "It was all some people could do to avoid laughing."[168]

Next to go was Karl Hand, a second-generation knight and Duke's second-in-command. In December 1979 Hand wrote Duke a five-page, single-spaced letter of resignation, fairly summarized in one line: "I am tired of seeing you hurt, abuse, use and deceive good white people in the name of the Klan."[169] Two months later, Hand and kleagle Aaron Morrison were charged with shooting up a black family's home in Barnegat, New Jersey. Both pled guilty, along with Hand's stepbrother, before Hand went on the lam, attempting suicide by drinking antifreeze. He survived to receive a six-month jail term, with three months suspended, in April 1981.[170]

In early 1980, Klan-watchers pegged Duke's membership around 1,000 to 1,200.[171] Many Alabama knights switched allegiance to the IEK because, as spokesman Willard Oliver explained, "Duke is a man of words, and we need a man of action. We need a leader who will get out in the streets with us." James Warner jumped ship at the same time, complaining, "People attracted to the Klan were just nigger haters. They were not intelligent and could not be educated to anything other than nigger hating. They had no grasp on Jews and could not be made to grasp it."[172]

On December 20, 1979, Duke incorporated a "new" organization—the National Association for the Advancement of White People (NAAWP)—whose name he lifted from five prior racist groups of the 1950s. In January 1980 he phoned Bill Wilkinson, seeking to discuss a matter "mutually profitable for both of us," as Wilkinson recalls. They met in Manchac, Louisiana, where Duke pitched his deal: for $65,000 he would sell Wilkinson his membership list, with a promise to abstain from Klan affairs for a decade. Wilkinson stalled for seven months, then agreed to pay $35,000. He met Duke again, this time in Cullman, Alabama, on July 20. Unknown to Duke, Wilkinson brought along reporters, who secretly videotaped the meeting, complete with Duke's endorsement of Wilkinson as "clearly the most effective and capable leader of the Ku Klux Klan." The upshot: a humiliating scandal and no cash in hand.[173]

Forced to resign, Duke named Don Black as his successor and withdrew—at least, in theory—to tend the fledgling NAAWP. In parting, he declared, "I want to leave no one with the impression that the Klan is a hopeless cause, or that I think it is essentially a negative force in America. The Klan is growing and improving all the time. Men like Louis Beam, Don Black, Chuck Bushong and many others are some of the very finest men America possesses. Additionally, I will never publicly denigrate the Ku Klux Klan, or its legitimate leaders. The last eight years in which I had various leadership roles in the Klan were the most fulfilling and exciting of my life. I want to wish Don Black and all Klanspeople the best of luck, and thank them for all their support in this sacred cause."[174]

Wilkinson's enjoyment of the Duke sting operation was short lived. Various members of his Klan had found themselves in court since January, when jurors convicted Clarence Brown of threatening Vietnamese fishermen in Alabama. The same month saw Klansmen Ricky Creekmore and Charles Puckett sentenced to a year each for assaulting black diners at a Muscle Shoals restaurant. In March, Duon Hogeland raided an interracial couple's home in Hayden, Alabama, receiving a six-month sentence and five years' probation. In April, IEK members Danny Foskey and Herschel Hall shot a nine-year-old black girl in Wrightsville, Georgia. Jurors convicted Hall of misdemeanor "reckless conduct." In September 1980 federal agents charged Illinois grand dragon James McKinney and Klansman Robert Hansen with stealing guns, explosives, and other items in burglaries spanning seven counties. McKinney received two three-year sentences, while Hansen got six months and paid a $1,000 fine.[175]

The worst was yet to come for Wilkinson. In August 1980 the Nashville *Tennessean* revealed that he had been an FBI informer since 1974. Wilkinson grudgingly confessed, insisting that he took no cash or favors from the feds, and that he only gave them "basic information," such as time and place of public rallies.[176] True or not, it was a grievous blow to Wilkinson's prestige. One thousand people still turned out to hear him in September, in Connecticut, but that number dropped by half for his next northern foray, to Pennsylvania in October. Nationwide, the *Tennessean* revelations sent IEK membership into a tailspin.[177]

Tom Metzger seemed to have the most luck after leaving Duke's order. His California Knights were active enough to spark counter protests by a new opposition group, People Against Racism, and Metzger also made the first Klan overture to youthful neo–Nazi "skinheads," offering guidance to Greg Withrow's White Student Union, later renamed the Aryan Youth Movement.[178] In June 1980 Metzger ran for Congress, stunning Democrats when he won their primary with 33,071 votes—37.1 percent of all ballots cast. November's election was something else, though, as Republican incumbent Clair Burgener claimed 298,815 votes to Metzger's 46,361.[179] Metzger claims to have survived the first of three assassination attempts during that campaign, then left the Klan before year's end to lead a new White American Political Association, subsequently renamed White Aryan Resistance.[180]

Blood and Thunder

Tom Metzger strikes a typically inflammatory pose (author's collection, date unknown).

Other Klans continued on their not-so-merry way in 1980. In Georgia, Edward Fields recruited Frank Shirley—an alumnus of Duke's Knights and an NAAWP member—as a national officer of the New Order Knights.[181] NSPA leader Harold Covington surprised the media in May, when he polled 56,017 votes—43.69 percent of the total—in a losing race to become North Carolina's attorney general.[182] Glenn Miller called that result "a fluke," claiming 98 percent of Covington's votes came from confused Republicans mistaking winner Keith Snyder for the Nazi candidate. Miller left the NSPA in December, founding the Carolina Knights of the Ku Klux Klan. From two dozen knights at the outset, he boosted membership to 150 by spring 1981, inviting Fields to address their first rally and adopting *The Thunderbolt* as his Klan's "official" publication. Backed by second-in-command Stephen Miller (no relation), Glenn declared that he "did not want to lead a small group of men in burning crosses and assaulting interracial couples or committing other illegal acts.... I must admit, however, that I never objected when other groups did, and was pleased when hearing they had."[183]

One group that pleased him was the Justice Knights of Tennessee. In April 1980 three members lit a cross in Chattanooga, then wounded four elderly black women in random drive-by shootings. Jurors acquitted Imperial Wizard Lyndon Church and another knight of attempted murder; Marshall Thrash, convicted on lesser charges, served one-third of a nine-month sentence. Other jurors were less lenient with the leaders of another local Klan. Caught with explosives in July 1980, Imperial Wizard Rocky Coker and Imperial Titan Larry Owens were sentenced to prison.[184] April's shooting victims, dissatisfied with Chattanooga justice, filed a civil suit against the Justice Knights, winning $535,000 in February 1982.[185]

West Virginia Klansmen launched a six-month reign of terror against the Rev. Michael Curry and his wife in June 1980, displeased by Curry's "liberal" stance on race. The couple fled their native state in January 1981, for a safe parish in Massachusetts.[186] In Muncie, Indiana, Klansmen Clifford and Samuel Redwine objected to a black family sharing their neighborhood. From stoning the house, they advanced to arson in June 1980, Clifford boasting afterward that he had "killed eight niggers." In fact, the family of six was safe, but loose lips sent the Redwines to federal prison with fellow Klansman Clifford Strong.[187] Farther north, in Detroit, five Klansmen fired shots at a black man in August 1980. Informed that they had missed him, they returned to shoot up his home.[188]

In the wake of the Greensboro acquittals, several previously hostile racist groups took their first halting steps toward unification. "Pastor Bob" Miles led the way, preaching his own brand of dualist Christian Identity, welcoming Klansmen, neo–Nazis, and members of the tax-loathing Posse Comitatus to his Mountain Church in Cohoctah, Michigan. Widely described as a "klanarchist," Miles endorsed the "Northwest Territorial Imperative," delineating the Pacific Northwest as a "White American Bastion" purged of minorities.[189]

Southern Strategies

Presidential politics loomed large in 1980. David Duke waged a halfhearted campaign for the Democratic nomination, then realized the Constitution barred him from the White House at age 30 and withdrew, complaining of "minimum entry age laws specifically designed to keep me off the ballot."[190] The Klan's best hope lay with Ronald Reagan, who pursued the Republican "Southern strategy" premiered by Richard Nixon 12 years earlier. As Reagan strategist Lee Atwater explained: "You start out in 1954 by saying, 'Nigger, nigger, nigger.' By 1968 you can't say 'nigger'—that hurts you. Backfires. So you say stuff like forced busing, states' rights and all that stuff. You're getting so abstract now you're talking about cutting taxes, and all these things you're talking about are totally economic things and a byproduct of them is blacks get hurt worse than whites. And subconsciously maybe that is part of it. I'm not saying that. But I'm saying that if it is getting that abstract, and that coded, that we are doing away with the racial problem one way or the other. You follow me? Because obviously sitting around saying, 'We want to cut this,' is much more abstract than even the busing thing, and a hell of a lot more abstract than 'Nigger, nigger.'"[191]

Klansmen got the message when Reagan delivered his first campaign speech in Tuscumbia, Alabama, headquarters of Don Black's Knights, then moved on to Mississippi's Neshoba County Fair, near the site of 1964's most notorious Klan murders. His "states' rights" speech won the Klan's endorsement, including a comment in the *Crusader* that the GOP's platform "reads as if it were written by a Klansman."[192] The result, given incumbent Jimmy Carter's troubled term, was probably inevitable. Reagan triumphed by a margin of 8.4 million votes, while John Rarick, bearing the AIP's standard, ran fifth in a field of eight third-party hopefuls.[193] No one outside Ohio noticed Dale Reusch's third failed bid to become Medina County's sheriff.[194]

In Georgia, J. B. Stoner lost another Senate race, proceeding to trial in May on church-bombing charges. Jurors convicted him on May 14, and Alabama's Supreme Court upheld that verdict in August 1982. Free on bond, Stoner fled into hiding but surrendered to begin serving his 10-year sentence on June 2, 1983.[195]

With Stoner otherwise engaged, the NSRP invited four Belgian neo–Nazis to Georgia in October 1980, but ADL protests to the State Department abbreviated their visit.[196] A month later, New Jersey police arrested James Slater with a cache of weapons and Klan paraphernalia. November also saw three Michigan Klansmen imprisoned for attempting to kill a black man who drank at a "white" saloon.[197]

New Decade, Old Tactics

Klansmen showed no inclination to mellow in 1981. Hoosier knights Philip Beach and Randall Sanders vandalized an Evansville synagogue in February, repeating the stunt at a Jewish cemetery in March. At trial in June, they were sentenced to pay the $5,000 cleanup bill.[198] Also in February 1981, police charged two Klansmen with kidnapping after they snatched suspected turncoat William Seward, covered him with yellow paint and feathers, then tossed him from a moving car.[199]

Mischief turned deadly in Alabama, where UKA titan Bennie Hays fumed over a black cop-killer's mistrial in Mobile. "If a black man can get away with killing a white man," Hays said, "we ought to be able to get away with killing a black man." Acting on his father's words in March 1981, Henry Hays and Klansman James Knowles chose 19-year-old Michael Donald at random, strangled him, cut his throat, and left his body hanging from a tree across the street from Hays's home. Police initially dismissed the lynching as a drug-related murder, until local activists pressured the FBI to investigate. Agents cracked the case in June 1983, arresting the killers, accomplice Benjamin Cox, Jr., and Bennie Hays. Knowles turned state's evidence, accepted a life sentence, and testified against Henry Hays, sending him to death row, where he was executed in June 1997. Cox also received a life term, while Bennie Hays escaped after a fashion. Granted a mistrial due to poor health in February 1988, he died before a new trial could convene.[200]

The story might have ended there, but Donald's mother pursued the Klan in civil court, aided by Morris Dees and the SPLC. Evidence against the UKA included James Knowles's testimony that Donald was killed "to show Klan strength in Alabama," and a cartoon from *The Fiery Cross,* depicting a black man with a noose around his neck and the caption "White people should give Blacks what they deserve." In February 1987 jurors ruled against the

UKA, ordering Robert Shelton's Klan to pay Beulah Donald $7 million. Unable to foot the bill, Shelton surrendered his Tuscaloosa headquarters, valued at $225,000, and effectively went out of business.[201]

Other knights ignored that message from the courts. In April 1981 jurors convicted New Jersey Klansmen of firing on a black family's home in Toms River.[202] A month later, ATF agents staged raids in Maryland, New Jersey, Delaware and Pennsylvania, arresting 10 knights on weapons charges and for conspiring to firebomb the NAACP's Baltimore office. Charles Sickles, leader of the Adamic Knights, was one of four knights indicted in June, receiving a five-year sentence in October 1981. Richard Savina, charged in the Baltimore plot, got 15 years.[203]

May also exposed a plot in Tennessee, where members of the Confederate Vigilante Knights planned to bomb a Nashville synagogue, television tower, and several pawnshops owned by Jews. The temple bomb backfired on the conspirators, landing six in federal custody. Jurors convicted two of the plotters, Gladys Girgenti and Bobby Joe Norton, sending them to prison for 15 and five years, respectively.[204]

In Texas, Louis Beam's knights fixed their sights on Vietnamese fishermen in 1981, harassing them with cross-burning, threats, and armed flotillas of Klansmen who shadowed their targets at sea. In April, aided by the SPLC, the Vietnamese Fishermen's Association sued Beam and company in federal court, winning a permanent injunction against further interference with their livelihood, plus an order closing Beam's paramilitary training camps in June 1982.[205] Beam reacted by challenging Morris Dees to a duel. He wrote:

> If you are the despicable, low-down, vile poltroon I think you are, you will of course decline, in which case my original supposition will have been proven correct and your lack of character verified. If, on the other hand, you agree to meet me, you will raise immeasurably the esteem others hold you in. Imagine: acquaintances, associates, supporters, friends, family—your mother— think of her; why I can just see her now, her heart bursting with pride as you, for the first time in your life, exhibit the qualities of a man and march off to the field of honor. (Every mother has the right to be proud of her son once.) You will be worse than a coward if you deny her this most basic of rights. Think of her. In closing, let me make it clear that I believe you so base a coward that you will be too timid to even place a pen in hand to answer this letter, for I know a craven anti–Christ Jew when I have seen him. Here's your chance to prove me wrong.[206]

"Operation Red Dog"

One of the more bizarre events in Ku Klux history occurred on April 27, 1981, when ATF agents in Louisiana arrested Don Black and eight other men on charges of conspiracy to violate U.S. neutrality laws by invading the Caribbean island nation of Dominica. Jailed with Black were American knights Danny Joe Hawkins and Mike Perdue, Canadian Klansmen James McQuirter and Wolfgang Droege, and Barbadian gunrunner Sydney Burnett-Alleyne. Nabbed before they could set sail, the group was caught with a cache of guns and explosives, plus a large Nazi flag. Their plan, according to the seven plotters who pled guilty, was to topple the regime of Prime Minister Eugenia Charles and return deposed predecessor Patrick John to office. John, a collaborator in the plot, was expected to grant his white allies sweeping power, including the right to own slaves.[207]

As pieced together by investigators, Droege initially proposed the invasion—targeting

Weapons and other items seized by ATF agents from Klansmen who planned to invade Dominica, ca. 1981 (National Archives).

Grenada, rather than Dominica—to David Duke in 1979. Duke arranged for $10,000 financing, then dropped out of the plot in 1980, by which time the goal had shifted. Canadian mafioso Charles Yanover bought into the scheme, envisioning Dominica as a gambling Mecca and drug transshipment point. The original ship captain chosen by Duke got cold feet, and his replacement tipped the ATF in time to make their April raid.[208]

Don Black's participation in the far-fetched scheme may have been sparked by his embarrassing electoral defeat in 1979. Campaigning to become Birmingham's mayor, he polled a paltry 2.5 percent of the vote, losing out to black candidate Richard Arrington, Jr.[209] In the wake of that humiliation, ruling a Caribbean island may have seemed irresistible. Sydney Burnett-Alleyne agreed to seating John as a figurehead ruler, but admitted "that was not the real reason behind my plan of action. I wanted to add the landmass of Dominica to that of Barbados and also to be able to undertake an industrial project of considerable size. South African resources, millions of dollars, were available to me to be used for such a project."[210]

In fact, John was arrested *before* the abortive invasion, later sentenced to 12 years in prison. Rational men might have scuttled their plan at that point, but Black's raiders forged ahead to their sorrow. While most of the frustrated warriors pled guilty, Black and Hawkins faced a jury that convicted them in June 1981, dispatching them to prison for three years. Prosecution of Droege and McQuirter left Droege's girlfriend in charge of the Canadian Klan, withered to a shadow of its former self when he was finally released in 1983.[211]

Don Black kept busy while appealing his conviction, planning a "Block Amnesty for Illegal Aliens" march on Washington, D.C., in March 1982, attending an Aryan Nations Congress with Louis Beam in July 1982, accepting leadership of a new Confederation of Klans in September, at a Stone Mountain rally hosted by James Venable. Also in attendance at that gathering were Edward Fields, Robert Miles, and "ex"–Klansman David Duke. Two months after his coronation, Black entered federal prison.[212]

Turbulent Empires

If Operation Red Dog prompted derision from critics, Klansmen still took themselves seriously. Bill Wilkinson brought his IEK to Connecticut in March 1981, founding one of the group's most active realms under Grand Dragon James Farrands, a Roman Catholic who opened Klan ranks to his coreligionists.[213] In Colorado, David Lane ran afoul of rival Fred Wilkins for distributing Nazi literature. As Wilkins told it, "I ran him out of the Klan because I didn't like his way of doing things."[214] Lane found a new home with the Aryan Nations, first as the group's Colorado organizer, then moved to Idaho as its "propaganda minister."[215]

More traditional Klansmen were marching in Georgia, around Cedartown, outraged by employment of Mexican immigrants at the Zartic Frozen Food plant. Edward Fields led his New Order Knights in protest, organizing angry Zartic workers—including some blacks—into a Klan-led "American Labor Union" that joined robed knights on the picket line, demanding ouster of "illegals."[216] Violence followed, including homicides of two Mexican workers. Jurors accepted self-defense pleas from white gunmen in both cases, in courtrooms packed with spectators wearing Klan insignia, and a prosecution witness from one trial died when arsonists torched his home.[217]

Alabama Klansmen not immersed in lynching or invasion plans expressed themselves in other ways, attempting to bomb Birmingham's Galilee Baptist Church in October 1980, shooting up a Tuscaloosa family's home in February 1981, and stabbing three black men in Talladega 10 months later.[218] Three Arizona knights plotted to kidnap one Klansman's children—removed from his custody by court order—but the plan sent them to prison.[219] Even the year's most notorious serial killings—the so-called Atlanta "child murders"—smacked of Klan involvement. Prosecutors convicted black defendant Wayne Williams of murdering two adult males, then "cleared" the slayings of 22 minors by blaming them on Williams without formal charges. Evidence collected (and suppressed) by the Georgia Bureau of Investigation linked a Klan/NSRP family to one of the killings blamed on Williams, and police chief Louis Graham reopened four of the "solved" cases in 2005, declaring that he never believed Williams guilty.[220]

Proving that there is no such thing as bad publicity for an extremist group, the Klans increased their membership to 13,000 during 1981, according to the ADL.[221] Bill Wilkinson claimed 2,500 of that total for his IEK, declaring that "we are the Klan today," but outside observers shaved a thousand members from his estimate.[222] Future leaders on the rise included Dennis Mahon, a Florida mechanic for Eastern Airlines who joined Duke's Knights in 1980, and Charles Howarth, a Colorado Posse Comitatus member who switched allegiance to the UKA after his May 1982 arrest for selling pipe bombs to undercover officers. Howarth pled guilty on one count in February 1983 and received a two-year prison term.[223]

Mississippi produced the first Klan headlines of 1982, when two members of the Mississippi Independent Knights, shot up the *Jackson Advocate*'s newspaper office.[224] Seven months later, Meridian police found teenager Beverly Parnell murdered in an abandoned warehouse, with "KKK" painted on the floor beside her corpse.[225] Between those crimes, in February, California klavern leader Michael Mendosa received a six-year sentence for firing at residents of a Richmond housing project.[226] In March, during a spate of cross-burnings, Baltimore police jailed two knights for pulling knives on black men in a tavern.[227]

North Carolina's knights confused Klan watchers in 1982. The SPLC counted 350 Klansmen statewide, while the ADL reported 750 collaborating with another 250 NSPA and NSRP members.[228] Glenn Miller hosted an April "Hitlerfest" in Benson, with David Duke, Don Black, Edward Fields and Robert Miles among the featured speakers.[229] That same month, Klansman William Moose shot a black motorist for driving too slowly in Draper. He received a death sentence, later commuted to life imprisonment, and was paroled in 2007.[230] Miller found himself "embarrassed" by a rally of Virgil Griffin's Christian Knights, with its sickly 12-foot fiery cross, and was amused when rival Joe Grady's White Knights of Liberty stole Griffin's Cadillac, smashing it in a car crusher. When not leading rallies, Miller organized a "special forces" arm of his Carolina Knights and pressured Johnston County's superintendent of education to move Miller's son from a "black-infested" school to a campus Miller deemed safer.[231]

Tom Metzger took another fling at politics in June 1982, entering California's Democratic senatorial primary. He ran fifth in a field of 11, but still logged 76,502 votes running as an avowed "Aryan" candidate. Moving on from there to television, he launched *Race and Reason* as a public access program, eventually airing in 13 states.[232] Another California knight, Fontana bus driver George Pepper, lost his bid to become the city's mayor.[233] In Florida's Palm Beach County, commissioner Dennis Koehler angrily rejected Klan endorsements of his congressional candidacy, but lost nonetheless.[234] Glenn Miller pursued a state senate seat, urging supporters to "Vote White," and polled 26 percent of the vote in a two-man race. Afterward, he frankly admitted that "75 percent of that 26 percent didn't realize they were voting for a Klansman, and wouldn't if they had."[235]

Klansmen remained immersed in violence through year's end. Police in Knoxville, Tennessee, accused UKA members of burning a black family's home in July.[236] Bill Wilkinson's knights scuffled with protesters in Jacksonville, Florida, and Wilkinson suffered a shower of eggs at a Boston rally, in October.[237] Georgia Klansmen whipped white Waco resident Peggy French for dating black men in November 1982, eluding justice until three were identified and convicted in 1984.[238] DeKalb County officers arrested Donald Terbeck in December, for firing at black restaurant patrons and wounding one. Terbeck denied Klan membership, but had previously passed out Ku Klux "calling cards" at the same diner and chose James Venable as his lawyer.[239]

CHAPTER 10

At War with "ZOG" (1983–1995)

Nineteen eighty-three began with more grim headlines for the Klan. Bill Wilkinson's IEK filed for bankruptcy in January, claiming $14,800 in assets versus liabilities of $42,019.74 and an overdue tax bill of $8,915.76.[1] That same month, Joe Grady and 14 of his knights tried to "bail out" a black rape suspect in Statesville, North Carolina, but the prisoner declined their generosity.[2] Grady escaped jail time, but Virgil Griffin drew a six-month sentence for burning a cross on private property. Prosecutors noted that Griffin had targeted the wrong address, and a sympathetic judge allowed him work release each day.[3] Cross-burnings and drive-by shootings kept black residents of Iredell and Alexander Counties in a state of fear.[4]

On February 9, 1983, masked Klansmen invaded an interracial couple's home in Tallapoosa, Georgia, leaving victim Warren Cokely with a fractured skull. FBI agents arrested five suspects in August 1984, linking two with Peggy French's 1982 flogging. Three months later, jurors convicted three Klansmen of civil rights violations and a fourth for perjury.[5] In April 1983, James Venable's National Knights, led by king kleagle Daniel Emery, joined a gay-bashing pastor's attempt to purge books with homosexual themes from a library in Kalamazoo, Michigan. The Rev. Vivian Varner welcomed Emery and 13 neo–Nazis to an abortive rally in May, before Emery was jailed for armed harassment of a Sturgis resident.[6]

J. B. Stoner's imprisonment left a power vacuum at NSRP headquarters, with leadership first devolving to R. B. Montgomery, then to Eugene Wilson.[7] Edward Fields, preoccupied with his New Order Knights, found himself expelled from the party in August, but salvaged control of *The Thunderbolt*. Membership plummeted, while Fields joined Stoner in a lawsuit to recover the party's assets, including Stoner's home.[8]

Counterattack

On July 28, 1983, Klansmen torched SPLC headquarters in Montgomery, Alabama. Morris Dees offered a $25,000 reward for capture of the arsonists, and FBI agents subsequently arrested three members of Don Black's Knights. Defendants Charles Bailey, Roy Downs, Jr., and Joe Garner pled guilty to federal charges on February 20, 1985, and were sentenced to prison, failures in their effort to derail pending anti–Klan lawsuits.[9]

One who rued that failure was Glenn Miller, named with his Carolina Knights as a defendant in October 1983, when Dees and company took the case of Bobby Person, a black prison guard whom Miller's knights had terrorized since May. The case would not reach court until 1986, when Miller found himself jailed for contempt after violating an injunction against paramilitary training sessions. It was, Miller later wrote, "the beginning of my downfall."[10] Miller suffered a personal loss in November 1983, when one of his klavern leaders murdered another after a rally in Siler City. The victim, David Wallace, had been one of Miller's earliest recruits and closest friends.[11]

James Venable hosted another Stone Mountain unity rally in September 1983, led by Thom Robb, but unity remained evasive.[12] Two months later, Southern California Klansmen boasted of beheading undocumented aliens. Spokesmen for the civil rights group Hermandad Mexicana Nacional took the claim seriously, noting several recent disappearances of migrant workers, but no bodies surfaced.[13] That same month, "ex"–Klansman Tom Metzger joined 20 knights to burn three crosses in Kagel Canyon, while hoisting their arms in Nazi salutes.[14] Texan Louis Beam graced Idaho's Aryan World Congress in 1983, sharing the rostrum with Robert Miles and Ralph Forbes of Arkansas, a former captain of the American Nazi Party.[15] Beam told his audience, "I didn't come here for your applause. I came here for your blood.... The old period is over and a new period is going to begin.... I'm here to tell you that if we can't have this country, as far as I'm concerned, no one gets it. The guns are cocked, the bullets are in the chamber.... We're going to fight and live or we're going to die soon. If you don't help me kill the bastards, you're going to be required to beg for your child's life, and the answer will be 'No.'"[16]

Rumors of War

Klansmen were listening to Beam and others as they called for war. In December 1983 the *Inter-Klan Newsletter & Survival Alert,* published from Aryan Nations headquarters in Idaho, carried a Ku Klux "declaration of independence" that read:

> When in the course of human events it becomes obvious to a people governed that their government is not ruling in their interest or behalf and is, in fact, carrying on in a manner opposed to and inimical to the expressed will of the people; when, in addition, a long train of abuse, injury, mistreatment, damage, and harm has been endured with patience and hope of relief through normal means and procedures to no avail; when to all intents and purposes whether by act, deed, legislation, or fiat a government seems bent on the destruction of the people, culture, heritage, folkways, and Christian faith of those who brought it into being, then it becomes the right and the sacred duty of the governed to dissolve their creation and form a new instrument to safeguard their rights, liberties, property, and culture.
>
> Therefore, we as descendants of the Founding Fathers and in accordance with their will and intent do hereby declare our independence of and separation from the despotism, tyranny, dictatorship, and oppression commonly referred to as the Federal Government. We hereby state our intent to return to the law of our fathers and of our God, Jesus the Christ. We declare that we owe no allegiance of any kind in fee or simple to the anti–God, alien-dominated, unconstitutional, illegal, Washington regime of usurpers, criminals, heathens, infidels, malefactors [*sic*], sodomites, culprits, and evildoers. We hereby state our intent and purpose to establish a new means of self-government as deemed necessary by ourselves in accordance with God's Laws, the Declaration of Independence of our forefathers, the Constitution of the United States, English

Common Law, and the rights of free men as granted in the Magna Carta and traditions of the Anglo-Saxon Race.

In all this, requesting and seeking the aid and help of our God Jesus the Christ in this the year of our Lord, Nineteen Hundred Eighty-three, the month of December, the third day. In the name of God. Amen.[17]

Two months before that declaration went to press, another group had taken steps to launch the war on "ZOG"—the neo–Nazi anagram for Washington's "Zionist Occupation Government." Ringleader Robert Jay Mathews had found his way from the John Birch Society to the Aryan Nations and National Alliance, receiving a standing ovation for his speech at the latter group's September 1983 convention in Virginia. Inspired by leader William Pierce's futuristic novel of Aryan revolution, *The Turner Diaries,* in October Mathews invited hand-picked friends to his home in Metalline Falls, Washington, to form a group known alternately as The Order and the *Brüder Schweigen* (Silent Brotherhood).[18] Charter members included past of present Klansmen David Lane, Thomas Martinez and Frank Silva; Richard Kemp and Bill Soderquist from the National Alliance; Thomas Bentley, Randolph Duey, Bruce Pierce and Gary Yarbrough from Richard Butler's Aryan Nations; with David Tate, Jackie Norton, Randall Rader and Jean Craig (mother of Mathews's pregnant girlfriend) from James Ellison's Arkansas-based Covenant, Sword, and Arm of the Lord (CSA). Later recruits included Richard Scutari, Andrew Barnhill, Ardie McBrearty, Kenneth Loff, and Denver Parmenter.[19]

Following the blueprint of *The Turner Diaries,* Mathews and company set out to finance their war via robbery and counterfeiting. The first heist, at a porn shop in Seattle, netted a disappointing $369. Fake 50-dollar bills printed at Aryan Nations headquarters proved no more successful, sending Bruce Pierce to jail in December. Two weeks later, Mathews pulled a solo bank holdup in Seattle, bagging $25,952. Next, Yarbrough and Pierce (free on bail) robbed an Idaho truck stop and stole $10,000 worth of electronics equipment from stores in Spokane. A January bank heist in Spokane collected $3,600, of which Mathews donated $100 to Richard Butler and $200 to Robert Miles. In March, Mathews led a four-man team that stole $43,345 from an armored truck in Seattle. Pierce pled guilty to federal counter-feiting charges in April 1984, expecting probation, but received a two-year prison term instead. Begging time to put his affairs in order, he was granted three weeks and skipped bail.[20]

On April 23 seven gunmen escaped with $230,379 from an armored car heist in Seattle. Mathews sent $40,000 to Butler, kept $85,000 to fund future operations, and divided the rest with his team. To celebrate, Pierce and Kemp firebombed a Boise, Idaho, synagogue six days later. The Order committed its first murder on May 27, silencing a loose-lipped Aryan Nations member in Idaho. Next they turned on "Jew rabble-rouser" Alan Berg, machine-gunning the radio host at his Denver home on June 18. On July 16, guided by tips from a National Alliance member employed by the Brink's security company, raiders stole $3.6 million from an armored truck near Ukiah, California. In the process, Mathews dropped a pistol registered to Andrew Barnhill, thus giving FBI agents their first clue that The Order existed.[21]

As before, Mathews dispersed large chunks of loot to fellow "Aryans," including Richard Butler, Robert Miles, Tom Metzger, William Pierce, Louis Beam, and Dan Gayman. Glenn Miller gratefully received $200,000 for his Carolina Knights, later describing Mathews as "an awesome man ... in the class with Hitler, Rommel, Stonewall Jackson, and Nathan Forest." Months later, Miller asked his second-in-command to ferry David Lane from North Carolina to Idaho, but federal heat aborted the mission.[22]

While Mathews charmed high-ranking racists, FBI agents pursued Andrew Barnhill, raiding his last known address in August 1984. They missed Barnhill but found a list of seven Order members, complete with phone numbers. In October, Thomas Martinez—facing trial for a June 1984 counterfeiting arrest—approached the FBI and agreed to serve as a double-agent within The Order. His first gift to Bureau handlers was a list of "Brüders Schweigen Staff" dividing the United States into six regions with provisional commanders: Robert Miles got the Midwest, Louis Beam took the West, Tom Metzger claimed California, Denver Parmenter had the Pacific Northwest, William Pierce got the Northeast, while Glenn Miller took Dixie. Agents nearly caught Yarbrough in October 1984, but he shot his way clear of the trap. Martinez laid another in Portland, Oregon, the following month, and while G-men bagged Yarbrough, Mathews escaped.[23] That near-miss inspired a formal declaration of war that read:

> We, the following, being of sound mind and under no duress, do hereby sign this document of our own free will, stating forthrightly and without fear that we declare ourselves to be in full and unrelenting state of war with those forces seeking and consciously promoting the destruction of our faith and our race. Therefore, for Blood, Soil, and Honor, for the future of our children, and for our King, Jesus Christ, we commit ourselves to Battle. Amen.[24]

Mathews signed the document, along with Duey, Scutari, Silva, Bruce Pierce, plus Klansmen Mark Jones and Michael Norris, new recruits Robert and Sharon Merki, and their son Ian Stewart. Instead of launching new offensives, though, the warriors went into hiding. Mathews, Duey and the Merkis fled to a bunker on Whidbey Island, in Puget Sound, while others scattered nationwide. FBI agents stormed Whidbey Island on December 7, 1984, killing Mathews and arresting his companions. Agents nabbed David Lane in March 1985, in Winston-Salem, North Carolina. Davie Tate, en route to Arkansas, shot two Missouri policemen on April 15. Feds captured Silva at an Arkansas campground the same day, then routed Tate from the CSA's compound five days later. James Ellison and seven CSA members later pled guilty to manufacturing illegal weapons; jurors convicted additional members on bombing and auto theft charges.[25]

In April 1985 federal prosecutors charged Order members with racketeering, conspiracy, and transporting stolen cash across state lines. Richard Scutari, the last man standing, eluded capture until March 1986, by which time his comrades were all in prison. Guilty pleas on state charges brought 13 Order associates sentences ranging from five to 20 years, while a Missouri judge handed David Tate a life sentence for murder. With nine others, Tate faced federal charges before year's end, all 10 convicted on December 30, 1985, drawing sentences from five to 60 years. Scutari pled guilty to the Ukiah holdup, receiving a 60-year sentence in June 1986. In November 1987 Tate and Bruce Pierce stood trial again, for violating Alan Berg's civil rights, receiving twin 150-year sentences. Jurors in that trial acquitted David Lane and Jean Craig.[26] While those cases wound through the courts, Alabama Klansman Bill Riccio was briefly detained in Birmingham, after claiming that Robert Mathews had approached him with plans to kill Morris Dees. Riccio demurred, he said, fearing that Mathews was an FBI informer.[27]

Business as Usual

Most Klansmen stopped short of overt rebellion in the 1980s, but they could not shed their addiction to violence of word and deed. In December 1983, Commonwealth Edison of Chicago dismissed employee Robert Schloneger from his post as a control panel operator at one of the company's nuclear plants, after he told the *Arlington Heights Herald,* "The bombs have to fall in 1984. If they don't, within 10 years I'm going to take a gun and start shooting people." CommEd spokesmen said psychological tests had proved Schloneger "mentally sound," and stressed that he was not fired for serving as "arch dragon" of Lake County's Order of the Fiery Cross.[28]

February 1984 found Colorado Klansman Fred Wilkins in court, sued by a black family for the "emotional horror" they suffered after renting a townhouse near his in 1980. Wilkins settled the case for $40,000.[29] Two months later, black teenager Timothy Carey rode his bicycle past a group of New Order Knights in Cedartown, Georgia. Klansman Randall Smith sprayed Carey with Mace and pummeled him with brass knuckles. Smith pled guilty to battery, then threatened Carey after his sentencing hearing. Carey filed suit against Smith and two other knights on conspiracy charges. Jurors in that case dismissed the most serious counts but awarded Carey $1,000 for "verbal assault."[30]

Elsewhere in Georgia, during May 1984, police charged Edward Fields with burglarizing NSRP headquarters, removing confidential files and office equipment worth $5,000. R. B. Montgomery also accused Fields of assault, claiming he brandished a pistol and threatened Montgomery's life. While those charges, and countersuits filed by Fields, were subsequently dismissed, they stymied expansion by his New Order Knights.[31]

In July 1983 the SPLC's latest anti–Klan lawsuit—spawned by riotous events in Decatur, Alabama, four years earlier—revealed evidence of conspiracy by Grand Dragon Roger Handley and his knights. Carlotta Berryhill, a former klavern officer from Huntsville, described a meeting convened by Handley before the melee, directing Klansmen to Decatur and warning them, "Whatever you do, don't ever say we weren't going to let the niggers march because we would be violating their civil rights."[32] FBI agents renewed their investigation, arresting Handley, Bill Riccio, and eight other knights in May 1984. Legal proceedings dragged on into 1989: nine Klansmen ultimately pled guilty to misdemeanor charges, serving short jail terms, while jurors convicted the tenth.[33] Bill Wilkinson announced his resignation from the IEK in September 1984, ceding his wizard's robe to Alabama grand dragon James Blair.[34]

Glenn Miller kept busy in 1984, gloating when North Carolinians Against Racist and Religious Violence claimed their state had the country's fastest-growing Klan population. In May, Miller sought the Democratic gubernatorial nomination, placing eighth in a field of 10 candidates with 5,790 votes. In October he renamed his Klan the Confederate Knights, planting "at least one den" in Tennessee, Georgia, Virginia, and South Carolina. The Palmetto State proved disappointing, convincing Miller that "there is a big difference between the two populations of white people," but he scored a coup of sorts by bringing the Klan back to Robeson County, with a rally held on November 20. Hours before that event, drive-by gunmen peppered Miller's home with buckshot, narrowly missing two of his children. In his spare time, Miller taped cable access interviews with Louis Beam, Robert Miles, and members of The Order.[35]

Richard Ford founded the Florida White Knights in 1984, later renaming it the

Fraternal White Knights. The Klan's recruiting center was a biker bar in Ormond Beach, the Iron Horse Tavern, managed by FWK officer Michael "Nazi Mike" Hawkwinds. The Klan's third corporate officer, mechanic Michael Lynn, boasted a rap sheet including charges of robbery, drug possession, aggravated battery on a police officer, resisting arrest, and fleeing to escape prosecution.[36] Competition from Mike Eddington's Knights of the White Camellia faltered when Eddington moved to Georgia, joining the Southern White Knights.[37]

In May 1984 the U.S. Supreme Court suspended J. B. Stoner from a list of lawyers authorized to speak before it. The court gave Stoner time to appeal, then permanently struck him from the roster when he failed to answer by October. Three months later the 11th Circuit Court of Appeals upheld Stoner's 10-year sentence.[38] Don Black left prison in November 1984 and instantly resumed racist activities.[39]

"Populism" Revived

Ronald Reagan faced no serious competition in his 1984 reelection bid, trouncing Democratic rival Walter Mondale by a margin of 16,878,120 votes in November. Of more interest to Klan-watchers were several contenders on the third-party front. Lyndon LaRouche, running as an independent with Mississippi's Billy Davis, employed Roy Frankhouser as a campaign advisor and polled 78,809 votes. Irregularities in that campaign later sent both LaRouche and Frankhouser to prison.[40]

Farther down the list, at number six with 66,168 votes, was "Pole Vaulting Parson" Robert Richards, a two-time Olympic gold medal winner nominated by the newly formed Populist Party. Founded by anti–Semite Willis Carto, the party displayed no overt racism in its first electoral outing, but later cast its lot with David Duke and fell under control by neo–Nazis.[41]

An even stranger entry to the list, placing 11th with 13,149 votes, was the American Party, running White House hopeful Delmar Dennis. A former member of the Mississippi White Knights, Dennis had turned informer for the FBI after Neshoba County's triple murder in June 1964, appearing three years later as a key prosecution witness against Samuel Bowers and company. His party was a splinter of the old George Wallace AIP from 1968, while his running mate, Traves Brownlee, led an outfit called Americans for Constitutional Taxation.[42]

In Mississippi, Klan ally and Nationalist Movement leader Richard Barrett faced three black rivals in a congressional race, which he described as a choice between "the cotton boll and three lumps of coal." Previously known for founding the National Youth Alliance, and for a 1982 memoir advocating resettlement of "those who were once citizens" to "Puerto Rico, Mexico, Israel, the Orient, and Africa," Barrett came in second with 9,500 votes.[43]

The More Things Change...

Glenn Miller's Confederate Knights staged their largest public march in January 1985, followed two months later by another name change, becoming the White Patriot Party (WPP). Miller discarded robes in favor of military fatigues, explaining that "the name 'Ku

A demonstration by Glenn Miller's White Patriot Party in North Carolina, ca. 1985–1986 (Southern Poverty Law Center).

Klux Klan' turned too many people off, and I was tired of apologizing for everything the media found wrong with it." In protest, many knights defected to Joe Grady's Klan, while Miller distracted himself with TV appearances, including a debate with CORE leader Floyd McKissick and a joint appearance with Don Black on *The Sally Jessy Raphael Show*.[44]

Ohio grand dragon and IEK imperial klaliff Van Loman quit the Klan in February 1985, announcing plans to seek a seat on Cincinnati's city council, but he would not actually make the effort until 1992.[45] The same month saw Bill Riccio jailed in Alabama for caching illegal weapons and compiling a "hit list of officials." Federal jurors convicted him in April, handing him a two-year sentence.[46] George Pepper, klavern leader in Fontana, California, resigned with an apology in March, declaring his intent to "preach the word of God."[47] April saw five UKA members arrested in St. Petersburg, Florida, for plotting to start a race war. Four knights received prison terms in 1986. Meanwhile, in August 1985, Ku Klux jail guard Barry Robinson pled guilty to assaulting black inmates in Escambia County, paying a $40,000 fine.[48]

Kentucky's Klan also made headlines during 1985. Klansmen harassed Robert Marshall's family after they bought a "white" home in Sylvania, then started a defense fund for the arsonists who torched the house in July. The Marshalls sued Klan leaders to expose the names of local members, including policemen, resulting in one Klan kop's conviction for contempt of court. The officer—Alex Young—was fired in November for lying to superiors and distributing 10,000 Klan pamphlets as a member of the Klan's "Confederate Officers Patriot Squad."[49]

Ripples from the Greensboro massacre continued in March 1985, as jurors in a civil trial found two Klansmen, three Nazis, two Greensboro police officers and an informer responsible for the wrongful death of one demonstrator and for injuries to two survivors. The panel awarded three plaintiffs $394,959.55 in compensatory damages, but as this book went to press, only one plaintiff had received payment.[50] In July, a member of the White Knights of Liberty turned state's evidence against nine komrades. Arrested for terrorizing black families in Iredell and Alexander Counties, the nine received prison terms in January 1987.[51] In Florida that month, Belle Glade police jailed nine more terrorists who had formed a WPP chapter "just for something to do," assaulting blacks on the streets and firing into their homes.[52]

In September 1985 a federal grand jury indicted Dale Reusch for illegal purchase and interstate transportation of firearms. He pled guilty in April 1986, paying a $5,000 fine with prison time suspended, later claiming he was "railroaded."[53] Also in September, federal agents arrested Coy Phelps for three bungled bombings in San Francisco. Phelps acted independently, but his van bore an IEK bumper sticker and his home was stocked with racist literature.[54]

Roy Frankhouser mimicked Tom Metzger in 1985, launching his own *Race and Reason* program on Berks Cable TV, while Metzger made news by addressing a Black Muslim rally, excoriating Jews and donating $100 to leader Louis Farrakhan.[55] Georgia's New Order Knights collapsed that year, while officials in Commerce, Georgia, canceled their Christmas parade to prevent a Klan float from joining.[56] In December, Dave Holland left James Venable's National Knights to lead his own Southern White Knights.[57]

Another new group on the scene, created in March 1985, was the Council of Conservative Citizens (CCC), founded by former Citizens' Council leader Gordon Baum and based in St. Louis, Missouri. Like its predecessor, the CCC initially presented a respectable façade, attracting many Southern politicians, but that veneer dissolved as racist statements from its leaders—calling blacks "a retrograde species of humanity," terming America's multi-cultural population a "slimy brown mass of glop"—went public. The CCC embraced David Duke, and some chapters went even further. At least one group reportedly displayed Nazi flags at its meetings, applauding a speech by DeWest Hooker—self-styled "best friend" of George Lincoln Rockwell—who advised, "Be a Nazi, but don't use the word."[58]

Organized racism discovered cyberspace in 1984, with establishment of the Aryan Nations Liberty Net, connecting extremists worldwide. Robert Miles posted predictions of new terrorist campaigns, modeled on those of the Irish Republican Army, while Louis Beam sold passwords for 10 dollars each. ADL spokesmen warned Congress of the network in January 1985, but it collapsed in November, its demise blamed by Richard Butler on "a technical failure with a computer disk drive."[59]

America marked its first observance of Martin Luther King, Jr. Day in January 1986, and the Klan could not resist protesting, with a demonstration led by Thom Robb in Pulaski, Tennessee. Over time, the annual rally evolved into a European American Heritage Festival and shifted to October.[60] In February 1986 police charged Edward Fields, Dave Holland and Frank Shirley with beating an anti–Klan activist in Marietta, Georgia. Jurors acquitted Holland, whereupon Fields and Shirley were discharged.[61] Georgia Klansman Daniel Carver launched a recruiting drive in March, briefly jailed for assaulting a black minister, but the episode earned him guest spots on TV talk shows hosted by Phil Donahue and Geraldo Rivera.[62]

On the Lam

Glenn Miller claimed 5,000 WPP members by 1986, touting his goal as "Southern independence, the creation of an all-white nation within the one million square miles of Mother Dixie."[63] To that end, he pursued a U.S. Senate seat in May's Republican primary, running third with 6,662 votes out of 209,825 ballots cast.[64] Cross-burnings and sporadic violence accompanied that campaign, and Miller threatened war against the state government if legislators ignored his unsolicited questionnaires.[65]

That stunt floundered as Miller found himself in court, denying charges of illegal paramilitary activity. With Stephen Miller, he was cited for contempt on July 25, both receiving six month jail terms, while Judge William Britt fined the WPP $2,000. The capper was Britt's order for the Millers to avoid all contact with their party and 28 similar groups for the next 40 months, until they discharged their probation. Rather than submit to exile, Glenn Miller sold his farm at a loss, left U.S. marine Cecil Cox in charge of the WPP (soon renamed the Southern National Front), and prepared to go underground with Douglas Sheets and Robert Jackson, two Posse Comitatus members who collaborated with the party.[66]

Legal problems multiplied in January 1987, with Stephen Miller's indictment on federal weapons charges.[67] Ten days later, gunmen executed three men at a gay bookstore in Shelby, North Carolina, leaving police briefly baffled.[68] In March, Glenn Miller drove to Oklahoma, collecting Sheets and Jackson with intent to "wage war against the Jews and the federal government." His declaration of war, dated April 6, demanded Stephen Miller's freedom, dismissal of Glenn's 1986 conviction, $888,000 in damages, and various other concessions. Miller mailed 2,000 copies to WPP members, other racist groups, Congress, the Justice Department, and sundry news agencies.[69] Instead of surrender, however, Miller received an indictment for sending threats by mail. U.S. marshals captured him with Jackson, Sheets, and cohort Tony Wydra in April 1987, at a Missouri trailer park.[70] With the four in custody, a WPP member named Sheets and Jackson as the January bookstore killers.[71] Weapons seized at their arrest prompted yet another indictment, in November 1987, charging Miller, Sheets and Jackson with firearms violations.[72]

Multiple trials ensued. Stephen Miller received a 10-year sentence, served nearly seven, then violated his parole and went back to prison.[73] Glenn Miller pled guilty to one count, receiving five years' probation and a 10-year suspended sentence, but still faced prison for his 1986 contempt conviction.[74] In September 1987 he struck a deal to testify against 14 white supremacist leaders charged with sedition, in exchange for leniency.[75] In April 1988 federal jurors convicted Sheets and Jackson on weapons charges, resulting in 20-year sentences.[76]

Sheets and Jackson faced trial for the bookstore murders in May 1989. Kirk Lyons, a Texas lawyer affiliated with Louis Beam and the Aryan Nations, represented Sheets in the muddled proceedings, including testimony from a blind shooting survivor and accusations from Glenn Miller that the defendants boasted to him of the killings. Black cellmates of the suspects echoed that contention, but their credibility was dubious. Sheets replied, under oath, that Miller himself was the slayer, enraged at paying $75,000 in blackmail to suppress compromising photographs. On May 26 jurors acquitted both men of all charges, leaving the murders unsolved.[77]

Trials and Tribulations

Kleagles labored to rejuvenate the Klan's Illinois realm in 1986, with mixed results. Zion's knights brawled with blacks at Illinois Beach State Park in June, and white gunman Joey Isbell shot a black youth at a July carnival, while shouting, "Klan! Klan! Klan!" Jurors found Isbell guilty but mentally ill, and police denied any Ku Klux connection, but spokesmen for Citizens Against the Klan told reporters, "It is not an isolated incident."[78] Chicago witnessed violence in June, when Klansmen and members of the neo–Nazi America First Committee rallied to hear keynote speaker Thom Robb at Marquette Park. Bat-wielding members of an International Committee Against Racism attacked the rally, sparking retaliation from some 3,000 whites. The melee left 11 persons injured and 17 in custody.[79]

Rain plagued IEK imperial wizard James Blair, when he tried to stage a Pennsylvania rally in July 1986, and counter-demonstrations by the NAACP angered Maryland Klansmen in August, leaving Grand Dragon Sam Royer to threaten, "If they want violence, we'll have violence."[80] Wizard Blair gave up the fight in September, ceding his office to James Farrands of Connecticut, the Klan's first northern wizard *and* first Roman Catholic. While skirting the religious issue in a *New York Times* interview—"If a Catholic could be president, then he could join the Klan"—Farrands held the line on Jews. "A very ticklish question," he said. "We don't take Jews. They're not Christians."[81]

Irregularities from 1984's presidential campaign surfaced in October 1986, as a federal grand jury indicted Lyndon LaRouche and 12 associates for credit card fraud and obstruction of justice, charging massive swindles in the form of loans LaRouche never meant to repay. Officers raided LaRouche's "heavily fortified" Virginia estate and an office in Massachusetts, seizing vanloads of evidence. Multiple trials sent LaRouche to prison for 15 years, while various codefendants drew terms ranging from one month to 77 years.[82] One of those charged, Pennsylvania Klansman Roy Frankhouser, bared LaRouche's indiscretions at his trial 1987, while LaRouche invoked the Fifth Amendment to avoid self-incrimination. Jurors convicted Frankhouser of obstructing federal investigations, handing him a three-year sentence and a $50,000 fine, then prosecutors granted him immunity on other charges in return for testimony against his cohorts at subsequent trials. That immunity did not prevent FBI agents from jailing Frankhouser on unrelated weapons charges in October 1988.[83]

As Frankhouser prepared himself for prison, J. B. Stoner won his freedom in November 1986, released for good behavior after serving 40 months of his 10-year sentence.[84] Edward Fields welcomed his old friend home, between speaking appearances at Robert Miles's Michigan farm and the Aryan Nations' Idaho compound.[85] In Texas that month, Grand Dragon Charles Lee promoted his White Camelia Knights with a write-in gubernatorial campaign.[86] Don Black pursued an Alabama U.S. Senate seat in 1986, running as a member of the Populist Party, but was rejected by voters.[87]

Sheets and Skins

Neo-Nazi "skinheads"—racist youth with close-cropped scalps—bridged the Atlantic from England in 1985, making their first appearance in Chicago. ADL observers estimated their total number at 1,500 in 12 states by 1988, expanding and stabilizing around 3,500 in

Racist skinheads like these, wearing KKK insignia on their jackets, have associated with the Klan since 1985 (Southern Poverty Law Center).

40 states five years later. Furious violence was their trademark, producing at least 37 murders by December 1994. Other crimes ranged from vandalism and arson to random assaults on Jews, nonwhites and gays.[88]

Skinhead involvement with the Klan dates from their first appearance in America, when members of Chicago's "Romantic Violence" gang joined other racists for a rally on Robert

Miles's farm.[89] Soon, "skins" were marching in Klan demonstrations and sporting Klan insignia beside swastikas and other Nazi symbols on their makeshift uniforms. Tom Metzger boasts, "I was the first in the country to recognize skinheads and befriend them," recruiting them for his White Aryan Resistance, ostensibly led by son John. Making the rounds of talk shows with young Nazis in tow, the Metzgers scored their greatest media coup in November 1988, brawling on-air with CORE leader Roy Innis and hostile audience members, leaving host Geraldo Rivera with a broken nose.[90] That same month, WAR recruiter Dave Mazella visited a gang of skins in Portland, Oregon, leading them in random street attacks. Assault led to murder on November 12, when three skins fatally beat Ethiopian graduate student Mulugeta Seraw. The SPLC and ADL sued WAR on behalf of Seraw's family, winning a $12.5 million judgment that forced Metzger to sell his home. Undaunted, he continued rousing skinheads nationwide, declaring, "We will put blood on the streets like you've never seen. And advocate more violence than both world wars put together."[91] Sacramento skinhead Richard Campos listened to Metzger's recorded rants on a daily basis in 1993, before he fire-bombed a city councilman's home, an NAACP office, a synagogue, the office of the Japanese American Citizens League, and a state anti-discrimination office.[92]

Elsewhere, Klan leaders recruited skinheads to fill slender ranks and serve as their "front line" soldiers. Wyoming's Casper Area Skinheads also called themselves Wyoming Knights of the KKK. Skins from Indianapolis hit the road in April 1990, to join a Klan rally at Oxford, Ohio. At least two skins were regulars at Kansas City outings of Missouri's White Knights. Pieter Van Gulden, leader of a skinhead gang on Long Island, was arrested at a New Jersey Klan rally in April 1990. Baltimore's American Resistance gang boasted close ties to Leo Rossiter's Maryland Knights, joining Rossiter in an April 1990 brawl with leftist pro-testers. In Orlando, Florida, John Baumgardner's Invisible Empire Knights welcomed members of the Florida Corps Skinheads, while Tony Bastanzio's Dixie Knights rallied with Youth Corps 87. On Florida's Treasure Coast, American Front member David Lynch collaborated with Bastanzio and with Tom Metzger's WAR. In Texas, the San Antonio South Skins maintained regular correspondence with Klansmen.[93] Shawn Slater, boss of the Denver Skins, allied his gang with John Abarr's Wyoming Knights in 1990. Two years later, he emerged as grand dragon of Thom Robb's Knights, telling reporters, "I hope to be the governor of Colorado someday."[94]

Georgia provided fertile soil for skinheads, as for Klans, though relations between the two were sometimes strained. Older knights took offense at the hard-rock music blared by 100 skins at a Stone Mountain rally in April 1989, while others strove to accommodate youth. Another gathering, in August 1991, found 200 skins mingling with members of the IEK, U.S. Klans, Southern White Knights, and the Populist Party. In January 1992 skins marched in Atlanta with the IEK, U.S. Klans, Winder Knights and Aryan White Knights to protest celebration of Martin Luther King's birthday. J. B. Stoner met with members of the Aryan Resistance League in May, and Bill Riccio came from Alabama in July, to address John Armstrong's Aryan White Knights in Conyers. The Aryan Resistance League also participated in a "summit" with John Pendergrass, grand dragon of the Royal Confederate Knights. Skins joined another IEK march through Gainesville, in September 1992, supporting imprisoned Idaho white supremacist Randall Weaver. In January 1993, John Edwards led skinhead members of the Christian Guard from Georgia to a Klan rally in Pulaski, Tennessee.[95]

Skinheads also felt at home in Alabama. Edward Fields, Thom Robb, Dave Holland and Frank Shirley talked strategy with Birmingham's skins in 1990, and skinheads joined Klansmen to march on SPLC headquarters in Montgomery, in March 1991. Eight months later, Grand Dragon Roger Handley staged an "Aryan Unity" rally at his Fultondale farm near Birmingham, accompanied by Holland, Bill Riccio, members of WAR and the SS of America. In April 1992, hours after Riccio staged a birthday celebration for Adolf Hitler, three Birmingham skins murdered a homeless man nearby. Riccio led a rally to support the killers in June, joined by skinheads and Aryan White Knights from Georgia, who cheered his threat to castrate any black men who seduced white women. Riccio's August arrest on federal weapons charges, with Handley and six others, put a damper on that month's Aryan Youth Jam in St. Clair County, where officers jailed a member of the Confederate Knights and two skins for carrying pistols. The federal bust—Riccio's fourth since 1979 on weapons and drug charges—sent him to prison for 15 months, but he returned to Birmingham upon release, doubling as a skinhead leader and imperial kludd of the North Georgia White Knights.

A 1993 HBO documentary, *Skinheads USA: Soldiers of the Race War*, quoted a young Nazi saying, "I wish Bill would have been my biological father. He is my father. He's all these youths' father, every single one of us." That ardor cooled over time: in 2007, five graduates of Riccio's crew accused him of sexual abuse, one leveling similar charges at Roger Handley. Neither Klansman has been indicted to date.[96]

Tennessee, birthplace of the KKK, witnessed its first collaboration between skins and Klansmen at Pulaski, in January 1991. Ten months later skinheads joined visiting members of the U.S. Klans and the Indiana-based Northwest Territory Knights for a rally in Springfield. A hundred skins returned to Pulaski in January 1993, marching with Klansmen and William West, from the National Alliance.[97]

Pennsylvania skins, organized as "White Justice," found a natural ally in Roy Frank-houser during 1990, and Riot Roy soon spread his influence farther afield. In July 1994 a federal grand jury in Massachusetts indicted four New Dawn Hammerskins for harassing blacks and Jews. Frankhouser—lately leading a Klan faction called the Pale Riders—harbored fugitive gang leader Brian Clayton for nine months, while advising other skins and their kin to destroy evidence. In February 1995 jurors convicted Frankhouser of conspiracy and obstructing justice, handing him a 25-month prison term.[98]

Washington State saw its first Klan-skinhead collaboration in June 1996, in Spokane. Knights gathered at an American Legion hall to induct 15 skinheads, but members of the United Front Against Fascism crashed their party, touching off a brawl. Bill Albers, imperial wizard of the American Knights, complained to reporters, "This was supposed to be a private function. We didn't want any of this. You don't see the Klan going out and causing problems."[99]

Fraternization between knights and skins continues in the 21st century. Louisville, Kentucky's short-lived SS Knights of the KKK, founded in 2001, was essentially a neo–Nazi Klan.[100] In 2002 members of Connecticut's White Wolves joined National Knights for a "White Unity Fest" in Indiana. Returning home, they were jailed with Connecticut White Knights grand titan Louis Wagner for assaulting saloon patrons.[101] In January 2004 Tom Metzger told attendees at a "hate rock" festival near Phoenix, "Don't operate like a battleship. Operate like a Nazi submarine! Use your periscope! We have to infiltrate! Infiltrate the military! Infiltrate your local governments! Infiltrate your school board! Infiltrate law enforcement! You are not domestic terrorists. You are freedom fighters."[102] In June 2005 the National Socialist Movement staged a rally in Yorktown, Virginia, attended by Teutonic Knights and other Klansmen. Virgil Griffin emailed rally organizer Jeff Schoep that police had kept his Cleveland Knights from turning up. Another NSM rally, held in Michigan in April 2006, featured robed knights and special guest Tom Metzger.[103] Skins from "Blood and Honor" organized a Nordic Fest with IEK leader Ron Edwards in September 2005, at his home in Dawson Springs, Kentucky, followed by a National Skinhead Council meeting in October.[104] In November, after racial scuffles at a local high school, white supremacist Hal Turner held a "rally against violence" that drew skins and Klansmen to Kingston, New York.[105]

Challenging History

Georgia's Forsyth County has a reputation for white racism dating from 1912, when two alleged rapes of white women by black men sparked a pogrom, driving all but 17 of the county's 1,100 African Americans out of the district.[106] Seeking to change that image, 50 civil rights activists staged a "walk for brotherhood" through Cumming, the county seat, on January 17, 1987. Four hundred Klansmen, warned by J. B. Stoner that "niggers bring crime and AIDS," pelted them with stones and bottles, injuring four, and the attack made international headlines. Frank Shirley told a reporter, "We sent a message today. We white people won and the niggers are on the run."[107]

In that, he was mistaken. Despite a rare snowfall, 12,000 marchers returned a week later, guarded by 2,300 police against 6,000 whites shouting, "Nigger, go home!" and "KKK is here to stay!" No violence occurred, but officers arrested David Duke, Don Black and Frank Shirley for obstructing traffic, later fining them 50 dollars each, while an editorial in Duke's *NAAWP News* hailed "Victory in Forsyth County." Shirley and Richard Barrett formed a Forsyth County Defense League to defend Klansmen charged with stoning marchers, Barrett traveling from Mississippi to serve as their lawyer.[108]

Local misdemeanor charges paled beside the civil lawsuit filed by SPLC attorneys in March 1987, naming the Southern White Knights, Invisible Empire Knights, and 12 specific Klansmen as conspirators in the January 17 attack. Jurors agreed at trial, in October 1988, assessing damages of $400,000 each against the two Klans, $50,000 against SWK grand dragon Dave Holland, and $1,000 to $30,000 against 10 other knights, for a total of $1 million. The Supreme Court upheld those verdicts in May 1990, but no payments on the Klans' debt were forthcoming. In June 1994, James Farrands struck a bargain with the SPLC on behalf of the IEK and its successor group, the Unified Klan, to cease operations, close the Klan's bank account and post office box, donate its office equipment to the NAACP, and shun "any white supremacy organization or activity" in the future.[109]

While that case wound through the courts, 13 Klansmen were jailed for an Augusta cross-burning, ordered to publicly apologize in April 1987.[110] In Alabama, Don Black reconsidered his alliance with the Klan. He left the order by year's end, and moved to Florida.[111]

Riot police on standby in Forsyth County, Georgia, January 1987, after a Klan attack on civil rights marchers (Library of Congress).

Swimming Upstream

While Georgia's knights made global headlines, other Klansmen struggled to stay relevant in 1987. A judge in Frederick, Maryland, banned public protests on Martin Luther King's birthday but allowed Grand Dragon Roger Kelly to burn a cross with 13 members on private property. In September, Kelly staged an unauthorized rally at a Carroll County farm and was indicted for illegal cross-burning.[112]

Between those incidents, in August, Illinois transplant Kim Badynski staged his first Klan rally in Spokane, Washington. Uninformed "experts," forgetting the 1920s, called Badynski's arrival "the first time a Klan leader has set up shop in the Pacific Northwest."[113] That same month, Dennis Mahon—now Missouri grand dragon for Stanley McCollum's Knights—sought permission to broadcast Tom Metzger's *Race and Reason* program on Kansas City's public access channel. Told that network rules required a locally-produced program, Mahon countered with plans to air *Klansas City Kable*. Rejected yet again, he sued the city council and won his case in 1989. Police arrested Mahon and 17 cohorts for disorderly conduct as the show's first episode was taping, but *Klansas City Kable* finally aired in April 1990.[114]

In September 1987 the Southern White Knights welcomed 300 Klansmen from various states to an "All Klans Conference" on James Venable's Stone Mountain property. Later that month, the Southern National Front—languishing without Glenn Miller's leadership—formally disbanded.[115] In October federal jurors acquitted two Florida Klansmen at their second trial for making firebombs. Both testified that prosecution witness Robert Fotheringham, a cashiered prison guard and owner of a substantial rap sheet, had recruited them for the Klan in 1983.[116] Around the same time, the leaderless NSRP disintegrated.[117] J. B. Stoner was busy elsewhere, addressing the faithful in California that November, where Glendale police protected his skinhead entourage from militant Jewish Defense League members. Los Angeles officials denied Stoner's request to lead another rally on Valentine's Day, touting his new Crusade Against Corruption with its slogan "Praise God for AIDS."[118]

Sedition

Federal prosecutors viewed The Order's crimes as more than a half-baked rebellion. Disbursing stolen cash to racist groups nationwide indicated conspiracy, and further investigation of the gang revealed more sinister plans. Agents claimed that three CSA leaders—James Ellison, Kerry Noble, and twice-convicted killer Richard Snell—planned in October 1983 to bomb Oklahoma City's Alfred P. Murrah Federal Building, and that they shared the plan with Robert Miles.[119] In April 1987 a federal grand jury in Fort Smith, Arkansas, indicted 14 men on sedition charges, for plotting to overthrow the federal government. Defendants included Miles, Richard Butler, and Louis Beam; Order members Andrew Barnhill, David Lane, Ardie McBrearty, Bruce Pierce and Richard Scutari; Richard Snell and four other CSA members; plus Arkansas gun dealer Robert Smalley, earlier convicted of falsifying records for sales to The Order.[120]

Forewarned of impending arrests, Beam fled to Mexico, allegedly aided by Texas chiropractor Neill Payne, while FBI agents bagged the few other defendants who were still at

J. B. Stoner (center, with microphone) enlists Klansmen to promote his "Crusade Against Corruption" in the late 1980s (Southern Poverty Law Center).

large. Before leaving the country as a "Top Ten" fugitive, Beam retained attorney Kirk Lyons to represent him if he was captured —as in fact he was, after a shootout with Mexican police in November 1987. FBI agents jailed Payne three weeks later, for harboring Beam, seizing guns, grenades, and three Nazi uniforms at his home. Prosecutors scheduled trial of the accused seditionists for February 1988. Attorney Lyons closed his Houston personal injury practice to join the racist movement full-time.[121]

The impending trial galvanized racist leaders. Edward Fields raised funds for the defense while promoting the National Democratic Front's White Unity Day in North Carolina.[122] Thom Robb initially quarreled with Missouri grand dragon Dennis Mahon over use of violence, then wound up raising cash for the defense and attending the trial as a show of support, while Mahon defected to lead his own White Knights in Kansas City.[123] Curiously no one was indicted for receiving stolen money from The Order, which left Tom Metzger and William Pierce at liberty.[124]

The trial, held in a courthouse ringed by demonstrators including Klansmen and skinheads, was a seven-week fiasco for the feds. Judge Morris Arnold directed an acquittal verdict for Robert Smalley on March 18, and jurors acquitted the other 13 of all charges on April 7. Thom Robb—whose teenage daughter testified in Louis Beam's defense—rushed to hug the accused, then told reporters, "The government was going to send a message to the movement. The movement sent a message to the government." Robert Miles, more circumspect, remarked, "What movement? What's left of it after this?" Richard Butler, feeling optimistic, said, "This means we still enjoy the freedom of speech, freedom of assembly, freedom of association and freedom of religion." Beam, combative as ever, declared, "I think ZOG has suffered a terrible defeat here today. I think everyone saw through the charade and saw that I was simply being punished for being a vociferous and outspoken opponent of ZOG."[125]

Glenn Miller was the trial's big loser, having soiled his warrior's reputation once again by testifying for the state against his comrades, detailing gifts of cash from The Order. He served three years in prison, followed by five years' parole forbidding him to live in any Southern state. Instead, he trained as a truck driver, preaching anti–Semitism to anyone who would listen on long hauls from coast to coast. "After prison," Miller wrote, "the freedom of the open road is gloriously exhilarating."[126]

Adrift

Richard Barrett returned to Georgia in January 1988, leading 40 robed knights and 25 plainclothes stragglers on a march through Cumming, pausing en route to collect signatures for a "Forsyth County Covenant" proclaiming that "America's heritage as a free, white, Christian, English-speaking democracy must be advanced" and that "all efforts to make us a bilingual, bi-sexual or bi-racial society must be defeated." Observers noted that only 12 of the marchers were locals.[127] The same week saw Florida grand dragon John Baumgardner arrested for burning a cross too close to an occupied home. Two jurists—one black, the other a Holocaust museum director—recused themselves before Baumgardner found a judge to hear his case. Jurors convicted him in July, imposing a $250 fine.[128]

In May 1988 IEK grand dragon Roger Kelly requested a permit to march through Thurmont, Maryland. Officials rejected his petition, and Kelly tried again in August and October, denied both times when no insurance company would sell the Klan a policy to compensate the town for any damages. The American Civil Liberties Union sued Thurmont in December, winning a judgment that the insurance demand was illegal.[129]

As 1988 wound down, with membership shrunken to an estimated 5,500 knights nationwide, competing Klans survived as best they could.[130] They did without Don Black—settled in Florida and married to the former Chloe Hardin, who had divorced first husband David Duke in 1984—and without Bill Wilkinson, who left the States entirely, settling in Belize and founding the San Pedro Crime Committee.[131] Inspired by J. B. Stoner's latest passion, some knights targeted gays, especially in Florida, where Klansmen donned rubber gloves to picket gay bars and events.[132] Kirk Lyons addressed the year's Aryan Nations World Congress, seeking backers for a new Patriot's Defense Foundation aimed at freeing racist "prisoners of conscience."[133]

Politics distracted some Klansmen in 1988. J. B. Stoner, Edward Fields and Richard Barrett tried to organize a march against the Democratic National Convention in Atlanta, but the notion died from apathy.[134] David Duke announced his presidential race in June 1987, but had trouble finding a party.[135] He won New Hampshire's obscure Democratic vice presidential primary in February 1988, burying two opponents with 99.69 percent of 10,564 ballots cast, then placed sixth in Louisiana's primary the following month, with 23,391 votes out of 625,019.[136] Nominated by the Populists in June 1988, Duke struggled to select a running mate. Ex-Green Beret James "Bo" Gritz volunteered, then withdrew when the Party chose

Duke as its standard bearer. Officially, the runner-up was Trenton Stokes of Arkansas, but ballots in some states—including Louisiana—listed Duke's would-be veep as Floyd Parker, a New Mexico physician. By November, Duke was on the ballot in 11 states, polling 47,047 votes nationwide (18,612 of them from Louisiana).[137] Delmar Dennis made his second presidential bid with the American Party, but secured barely one-third of his former tally, with 3,475 votes.[138]

In local races, Tony Bastanzio sought the sheriff's office in Lake County, Florida, until Governor Bob Martinez declined to restore his civil rights, lost to a 1979 felony drug conviction.[139] Grand Dragon Ken Taylor ran for coroner in Montgomery County, Indiana—a post requiring no medical knowledge—but lost to a mortician.[140]

"It's a White Revolution"

Georgia's Forsyth County spawned more controversy in January 1989, as Richard Barrett sought to lead a march on Martin Luther King's birthday. Since 1987 local officials had passed an ordinance requiring payment of $1,000 per day for public demonstrations. Barrett sued and won his case in June 1992, when the Supreme Court declared the ordinance "facially unsonstitutional."[141]

While Barrett fought for the right to march, David Duke scored his only political triumph, winning election to Louisiana's House of Representatives in February 1989, in a special election to replace Charles Cusamano, lately elevated to a judgeship. Duke's win was narrow, shading rival John Treen by a mere 227 votes, but it was a victory nonetheless.[142] Plastic surgery helped, as noted by colleague Ron Gomez, who recalled meeting Duke for the first time in 1975.

> He was still in his mid–20s and very non-descript. Tall and slimly built, he had a very prominent nose, flat cheek bones, a slightly receding chin and straight dark brown hair. The interview turned out to be quite innocuous, and I hadn't thought about it again until Duke came to my legislative desk, and we shook hands. Who was this guy? Tall and well-built with a perfect nose, a model's cheek bones, prominent chin, blue eyes and freshly coiffed blond hair, he looked like a movie star.[143]

In action, Gomez described Duke as "so single minded, he never really became involved in the nuts and bolts of House rules and parliamentary procedure. It was just that shortcoming that led to the demise of most of his attempts at lawmaking." Gomez described Duke's tenure in the House as "short and uninspired. Never has anyone parlayed an election by such a narrow margin to such a minor position to such international prominence."[144] Despite attempts to shed his racist image, Duke continued selling neo–Nazi literature from his office, telling those who would listen that "Jews are trying to destroy all other cultures."[145]

By March 1989 Tom Metzger was promoting his own brand of politics, dubbed the "Third Position." A revolutionary nationalist movement billed as being "beyond left and right," Third Positionism actually represents an extreme form of neo-fascism.[146] Metzger aired his new creed at a poorly attended "Aryan Woodstock" in Napa, California, telling 50 tipsy skinheads, "The right wing is dead. The Marxists are dead. It's a white revolution."[147]

Two days after Metzger's speech, 16 members of the Christian Knights marched through Philadelphia, Mississippi, chanting, "White power for America!" Grand Dragon Jordan

Gollub led the demonstration, then was fired by Virgil Griffin in May, upon exposure of his Jewish ancestry. Gollub, a Pennsylvania native, admitted being born to Jewish parents, but insisted, "I was not raised in any Jewish religious background. The only thing my parents believed in was the state of Israel. I was never bar mitzvahed. I'm anti–Zionist. I believe in Christianity." To prove it, he founded his own Southern Knights of the Great Forest, saying, "We will be marching in Mississippi. People will see we are organized. We are not just a bunch of bull."[148]

In August 1989 police arrested Klansman Buddy Hernandez for wearing his hood on a stroll through Fredericksburg, Virginia. At trial for violating the state's anti-mask law, Hernandez called the hood "part of the symbolic symbol of the Klan." His judge disagreed, ruling that Klansmen could express their views as well without a mask. He lost on appeal, in 1991, when the state's Court of Appeals held that "[t]he incidental effect of preventing a Klansman from wearing his 'full costume' is minor when compared to the government's interest in keeping communities safe and free from violence."[149]

Stanley McCollum retired from the Klan in 1989, ceding control of his Knights to Thom Robb. Robb moved headquarters to his home in Harrison, Arkansas, attempting to follow Duke's lead in courting national media, but like Duke, his anti–Semitism shone through. "I hate Jews," he said. "I hate race-mixing Jews. We've let Antichrist Jews into our country and we've been cursed with abortion, inflation, homosexuality, and the threat of war."[150] As for African Americans, he wrote, "When the Negro was under the natural discipline of white authority, white people were safe from the abuse and violence of the Negro, but the Negro was also safe from himself."[151]

Out west, in April 1989, Los Angeles attorney William Daniel Johnson briefly moved to Wyoming, hoping to win the congressional seat vacated by secretary of defense nominee Dick Cheney. Best known as the author of a failed constitutional amendment limiting U.S. citizenship to persons with "no ascertainable trace of Negro blood, nor more than one-eighth Mongolian, Asian, Asia Minor, Middle Eastern, Semitic, Near Eastern, American Indian, Malay or other non–European or non-white blood," Johnson chose Klansman John Abarr as his campaign manager. Defeated in that race, with less than 1 percent of the vote, Johnson returned to California, where someone bombed his League of Pace Amendment Advocates office in August. Discouraged, Johnson left the League for other racist pursuits, replaced as its leader by former Texas grand dragon Jesse Johnson.[152]

In other news, former Duke bodyguard Johnny Clary—better known since 1983 as professional wrestler "Johnny Angel," Arkansas heavyweight champion for 1986–88—ascended to lead a new White Knights splinter Klan in 1989. Doubling as "Heartland Director" of Tom Metzger's WAR, Clary strove to unite Klansmen, Nazis and skinheads, turning up on talk shows chaired by Oprah Winfrey and Morton Downey, Jr., but an arrest on weapons charges and the revelation that his girlfriend was an FBI informer sapped his will to agitate for white supremacy. In 1990 Clary burned his robes, founded "Operation Colorblind," and emerged by 1995 as a spokesman for CORE.[153]

In July 1989, stricken with Alzheimer's disease, James Venable surrendered his Georgia law license. Mental incapacity did not bar him from leading the National Knights, however, and he hosted the annual Stone Mountain rally on Labor Day weekend.[154] Two months later, Cobb County authorities arrested True Knights imperial secretary Neva Veitch for the November 1987 murder of her husband. Previously, Veitch had blamed the slaying on two black men whom, she claimed, also raped her. The case broke when her new lover, Klan leader David Craig, betrayed Veitch, now worried that she might hire someone to kill *him*. Prosecutors charged Craig as an accomplice; he received a life sentence in March 1990 and hanged himself in prison three months later. Veitch pled guilty and received her life sentence in August 1990.[155]

In November 1989 Georgia Klansmen Dave Holland and Frank Shirley planned a demonstration in Montgomery, Alabama, protesting the SPLC's unveiling of a monument to civil rights martyrs, whom the knights dubbed "communists." As a precaution, they arranged for bondsman Sonny Livingston to bail out any Klansmen jailed that day, but it was wasted effort, as a federal injunction banned the march.[156]

In December 1989 ex-policeman and Klan infiltrator Douglas Seymour told California's Fair Employment Housing Commission that San Diego's klavern remained "one of the strongest chapters in the country." Seymour—winner of a recent $531,000 lawsuit against the San Diego Police Department—also testified that his superiors "ordered him to lie to the FBI, the county grand jury, Escondido police officers, and Palomar Hospital, who treated him for a gunshot wound."[157] Later that month, in Newfields, New Hampshire, Officer Thomas Herman lost his badge over involvement with the Klan.[158]

"O Klanada!"

Canada's Klan languished in the wake of Operation Red Dog. James McQuirter left prison for a Toronto halfway house in 1989, and rebuffed overtures from Wolfgang Droege to join the Heritage Front in 1991, declaring that he had "no desire to get involved in racist politics."[159] By 1990 Thomas Herman, an ex-policeman from Maine, presided over klaverns in Ontario, Québec, and the Maritime provinces, but French Canada proved troublesome. Federalist Eric Vachon lost control of the Sherbrooke klavern when separatist Michel Larocque led a walkout, founding the Longitude 74 Ku Klux Klan, named for Montreal's map coordinates.[160] Alleged top Klansman and avowed nonracist Teàrlach Mac a' Phearsoin received a two-year prison term in 1994, based on accusations from his latest gay partner, but maintained his innocence—born out, perhaps, by a subsequent pardon.[161] Infighting aside, Klan activities were limited by provisions of Canada's Criminal Code, imposing fines and prison time for "hate propaganda" targeting "any section of the public distinguished by color, race, religion, ethnic origin or sexual orientation."[162]

One Klansman who ran afoul of that law was William Harcus, founder in 1990 of the Modern Manitoba Knights. In December 1991 prosecutors charged Harcus and two other knights with advocating genocide of blacks through telephone recordings. That case dissolved at trial, in September 1992, when an undercover officer admitted using illegal wiretaps against the defendants.[163] Even so, complaints from B'nai B'rith and other groups prompted Canada's Human Rights Commission to ban telephone hate lines in December 1992.[164] Dennis Mahon entered Canada in January 1993, welcomed by members of the Heritage Front, but immigration officers deported him on grounds that he was likely to violate laws banning hate speech.[165]

While most Canadians ignored the modern Klan, a murder in Saskatchewan brought the order unwelcome attention in 1991. On January 28 Cree trapper Leo LaChance entered

Northern Pawn & Gun in Prince Albert, a hangout for off-duty police and prison guards. Moments later he was dead, shot with a military-style rifle at close range. The shop's proprietor, Carney Nerland—a Klansman and Saskatchewan leader of the Aryan Nations—pled guilty to manslaughter and received a four-year sentence. On December 15, 1993, he left prison, stepped into a Royal Canadian Mounted Police car, and vanished into the federal witness protection program.[166]

That much is known, but the case still poses many unanswered questions. For starters, Nerland seemed an unlikely Nazi, married to a Chilean immigrant, partnered with an Indian, renting shop space from a Jewish landlord. Prince Albert police truncated their investigation, pleading "budget restrictions," and testimony from eyewitnesses to the shooting—two prison guards—conflicted with forensic evidence. Licensed to sell guns despite his criminal record, Nerland enjoyed a remarkable cash flow and befriended numerous policemen, including a Regina-based RCMP officer who visited him in jail soon after his arrest. Prosecutors took a lenient stance on sentencing, despite Nerland telling an officer, "If I am convicted of killing that Indian, they should give me a medal and you should pin it on me." A commission of inquiry criticized police and prosecutors for lack of "diligence," while skirting the question of informers in the Klan. Various comments from Nerland remain unexplained. A reference to Klan ideology as a "rape of my soul and mind," remarks that his "field of operations were [*sic*] specific," and a claim that "If I was for real, I could have organized a serious Klan in Saskatchewan," suggest his possible employment as a double-agent.[167]

"We're Not a Hate Group"

The Klan's struggle for relevancy took various forms in 1990. Donald Spivey's Florida Knights sought to purge Lakeland of narcotics in January, reporting that "We have come into contact with several drug dealers and have dealt with them accordingly. We talked to them and prayed with them a little bit, and they moved to Tampa."[168] Georgia's Forsyth County embarrassed itself again in February, as 20,000 civil-rights supporters marched through Cumming under a shower of peanuts, distributed by Klansman Ed Stephens to "throw at the monkeys."[169]

And Klanfolk kept getting in trouble. In March 1990 commanders at Carswell Air Force Base discharged five IEK members serving as military police. One of them—Sgt. Timothy Hall, the state's king kleagle—also lost his part-time job as a county sheriff's deputy, with two more Klan recruits. Sixteen Klansmen picketed the base, Louisiana grand titan Wayne Pierce, complaining, "We're not a hate group. We do have a right to serve our country, which involves military service."[170] In May, Jerry Byrd of the Royal Confederate Knights took a fall for criminal trespass, while his wife was booked on a behavior warrant.[171] Tennessee grand dragon Leonard Armstrong fired on a Nashville synagogue in June, facing federal charges with Aryan Nations accomplice Jonathan Brown.[172]

Kirk Lyons did his best to keep violent racists out of prison. In May 1990 he defended Aryan Nations member Stephen Nelson, accused of plotting to bomb a Tacoma gay bar, but Nelson received an eight-year sentence.[173] Five months later, Lyons's Patriot's Defense Foundation represented Georgia Klansmen seeking to overturn the state's anti-mask law.[174] Between those trials, in September, Lyons married imprisoned Order member David Tate's sister, with Richard Butler presiding at the Aryan Nations' Idaho compound. Louis Beam served as best man.[175]

Politics, as usual, enticed some knights. J. B. Stoner made his last bid for office in June, supported by Frank Shirley, the IEK, and the Royal Confederate Knights. He ran seventh in a field of nine candidates for lieutenant governor, polling 30,084 votes out of 949,391 ballots cast.[176] In Florida, former UKA grand dragon John Rogers lost his July campaign to become secretary of state.[177] In Arkansas, Ralph Forbes polled 33,185 votes—46 percent of the total—in May's Republican primary for lieutenant governor.[178] David Duke was more ambitious, striving to unseat Louisiana senator Benner Johnston, Jr. Running as a Republican in October's primary, supported by John Rarick and dogged by a hastily organized Louisiana Coalition Against Racism and Nazism, Duke lost the race but still collected 607,091 votes, 43.51 percent of the total.[179]

The year ended badly for Louisiana knights, as federal agents jailed Grand Dragon Wayne Pierce on firearms charges, in November. Jurors convicted him in February 1991, but Pierce remained free on bond pending sentencing in May. While still at liberty, he led other knights in several cross-burnings, resulting in more indictments for civil rights violations. Pierce pled guilty to those charges in December 1991, receiving a six-year sentence.[180]

A month before Pierce's arrest, Virginia white supremacist Jared Taylor founded the New Century Foundation, a pseudo-scientific "think tank" that purports to demonstrate black inferiority through its Web site and *American Renaissance* magazine. It also sponsors biennial American Renaissance conferences, welcoming Klansmen and fascists of all persuasions. In March 2009 Virginia's state police would list American Renaissance as a neo–Nazi extremist group in its annual terrorism threat assessment.[181]

More disturbing was the November arrest of four men, including two active-duty soldiers, on multiple weapons charges. An indictment filed in January 1991 charged Green Beret Sgt. Michael Tubbs, his brother John, Warrant Officer Jeffrey Jennett, and Stephen Fussell with stealing military weapons and explosives while plotting a reign of terror against blacks and Jews. The crime spree dated from January 1987, when Tubbs and Jennett stole rifles from two other soldiers at Fort Bragg, North Carolina, telling their victims, "This is for the KKK." Calling themselves Knights of the New Order, self-styled "lifeguards of the gene pool," the quartet stockpiled automatic rifles, an anti-aircraft machine gun, a 40-millimeter grenade launcher, land mines, hand grenades, other explosives, and huge quantities of ammunition. Betrayed by Tubbs's wife while he was overseas, the four were captured with their arsenal, reams of hate literature, and recorded speeches by Adolf Hitler. Fussell and Jennett pled guilty in February 1991, followed by the Tubbs brothers and two other accomplices in April.[182]

"White Rights Survival"

Klansmen endured more travails in 1991, ranging from trivial to serious. Police in Rome, Georgia, jailed Royal Confederate Knight Bryan Cromer in February, for multiple violations of the vehicular code.[183] Two weeks later, a New Jersey grand jury indicted IEK grand dragon Joseph Doak, his wife, and four Klansmen for plotting to kill two Klansmen who criticized their leaders. Doak, his wife, and a third defendant pled guilty in July 1992, the ex-dragon receiving a three-year sentence.[184]

Four Klans joined the Georgia National Socialist Alliance in March, addressed by Edward Fields, Dave Holland and Frank Shirley as they rallied outside SPLC headquarters in Montgomery, Alabama. Two weeks later, in Somerville, U.S. Klans imperial wizard Keith Smith chaired a "summit" including delegates from the Alabama Knights, Confederate Knights, and Royal Confederate Knights.[185] That same month, Georgia Klansman Donald Shedd ducked theft charges, while pleading guilty to drunk driving. Roy Roaderick and wife Katheryn also logged the first in a series of Floyd County arrests: Roy for writing bad checks, trespassing, brandishing pistols, public drunkenness, terroristic threats and aggravated assault; Katheryn for fraud and causing repeated disturbances at the county jail. Their antics proved so embarrassing that both were banished from the Royal Confederate Knights in December 1992.[186]

Dave Holland, national director of the Southern White Knights, faced his own problems in Georgia. A federal grand jury charged him with perjury in March, while Newton County prosecutors hit him with a charge of using "fighting words." Convicted on the perjury charge in March 1992, Holland was sentenced to six months' house arrest, 250 hours of community service, and two years' probation, while paying $911.50 in fines.[187]

Georgia's Klans remained the most visible in 1992: heckling a Gainesville performance of the satirical play "Coup Clucks," protesting selection of a black valedictorian at Newton County High School, drawing rifle fire at a Covington rally, and infiltrating Blakely's fire department until lawsuits cost three knights their jobs. In May, Gainesville police jailed two IEK members for inciting a riot and violating anti-mask laws. On May 18 various Klans rallied at Daniel Carver's Oakwood farm, where Grand Dragon James Spivey ejected two knights for waving Nazi flags.[188] Carver's wife, Darlene, made klannishness "a family thing," naming her proudest moment as the day her grandchild first said, "Nigger."[189]

Edward Fields, approaching 60, remained one of the Klan's busiest networkers in 1991, staging rallies with Thom Robb, touring the country with British fascist John Tyndal, and publishing *The Truth at Last,* successor to *The Thunderbolt.*[190] Kirk Lyons tried to keep up, changing his PDF's name to CAUSE—Canada, Australia, the United States, South Africa and Europe—described as "America's only pro–White law firm." He soon left Texas for North Carolina, but was haunted by rumors of FBI collaboration. Speaking to *The Klansman* in 1991, Lyons begged knights to believe that he was not an agent of ZOG.[191]

Another rising star of the radical right, Bo Gritz, struggled to disassociate himself from racism while embracing Christian Identity. In 1991 Gritz promoted real estate deals in two Idaho "Christian Covenant Communities" he dubbed "Shenandoah" and "Almost Heaven." He also addressed North Carolina's First National Identity-Christian Conference in July, sharing the stage with Confederate Knights imperial wizard Terry Boyce.[192] Dennis Mahon, ever restless, visited Germany in September 1991, finding it "very inspiring" to walk in Hitler's footsteps at the Reichstag. He also stopped at Sachsenhausen's death camp, where he "had a real laugh at the wild stories and oversize photos of the 'victims.'"[193]

Back in Georgia that month, Edward Fields and Clyde Harrelson, both fresh from a Klan rally at Stone Mountain, chaired a Populist Party meeting in Calhoun. In October, at Stone Mountain, Fields led a National Unity Convention of "over 200 small independent local Patriotic groups in America." Ricky Terrell, lately defected from the Southern White Knights to the Conyers-based Confederate Forces, called the assembly a "white rights survival group."[194]

David Duke sought to energize the racist right once more in 1991, with a bid to become Louisiana's governor. Edward Fields raised money for the effort in Georgia, while aged John Crommelin served as Duke's campaign manager. Duke ran as a Republican, despite repudiation by the party and personal slams from President George H. W. Bush, declaring himself the voice of America's "white majority." His opponent, ex-governor Edwin Edwards, had a slew of Mafia-related scandals on his record, but Duke opponents still found him more palatable than a Nazi, printing thousands of bumper stickers that read: "Better a lizard than a wizard" and "Vote for the crook. It's important." Edwards failed to win a clear majority in October, polling 523,096 votes to Duke's 491,342, while other candidates claimed 534,817. In November's runoff, however, Edwards triumphed with 1,057,031 votes to Duke's 671,009. Undismayed, Duke told reporters, "I won my constituency. I won 55 percent of the white vote."[195]

Tom Metzger's legal turmoil continued in May 1991, with an injunction barring him from depicting cartoon character Bart Simpson on T-shirts with the caption "Total Nazi Dude." Five months later, jurors convicted Metzger for his role in a December 1983 cross-burning, imposing a six-month prison term and 200 hours of community service working with minorities. Released after 46 days to tend his dying wife, Metzger was barred from leaving California, but he found the ban impossible to bear.[196]

The week after Metzger's conviction, 170 persons attended an "Aryan Unity Rally" in Fultondale, Alabama, organized by Dave Holland and Miles Dowling, from the SS of America. Celebrants burned a cross and swastika, while firing guns into the air. A month later, Gainesville canceled its Christmas parade when Klansmen announced plans to enter a float titled "I'm Dreaming of a White Christmas."[197]

On the day that announcement was made, December 6, Kentucky Klansmen burned the Bowling Green Baptist Church, seeking to punish the pastor of that all-white congregation for calling the Klan "a putrid cancer on the body politic of society." The raid's leader, Grand Dragon Brian Tackett, had previously castrated a man on orders from Imperial Wizard Ernest Pierce, who suspected the victim of raping a teenage girl. Tackett obeyed, though convinced of the target's innocence. Federal jurors convicted Pierce and Tackett of arson in April 1993, while acquitting Tackett's mother of supplying the gasoline.[198]

Mississippi Turning

Byron De La Beckwith had retired to Signal Mountain, Tennessee, by the time Mississippi prosecutors filed a new indictment against him in December 1990, for murdering Medgar Evers. Arrested at home on December 17, he made bail, then was jailed again without bond on December 30, pending extradition. Agitation for another trial in Jackson had stalled for lack of evidence until Myrlie Evers supplied a transcript from Beckwith's original trial and assistant district attorney Robert DeLaughter found the murder weapon in storage. Tennessee's Criminal Court of Appeals blocked extradition in January 1992, but Beckwith finally returned to Mississippi 10 months later. In December 1992 Mississippi's Supreme Court narrowly approved Beckwith's retrial, by a vote of four to three.[199]

Proving the case after 29 years posed a challenge. One witness, former FBI informer Delmar Dennis, was initially afraid to testify but finally relented, describing Beckwith's public boasts of the slaying. Mary Adams recalled being introduced to Beckwith as Evers's killer; when she refused to shake his hand, Beckwith told her "he had not killed a man, but a damn chicken-stealing dog—and you know what you have to do when a dog has tasted blood." Louisiana prison guard Mark Reiley described Beckwith's altercation with a black nurse in 1979, shouting that "if he could get rid of someone like Evers, he would have no problem getting rid of her." A retired Greenville policeman repeated his false alibi for Beckwith, but jurors dismissed it, convicting Beckwith on February 5, 1994. The court imposed a life sentence without parole.[200]

While Richard Barrett petitioned Governor Kirk Fordyce for a pardon, calling Beckwith "the prisoner of an affirmative-action jury" and leading Alabama Klansmen to protest the verdict, Beckwith appealed his sentence.[201] Mississippi's Supreme Court upheld the conviction in December 1997, and the U.S. Supreme Court declined to review that decision. Beckwith died in prison on January 21, 2001.[202]

"Let's Go Get Them!"

The Klan persevered in 1992, drawing 150 knights to hear Edward Fields, Frank Shirley, Daniel Carver, and Louis Beam at Pulaski's annual January rally. "I spit on you!" Beam raged at federal authorities. "You're dogs! You're scum! We're gonna dance on your graves. The enemy is on the hill of power in America. Their guns are in place. And they're waiting for you. Let's go get them! We're going to have to take America back. White victory!" In February's issue of *The Seditionist,* Beam wrote: "Those who join organizations to play 'let's pretend' or who are 'groupies' will be quickly weeded out. All individuals and groups operate independently of each other and never report to a central headquarters or single leader for direction or instruction.... Participants in a program of Leaderless Resistance through phantom cell or individual action must know exactly what they are doing, and exactly how to do it." Tom Metzger echoed Beam's call for "lone wolf" attacks, as did Internet Nazi Alex Curtis, prior to his conviction on federal conspiracy charges.[203]

Colorado witnessed a Klan revival of sorts in the early 1992, led by Shawn Slater. A Nazi since his high school years in Aurora, Slater staged his first Klan rally on Hitler's birthday in 1991, rising to the rank of exalted cyclops in Thom Robb's Knights before year's end. He furnished children with T-shirts reading "Klan Kids Kare," as part of what he called an "education program," peddling the line "Equal rights for all; special privileges for nobody." In January 1992 he won a Denver court's permission to rally his knights on Martin Luther King's birthday. As black opponents scuffled with police and smashed store windows, Slater gloated that it was "a million dollars worth of publicity." When his Klansmen dropped *The White Patriot* on local doorsteps, "Somebody usually gets mad and makes a few calls. And bingo! We're back on television."[204]

Georgia's Southern White Knights, already wounded by Dave Holland's perjury conviction, suffered more troubles in 1992. Grand Dragon Greg Walker received probation for firing his shotgun at a man in Conyers, then was jailed in May on drug and weapons charges, prompting his replacement with Tony Hedgewood. Douglas Shedd of the Royal Confederate Knights got off easy by comparison, sentenced to alcohol counseling after his March guilty plea to drunk driving.[205] Clyde Harrelson left the Populist Party in April for a new venture—

the Committee to Save Our State Flag—then quit that in turn when his racist ties were exposed. Over the next year he remained a fixture at Klan rallies, celebrated Hitler's birthday, and finally emerged as treasurer of a newly minted America First Party.[206]

Dennis Mahon moved again in 1992, this time to Tulsa, where he launched his *Oklahoma Excalibur* newsletter in March, doubling as a spokesman for WAR.[207] West Virginians speculated on Klan connections to the April 30 murder of Hampshire County newspaper publisher Warren Duliere, closely following his challenge for Klansmen to "come out from behind their robes, hoods and masks," but the crime remains unsolved.[208] In New York, long-time grand dragon William Hoff lost his job at Third World Personnel Services when members of the Jewish Defense League tipped his black employer to Hoff's Klan affiliation.[209]

In Georgia, that June, federal prosecutors indicted three IEK members for a series of cross-burnings in Early County. Georgia's main controversy centered on attempts to strip the Confederate flag from a corner of the state banner, an affront that prompted Klansmen and skinheads to rally in Atlanta, cheering when Populist Party members unveiled a bust of Governor Zell Miller painted black. In August, IEK leader Willie Jackson—an exterminator by trade—found himself at the eye of a storm when state representative Mary Young-Cummings protested a Klansman "going in and out of the houses of blacks using poisonous chemicals." Florida grand dragon John Baumgardner, incensed on Jackson's behalf, threatened to picket Young-Cummings's office.[210]

The death of Tom Metzger's wife in March 1992 precipitated a new round of racist activity. Metzger entered California's Democratic Senate primary in June, receiving 75,593 votes (2.8 percent of the total), then violated his probation in July by taking son John to address Toronto's Heritage Front. Canadian authorities jailed the Metzgers for five days, then deported them for seeking "to promote race hatred."[211]

Northern Klans grabbed their share of headlines in August 1992. Geraldo Rivera had his second brawl with bigots in Janesville, Wisconsin, facing off against Illinois knight John McLaughlin at a white power rally. "He first called me a 'spic,' then a dirty Jew, then threw something at me and kicked me in the left leg," Rivera said. "Then I hit him back. Then we fell to the ground and I got on top and we were both arrested."[212] Klansmen chuckled over that, but mourned the loss of Robert Miles, killed by a stroke in Michigan the day before Rivera's Janesville brawl.[213]

"Stop the Persecution"

On August 21, 1992, U.S. marshals tried to arrest Randall Weaver—an Aryan Nations associate, indicted in December 1990 for selling illegal weapons to ATF agents—at his isolated home on Ruby Ridge, in the Idaho Panhandle. An initial skirmish killed one marshal and Weaver's teenage son, then FBI agents moved in, wounding Weaver and killing his wife on August 22. Bo Gritz joined in negotiations for Weaver's surrender, accomplished on August 31. At trial in April 1993 jurors acquitted Weaver of murder and related charges, while convicting him of jumping bail and failure to appear in court. The FBI settled Weaver's wrongful death claims out of court, for $3.1 million.[214]

Outrage at the Weaver case spanned the political spectrum, but it boiled most fiercely on the radical right. In October 1992 Christian Identity minister Peter Peters convened a

"Rocky Mountain Rendezvous" in Estes, Colorado, drawing leaders from the racist fringe to protest Weaver's treatment by ZOG. In 1983 members of The Order had frequented Peters's church in Colorado. At Estes, he welcomed guest speakers Richard Butler, Louis Beam, Kirk Lyons, and Larry Pratt, spokesman for Gun Owners of America. Lyons briefly represented Weaver after his arrest, but was discarded in favor of celebrity attorney Gerry Spence. At Estes Park, Lyons proposed filing a class action lawsuit "on behalf of all Identity believers against this government to stop the persecution," but nothing came of it. While the Colorado gathering accomplished little, observers generally view it as the launching pad for America's "patriot militia" movement of the 1990s.[215]

Matters were less dramatic in Georgia. Daniel Carver was ejected from a Jackson County flea market for selling Klan paraphernalia, then canceled plans for a float in Gainesville's Christmas parade. British Holocaust denier David Irving spoke in Smyrna, in October, his 40-member audience including Edward Fields, Dave Holland, Clyde Harrelson and Frank Shirley. Between November 1992 and February 1993, Charles Stoner, a knighthawk for the Royal Confederate Knights, logged arrests for wife-beating, driving drunk on a suspended license, theft, and obstructing police.[216]

Barry Black, a trucker whose rap sheet dated from 1968, founded Pennsylvania's Keystone Knights in 1992. Rather surprisingly, he also found employment as a Cambria County constable, serving three months before he was accused of tampering with mail and lecturing prisoners on the principles of klannishness. The district attorney belatedly discovered Black's record—including guilty pleas to burglary, larceny and receiving stolen property—and stripped him of his badge.[217] In Cincinnati, vandals knocked down a cross erected by U.S. Knights on four occasions, before vice president Ron Lee found one reinforced with steel. Eight of the miscreants were jailed, while Lee threatened to sue the city.[218]

"Democracy Is a Farce and a Failure"

Presidential politics frustrated Klansmen in 1992. They viewed incumbent George H. W. Bush as the architect of an apocalyptic "New World Order," and Democratic rival Bill Clinton was no better, a liberal admirer of the Kennedys. GOP leaders banned David Duke from Georgia's primary in January, but he made the ballot in Louisiana two months later, polling 11,956 votes out of 134,893 ballots cast.[219] Forging ahead in other primaries, ironically endorsed by civil rights icon James Meredith, Duke collected 119,115 votes nationwide but claimed no delegates at the Republican convention. Along the way, he denied providing Colorado Klansman Shawn Slater with a donor list and said, "We do not seek the Klan support. We do not want the Klan support. We repudiate Klan support. It's as simple as that."[220] His abortive campaign inspired a mocking song by the punk band Skankin' Pickle.[221]

Other presidential contenders in 1992 included journalist and former Nixon White House staffer Patrick Buchanan, running as a Republican, and Bo Gritz representing the Populist Party. Despite his affiliation with Georgia's Populists, Edward Fields gave Buchanan front-page coverage in *The Truth at Last,* presaging white supremacist support for Buchanan in 1996 and 2000.[222]

Gritz's denials aside, racists infested the Populist Party. Washington state chairman Kim Badynski hailed the swastika as "an early Christian symbol," while Homer Brand, leader of Washington's violently anti–Semitic "Duck Club," secured the party's nomination for state attorney general in 1992. Ralph Forbes, a "former" American Nazi, served as the party's Arkansas chairman while running for Congress. Jerry Pope of the NSRP was party chairman in Kentucky. Ohio chairman Van Loman was a former grand dragon. California Klansman Dennis Hilligoss ran the party's San Fernando/Simi Valley chapter, and WAR associate Joe Fields sat on its national committee.[223] Kirk Lyons addressed a party gathering that year, proclaiming "a global struggle that European people will not perish from the face of the earth." Soon afterward, he told a German neo–Nazi magazine, "Democracy is a farce and a failure. It would be good if the Klan followed the advice of former Klansman Robert Miles: 'Become invisible.' Hang the robes and hoods in the cupboard and become an underground organization. This would make the Klan stronger than ever before."[224]

Gritz did not expect to win in 1992, but he polled 107,014 ballots nationwide—.001 per cent of the popular vote. It was the party's last hurrah: the Populists dissolved soon afterward and ran no candidates in 1996.[225] Thom Robb craved a state legislative seat in Arkansas, filing as a Republican in 1992, but state party leaders rebuffed him.[226]

"Bloody Vidor"

In September 1992 U.S. District Judge William Justice ordered desegregation of public housing complexes in 36 Texas counties. That included Vidor Villas, in all-white "Bloody Vidor," near Louisiana's border. Klansmen rallied to Vidor's defense, posting warnings to "Keep Vidor White" and touring Vidor Villas in a bus with automatic weapons bristling from its windows. One knight offered 50 dollars to any white youths who assaulted black children.[227] The tactic seemed to work, as Vidor's "last black"—one Bill Simpson—fled the town in August 1993, only to be murdered in Beaumont.[228]

Texas Knights grand dragon Mike Lowe was pleased. "Vidor has always been known as Klan country," he told reporters. "We've had members there, but we never had occasion to work the area. We waited until a good issue came up." Grand Dragon Charles Lee was equally proud of work done by his White Camelia Knights, but this time Vidor surprised Klansmen. Mayor Ruth Woods hailed integration of Vidor Villas as "morally right," while locals slammed invading knights as outside agitators. The Texas Commission on Human Rights subpoenaed Klan membership lists, seeking to identify persons who harassed Vidor Villas residents. Both dragons were jailed in July, for refusing to furnish their rosters: Lee escaped trial by claiming he kept no records; Lowe was fined $13,000 and sentenced to six months in jail. Federal authorities supervised integration of Vidor Villas in January 1994, while incidents continued. TCHR director William Hale obtained injunctions against both Klans, barring them from the project under penalty of $50,000 fines and unlimited damages.[229]

FBI agents finally cracked down in Vidor, not for Klan terrorism against blacks, but for an incident involving a white minister. The Rev. Dennis Turbeville had spoken out against the Klan in November 1992, prompting member Judith Foux to place a card on the door of his church, reading: "You have just been paid a friendly visit by the Ku Klux Klan. Don't make the next visit your worst nightmare." Son Steven Foux subsequently perjured himself before a federal grand jury investigating that incident, while his brother Carl harassed a prosecution witness. In September 1994 the three Fouxs pled guilty to violating the 1968 Fair Housing Act.[230]

Elusive Unity

Various Klans remained at odds with one another during 1993, extending even to the annual Pulaski march in January. Clyde Harrelson joined skinheads and Richard Ford's Florida-based Fraternal White Knights for the first parade, on January 9, while Thom Robb's Knights and the IEK marched two weeks later. Between those demonstrations, on January 18, James Venable died at a Georgia nursing home, succeeded by Hoosier wizard Railton Loy, who moved National Knights headquarters to South Bend, Indiana, and christened the order a "church."[231]

Elsewhere, sponsors of Boston's annual St. Patrick's Day parade barred Klansmen and gays alike from the procession, citing its "family theme." In Georgia, Daniel Carver and his sons were jailed for assaulting sheriff's deputies called out to a domestic melee at their home. Roy Frankhouser faced trial in Pennsylvania, for stabbing a Klan security guard at an IEK meeting in 1992, but jurors accepted his self-defense plea in April 1993.[232]

April's big news came from Texas, where a two-month federal siege of a religious cult's compound at Waco ended in flames and tragedy. The drama began on February 28, with a bungled ATF raid that left four agents and five cult members dead. Negotiations dragged on until April 19, when FBI agents moved in with armored vehicles and tear gas, sparking a conflagration that claimed 76 lives, including 20 children.[233] Controversy persists to this day over the fire's point of origin, but radical rightists had no doubts: the case became an instant symbol of "federal tyranny."

Kirk Lyons played a small role in the siege before it turned to ashes, filing what he called "a historic, never before filed, [request for a] temporary restraining order" asking federal agents to stand down. Rejected in court, he staged a press conference, claiming that such standoffs typically end "in injury and death, mostly by fire." When his prediction came true, Lyons told reporters, "We knew what these dangerous, cultist maniacs in the government were going to do." CAUSE sued the government on behalf of three survivors and relatives of 23 who died, but that action was consolidated into a larger case, dismissed in July 2000.[234]

Louis Beam was also at Waco, posing as a journalist, reporting on "police state terrorism." In the process, he managed to conflate the standoff with the Holocaust. "Raised in small town America," he wrote, "I learned from television while still but a child about the terrible gassing and executions alleged to have happened in Germany during World War II. I would be 34 years old before I researched the matter and found out that it was just wartime propaganda carried over to peace time by Jewish organizations like the ADL. The absence of the Jewish holocaust in my life over the last 10 years has created a void that the federal government filled on April 19, 1993. A shattered Jewish fable has been replaced with a reality that I and 25 million other Americans were witness to."[235]

While outraged "Christian patriots" organized "militias" nationwide, Edward Fields pursued his goal of uniting all Klans under one umbrella. Dissolving his ineffectual Emergency Committee to Suspend Immigration, he joined Clyde Harrelson and former Populist Party leader A. J. Barker in June to launch the America First Party. Barker served as chairman,

Fields as secretary, and Harrelson as treasurer, while aging Columbian Emory Burke addressed the party's first convention. Others present included Kirk Lyons and ex-wizard Don Black. Barker doubled as North Carolina's state chairman of the Council of Conservative Citizens. Attendees at later AFP meetings included David Duke and Richard Butler. In November the AFP threw a Christmas party in collaboration with the Southern White Knights. When not engaged in party business, Fields joined Lyons, Thom Robb and Klansman William Hoff, Jr., to protest construction of the U.S. Holocaust Museum in Washington.[236]

Other attempts to unify the Klans were strictly small-time. A July parade through Rome, Georgia, featured five factions but drew only 40 marchers. Three weeks later, Imperial Wizard Donnie Allen disbanded the Royal Confederate Knights, while ex-convict Johnny Pendergrass welcomed the group's handful of members into his new Southern Confederate Knights. Police in Rome jailed Robert Pendergrass, an officer of his brother's Klan, for underage drinking in September.[237] Cincinnati officials banned further displays of Klan crosses at Christmas, while Louisiana barred Darrell Flinn's White Camelia Knights from "adopting" a stretch of Highway 90 as a recruiting ploy.[238]

At year's end, the Klan remained media-conscious as ever. Templar Knights imperial wizard J. D. Alder wangled a guest spot on Phil Donahue's talk show, while David Duke tried radio, hosting the "David Duke Conservative Hotline." Kim Badynski nominated Thom Robb's daughter, Rachel Pendergraft, for a seat on the Knights' grand council, quickly approved by her father. Once installed as National Membership Coordinator, she launched radio's "Global Minority Report," co-hosted a weekly Internet program called "This is the Klan," and published *An Easy Guide to Home Schooling for the Racially Conscious Family*.[239]

January 1994 brought more confusion and disappointment for Klansmen. Don Taylor, self-styled "Preacher/Instructor" of Georgia's True Knights, renamed his tiny clique the Invisible Empire National Knights, maintaining cordial relations with Clyde Harrelson, the Christian Guard, and the Aryan Resistance League.[240] Snow kept most spectators from a Klan rally protesting Martin Luther King's birthday in Springfield, Illinois, but police still jailed eight persons for assault and disorderly conduct.[241]

Last Hurrah

James Farrands tried to salvage his IEK after a federal court ordered the Klan's disbandment in May 1993. A month later, in Georgia, he announced creation of a "new" Unified Klan to replace the old order. SPLC lawyers closed ranks, filing petitions that would scotch the clumsy evasive effort in July 1994, but while it lasted the UK caused trouble. Georgia's realm defected en masse, to become the Klavelier Knights under Imperial Wizard James Spivey, but the worst shock came from New England.[242]

In January 1994 ATF agents arrested seven UK members—including William Dodge, grand dragon of Connecticut, Massachusetts and Rhode Island—for possession of explosives, silencers, and automatic weapons. Klansman George Steele pled guilty in April, then killed himself prior to sentencing. Dodge and knight Stephen Gray pled guilty in May, while jurors convicted Klansman Edmund Borkoski of conspiracy in July. That same month, as the UK disbanded for good, Dodge received a 65-month prison term, followed by three years' supervised release. In September, Scott Palmer and Edmund Borkoski were sentenced to 63 and

54 months, respectively, with fines of $10,000 and $7,500, while Stephen Gray got six months in a halfway house. Kleagle Ronald Akia, left in charge of the shattered New England realm, could only complain from the sidelines.[243]

"The Best Possible Light"

Klansmen found little to celebrate in 1994. Georgia's Rebel Knights welcomed J. B. Stoner to a rally in Cumming, while Richard Ford banished Peach State spokesman Kerry Mayhew from the Fraternal White Knights.[244] Federal jurors in Indiana convicted Klansman Robert Rogers of assaulting a black couple in 1992, imposing a 22-year sentence; five other knights had already pled guilty.[245] Michigan Klansman David Neumann, announcing an April rally in Lansing, told reporters, "We're trying to portray ourselves in the best possible light," but authorities still erected six-foot fences to restrain opponents, while declaring the site a temporary no-fly zone.[246] Disorders at that gathering moved Lansing's mayor to ban a second rally, scheduled for July.[247]

The Midwestern realms of Thom Robb's Knights suffered successive schisms in 1994. That April, Illinois grand dragon Ed Novak led dissident knights into a new Chicago-based Federation of Klans. Four months later, David Neumann led another walkout, claiming the original Knights' label for his Michigan faction. Neumann explained the break by saying, "Thom Robb is a poor example of a Klansman. He comes off as a young Republican, not as a racialist." A collateral charge accused Robb of embezzling telephone hotline funds and a donor's $20,000 contribution to the Klan.[248]

Kleagle John Abarr's Northwest Knights maintained a tenuous foothold in Wyoming, expanding from Great Falls to peddle leaflets in Billings, "promoting against political correctness" with help from local skinheads. The results included vandalism at a Jewish cemetery, bomb threats to a synagogue, and libel suits against the Klan from targets of its hate sheets, including Billings police chief Wayne Inman.[249]

October 1994 was a hectic month for Klansmen. First, Romie Young was jailed for plotting to blow up a dam near Huntingdon, Pennsylvania, then charges were dropped when informer Gene Fouse said FBI agents had scripted his conversations with Young. Nine days later, Maryland police arrested Pennsylvania Klansman Michael Birkl following a six-hour siege at a doctor's office, staged to "get his message out." On the 24th, Georgia police arrested four knights for killing komrade William Tucker, after he botched the burning of a crack house. Defendant William Mize demanded a death sentence at his trial, in December 1995, and jurors obliged. Triggerman Eric Hattrup pled guilty and was sentenced to life without parole.[250]

The "Pro-Life" Klan

Klansmen reacted slowly to the Supreme Court's 1973 decision in *Roe v. Wade*, legalizing abortions, but they caught up with a vengeance in the 1990s. The Aryan Nations blamed Jews for abortion—"the real holocaust!!!!!"—and Tom Metzger agreed, declaring, "Abortion makes money for Jews. Almost all abortion nurses are lesbians. Jews must be punished for this holocaust and murder of white children along with their perverted lesbian nurses."[251]

Klansmen climbed aboard the bandwagon. In August 1994, after gunman Paul Hill murdered Dr. John Baynard and clinic escort James Barrett in Pensacola, Florida's Templar Knights staged a rally supporting Hill. Grand Dragon John Baumgardner called for demonstrations at Melbourne's clinic, protesting the "misuse" of federal marshals assigned as guards, but the nine knights who answered his call were led by J. D. Alder, lately calling himself imperial wizard of a United Florida Klan.[252] Adler told reporters, "Abortion is racial suicide for the white race. Men such as Paul Hill are heroes for eliminating baby killers and saving the lives of unborn beautiful white babies. We of the Klan would be willing to pay higher taxes to pay for tar baby abortions if it meant a whiter and brighter future for our people. Baby killers need to know that the Klan is not asleep."[253]

Pensacola was Florida's focus of "pro-life" violence, much of it linked to John Burt, an ex–Klansman who launched a street ministry in 1978 and opened Our Father's House, a refuge for pregnant teens, in 1981. Soon afterward, he joined the anti-abortion crusade, emerging as its local leader. Burt served as "spiritual advisor" to serial clinic bombers Matt Goldsby and Jimmy Simmons, picketing their trial in 1984.[254] Asked about his link to the bombings, Burt said, "We're in a battle between good and evil. I can't help it if what I do inspired someone to go off the deep end."[255]

Indeed, Burt's congregants displayed a marked tendency toward violence. He "counseled" Paul Hill, and before him, Michael Griffin, murderer of Dr. David Gunn in 1993. Burt's influence on Griffin inspired defense attorneys to claim "brainwashing" at trial, but jurors rejected the argument.[256] In May 1988 police caught terrorist John Brockhoeft leaving Burt's house with explosives in his car, intended for a local women's clinic. Burt denied knowledge of the plot, but was sentenced to two years' house arrest.[257] It all sounded rather klannish, and Burt seemed to harbor nostalgia for his old order. "Get rid of the Klan's violence and racial bigotry," he said, "and I could work with those people. Fundamentalist Christians and those people are pretty close, scary close, fighting for God and country. Some day we may all be in the trenches together in the fight against the slaughter of unborn children."[258]

Burt's crusade ended in June 2003, with charges of molesting a minor at Our Father's House. He fled Pensacola and was caught in Gadsden County, after bungling a suicide attempt. In April 2004 jurors convicted Burt on five felony counts, resulting in an 18-year prison term.[259] He died in custody nine years later, eulogized online by convicted clinic bomber Michael Bray as an "honest soldier."[260]

Dixie Rising

Southern nostalgia for slavery had never faded after Appomattox, but the first calls for a new secession came in 1994, when Michael Hill—a professor of Celtic history at Tuscaloosa's historically black Stillman College—founded the Southern League, soon renamed League of the South. Thus began the "neo–Confederate" movement, lionizing the South's "Anglo-Celtic" heritage and adding strong doses of Christian fundamentalism. Initially proud that the SPLC did not consider it a hate group, the LOS soon veered into radical territory, aligning itself with the white supremacist CCC and losing most of its academic founders in the process. Hill resigned his teaching post to run the growing organization full-time. Within four years of its foundation, LOS board member Jack Kershaw would declare, "Somebody needs to say a good word for slavery. Where in the world are the Negroes better off today than in America?"[261]

For the LOS, it was a short step from praising segregation and secession to endorsing the Klan. In May 2000, after a brawl between Klansmen and blacks in Decatur, Alabama, LOS member Soiren Dresch wrote online, "Sounds like Decatur needs a response to the blacks who think the world is their oyster. I hope the next group is armed and ready to hit an afro between the eyes." A month later, after disturbances at Biloxi's "Black Spring Break," Tuscaloosa member David Cooksey wrote, "You see the day is coming when we will NEED a new type of Klan. Yes I said Klan!! If push comes to shove I'm for it! Time has come to stop this crap now! Or would you all like to see your daughters raped???" Michael Hill added, "It is time for us, as Southern whites, to look to our own well being and defense against these thugs. Moreover, it is time we demand that respectable members of the 'minority community' control their debased 'brothers and sisters.' If they refuse, then we can only believe that they secretly condone such behavior. Let us not flinch when our enemies call us 'racists'; rather, just reply with, 'So, what's your point?'"[262]

While the CCC and LOS formed two legs of the neo–Confederate stool, a third—the venerable Sons of Confederate Veterans—took longer to join the party. Founded as an ostensibly apolitical fraternity in 1896, the SCV had been frankly racist at first, praising the original Klan in its *Confederate Veteran* newsletter, declaring the United States a nation "for white people," opining that "when a Negro has learned to read he ceases to work," and supporting segregation through the 1960s, but in 1989 the group condemned use of Confederate flags by anyone espousing "political extremism or racial superiority." In 1993 one SCV "camp" marched in protest against a Klan demonstration, and the board expelled "Chief of Heritage Defense" Charles Lunsford the following year, for addressing a CCC gathering. In response, Lunsford groused, "The SCV will no longer be fighting the fight for Southern heritage, and those of us who made the SCV famous by fighting these battles and swelling the ranks are being purged." A 1996 SCV ban on emails praising secession drove executive council member Walter Kennedy to resign, fuming, "If it was 'Right' in 1861, why is it 'Wrong' today?"[263]

Racists remained within the SCV, of course. A prominent example, Leonard Wilson, first drew attention in 1956, as a leader of riots against Autherine Lucy's admission to the University of Alabama. A longtime Citizens' Council member, Wilson was also a founder of the CCC and leader of the SCV's Alabama division, whose official bio describes him simply as "a political activist since junior high school."[264] With such men in charge, a purge of extremists could only go so far, and it stopped dead in collision with Kirk Lyons.

In January 1992, at the invitation of reclusive Populist Party member and David Duke financier Herbert Horton, Lyons moved from Texas to Black Mountain, North Carolina, living in one house owned by Horton and running his CAUSE legal firm from another. Close behind him came in-laws Charles and Betty Tate, with chiropractor Neill Payne—arrested for harboring Louis Beam in 1987, wed to Laura Tate three years later in the same Aryan Nations ceremony where Lyons married sister Brenna. Lyons confused some supporters in January 1994, attending a prayer breakfast for Martin Luther King and singing "We Shall Overcome," but that was an aberration. In the same month, he founded SCV Camp No. 758 in Black Mountain and installed himself as its commander. In May 1995 he waffled again, following a local Klan march, branding demonstration leader Virgil Griffin a "world-class moron." The following year, Lyons renamed CAUSE the Southern Legal Resource Center, installing fellow SCV member Neill Payne as executive director. By September 1997 Lyons billed himself as the SCV's "Chief of Staff of the Army of Northern Virginia."[265]

In 1998 the SCV revised its ban on racist groups, requiring only that members should not "endorse the activities or goals of organizations with explicit or implicit racial motives *during meetings or events of the Sons of Confederate Veterans*" (emphasis added). LOS chief Michael Hill enthused that the shift permitted SCV members "to cooperate with the League in non-political matters. Gauging from the actions of the latest SCV national convention in early August, the old guard there is on the way out." Soon, issues of *Confederate Veteran* carried the League's Web address, ads for Susan Davis's 1924 *Authentic History of the Ku Klux Klan,* and photos of CCC boss Gordon Baum founding an SCV camp in Missouri.[266]

Lyons, meanwhile, pushed for consolidation of the neo–Confederate movement. In April 2000 he shared the stage with David Duke at a Virginia meeting of the neo–Nazi American Friends of the British National Party. After praising Duke as a "white knight," Lyons said he had spent most of his two decades as an SCV member "cursing the organization for spinelessness and cowardice" in excluding Klansmen. He jeered the "granny" faction who "hide in their shirts at the mention of the R-word [racism]," reporting that "unreconstructed Southerners" like himself were pushing the SCV toward white nationalism. Under the new rule, he said, "Theoretically, it's a citizen's coalition, anybody can join." Applause greeted his comment that "[t]he civil rights movement I am trying to form seeks a revolution. We seek a return to a godly society with no Northernisms attached to it—a majority European-derived society." Four months later, after Lyons addressed another Nazi audience in Washington, he won election to the SCV's national executive council. That same vote installed as "chaplain-in-chief" John Weaver, who claims Africans "blessed the Lord for allowing them to be enslaved and sent to America."[267]

The SCV's hard-right shift displeased many members, causing 11,000 to resign by December 2001. Lyons welcomed the exodus, declaring that "the slackers and the grannies have been purged from our ranks." He then announced his candidacy for commander-in-chief of the Army of Northern Virginia Department, prompting opponent Charles Hawks to say, "I'm afraid that if he's elected we will be considered racist because we elected him." Gilbert Jones, a longtime SCV member in North Carolina, wrote, "The SCV has come to a decisive fork in the road. The elections of 2002 will decide the fate of the Sons of Confederate Veterans. I think we ought to take the neo–Nazis, the white supremacists, and the skinheads and show them to the door."[268]

That vote went against moderation, choosing Lyons ally Ron Wilson as commander-in-chief. Wilson suspended some 300 members who opposed his efforts to revise the group's constitution, filling it with amendments drafted by Lyons, then was scandalized when Florida leader John Adams surreptitiously signed up SPLC staff writer Heidi Beirich for Internet porn sites. Wilson lost his bid for a second term as commander, but was replaced by equally radical leader Denne Sweeney. By then, banished North Carolina SCV leader Anthony Hodges complained that members of "racial groups" held "key leadership positions" in the SCV. Examples included chief of staff Ronald Casteel from the LOS and chaplain-in-chief Rondel Rumberg from the CCC. Sweeney described those organizations as "borderline groups," saying he was only opposed to groups that "espouse[d] violence and overthrow and killing of black people"[269]

Oddly, he had no objection to recruiting Michael Tubbs, ex–Green Beret and ex-convict, imprisoned in 1991 for stealing army weapons to outfit his New Order Knights in North Carolina. In 2004 Tubbs emerged as Florida leader of both the SCV and LOS, whose leader, Michael Hill, proclaimed him "a reformed man." In December 2005 Sweeney suspended the entire Oklahoma division, replacing its leaders with some of his allies. Two months later, he banished Kansas division commander Charles Walthall from the SCV's e-list, as Walthall put it, "for taking exception to the racist, pro–Nazi, pro-assassination, and political extremist rhetoric being bantered about by members of the list. So I consider my removal from the list of low-lifes as an honor." In order to survive, he wrote, the SCV "has got to move away from the racial, secessionist, anti–American agenda being preached."[270]

Still nothing changed for the better. In February 2006 Sweeney proposed a new constitution, essentially written by Lyons, deleting the original's mentions of a reunited America and its Pledge of Allegiance. That move prompted a resolution from Mississippi's largest SCV camp, urging the group's executive council to pass resolutions "expressively stating that membership in any organization such as the Ku Klux Klan or support for or sympathy with that organization is not compatible with membership in the SCV"; to "immediately establish a written policy that no person can serve as an officer of the SCV in any capacity who maintains membership in or gives aid and encouragement to any racist group, white-supremacist group, neo–Nazi group, anti–Semitic group or neo-secessionist group"; and "to disavow and terminate any association, patronage, or financial support of Kirk Lyons or the Southern Legal Resource Center, and to take prompt steps to terminate Mr. Lyon's membership in the SCV."[271]

Those demands fell on deaf ears, as the SCV approved Sweeney's constitution and chose hand-picked successor Chris Sullivan as the next commander. Ed Butler, picked to lead the Army of Tennessee, cheered that "[t]he Sons of Confederate Veterans have endorsed a radical direction. We should all resolve to work to defeat the Marxist Socialists that are waging war on Southern culture." The SLRC served as the SCV's de facto legal department, bankrolled with $10,000 under Sweeney, while two SCV leaders sat on its board of directors. Neill Payne completed the cross-pollination, joining the SCV's Amendments and Resolutions Committee. In 2011 the SCV's Mississippi Division campaigned for state license plates honoring Klan grand wizard Nathan Bedford Forrest.[272]

"Hell Has Victory"

A decade after its demise, The Order was reborn after a fashion, on the Pennsylvania farm of longtime Klansman, Aryan Nations member and Posse Comitatus leader Mark Thomas. Inspired by Robert Mathews, self-styled guerrillas Peter Langan and Richard Guthrie, Jr., had swindled stores of some $250,000 by returning stolen merchandise, then turned to robbing banks, netting more than $30,000 between January and October 1994. When they solicited advice on future raids from Thomas, he drove them to Arkansas, introducing them to Philadelphia skinhead musicians Kevin McCarthy and Scott Stedeford, then living at Elohim City, Oklahoma.[273]

Elohim City—"City of God"—is a settlement of Christian Identity "purists," founded in 1973 by Robert Millar. Millar mediated CSA leader James Ellison's surrender to FBI agents in 1985 and testified as a character witness for member Richard Snell at his trial for killing an Arkansas policeman. Klansman Dennis Mahon kept a trailer there in 1994–95, and other extremists visited frequently. Meeting Thomas and friends at a nearby restaurant, McCarthy and Stedeford eagerly joined their budding "Aryan Republican Army." Thinking beyond robberies, Thomas—the gang's "designated spiritual leader"—advised that if the crew "attacked various places like utilities, railways, communications and even government installations, ARA would become a force that the government would have to reckon with." Their ambitious goal: replacing ZOG with an all-white nation ruled under Bible-based laws.[274]

First, however, there would be more holdups, executed with near-military precision. The gang worked in disguise—ski masks or Halloween masks of American presidents, once dressing as FBI agents with bogus raid jackets—and spoke gibberish to confuse bank staffers, typically leaving dummy bombs behind to stall pursuit. As a prank, they sometimes rented getaway cars in the names of real-life federal agents, using fake I.D. In their first three outings as a foursome they stole $67,050 from banks in Iowa, Ohio and Missouri.[275]

Somewhere along the way, ARA members may have met a young ex-soldier, Timothy McVeigh. Obsessed with guns from childhood, McVeigh joined the army in 1988 and was reprimanded for wearing a Klan T-shirt at Fort Benning, to protest perceived "black power" displays by African American soldiers. He served in Operation Desert Storm and left the service with a Bronze Star in December 1991, adopting a transient lifestyle. He read *The Turner Diaries,* attended Klan meetings in Texas, and briefly joined the order, then dropped out, deeming it insufficiently zealous on Second Amendment issues. In 1992 girlfriend Catina Lawson saw McVeigh with illegal German immigrant Andreas Strassmeir. That same year, Strassmeir fraudulently obtained a Tennessee driver's license, claiming a Knoxville address supplied by his lawyer, Kirk Lyons. In 1993 Lyons arranged for Strassmeir to live at Elohim City, serving as the compound's security chief and training "Aryan warriors." In September 1994 compound dwellers saw McVeigh on the settlement's gun range with Dennis Mahon, a close friend of Mark Thomas.[276]

Did McVeigh join the ARA? McVeigh and friend Terry Nichols were in Fayetteville, Arkansas, on October 11–12, 1993, when Langan and Guthrie aborted an armored car robbery there; McVeigh also received a traffic citation on October 12 in Crawford, four miles from Elohim City. In October and December 1993 McVeigh penned letters to his sister, referring to "a network of friends who share [my] beliefs" and calling bank holdups "a kind of Robin Hood thing." In November 1994 McVeigh looted the Arkansas home of a gun show acquaintance, stealing $60,000 worth of gold, silver, jewelry and firearms. A month later he gave his sister three $100 bills, allegedly proceeds from helping plan a bank heist, and asked her to exchange them for "clean" money.[277] Hardly proof positive, and yet....

In January 1995 the ARA quartet drove from Missouri to Arizona, remaining there through February. They planned another armored car holdup, but as before, scrubbed the mission. McVeigh and Terry Nichols were also in Arizona, visiting survivalist Steven Colbern in Kingman, then home to another friend of McVeigh's, Michael Fortier. Colbern, a chemist who specialized in homemade explosives, later admitted knowing McVeigh as "Tim Tuttle." On February 21, 1995, an ammonium nitrate bomb exploded at the Kingman home of Rocky

McPeak, believed to be the handiwork of Colbern and loan shark Clark Vollmer. When McPeak confronted Vollmer at home, the next day, he saw McVeigh there with an unidentified male companion.[278]

March 1995 found ARA members back in the Midwest, stealing $28,225 from a bank in Des Moines on the 29th. Before that holdup, Stedeford bought a used car, using a counterfeit driver's license. FBI agents got their first photo of Stedeford when they obtained a copy of that license from the dealer. On April 1 Mark Thomas drove to Elohim City with Stedeford and McCarthy, to await the execution and funeral of Richard Snell. Dennis Mahon, also present for the service, abruptly left with the other three on April 17, two days prior to Snell's death. Mahon went to Illinois, while Thomas returned to Pennsylvania; Stedeford and McCarthy's whereabouts are unknown until they joined Langan in Pittsburg, Kansas, on April 20.[279]

Meanwhile, Timothy McVeigh was busy. On April 5 he phoned Andreas Strassmeir at Elohim City. Three days later, McVeigh and two other men visited a Tulsa strip club. Security cameras caught McVeigh telling a dancer, "On April 19, 1995, you'll remember me for the rest of your life." Five dancers identified his companions, from photos, as Strassmeir and Michael Brescia, an Elohim City resident engaged to marry Robert Millar's stepgranddaughter. By April 10 McVeigh was in Herrington, Kansas, at the home of Terry Nichols. There, on April 17, he rented a Ryder moving van. The next day, he phoned Black Mountain, North Carolina, speaking for 20 minutes to Dave Holloway, assistant director of CAUSE under Kirk Lyons.[280]

On April 19, 1995, McVeigh parked the truck near Oklahoma City's Alfred P. Murrah Federal Building. Its cargo exploded at 9:02 a.m. killing 167 identified victims and wounding 684. Police also found a severed leg, belonging to a 168th victim who remains unidentified. Ninety minutes after the blast, a state trooper arrested McVeigh near Perry, Oklahoma, armed with a pistol and driving a car with no license plates. Booked as "John Doe," McVeigh listed a home address in Michigan occupied by James Nichols, Terry's brother. FBI agents found the Ryder truck's axle on April 20, traced it to McVeigh, and arrested him on April 21, as he was about to post bail on local charges.[281]

Richard Snell died on schedule in Missouri, eight minutes after the Murrah bombing. Informed of the blast, he chose his last words carefully: "Governor Tucker, look over your shoulder. Justice is on the way. I wouldn't trade places with you or any of your political cronies. Hell has victory. I am at peace." Terry Nichols surrendered to Kansas police on April 21. FBI agents nabbed brother James on April 25, then released him for lack of evidence on May 24. Michael and Lori Fortier, jailed as accomplices, agreed to testify against McVeigh and Terry Nichols.[282]

The ARA resumed action in May 1995, stealing $49,000 from three banks by mid-August. Michael Brescia joined the team for a $9,845 heist in Wisconsin, on August 30, then returned to Elohim City. In November the gang stole $2,500 from a St. Louis bank. McCarthy quit the group in December, over a quarrel on tactics, leaving Langan, Guthrie and Stedeford to rob an Ohio bank on the 19th. Guthrie pulled a solo robbery in Philadelphia, then walked into an FBI trap on January 15, 1996. With his help, agents cornered Langan three days later, wounding him in a shootout before he surrendered. Mark Thomas warned Kevin McCarthy of the arrests, but his days were numbered. Feds captured him and Stedeford on May 24, in different cities.[283]

Other agents, meanwhile, pursued loose ends in the Murrah bombing. Dennis Mahon came under close scrutiny, described at an April 1995 FBI briefing as known for "targeting federal installations for destruction through bombings, such as the IRS Building, the Tulsa Federal Building, and the Oklahoma City Federal Building." An ATF informer testified that Mahon and Andreas Strassmeir traveled to Oklahoma City three times between November 1994 and January 1995. Though never charged, Mahon told a racist audience in 2004, "I knew Timothy McVeigh quite well. In fact, I knew him back when he was named Timothy Tuttle, and he and I were involved in quite a few bom— Let's just say he and I did some serious business together. And after Oklahoma City, the feds came after me big-time, boy, but they never proved a thing."[284]

Strassmeir fled Elohim City in July 1995, hiding out in Black Mountain, North Carolina, until January 1996, when he escaped to Berlin with aid from CAUSE assistant director Dave Holloway—or Germany's elite GSG-9 counterterrorism unit, according to Kirk Lyons. In 2007 former FBI Terrorist Task Force director Daniel Coulson called for a new investigation of the Murrah bombing, claiming Strassmeir was "working for the German government and the FBI" at Elohim City. Strassmeir's present whereabouts are unknown.[285]

Timothy McVeigh's lawyer subpoenaed Kirk Lyons as a defense witness in February 1996, but he was not called to testify at trial in 1997. Richard Guthrie pled guilty to 19 bank robberies, then hanged himself in jail, in July 1996. Kevin McCarthy admitted six holdups and testified against Peter Langan, resulting in his February 1997 conviction. A month before that verdict, prosecutors charged Michael Brescia with helping the ARA rob a Wisconsin bank in 1995. Brescia pled guilty and agreed to cooperate with authorities in May 1997. In February 1997 Mark Thomas pled guilty to plotting seven holdups and agreed to aid investigators. Richard Butler professed himself "shocked," while Dennis Mahon groused, "He'll drop everyone's name. I believe he'll drop my name." Still, no further indictments emerged.[286]

In June 1997 federal jurors convicted Timothy McVeigh on 11 counts of murder and conspiracy. He died by lethal injection in June 2001. Terry Nichols received a federal sentence of life without parole in June 1998, matched by an identical state prison term in August 2004. Michael Fortier testified against both former friends and received a 12-year sentence in May 1998. He left prison in January 2006, entering the federal witness protection program.[287]

Business as Usual

While many Klansmen cheered the Oklahoma City bombing, most concerned themselves primarily with local matters. In January 1995 Denver police jailed 21 knights and neo-Nazis on charges of robbery and vandalism, seizing numerous weapons. Two months later, Don Black launched his Stormfront Web site, described as "a resource for those courageous men and women fighting to preserve their White Western culture, ideals, and freedom of speech and association—a forum for planning strategies and forming political and social groups to ensure victory." In 1996 Black said, "We're reaching tens of thousands of people who never before had access to our point of view." Featuring blogs by David Duke, William Pierce, and other neo-Nazi leaders, Stormfront claimed 52,000 subscribers by 2005, and boasted of 500 more joining monthly.[288]

In April 1995 the Department of Defense reissued its rule barring members of the armed forces from groups that "espouse supremacist causes."[289] Ministers united to oppose two Illinois rallies by Thom Robb's Knights in May, prompting Rachel Pendergraft to say, "It doesn't bother me. This is a free country." A requirement for $1 million insurance stalled those plans in June, but Grand Dragon Dennis McGiffen obtained permission in July.[290]

In South Carolina, on June 20–21, 1995, arsonists leveled two black churches in Manning and Greeleyville. The fires appeared to fit a pattern, with 670 church arsons or bombings logged between January 1995 and September 1998, and while a National Church Arson Task Force found no evidence of conspiracy, Klansmen *were* behind the Carolina fires.[291] Christian Knights members Gary Cox and Timothy Welch pled guilty in August 1996, followed by Arthur Haley and Hubert Rowell in December. All received prison terms, while the SPLC sued the Christian Knights for damages, winning a $37.8 million judgment in July 1998 (reduced on appeal to $21.5 million).[292]

CHAPTER 11

"Yesterday, Today, Forever"
(1996–2014)

The approach of a new century found some Klansmen mired in the past, while others explored new frontiers. Louisiana knight Darrell Flinn mimicked others with his cable access show *The Klan in Acadiana,* launched in 1994, but it brought him to court in February 1996, when authorities belatedly noted Klansmen wearing masks for the broadcasts. Prosecutor Floyd Johnson deemed it a violation of the state's anti-mask law, while Flinn challenged that the 1924 statute did not anticipate television. Flinn quit the Klan when reporters discovered his black live-in girlfriend.[1]

A similar case troubled California wizard Bill Albers in February 1996. While police respected his right to burn crosses in private, with permits from Modesto's fire department, a new Unified Air Pollution Control District banned the practice. Albers defiantly proceeded, logging $100,000 in citations.[2] June found Albers in Auburn, Washington, scuffling with protesters at an American Legion hall where the wizard staged an initiation ceremony for local teens. "We got kids coming out in droves," Albers said. "They don't have no following to go to." George Kelly, fined for breaking a reporter's camera, said, "Hell, I'd do it again, man."[3]

Risky Business

Eric Lane, imperial wizard of the Dixieland White Knights in Texas, had more serious problems with an October 1996 initiation ritual, when he blindfolded two 14-year-old girls, stripped them, then ordered them to have sex with each other before servicing him. The result: a 10-year prison term imposed in May 1998.[4]

Later that October, Christian Knights members Joshua England and Clayton Spires, Jr., attended a Klan turkey shoot, followed by a CCC rally in Lexington County, South Carolina. While driving home, they strafed a black nightclub with rifle fire, wounding three persons. Both pled guilty in federal court, receiving 26-year prison terms, then were hit with matching sentences on state charges in 1999.[5]

In November 1996 a half-dozen Christian Identity zealots met in Montana to charter the Church of True Israel, led by former Aryan Nations state leader Charles Mangels. Other founders included ex-wizard Stanley McCollum, former Colorado Klansman Charles

Howarth, Aryan Nations defector John Burke, and Edward Dosh, fundraising director for the Militia of Montana. Howarth died in November 2000, before the new sect attracted many members, but a full-scale exodus from Richard Butler's camp began in early 2001, after the Aryan Nations compound was sold to satisfy a judgment from another SPLC lawsuit. Dropping overt Nazi trappings, the cult recruited "working-class people with white, Christian values," specifically excluding "Jews, Orientals, Mexicans, Negroes or any other combination of Mongrels."[6]

Another presidential race absorbed Klansmen in 1996. Ralph Forbes made an appealing candidate, running with self-styled anti-abortion "fanatic" Pro-Life Anderson (né Charles) on the America First Party ticket, claiming 184,820 votes nationwide out of 96,275,640 ballots cast.[7] Nearly as appealing, Republican contender Pat Buchanan had lapsed into Holocaust denial, writing that Treblinka's gas chambers "do not emit enough carbon monoxide to kill anybody," praising Hitler as "an individual of great courage, a soldier's soldier in the Great War, a political organizer of the first rank, a leader steeped in the history of Europe, who possessed oratorical powers that could awe even those who despised him."[8] His supporters included campaign co-chair Larry Pratt, forced to resign in February 1996 over ties to Kirk Lyons; co-chairman Michael Farris, attendee of a "White Rose Banquet" honoring anti-abortion terrorists; Florida chairwoman Susan Lamb, a member of David Duke's NAAWP; Louisiana delegate Vincent Bruno, formerly with Duke's gubernatorial campaign staff in 1991; and William Carter, a member of Buchanan's South Carolina steering committee, fired when reporters exposed his role in Duke's 1992 presidential campaign.[9]

As for Duke, he tried once more for a U.S. Senate seat, running last in a field of four candidates with 141,489 votes out of 978,683 ballots cast.[10] J. D. Alder closed the year with a December visit to *The Jerry Springer Show,* telling the audience, "We're all gathered here tonight to celebrate a white Christmas, a Ku Klux Klan Christmas, a Christmas with multi-colored lights instead of the damned Jew product of light bushes that we've got in the department stores. And Klanta Claus will be here to give all the good Klansmen some real nice stocking stuffers and lumps of coal for the little nigger kids because we're having a white Christmas."[11]

Other knights preferred bullets to ballots. On January 22, 1997, police raided the Illinois home of Klansman Ricky Salyers, seizing grenades, artillery shells, and 35,000 rounds of ammunition.[12] Six days later, in North Carolina, arsonists torched the home of a mixed race couple previously threatened by the Klan.[13]

Kentucky grand dragon Ronald Edwards founded the Imperial Klans of America, relocating headquarters to Decatur, Illinois, before year's end. Legal problems distracted Edwards in 2002, allowing Dale Fox and his Ohio-based Brotherhood of Klans to raid the IKA's membership, but Edwards rebounded the following year, reclaiming most of his former knights. A heart attack killed Fox in November 2006, passing power to former skinhead and Aryan Nations webmaster Jeremy Parker.[14]

"The Solution Is White Revolution"

Edward Foster's Keystone Knights rallied in Pittsburgh, in April 1997, joined by Jeff Berry and a contingent of his Indiana-based American Knights. While police jailed three rowdy protesters, Berry told the crowd, "The solution is white revolution."[15]

Something like it was brewing in Texas, where FBI agents arrested four Kluxers on April 23. Betrayed by one of their own, the four had planned to bomb a natural gas refinery outside Fort Worth, using the disaster as cover for an armored car holdup. Ringleader Edward Taylor, Jr., pled guilty in October, followed by conviction of his three accomplices. Sentenced in January 1998, Taylor received 262 months, while his codefendants drew terms ranging from 110 to 168 months.[16]

Fourteen years of legal wrangling began in Laurens, South Carolina, in April 1997, when ex-grand dragon Michael Burden sold his Echo Theater to the Rev. David Kennedy, a black civil rights activist. Kennedy wanted the site for his church, but agreed that Burden could retain ownership until his death. On the sly, Burden sold the Echo to Klansman John Howard, who transformed it into a "Redneck Shop," peddling racist paraphernalia and hosting a backroom Klan museum. Kennedy's efforts to evict Howard dragged on through 2011, when he finally acquired clear title to the property. A court ordered Howard to pay Kennedy's $3,300 legal tab.[17]

Portage, Indiana, Klansmen targeted a Latino woman's newly purchased mobile home in July 1997, dressing in full regalia to assault the dwelling with bats, clubs and bricks. Federal prosecutors indicted two knights, Randolph Benwell II and Darrell Blanchard, on civil rights charges in January 1998. Both pled guilty and were sentenced in September 1998, Benwell to one year in prison, Blanchard to four months followed by a matching period of home confinement.[18]

In August 1997 Michael Cuffley, kleagle for Thom Robb's Missouri realm, applied to "adopt" a stretch of Interstate 55 near St. Louis, exchanging litter cleanup for posting of a sign that advertised the Klan. Rejection spawned litigation and successive appeals by the state, but Cuffley fought his case all the way to the Supreme Court, defeating Missouri's Highway and Transportation Commission at each level.[19] Another case from August offset Cuffley's triumph in the public mind. Kentucky police arrested Tony Gamble, imperial wizard of the Tri-state Knight Riders, for repeatedly raping and sodomizing two young girls between 1992 and 1994. Convicted at trial, Gamble received a 55-year prison term in March 1998.[20]

Even former Klansmen, long retired, were bad news for the order. In Salem, Virginia, where a car-bombing killed a toddler and wounded her father in 1975, prosecutors finally caught up with ex-knight Frank Helvestine III, betrayed by his son-in-law. Helvestine supplied the explosives for another Klansman—long deceased—to wreck an interracial couple's car. The victims, simple passersby, had not been targeted. Helvestine's advanced age and failing health would not spare him from a 12-year prison term in September 1997.[21]

A month later, in Wilkesboro, North Carolina, four knights assaulted Calvin Cothern when he tried to quit their klavern. In July 1998 three of the attackers received jail terms ranging from three to six months.[22] The case of Tarheel grand dragon J. J. Jones was less dramatic. Police nabbed him after a Carthage rally, in November, for writing bad checks in Virginia.[23] The crowning insult came two days later, when Stone Mountain, Georgia, elected its first black mayor.[24] On November 13, Klansman and Aryan Nations member Matthaeus Jaehnig led Denver police on a wild chase following a burglary, then killed one officer before committing suicide.[25] The year ended with threats in North Carolina, as American Knights grand cyclops Robert Moore challenged opponents in Asheville. "It's going to be another Greensboro if they throw rocks," he declared—and thereby lost the Klan's parade permit.[26]

Roy Frankhouser faced more criminal charges as 1997 drew to a close. Speaking once

Klansmen fought and won a legal battle for the right to "adopt" a Missouri highway, ca. March 2001 (author's collection).

more for the UKA, he had harassed and threatened "race traitor" Bonnie Jouhari, a fair housing advocate, along with her daughter. In 1998 the SPLC sued Frankhouser and neo–Nazi Ryan Wilson's Alpha HQ Web site, securing a $1 million judgment against Wilson. Frankhouser's penalty was different: he agreed to 80 hours of sensitivity training and 1,000 hours of community service, plus airing public apologies to his victims with fair housing public service announcements on his *White Forum* cable access program. The capper was financial, granting the Jouharis 10 percent of Frankhouser's income for a decade.[27]

New Orders, Old Tactics

Klansmen continued to make headlines in 1998. Robert Moore resumed his threats in January, targeting an Asheville businesswoman who procured an injunction against his latest rally, warning that "she better keep her eyes open behind her head every day she walks down those streets."[28] Indiana spokesmen for a previously unknown group, Imperial Empire Wizards of the KKK, sued Rockville's historic Billie Creek Village for excluding the Klan from its annual Civil War reenactments, claiming damages of $500,000.[29]

Between February 23 and March 16, 1998, FBI agents arrested Dennis McGiffen and five other "New Order" Klansmen on conspiracy charges, including robberies and sale of illegal weapons to bankroll a terrorist campaign against targets including the ADL, SPLC, and California's Simon Wiesenthal Center. Defendant Wallace Weicherding told a police informer, "The building in Oklahoma, when we get moving, that ain't nothing." By May, McGiffen and four codefendants had pled guilty on various charges, drawing sentences that ranged from 20 months to seven years. Jurors convicted Weicherding in August 1998, resulting in a six-year sentence.[30]

While the New Order knights sat in jail, Kirk Lyons struggled with his public image, denying charges of racism even as he told reporters interracial marriage was "like taking rainbow ice cream and putting it in a blender. What you get is this gray mush not fit to eat." He defended public displays of Confederate flags as "a civil rights issue" and lunched with Asheville's NAACP leader, prompting calls for that officer's resignation.[31] Jeff Berry's American Knights tried a new trick, inserting fliers into free newspapers, sparking complaints from publishers in half a dozen states. "They can tell us to stop, but until they show us a law, we're not," Berry said.[32]

In April 1998 Kim Badynski's Northwest Knights provided security for British Holocaust denier David Irving, for a speech in Seattle.[33] Jeff Berry suffered a setback that month, when a federal judge dismissed his $8 million lawsuit against Ann Arbor, Michigan, for failure to protect the Klan's rights at a rally two years earlier.[34] One month later, David Neumann, Michigan coordinator of Thom Robb's Knights, lost his lawsuit to compel a rally in Lansing.[35] May brought more trouble to North Carolina, as police jailed two Klansmen for firing at a black couple's home in Rutherford County.[36]

Barry Black faced charges of his own in August 1998, for violating Virginia's cross-burning statute. Convicted in June 2001, he appealed to the state's supreme court and won there, by a narrow vote of four to three that ruled the law unconstitutional. The U.S. Supreme Court affirmed that decision, on appeal by the state, in April 2003, but approved the jailing of two knights who lit a cross at a black couple's home in May 1998.[37]

Road Rage

On June 7, 1998, three white men offered black hitchhiker James Byrd, Jr., a ride in Jasper, Texas. They drove him out of town, beat him on a lonely road, then dragged him for three miles behind their pickup truck, until he was beheaded and dismembered. The clumsy killers dropped a wrench and cigarette lighter which led FBI agents to suspects Shawn Berry—heavily tattooed member of a prison gang, the Confederate Knights of America—and John King; accomplice Lawrence Brewer soon joined them in jail.[38] At parolee Brewer's home, investigators found large quantities of Klan and neo–Nazi literature, including *The Turner Diaries*.[39] Darrell Flinn's White Camelia Knights rallied twice in the killers' defense, in June and October, joined on the first march by Thom Robb's Knights. Jeff Berry—no relation to Shawn—led his own rally in October 1998, shouting at a hostile audience, "We hate Jews. We hate niggers. I'm a Yankee and I have never heard the word thank you in the nigger vocabulary. We don't like you niggers. Tell me one thing your race has accomplished."[40]

None of it helped the three defendants. Jurors convicted King in February 1999 and sentenced him to die. Brewer received an identical sentence in September. Berry was luckier, wearing a "What Would Jesus Do?" bracelet to court in November 1999, when he received a life sentence with 40 years to serve before parole. Brewer died by lethal injection in September 2011, after declaring, "I have no regrets. No, I'd do it all over again, to tell you the truth." King remained on death row as this book went to press.[41] In October 1999 Congress passed a federal hate crime statute named for James Byrd and gay murder victim Matthew Shepard, expanding federal jurisdiction over crimes motivated by bias.[42]

And Ku Klux violence continued. In July 1998, California police jailed Klansman John Varela for assaulting a witness at a hate crime trial.[43] Two weeks later, four Keystone Knights menaced a Pennsylvania state trooper with guns as he sat in a tree, watching a "White Pride Day" rally. By July 1999 three of the defendants were caged with sentences ranging from six to 30 months, while jurors acquitted the fourth.[44] In October 1998 Klansman Joseph Holleran painted swastikas and other racist symbols on a Pennsylvania synagogue, earning a 27-month prison term.[45] That same month, ex–Klansman E. H. Hennis brought a fake bomb to a Guilford County Commission meeting in North Carolina, warning panel members, "My way of getting you, you won't be carried off in stretchers. And I'm not making a threat, I'm just telling you facts. Your body parts can be picked up and put in a body bag." Police raided Hennis's farm, seizing three tons of ammonium nitrate. Convicted in January 2000, Hennis received a suspended jail term and three years' probation. The aging knight's campaign to join the commission, in 2008, ended in humiliation at the polls.[46]

Churches of Hate

As the century closed, Klansmen increasingly cloaked themselves in religion. Observers ranked Jeff Berry's Church of the American Knights as the country's most active faction, but others tried to keep pace.[47] Imperial Wizard Jimmy Ray Shelton led North Carolina's Church of Confederate Ghost Knights, but he ran into trouble while visiting Texas in March, with Klansman Eddie Bradley. Bastrop police tried to stop them for speeding, drawing gunfire in a high-speed chase that left both Klansmen jailed on charges of attempted capital murder. Their vehicle contained five guns, seven knives, brass knuckles, detonation cord, methamphetamine, and $1,500 in cash. Convicted in September, Shelton drew a 99-year sentence.[48]

In April 1999 ATF and FBI agents raided a Klansman's farm at Oregonia, Ohio, arresting ex-convict Aryan Nations member Kale Kelly on weapons charges. Authorities had tracked his meetings with IKA imperial wizard Ron Edwards, and searched a Klan compound in Greenville, Kentucky, asking Edwards if Kelly had mentioned plans to bomb a federal building. Kelly pled guilty to illegal gun possession as a convicted felon, receiving a four-year sentence and a $9,000 fine in July. His Ohio benefactor, Klansman Ed Ingram, attended the hearing with his daughter (Kelly's girlfriend), telling reporters, "You win some, you lose some."[49]

David Duke tried another run for office in May 1999, campaigning for Congress as a Republican. He placed fourth in a field of nine candidates, polling 28,059 among 146,498 ballots cast.[50] A month later, in Fort Payne, Alabama, police jailed five Klansmen for bringing concealed weapons to a courthouse rally. More knights rushed the jail, repelled by officers in riot gear. Jurors convicted three defendants, resulting in six-month suspended jail terms.[51] In July, Delta Knights kleagle Greg David faced charges of stealing $6,700 from his girlfriend's family. A separate indictment accused him of raping a black man in 1997.[52] In October, Charleston, South Carolina's city council passed a resolution branding the Klan a domestic terrorist organization and condemning any group "whose purpose is to encourage hate of any individual, race, religion, culture or way of life."[53]

David Duke addresses the Friends of the British National Party in 1999, flanked by Ray Armstrong (left) and Nick Griffin (Southern Poverty Law Center).

November 1999 saw North Carolina Klansmen Robert Guffey and son Andrew charged with possession of bombs, stolen property, and illegal drugs.[54] That same month, in Indiana, Jeff Berry held two reporters at gunpoint during an interview at his home. The reporters filed suit in January 2000, winning a $120,000 judgment in December. That verdict spurred authorities to slap Berry with five felony charges in 2001. He pled guilty in October and received a seven-year sentence.[55]

The year ended badly for Keystone Knights leader Edward Foster, charged in December with burning the home his wife won in their divorce settlement. Aside from arson, prosecutors charged him with insurance fraud.[56]

Klans and Militias

The latter 1990s witnessed a groundswell of "patriot militias" nationwide, inspired by events at Ruby Ridge and Waco, arming in defense against their government and a poorly defined "New World Order." Observers counted 858 such groups in 1996.[57] Most denied any taint of racism, but at least 137 recruited Klansmen and Nazis, as had the Minutemen three decades earlier.[58]

Kirk Lyons, present at the Rocky Mountain Rendezvous that launched the movement, served as an "unofficial legal advisor for militia leaders." In June 1995 he said, "They call me all the time. I tell them this. I tell everybody this. If you want to stay out of jail, keep your damn mouths shut because there's a good chance you're going to get infiltrated."[59] Larry Pratt's Gun Owners of America helped bankroll CAUSE, while *Soldier of Fortune* magazine urged all "patriots, militiamen, and everyone else concerned over what happens to our freedom" to support Lyons.[60]

Other knights had more direct involvement in the movement. Ex-Klansman August Kreis founded and led Pennsylvania's Messiah Militia, telling reporters that any future showdowns with the government "won't be like Waco. They won't have to wonder who shot first. It will be us."[61] Aging dragon Robert Scoggin claimed alliance with the South Carolina Civilian Militia, but its spokesmen denied any ties.[62] Montana militia leaders John Trochmann and Rick Hill were cohorts of Richard Butler's Aryan Nations.[63]

Dennis Mahon's Oklahoma Klan "completely collapsed" after the Murrah bombing, leaving him committed to "small cells and lone wolfism." He moved to Arizona, telling a 2004 Aryan Fest audience, "You nuke D.C., you're going to wipe out most of the politicians, plus a couple million crack-head niggers. It's a win-win. And I think it's the only way, I really do. Terrorism works. We did a lot of terrorism in Tulsa in the 1980s. We put heads in the road, and people paid attention."[64] Following his own advice, though on a smaller scale, would soon send him to prison.

President Barack Obama's election in 2008 revived the flagging "patriot" movement, with increased doses of paranoia and outright racism. The Konfederate Klavaliers Arkansas Volunteer Militia Kavalry, affiliated with the Orion Knights, declares that "America was founded and built by white men, for white men and women and their posterity! Only members of the white Adamic race are true Americans! This land is our land, and we intend to take it back!" That said, the group warns potential recruits that "We do NOT promote, and neither do we condone ANY criminal behavior unlawful or illegal acts whatsoever!!!"[65]

Reheating Cold Cases

While militias spread, Southern prosecutors revisited more of their unsolved racist murders from the civil rights era. Forty years after the fact, Montgomery, Alabama's district attorney reopened Willie Edwards's case, changing his cause of death from "unknown" to homicide. That gesture floundered in 1999, when a grand jury declined to indict any surviving suspects.[66]

Mississippi was more successful with Sam Bowers and the White Knights. Investigation of Bowers for illegal gambling, in 1997, evolved into reopening the Dahmer case from 1966.[67] In the process, Jackson newsman Jerry Mitchell learned that Billy Pitts, convicted of Dahmer's slaying in 1968, had yet to serve a day of his life sentence. Issuance of an arrest warrant persuaded Pitts to testify against his former komrades, whereupon police arrested Bowers, Deavours Nix, and Charles Noble in May 1998.[68] Ancient FBI files revealed evidence that Klansmen contacted three jurors in Bowers's 1968 murder trial, of whom one "said yes" to fixing the verdict.[69] Nix made his court appearance in a wheelchair, pleading terminal illness, but detectives caught him playing golf soon afterward. Noble denied killing Dahmer, or even joining the Klan.[70]

Old friends rallied for the defense. Edward Fields, in *The Truth at Last,* declared, "There is no doubt that Sam Bowers is the greatest and most heroic defender of White people's rights of this era." Anonymous "Free Sam Bowers" fliers littered driveways in Jackson.[71] Against them was sworn testimony from Pitts and another ex–Klansman, Bob Stringer, who recalled a meeting where Bowers ordered a "Number Four" project—murder—directed at Dahmer.[72]

Bowers faced trial alone in August 1998, sitting through descriptions of the fatal raid from Dahmer's children. Pitts, Stringer and Webber Rogers—another ex–Klansman who joined in a "dry run" rehearsal for Dahmer's murder—told their stories to the jury. Deavours Nix appeared for the defense, describing the Klan as a benevolent charity group, calling Bowers a patriot. "He did not use profane language and I never heard him use a racial slur," Nix said. Jurors saw through the smoke and convicted Bowers on August 21. Bowers received a life sentence and died in prison, in November 2006. Nix never made it to trial, killed by cancer in September 1998. Jurors failed to reach a verdict on Charles Noble at his trial, in June 1999.[73]

Invisible Empire Worldwide

William Simmons claimed the whole world for his empire in 1915, but the Klan only approached that goal in the 1990s. Canadian knights continued to struggle for traction, losing Teàrlach Mac a' Pheasron to social work and a religious ministry in 1997.[74] British Columbian Klansman William Nicholson—arrested in 2001 for possession of weapons, explosives, and marijuana—emerged from prison a year later, apologetic and vowing "to burn my robes."[75] In 2007, Jeremy Parker expanded his Ohio-based Brotherhood of Klans to plant klaverns in Calgary, Alberta, and Regina, Saskatchewan, claiming 250 members.[76] Presently, Chris Waters, imperial wizard of the home-grown Aryan Nations Knights, claims to lead "the largest growing Klan in Canada," working closely "with our Brothers in the States."[77]

Americans in Panama had formed a klavern in the 1920s, but the next Klansman seen in the country, eight decades later, was Canadian James McQuirter. Abandoning his birth name when he renounced white supremacy, McQuirter entered the self-help field as "James Alexander," published *Realm of Wealth: The 9 Cycles of Prosperity*, and took his act on the road. Tracked by a Canadian reporter to Panama's Gamboa Resort in 2008, McQuirter was the front man for Emerald Passport, an apparent pyramid scheme billed in its ads as "one of the most profitable income opportunities in the world today." Emerald Passport president Jaime Figueroa claimed ignorance of "Alexander's" history as Canada's top Klansman.[78]

In November 2007 an Internet posting from the European White Knights claimed active units in Austria, Belgium, Denmark, England, Estonia, France, Germany, Ireland, the Netherlands, Norway, Poland, Scotland, Sweden, and Wales.[79] The next European Klan news came from a rival group, the United Northern and Southern Knights, in August 2009. That faction, based in Chicago, claimed units in Britain and Croatia, while offering Web blogs in Flemish, French, German and Italian.[80]

Britain certainly felt stirrings. Convicted child molester Allen Beshella, once an aide to James Farrands, sought to colonize Wales for the Klan in the late 1980s, teaming with skinheads to launch a minor reign of terror in Caerau. They posed in robes, burned crosses, sent threatening letters to "white niggers," and beat victim Leighton Evans so badly that he

Allen Bashela, second from right, leads a racist demonstration in Wales (author's collection).

required plastic surgery. Alan Winder replaced Beshella as Britain's top Klansman by 1998, but Beshella remained active until his imprisonment for promoting race hatred, in 2002. By then, the Klan had spread to Scotland and the British Midlands, targeting Asians and other nonwhite immigrants. Welsh police jailed three knights in February 1999, for assaulting Dr. Sajal Sengup in Maerdy. In 2009 Britain's Home Office added ex-wizard Don Black to a list of racists banned from entering the country. Two years later, London's *Daily Mirror* named biker Chris Hopgood as Britain's grand dragon, affiliated with the European White Knights of the Burning Cross. In October 2013, Welsh resident Christopher Philips pled guilty to donning Klan robes for the Swansea mock lynching of a black "golliwog" doll.[81]

Germany harbored Klansmen before Adolf Hitler's ascendancy, and the order returned in 2000, promoted in Baden-Württemberg by a state security officer calling himself "Ryan Davis." Known for years prior as a Nazi and skinhead musician, Davis styled himself grand dragon, with a charter from a Mississippi faction, and led his knights into alliance with the violent National Socialist Underground. NSU members attended Klan cross-burnings and launched a terror spree that climaxed with a police officer's murder in April 2007. By then, other cops had joined the Klan, including one—commanding a riot control squad—who was still on the job when *Der Spiegel* broke the story in August 2012.[82]

In the Balkans, Serbian knights donned hoods to chant with neo–Nazis at a Belgrade soccer game in January 2007.[83] A similar scene played out in Asenovgrad, Bulgaria, when brownshirts and white robes gathered for a Nazi rock concert at the town's library, in August 2009.[84]

If Europe, with its fascist past, seemed fertile ground for klannishness, the order's expansion Down Under surprised some observers. Peter Coleman, an exalted cyclops of the Kentucky-based Imperial Klans, claimed klaverns in Australia's three eastern states by June 1999, with a total of 70 members. "Our aim," he said, "is for a white Australia, a fair Australia." The nation's Aborigines, in his view, were "beyond help ... the worst of the whites mixed in with the black." Expelled by Australia's right-wing One Nation party, Coleman faced competition from Missouri's New Order Knights, but an ADL spokesman seemed unconcerned, telling reporters, "Just because there are three guys running around in hoods doesn't mean we have to rush to the barricades." Still, Defense Minister John Moore ordered an investigation of Coleman's claim to members in the military, while the Australian Secret Intelligence Organization was "deeply concerned."[85]

The still-unsolved January 2000 murder of teacher Bjarne Carlsen at Brewarrina, New South Wales, justified that concern when police found "KKK" scrawled on the corpse. Nine months later, white soldiers dressed as Klansmen harassed black recruits at Queensland's Lavarack Barracks. Threatening letters frightened Aboriginal families in Lismore, New South Wales, in 2006. The following year, in July, Queensland teacher Graeme McNeil complained to one of his high school students, Anthony Rowlingson, that Anthony's brother had "taken liberties with my laptop," revealing McNeil's double life as a Klansman. Rowlingson shot his brother and received a life sentence. McNeil got eight years in 2010, for helping conceal the body.[86]

The outback Klan's nearest brush with legitimacy comes through its alliance with the far-right Australia First Party, founded in 1996. The party's Web site has displayed Klan symbols and raised no protest when self-described imperial wizard David Palmer told reporters, in 2009, that several knights had "secretly joined" the AFP. "We aren't interested in actually registering as a party," Palmer explained. "[The Klan] is a white pressure group; a white social group for white families. But also a reserve in case the ethnics get out of hand and they need sorting out. Members don't necessarily have to be Christian. As long as they're white it's OK."[87]

"You Know Who We Are"

The advent of a new millennium agitated paranoid extremists, filling their minds and Web sites with predictions of global disaster, but Klansmen faced the same old problems after "Y2K." As Edward Foster told reporters, "The [Klan's] legacy is that we've had a lot of hangings, a lot of bombings, a lot of shootings. That don't bother me at all. If somebody wants to go out here and kill a nigger or something.... They're not our equal, they have got no right to breathe free air in America. This is not the Boy Scouts; this is the Ku Klux Klan. You know who we are, and you know what our history is."[88]

In January 2000, Klansman Dennis Adamson received a one-year sentence for terrorizing black neighbors in Ball Ground, Georgia. Three weeks later, police raided South Mississippi Ku Klux Klan wizard Jimmie Maxey's home, seizing his computer, after he posted threats to the state's attorney general online.[89] April saw Jimmy Crawford, founder of the South Carolina Ghost Riders, jailed for recruiting teens to firebomb a black church in Bishopville. In June 2000 North Carolina Klansman Jacob Stull pled guilty to shooting up a black family's home, receiving a 54-month prison term. That same month, arsonists leveled Fern Creek, Kentucky's Heart of Fire Christian Church, after its pastor criticized Klansmen. Three days later, Maryland jurors convicted Klan-affiliated brothers Daniel and David Starkey of murdering a black woman in 1999. On the same day, June 15, Connecticut knight Scott Palmer pled guilty to intimidation based on bigotry, facing terms in both state and federal prison.[90]

Kirk Lyons tried a new twist with his SLRC in 2000, appointing H. K. Edgerton as chairman of the board. The surprise: Edgerton was black, a former president of Asheville, North Carolina's NAACP chapter, suspended in December 1998 for noncompliance with the organization's rules. He soon became a fixture at functions staged by the Sons of Confederate Veterans, clad in Confederate gray and toting the South's vanquished battle flag. When not engaged in SLRC business, Edgerton served as president of Southern Heritage 411, a corporation "founded to inform the public about Southern Heritage from the perspective of the hundreds of thousands of black people who love and support the South, its people, its customs, and its history."[91]

In August 2000 Oklahoma Klansmen Dillon Bell and Jonathan Duke vandalized Jewish headstones at Tulsa's Rose Hill Memorial Park. Arrested in September, both pled guilty, receiving seven-year prison terms (with five years suspended for Bell).[91] Two months later, following a Klan rally in Skokie, Illinois, National Alliance member Eric Hanson assaulted a black woman, then fled to Lindenhurst, where he died in a shootout with police, in June 2001.[92]

On the political front, Pat Buchanan left the Republican Party in October 1999, staking his presidential hopes on billionaire Ross Perot's Reform Party. In March 2000, at a banquet in Virginia, David Duke, Don Black, and National Alliance spokesman Sam van Rensburg joined RP state coordinator Peter Gemma in stressing the "importance of getting Pat Buchanan on the ballot in all 50 states." Three weeks later, still in Virginia, Buchanan staffers held another meeting with Kirk Lyons, *American Renaissance* editor Jim Lubinskas, and Nick Griffin from the American Friends of the British National Party. At the time, AF-BNP leader Mark Cotterill, an expatriate British fascist, worked at Buchanan's Virginia campaign headquarters. In June, Buchanan addressed an Illinois meeting jointly sponsored by the CCC and the Rockford Institute, a "think tank" devoted to preserving white America's "overt racial identity."[93]

Buchanan stunned those supporters in August 2000, when he chose black female activist Ezola Foster as his running mate. Mark Cotterill told reporters, "Buchanan is now part of the problem, and not part of the solution." In November, Buchanan polled a paltry 449,181 votes out of 105,425,985 ballots cast, and promptly reneged on his promise to remain with the Reform Party for five years, building it into a national force.[94]

In lesser contests, Ralph Forbes failed to qualify for a congressional race with his newly formed Freedom Party of Arkansas, but mounted a write-in campaign, polling 393 votes out of 91,142 ballots cast in the state's 3rd District.[95]

"Y2Kaos"

The 21st century properly began in 2001, but little changed for Klansmen. Railton Loy's National Knights scuffled with protesters at a South Bend, Indiana rally in May, then required police aid to locate their cars. A month later, in Williamson County, Texas, two sheriff's deputies were fired for serving as kleagles.[96] Later in June, Klansman Steven Heldenbrand joined Midland Hammerskins to attack black diners at a restaurant in Springfield, Missouri. All pled guilty, drawing prison terms ranging from two to four years.[97] Railton Loy made new headlines in September, convicted of telephone harassment, sentenced to six months and a $150 fine. His Klan finally inspired St. Joseph County to ban all "hate activities" in July 2003.[98]

The catastrophic terrorist attacks of September 2001 galvanized right-wing extremist groups throughout America. Illinois Klansman Basil Sitzes counseled moderation, claiming, "I have nothing against Jews, they're pretty good allies. And I've got nothing against Muslims and blacks. Only thing is, I believe the races shouldn't intermarry." Other racist leaders were more combative, capitalizing on national rage. Joe Roy, director of the SPLC's Intelligence Project, warned, "Don't judge too much by Basil's KKK. He's kind of a has-been. There was a 12 percent increase in these groups throughout the country last year."[99] At year's end, Baton Rouge police investigated claims that Circle Six Knights imperial wizard Scott Ayers had killed himself. Instead of a corpse, they found guns, bombs, and marijuana at his home, along with Klan paraphernalia. Ayers remained missing, while two of his knights went to jail for bomb making and passing bad checks.[100]

Settling Old Scores

Black residents of Birmingham were cautiously optimistic in 1997, when FBI agents and local police reopened their 1963 "Bapbom" investigation. While battling its reputation for obstructionism, the Bureau still appeared to drag its feet. Three more years elapsed before a grand jury indicted aging Cahaba Boys Bobby Cherry and Thomas Blanton, Jr., for their role in the bombing, in May 2000, and Cherry's case was quickly sidelined with a judgment of mental incompetence.[101] Blanton faced trial alone in April 2001, haunted by his own words caught on tape in 1963. Jurors convicted him on May 1, resulting in four life sentences.[102]

Another year passed before psychologists deemed Cherry fit for trial. Seemingly amused by the proceedings, smirking while jurors viewed old footage of him beating Fred Shuttlesworth. The smile dropped when Cherry's son recalled his boasts of planting the church bomb, and Cherry seemed outraged by the jury's guilty verdict. "This whole bunch lied all the way through this thing," he protested. "Now, I don't know why I'm going to jail for nothing." He died there, at 74, in November 2004. Blanton remained in prison as this book went to press.[103]

In November 1999 FBI agents reopened their file on Ben White, murdered on federal land in 1966. Klan killer James Jones was dead, but his confession survived on paper, supporting the indictment of accomplice Earl Avants in June 2000. Legal maneuvers stalled the trial until February 2003, when jurors convicted Avants of aiding and abetting White's murder, handing him a sentence of life imprisonment without parole. Avants died in prison at 72, in June 2004.[104]

"I'll Have His Head"

Railton Loy's National Knights kept making headlines of the wrong sort through 2002. At New Year's, FBI agents raided the home of Loy's son—Indiana grand dragon Richard Loy—to arrest an Oregon skinhead wanted on kidnapping charges. In December, at the Klan's "Christmas unity rally," the Loys appalled Christian Identity attendees by serving them pork. Richard followed that faux pas with a turn as "Klanta Klaus," sporting bloody lips and missing teeth from a firearms accident, then led disappointed knights in a botched cross-and-swastika burning where both "sacred" symbols collapsed.[105]

Laughter did not suit North Carolina's Nation's Knights, led by Charles Barefoot, Jr. Johnston County deputies raided Barefoot's home in July 2002, seizing machine guns and explosives, allegedly intended for a blitz against the sheriff's office. Officers also charged Barefoot and his son with two counts of arson, for burning a barn and a bus. Barefoot's grudge against Sheriff Steve Bizzell stemmed from 2001, when Bizzell barred the Klan from Benson's "Mule Days" parade," whereupon Barefoot vowed, "I'll have his head." While that case was pending, in January 2003, officers seized a bloodstained van from Barefoot's estranged wife, linking it to the murder of an unidentified man found days earlier, in Sampson County. The Barefoots and two other Klansmen faced murder charges, stalled by Charles spouting "gibberish" and "kooky stuff" before a judge who found him mentally incompetent. That would not save him from the weapons charges, though: Barefoot pled guilty in that case and received a 27-month term in state prison. Federal charges from the same arrest earned him another 15 years, in February 2013.[106]

In April 2002 David Fuselier, great titan of America's Invisible Empire, led four other knights in burning a cross at a black family's home in Longville, Louisiana. Police jailed Fuselier and his girlfriend on drug charges in October, followed by a federal indictment for racial intimidation in November. Fuselier pled guilty, then appealed his 13-year sentence as "too severe," an argument rejected by the Fifth Circuit Court of Appeals in 2004.[107]

Jordan Gollub focused his attention on parades in 2002, with mixed results. After obtaining a permit to march through York, Alabama, he canceled the July event and turned instead to three September demonstrations in Mississippi, including one at Philadelphia. "Neshoba has history, of course, with the killings," Gollub said, "but we want to make it clear that's not the type of behavior we condone. We believe in racial separation, among other things, but we certainly denounce the violent behavior that a lot of people associate with us."[108]

People such as David Hull, leader of the Pennsylvania-based White Knights, arrested in February 2003 for witness tampering, weapons charges, and instructing others to build bombs for use against abortion clinics. Convicted on seven counts in February 2005, Hull received a 12-year sentence, followed by three years' probation.[109]

Or people like twin brothers Dennis and Daniel Mahon. Daniel—a self-described "domestic terrorist"—was fired by American Airlines in May 1999, for starting a "Caucasian Employee Resource Group" among coworkers. Tom Metzger rose to his defense in 2001, telling readers of *Aryan Update* that "the Mahon family is under assault." And with good reason. On February 26, 2004, a mail bomb severely wounded Donald Logan, the black director of Scottsdale, Arizona's Office of Diversity and Dialogue. Federal agents tracked the Mahons to Illinois, arresting them for the bombing in June 2009. Jurors acquitted Daniel at trial, in May 2012, but convicted Dennis on three counts, handing him a 40-year sentence.[110]

Little changed for the Klan as the decade wore on. In February 2003, three Kentucky Klansmen pled guilty to charges of harassing a black family until the victims fled their West Covington home. In July the defendants received sentences ranging from 46 to 87 months, while the mother of one knight drew 24 months. Devlin Burke served his time in that case, then attacked a group of strangers outside a Covington gay bar in August 2010, slashing them with a razor. That assault earned him a 17-year sentence in April 2011.[111]

In November 2003, Tennessee members of America's Invisible Empire nearly killed prospective Klansman Karl Mitchell III, when a participant in his initiation shot him with a pistol, rather than a paintball gun.[112] Police in Coarsegold, California, arrested Bobby and Donna Hubbard in April 2005, for assaulting a Jewish woman, telling their victim, "You should have burned in the oven with the rest of the Jews." At their home, officers found guns, Klan robes, and photos of cross-burnings. Donna—a high school teacher of "health careers"—pled no contest in February 2007 on charges of battery and possessing assault weapons.[113] In August 2005, North Georgia White Knights member Daniel Schertz pled guilty to building pipe bombs, intended for use on buses transporting immigrant workers from Tennessee to Florida. In November Schertz received a 170-month prison term.[114]

White Knights Falling

In 2002 a Chicago high school teacher, Barry Bradford, joined forces with Mississippi journalist Jerry Mitchell to reopen the Neshoba County murder case from 1964. Filming a documentary on the crime, Bradford's students caught longtime suspect Edgar Killen off-guard in a recorded interview, taping various incriminating comments, while Mitchell identified the late "Mr. X" who directed FBI agents to the Klan's burial ground.[115] As a result, in January 2005, a local grand jury indicted Killen on three counts of murder. A logging accident crushed Killen's legs and stalled his trial until June, when jurors convicted him on reduced charges of manslaughter. It hardly mattered, since his 60-year sentence meant Killen would die in prison. The Supreme Court rejected his appeal in November 2013.[116]

Two weeks after Killen's conviction, Thomas Moore visited Meadville, Mississippi, with a Canadian film crew, seeking new leads in the murder of his brother Charles, with friend Henry Dee, in May 1964. They reached suspect Charles Edwards, who declined an interview, and relatives of James Seale, who claimed he was dead. That lie unraveled in January 2007, when FBI agents nabbed Seale in Roxie, charging him with kidnapping. At trial, Seale's ancient confession returned to haunt him, resulting in a June conviction and three life prison terms. The Fifth Circuit Court of Appeals overturned Seale's conviction in 2008, then reversed itself in 2009. The Supreme Court declined to review that decision in 2010, shortly after Franklin County officials settled a lawsuit filed by surviving relatives of the two victims, alleging that sheriff's deputies aided and abetted the killers. Seale died in prison, in August 2011.[117]

"They're Still Around"

Bad luck dogged Klansmen through the latter 2000s. In March 2006 veteran Nebraska State Patrol officer Robert Henderson lost his job over membership in the White Knights. He appealed to the state supreme court, which affirmed his dismissal in 2009, saying, "One cannot simultaneously wear the badge of the Nebraska State Patrol and the robe of a Klansman without degrading what that badge represents when worn by any officer."[118]

In July 2006 Jeff Berry quarreled with son Anthony in Spencerville, Indiana, and the argument turned bloody, leaving Jeff in critical condition while Anthony was booked for aggravated battery. Brain-damaged and given a 50-percent chance of survival, the ex-wizard pulled through with physical impairments. Anthony pled guilty to reduced charges in July 2007, while a Klansman-accomplice departed for army boot camp to "straighten him out."[119]

On July 30, 2006, two Imperial Klans members attacked a youth of Panamanian descent at a carnival in Brandenburg, Kentucky, leaving him severely injured. Defendants Jarred Hensley and Andrew Watkins pled guilty, receiving three-year sentences, while SPLC lawyers sued their Klan and Imperial Wizard Ron Edwards, winning a $2.5 million judgment in November 2008, affirmed on appeal by Kentucky's Supreme Court in March 2012.[120]

Gordon Young, ex-wizard of the World Knights of the KKK, faced Maryland child molestation charges in February 2007, but jurors acquitted him in July, discounting vague testimony from the alleged victim.[121] Raymond Foster, imperial wizard of the Sons of Dixie Knights, was less fortunate in Bogalusa, Louisiana. Police arrested Foster, his son, and five other knights in November 2008, on various charges linked to the murder of Cynthia Lynch, a white woman slain when she had second thoughts in the midst of an initiation ceremony. Some Bogalusans were surprised to find the Klan still active in their midst, but an old-timer said, "They're still around, but they don't force it on you like the blacks do with Martin Luther King." Foster initially claimed self-defense, then pled guilty to second-degree murder in May 2010, receiving a life sentence.[122]

Web of Hate

When Don Black launched his Stormfront Web site in 1995, he told a reporter, "It's about building a community and attracting hard-core supporters. We don't use the 'nigger, nigger' type of approaches. We don't want to present the Jerry Springer or Geraldo Rivera image of rabid racists. There are a lot of people who want to agree with us. They just don't want to be associated with that."[123]

That said, within two years of startup Black was featuring the work of Adolf Hitler, David Duke, William Pierce, Edward Fields, and lesser scribes such as Alexander Winchell ("Proof of Negro Inferiority") and Willie Martin ("1001 Quotes by and About Jews"). A collateral site run by Black, White Singles, arranged contacts for subscribers certified as "heterosexual, white gentiles only." Another Black operation, Blitzcast, served seekers of audio podcasts.[124]

Black's success spawned competition, ranging from relatively "high class" racist Web sites to the depths of crudity. Adrian Marlow collaborated with Black to launch White Pride World Wide, cross-pollinating with Stormfront until the two virtually merged in 1998.[125]

Knights Party director Thom Robb (right) with Canadian fascist Paul Fromm (center) and unidentified companion (Southern Poverty Law Center).

Jew Watch, established in 1998 by National Alliance member Frank Weltner, peddles Weltner's book *My Dead America* alongside thousands of articles comprising "an oasis of news for Americans who presently endure the hateful censorship of Zionist occupation."[126] David Duke also embraced the Internet, promoting his NAAWP and its successor, EURO (the European-American Unity and Rights Organization), soliciting donations to defend the rights of "European and Americans wherever they may live."[127]

By 1999, no self-respecting racist group felt complete without a Web site. Thom Robb's Knights produced the first Klan site, pushing a "kinder, gentler" image, stressing that whites "have a right to be proud of their race." Individual realms of the Knights followed suit, claiming "dramatic" growth in membership as a result of online applications.[128] Later renamed the Knights Party, with Rachel Pendergraft at the helm, Robb's Klan saw itself "Bringing a Message of Hope and Deliverance to White Christian America! A Message of Love NOT Hate!"[129]

Other factions followed Robb's example, but with less finesse. The White Camelia Knights proclaim themselves "White Christian Men and Women dedicated to the advancement and protection of the same Christian beliefs that were the foundation of this once great nation," warning visitors that "[r]acial suicide all in the name of equality is insane.... Why are so many people bent on promoting race-mixing and racial equality? Because, it is

Satan's goal to have us violate our Heavenly Father's law on mixing our seed with the other people of the world."[130] The Loyal White Knights present themselves as "a law abiding Christian Organization. We stand for pride in our race; and what our people have done past, present and future."[131] The Imperial Klans of America declare: "Our aims include fighting for White Civil Rights, educating our people concerning the problems that face our race, culture, and civilization, and uniting and organizing those of our people who are still resistant towards the ever-increasing anti–White hysteria that is plaguing the entire white world."[132] Imperial Wizard Jeff Jones, speaking for the Knight Riders, writes: "The uncivilized hoards [*sic*] who liberals call Minorities make up the majority of welfare recipients. With that said, I'll get straight to the point. The Blacks and Mexicans who believe entitlements are owed to them are held at bay only for as long as they receive welfare benefits.... White America, this is your wake up call. Many of us have been preparing for this, but for those of you who have not, your life and property may be at stake."[133]

By 2005 the Simon Wiesenthal Center found more than 5,000 racist and anti–Semitic Web sites online. In March of that year, Brian Levin, director of the Center for the Study of Hate and Extremism at California State University in San Bernardino, told NBC's George Lewis, "The key here is not the number of hate groups, but the fact that the technology can deliver messages of hate and instructions on who should be targeted straight to people who are ticking time bombs."[134] Seven years later, the Internet hacking collective known as Anonymous announced "Operation Blitzkrieg" against Klan and neo–Nazi sites online. It began with Stormfront, claiming 240,000 registered members, and briefly disabled that Web site in February 2012.[135]

Despite such opposition, hate sites still proliferate. The SPLC's last tabulation, in 2011, found 49 Klan sites online (seven linked to Thom Robb), competing for attention with 287 other white racist groups.[136] Robb, still a trend-setter in the field, offers "White Pride TV" online, with video clips from Don Black, Willis Carto, J. B. Stoner, Edward Fields, Richard Butler, Louis Beam, Ralph Forbes, and other heroes of the movement. Daughter Rachel hosts "The White Women's Perspective," while blond grandson Andrew Pendergraft stars in "The Andrew Show." As mom Rachel explains, Andrew "is proud to be a white Christian boy in America, but he knows that because of his minority status, the odds might be stacked against his people."[137]

Empires in Flux (2004–2007)

Offline, Klansmen and their allies pursued the futile quest for unity. One step in that direction, in May 2004, was the "New Orleans Protocol," conceived by David Duke and hailed by signatories as "a historical [*sic*] agreement about future conduct in the post–September 11 era." "Founding endorsers" included Duke, Don Black, Edward Fields, Willis Carto, British National Party founder John Tyndall, CCC board member Sam Dickson, National Alliance spokesmen David Pringle and Kevin Strom, and Klan ally Paul Fromm, from the Canadian Association for Free Expression.[138] Considering its authors and their histories, the agreement's terms seemed ludicrous:

1. Zero tolerance for violence.
2. Honorable and ethical behavior in relations with other signatory groups. This

includes not denouncing others who have signed this protocol. In other words, no enemies on the right.

    3. Maintaining a high tone in our arguments and public presentations.[139]

    Outsider Alex Linder, owner-operator of the Vanguard News Network ("No Jews. Just Right."[140]) shredded the protocol online, correcting its grammar, mocking its vow of nonviolence—"ARYANS PROMISE TO SHOW UP WITH KNIFE AT GUNFIGHT"—and concluding that "SLURS ARE NOT THE PROBLEM AND HYPOCRITES IN BUSINESS SUITS ARE NOT THE SOLUTION."[141] Others who missed the meeting largely ignored it, proceeding with business as usual. In 2004, Ray Armstrong—a longtime Duke associate, roommate and bodyguard—ran for Congress from Louisiana's First District, with Duke as his chief advisor. Armstrong placed second in a field of six candidates, with 19,266 votes (6.69 percent of the total).[142]

    ADL observers noted a Ku Klux "resurgence" in 2006, citing strenuous recruiting drives across the Great Plains, in the Mid-Atlantic states, and on the Pacific Coast. Kleagles stressed conservative social issues, opposing abortion, gay marriage, and immigration. Members of the World Knights rallied at Civil War battlefields in June, and joined other groups in August at Harper's Ferry, Virginia, protesting a commemoration of the Niagara Movement (forerunner of the NAACP). Their reward was a factional rift in November, wizard Gordon Young leading some of his knights into the National Socialist Movement, while others joined an NSM splinter group, the American National Socialist Workers Party.[143] At year's end, the ADL found 39 Klans vying for members in 22 states. Most were one-state operations, though Railton Loy's National Knights had klaverns in 20 states, trailed closely by the Empire Knights with 18.[144]

    The SPLC's tally of Klans for 2006 differed: 35 distinct groups with klaverns scattered

Members of the National Socialist Movement welcomed Gordon Young's Klansmen in 2006 (Southern Poverty Law Center).

over 32 states and the District of Columbia. The National Knights led that list as well, with dens in 20 states, while the Brotherhood of Klans had colonized 18.[145]

One cheap method of recruiting, pioneered by Jeff Berry's American Knights a decade earlier, was the insertion of Klan fliers inside free throwaway newspapers. Many publishers complained of the tactic, but North Carolina's *Rhino Times* was first to sue Robb's Knights Party for hijacking their paper in September 2006. Robb responded with a defamation charge against the newspaper (dismissed), then agreed to cease the practice in October 2007. The ink was barely dry on that agreement when Robb told Web site readers, "Wrapping literature around discarded sheets of newsprint as an economical means of sharing information with the general public, whether that newsprint is the New York Times, the circular from a department store, or the Rhino Times of Greensboro, North Carolina was and continues to be fully legal. You can use your week old issue of The Wall Street News [*sic*], or Rhino Times to line a drawer, polish a window, pack a gift, or to wrap a KKK leaflet around." The *Rhino Times* sued again, this time for breach of contract, and won $25,000 in June 2009.[146]

Black Man in the White House

Politics continues to draw past and present Klansmen. Declaring that "federal elections offer public speaking opportunities we can't afford to pass up," Glenn Miller ran for Congress in Missouri, in 2006, wangling interviews on various national TV shows before election day, when he claimed 23 of 241,072 ballots cast.[147]

The race that mattered, though, was 2008's presidential contest, pitting white Republican senator John McCain against black Illinois senator Barack Obama. IKA wizard Ron Edwards grudgingly endorsed McCain, while branding Obama "a piece of shit" and opining that "anything is better than Hillary Clinton."[148] Satirical rumors of Klan support for Obama prompted the Knights Party to post a headline on its Web site reading "Ku Klux Klan DOES NOT Endorse Barack Obama for President." Thom Robb warned of "a backlash" or "race war" if Obama carried the election, but daughter Rachel was more pragmatic, telling reporters, "There's no such thing as bad press."[149]

Don Black donated money to Republican Ron Paul's campaign, while telling the *Washington Post,* "I get nonstop E-mails and private messages from new people who are mad as hell about the possibility of Obama being elected. White people, for a long time, have thought of our government as being for us, and Obama is the best possible evidence that we've lost that. This is scaring a lot of people who maybe never considered themselves racists, and it's bringing them over to our side."[150] The campaign turned a spotlight on Black's family, as son Derek won election to Palm Beach County's Republican Executive Committee, then was refused his seat, allegedly for failing to sign a loyalty oath.[151] Meanwhile, reporters noticed that Chloe Black worked for Florida sugar baron Jose Fanjul, as a spokesperson for Glades Academy, a school devoted to educating children of impoverished black and Hispanic migrant workers. That apparent conflict of interest sparked cries of outrage, countered when Chloe told reporters she had played no role in the white supremacist movement "in 30 years." Glades Academy, meanwhile, declined to "comment on the private lives of our employees." Another two years passed before Fanjul's Florida Crystals confirmed that Chloe's job was secure. "We will not discriminate against anybody," a spokesperson said, "and that has been our policy forever."[152]

Obama defeated McCain by 9.5 million votes in November, and racists turned their attention to protesting his inauguration, urging whites to fly Confederate flags on January 20, 2009, or turn their "Yankee flags" upside-down as a symbol of "dire distress." The plan was hatched on Stormfront, by a Tennessee Klansman urging a "Day of the Flag" to "take our message of Race and Nation out to the streets." Jeremy Eastwood, writing from New Jersey for the United Realms of America Knights, urged Klansmen to "get out there and Recruit Recruit Recruit. We must take bake [sic] our nation that is being taking [sic] away."[153]

Inauguration Day passed without any mass protests, and Klansmen settled back into their normal routine, joining skinheads and the National Socialist Movement to celebrate Hitler's birthday in St. Louis, in April 2009.[154] Six months later, in Nevada, former David Duke aide Jamie Kelso helped organize the American Third Position Party, a vehicle pursuing "an America that is recognizable to us, one that we can feel comfortable in." Directors included Cal State Long Beach psychology professor Kevin MacDonald, whose anti–Semitism prompted the school to disassociate itself from his published work. Duke, in *My Awakening* (1998), cites MacDonald's writings as central to his views of the Jewish menace.[155]

Modern law enforcement officers risk their jobs by flirting with the Klan. In Florida, Fruitland Park policeman James Elkins was fired in January 2009, for joining the National Aryan Knights. Twelve months later, in Alachua County, jailer Wayne Kerschner got his pink slip when superiors learned that he and his wife belonged to the United Northern and Southern Knights.[156] Undiscouraged, UNSK imperial wizard Cole Thornton admitted that other cops also belonged to his Klan. "They like the fact that we support law enforcement," he said. "These guys are out there putting their lives on the line, and we back them." Joining a "traditional Klan," Thornton added, "makes them a better cop."[157] Finding *any* members was a chore in South Carolina, where National Knights grand dragon Tim Bradly staged a "rally" in March 2010 and found himself the only Klansman present.[158]

That same month, Tom Metzger announced his latest run for Congress in Warsaw, Indiana. He had returned to his home state in 2006, occupying his late mother's home, and endured an ATF search in June 2009, related to Dennis Mahon's Arizona arrest. Mahon's bombing indictment charged that he was acting "to promote racial discord on behalf of" WAR, but agents found no evidence of Metzger playing any part in the attack. Metzger's goal, if elected, was simple: "I'd go to Washington and have a fistfight every day." His campaign Web site called him an "independent worker candidate," appealing to others like himself, "who are not tied to transnational corporations or the super rich." Metzger failed to make the ballot in that contest.[159]

In June 2010, Fraternal White Knights kleagle Billy Ash used Stormfront to announce the banishment of ex-imperial wizard Douglas Sadler for "conduct unbecoming of a Klansman." Sadler's wife wrote back to "defend his honor," noting that difficulties in her latest pregnancy forced Sadler to miss an initiation ceremony in Virginia.[160] Later that month, FBI agents stung ex–Missouri grand dragon Neal Schmidt, luring him to Georgia for sex with two mythical underage girls. Schmidt pled guilty in April 2011, receiving a 20-year sentence.[161] Also in June, police in Louisiana arrested Klansman Jason Fallon for aggravated assault, illegal use of a weapon, and threatening a black man's life.[162]

In August 2010, Klansmen joined the National Socialist Movement, SS Action Group,

Tom Metzger remains a political activist and spokesman for white nationalist causes (author's collection).

and Confederate Hammerskins for a march in Knoxville, Tennessee.[163] December logged a fresh arrest for onetime Osceola County, Florida Klan leader George Hixon—imprisoned in the 1980s for possessing an unregistered machine gun—after he punched his girlfriend and fired shots at her, in a quarrel over who got to drink "the good beer."[164]

Klansmen continued to blunder their way through 2011. In March, the White Reference Web site crowed that "anti-racist turncoat" Johnny Clary had been banned from speaking at two Australian high schools, based on his public statements panning gays and Muslims.[165] In May, 10 members of Virginia's Southern Cross Soldiers of the Ku Klux Klan turned out to picket gay-bashing acolytes of the Westboro Baptist Church, marching at Arlington National Cemetery with their trademark placards reading "God Hates Fags."[166] In September, Arkansas neo–Nazi Billy Roper disbanded his White Revolution group and pledged allegiance to Thom Robb's Knights Party.[167] In Louisiana, four months later, persons unknown tried to settle old debts by torching the home of Barbara Hicks Collins, widow of 1960s Deacons for Defense leader Robert Hicks. Failing at that, they burned her car instead.[168]

Four More Years

The prospect of Barack Obama's reelection in 2012 whipped Klansmen into a frenzy. Mega-rich Republican Mitt Romney offered nothing to working class knights, and while

CCC member Merlin Miller was attractive, running for the American Third Position Party, he had no hope of victory.[169] Without a candidate to call their own, Klansmen could only vote their hopes and pray for a truly White House in 2013.

In late March 2012, Thom Robb convened a National Faith and Freedom Conference at the Knights Party's compound in Harrison, Arkansas. Speakers included Merlin Miller ("The Jews did not win America. They stole it while we slept."), Billy Roper ("We are conquerors. We don't need therapy. We just need more territory to conquer."), Paul Fromm ("We didn't come here with Columbus, we didn't come here with the Vikings. We were here 10,000 years ago. We're coming back."), and Rachel Pendergraft ("The Jews are very smart. They know the best way to undermine a nation is by integration."). Coyly referring to Hitler, Pendergraft said, "Let me quote from a great German statesman. I won't say his name, but I admire him very much."[170] No unity resulted, but the faith was reaffirmed.

Trouble simmered during the campaign. In South Carolina, Anderson County Councilman Eddie Moore admitted joining the Klan in "my early younger days," as a deputy sheriff, but said, "I don't recall owning a hood."[171] In North Carolina, members of Charlotte's Latin American Coalition dressed as clowns to heckle a Klan rally.[172] Virginia knights used Obama's reelection as a recruiting tool, telling reporters, "Since Obama's first term our numbers have doubled and now that we're headed to a second term it's going to triple, this is going to be the biggest resurgence of the Klan since 1915."[173]

Klan critics in Memphis fought back by vandalizing a statue of Nathan Bedford Forrest and pressuring the city council to remove a half-ton granite slab, planted without permission by the SCV, which designated its location "Forrest Park." Workers uprooted the marker in January 2013, and a February council vote formally changed the site's name to Health Sciences Park. Chris Barker's Loyal White Knights traveled from North Carolina to protest the change, drenched by cold rain on the appointed day, while police kept hecklers at a distance.[174]

Other Klan activities in 2013 ranged from mundane to bizarre. In March, Bradley Jenkins, chief of a resuscitated UKA, staged a meeting with a black street gang, the Grape Street Crips, in Memphis.[175] That same month, Klansman Kevin Lynch logged his 18th arrest in South Daytona, Florida, for stockpiling illegal weapons.[176] The most peculiar case involved Klansman Glendon Scott Crawford, a mechanic for General Electric in Albany, New York, arrested by FBI agents in June, while seeking radioactive materials for a "death ray." Displaying remarkable impartiality, Crawford suggested that his weapon could be used on President Obama and for "killing Israel's enemies while they slept." Crawford claimed membership in the United Northern and Southern Knights, but had gone in search of Jewish backers when the Klan turned him down.[177]

While Crawford awaited psychiatric analysis, Thom Robb announced plans for an August "Soldiers of the Cross Training Institute" in the Ozark Mountains, charging campers $500 each to learn the "HOLY mission of White Christian Revival." Graduates, he hoped, would emerge to lead a "New Crusade for race, faith and homeland," aided by faculty members Paul Fromm, Billy Roper, and Tomislav Sunic, a Croatian neo–Nazi. Weary of public association with Robb's Klan, officials in Harrison debated spending $30,000 on a diversity Web site to salvage their town's reputation.[178]

Bad publicity continued through August 2013, as Allen Morgan, an Iraq war veteran in Munford, Alabama, tried to put a Klan murder contract on a black neighbor whom he suspected of raping his wife. The knight he approached with plans for a "slow painful death" was an undercover agent, who arrested him. Morgan pled guilty to federal charges in October, facing 10 years in prison.[179] In September, Wyoming UKA leader John Abarr met with NAACP officials and joined their organization, without forsaking the Klan. "I like it," he said, "because you wear robes, and get out and light crosses, and have secret handshakes. I sort of like it that people think I'm some sort of outlaw."[180]

The Klan's first wizard came under attack once more in September 2013, this time in Jacksonville, Florida. Petitions to rename Nathan Bedford Forrest High School had circulated since 2006, always rejected by school board officials, but the latest effort collected more than 176,000 signatures, reminding administrators that 54 percent of the school's student body was black. In November the board voted unanimously to choose a new name, at some undetermined future date.[181]

Nothing changed for Klansmen as the year wound down. Sky View High School's principal, in Smithfield, Utah, suspended two students who donned Klan regalia for Halloween.[182] Police in Panama City, Florida, jailed Klansman David Kelley for threatening them with a BB gun.[183] Elsewhere in Florida, confused members of the Loyal White Knights scattered recruiting fliers around a black neighborhood in New Smyrna Beach and a Latino section of Rockledge. Questioned by reporters, leader Robert Jones explained, "We don't have no way of judging where we're putting the fliers at."[184] A week later, federal prosecutors in Alabama charged ex–exalted cyclops Steven Dinkle with multiple felonies, related to a 2009 cross-burning in Ozark.[185] Sean Sergeant, chief of Owensburg, Indiana's fire department, resigned in December after posting Facebook urgings to "Join here and support your local Klan!! I did!!"[186] Eight days later, in Maryland, Confederate White Knights imperial wizard Richard Preston called for a rally to impeach President Obama, declaring, "It's time for the American people to stand up."[187] Georgia Klansman Michael Fullmore received a 52-month prison term on December 19, 2013, for providing arms to a convicted felon, part of a plot to burn a Catholic church in Claxton.[188]

On April 13, 2014—the eve of Passover—a drive-by gunman shot five persons, killing three, outside two Jewish facilities in Overland Park, Kansas. The dead, none of them Jewish, included a physician and his grandson, shot at the city's Jewish Community Center, and a woman slain outside the Village Shalom senior living home. Soon after the shootings, police arrested 73-year-old Frazier Glenn Cross of Aurora, Missouri, who shouted "Heil Hitler!" as he was taken into custody.[189]

The Southern Poverty Law Center quickly identified "Cross" as Frazier Glenn Miller, notorious 1980s leader of the KKK and White Patriot Party in North Carolina. Further investigation revealed that Cross received his new surname in 1990, from the U.S. Marshals Service, after leaving federal prison to enter the witness protection program. The shootings followed warnings from the Anti-Defamation League that the convergence of Passover and Adolf Hitler's birthday (April 20) were likely to produce outbreaks of anti–Semitic violence. Police booked Frazier/Cross on three counts of murder and various other charges, holding him in lieu of $10 million bail, while Chief John Douglass declared himself "unquestionably determined" that the shootings were hate crimes.[190]

In Marionville, Missouri, aging mayor Dan Clevenger—an acquaintance of Miller— told reporters, "It was kind of shocking at first. But then reading the article and thinking about it, I thought 'yeah that sounds like something he would do.'"[191] Clevenger felt compelled to go further, adding, "I am a friend of his, helping to spread his warnings. The Jew-run medical industry has succeeded in destroying the United States' workforce. I don't think the government is run by Jews. We are still a democracy. Sure there are Jews in government. I mean, Nancy Pelosi, she is a Jew. And she brags about it." (In fact, Pelosi—as with Miller's victims—is not Jewish.) Those sentiments cost Clevenger his job, as Marionville residents demanded and received his resignation on April 21.[192]

Frazier, meanwhile, remained in custody as this book went to press, seeming pleased with his new notoriety. Former colleagues were less impressed. Don Black, ex-grand dragon and Stormfront Web site founder, told reporters, "I think Glenn had gone insane, completely insane in recent years, probably because of the alcohol. But whatever it was, he did us a lot of damage this weekend."[193]

Leaderless Persistence

One major problem of the modern Invisible Empire is its lack of charismatic leadership. Across the country, once-dynamic wizards and dragons have fallen by the wayside over the past two decades.

Louis Beam stopped attending Aryan Nations conferences in 1996, after Richard Butler bypassed him to choose successor Neuman Britton. Beam penned a letter to his fans that read, in part, "It is now almost 10 years since my arrest, trial and subsequent release at Fort Smith, Arkansas, for sedition. Since 1969, I have been in the struggle.... I intend to give my family the next years of my life.... Additionally, as a result of exposure to Agent Orange while in Vietnam, my health declines. I have concealed this for years but now find myself less than fit to continue as in days before. I have for 30 years given my all. I pray others will do the same."[194]

Edward Fields remained a fixture of Klan "unity" meetings at the turn of the century, attended Byron De La Beckwith's funeral in 2001, and joined the National Alliance in 2003. In April 2013, aged 80, he placed a wreath on Mary Phagan's grave in Atlanta.[195] While always busy, his dream of leading another great Klan proved elusive.

David Duke pled guilty to federal charges of mail fraud and filing false tax returns in December 2002, receiving a 15-month prison term and a $10,000 fine.[196] Upon release, he traveled extensively through Russia and Eastern Europe, peddling revised editions of *My Awakening*. Police in Prague jailed Duke in April 2009, for denying the Holocaust, then expelled him from the Czech Republic.[197] He settled next in a village near Salzburg, Austria, ostensibly supporting himself through sales of wildlife photographs.[198] Still there in 2011, Duke drew increasing heat from the liberal Austrian Green Party, whose leader complained, "It seems that an American Nazi is welcome here anytime. Duke would have no chance to mutter a word before he was thrown out of the Schengen zone were he a migrant worker."[199] A side trip to Germany saw Duke jailed again, in Cologne, slapped with orders "to leave German territory without delay."[200] He next tried Milan, lasting 18 months before a court expelled him from Italy in December 2013.[201] Wherever he lands next, there seems to be no future for him as a movement leader in the States.

Death called on many aged wizards in the early 21st century. Horace King, "reformed" leader of South Carolina's Christian Knights, died in January 2002.[202] A heart attack killed

Robert Shelton in March 2003, followed 12 days by Robert Scoggin.[203] Paralyzed by a stroke, J. B. Stoner died from pneumonia at a Georgia nursing home, in April 2005.[204] David Lane, imprisoned author of the Klan-venerated "Fourteen Words"—"We must secure the existence of our people and a future for White Children"—died in custody on May 28, 2007.[205] Relatives released no cause of death for Virgil Griffin, in February 2009.[206] Riot Roy Frankhouser survived Griffin by two months, leaving no known kin when he died at a Pennsylvania nursing home in May 2009.[207] Dale Reusch passed in January 2011, at Akron's Select Specialty Hospital.[208] Jeff Berry reconciled with son Anthony after their near-fatal brawl. His passing, in May 2013, barely caused a ripple in the Klan or in the media.[209]

Other leaders of the Klan professed to be "reformed." James Roesch, once Texas wizard of the Knights of the White Kamelia, "came to Christ" before he left the order, then discovered a fascination with soccer. "I had a religious awakening," he said in 2008. "I realized the path that I was on wasn't the path that people should be taking."[210] If Roesch seemed genuine, observers had their doubts about Bill Riccio. Released from jail in 2005, Riccio regained his right to vote in 2006, then was granted a "certificate of pardon" by Alabama's Board of Pardons and Paroles in April 2008, for having "conducted himself as to demonstrate his reformation and to merit pardon with restoration of civil rights." Oddly, in 2007, Riccio told a reporter that he was still recruiting young men for the cause of white supremacy. ATF agent Bart McIntire told the SPLC, "To believe he is reformed would be naïve. He is a chameleon and will disguise his true colors of hatred and anti-government belief."[211]

In May 2010 FBI agents arrested former IKA wizard Ron Edwards, girlfriend Christine Gillette, and a third suspect on drug charges, including trafficking in methamphetamine and painkillers. Edwards and Gillette pled guilty in March 2011. Two months later, Edwards received a four-year sentence, while Gillette was sentenced to 366 days. Edwards's son remained at liberty, leading a skinhead group called Supreme White Alliance.[212]

In September 2010 the National Knights staged a two-day celebration to honor Railton Loy's half-century of service to the Klan. The group's Web site carried the message "KKKongrats. God Bless Your Lordship and may you rule for many years to come." In April 2012, stricken with diabetes at 74, Loy announced his impending retirement, assuming the title of "emperor" while Jon Welch of upstate New York replaced him as imperial wizard.[213]

Only Thom Robb remains as a Klansman of national stature, beset by critics both inside and outside the Klan. Wizard-turned-evangelist Johnny Clary writes online that hostile Klansmen have dubbed him "Thom Slobb," accusing Robb of playing fast and loose with Klan finances, even publishing a cartoon strip in *The Separatist* depicting Robb as a homosexual with Jewish lovers.[214] Edward Fields holds a different view, telling readers of *The Truth at Last,* "Today there are numerous Klan groups. Some only existing in a single community, others state wide or operating in several states. There is one Klan leader who has built a true national Klan organization. This is Pastor Thom Robb. Today he carries on more wide spread activity than any other KKK leader we know of. Robb is an excellent speaker and leader. He is a true man of God—we wholeheartedly and unreservedly endorse Pastor Robb. I want to urge all independent and local Klan groups who are considering affiliation with a national body to contact this sterling leader who has accomplished so much good for his race and the Klan."[215]

The Empire Today

In 2013 the SPLC counted 26 Klans nationwide, with 163 klaverns active in 33 states.[216] Single-klavern operations included the Alabama Knights, Dixie Rangers Knights (Louisiana), Knights of the Holy Cross (Ohio), Ku Klux Klan LLC (Arkansas), Lone Wolf Brigade Knights (Texas), North Louisiana White Knights, True Invisible Empire Knights (Missouri), and True White Knights of the Christian Cross (Alabama). Slightly larger Klans, with two klaverns each, included the Aryan Nations Knights (Louisiana and Oklahoma), Rebel Brigade Knights (Pennsylvania and Virginia), and the White Camelia Knights in Texas.

Thom Robb's Knights Party, despite its domination of the Internet, claimed only three klaverns in 2013: two in Arkansas, and one in Tennessee. Other three-klavern Klans included the Empire Knights, Original Knight Riders Knights, and True Invisible Empire Tradition-alist American Knights. The International Keystone Knights boasted four chapters in three states. Mississippi's Original Knights of America claimed five klaverns statewide, while the Southern Kalvary Knights had five chapters scattered over as many states. Two Klans—the Knight Riders Knights and United Northern and Southern Knights—each claimed seven klaverns spread over seven states.

The top six Klans in 2013 were the reborn United Klans of America (32 klaverns in 18 states), the United White Knights (27 chapters in four states), the Loyal White Knights (16 dens in 14 states), the Mississippi White Knights (11 chapters statewide), the Fraternal White Knights and Ku Klos Knights (each with 10 klaverns spread over 10 states).

Geographically, Klan strength had its greatest concentration in the former Confederacy, where 11 states harbored 102 klaverns of 24 different factions. Texas led the pack, boasting seven Klans with 26 chapters. Mississippi came next, with 17 klaverns representing three Klans. Georgia divided its 11 klaverns among five Klans, dominated by the Knight Riders Knights. Tennessee, birthplace of the order, had seven Klans with nine klaverns. Alabama, Louisiana and Virginia each hosted five Klans, with eight, seven, and eight klaverns, respec-tively. Among Arkansas's four Klans, only Thom Robb's Knights claimed two klaverns. Florida and once-mighty North Carolina harbored three Klans each, with four and five klav-erns, respectively. South Carolina, a shadow of its former self, hosted single klaverns of two rival factions.

Moving to the Border South, Klan strength began to fade. Oklahoma, where Klansmen once impeached a governor, claimed eight klaverns, all but two representing the United White Knights. Kentucky, Missouri and West Virginia each nurtured three klaverns, estab-lished by six rival Klans. Maryland harbored two Klans, with one klavern apiece. Delaware's Loyal White Knights were lonely in their solitary den.

Recruitment lagged in the Northeast, where Klansmen and Catholics battled by torch-light during the 1920s. Six Klans claimed outposts in the region during 2013, with four rivals in Pennsylvania, manning one klavern each. Single chapters of separate Klans clung to life in New York, New Hampshire, and Rhode Island.

The Midwest, 1920s bastion of the Klan's political strength, claimed 25 klaverns of nine Klans in 2013, spread across seven states. Ohio hosted six factions, with one klavern each. Illinois came close behind, with five single-klavern factions. Indiana also showed diver-sity, with four rival Klans manning one chapter each. The UKA claimed three Michigan klaverns, with one each for two competing groups. Iowa and South Dakota each welcomed

The Klan endures, "Yesterday, Today, Forever." Photograph ca. early 1960s (Florida State Archives).

two klaverns from different Klans, while the Southern Kalvary Knights stood alone in Wisconsin.

In the West, kleagles found slim pickings. Arizona, Colorado and New Mexico each had a single klavern struggling to survive. Montana and Washington both claimed dual chapters of the UKA, clinging to tenuous life. In California, scene of so much action from 1921 through the 1980s, Klan-watchers found no klaverns at all.

According to SPLC estimates, the Invisible Empire greeted 2013 with 5,000 to 8,000 members, a drop in the bucket of some 313 million known U.S. residents.[217] It is tempting to write the order's obituary, but thus far, all such declarations of its death have been distinctly premature. The Klan survives today—and will survive, as long as it finds safety in the First Amendment—because bigotry never dies. It finds new targets and new angles of attack, but no one yet has found a means of purging it from humankind. To that extent, at least, Klansmen are truthful in their boast from glory days, nearly a century ago.

> Yesterday, Today, Forever,
> Since Eighteen Hundred and Sixty-Six,
> the KU KLUX KLAN
> has been riding and will
> continue to do so as long as
> the WHITE MAN LIVETH.[218]

Chapter Notes

References drawn from sources in the selected bibliography are presented in shortened form. Others provide full bibliographic information.

Introduction

1. Russell Howe, "A Talk with William Faulkner," *The Reporter* (March 22, 1956), pp. 18–20.
2. William Faulkner in *The Reporter* (April 19, 1956), p. 5.
3. Quoted by Max Brantley, Arkansas Blog (Oct. 6, 2012), http://www.arktimes.com/ArkansasBlog/archives/2012/10/06/loy-mauch-update-the-republican-rep-is-on-record-on-slavery-too (accessed Feb. 28, 2013).
4. Variant lyrics for "Good Ole Rebel," by Major Innes Randolph, circa 1866: Kennedy, *After Appomattox*, pp. 24–25; Jan Fortune, *Fugitives* (New York: Signet, 1968), pp. xvii–xviii.

Chapter 1

1. "Casualties and Costs of the Civil War," Digital History, http://www.digitalhistory.uh.edu/historyonline/us20.cfm (accessed March 5, 2013).
2. "Selected Statistics on Slavery in the United States," Causes of the Civil War, http://civilwarcauses.org/stat.htm (accessed March 5, 2013).
3. Horn, *Invisible Empire,* pp. 8–9; Trelease, *White Terror,* pp. 3–4.
4. Michael Lewis and Jacqueline Serbu, "Kommemorating the Klan," *The Sociological Quarterly* 40 (Winter 1999): 139.
5. Trelease, pp. 3, 430; *Constitution and Laws of the United Klans of America, Inc., Knights of the Ku Klux Klan* (September 1964), p. 53.
6. Fry, *Night Riders,* p. 21.
7. William Rose, "Some Notes on Theta's History," *The Phi Gamma Delta* 2 (November 1930): 106–111; Trelease, pp. 4–5, 21.
8. Wade, *Fiery Cross,* pp. 39–40; Carlton Beals, *Brass-Knuckle Crusade: The Great Know-Nothing Conspiracy, 1820–1860* (New York: Hastings House, 1960), pp. 165–7, 293–294.

9. Fry, pp. 69–73, 85–9, 102–6, 112–13; "The Slave Laws of Tennessee," Tennessee Trails, http://genealogytrails.com/tenn/slavelaws.html (accessed March 9, 2013).
10. "Second Inaugural Address of Abraham Lincoln," Yale Law School, http://avalon.law.yale.edu/19th_century/lincoln2.asp (accessed March 9, 2013).
11. Eric Foner, *Reconstruction: America's Unfinished Revolution, 1863–1877* (New York: HarperCollins, 1988), pp. 181–184.
12. Ibid., 199–201, 207–9.
13. Trelease, p. xliv; Kennedy, *After Appomattox,* pp. 58–59; Newton, *Ku Klux Klan in Mississippi,* pp. 7, 12; George Wright, *Racial Violence in Kentucky, 1865–1940* (Baton Rouge: Louisiana State University Press, 1990), p. 38.
14. Foner, pp. 271–91; "The Reconstruction Acts: 1867," Texas State Library and Archives Commission, https://www.tsl.state.tx.us/ref/abouttx/secession/reconstruction.html (accessed March 9, 2013).
15. Horn, p. 10; Trelease, pp. 4–5; Wade, p. 34.
16. Wade, p. 34.
17. Hattie Magee, "Reconstruction in Lawrence and Jefferson Counties," *Publications of the Mississippi Historical Society* 11 (1910): 194–195.
18. Haas, *KKK,* p. 25; Horn, pp. 32–3, 312–313; Hurst, pp. 285–7; Trelease, pp. 14–15.
19. Horn, pp. 383–389.
20. Ibid., p. 397.
21. Trelease, p. 21; Horn, pp. 387–388, 391.
22. Horn, p. 216.
23. "Ku Klux Klan in Alabama During the Reconstruction Era," Encyclopedia of Alabama, http://www.encyclopediaofalabama.org/face/Article.jsp?id=h-2934 (accessed March 1, 2013).

24. Haas, p. 26; Horn, pp. 245–7, 250, 335–7; Wade, p. 58; J. C. Lester and D. L. Wilson, *Ku Klux Klan: Its Origin, Growth and Disbandment* (New York: Neale, 1905), p. 27; "Albert Pike Did Not Found the Ku Klux Klan," Grand Lodge of British Columbia and Yukon, http://freemasonry.bcy.ca/anti-masonry/kkk.html (accessed March 9, 2013).
25. Trelease, p. 20.
26. Davis, *Authentic History*, p. 217.
27. Haas, p. 26; Hurst, p. 345.
28. Davis, p. 236.
29. Kennedy, *After Appomattox,* p. 80.
30. Davis, p. 254.
31. Hurst, pp. 15–17.
32. Ibid., pp. 31–67.
33. Ibid., pp. 71–164.
34. "Proclamation by the Confederate President," Freedmen & Southern Society Project, http://www.history.umd.edu/Freedmen/pow.htm (accessed March 11, 2013).
35. Hurst, pp. 165–181.
36. Richard Fuchs, *An Unerring Fire: The Massacre at Fort Pillow* (Mechanicsburg, PA: Stackpole, 2002), p. 14.
37. Hurst, pp. 271–275.
38. Ibid., pp. 284–285.
39. Newton, *The Ku Klux Klan,* p. 68.
40. Ibid., p. 213.
41. Horn, p. 397.
42. Wade, p. 47.
43. Wright, pp. 41–42, 311.
44. Newton, *The Ku Klux Klan,* p. 211.
45. Davis, p. 268; Elliott Coues, *History of the Expedition Under the Command of Lewis and Clark* Vol. 1 (New York: Francis P. Harper, 1893), p. lxxv.
46. Trelease, pp. 65–67.
47. Davis, pp. 29–30.
48. Hurst, pp. 300–301; Kennedy, *After Appomattox,* p. 80.
49. Hurst, pp. 301–302.
50. The Grant Gallery, Item No. 830, http://www.railsplitter.com/sale10/images/714.jpg (accessed March 4, 2013).

51. Foner, pp. 340–341.

52. Trelease, p. 135; Richard Hofstadter and Michael Wallace, *American Violence: A Documentary History* (New York: Vintage, 1970), pp. 223–224.

53. Trelease, p. 138.

54. Ibid., p. 29.

55. Ibid., pp. 115–117.

56. Ibid., pp. 76–78, 114–115, 117.

57. Ibid., p. 121.

58. Horn, pp. 150–151.

59. Trelease, pp. 149–174.

60. "Presidential Election 1868 Popular Vote," HistoryCentral.com, http://www.historycentral.com/elections/1868Pop.html (accessed March 15, 2013).

61. "Interview with General N. B. Forrest," Cincinnati *Commercial*, Aug. 28, 1868.

62. Ibid.

63. Newton, *Ku Klux Klan in Mississippi*, pp. 12–13.

64. Trelease, pp. 79–80; Horn, pp. 266–268.

65. Trelease, pp. 92–94, 136, 173–174; Horn, pp. 343–345.

66. Trelease, pp. 137–148.

67. Ibid., pp. 68–69, 189–193, 219–220.

68. Ibid., pp. 26–27, 30; Kennedy, *After Appomattox,* pp. 216–217; Horn, pp. 346–348.

69. Horn, pp. 348–51; Trelease, pp. 34, 70–71, 73, 115, 82, 92–93, 127–9, 151, 245, 338.

70. Trelease, pp. 175–185; Horn, pp. 107–113.

71. Davis, pp. 125–126.

72. Ibid., pp. 126–127.

73. Trelease, pp. 67–68, 185.

74. Ibid., pp. 278–280.

75. Ibid., pp. 246–273, 302–310.

76. Ibid., pp. 274–278, 287–301.

77. Ibid., pp. 226–245, 318–335.

78. Ibid., p. 311.

79. Ibid., pp. 189–225, 336–348.

80. Ibid., pp. 349–369.

81. Horn, pp. 265–269.

82. "Enforcement Act of 1871 (third act)," Wikipedia, http://en.wikipedia.org/wiki/Enforcement_Act_of_1871_(third_act) (accessed March 19, 2013).

83. "The Ku Klux Klan Act," HarpWeek, http://education.harpweek.com/KKKHearings/AppendixA.htm (accessed March 19, 2013).

84. Horn, pp. 296–299.

85. Ibid., pp. 299–300.

86. Kennedy, *After Appomattox,* p. 211.

87. Ibid., pp. 211–213.

88. Ibid., pp. 213–217.

89. Ibid., p. 217.

90. Horn, p. 300.

91. Hurst, p. 331.

92. "The Kuklux: Proclamation of Martial Law in South Carolina," *New York Times,* Oct. 17, 1871.

93. Newton, *The Ku Klux Klan,* p. 9; Stephen Budiansky, *The Bloody Shirt: Terror After the Civil War* (New York: Plume, 2008), p. 139.

94. Chalmers, *Hooded Americanism,* p. 2.

95. Newton, *The Ku Klux Klan,* p. 276.

96. Horn, p. 375.

Chapter 2

1. "United States Presidential Election, 1872," Wikipedia, http://en.wikipedia.org/wiki/United_States_presidential_election,_1872#Campaign (accessed March 23, 2013).

2. Kim Gravelle, *Fiji's Times: A History of Fiji* (Suva: The Fiji Times, 1988), pp. 120–124.

3. Ibid.

4. *Slaughter-House Cases,* 83 U.S. 36 (1873).

5. Foner, p. 437; Charles Lane, *The Day Freedom Died: The Colfax Massacre, the Supreme Court, and the Betrayal of Reconstruction* (New York: Henry Holt, 2008), pp. 88–109.

6. *United States v. Cruikshank* 92 U.S. 542 (1876).

7. Adolph Reed, Jr., "The Battle of Liberty Monument," *The Progressive* 57 (June 1, 1993), http://www.thefreelibrary.com/The+battle+of+Liberty+Monument.-a013773324 (accessed March 27, 2013).

8. George Rable, *But There Was No Peace: The Role of Violence in the Politics of Reconstruction* (Athens: University of Georgia Press, 1984), p. 132.

9. Foner, pp. 550–551.

10. Hofstadter and Wallace, pp. 101–105.

11. Wright, pp. 28–33.

12. Horn, p. 280.

13. Newton, *The Ku Klux Klan,* p. 200.

14. Newton, *KKK in Mississippi,* p. 38.

15. Ibid., pp. 39–40.

16. Ibid., pp. 41–42.

17. Civil Rights Act of 1875 (18 Stat. 335–337); *Civil Rights Cases,* 109 U.S. 3 (1883).

18. Hall, "The Ku Klux Klan in Southern Illinois in 1875," pp. 364–5.

19. Ibid., p. 365.

20. Ibid., pp. 366–72.

21. C. Vann Woodward, *Reunion and Reaction: The Compromise of 1877 and the End of Reconstruction* (New York: Oxford University Press, 1951), p. 195.

22. "Democratic Party Platform of 1876," The American Presidency Project, http://www.presidency.ucsb.edu/ws/?pid=29581 http://www.presidency.ucsb.edu/ws/?pid=29581 (accessed April 6, 2013).

23. Newton, *KKK in Mississippi,* pp. 42–43.

24. Budiansky, pp. 221–254.

25. Alfred Williams, *Hampton and His Red Shirts: South Carolina's Deliverance in 1876* (Charleston, SC: Walker, Evans and Cogswell, 1935), p. 126.

26. John Reynolds, *Reconstruction in South Carolina* (New York: Negro University Press, 1969), p. 380.

27. "South Carolina Gubernatorial Election, 1876," Wikipedia, http://en.wikipedia.org/wiki/South_Carolina_gubernatorial_election,_1876 (accessed April 6, 2013).

28. "John B. Gordon (1832–1904)," The New Georgia Encyclopedia, http://www.georgiaencyclopedia.org/nge/Article.jsp?id=h-2805 (accessed April 7, 2013).

29. Patrick Riddleberger, "The Radicals' Abandonment of the Negro During Reconstruction," *Journal of Negro History* 45 (1960): 88–102.

30. Davis, pp. 291–293.

31. William Gillette, *Retreat from Reconstruction, 1869–1879* (Baton Rouge: Louisiana State University Press, 1979), pp. 314–315.

32. *Hall v. DeCuir* 95 U.S. 485 (1877).

33. *Louisville, New Orleans and Texas Railway Company v. Mississippi* 133 U.S. 587 (1890).

34. *Plessy v. Ferguson* 163 U.S. 537, 16 S. Ct. 1138, 41 L. Ed. 256 (1896).

35. "List of Jim Crow Law Examples by State," Wikipedia, http://en.wikipedia.org/wiki/List_of_Jim_Crow_law_examples_by_State (accessed May 12, 2013).

36. William Craigie and James Hulbert, eds., *A Dictionary of American English on Historical Principles*, 4 vols. (Chicago: University of Chicago Press, 1938–1944).

37. *Minor v. Happersett* 88 U.S. 162 (1875).

38. *Williams v. Mississippi* 170 U.S. 213 (1898).

39. *James v. Bowman* 190 U.S. 197 (1903).

40. "Disfranchisement After the Reconstruction Era," Wikipedia, http://en.wikipedia.org/wiki/Disfranchisement_after_Reconstruction_era#White_primary (accessed May 12, 2013).

41. Lynchings: By Year and Race, http://law2.umkc.edu/faculty/projects/ftrials/shipp/lynchingyear.html (accessed May 12, 2013).

42. National Association for the Advancement of Colored People, *Thirty Years of Lynching in the United States, 1889–1918* (New York: Negro Universities Press, 1919), p. 29.

43. "Lynching in the United States," Wikipedia, http://en.wikipedia.org/wiki/Lynching_in_the_United_States#Reconstruction_.281865.E2.80.931877.29 (accessed May 12, 2013).

44. Herbert Bob, "The Blight That Is Still with Us," *New York Times,* Jan. 22, 2008.

45. NAACP, *Thirty Years of Lynching*, pp. 43–105.

46. "Danville Riot," History Engine, http://historyengine.richmond.edu/epi sodes/view/506 (accessed May 18, 2013).

47. "Black Laborers Attacked," History Engine, http://historyengine.rich mond.edu/episodes/view/189 (accessed May 18, 2013).

48. The "Carrollton Massacre," http://www.vaiden.net/carrollton_massacre. html (accessed May 18, 2013).

49. 1898 Wilmington Race Riot Commission, http://www.history.ncd cr.gov/1898-wrrc (accessed May 18, 2013).

50. Charles Crowe, "Racial Massacre in Atlanta: September 22, 1906," *Journal of Negro History* 54 (April 1969): 150–75.

51. Richard Maxwell Brown, "The American Vigilante Tradition," in *Violence in America: Historical and Comparative Perspectives* (New York: Bantam, 1969), pp. 154–226.

52. Richard Maxwell Brown, "Historical Patterns of Violence in America," in *The History of Violence in America* (New York: Bantam, 1969), p. 70.

53. Ibid.

54. Holmes, "Whitecapping: Anti-Semitism in the Populist Era."

55. Holmes, "Moonshining and Collective Violence: Georgia, 1889–1895."

56. NAACP, *Thirty Years of Lynching*, pp. 45, 49, 57, 59, 63, 66, 80–2, 92–3, 97, 102.

57. Maxwell, "American Vigilante Tradition," p. 224.

58. Holmes, "Whitecapping in Georgia," p. 388.

59. Ibid., p. 309; Holmes, "Whitecapping: Agrarian Violence in Mississippi," p. 184.

60. "The American Protective Association," New Advent, http://www.newadvent.org/cathen/01426a.htm (accessed May 25, 2013).

61. Michael Williams, *The Shadow of the Pope* (New York: McGraw-Hill, 1932), pp. 103–4.

62. "The American Protective Association," New Advent.

63. David Sarasohn, *The Party of Reform: Democrats in the Progressive Era* (Jackson: University Press of Mississippi, 1989), p. 177.

64. Matthew Hild, *Greenbackers, Knights of Labor, and Populists, Farmer-Labor Insurgency in the Late-Nineteenth-Century South* (Athens: University of Georgia Press, 2007), p. 123.

65. James Hunt, *Marion Butler and American Populism* (Chapel Hill: University of North Carolina Press, 2007), pp. 3–7.

66. Thomas E. Watson, "The Negro Question in the South," *The Arena*, 6 (October 1892): 540–550.

67. Hunt, *Marion Butler and American Populism*, pp. 3–7.

68. "United States Presidential Election, 1896," Wikipedia, http://en.wiki pedia.org/wiki/United_States_presi dential_election,_1896 (accessed May 25, 2013).

69. Dave Leip's Atlas of U.S. Presidential Elections, http://uselectionatlas.org (accessed May 25, 2013); "Thomas E. Watson (1856–1922)," The New Georgia Encyclopedia, http://www.georgia encyclopedia.org/nge/Article.jsp?id=h-2540 (accessed May 25, 2013).

70. 1898 Wilmington Race Riot Commission, http://www.history.ncd cr.gov/1898-wrrc/report/report.htm (accessed May 25, 2013).

71. Stephen Kantrowitz, *Ben Tillman and the Reconstruction of White Supremacy* (Chapel Hill: University of North Carolina Press, 2000), pp. 61, 63–7, 74–9, 102–4, 120–1.

72. Rayford Logan, *The Betrayal of the Negro, from Rutherford B. Hayes to Woodrow Wilson* (New York: Da Capo, 1965), p. 91.

73. Edmund Morris, *Theodore Rex* (New York: Random House, 2002), p. 55.

74. *New York Times*, Nov. 8, 1872.

75. Wright, *Racial Violence in Kentucky*, pp. 311–16.

76. Luntz, *Forgotten Turmoil*, pp. 15, 36.

77. Ibid., pp. 15, 28.

78. Ibid., pp. 731–32.

79. Ibid., pp. 733–34.

80. Ibid., pp. 734–35.

81. Ibid., pp. 735–36.

82. David Burrell, "Dunning, William A.," in *Encyclopedia of Historians & Historical Writing*, Vol. 1 (London: Fitzroy Dearborn, 1999), p. 330.

83. William Dunning, "The Undoing of Reconstruction," in *Reconstruction in Retrospect* (Baton Rouge: Louisiana State University Press, 1969), p. 136.

84. Peter Novick, *That Noble Dream: The "Objectivity Question" and the American Historical Profession* (Cambridge: Cambridge University Press, 1988), p. 73.

85. E. Merton Coulter, *The South During Reconstruction, 1867–1877* (Baton Rouge: Louisiana State University Press, 1947), pp. 60, 141.

86. Claude Bowers, *The Tragic Era: The Revolution After Lincoln* (New York: Houghton Mifflin, 1929), p. 345.

87. Woodrow Wilson, *A History of the American People*, Vol. 5 (New York: Harper, 1903), pp. 60–62.

88. Charles Carroll, "*The Negro a Beast*" or "*In the Image of God*" (St. Louis: American Book and Bible House, 1900).

89. William Calhoun, *The Caucasian and the Negro in the United States* (Columbia, SC: R. L. Bryan, 1902).

90. William Smith, *The Color Line; A Brief of Behalf of the Unborn* (New York: McClure, Phillips, 1905): p. ix.

91. Robert Shufeldt, *The Negro: A Menace to American Civilization* (Boston: Richard G. Badger, 1907), pp. 176–77.

92. "Robert Charles Riots (1900)," BlackPast.org, http://www.blackpast.org/?q=aah/robert-charles-riots-1900 (accessed May 26, 2013).

93. "Atlanta Race Riot of 1906," The New Georgia Encyclopedia, http://www.georgiaencyclopedia.org/nge/Art icle.jsp?id=h-3033 (accessed May 26, 2013).

94. James Crouthamel, "The Springfield Race Riot of 1980," *Journal of Negro History* 45 (July 1960): 164–181.

95. Samuel Roberts, "Kelly Miller and Thomas Dixon, Jr. on Blacks in American Civilization," *Phylon* 41 (1980): 202–9.

96. Raymond Cook, *Thomas Dixon* (Woodbridge, CT: Twayne, 1974), pp. 25, 34, 36–9, 40–2.

97. Wade, p. 123.

98. Thomas Dixon, *The Clansman: An Historical Romance of the Ku Klux Klan* (New York: Grossett and Dunlap, 1905), p. 326.

99. "Thomas Woodrow Wilson," Nobelprize.org, http://www.nobelprize.org/nobel_prizes/peace/laureates/1919/wilson-bio.html (accessed May 26, 2013).

100. Henry Blumenthal, "Woodrow Wilson and the Race Question," *Journal of Negro History* 48 (1963): 1–21.

101. Woodrow Wilson to Bishop Alexander Walters, Oct. 16, 1912, published in *The Freeman* (Indianapolis), Nov. 2, 1912.

102. Nancy Weiss, "The Negro and the New Freedom: Fighting Wilsonian Segregation," *Political Science Quarterly* 84 (1969): 64, 67, 118; Kathleen L. Wolgemuth, "Woodrow Wilson and Federal Segregation," *Journal of Negro History* 44 (1959): 159, 162.

103. "Missed Manners: Wilson Lectures a Black Leader," History Matters, http://historymatters.gmu.edu/d/5719 (accessed May 26, 2013).

104. Bruce Bartlett, *Wrong on Race: The Democratic Party's Buried Past* (New York: Palgrave Macmillan, 2008), pp. 108–10.

105. "Calvin Henry Simmons (1837–1893)," Ancestry.com, http://records.ancestry.com/Calvin_Henry_Simmons_records.ashx?pid=105188624 (accessed May 28, 2013).

106. Ibid.; Chalmers, *Hooded Americanism*, pp. 28–9.

107. Wade, pp. 140–3.

108. Chalmers, *Hooded Americanism*, pp. 28–9.

109. Greenhaw, *Fighting the Devil*, p. 49; Haas, pp. 42–3; Wade, pp. 140–3.

110. Patrick McSherry, "A Brief History of the 1st Alabama Volunteer Infantry," The Spanish American War Centennial Website, http://www.spanamwar.com/1stalabama.html (accessed May 28, 2013).

111. Jackson, *Ku Klux Klan in the City,* pp. 5–6.

112. Alexander; Gross. *A History of the Methodist Church, South in the United States* (New York: Christian Literature, 1907), pp. 15–37.

113. Chalmers, *Hooded Americanism,* pp. 28–9; Wade, pp. 140–3.

114. Haas, pp. 42–3.

115. Rice, *Ku Klux Klan in American Politics,* pp. 1–2; Morningside/Lenox Park Association Archive, http://tk-jk.net/mlpadotorg/History/fog0000000080.html (accessed May 28, 2013).

116. Chalmers, *Hooded Americanism,* pp. 28–9; Haas, *KKK,* pp. 42–3; Wade, pp. 140–3.

117. Wade, pp. 140–3.

Chapter 3

1. Wade, p. 143.

2. "Temperance Movement," The New Georgia Encyclopedia, http://www.georgiaencyclopedia.org/nge/Article.jsp?id=h-828 (accessed July 7, 2013).

3. Gillette and Tillinger, *Inside Ku Klux Klan,* p. 28.

4. Ibid.

5. Ibid., p. 29.

6. C. Vann Woodward, *Tom Watson: Agrarian Rebel* (New York: Oxford University Press, 1963), pp. 426–7.

7. Ibid., p. 432.

8. Ibid., pp. 422–3.

9. *The Guardian of Liberty,* Vol. III, no. 24 (July 1915): 446.

10. Gillette and Tillinger, p. 28.

11. Steve Oney, "The Lynching of Leo Frank," *Esquire* (September 1985), http://archive.org/stream/steveOneyTheLynchingOfLeoFrankEsquireMagazineSeptember1985/LeoFrankEsquire#page/n0/mode/2up (accessed July 7, 2013).

12. Russell Aiuto, "The Lynching of Leo Frank," Crime Library, http://www.trutv.com/library/crime/notorious_murders/not_guilty/frank/1.html (accessed July 7, 2013).

13. Woodward, *Tom Watson,* p. 381.

14. Ibid., p. 382.

15. Wade, p. 144.

16. Woodward, *Tom Watson,* p. 446.

17. Wade, p. 146.

18. Ibid., pp. 119–25.

19. Ibid., pp. 125–6.

20. Chalmers, *Hooded Americanism,* pp. 26–7.

21. Ibid., p. 27.

22. Wade, p. 127.

23. Newton, *The Ku Klux Klan,* p. 248.

24. *"The Birth of a Nation,"* Wikipedia, http://en.wikipedia.org/wiki/The_Birth_of_a_Nation (accessed July 8, 2013).

25. Ibid.

26. "D. W. Griffith's *The Birth of a Nation* (1915)," The Rise and Fall of Jim Crow, http://www.pbs.org/wnet/jimcrow/stories_events_birth.html (accessed July 8, 2013).

27. Chalmers, *Hooded Americanism,* p. 30; Wade, pp. 146–7.

28. Wade, p. 47.

29. Jackson, *KKK in the City,* pp. 6–7.

30. "American Protective League," Wikipedia, http://en.wikipedia.org/wiki/American_Protective_League (accessed July 22, 2013).

31. Jackson, *KKK in the City,* p. 6.

32. Feldman, *Politics, Society, and the Klan,* p. 29.

33. Wade, p. 150.

34. Rice, p. 6.

35. Wade, pp. 153–4.

36. Ibid.

37. Ibid., pp. 155–7.

38. Ibid., pp. 148, 151–2.

39. The *"Knights of Liberty" Mob and the I.W.W. Prisoners at Tulsa, Okla.* (November 9, 1917). New York: National Civil Liberties Bureau, 1918.

40. Wade, p. 159.

41. *New York World,* Sept. 6, 1921.

42. Ibid., Sept. 7, 1921.

43. Ibid., Sept. 8, 1921.

44. Ibid., Sept. 10–12, 1921.

45. Ibid., Sept. 14–15, 1921.

46. Ibid., Sept. 18–21, 1921.

47. *Atlanta Constitution,* Sept. 9, 1921.

48. Wade, pp. 158–9.

49. Ibid., p. 159.

50. U.S. House of Representatives, Committee on Rules. *The Ku Klux Klan,* pp. 3–14.

51. Ibid., pp. 20–29.

52. Ibid.

53. Ibid.

54. Ibid., pp. 40–44.

55. Don Whitehead, *The FBI Story* (New York: Random House, 1956), p. 61.

56. Ibid., pp. 56–9.

57. U.S. House of Representatives, Committee on Rules. *The Ku Klux Klan,* pp. 45–9.

58. Ibid., pp. 50–4.

59. Ibid., pp. 60–4.

60. Ibid., pp. 65–9.

61. Ibid.

62. Ibid.

63. Ibid.

64. Ibid.

65. Ibid., pp. 70–4.

66. Ibid.

67. Ibid.

68. Jackson, *KKK in the City,* p. 83.

69. U.S. House of Representatives, Committee on Rules. *The Ku Klux Klan,* pp. 75–94.

70. Ibid., pp. 155–169.

71. Ibid., p. 138.

72. Chalmers, *Hooded Americanism,* p. 38.

Chapter 4

1. Jackson, *KKK in the City,* p. 237.

2. *Washington Post,* Nov. 2, 1930.

3. *New York Times,* Dec. 15, 1921.

4. Chalmers, *Hooded Americanism,* pp. 100–1.

5. Wade, pp. 187–8.

6. Ibid., pp. 189–90.

7. *New York Times,* Oct. 5 and Nov. 29, 1922.

8. Wade, p. 190.

9. *Evening Independent* (St. Petersburg, FL), Dec. 22, 1923.

10. Wade, p. 191.

11. Ibid.

12. *Bakersfield Californian,* March 10, 1924.

13. *New York Times,* Feb. 13, 1924.

14. William J. Simmons, *The Kloran* (Atlanta: n.p., 1915).

15. Blee, pp. 24–6, 28; Sarah Doherty, "'Aliens Found in Waiting': The Women of the Ku Klux Klan in Suburban Chicago, 1870–1930," Ph.D. dissertation, Loyola University, 2012, pp. 4–5.

16. Blee, pp. 26–8.

17. Ibid., pp. 29–31.

18. Ibid., pp. 157–60.

19. Kathleen Blee, "Mothers in Race-Hate Movements," in *The Politics of Motherhood: Activist Voices from Left to Right* (Hanover, NH: Dartmouth College Press, 1997), p. 248.

20. *The Daily Mail* (London), March 6, 2012.

21. Trevor Giffey, "Non-Citizen Klan: Royal Riders of the Red Robe," Seattle Civil Rights and Labor History Project, http://depts.washington.edu/civilr/kkk_rrrr.htm (accessed Dec. 12, 2013); *New York Times,* Nov. 28, 1922.

22. American Krusaders, *Ritual: Supreme Headquarters, Little Rock, Arkansas* (Little Rock: American Krusaders, 1924).

23. "Ahepa's 75th Anniversary: Forgotten History: The Klan vs. Americans of Hellenic Heritage in an Era of Hate," The Odyssey Charter School, http://www.greece.org/AHEPA/99000his.html (accessed Dec. 12, 2013).

24. Blee, p. 169; *New York Times,* Oct. 19, 1924.

25. "Ku Klux Klan," The Canadian Encyclopedia, http://www.thecanadianencyclopedia.com/articles/ku-klux-klan; Karen Magill, "Canadian KKK," Vancouver Vagabond, http://karen-magill.blogspot.com/2013/04/canadian-kkk.html; Foreign Branches of the 1915–1944 Ku Klux Klan, http://www.kkklan.com/foreignklan.htm (all accessed Dec. 15, 2013).

26. Magill, "Canadian KKK"; *Leader-*

Post (Regina, SK), Aug. 24, 2007; *Moose Jaw Times Herald,* Feb. 26, 2010; "Ku Klux Klan," The Encyclopedia of Saskatchewan, http://esask.uregina.ca/entry/ku_klux_klan.html (accessed Dec. 15, 2013).

27. Newton, *Ku Klux Klan,* p. 225; "Remembering the St. Boniface Fire," West End Dumplings, http://westend-dumplings.blogspot.com/2009/12/remembering-st-boniface-college-fire.html (accessed Dec. 15, 2013).

28. "Explosion on the Kettle Valley Line," Great Unsolved Mysteries in Canadian History, http://www.canadianmysteries.ca/sites/verigin/home/indexen.html (accessed Dec. 15, 2013).

29. Foreign Branches of the 1915–1944 Ku Klux Klan, http://www.kkklan.com/foreignklan.htm.

30. Ibid.

31. *New York Times,* Nov. 30, 1924.

32. Ibid., July 15, 1928.

33. Ibid., Aug. 27, 1923.

34. Ibid., Aug. 28, 1923.

35. William Mahoney, *Some Ideals of the Ku Klux Klan* (Atlanta: KKK, n.d.).

36. Wade, p. 171.

37. Randall Balmer, *Encyclopedia of Evangelicalism,* (London: Westminster, 2002), p. 527.

38. Daniel Cady, "Robert Shuler and the Ku Klux Klan," in *Race, Religion, Region: Landscapes of Encounter in the American West* (Tucson: University of Arizona Press, 2006), pp. 47–9.

39. A. Cyrus Hayat, "Billy Sunday and the Masculinization of American Protestantism, 1896–1935," Master's thesis, Indiana University, 2008.

40. R. K. Johnson, *Builder of Bridges: The Biography of Dr. Bob Jones, Sr.* (Murfreesboro, TN: Sword of the Lord, 1969), p. 138; *El Paso Times,* September 30, 1922; Bob Jones, *The Perils of America* (pamphlet, 1934).

41. "Bob Jones University Apologizes for Its Racist Past," *Journal of Blacks in Higher Education* 23 (Spring 1999): 72.

42. Daniel Turner, *Standing Without Apology: The History of Bob Jones University* (Greenville, SC: Bob Jones University Press, 1997), pp. 226–227; "Bob Jones University Drops Interracial Dating Ban," *Christianity Today,* March 1, 2000.

43. *The Good Citizen* 11 (February 1923).

44. "Klan Buys College Close to Princeton," *The Harvard Crimson,* Oct. 31, 1923.

45. Alma White, *The Ku Klux Klan in Prophecy* (Zarephath, NJ: Pillar of Fire Church, 1925).

46. Alma White, *Heroes of the Fiery Cross* (Zarephath, NJ: Pillar of Fire Church, 1928).

47. *New York Times,* May 2–3, 1923.

48. Alma White, *Guardians of Liberty* Vol. 1 (Zarephath, NJ: Pillar of Fire Church, 1926), pp. 119–120.

49. Ibid. Vol. 3, p. 103.

50. *Home News Tribune* (Middlesex County, NJ), April 24, 1997.

51. *New York Times,* July 14, 1924; Berkeley *Daily Tribune,* April 26, 2013.

52. William Kunstler, *The Hall-Mills Case: The Minister and the Choir Singer* (New Brunswick, NJ: Rutgers University Press, 1980), pp. 39, 69–70, 323–33.

53. Barkun, pp. 22–5, 160–2.

54. Carroll, *"The Negro a Beast" or "In the Image of God."*

55. Barkun, p. 183.

56. *New York World,* Sept. 19, 1921.

57. "Ku Klux Klan in Virginia," Encyclopedia Virginia, http://www.encyclopediavirginia.org/Ku_Klux_Klan_in_Virginia#start_entry (accessed December 13, 2013).

58. Chalmers, *Hooded Americanism,* p. 58.

59. Ibid., p. 67.

60. Ibid., p. 93.

61. Ibid., p. 130.

62. Ibid., pp. 41–2.

63. Ibid., pp. 49–54.

64. Ibid., pp. 73–4.

65. Ibid., pp. 79–83.

66. Ibid., pp. 237–8.

67. Newton, *Ku Klux Klan,* p. 196.

68. Ibid., p. 205.

69. Ibid., p. 207.

70. Chalmers, *Hooded Americanism,* p. 259.

71. "The Ku Klux Klan in Williamson County, Part 2," Marion Illinois History Preservation, http://www.mihp.org/2013/09/the-ku-klux-klan-in-williamson-county-part-two/#; Edward McClelland, "The 12 Most Corrupt Public Officials in Illinois History: S. Glenn Young," NBC Chicago, http://www.nbcchicago.com/blogs/wardroom/The-12-Most-Corrupt-Public-Officials-In-Illinois-History-S-Glenn-Young-136674698.html (both accessed Dec. 14, 2013).

72. Chalmers, *Hooded Americanism,* pp. 119–20.

73. *Los Angeles Times,* April 24–29, Aug. 6–27, 1922, and Feb. 20, 1925.

74. Rice, pp. 35–6.

75. Ibid., pp. 45–7, 58–64.

76. Feldman, *Politics, Society, and the Klan in Alabama,* pp. 63–91.

77. Rice, pp. 48–9; Laura Bradley, "Protestant Churches and the Ku Klux Klan in Mississippi During the 1920s," Masters thesis, University of Mississippi (1962), pp. 22–3.

78. Newton, *KKK in Mississippi,* pp. 82–3, 102.

79. "Miriam Amanda Wallace Ferguson," Texas State Historical Association, https://www.tshaonline.org/handbook/online/articles/ffe06; "Dale James Moody, Jr.," Texas State Historical Association, https://www.tshaonline.org/handbook/online/articles/fmo19; "Earle Bradford Mayfield," Texas State Historical Association, https://www.tshaonline.org/handbook/online/articles/fma91 (all accessed Dec. 14, 2013).

80. Newton, *Ku Klux Klan,* pp. 198–9.

81. Ibid., p. 217; Finn John, "Corruption, Hypocrisy Brought Down Ku Klux Klan in 1920s," NorthCoast Oregon, http://www.northcoastoregon.com/2013/06/24/corruption-hypocrisy-brought-down-ku-klux-klan-in-1920s (accessed Dec. 14, 2013).

82. Wade, p. 165.

83. Newton, *Invisible Empire,* pp. 59, 61.

84. Newton, *Ku Klux Klan,* p. 237.

85. Rice, 74–84; Chalmers, *Hooded Americanism,* pp. 202–12.

86. Ibid.

87. "The Immigration Act of 1924," U.S. Department of State, Office of the Historian, http://history.state.gov/milestones/1921-1936/immigration-act (accessed Dec. 15, 2013).

88. Wade, p. 191.

89. Chalmers, *Hooded Americanism,* pp. 286–8.

90. Ibid., pp. 289–90.

91. Don Whitehead, *The FBI Story: A Report to the People* (New York: Random House, 1956), p. 61.

92. *New York Times,* Dec. 26–27, 1922; "Filmore Watt Daniel," Find a Grave, http://www.findagrave.com/cgi-bin/fg.cgi?page=gr&GRid=68143589; "Thomas Fletcher Richard," Find a Grave, http://www.findagrave.com/cgi-bin/fg.cgi?page=gr&GRid=44235131 (both accessed Dec. 15, 2013).

93. Federal Bureau of Investigation, "A Byte Out of FBI History: Imperial Kleagle of the Ku Klux Klan in Kustody," http://www.fbi.gov/news/stories/2004/march/kkk031104 (accessed Dec. 15, 2013).

94. Newton, *Ku Klux Klan,* p. 372; *Daily Times* (Beaver, PA), March 10, 1924.

95. "Florida Lynchings," Roots Web, http://www.rootsweb.ancestry.com/~flttttp/lynchings.htm (accessed Dec. 16, 2013).

96. *Orlando Sentinel,* March 7, 1993.

97. Newton, *Invisible Empire,* pp. 49–50.

98. Ibid., pp. 51–2.

99. Ibid., pp. 53–6.

100. Ibid., pp. 54–6.

101. *Tampa Bay Times,* Oct. 19, 2012.

102. Newton, *Invisible Empire,* pp. 59–60.

103. Chalmers, *Hooded Americanism,* pp. 162–5.

104. Max Harrison, "Gentlemen from Indiana," *Atlantic Monthly* 141 (1928): 676–86.

105. Ibid.

106. Ibid.

107. Chalmers, *Hooded Americanism,* p. 171.

108. Harrison, "Gentlemen from Indiana"; "'Murder Wasn't Very Pretty': The Rise and Fall of D. C. Stephenson," *Smithsonian* (Aug. 30, 2012), http:// blogs.smithsonianmag.com/history/ 2012/08/murder-wasnt-very-pretty-the-rise-and-fall-of-d-c-stephenson (accessed Dec. 16, 2013).

109. "'Murder Wasn't Very Pretty.'"

110. Ibid.

111. "The D. C. Stephenson Trial: A Chronology," University of Missouri–Kansas City School of Law, http://law 2.umkc.edu/faculty/projects/ftrials/ste phenson/stephensonchrono.html (accessed Dec. 16, 2013).

112. *Niagara Falls Gazette,* May 28, 1926; *Muskegon Chronicle,* March 22, 2010.

113. *Muskegon Chronicle,* March 22, 2010.

114. Newton, *KKK in Mississippi,* pp. 91–1.

115. Ibid., p. 92.

116. Ibid., pp. 92–4.

117. Joseph Cummins, "Dirty Campaigning in the Roaring Twenties: Herbert Hoover vs. Al Smith," Mental Floss, http://mentalfloss.com/article/19897/ dirty-campaigning-roaring-twenties-herbert-hoover-vs-al-smith (accessed Dec. 16, 2013).

118. "Democratic National Convention of 1928," Texas State Historical Association, http://www.tshaonline.org/ handbook/online/articles/wbd01 (accessed Dec. 16, 2013).

119. Rice, p. 86.

120. Chalmers, *Hooded Americanism,* p. 291.

121. Arthur Goldwag, *The New Hate: A History of Fear and Loathing on the Populist Right* (New York: Random House, 2012), p. 230.

122. Rice, pp. 87–8.

123. Ibid., pp. 88–9.

124. Cummins, "Dirty Campaigning in the Roaring Twenties."

125. Ibid.

126. "1928 Anti-Smith Flier," Presidential Campaign Rhetoric, http:// campaignrhetoric.wordpress.com/2011/ 04/24/1928-anti-smith-flier-teddy-powers (accessed Dec. 16, 2013).

127. Rice, p. 90.

128. "1928 Presidential General Election Results," Dave Leip's Atlas of U.S. Presidential Elections, http://uselec tionatlas.org/RESULTS/national. php?year=1928 (accessed Dec. 16, 2013).

129. John Craig, "'There's Hell Going On Up There': The Carnegie Klan Riot of 1923," *Pennsylvania History* 72 (Summer 2005): 322–46.

130. *Pittsburgh Post-Gazette,* April 11, 2004.

131. Chalmers, *Hooded Americanism,* p. 241.

132. Ibid., pp. 241–2.

133. *Arkansas Catholic,* April 21, 1928.

134. Ibid.

135. Ibid.

136. Ibid.; *Lewiston* (ME) *Evening Journal,* April 10, 1928.

137. *Reading* (PA) *Eagle,* April 10, 1928; *Arkansas Catholic,* April 21, 1928.

138. *Arkansas Catholic,* April 21, 1928; *Pittsburgh Press,* Sept. 22, 1928.

139. *Arkansas Catholic,* April 21, 1928.

140. *Jewish Daily Bulletin,* April 14, 1928.

141. *Pittsburgh Press,* Aug. 14, 1929.

Chapter 5

1. Wade, p. 257.

2. Feldman, *Politics, Society, and the Klan,* pp. 199–210.

3. Ibid., pp. 212–13, 221–9, 239, 244.

4. Wade, pp. 258–9.

5. Newton, *Ku Klux Terror,* p. 31; Feldman, *Politics, Society, and the Klan,* pp. 224, 243; Wade, p. 258.

6. Feldman, *Politics, Society, and the Klan,* pp. 240–1.

7. Ibid., pp. 241–2.

8. Ibid., pp. 244–5.

9. Chalmers, *Hooded Americanism,* p. 307.

10. Wade, p. 259.

11. "United States Presidential Election, 1932," Wikipedia, http://en.wiki pedia.org/wiki/United_States_presiden tial_election,_1932 (accessed July 25, 2013).

12. Joseph Kane, *Presidential Fact Book* (New York: Random House, 1998), p. 201.

13. Wade, p. 259.

14. Chalmers, *Hooded Americanism,* p. 307; Rice, p. 102.

15. Chalmers, *Hooded Americanism,* p. 307; Sims, *The Klan,* p. 3.

16. Gerald Dunne, *Hugo Black and the Judicial Revolution* (New York: Irvington, 1977), pp. 116, 118, 121; Feldman, *Politics, Society, and the Klan,* pp. 127–8.

17. Wade, p. 260.

18. Ibid.

19. Thomas Brooks, *Toil and Trouble: A History of American Labor* (New York: Delacorte, 1971), p. 368.

20. Hofstadter and Wallace, *American Violence: A Documentary History,* pp. 175–9.

21. Robert Ingalls, "The Tampa Flogging Case, Urban Vigilantism," *Florida Historical Quarterly* 56 (July 1977): 13–27.

22. "Congress of Industrial Organizations," The Gilder Lehrman Institute of American History, http://www.gil derlehrman.org/history-by-era/new-deal/timeline-terms/congress-indus trial-organizations (accessed July 25, 2013).

23. Sharon Smith, "The 1930s: Turning Point for U.S. Labor," *International Socialist Review* Issue 25, September–October 2002.

24. Wade, pp. 262–3.

25. Chalmers, *Hooded Americanism,* pp. 306, 320–1.

26. Jeremy Brecher, *Strike!* (Boston: South End, 1997), p. 198.

27. Constance Backhouse, *Colour Coded: A Legal History of Racism in Canada, 1900–1950* (Toronto: University of Toronto Press, 1999), pp. 173–225.

28. Stephen Dorril, *Blackshirt: Sir Oswald Mosley and British Fascism* (London: Penguin, 2007), pp. 425–6, 465, 493; Richard Thurlow, *Fascism in Britain: A History, 1918–1985* (Oxford: Basil Blackwell, 1987), pp. 80–3.

29. "Kormack's Kaledonian Klan," Metapedia, http://en.metapedia.org/ wiki/Kormack%27s_Kaledonian_Klan; "Foreign Branches of the Ku Klux Klan," http://www.kkklan.com/foreignklan. htm (both accessed Aug. 18, 2013).

30. Richard Bak, "The Dark Days of the Black Legion," *Detroit Hour,* http:// www.hourdetroit.com/Hour-Detroit/ March-2009/The-Dark-Days-of-the-Black-Legion (accessed July 26, 2013).

31. Ibid.

32. Ibid.; Frank Donner, *Protectors of Privilege* (Berkeley: University of California Press, 1990), pp. 55–6.

33. Bak, "The Dark Days of the Black Legion."

34. Ibid.

35. *Sarasota Herald-Tribune,* May 27, 1936.

36. Wade, p. 262.

37. Feldman, *Politics, Society, and the Klan,* pp. 229–37; Chalmers, *Hooded Americanism,* pp. 313–16.

38. Ibid.

39. Howard Ball, *Hugo L. Black: Cold Steel Warrior* (Oxford: Oxford University Press, 1996), p. 16; Roger Newman, *Hugo Black: A Biography* (New York: Fordham University Press, 1997), pp. 87, 104.

40. *Alexander v. Holmes County Board of Education,* 396 U.S. 19 (1969).

41. "Dixie Bibb Graves," Wikipedia, http://en.wikipedia.org/wiki/Dixie_ Bibb_Graves (accessed July 26, 2013).

42. Rice, p. 98.

43. Chalmers, *Hooded Americanism,* pp. 80–3.

44. Harry Ashmore, *Civil Rights and Wrongs: A Memoir of Race and Politics, 1944–1996* (Columbia: University of South Carolina Press, 19979), p. 26.

45. Rice, pp. 79–80, 98–9.

46. Carlos M. Larralde and Richard Griswold del Castillo, "San Diego's Ku

Klux Klan 1920–1980," *The Journal of San Diego History* 46 (Spring/Summer 2000), http://www.sandiegohistory.org/journal/2000-2/klan.htm (accessed Sept, 26, 2013).

47. Haas, pp. 88–9; Wade, p. 265.
48. Wade, p. 264.
49. Ibid., p. 265.
50. Harold Henderson, *The Politics of Change in Georgia: A Political Biography of Ellis Arnall* (Athens: University of Georgia Press, 1991), pp. 26–8.
51. *Texas State Handbook Online*, Texas State Historical Association, http://www.tshaonline.org/handbook/online/articles/fev17 (accessed July 26, 2013).
52. Haas, p. 89.
53. *Atlanta Constitution*, July 11, 1939.
54. U.S. Congress, *The Present-Day Ku Klux Klan Movement*, p. 8.
55. Wade, p. 266.
56. Chalmers, *Hooded Americanism*, p. 321.
57. Feldman, *Politics, Society, and the Klan*, pp. 243–58.
58. Wade, pp. 263–6.
59. *Washington Post*, June 19, 2005; "Robert Byrd," Wikipedia, http://en.wikipedia.org/wiki/Robert_Byrd (accessed Aug. 11, 2013).
60. Wade, pp. 267–8.
61. Ibid., p. 268.
62. Ibid.
63. Newton, *Invisible Empire*, p. 102.
64. Chalmers, *Hooded Americanism*, p. 322; "Leslie Fry," Wikipedia, http://en.metapedia.org/wiki/Leslie_Fry (accessed July 27, 2013).
65. Chalmers, *Hooded Americanism*, p. 322.
66. Ibid.; "German American Bund," Wikipedia, http://en.wikipedia.org/wiki/German_American_Bund (accessed July 27, 2013).
67. Wade, p. 271.
68. *The Evening News* (Sault Ste. Marie, MI), April 5, 1940; Jewish Telegraphic Agency, http://www.jta.org/1940/04/03/archive/dies-orders-subpoenas-for-michigan-klan-leaders-as-dickstein-calls-anti-semites-traitor (accessed July 27, 2013).
69. *Baltimore Afro-American*, April 18, 1942.
70. Haas, p. 90.
71. Newton, *Invisible Empire*, pp. 103–4.
72. Haas, p. 90.
73. "History of the Ku Klux Klan in New Jersey," Wikipedia, http://en.wikipedia.org/wiki/History_of_Ku_Klux_Klan_in_New_Jersey (accessed Sept. 26, 2013).
74. Alma Bridwell White, *Guardians of Liberty* (Zarephath, NJ: Pillar of Fire Church, 1943).
75. Haas, p. 91.
76. Wade, p. 275.
77. Haas, p. 91.

78. Newton, *Invisible Empire*, p. 105.
79. Ibid.
80. Ibid.
81. Wade, p. 196; Rice, p. 101.
82. Thomas Borstelmann, *Apartheid's Reluctant Uncle: The United States and Southern Africa in the Early Cold War* (New York: Oxford University Press, 1993), p. 38.
83. *Seattle Times*, Nov. 3, 1991.
84. "Harry S. Truman," Wikiquote, http://en.wikiquote.org/wiki/Harry_S._Truman.
85. Rice, pp. 99–100.
86. "California's 15th Congressional District," Wikipedia, http://en.wikipedia.org/wiki/California%27s_15th_congressional_district (accessed July 27, 2013).

Chapter 6

1. House Committee on Un-American Activities, *The Present-Day Ku Klux Klan Movement*, p. 9. Hereafter cited as "HCUA."
2. "Ku Klux Klan in Virginia," Encyclopedia Virginia.
3. Newton, *Invisible Empire*, p. 106.
4. Newton, *Ku Klux Klan*, p. 67.
5. "Ku Klux Klan," Metapedia, http://en.metapedia.org/wiki/Ku_Klux_Klan (accessed Aug. 11, 2013).
6. "Stone Mountain," Wikipedia, http://en.wikipedia.org/wiki/Stone_Mountain (accessed Aug. 11, 2013); *New York Times*, Jan. 21, 1993.
7. "The Contemporary Ku Klux Klan," in *Assassination and Political Violence* (New York: Bantam, 1970), p. 362.
8. HCUA, *The Present-Day Ku Klux Klan Movement*, p. 10.
9. "Association of Georgia Klans," Wikipedia, http://en.wikipedia.org/wiki/Association_of_Georgia_Klans (accessed Aug. 11, 2013).
10. *Washington Post*, June 19, 2005; "Robert Byrd," Wikipedia.
11. "Association of Georgia Klans," Wikipedia; HCUA, *The Present-Day Ku Klux Klan Movement*, p. 10.
12. Haas, p. 95.
13. Newton, *Ku Klux Klan*, p. 383; "Association of Georgia Klans," Wikipedia.
14. Newton, *Ku Klux Klan*, p. 254.
15. "Three Governors Controversy," The New Georgia Encyclopedia, http://www.georgiaencyclopedia.org/nge/Article.jsp?id=h-591 (accessed Aug. 11, 2013).
16. Rice, pp. 109–12.
17. Weinburger, "The Columbians, Inc."
18. "The Columbians," Metapedia, http://en.metapedia.org/wiki/The_Columbians (accessed Aug. 11, 2013).
19. "Columbians," The New Georgia Encyclopedia, http://www.georgiaency-

clopedia.org/nge/Article.jsp?id=h-3605 (accessed Aug. 11, 2013).
20. "The Columbians," Metapedia.
21. Wade, pp. 282–3.
22. Weinburger, "The Columbians, Inc."
23. "J. B. Stoner," Metapedia, http://en.metapedia.org/wiki/J._B._Stoner (accessed Aug. 11, 2013).
24. McWhorter, *Carry Me Home*, p. 75.
25. Wade, p. 263.
26. Ibid., pp. 277–8.
27. Chalmers, *Hooded Americanism*, pp. 330–1.
28. Newton, *Ku Klux Terror*, pp. 42–3, 51–5, 128.
29. *Birmingham News*, July 16, 2000.
30. Charles Abrams, "Invasion and Counterattack," in *Violence in America* (New York: Vintage, 1959).
31. Newton, *Ku Klux Klan*, p. 386; *Jet Magazine*, Feb. 14, 1952.
32. Wade, p. 289.
33. "Federated Knights of the Ku Klux Klan," Metapedia, http://en.metapedia.org/wiki/Federated_Knights_of_the_Ku_Klux_Klan (accessed August 11, 2013).
34. "Original Southern Klans," Metapedia, http://en.metapedia.org/wiki/Original_Southern_Klans (accessed Aug. 11, 2013).
35. "Southern and Northern Knights of the Ku Klux Klan (1949)," Metapedia, http://en.metapedia.org/wiki/Southern_and_Northern_Knights_of_the_Ku_Klux_Klan_%281949%29 (accessed Aug. 11, 2013).
36. "Federated Klans of Alabama," Metapedia, http://en.metapedia.org/wiki/Federated_Klans_of_Alabama (accessed Aug. 11, 2013).
37. *Mexia* (TX) *Weekly Herald*, Aug. 22, 1946.
38. "Beauford H. Jester," Wikipedia, http://en.wikipedia.org/wiki/Beauford_H._Jester (accessed Aug. 11, 2013).
39. "Association of Georgia Klans," Wikipedia.
40. John Warren, *Duck: A Legal History of Robert Mallard's Murder* (Boston: Northeastern University School of Law, 2011), p. 6.
41. Ibid., pp. 6–7.
42. "Isaiah Nixon," Northeastern University, http://nuweb9.neu.edu/civilrights/isaiah-nixon (accessed Aug. 15, 2013).
43. "Georgia Gubernatorial Special Election, 1948," Wikipedia, http://en.wikipedia.org/wiki/Georgia_gubernatorial_special_election,_1948 (accessed Aug. 15, 2013).
44. Warren, *Duck*, pp. 7–8.
45. Ibid., pp. 14–19.
46. Ibid., pp. 29–36.
47. Michael Klarman, *From Jim Crow to Civil Rights: The Supreme Court and the Struggle for Racial Equality* (New

York: Oxford University Press, 2004), p. 250.

48. Newton, *Ku Klux Terror*, pp. 44–5.

49. Ibid., p. 46.

50. Ibid., p. 47; "Association of Georgia Klans," Wikipedia; *Toledo Blade*, May 27, 1949.

51. "The Contemporary Ku Klux Klan," p. 363.

52. Newton, *Invisible Empire*, pp. 116–17.

53. Ibid., pp. 119–22.

54. *Indianapolis Recorder*, Aug. 6, 1949.

55. *St. Petersburg Times*, Aug. 4, 1949.

56. "The Contemporary Ku Klux Klan," p. 363.

57. *St. Petersburg Times*, Aug. 4, 1949.

58. *Kokomo Tribune*, March 10, 1950.

59. Wade, *Fiery Cross*, p. 297.

60. "Unmasking the Klan," Weld for Birmingham, http://weldbham.com/blog/2012/07/18/unmasking-the-klan-late-1940s-coalition-against-racial-violence (accessed Aug. 15, 2013).

61. Wade, p. 290; Newton, *Ku Klux Klan*, p. 106.

62. Feldman, *Politics, Society, and the Klan*, p. 308; Newton, *Ku Klux Klan*, pp. 79, 106.

63. *Birmingham News*, July 16, 2000.

64. Feldman, *Politics, Society, and the Klan*, p. 308.

65. "Unmasking the Klan."

66. "Sam Roper," Metapedia, http://en.metapedia.org/wiki/Samuel_W._Roper (accessed Aug. 15, 2013); Haas, pp. 103–4.

67. Newton, *Ku Klux Klan*, p. 85.

68. Gillette and Tillinger, p. 74.

69. Ibid., pp. 78–83.

70. Rice, pp. 117–18.

71. "Thomas Lemuel Hamilton and the Ku Klux Klan," the Carter-Klan Documentary Project, http://www.carter-klan.org/Hamilton.html (accessed Aug. 22, 2013).

72. Ibid.

73. *St. Petersburg Times*, Nov. 23, 1949.

74. "Thomas Lemuel Hamilton and the Ku Klux Klan."

75. Ibid.

76. Ibid.

77. Ibid.

78. Ibid.; Timothy Tyson, *Blood Done Sign My Name* (New York: Random House, 2007), pp. 54–5.

79. "Thomas Lemuel Hamilton and the Ku Klux Klan."

80. *St. Petersburg Times*, March 1, 1950, and Oct. 14, 1952; *The Courier News* (Blytheville, AR), March 14, 1950; Newton, *Ku Klux Klan*, p. 281.

81. "John G. Crommelin," Metapedia, http://en.metapedia.org/wiki/John_G._Crommelin; American National Biography Online, http://h-net.msu.edu/cgi-bin/logbrowse.pl?trx=vx&list=h-

us1918-45&month=0309&week=d&msg=LoOZbD9KIfUdKMPEVCP5RA&user=&pw= (both accessed Aug. 22, 2013).

82. Newton, *Invisible Empire*, pp. 126–7.

83. Ibid., pp. 130–5, 137–8.

84. Ibid., p. 137.

85. "Ku Klux Klan in Virginia," Encyclopedia of Virginia, http://www.encyclopediavirginia.org/Ku_Klux_Klan_in_Virginia#start_entry (accessed Aug. 25, 2013).

86. "Robert Byrd," Wikipedia; *Washington Post*, June 19, 2005.

87. "Edward Fields," ADL Archives, http://archive.adl.org/learn/ext_us/Fields.asp?xpicked=2&item=Fields (accessed Aug. 25, 2013).

88. "United Klan," Metapedia, http://en.metapedia.org/wiki/United_Klan (accessed Aug. 25, 2013).

89. *The News and Courier* (Charleston, SC), Jan. 6, 1952; HCUA, p. 11.

90. "U.S. Klans," Wikipedia, http://en.wikipedia.org/wiki/U.S._Klans (accessed Aug. 25, 2013).

Chapter 7

1. *Brown v. Board of Education*, 347 U.S. 483 (1954).

2. Alex Alston Jr. and James Dickerson, *Devil's Sanctuary: An Eyewitness History of Mississippi Hate Crimes* (Chicago: Chicago Review, 2009), p. 28.

3. Tom Brady, "A Review of Black Monday," address delivered to the Indianola (MS) Citizens' Council, Oct. 28, 1954.

4. "White Citizens' Council," Wikipedia, http://en.wikipedia.org/wiki/White_Citizens%27_Council (accessed Aug. 29, 2013).

5. "William James Simmons," Metapedia, http://en.metapedia.org/wiki/William_James_Simmons (accessed Aug. 29, 2013).

6. "Roy V. Harris (1895–1985)," New Georgia Encyclopedia, http://www.georgiaencyclopedia.org/articles/history-archaeology/roy-v-harris-1895-1985 (accessed Aug. 29, 2013).

7. Mendelsohn, pp. 1–20.

8. Ibid., pp. 15–16.

9. Newton, *Ku Klux Klan*, p. 171.

10. Charles Payne, *I've Got the Light of Freedom: The Organizing Tradition and the Mississippi Freedom Struggle* (Berkeley: University of California Press, 2007), pp. 34–35.

11. Wade, p. 300.

12. George Thayer, *The Father Shores of Politics: The American Political Fringe Today* (New York: Simon and Schuster, 1967) pp. 107–123.

13. Newton, *Ku Klux Klan*, p. 171.

14. HCUA, p. 11.

15. "U.S. Klans," Wikipedia; "U.S. Klans, Knights of the Ku Klux Klan,"

Metapedia, http://en.metapedia.org/wiki/U.S._Klans,_Knights_of_the_Ku_Klux_Klan (accessed August 29, 2013).

16. "U.S. Klans, Knights of the Ku Klux Klan," Metapedia.

17. "Ku Klux Klan in Virginia," Encyclopedia of Virginia.

18. *Washington Post*, Oct. 21, 1955.

19. Cook, *The Segregationists*, pp. 119–20.

20. David Rose, *The Big Eddy Club: The Stocking Stranglings and Southern Justice* (New York: New, 2011), pp. 141–2.

21. "White Brotherhood," Metapedia, http://en.metapedia.org/wiki/White_Brotherhood (accessed Aug. 29, 2013).

22. *The Argus* (Melbourne, Australia), Aug. 23, 1956.

23. "Montgomery Bus Boycott," Encyclopedia of Alabama, http://www.encyclopediaofalabama.org/face/Article.jsp?id=h-1567 (accessed Aug. 29, 2013).

24. "Asa Carter (Forrest Carter)," Encyclopedia of Alabama, http://www.encyclopediaofalabama.org/face/Article.jsp?id=h-2427 (accessed Aug. 29, 2013); "Asa Earl Carter," Wikipedia, http://en.wikipedia.org/wiki/Asa_Earl_Carter (accessed Aug. 29, 2013); *New York Times*, Oct. 4, 1991.

25. Webb, *Rabble Rousers*, p. 113; "Original Ku Klux Klan of the Confederacy," Wikipedia, http://en.wikipedia.org/wiki/Original_Ku_Klux_Klan_of_the_Confederacy (accessed Aug. 29, 2013).

26. "Autherine Lucy," Encyclopedia of Alabama, http://www.encyclopediaofalabama.org/face/Article.jsp?id=h-2489 (accessed Aug. 29, 2013); McWhorter, pp. 18–19, 103.

27. Brian Ward, "Civil Rights and Rock and Roll: Revisiting the Nat King Cole Attack of 1956." *OAH Magazine of History* 24 (2010): 21–24; *New York Times*, April 19, 1956.

28. Webb, *Rabble Rousers*, pp. 111–16.

29. Ibid., pp. 49–51.

30. Ibid., pp. 50–4; *Rome* (GA) *News-Tribune*, March 13, 1957.

31. "Clinton Desegregation Crisis," The Tennessee Encyclopedia of History and Culture, http://tennesseeencyclopedia.net/entry.php?rec=279 (accessed Aug. 30, 2013); Webb, *Rabble Rousers*, pp. 48–9.

32. *Rome* (GA) *News-Tribune*, March 13, 1957.

33. Newton, *Ku Klux Klan*, p. 156.

34. *Nashville Post*, Sept. 7, 2007.

35. Parker, *Violence*, p. 6; Webb, *Rabble Rousers*, p. 80.

36. "The 54th Anniversary of the Dynamite Bombing of Hattie Cotton Elementary," Enclave, http://enclave-nashville.blogspot.com/2011/09/54th-anniversary-of-dynamite-bombing-of.html (accessed Aug. 31, 2013).

37. Webb, *Rabble Rousers,* pp. 84, 95–6.

38. Newton, *Ku Klux Klan,* p. 156.

39. "Montgomery Bus Boycott Timeline," Southern Polytechnic State University, http://students.spsu.edu/asemenov/timeline.html (accessed Aug. 31, 2013).

40. *Birmingham News,* July 16, 2000.

41. Greenhaw, *Fighting the Devil,* p. 31.

42. "Montgomery Bus Boycott Timeline."

43. Greenhaw, *Fighting the Devil,* pp. 9–16.

44. "Original Ku Klux Klan of the Confederacy," Wikipedia; Christopher Hewitt, *Political Violence and Terrorism in Modern America: A Chronology* (Westport, CT: Greenwood, 2005), p. 4; "Asa Earl Carter," Wikipedia.

45. Hewitt, *Political Violence,* p. 4; *Birmingham News,* July 16, 2000.

46. "Asa Earl Carter," Wikipedia.

47. Nunnelly, pp. 55–9.

48. "Eldon Edwards: The Mike Wallace Interview," Harry Ransom Center, University of Texas at Austin, http://www.hrc.utexas.edu/multimedia/video/2008/wallace/edwards_eldon_t.html (accessed Aug. 31, 2013).

49. Ibid.

50. Ibid.

51. Ibid.

52. Ibid.

53. Mary Stanton, *Journey Toward Justice: Juliette Hampton Morgan and the Montgomery Bus Boycott* (Athens: University of Georgia Press, 2006), p. 193.

54. Ibid.; *Port Angeles* (WA) *Evening News,* May 31, 1957.

55. Parker, *Violence,* p. 6.

56. Ibid., pp. 6–7; Huie, *Three Lives,* pp. 12–15.

57. Huie, *Three Lives,* pp. 15–17; McWhorter, pp. 25–6.

58. McWhorter, pp. 127–8; *Birmingham News,* Sept. 17, 2010; Jackson (MS) *Clarion Ledger,* Oct. 24, 2011.

59. Hewitt, *Political Violence,* p. 5.

60. "Desegregation of Central High School," The Encyclopedia of Arkansas History and Culture, http://www.encyclopediaofarkansas.net/encyclopedia/entry-detail.aspx?entryID=718 (accessed Sept. 1, 2013).

61. Parker, *Violence,* p. 9; *Arkansas Gazette,* Jan. 1, 1960.

62. Newton, *Ku Klux Klan,* p. 391; McMillen, *Citizens' Council,* pp. 283–4.

63. McMillen, *Citizens' Council,* p. 284; Newton, *Ku Klux Klan,* p. 107; Roy Reed, *Faubus: The Life and Times of an American Prodigal* (Fayetteville: University of Arkansas Press, 1997), pp. 256–7.

64. Knebel and Mollenhoff, "Eight Klans," p. 66; *Miami News,* April 23, 1957; HCUA, p. 12.

65. "U.S. Klans," Wikipedia.

66. "Horace Sherman Miller," Texas State Historical Association, http://www.tshaonline.org/handbook/online/articles/fmi93 (accessed Sept. 1, 2013); Morris Fine and Milton Himmelfarb, *American Jewish Yearbook 60* (New York: American Jewish Committee, 1959), p. 50.

67. "U.S. Klans," Wikipedia; HCUA, p. 20.

68. "U.S. Klans," Wikipedia; *Tuscaloosa News,* June 7, 1957; *Time,* June 17, 1957; *Reading* (PA) *Eagle,* June 11, 1957; *Gadsden Times,* Oct. 1, 1958.

69. Anti-Defamation League, "The Ku Klux Klan Revival," *Facts* (November-December 1956): 93; *Miami News,* April 23, 1957; *Concordia* (LA) *Sentinel,* Dec. 17, 2009; HCUA, pp. 12, 15; Bartley, *Rise of Massive Resistance,* p. 203; Newton, *Ku Klux Klan in Mississippi,* p. 116; "Lineage of Ku Klux Klan Organizations," Metapedia, http://en.metapedia.org/wiki/Lineage_of_Ku_Klux_Klan_organizations (accessed Sept. 1, 2013).

70. James William Cole Papers, East Carolina University, http://digital.lib.ecu.edu/special/ead/findingaids/0040; "James W. 'Catfish' Cole," Wikipedia, http://en.wikipedia.org/wiki/James_W._%22Catfish%22_Cole (both accessed Sept. 1, 2013).

71. Newton, *Ku Klux Klan,* pp. 389–90.

72. Dan Morrill, "A History of Charlotte and Mecklenburg," Charlotte-Mecklenburg Historic Landmarks Commission, http://www.cmhpf.org/Morrill%20Book/CH12.htm (accessed Sept. 1, 2013).

73. "James W. 'Catfish' Cole," Wikipedia; "Robert F. Williams," Wikipedia, http://en.wikipedia.org/wiki/Robert_F._Williams (accessed Sept. 1, 2013).

74. Newton, *Ku Klux Klan,* pp. 389–90.

75. "Triracial Segregation in Robeson County," Learn NC, http://www.learnnc.org/lp/editions/nchist-newcentury/5816 (accessed Sept. 1, 2013).

76. Newton, *Ku Klux Klan,* p. 90; "James W. 'Catfish' Cole," Wikipedia; Tyson, *Blood Done Sign My Name,* p. 56.

77. *Fayetteville Observer,* Jan. 18, 2008; "The Lumbees Face the Klan," Learn NC, http://www.learnnc.org/lp/editions/nchist-postwar/6068 (accessed Sept. 1, 2013).

78. Newton, *Ku Klux Klan,* pp. 390–1; *Raleigh* (NC) *News and Observer,* Feb. 17, March 19, and March 21, 1958.

79. "John G. Crommelin," Metapedia, http://en.metapedia.org/wiki/John_G._Crommelin (accessed Oct. 22, 2013).

80. "Alabama Gubernatorial Election, 1958," Wikipedia, http://en.wikipedia.org/wiki/Alabama_gubernatorial_election,_1958 (accessed Sept. 2, 2013).

81. "John M. Patterson (1959–63)," Encyclopedia of Alabama, http://www.encyclopediaofalabama.org/face/Article.jsp?id=h-1431 (accessed Sept. 2, 2013).

82. Cook, *The Segregationists,* p. 129.

83. Ibid., p. 130.

84. Marshall Frady, *Wallace* (New York: Random House, 1996), p. 126.

85. "George C. Wallace," Encyclopedia of Alabama, http://www.encyclopediaofalabama.org/face/Article.jsp?id=h-1676 (accessed Sept. 2, 2013).

86. *Tuscaloosa News,* Dec. 18, 1994.

87. "Alabama Gubernatorial Election, 1958," Wikipedia.

88. Carter, *Politics of Rage,* p. 96.

89. Cook, *The Segregationists,* p. 130.

90. "Asa Earl Carter," Wikipedia.

91. FBI memo dated Feb. 5, 1958.

92. *Tuscaloosa News,* Dec. 4, 1958; "List of Nationalist Conferences and Meetings in America," Metapedia, http://en.metapedia.org/wiki/List_of_nationalist_conferences_and_meetings_in_America (accessed Sept. 5, 2013).

93. "National States Rights Party," Metapedia, http://en.metapedia.org/wiki/National_States_Rights_Party (accessed Sept. 5, 2013).

94. "National States Rights Party," Metapedia.

95. Newton, *Ku Klux Klan,* p. 388.

96. Abrams, "Invasion and Counterattack," pp. 189–90.

97. Newton, *Ku Klux Klan,* pp. 387–91; Hewitt, *Political Violence,* pp. 2–6.

98. Newton, *Ku Klux Klan,* pp. 390–1.

99. Newton, *Invisible Empire,* pp. 153–4; Newton, *Ku Klux Terror,* pp. 79–80.

100. Newton, *Ku Klux Terror,* pp. 80–4.

101. Ibid., pp. 84–6.

102. Ibid., pp. 86–7.

103. Ibid., pp. 97–8; "Temple Bombing," New Georgia Encyclopedia, http://www.georgiaencyclopedia.org/articles/arts-culture/temple-bombing (accessed Sept. 5, 2013).

104. *Atlanta Constitution,* May 20, 1960; FBI memo dated May 26, 1960; FBI interview transcripts dated Feb. 18, 2009.

105. William McCord, *Mississippi: The Long, Hot Summer* (New York: W. W. Norton, 1965), p. 37; Maryann Vollers, *Ghosts of Mississippi* (Boston: Little, Brown, 1995), p. 52; Ira Harkey, *The Smell of Burning Crosses* (Jacksonville, MS: Harris-Wolfe, 1967), p. 104; Massengill, *Portrait of a Racist,* pp. 149–50.

106. Newton, *Ku Klux Klan in Mississippi,* pp. 111–12.

107. "Clinton Melton," Northeastern University School of Law, http://nuweb9.neu.edu/civilrights/clinton-melton (accessed Sept. 5, 2013).

108. Newton, *Ku Klux Klan in Mississippi*, pp. 115–18.

109. Ibid., pp. 116–17.

110. "Louisiana Gubernatorial Election of 1959–60," Wikipedia, http://en.wikipedia.org/wiki/Louisiana_gubernatorial_election,_1959-60 (accessed Sept. 26, 2013).

111. Parker, *Violence*, pp. 13–16.

112. "The Ku Klux Klan: Legacy of Hate," ADL Archives, http://archive.adl.org/issue_combating_hate/uka/rise.asp (accessed Sept. 6, 2013).

113. Newton, *Ku Klux Klan*, pp. 391–2; "Robert Shelton," Wikipedia.

114. Forster and Epstein, *Report*, p. 21.

115. "U.S. Klans," Wikipedia.

116. Newton, *Invisible Empire*, p. 157.

117. Ibid.; Parker, *Violence*, p. 18.

118. Joseph Kane, *Presidential Fact Book* (New York: Random House, 1998), p. 227.

119. *Washington Post*, June 19, 2005.

120. Newton, *Invisible Empire*, p. 159.

121. Stephen Fox, *Blood and Power: Organized Crime in Twentieth-Century America* (New York: Penguin, 1989), pp. 333–4.

122. "Transcript: JFK's Speech on His Religion," National Public Radio, http://www.npr.org/templates/story/story.php?storyId=16920600 (accessed Sept. 8, 2013).

123. "October 13, 1960 Debate Transcript," Commission on Presidential Debates, http://www.debates.org/index.php?page=october-13-1960-debate-transcript (accessed Sept. 8, 2013).

124. Newton, *Invisible Empire*, p. 159.

125. *Los Angeles Times*, Dec. 15, 1988.

126. Kane, *Presidential Fact Book*, 228; "John G. Crommelin," Metapedia.

127. Forster and Epstein, *Report*, p. 20.

128. HCUA, p. 48.

Chapter 8

1. Parker, *Violence*, p. 25; Newton, *Ku Klux Klan*, p. 63; "Charlayne Hunter-Gault," New Georgia Encyclopedia, http://www.georgiaencyclopedia.org/articles/arts-culture/charlayne-hunter-gault-b-1942 (accessed Sept. 12, 2013).

2. HCUA, p. 21.

3. *Morgan v. Commonwealth of Virginia*, 328 U.S. 373 (1946).

4. *Boynton v. Virginia*, 364 U.S. 454 (1960).

5. Parker, *Violence*, p. 18; "Timeline," Equal Justice Initiative, http://racialjustice.eji.org/timeline (accessed Sept. 12, 2013).

6. Newton, *Ku Klux Terror*, pp. 105–3.

7. Ibid., p. 108.

8. Ibid., p. 109.

9. Ibid., p. 111; "Timeline," Equal Justice Initiative.

10. Newton, *Ku Klux Terror*, p. 112; *Old Gold and Black* (Wake Forest University newspaper), Feb. 14, 2013.

11. Newton, *Ku Klux Terror*, pp. 110–11.

12. Ibid., p. 113.

13. Ibid., pp. 113–14; McWhorter, *Carry Me Home*, p. 199.

14. Newton, *Ku Klux Terror*, p. 114.

15. Ibid.

16. Ibid., p. 115.

17. *United States v. U.S. Klans, Knights of Ku Klux Klan, Inc.* Civ. A. No. 1718-N., 194 F. Supp. 897 (1961).

18. Parker, *Violence*, p. 20; Newton, *Ku Klux Klan*, p. 300.

19. Robert Williams, *Negroes with Guns* (Detroit: Wayne State University Press, 1962), pp. 48–9.

20. Wilmington (NC) *Morning Star*, Jan. 17, 1976.

21. *Kokomo Tribune*, June 22, 1961.

22. HCUA, pp. 22–8.

23. "Albany Movement," New Georgia Encyclopedia, http://www.georgiaencyclopedia.org/articles/history-archaeology/albany-movement (accessed Sept. 15, 2013).

24. Newton, *Ku Klux Klan*, pp. 204, 393.

25. Christopher Strain, *Pure Fire: Self-Defense as Activism in the Civil Rights Era* (Athens: University of Georgia Press, 2005), pp. 75–6.

26. Andrew Tully, *The FBI's Most Famous Cases* (New York: Dell, 1965), p. 222.

27. "Albany Movement," New Georgia Encyclopedia.

28. Parker, *Violence*, pp. 26–7.

29. Newton, *Ku Klux Klan*, p. 393.

30. "The Contemporary Ku Klux Klan," in *Assassination and Political Violence*, p. 368.

31. Newton, *KKK in Mississippi*, p. 117.

32. Ibid., p. 120; Parker, *Violence*, p. 24.

33. Newton, *KKK in Mississippi*, p. 122.

34. Ibid.; "National States Rights Party," Harold Weisburg Collection, N Disk.

35. Newton, *KKK in Mississippi*, pp. 122–3.

36. Ibid., pp. 123–4.

37. Ibid., pp. 124–6; *Concordia Sentinel*, Sept. 17, 2009.

38. Newton, *Ku Klux Terror*, pp. 119–20.

39. "Alabama Gubernatorial Election, 1962," Wikipedia, http://en.wikipedia.org/wiki/Alabama_gubernatorial_election,_1962 (accessed Sept. 22, 2013).

40. Newton, *Ku Klux Terror*, pp. 121–4.

41. Ibid., pp. 122–3.

42. "John G. Crommelin," Metapedia.

43. HCUA, pp. 20, 339–42.

44. Ibid., p. 50; "Butterworth, Wally (1901–1974)," University of Virginia Social Networks and Archival Context Project, http://socialarchive.iath.virginia.edu/xtf/view?docId=butterworth-wally-1901-1974-cr.xml (accessed Sept. 22, 2013).

45. HCUA, pp. 50–1.

46. George McMillan, "New Bombing Terrorists of the South Call Themselves NACIREMA," *Life* (Oct. 11, 1963): 39–40.

47. HCUA Testimony, Part 2, pp. 2215–16, 2222–29.

48. Ibid., pp. 2098–9, 2123.

49. "Edward Fields," Anti-Defamation League; "National States Rights Party," Harold Weisburg Collection, N Disk.

50. *Birmingham News*, July 16, 2000.

51. *Los Angeles Times*, Oct. 27, 2002; McWhorter, pp. 212–13.

52. *Los Angeles Times*, Oct. 27, 2002; Mary Stanton, *Freedom Walk: Mississippi or Bust* (Oxford: University Press of Mississippi, 2003), pp. 5–6.

53. *Los Angeles Times*, Oct. 27, 2002; Stanton, *Freedom Walk*, pp. 66–9, 74; Mendelsohn, p. 60.

54. Stanton, *Freedom Walk*, pp. 76–9, 214–15; *Los Angeles Times*, Oct. 27, 2002.

55. Newton, *Ku Klux Terror*, pp. 124–5.

56. Ibid., pp. 126–7.

57. Ibid., pp. 127–8.

58. Ibid., p. 128.

59. Ibid., pp. 128–9.

60. Ibid., pp. 129–30,

61. "John F. Kennedy Civil Rights Address," American Rhetoric, http://www.americanrhetoric.com/speeches/jfkcivilrights.htm (accessed Sept. 26, 2013).

62. Newton, *Ku Klux Klan in Mississippi*, p. 132.

63. Ibid., pp. 132–3.

64. Ibid., p. 133.

65. Ibid., pp. 129–30.

66. Ibid., pp. 127–8.

67. HCUA, p. 97.

68. Newton, *Ku Klux Klan in Mississippi*, pp. 138–9.

69. *Birmingham News*, July 16, 2000.

70. Newton, *Ku Klux Terror*, p. 131.

71. *Tuscaloosa News*, Aug. 26, 1963.

72. Newton, *Ku Klux Terror*, pp. 133–6.

73. Ibid., p. 138.

74. Ibid., pp. 139–43.

75. HCUA, pp. 27–8, 160–1.

76. Robert E. Scoggin Papers, J. Murrey Atkins Library, University of North Carolina; Newton, *Ku Klux Klan*, p. 395.

77. HCUA, pp. 77, 153–9; David Cunningham, *Klanville, U.S.A.: The Rise and Fall of the Civil Rights-Era Ku Klux Klan* (New York: Oxford University Press, 2012), p. 255.

78. Newton, *Ku Klux Klan*, pp. 394–5, 398.

79. Newton, *Ku Klux Klan in Mississippi*, p. 128.

80. Newton, *Ku Klux Klan*, p. 77.

81. "List of Nationalist Conferences and Meetings in America," Metapedia.

82. Cuban Information Archives, http://cuban-exile.com/doc_101-125/doc0122.html (accessed Sept. 29, 2013).

83. "Lt. George Butler," Spartacus Educational, http://www.spartacus.schoolnet.co.uk/JFKbutler.htm (accessed Sept. 29, 2013).

84. "The Serpentine Trail of Roy Frankhouser," http://laroucheplanet.info/pmwiki/pmwiki.php?n=Library.PalimpsestWorld (accessed Sept. 29, 2013).

85. Ibid.

86. Dave Reitzes, "Jim Garrison's Klansman," Kennedy Assassination Home Page, http://mcadams.posc.mu.edu/kimble.htm (accessed Sept. 29, 2013); Michael Benson, *Who's Who in the JFK Assassination: An A to Z Encyclopedia* (New York: Citadel, 1993), pp. 237–8.

87. *New Orleans Times-Picayune*, February 16, 1968.

88. Newton, *Ku Klux Klan in Mississippi*, pp. 121–2, 136.

89. "Julius Harper," Metapedia, http://en.metapedia.org/wiki/Julius_Harper (accessed Sept. 29, 2013).

90. "Samuel Bowers," Wikipedia, http://en.wikipedia.org/wiki/Samuel_Bowers (accessed Sept. 29, 2013).

91. Newton, *Ku Klux Klan in Mississippi*, p. 115; Newton, *Ku Klux Klan*, p. 59.

92. Newton, *Ku Klux Klan in Mississippi*, p. 129.

93. Jackson (MS) *Clarion-Ledger*, July 21, 2012.

94. *Concordia Sentinel*, July 3, 2008; HCUA, p. 131.

95. Newton, *Ku Klux Klan in Mississippi*, p. 138.

96. *Jackson Free Press*, Jan. 31, 2007; "James Ford Seale," Wikipedia, http://en.wikipedia.org/wiki/James_Ford_Seale (accessed Sept. 29, 2013).

97. Newton, *Ku Klux Klan in Mississippi*, pp. 140–1.

98. Ibid., pp. 141–3.

99. Ibid., p. 143.

100. Ibid., 145–7.

101. *Concordia Sentinel*, Jan. 22, June 11, and Oct. 22, 2009.

102. Ibid., July 3 and Oct. 23, 2008; Jan. 15, 2009; May 6, 2010.

103. Ibid., July 3, 2008.

104. Newton, *Ku Klux Klan in Mississippi*, p. 152.

105. HCUA, pp. 29–30.

106. *Concordia Sentinel*, July 3, 2008.

107. Newton, *Invisible Empire*, p. 163.

108. HCUA, p. 149.

109. Gillette and Tillinger, p. 118.

110. Newton, *Invisible Empire*, p. 166.

111. Ibid., pp. 164–8.

112. Ibid., pp. 169–72.

113. Ibid., pp. 172–4.

114. Newton, *Ku Klux Klan in Mississippi*, pp. 152–4.

115. Ibid., p. 132.

116. John Drabble, "The FBI, COINTELPRO-WHITE HATE, and the Decline of Ku Klux Klan Organizations in Alabama, 1964–1971." Alabama Review 61 (January 2008): 3–47.

117. Newton, *Ku Klux Klan in Mississippi*, pp. 154–8.

118. HCUA, pp. 119–20, 151; Andrew Tully, *The FBI's Most Famous Cases* (New York: Dell, 1965), p. 213.

119. Parker, *Violence*, p. 70.

120. HCUA, p. 120; Gillette and Tillinger, pp. 135–6.

121. Gillette and Tillinger, p. 138.

122. HCUA, pp. 52, 67; Parker, *Violence*, pp. 112–13.

123. Parker, *Violence*, p. 71.

124. HCUA, p. 153.

125. Kane, *Presidential Fact Book*, p. 236.

126. Stephan Lesher, *George Wallace: American Populist* (Reading, MA: Addison-Wesley, 1994), p. 273.

127. Ibid., pp. 303–4.

128. Chalmers, *Hooded Americanism*, pp. 382–4; Sherrill, "A Look Inside," p. 22.

129. Kane, *Presidential Fact Book*, p. 237.

130. Chalmers, *Hooded Americanism*, p. 384.

131. Sherrill, "A Look Inside," p. 29.

132. Drabble, "The FBI ... Alabama."

133. "Louisiana Gubernatorial Election, 1963–64," Wikipedia, http://en.wikipedia.org/wiki/Louisiana_gubernatorial_election,_1963%E2%80%9364 (accessed Oct. 6, 2013).

134. *Concordia Sentinel*, March 25, 2010.

135. Drabble, "The FBI ... Alabama"; HCUA, pp. 106–7.

136. *Concordia Sentinel*, Jan. 12, 2011.

137. Ibid., March 25, 2010; "Frank Morris Case," The Civil Rights Cold Case Project, http://coldcases.org/cases/frank-morris-case (accessed Oct. 6, 2013).

138. *Concordia Sentinel*, Jan. 15, 2009; Jan. 12, 2011; "Frank Morris Case," The Civil Rights Cold Case Project.

139. Larry Keller, "Battling the Klan in the 1960s," SPLC *Intelligence Report*, Summer 2009; Drabble, "The FBI ... Alabama."

140. *The Militant*, March 19, 2012, http://www.themilitant.com/2012/7611/761150.html (accessed Oct. 6, 2013).

141. Hill, "Deacons," pp. 137–58.

142. Drabble, "The FBI ... Alabama"; Hague, "Niggers Ain't Gonna Run."

143. Drabble, "The FBI ... Alabama."

144. Ibid.; Hague, "Niggers Ain't Gonna Run"; Hill, "Deacons," p. 192.

145. Hague, "Niggers Ain't Gonna Run."

146. HCUA, p. 124 and Vol. 3, p. 2449; *Los Angeles Times*, June 26, 2002; Kristine Denholm, "Chasing Ghosts in a Civil Rights Era Cop Killing," *Police: The Law Enforcement Magazine*, Oct. 22, 2010.

147. Hague, "Niggers Ain't Gonna Run"; Larry Keller, "Klan Murder Shines Light on Bogalusa, La.," SPLC *Intelligence Report*, Summer 2009.

148. *United States of America v. Original Knights of the Ku Klux Klan, et al.* 250 F.Supp. 330 (1965).

149. "Selma to Montgomery March," Encyclopedia of Alabama, http://www.encyclopediaofalabama.org/face/Article.jsp?id=h-1114 (accessed Oct. 10, 2013); Newton, *Ku Klux Klan*, p. 400.

150. HCUA, p. 149.

151. "Modern Ku Klux Klan in Alabama," Encyclopedia of Alabama, http://www.encyclopediaofalabama.org/face/Article.jsp?id=h-3291 (accessed Oct. 10, 2013).

152. Aimee Edmonson, "In Sullivan's Shadow: The Use and Abuse of Libel Law During the Civil Rights Movement," Ph.D. dissertation, University of Missouri, 2008, pp. 11, 120–5.

153. Flowers, "Southern Plain Talk," p. 40.

154. "Jimmy Lee Jackson," Encyclopedia of Alabama, http://www.encyclopediaofalabama.org/face/Article.jsp?id=h-2011 (accessed Oct. 10, 2013).

155. "Selma to Montgomery March," Encyclopedia of Alabama.

156. *Boston Globe*, July 17, 2011.

157. Ibid.; Newton, *Ku Klux Klan*, p. 290; Mendelsohn, pp. 172–3.

158. "Selma to Montgomery March," Encyclopedia of Alabama; *Birmingham News*, July 16, 2000; "The Contemporary Ku Klux Klan," in *Assassination and Political Violence*; *Los Angeles Times*, Oct. 27, 2002.

159. "Selma to Montgomery March," Encyclopedia of Alabama; Parker, *Violence*, p. 99.

160. Parker, *Violence*, pp. 99–100; Newton, *Ku Klux Klan*, p. 285.

161. Newton, *Ku Klux Terror*, pp. 155–60.

162. Parker, *Violence*, p. 101; *Anniston Star*, March 22–24, 2009.

163. Newton, *Ku Klux Terror*, pp. 156–7.

164. Newton, *Ku Klux Klan*, p. 278.

165. Newton, *Ku Klux Terror*, pp. 159–60.

166. HCUA, pp. 37, 62, 147; Newton, *Ku Klux Klan*, p. 216.

167. HCUA, pp. 35–6; Newton, *Ku Klux Klan*, pp. 60–1, 98.

168. HCUA, pp. 34–5; *The Morning Call* (Allentown, PA), Jan. 18, 1987; Newton, *Ku Klux Klan*, p. 94.

169. HCUA, p. 37.

170. *Detroit News,* July 30, 2009.
171. HCUA, p. 2.
172. Ibid., pp. 2, 25, 28, 39–40, 125–33.
173. Greene, *The Temple Bombing,* pp. 162–3.
174. HCUA, pp. 18, 60–2.
175. *Deschler's Precedents,* Volume 4 (Washington, DC: U.S. Government Printing Office, 1966), p. 2462.
176. U.S. Department of Justice, *United States Attorneys Bulletin* 14 (Dec. 23, 1966), p. 528.
177. CBS Evening News, March 14, 1969.
178. KUAC-TV, Channel 9 (Fairbanks, AK), May 3, 2013.
179. *Concordia Sentinel,* Oct. 22, 2009.
180. Ibid., July 3, 2008; Sept. 17, 2009.
181. Ibid., Feb. 26, 2009.
182. *United States v. Cecil Price, et al.* (383 U.S. 787).
183. Newton, *Ku Klux Klan in Mississippi,* pp. 166–9.
184. Ibid.
185. "'Holy War' on Beatles 1966," The Lennon Prophecy, http://www.nonnelnhoj.com/_wsn/page3.html (accessed Oct. 13, 2013).
186. *City of Tupelo v. Walton, et ux.,* Jan. 11, 1960.
187. Newton, *Ku Klux Klan in Mississippi,* p. 170.
188. Ibid., p. 171.
189. Ibid., pp. 171–2; *Concordia Sentinel,* Oct. 22, 2009.
190. Parker, *Violence,* pp. 169–71; Newton, *Ku Klux Klan in Mississippi,* p. 172.
191. "Ku Klux Klan in Virginia," Encyclopedia of Virginia; Parker, *Violence,* p. 175.
192. Parker, *Violence,* pp. 112–14.
193. Ibid., p. 121.
194. James William Cole Papers, East Carolina University.
195. Cunningham, *Klanville, U.S.A.,* pp. 200–1, 209.
196. Parker, *Violence,* pp. 143–4; *Lynch v. Maryland,* Court of Special Appeals of Maryland, Dec. 6, 1967.
197. "St. Marks [*sic*] Church Target of Klan in 1967," http://www.flickr.com/photos/washington_area_spark/8305491936 (accessed Oct. 13, 2013).
198. Parker, *Violence,* p. 173; HCUA p. 115.
199. "New Orleans Mayoral Election, 1965," Wikipedia, http://en.wikipedia.org/wiki/New_Orleans_mayoral_election,_1965 (accessed Oct. 17, 2013).
200. "Louisiana-Racism-Ku Klux Klan," East Baton Rouge Parish Library, http://ref-raff.wikispaces.com/Louisiana+-+Racism+-+Ku+Klux+Klan (accessed Oct. 17, 2013).
201. *Concordia Sentinel,* April 22 and July 16, 2009.
202. Keller, "Klan Murder Shines

Light on Bogalusa, La."; "Triggs, Clarence (1942–1966)," American Government Blog, http://govnoblog.biz/triggs-clarence-1942-1966 (accessed Oct. 17, 2013).
203. Sherrill, "A Look Inside the Invisible Empire," pp. 4–5; Kannapolis (NC) *Daily Independent,* Nov. 6, 11 and 15, 1966; "Rowan County Sheriff's Office (North Carolina)," Wikipedia, http://en.wikipedia.org/wiki/Rowan_County_Sheriff%27s_Office_%28North_Carolina%29 (accessed Nov. 16, 2013).
204. "Asa Earl Carter," Texas State Historical Association, http://www.tshaonline.org/handbook/online/articles/fcaak (accessed Oct. 17, 2013).
205. "1966 Gubernatorial Democratic Primary Election Results—Alabama," U.S. Election Atlas, http://uselectionatlas.org/RESULTS/state.php?fips=1&year=1966&f=0&off=5&elect=1 (accessed Oct. 17, 2013).
206. "John G. Crommelin," Metapedia.
207. "Lester Maddox," Wikipedia, http://en.wikipedia.org/wiki/Lester_Maddox; "Georgia Gubernatorial Election, 1966," Wikipedia, http://en.wikipedia.org/wiki/Georgia_gubernatorial_election,_1966 (both accessed Oct. 17, 2013).
208. Sherrill, "A Look Inside the Invisible Empire," p. 12.
209. Ibid., p. 19; "Arkansas Gubernatorial Election, 1966," Wikipedia, http://en.wikipedia.org/wiki/Arkansas_gubernatorial_election,_1966 (accessed Oct. 17, 2013).
210. "John Rarick," Wikipedia, http://en.wikipedia.org/wiki/John_Rarick (accessed Oct. 17, 2013); Sherrill, "A Look Inside the Invisible Empire," pp. 9–10; Michael Newton, *Ku Klux Klan,* p. 245.
211. *Concordia Sentinel,* June 5, 2008; Aug. 5, Sept. 3 and Oct. 22, 2009.
212. Newton, *Ku Klux Klan,* pp. 404–5; Newton, *Ku Klux Klan in Mississippi,* pp. 177–9.
213. Newton, *Ku Klux Klan in Mississippi,* p. 178; "Thomas Tarrants," Metapedia, en.metapedia.org/wiki/Thomas_Tarrants (accessed Oct. 17, 2013).
214. Newton, *Ku Klux Klan in Mississippi,* p. 177; "Kathy Ainsworth," Metapedia, en.metapedia.org/wiki/Kathy_Ainsworth (accessed Oct. 17, 2013).
215. Newton, *Ku Klux Klan in Mississippi,* pp. 178–9.
216. Ibid., pp. 174–5; *New York Times,* Sept. 11, 1969; *Concordia Sentinel,* Oct. 22, 2009.
217. Newton, *Ku Klux Klan in Mississippi,* pp. 175–8.
218. *New Orleans Times-Picayune,* Feb. 20, 1967.

219. "African Americans of Florida Parishes, Louisiana, Demand Civil Rights Protection, 1967," Global Nonviolent Action Database, http://nvdatabase.swarthmore.edu/content/african-americans-florida-parishes-louisiana-demand-civil-rights-protection-1967; "Louisiana—Civil Rights—Bogalusa March," East Baton Rouge Parish Library, http://ref-raff.wikispaces.com/Louisiana+-+Civil+Rights+-+Bogalusa+March (both accessed Oct. 20, 2013).
220. "Louisiana Gubernatorial Election, 1967," Wikipedia, http://en.wikipedia.org/wiki/Louisiana_gubernatorial_election,_1967 (accessed Oct. 20, 2013); "John Rarick," Wikipedia.
221. Newton, *Ku Klux Klan in Mississippi,* pp. 180–1.
222. Ibid., p. 180.
223. "Kathy Ainsworth," Metapedia.
224. Dan Christensen, "King Assassination: FBI Ignored Its Miami Informer," Cuban Information Archives, http://cuban-exile.com/doc_101-125/doc0114.html (accessed Oct. 20, 2013).
225. Newton, *Ku Klux Klan in Mississippi,* p. 179.
226. Michael Newton, *A Case of Conspiracy: James Earl Ray and the Assassination of Martin Luther King, Jr.* (Los Angeles: Holloway House, 1980), pp. 173–213.
227. John Edginton and John Sergeant, "The Murder of Martin Luther King, Jr.," *Covert Action Information Bulletin* 34 (Summer 1990): 21–7.
228. Wexler and Hancock, *Awful Grace,* pp. 30–1, 33–4; HSCA, pp. 497–8, 501–2.
229. *Chicago Sun-Times,* Dec. 28, 1967, and March 1, 1968; *The Blade* (Toledo, OH), March 2, 1968.
230. *Dallas Morning News,* Sept. 133, 1968; "Extremism and the Military: A Timeline," SPLC, http://legacysplc.www.splcenter.org/intel/news/item.jsp?sid=23&printable=1 (accessed Oct. 20, 2013).
231. "Asa Carter (Forrest Carter)," Encyclopedia of Alabama; Sherrill, "A Look Inside the Invisible Empire," p. 9; Newton, *Ku Klux Klan,* p. 256.
232. "1968 Presidential Election Results," U.S. Election Atlas, http://uselectionatlas.org/RESULTS/national.php?year=1968 (accessed Oct. 20, 2013).
233. "American Party (1969)," Wikipedia, http://en.wikipedia.org/wiki/American_Party_%281969%29; "National Alliance," SPLC, http://www.splcenter.org/get-informed/intelligence-files/groups/national-alliance (both accessed Oct. 20, 2013).
234. "John Rarick," Wikipedia.
235. *Akron Beacon Journal,* Jan. 29, 2011.
236. "Robert Shelton (Ku Klux Klan)," Wikipedia, http://en.wikipedia.

org/wiki/Robert_Shelton_%28Ku_Klux_Klan%29 (accessed Oct. 20, 2013).

237. *The News and Courier* (Charleston, SC), April 29, 1968.

238. *New York Times,* Feb. 15, 1969; Robert E. Scoggin Papers, J. Murrey Atkins Library.

239. "Richmond Flowers," Alabama Department of Archives and History, http://www.archives.alabama.gov/conoff/flowers.html (accessed Oct. 20, 2013).

240. "A. Roswell Thompson," Conservapedia, http://www.conservapedia.com/A._Roswell_Thompson (accessed Oct. 20, 2013).

241. *The News and Courier* (Charleston, SC), July 20, 1969.

242. *New York Times,* Sept. 17, 1969,

243. John Drabble, "The FBI, COINTELPRO-WHITE HATE, and the Ku Klux Klan in North Carolina, 1964–1971," John Hope Franklin Center Lecture Series, Duke University, Sept. 24, 2003.

244. *New Orleans States Item,* Sept. 10 and 11, 1969; *New Orleans Times Picayune,* Sept. 11, 1969; *New York Times,* Sept. 11, 1969; John Hailman, *From Midnight to Guntown: True Crime Stories from a Federal Prosecutor in Mississippi* (Oxford: University Press of Mississippi, 2013), pp. 262–7.

Chapter 9

1. *New York Times,* April 24, 1998.

2. Drabble, "The FBI, COINTELPRO-WHITE HATE, and the Decline of Ku Klux Klan Organizations in Mississippi."

3. *Concorida Sentinel,* Oct. 22, 2009.

4. Drabble, "The FBI, COINTELPRO-WHITE HATE, and the Decline of Ku Klux Klan Organizations in Alabama."

5. "Far Right Timeline (1965–1975)," Larouche Planet, http://laroucheplanet.info/pmwiki/pmwiki.php?n=Library.UnityNow5 (accessed Oct. 24, 2013).

6. Robert E. Scoggin Papers, J. Murrey Atkins Library.

7. *Washington Post,* Sept. 18, 1970.

8. Sims, *The Klan,* p. 9.

9. FBI memos dated June 12, 19, 23 and 30, 1970.

10. FBI memo dated July 20, 1970.

11. "Frank Collin," Wikipedia, http://en.wikipedia.org/wiki/Frank_Collin (accessed Oct. 24, 2013).

12. *Birmingham News,* Aug. 28, 1970.

13. "KPFT," Wikipedia, http://en.wikipedia.org/wiki/KPFT (accessed Oct. 24, 2013).

14. *New York Times,* June 12, 1971; Thorne Dreyer, "The KKK in the News Again," The Rag Blog, http://therag blog.blogspot.com/2009/02/thorne-dreyer-kkk-in-news-again-and.html (accessed Oct. 24, 2013); *Houston Chronicle,* Oct. 6, 2010.

15. Dreyer, "The KKK in the News Again"; *Arizona Republic,* Jan. 17, 1971.

16. "Louis Beam," ADL Archives, http://archive.adl.org/learn/ext_us/beam.asp?xpicked=2&item=beam (accessed Oct. 24, 2013).

17. *Arizona Republic,* Jan. 17, 1971; "The Bombing of KPFT," Arcane Radio Trivia, http://tenwatts.blogspot.com/2006/02/bombing-of-kpft.html (accessed Oct. 24, 2013).

18. *New York Times,* June 12, 1971.

19. *San Francisco Chronicle,* Oct. 13, 1971.

20. Gavin Daffy, "Kloak and Dagger," Internet Archive Digital Library, http://archive.org/stream/fokpft197509ia/fokpft197509ia_djvu.txt (accessed Oct. 24, 2013), p. 421.

21. Ron Laytner, "Ku Klux Klan Revealed," Edit International, http://www.editinternational.com/read.php?id=4819db071deb7 (accessed Oct. 24, 2013).

22. George Green, *The Establishment in Texas Politics: The Primitive Years, 1938–1957* (Norman: University of Oklahoma Press, 1984), p. 6; Dreyer, "The KKK in the News Again."

23. "Alabama Gubernatorial Election, 1970," Wikipedia, http://en.wikipedia.org/wiki/Alabama_gubernatorial_election,_1970 (accessed Oct. 24, 2013).

24. Ibid.

25. "Asa Earl Carter," Wikipedia.

26. Georgia Gubernatorial Election, 1970," Wikipedia, http://en.wikipedia.org/wiki/Georgia_gubernatorial_election,_1970; "Jesse Benjamin 'J.B.' Stoner," Our Campaigns, http://www.ourcampaigns.com/CandidateDetail.html?CandidateID=76937 (both accessed Oct. 24, 2013).

27. "John Rarick," Wikipedia.

28. *New York Times,* Oct. 6 and 7, 1971; Michael Meyerson, *Nothing Could Be Finer* (New York: International, 1978), pp. 65–6, 79–80, 84, 92–3.

29. Thomas Parker ed. *Violence in the U.S. Vol. 2, 1968–1971* (New York: Facts on File, 1974), p. 219.

30. "Grand Jury Refuses to Indict Klansman for Killing of Black Man," *Black Panther* 6 (May 15, 1971): 5.

31. Deposition of Virgil Griffin in the case of *James Waller et. al v. Bernard Butkovitch et. al.,* Civ. Action C-80-603-G, U.S. District Court, Middle District of North Carolina, Greensboro Division.

32. FBI memo dated Nov. 25, 1971.

33. Drabble, "The FBI, COINTELPRO-WHITE HATE, and the Decline of Ku Klux Klan Organizations in Alabama."

34. *New Orleans States Item,* Jan. 19, 1972.

35. "John Rarick," Wikipedia.

36. Bob Simpson, "Standing Against the Maryland Klan 1971: A Personal Memory," *Washington Area Spark,* Jan. 2, 2013.

37. Mark Sagor, "My Boss Was Tarred and Feathered by the KKK," Cognoscenti, http://cognoscenti.wbur.org/2013/01/21/mlk-mark-sagor (accessed Oct. 24, 2013).

38. *New York Times,* May 22, 1973; "Robert E. Miles," Metapedia, http://en.metapedia.org/wiki/Robert_E._Miles (accessed Oct. 24, 2013).

39. *Detroit News,* July 30, 2009.

40. "Mississippi Gubernatorial Election, 1971," Wikipedia, http://en.wikipedia.org/wiki/Mississippi_gubernatorial_election,_1971 (accessed Oct. 24, 2013).

41. "SPLC History," Southern Poverty Law Center, http://www.splcenter.org/who-we-are/splc-history; "Morris Dees," Wikipedia, http://en.wikipedia.org/wiki/Morris_Dees; "The Intelligence Project," SPLC, http://legacysplc.wwwsplcenter.org/intel/history.jsp (all accessed Oct. 27, 2013).

42. *The Elkhart* (IN) *Truth,* April 16, 2012.

43. *The Afro American,* Feb. 26, 1972.

44. *White Nationalist,* June 1972; Wheaton, *Greenkil,* p. 43.

45. "Roy Frankhouser," Metapedia, http://en.metapedia.org/wiki/Roy_Frankhouser (accessed Oct. 27, 2013); "Far Right Timeline (1965–1975)."

46. "Far Right Timeline (1965–1975)."

47. "United States Presidential Election, 1972," Wikipedia, http://en.wikipedia.org/wiki/United_States_presidential_election,_1972 (accessed Oct. 27, 2013).

48. "Jesse Benjamin 'J.B.' Stoner," Our Campaigns; "Edward Fields," ADL Archives, http://archive.adl.org/learn/ext_us/Fields.asp?xpicked=2&item=Fields (accessed Oct. 27, 2013).

49. *Akron Beacon Journal,* Jan. 29, 2011; "John Rarick," Wikipedia.

50. "Far Right Timeline (1965–1975)"; Associated Press, Aug. 31, 1973; *Williamsport* (PA) *Sun-Gazette,* Oct. 17, 1973.

51. *The Elkhart Truth,* April 16, 2012.

52. Newton, *Ku Klux Klan in Mississippi,* p. 186.

53. *Concordia Sentinel,* Oct. 22, 2009.

54. "A. Roswell Thompson," Conservapedia; *Gadsden* (AL) *Times,* Aug. 12, 1973; Drabble, "The FBI, COINTELPRO-WHITE HATE, and the Decline of Ku Klux Klan Organizations in Alabama."

55. *Thunderbolt* No. 166, November 1973.

56. *Durham Sun,* Oct. 24, 1974.

57. Robert E. Scoggin Papers, J. Murrey Atkins Library.

58. "Asa Carter (Forrest Carter)," En-

cyclopedia of Alabama; "Asa Earl Carter," Texas State Historical Association; *New York Times*, Oct. 4, 1991.

59. "Dan Gayman," ADL Archives, http://archive.adl.org/learn/ext_us/gayman.asp?xpicked=2&item=gayman; "National Emancipation of Our White Seed," Wikipedia, http://en.wikipedia.org/wiki/National_Emancipation_of_our_White_Seed (both accessed Oct. 27, 2013).

60. Laytner, "Ku Klux Klan Revealed."

61. "Foreign Branches of the Ku Klux Klan," An Educational, Historical Study of the Ku Klux Klan, http://www.kkklan.com/foreignklan.htm; "Factual Information About Rev. Teàrlach Barra Eoin Ròs Dunsford Mac a' Phearsoin," http://thetruthabouttearlach.org (both accessed Oct. 27, 2013).

62. "Foreign Branches of the Ku Klux Klan"; "James Alexander McQuirter," Wikipedia, https://en.wikipedia.org/wiki/James_Alexander_McQuirter; Matthew Lauder, "Operation Red Dog," Internet Archive, http://web.archive.org/web/20030902120245/http://canadiancontent.ca/articles/031401reddog.html (both accessed Oct. 27, 2013).

63. Cobb Citizens Coalition, *The Shadow of Hatred* (Atlanta: Neighbors Network, 1994).

64. Robert Douglas, "The Ku Klux Klan in Britain," *Sunday People* (London), Feb. 17, 1980.

65. Levitas, *The Terrorist Next Door*, p. 136.

66. "List of Nationalist Conferences and Meetings in America," Metapedia.

67. "Far Right Timeline (1965–1975)."

68. United Klans of America Collection, Michigan State University Libraries Special Collections, MSS 202.

69. FBI memos dated Jan. 20, Sept. 25 and Oct. 6, 1975, and July 15, 1976.

70. Trey Kay, "Great Kanawha County Textbook War," West Virginia Division of Culture and History, http://www.wvculture.org/goldenseal/Fall11/textbookwar.html; "The Great Textbook War," American RadioWorks, http://americanradioworks.publicradio.org/features/textbooks/books_and_beliefs.html (both accessed Oct. 27, 2013).

71. *New Orleans Times Picayune*, Nov. 2, 1974; "Gary Tyler," Wikipedia, http://en.wikipedia.org/wiki/Gary_Tyler (accessed Oct. 27, 2013).

72. "Ohio Gubernatorial Elections," Wikipedia, http://en.wikipedia.org/wiki/Ohio_gubernatorial_elections (accessed Oct. 27, 2013).

73. "John Rarick," Wikipedia.

74. "Jesse Benjamin 'J.B.' Stoner," Our Campaigns.

75. Glenn Miller, *A White Man Speaks Out*, http://whitenationalist.org/lindstedt/gm_index.html (accessed Oct. 31, 2013).

76. Bridges, *Rise of David Duke*, p. 55.

77. FBI memo dated May 17, 1967.

78. Bridges, p. 55.

79. "David Duke," ADL Archives, http://archive.adl.org/learn/ext_us/david_duke/default.asp; "David Duke," Wikipedia, http://en.wikipedia.org/wiki/David_Duke (both accessed Oct. 27, 2013).

80. "David Duke," Wikipedia; Bridges, *Rise of David Duke*, p. 79.

81. Bridges, pp. 32–33.

82. "Johnny's Story," Preach the Cross, http://preachthecross.net/about-johnny-clary/johnnys-story (accessed Oct. 31, 2013).

83. Sims, *The Klan*, pp. 112, 173–223.

84. *New York Times*, Nov. 10, 1991.

85. "Louis Beam," ADL Archives, http://archive.adl.org/learn/ext_us/beam.asp?xpicked=2&item=beam (accessed Oct. 31, 2013).

86. "Don Black," SPLC, http://www.splcenter.org/get-informed/intelligence-files/profiles/don-black (accessed Oct. 31, 2013).

87. "James K. Warner," Metapedia, http://en.metapedia.org/wiki/James_K._Warner; "Jerry Dutton," Metapedia, http://en.metapedia.org/wiki/Jerry_Dutton (both accessed Oct. 31, 2013).

88. *St. Petersburg Times*, March 7, 1978; *St. Petersburg Independent*, Nov. 1, 1978.

89. *Eugene* (OR) *Register-Guard*, June 10, 1979; *Pea Ridge Graphic*, Aug. 29, 1979.

90. "About National Director Pastor Thomas Robb," The Knights Party, http://www.kkk.bz/nationalleaders.htm; Johnny Lee Clary, "The Truth About Thom Robb," Preach the Cross, http://preachthecross.net/the-truth-about-thom-robb; "Thomas Robb," Wikipedia, http://en.wikipedia.org/wiki/Thomas_Robb (all accessed Oct. 31, 2013).

91. Mary Ellen Mark, "Girls in the Hood," *Elle UK*, March 1995; "About Rachel Pendergraft, National Membership Coordinator and Spokeswoman for The Knights," The Knights Party, http://www.kkk.bz/nationalleaders.htm; "Rachel Pendergraft," My Life, http://www.mylife.com/rachel-pendergraft (both accessed Oct. 31, 2013).

92. "Tom Metzger," SPLC, http://www.splcenter.org/get-informed/intelligence-files/profiles/tom-metzger; "David Duke," SPLC, http://www.splcenter.org/get-informed/intelligence-files/profiles/david-duke (both accessed Oct. 31, 2013); "Former Klansmen Tom Metzger and Bill Riccio Encourage Skinheads to Cooperate," SPLC *Intelligence Report*, Fall 2006, Issue 123.

93. "David Lane," ADL Archives, http://archive.adl.org/learn/ext_us/lane.asp?xpicked=2&item=lane; "David Lane (White Nationalist)," Wikipedia, http://en.wikipedia.org/wiki/David_Lane_%28white_nationalist%29 (both accessed Oct. 31, 2013); Flynn and Gerhardt, *Silent Brotherhood*, p. 216.

94. Bridges, p. 74.

95. Ibid., pp. 58–65.

96. Ibid., pp. 47–8.

97. Ibid., pp. 52–3.

98. "Our Community—Bill Wilkinson—'The Sailor of the Seven Seas,'" *The Island Newspaper* (Ambergris Caye, Belize), Nov. 14, 2002; "Knights of the Ku Klux Klan," SPLC, http://www.splcenter.org/get-informed/intelligence-files/groups/knights-of-the-ku-klux-klan (accessed Oct. 31, 2013).

99. "Jerry Dutton," Metapedia; Bridges, p. 75.

100. *New York Times*, April 24, 1998; Calvin Fred Craig Papers, 1953–1979, Emory University Manuscript, Archives, and Rare Book Library.

101. *Frederick* (MD) *News-Post*, May 27, 1975.

102. *The Elkhart Truth*, Sept. 22, 1975.

103. Illinois Legislative Investigating Commission, *Ku Klux Klan*, pp. 53–64.

104. Raleigh *News and Observer*, Oct. 10, 1975; *Greensboro Daily News*, Oct. 23, 1979; ADL, "The Ku Klux Klans: 1978," *Facts* 24 (March 1978): 6; "James Venable," Metapedia, http://en.metapedia.org/wiki/James_Venable (accessed Nov. 3, 2013).

105. *The Indiana Gazette*, Jan. 12, 1976; "88 Seconds in Greensboro," *Frontline* (PBS), Jan. 24, 1983.

106. HSCA, *The Final Assassinations Report*, pp. 375–405.

107. "John Rarick," Wikipedia; Kane, *Presidential Fact Book*, p. 263.

108. *Akron Beacon Journal*, Jan. 29, 2011.

109. "National States Rights Party," Metapedia.

110. Miller, *A White Man Speaks Out*.

111. *United States v. Chaney*, 559 F.2d 1094 (1977); William M. Chaney Oral History Transcript, Indiana State Library; ADL, "The Ku Klux Klans: 1978."

112. *United States v. Kimble*, 719 F.2d 1253 (1983).

113. *New Orleans Times-Picayune*, July 25 and Nov. 28, 1976; Aug. 14, 1977.

114. *New York Times*, Nov. 6, 2006; Drabble, "The FBI, COINTELPRO-WHITE HATE and the Decline of Ku Klux Klan Organizations in Mississippi"; C. S. Lewis Institute, http://www.cslewisinstitute.org/Following_Jesus_Christ_Tarrants_page_7 (accessed Nov. 3, 2013).

115. FBI memo dated Jan. 13, 1976.

116. Drabble, "The FBI, COINTELPRO-WHITE HATE, and the Ku Klux Klan in North Carolina, 1964–1971."

117. Ibid.

118. *Greensboro Daily News*, March 6, 1977; *Charlotte Observer*, July 17, 1977.

119. "Asa Carter (Forrest Carter)," Encyclopedia of Alabama; "Asa Earl Carter," Texas State Historical Association; "Asa Earl Carter," Wikipedia; *New York Times*, Oct. 4, 1991.

120. ADL, "The Ku Klux Klans: 1978," p. 8.

121. Ibid.; ADL, *Hate Groups in America* (New York: ADL, 1982), p. 5.

122. "Joseph Paul Franklin," Wikipedia, http://en.wikipedia.org/wiki/Joseph_Paul_Franklin (accessed Nov. 8, 2013).

123. Ibid.

124. Ibid.; *USA Today*, Oct. 27, 2013.

125. "Joseph Paul Franklin," Wikipedia.

126. Dr. Mike Aamodt, "James Clayton Vaughn, Jr.," Radford University Department of Psychology, http://maamodt.asp.radford.edu/Psyc%20405/serial%20killers/Franklin,%20Joseph%20Paul.pdf (accessed Nov. 8, 2013).

127. Ibid.; *Washington Post*, Nov. 20, 2013.

128. "*Hunter* (Pierce Novel)," Wikipedia, http://en.wikipedia.org/wiki/Hunter_%28Pierce_novel%29 (accessed Nov. 8, 2013).

129. "Bill Baxley," Wikipedia, http://en.wikipedia.org/wiki/Bill_Baxley (accessed Nov. 3, 2013).

130. *New York Times*, Sept. 4, 1993.

131. Sims, *The Klan*, pp. 141–66.

132. "Bill Baxley," Wikipedia.

133. "Viola Gregg Liuzzo," Encyclopedia of Alabama, http://encyclopediaofalabama.org/face/Article.jsp?id=h-1377 (accessed Nov. 3, 2013); *Gary Thomas Rowe v. Carl Griffin*, 676 F.2d 524 (1982).

134. *Liuzzo v. United States*, Civ. A. No. 79-72564, 485 F.Supp. 1274 (1980).

135. Vanessa Gallman, "The Continuing Saga of the KKK," *Southern Changes* 2 (1979): 18–21; "The Decline of the United Klans of America," ADL Archives, http://archive.adl.org/issue_combating_hate/uka/decline.asp (accessed Nov. 3, 2013).

136. Brenda Russell, "Southern Justice: 1978," *Harvard Crimson*, Oct. 21, 1978.

137. Gallman, "The Continuing Saga of the KKK."

138. *New York Times*, July 5, 1983.

139. Gallman, "The Continuing Saga of the KKK."

140. Stanton, *From Selma to Sorrow*, p. 31; ABC Evening News, Aug. 12, 1979; ADL, "The Ku Klux Klan Tries for a Comeback," *Facts* 25 (November 1979): 5.

141. *Bernice Brown v. Invisible Empire, Knights of the Ku Klux Klan*, CV-80-1449; *Orlando Sentinel*, July 27, 1989.

142. "GA Governor—D Primary," Our Campaigns, http://www.ourcampaigns.com/RaceDetail.html?RaceID=382406 (accessed Nov. 3, 2013).

143. "Ohio Gubernatorial Elections," Wikipedia, http://en.wikipedia.org/wiki/Ohio_gubernatorial_elections (accessed Nov. 3, 2013).

144. Associated Press, March 23, 1978.

145. ADL, *Hate Groups in America* (New York: ADL, 1982), p. 5.

146. "United League (Social Organization)," Wikipedia, http://en.wikipedia.org/wiki/United_League_%28social_organization%29; "KKK/United League March," Mississippi Civil Rights Project, http://mscivilrightsproject.org/index.php?option=com_content&view=article&id=96:kkkunited-league-march&catid=484:event&Itemid=49 (both accessed Nov. 8, 2013).

147. *Ocala* (FL) *Star-Banner*, May 23, 1978.

148. *Logansport* (IN) *Pharos-Tribune*, June 25, 1978.

149. ADL, "The Ku Klux Klan Tries for a Comeback," pp. 4–5.

150. Miller, *A White Man Speaks Out*.

151. Gallman, "The Continuing Saga of the KKK."

152. Wheaton, *Greenkil*, pp. 135–48.

153. "The Greensboro Massacre," Press Action, http://www.pressaction.com/news/weblog/full_article/hand11182004 (accessed Nov. 8, 2013).

154. *New York Times*, Feb. 17, 2009.

155. "The Greensboro Massacre," Press Action.

156. Ibid.; *Toledo Blade*, Nov. 18, 1980.

157. "Civil Rights Greensboro," University of North Carolina at Greensboro, http://library.uncg.edu/dp/crg/topicalessays/GreensMassacre.aspx (accessed Nov. 8, 2013).

158. *Gainesville Sun*, April 16, 1984.

159. NBC Evening News, Dec. 3, 1976; "Pendleton Marines Released," *The Veteran* (April 1977), http://www.vvaw.org/veteran/article/?id=1649 (accessed Nov. 9, 2013).

160. ADL, "The Ku Klux Klan Tries for a Comeback," p. 8.

161. Ibid., pp. 8–9; "Q&A on Fayetteville Murders and Hate and the Military," ADL Archives, http://archive.adl.org/presrele/DiRaB_41/2627_41.asp (accessed Nov. 9, 2013).

162. ADL, "The Ku Klux Klan Tries for a Comeback," pp. 2–3, 9–10.

163. Ibid., p. 13.

164. Ibid., p. 6.

165. Steve Gerkin, "Watts and Clary," *This Land* 4 (Aug. 15, 2013).

166. "David Duke," SPLC.

167. Bridges, p. 106.

168. Ibid., p. 76; "Tom Metzger: 'White Rights' Activist—Unapologetic and Uncensored," from the G-man, http://fromthegman.blogspot.com/2011/06/tom-metzger-white-rights-activist.html (accessed Nov. 9, 2013).

169. Bridges, p. 75.

170. ADL, *Hate Groups in America* (1982), p. 10; ADL, *Extremism on the Right: A Handbook* (New York: ADL, 1983), p. 92.

171. ADL, *Extremism on the Right*, p. 73.

172. Bridges, p. 84.

173. Ibid., pp. 85–7; Newton, *Ku Klux Klan*, p. 180.

174. "David Duke: In His Own Words," ADL Archives, http://archive.adl.org/special_reports/duke_own_words/on_kkk.asp (accessed Nov. 9, 2013).

175. ADL, *Hate Groups in America* (1982), pp. 6–7, 10; *Lakeland* (FL) *Ledger*, Oct. 2, 1981.

176. Bridges, pp. 88–9.

177. ADL, *Extremism on the Right*, pp. 17, 154.

178. *The Press-Enterprise* (Riverside, CA), April 13, 1997; "Former Klansmen Tom Metzger and Bill Riccio Encourage Skinheads to Cooperate," SPLC *Intelligence Report*, Fall 2006.

179. "Tom Metzger (White Supremacist)," Wikipedia, http://en.wikipedia.org/wiki/Tom_Metzger_%28white_supremacist%29 (accessed Nov. 9, 2013).

180. "Tom Metzger's Long March of Hate," The Nizkor Project, http://www.nizkor.org/hweb/orgs/american/adl/tom-metzger; "Tom Metzger: 'White Rights' Activist—Unapologetic and Uncensored" (both accessed Nov. 9, 2013).

181. Leonard Zeskind, *Blood Politics: The History of the White Nationalist Movement from the Margins to the Mainstream* (New York: Macmillan, 2009), p. 138; Cobb Citizens Coalition, *The Shadow of Hatred*.

182. "NC Attorney General—R Primary," Our Campaigns, http://www.ourcampaigns.com/RaceDetail.html?RaceID=274478&WhenStart=2013-05-17+13%3A41%3A09 (accessed Nov. 9, 2013).

183. Miller, *A White Man Speaks Out*.

184. ADL, *Hate Groups in America* (1982), pp. 6–7.

185. *New York Times*, Feb. 28, 1982.

186. Ibid., Jan. 12, 1981.

187. *U.S. v. Redwine*, 715 F.2d 315 (7th Cir. 1984).

188. Lutz, *They Don't All Wear Sheets*, p. 56.

189. "Robert E. Miles," Wikipedia, http://en.wikipedia.org/wiki/Robert_E._Miles (accessed Nov. 13, 2013).

190. Bridges, pp. 82–3.

191. *New York Times*, Oct. 6, 2005.

192. Ibid., Nov. 13, 2007; "Did David Brooks Tell the Full Story About Reagan's Neshoba County Fair Visit?" History News Network, http://hnn.us/article/44535; "Reagan's Infamous

Speech in Philadelphia, Mississippi," *The Volokh Conspiracy,* http://www.volokh.com/2011/08/16/reagans-infamous-speech-in-philadelphia-mississippi (both accessed Nov. 13, 2013).

193. "United States Presidential Election, 1980," Wikipedia, http://en.wikipedia.org/wiki/United_States_presidential_election,_1980 (accessed Nov. 13, 2013).

194. *Akron Beacon Journal,* Jan. 29, 2011.

195. "Jesse Benjamin 'J.B.' Stoner," Our Campaigns; *New York Times,* Aug. 14, 1982; CBS Evening News, June 2, 1983.

196. ADL, *Extremism on the Right,* p. 136.

197. ADL, *Hate Groups in America* (1982), p. 7.

198. Evansville (IN) *Courier and Press,* March 8 and 11, 1981, and June 19, 1981.

199. ADL, *Hate Groups in America* (1982), p. 8.

200. B. J. Hollars, *Thirteen Loops: Race, Violence, and the Last Lynching in America* (Tuscaloosa: University of Alabama Press, 2011), pp. 71–184.

201. *Donald v. United Klans of America* (S.D. Ala., filed June 14, 1984), No. 84-0725-CA.

202. Lutz, p. 62.

203. ADL, *Hate Groups in America* (1982), p. 9.

204. Ibid.; *U.S. v. Bobby Joe Norton and Gladys Girgenti,* 700 F.2d 1072 (1983).

205. *Vietnamese Fishermen's Association v. Knights of the Ku Klux Klan,* 543 F.Supp. 198 (1982).

206. Morris Dees, *Gathering Storm: America's Militia Threat* (New York: HarperCollins, 1996), pp. 35–6.

207. Matthew Lauder, "Operation Red Dog," Amnesty International, http://web.archive.org/web/200309021202 45/http://canadiancontent.ca/articles/031401reddog.html (accessed Nov. 14, 2013).

208. Ibid.

209. *Gadsden* (AL) *Times,* Oct. 11, 1979.

210. *Barbados Nation Newspaper,* Feb. 13, 1984.

211. *New York Times,* June 21, 1981.

212. ADL, *Extremism on the Right,* pp. 1, 20, 57–8, 74, 144, 155.

213. "Extremism in Connecticut," ADL Archives, http://archive.adl.org/learn/ext_us/ct (accessed Nov. 14, 2013); Meriden (CT) *Record-Journal,* March 18, 2011.

214. Flynn and Gerhardt, *Silent Brotherhood,* p. 216.

215. "David Lane," ADL Archives.

216. Cobb Citizens Coalition, *The Shadow of Hatred.*

217. Ibid.; *Palm Beach Post,* Nov. 28–

30, 1981; *Rome* (GA) *News-Tribune,* Oct. 3, 1983; Lyn Wells, "The Cedartown Story: The Ku Klux Klan & Labor in the 'New South,'" *Labor Research Review* 1 (1986): 69–79.

218. Lutz, pp. 20–1.

219. Ibid., p. 22.

220. *Orlando Sentinel,* Oct. 9, 1991; Associated Press, May 15, 2005; *The Free Lance-Star* (Fredericksburg, VA), Aug. 6, 2005.

221. *New York Times,* Feb. 14, 1987.

222. *Sarasota Herald-Tribune,* Jan. 3, 1981.

223. Leonard Zeskind, "Backgrounder: Arizona Mail Bomber Dennis Mahon to Be Sentenced," Institute for Research & Education on Human Rights, http://www.irehr.org/issue-areas/race-racism-and-white-nationalism/item/413-back grounder-arizona-mail-bomber-dennis-mahon-to-be-sentenced (accessed Nov. 14, 2013); Levitas, *The Terrorist Next Door,* pp. 185–6, 370; ADL, *Hate Groups in America* (1988), p. 14.

224. *Larry Walker v. State of Mississippi,* 473 So.2d 435 (1985).

225. Lutz, p. 58.

226. ADL, *Hate Groups in America* (1982), p. 9.

227. Lutz, p. 52.

228. Raleigh *News and Observer,* Aug. 22, 1982.

229. Folder 351 and 373, Greensboro Civil Rights Fund Records, 1979–1986, Collection #4630, Southern Historical Collection, University of North Carolina Chapel Hill.

230. Lutz, *They Don't All Wear Sheets,* p. 69; "William D. Moose," North Carolina Department of Public Safety, http://webapps6.doc.state.nc.us/opi/viewoffender.do?method=view&offenderID=0291193 (accessed Nov. 14, 2013).

231. Miller, *A White Man Speaks Out.*

232. "Tom Metzger (White Supremacist)," Wikipedia; "Tom Metzger's Long March of Hate," The Nizkor Project.

233. *Los Angeles Times,* March 3, 1985.

234. *Palm Beach Post,* June 26, 1982.

235. Miller, *A White Man Speaks Out.*

236. Lutz, p. 80.

237. ADL, *Extremism on the Right,* p. 155.

238. *Gadsden Times,* Aug. 12, 1984; *New York Times,* Nov. 10, 1984.

239. Lutz, p. 39.

Chapter 10

1. ADL, *Extremism on the Right,* p. 155.

2. Lutz, p. 69; Miller, *A White Man Speaks Out.*

3. Miller, *A White Man Speaks Out.*

4. Lutz, p. 69.

5. *United States v. Mailon Paul Wood, Kenneth E. Davis, William L.*

Deering and Winford "Billy" Wood, 780 F.2d 955 (1986).

6. *Kalamazoo Gazette,* Feb. 20, 2008; Lutz, p. 45.

7. ADL, *Extremism on the Right,* pp. 39–40, 137.

8. "Edward Fields," ADL Archives; Cobb Citizens Coalition, *The Shadow of Hatred.*

9. *New York Times,* July 31, 1983; Feb. 21, 1985.

10. *Person v. Carolina Knights of the Ku Klux Klan,* No. 84534-CIV-5 (D.N.C. Jan. 18, 1985); Miller, *A White Man Speaks Out.*

11. Miller, *A White Man Speaks Out.*

12. ADL, *Extremism on the Right,* pp. 21, 144.

13. "San Diego's Ku Klux Klan 1920–1980," *The Journal of San Diego History.*

14. *Los Angeles Times,* Oct. 29, 1991.

15. ADL, *Extremism on the Right,* pp. 1, 82.

16. "Louis Beam," ADL Archives.

17. *Inter-Klan Newsletter and Survival Alert,* Issue No. 4, December 1983.

18. "US Domestic Terrorism," History Commons, http://www.cooperativeresearch.org/timeline.jsp?timeline=us_domestic_terrorism_tmln&haitian_elite_2021_organizations=us_domestic_terrorism_tmln_the_order (accessed Nov. 16, 2013).

19. Michael Newton, *The Encyclopedia of Robberies, Heists and Capers* (New York: Facts on File, 2003), pp. 227–31.

20. Ibid.

21. Ibid.

22. Miller, *A White Man Speaks Out.*

23. Newton, *The Encyclopedia of Robberies, Heists and Capers,* pp. 27–31.

24. Ibid.

25. Ibid.

26. Ibid.; *New York Times,* June 7, 1986; "David Lane," ADL Archives.

27. *Los Angeles Times,* Feb. 10, 1985.

28. "Nuclear Klansman," *Death to the Klan* 3 (Winter 1983): 2.

29. ADL, *Hate Groups in America* (1988), p. 14.

30. *Carey v. Rudeseal,* Civ. A. No. 4: 85-cv-358-HLM, 703 F.Supp. 929 (1988).

31. Cobb Citizens Coalition, *The Shadow of Hatred.*

32. *New York Times,* July 5, 1983.

33. Associated Press, Nov. 23, 1988; *New York Times,* Jan. 10, 1989.

34. *New York Times,* Sept. 2, 1984; *Tuscaloosa News,* Feb. 28, 1984.

35. Miller, *A White Man Speaks Out;* "Frazier Glenn Miller, Jr.," Wikipedia, http://en.wikipedia.org/wiki/Frazier_Glenn_Miller_Jr. (accessed Nov. 17, 2013).

36. Fort Lauderdale *Sun-Sentinel,* May 13, 1989; "History and IW's," Fraternal White Knights of the Ku Klux Klan, http://www.fraternalwhiteknights.com/History_and_IW_s.html (accessed Nov. 17, 2013).

37. ADL, *The KKK and the Neo-Nazis,* p. 4; *New York Times,* Jan. 23, 1987.

38. *New York Times,* Oct. 4, 1984; *Los Angeles Times,* Jan. 17, 1985.

39. Inmate Locator, Federal Bureau of Prisons, http://www.bop.gov/iloc2/InmateFinderServlet?Transaction=NameSearch&needingMoreList=false&FirstName=stephen&Middle=d&LastName=black&Race=W&Sex=M&Age=&x=54&y=12 (accessed Nov. 17, 2013).

40. "United States Presidential Election, 1984," Wikipedia, http://en.wikipedia.org/wiki/United_States_presidential_election,_1984 (accessed Nov. 17, 2013).

41. Kane, *Presidential Fact Book,* p. 272; "Populist Party (United States, 1984)," Wikipedia, http://en.wikipedia.org/wiki/Populist_Party_%28United_States,_1984%29 (accessed Nov. 17, 2013).

42. "American Party (1969)," Wikipedia; *New York Times,* June 7, 1996; *Christian Science Monitor,* Oct. 12, 1984.

43. "Richard Barrett," ADL, http://archive.adl.org/learn/ext_us/barrett.asp?xpicked=2&item=barrett; "Richard Barrett (Lawyer)," Wikipedia, http://en.wikipedia.org/wiki/Richard_Barrett_%28lawyer%29 (both accessed Nov. 17, 2013).

44. Miller, *A White Man Speaks Out.*

45. *Toledo Blade,* Feb. 5, 1985; People Against Racist Terror, "Front Man for Fascism: 'Bo' Gritz and the Racist Populist Party," The Anomalies Channel, http://www.anomalies.net/archive/Fringe-Political_Belief/GRITZKKK.TXT (accessed Nov. 19, 2013).

46. ADL, *Hate Groups in America* (1988), p. 15.

47. *Los Angeles Times,* March 3, 1985.

48. ADL, *Hate Groups in America* (1988), p. 15.

49. *Marshall v. Bramer,* No. 86-5633, 828 F.2d 355 (1987); ADL, *Hate Groups in America* (1988), p. 17.

50. *Chicago Tribune,* March 7 and June 9, 1985; "Civil Rights Greensboro," University of North Carolina at Greensboro.

51. ADL, *Hate Groups in America* (1988), p. 15; Lutz, p. 67.

52. Lutz, pp. 32–3.

53. ADL, *Hate Groups in America* (1988), p. 15; *Akron Beacon Journal,* Jan. 29, 2011.

54. *Los Angeles Times,* Sept. 21, 1985; Lutz, *They Don't All Wear Sheets,* p. 24.

55. *Reading* (PA) *Eagle,* May 16, 2009; "Tom Metzger," SPLC.

56. Cobb Citizens Coalition, *The Shadow of Hatred*; "Daniel Carver," One People's Project, http://onepeoplesproject.com/index.php?option=com_content&view=article&id=67%3Adaniel-carver&catid=3%3Ac&Itemid=3&lang=en (accessed Nov. 19, 2013).

57. Cobb Citizens Coalition, *The Shadow of Hatred.*

58. "Council of Conservative Citizens," SPLC, http://www.splcenter.org/get-informed/intelligence-files/groups/council-of-conservative-citizens; "Gordon Baum," SPLC, http://www.splcenter.org/get-informed/intelligence-files/profiles/gordon-baum (both accessed Nov. 19, 2013); "Racist Council of Conservative Citizens Finds Home in Mainstream Politics," SPLC *Intelligence Report,* Winter 1999.

59. *Chicago Tribune,* Nov. 21, 1985; ADL, *Computerized Networks of Hate* (New York: ADL, 1985).

60. "Thomas Robb," Wikipedia.

61. Cobb Citizens Coalition, *The Shadow of Hatred.*

62. "Daniel Carver," One People's Project.

63. Ridgeway, *Blood in the Face,* p. 119.

64. "Frazier Glenn Miller, Jr.," Wikipedia.

65. Lutz, *They Don't All Wear Sheets,* p. 66; Miller, *A White Man Speaks Out.*

66. *Person v. Carolina Knights of the Ku Klux Klan*; Miller, *A White Man Speaks Out.*

67. *United States v. Stephen Samuel Miller et al.* (87-2-01 thru 05 CR-3), U.S. District Court, Eastern District of North Carolina.

68. *The Robesonian,* Jan. 20, 1987.

69. Miller, *A White Man Speaks Out.*

70. *United States v. Frazier Glenn Miller, Jr.* (87-31-01-CR-5), U.S. District Court, Eastern District of North Carolina.

71. Mab Segrest, *Memoir of a Race Traitor* (Boston: South End, 1994), pp. 144–5.

72. *United States v. Robert Eugene Jackson et al.* (87-CR-57-01-5), U.S. District Court, Eastern District of North Carolina.

73. "USA v. Stephen Samuel Miller et al: 87-CR-2-3," MIPT Terrorism Knowledge Base, http://web.archive.org/web/20070315061718/http://www.tkb.org/CaseHome.jsp?caseid=303 (accessed Nov. 19, 2013).

74. "USA v. Robert Eugene Jackson et al: 87-CR-57-01-5," MIPT Terrorism Knowledge Base, http://web.archive.org/web/20070314064942/http://www.tkb.org/CaseHome.jsp?caseid=304 (accessed Nov. 19, 2013).

75. ADL, *Hate Groups in America* (1988), p. 17.

76. Segrest, *Memoir of a Race Traitor,* p. 147.

77. Ibid., pp. 154–61.

78. *Chicago Tribune,* July 20, 1986; Lutz, p. 43; *People v. Isbell* No. 2-86-1197, 177 Ill. App.3d 854 (1988), 532 N.E.2d 964.

79. *Chicago Tribune,* June 29, 1986; Fort Lauderdale *Sun-Sentinel,* June 29, 1986.

80. *Philadelphia Inquirer,* July 21, 1986; Associated Press, Aug. 14, 1986.

81. *Montreal Gazette,* Sept. 2, 1986; *Ocala Star-Banner,* Sept. 28, 1986; "Extremism in Connecticut," ADL Archives; *New York Times,* July 22, 2013.

82. *Chicago Tribune,* Oct. 12, 1986; *Los Angeles Times,* Oct. 19, 1986, and Jan. 27, 1989; *Washington Post,* Dec. 17, 1988; *U.S. v. LaRouche,* 896 F.2d 815 (4th Cir. January 22, 1990).

83. *U.S. v. Frankhauser* [*sic*], 878 F.2d 1571 (4th Cir. July 4, 1989); *Boston Globe,* Nov. 17, 1987; *New York Times,* Dec. 10 and 11, 1987; *The Morning Call* (Allentown, PA), Oct. 6, 1988.

84. *New York Times,* Nov. 6, 1986.

85. "Edward Fields," ADL Archives.

86. ADL, *Hate Groups in America* (1988), p. 10.

87. "Don Black," SPLC; Fort Lauderdale *Sun-Sentinel,* April 16, 1990.

88. ADL, "Neo-Nazi Skinheads: A 1990 Status Report," *Terrorism* 13 (1990): 243; ADL, *The Skinhead International: A Worldwide Survey of Neo-Nazi Skinheads* (New York: ADL, 1995).

89. ADL, "Neo-Nazi Skinheads: A 1990 Status Report," p. 243.

90. *New York Times,* Nov. 4, 1988.

91. "Tom Metzger," SPLC.

92. *Sacramento Bee,* July 7, 2003; "Former Klansmen Tom Metzger and Bill Riccio Encourage Skinheads to Cooperate," SPLC *Intelligence Report,* Fall 2006, Issue Number 123.

93. ADL, "Neo-Nazi Skinheads: A 1990 Status Report," pp. 252–3, 255–6, 258, 262, 266, 268.

94. Ibid., p. 252; *New York Times,* Feb. 23, 1992.

95. ADL, "Neo-Nazi Skinheads: A 1990 Status Report," p. 254; Kelly, *Hatred in Georgia, 1991,* p. 37; Kelly, *Hatred in Georgia, 1992,* pp. 2, 22; Cobb Citizens Coalition, *The Shadow of Hatred.*

96. ADL, "Neo-Nazi Skinheads: A 1990 Status Report," p. 247; Kelly, *Hatred in Georgia, 1991,* pp. 8, 19, 46; Kelly, *Hatred in Georgia, 1992,* pp. 13, 20; "Former Klansmen Tom Metzger and Bill Riccio Encourage Skinheads to Cooperate"; "Former Followers Expose Neo-Nazi Skinhead, Former Klan Leader Bill Riccio for Sexual Harassment, Abuse," SPLC *Intelligence Report,* Fall 2007, Issue Number 127.

97. Kelly, *Hatred in Georgia, 1991,* pp. 15, 44; Cobb Citizens Coalition, *The Shadow of Hatred.*

98. ADL, "Neo-Nazi Skinheads: A 1990 Status Report," p. 263; ADL, *The Skinhead International*; *Reading* (PA) *Eagle,* May 16, 2009. ADL, "'Retro' Calendar of Conspiracy: A Chronicle of Anti-Government Extremist Criminal Activity for the Year 1994," Militia Watchdog, http://archive.adl.org/mwd/retro1994.asp (accessed Nov. 21, 2013).

99. Spokane *Spokesman-Review,* June 16, 1996.

100. "SS Knights of the KKK," Metapedia, http://en.metapedia.org/wiki/SS_Knights_of_the_KKK (accessed Nov. 21, 2013).

101. "Connecticut White Wolves," ADL Archive, http://archive.adl.org/learn/news/white_wolves.asp (accessed Nov. 21, 2013).

102. "Former Klansmen Tom Metzger and Bill Riccio Encourage Skinheads to Cooperate."

103. "The National Socialist Movement," ADL Archives, http://archive.adl.org/Learn/Ext_US/nsm/default.asp?LEARN_Cat=Extremism&LEARN_SubCat=Extremism_in_America&xpicked=3&item=nsm (accessed Nov. 21, 2013).

104. "Racist Skinhead Project," ADL, http://archive.adl.org/racist_skin heads/wsgwssm.asp; "Racist Skinhead Group Vinlanders Social Club on the Decline," SPLC *Intelligence Report,* Winter 2008, Issue Number 132 (both accessed Nov. 21, 2013).

105. ADL, "Hal Turner, White Supremacists Exploit Tensions in Kingston, NY," http://archive.adl.org/main_extremism/turner_051117.htm (accessed Nov. 21, 2013).

106. "Forsyth County," New Georgia Encyclopedia, http://www.georgiaencyclopedia.org/articles/counties-cities-neighborhoods/forsyth-county (accessed Nov. 22, 2013).

107. *New York Times,* Jan. 18, 1987.

108. *New York Times,* Jan. 23 and 25, 1987; ADL, *Hate Groups in America* (1988), p. 16; Cobb Citizens Coalition, *The Shadow of Hatred.*

109. *McKinney et al. v. Southern White Knights et al.,* No. 1:87-565-CAM (N.D. Ga., filed March 24, 1987); *Gainesville Sun,* Oct. 26, 1988; *Daily News* (Bowling Green, KY), May 29, 1990.

110. ADL, *Hate Groups in America* (1988), p. 17.

111. David Abel, "The Racist Next Door," *New Times,* Feb. 19, 1998.

112. Associated Press, Jan. 20, 1987; *Washington Post,* Oct. 2, 1987.

113. Spokane *Spokesman-Review,* Aug. 10, 1987.

114. 114. Ellen Alderman and Caroline Kennedy, *In Our Defense: The Bill of Rights in Action* (New York: William Morrow, 1991), pp. 25–36; Zeskind, "Backgrounder: Arizona Mail Bomber Dennis Mahon to Be Sentenced."

115. ADL, *Hate Groups in America* (1988), pp. 5, 9–10.

116. *Orlando Sentinel,* Oct. 16, 1987.

117. "National States Rights Party," Metapedia.

118. *Los Angeles Times,* Nov. 20, Nov. 23, and Dec. 19, 1987.

119. "Profile: Robert E. Miles," History Commons, http://www.historycommons.org/entity.jsp?entity=robert_e_miles_1 (accessed Nov. 22, 2013).

120. Newton, *Ku Klux Klan,* p. 28.

121. "Kirk Lyons Steps Up as Leader of Neo-Confederate Movement," SPLC *Intelligence Report,* Summer 2000, Issue Number 99; "Wilson's Actions Once Again Fail to Back His Words," Save Confederate History from the Sons of Confederate Veterans, http://www.savethescv.org/Actions%20Fail%20Words.htm (accessed Nov. 22, 2013); "Louis Beam," ADL Archives; *The Victoria* (TX) *Advocate,* Nov. 26, 1987.

122. "Edward Fields," ADL Archives.

123. Zeskind, "Backgrounder: Arizona Mail Bomber Dennis Mahon to Be Sentenced"; Clary, "The Truth About Thom Robb."

124. Zeskind, *Blood Politics,* p. 147.

125. *Los Angeles Times,* March 19 and April 7, 1988; *New York Times,* April 8, 1988; "Louis Beam," ADL Archives; "About Rachel Pendergraft," The Knights Party.

126. Miller, *A White Man Speaks Out.*

127. "Richard Barrett," ADL Archives.

128. *Orlando Sentinel,* March 14 and July 26, 1989.

129. *Invisible Empire, KKK v. Mayor et al. of Thurmont,* Civ. No. B-88-2577, 700 F.Supp. 281 (1988).

130. ADL, *Hate Groups in America* (1988), p. 4.

131. "Stormfront Founder's Wife Fronts for Minority School," SPLC *Intelligence Report,* Fall 2008, Issue Number 131; "Our Community—Bill Wilkinson—'The Sailor of the Seven Seas,'" *The San Pedro Sun* (Belize), Nov. 14, 2002.

132. *Orlando Sentinel,* June 27, 1988.

133. "Kirk Lyons Steps Up as Leader of Neo-Confederate Movement."

134. "Richard Barrett," ADL Archives.

135. ADL, *Hate Groups in America* (1988), p. 16.

136. "NH US Vice President—D Primary," Our Campaigns, http://www.ourcampaigns.com/RaceDetail.html?RaceID=393638; "Electoral history of David Duke," Wikipedia, http://en.wikipedia.org/wiki/Electoral_history_of_David_Duke (both accessed Nov. 23, 2013).

137. Kane, *Presidential Fact Book,* p. 283; "Electoral History of David Duke," Wikipedia "Populist Party (United States, 1984)," Wikipedia, http://en.wikipedia.org/wiki/Populist_Party_%28United_States,_1984%29 (accessed Nov. 23, 2013).

138. "American Party (1969)," Wikipedia.

139. *Orlando Sentinel,* May 7 and June 2, 1988.

140. Ibid., Nov. 8, 1988.

141. *Forsyth County v. Nationalist Movement,* 505 U.S. 123 (1992).

142. "Electoral History of David Duke," Wikipedia.

143. Ron Gomez, *My Name Is Ron and I'm a Recovering Legislator: Memoirs of a Louisiana State Representative* (Lafayette, LA: Zemog, 2000), p. 228.

144. Ibid., pp. 230–231.

145. "Hate on the Internet: The Anti-Defamation League Perspective," statement presented to the U.S. Senate Judiciary Committee on Sept. 14, 1999.

146. Spencer Sunshine, "Rebranding Fascism: National-Anarchists," Public Research Associates, http://www.publiceye.org/magazine/v23n4/rebranding_fascism.html (accessed Nov. 23, 2013).

147. *Orlando Sentinel,* March 5, 1989; "Tom Metzger," SPLC.

148. *Orlando Sentinel,* March 6, 1989; *Philadelphia Inquirer,* May 12, 1989.

149. *Hernandez v. Commonwealth of Virginia,* Record No. 0353-90-2, 406 S.E.2d 398 (1991).

150. "Knights of the Ku Klux Klan," SPLC.

151. "Thom Robb and the Knights of the Ku Klux Klan," The Nizkor Project, http://www.nizkor.org/hweb/orgs/american/adl/paranoia-as-patriotism/thom-robb-kkk.html (accessed Nov. 23, 2013).

152. "William Daniel Johnson," SPLC, http://www.splcenter.org/get-informed/intelligence-files/profiles/william-daniel-johnson; "William Daniel Johnson," Wikipedia, http://en.wikipedia.org/wiki/William_Daniel_Johnson (both accessed Nov. 23, 2013).

153. Gerkin, "Watts and Clary"; Johnny Lee Clary, "Johnny's Story," Preach the Cross, http://preachthecross.net/about-johnny-clary/johnnys-story.

154. Kelly, *Hatred in Georgia, 1989,* pp. 24, 30.

155. Ibid., pp. 31, 35; *New York Times,* March 29, 1990; *Marietta* (GA) *Daily Journal,* Aug. 10, 1990.

156. Kelly, *Hatred in Georgia, 1989,* p. 34.

157. "San Diego's Ku Klux Klan 1920–1980," *The Journal of San Diego History.*

158. *Los Angeles Times,* Dec. 13, 1989.

159. *National Post* (Ontario), Nov. 13, 2008.

160. "Foreign Branches of the Ku Klux Klan."

161. "Factual Information About Rev. Teàrlach Barra Eoin Ròs Dunsford Mac a' Phearsoin."

162. "Hate Speech Laws in Canada," Wikipedia, http://en.wikipedia.org/wiki/Hate_speech_laws_in_Canada#The_Criminal_Code_of_Canada (accessed Nov. 23, 2013).

163. *The Jewish Post & News* (Winnipeg), Sept. 16, 1992.

164. *B'nai B'rith v. W. J. Harcus,* Human Rights Tribunal, Dec. 16, 1992.

165. "Dennis Mahon," ADL Archives, http://archive.adl.org/learn/ext_us/ma

hon-brothers/default.asp?LEARN_Cat=Extremism&LEARN_SubCat=Extremism_in_America&xpicked=2&item=mahon_bros (accessed Nov. 23, 2013).

166. *Leader-Post* (Regina, SK), Aug. 24, 2007; "Book on Leo LaChance Murder Leaves Questions Unanswered," Aboriginal Multi-Media Society, http://205.186.158.152/publications/windspeaker/book-leo-lachance-murder-leaves-questions-unanswered (accessed Nov. 23, 2013).

167. "Book on Leo LaChance Murder Leaves Questions Unanswered"; Ron Bourgeault, "The Killing of Leo La-Chance," *Canadian Dimension* 28 (March/April 1994): 21.

168. *Orlando Sentinel,* Jan. 14, 1990.

169. *Chicago Tribune,* March 31, 1991.

170. "Extremism and the Military: A Timeline," SPLC; "Klan Protests Dismissal of Airman," NewsOK, http://newsok.com/klan-protests-dismissal-of-airmen/article/2310222 (accessed Nov. 24, 2013).

171. Kelly, *Hatred in Georgia, 1993,* p. 25.

172. *Orlando Sentinel,* Dec. 21, 1990.

173. *Seattle Times,* May 15, 1990, and April 2, 1992.

174. Cobb Citizens Coalition, *The Shadow of Hatred.*

175. "Kirk Lyons Steps Up as Leader of Neo-Confederate Movement."

176. *Rome News-Tribune,* June 17, 1990; Kelly, *Hatred in Georgia, 1990,* pp. 28, 30; "GA Lt. Governor—D Primary," Our Campaigns, http://www.ourcampaigns.com/RaceDetail.html?RaceID=500104 (accessed Nov. 24, 2013).

177. *Orlando Sentinel,* Aug. 29, 1990.

178. Coalition for Human Dignity, *Northwest Update* (Oct. 15, 1996), p. 3.

179. "David Duke," ADL Archives; "John Rarick," Wikipedia; "Electoral History of David Duke," Wikipedia.

180. *United States v. Wayne A. Pierce,* No. 92-4232, United States Court of Appeals, Fifth Circuit, Oct. 14, 1993.

181. "American Renaissance," SPLC, http://www.splcenter.org/get-informed/intelligence-files/groups/american-renaissance; "About Us," American Renaissance, http://www.amren.com/about (both accessed Nov. 24, 2013); Commonwealth of Virginia Department of State Police, *2009 Virginia Terrorism Threat Assessment* (Richmond: Virginia Fusion Center, 2009), pp. 21, 73.

182. *New York Times,* Nov. 19, 1990, and Jan. 28, 1991; *Fayetteville Observer,* Feb. 16 and 20, 1991; *Gainesville Sun,* April 12, 1991; Mark Potok, "C-4 and the Confederacy," SPLC *Intelligence Report,* Fall 2004, Issue Number 115.

183. Kelly, *Hatred in Georgia, 1991,* p. 24.

184. *Orlando Sentinel,* Feb. 24, 1991; *Philadelphia Inquirer,* Aug. 29, 1992.

185. Kelly, *Hatred in Georgia, 1991,* p. 20.

186. Kelly, *Hatred in Georgia, 1993,* pp. 8, 23, 25.

187. Cobb Citizens Coalition, *The Shadow of Hatred.*

188. Kelly, *Hatred in Georgia, 1991,* pp. 24–7.

189. *Chicago Tribune,* March 31, 1991; *Washington Post,* April 7, 1991.

190. "Edward Fields," ADL Archives; Cobb Citizens Coalition, *The Shadow of Hatred.*

191. "Kirk Lyons Steps Up as Leader of Neo-Confederate Movement"; "Update on Kirk Lyons, CAUSE, and Other White Supremacist/Militia Activity in Western North Carolina," Mountain Area Information Network, http://www.main.nc.us/wncceib/96whole.htm (accessed Nov. 24, 2013).

192. Lewis Loflin, "History of Christian Identity," http://www.sullivancounty.com/id3/identity_history.htm (accessed Nov. 24, 2013).

193. Zeskind, "Backgrounder: Arizona Mail Bomber Dennis Mahon to Be Sentenced."

194. Kelly, *Hatred in Georgia, 1991,* p. 40; Cobb Citizens Coalition, *The Shadow of Hatred.*

195. "Electoral History of David Duke," Wikipedia; Kelly, *Hatred in Georgia, 1991,* p. 44; *New York Times,* Nov. 10, 1991; Bill Hewitt, "An Ex-Klansman Cools His Image," *People Magazine* 36 (Nov. 18, 1991).

196. "Tom Metzger," SPLC; "Tom Metzger (White Supremacist)," Wikipedia; *Los Angeles Times,* Oct. 29, 1991.

197. Kelly, *Hatred in Georgia, 1991,* pp. 46–7.

198. *Orlando Sentinel,* April 4, 1993; *United States v. Ernest Glenn Pierce, Sr. and Brian Grayson Tackett,* Nos. 94-5841, 94-6234, United States Court of Appeals, Sixth Circuit (1985); Andy Ross, "Trial by Fire," *Memphis: The City Magazine* (September 2009), http://www.memphismagazine.com/September-2009/Trial-By-Fire (accessed Nov. 24, 2013).

199. *Los Angeles Times,* Dec. 19 and 31, 1990; Jan. 16 and 22, 1991; Oct. 4, 1991; Dec. 17, 1992.

200. Ibid., May 25, 1991; Feb. 1, 2, 3 and 6, 1994.

201. "Richard Barrett," ADL Archives.

202. *Los Angeles Times,* Dec. 23, 1997, and Jan. 24, 2001; *De La Beckwith v. State of Mississippi,* 707 So. 2d 547 (Miss. 1997), cert. denied, 525 U.S. 880 (1998).

203. Kelly, *Hatred in Georgia, 1992,* p. 2; "Louis Beam," ADL Archives.

204. Milton Kleg, *Hate Prejudice and Racism* (Albany, NY: SUNY Press, 1993), pp. 240–1; *New York Times,* Feb. 23, 1992.

205. Kelly, *Hatred in Georgia, 1991,* p. 7; Kelly, *Hatred in Georgia, 1992,* pp. vi, 6, 7, 11; Kelly, *Hatred in Georgia, 1993,* p. 23.

206. Cobb Citizens Coalition, *The Shadow of Hatred.*

207. Zeskind, "Backgrounder: Arizona Mail Bomber Dennis Mahon to Be Sentenced."

208. *Los Angeles Times,* May 17, 1992.

209. *Orlando Sentinel,* May 23, 1992.

210. Kelly, *Hatred in Georgia, 1992,* pp. 14, 19.

211. "Tom Metzger," SPLC; "Tom Metzger's Long March of Hate," The Nizkor Project; "Tom Metzger," ADL Archives, http://archive.adl.org/learn/ext_us/tom-metzger/background.asp?LEARN_Cat=Extremism&LEARN_SubCat=Extremism_in_America&xpicked=2&item=7 (accessed Nov. 25, 2013).

212. *Los Angeles Times,* Aug. 17, 1992.

213. *Orlando Sentinel,* Aug. 20, 1992.

214. David Lohr, "Randy Weaver: Siege at Ruby Ridge," Crime Library, http://www.trutv.com/library/crime/gangsters_outlaws/cops_others/randy_weaver/1.html (accessed Nov. 25, 2013).

215. "Louis Beam," ADL Archives; Loflin, "History of Christian Identity"; "Kirk Lyons Steps Up as Leader of Neo-Confederate Movement."

216. Kelly, *Hatred in Georgia, 1992,* pp. ix, 23, 25; Kelly, *Hatred in Georgia, 1993,* pp. 2, 4, 24.

217. "Barry Black," SPLC, http://www.splcenter.org/get-informed/intelligence-files/profiles/barry-black (accessed Nov. 25, 2013).

218. *Los Angeles Times,* Dec. 28, 1992; *Orlando Sentinel,* Dec. 29, 1992.

219. Kelly, *Hatred in Georgia, 1992,* p. 3; "Electoral History of David Duke," Wikipedia.

220. "David Duke," ADL Archives; *Chicago Tribune,* Jan. 27, 1992.

221. "David Duke Is Running for President," Skankin' Pickle, *Fever,* Beach Recordings.

222. Cobb Citizens Coalition, *The Shadow of Hatred.*

223. "Neo-Nazis Dominate Washington Populist Party," The Nizkor Project, http://www.nizkor.org/ftp.cgi/orgs/american/ftp.cgi?orgs/american//washington/populist.001; "Front Man for Fascism: 'Bo' Gritz and the Racist Populist Party," The Anomalies Channel, http://www.anomalies.net/archive/Fringe-Political_Belief/GRITZKKK.TXT (both accessed Nov. 25, 2013).

224. "Kirk Lyons Steps Up as Leader of Neo-Confederate Movement."

225. "Populist Party (United States, 1984)," Wikipedia; "1992 Presidential General Election Results," U.S. Election Atlas, http://uselectionatlas.org/RESULTS/national.php?year=1992 (accessed Nov. 25, 2013).

226. "Thom Robb and the Knights of the Ku Klux Klan," The Nizkor Project.

227. *Los Angeles Times,* Feb. 9, 1993; "Anti-Semitism in the United States: Hate Groups," Jewish Virtual Library, http://www.jewishvirtuallibrary.org/jsource/anti-semitism/KKK.html (accessed Nov. 26, 2013).

228. *Baltimore Sun,* Sept. 3, 1993.

229. *Los Angeles Times,* Feb. 9, 1993; *Orlando Sentinel,* Aug. 6, 1993; *Christian Science Monitor,* March 1, 1994.

230. *Galveston Daily News,* Sept. 17, 1994.

231. Kelly, *Hatred in Georgia, 1993,* pp. 9–10; *New York Times,* Jan. 21, 1993; "National Knights of the KKK Honor Grand Wizard," SPLC *Intelligence Report,* Winter 2010, Issue Number 140; "Church of the National Knights of the Ku Klux Klan," SPLC, http://www.splcenter.org/get-informed/intelligence-files/groups/church-of-the-national-knights-of-the-ku-klux-klan (accessed Nov. 26, 2013).

232. *Orlando Sentinel,* Feb. 2, 1993; Kelly, *Hatred in Georgia, 1993,* p. 8; *Reading* (PA) *Eagle,* May 16, 2009.

233. *Report of the Department of the Treasury on the Bureau of Alcohol, Tobacco, and Firearms Investigation of Vernon Wayne Howell Also Known as David Koresh.* Washington, DC: U.S. Government Printing Office, 1993.

234. "Kirk Lyons Steps Up as Leader of Neo-Confederate Movement."

235. "Louis Beam," ADL Archives.

236. Kelly, *Hatred in Georgia, 1993,* pp. v, vii, 13, 22; "Edward Fields," ADL Archives.

237. Kelly, *Hatred in Georgia, 1993,* pp. 15, 16, 19.

238. *Orlando Sentinel,* Oct. 8 and 29, 1993.

239. *Broward/Palm Beach New Times,* June 21, 2001; "Hate on the Internet: The Anti-Defamation League Perspective"; "About Rachel Pendergraft," The Knights Party.

240. Kelly, *Hatred in Georgia, 1993,* pp. v, 2, 13.

241. *Chicago Tribune,* Jan. 17, 1994.

242. Kelly, *Hatred in Georgia, 1993,* pp. v, 13.

243. "'Retro' Calendar of Conspiracy: A Chronicle of Anti-Government Extremist Criminal Activity for the Year 1994," Militia Watchdog; *The Courant* (Hartford, CT), July 16 and Sept. 29, 1994; *New York Times,* July 29, 1994; "Extremism in Connecticut," ADL Archives.

244. Kelly, *Hatred in Georgia, 1993,* p. vi.

245. "'Retro' Calendar of Conspiracy: A Chronicle of Anti-Government Extremist Criminal Activity for the Year 1994," Militia Watchdog.

246. *Ludington* (MI) *Daily News,* April 22, 1994.

247. *Mayor, City of Lansing v. Knights of the Ku Klux Klan,* Docket No. 187765, 564 N.W.2d 177 (1997).

248. "Thom Robb and the Knights of the Ku Klux Klan," The Nizkor Project; "Knights of the Ku Klux Klan," SPLC.

249. *High Country News* (Paonia, CO), June 27, 1994.

250. *Beaver County* (PA) *Times,* Oct. 5, 1994; *Baltimore Sun,* Oct. 15, 1994; *Augusta* (GA) *Chronicle,* Sept. 22, 1997; Affidavit of Christopher Eric Hattrup, Aug. 17, 2000.

251. Floyd Cochran and Loretta J. Ross, *Procreating White Supremacy: Women and the Far Right* (Atlanta: Center for Democratic Renewal, 1993).

252. Newton, *Invisible Empire,* p. 197.

253. "Ku Klux Klan," Pensapedia, http://www.pensapedia.com/wiki/Ku_Klux_Klan (accessed Nov. 27, 2013).

254. "John Burt," Pensapedia, http://www.pensapedia.com/wiki/John_Burt (accessed Nov. 27, 2013).

255. *New York Times,* March 5, 1994.

256. Ibid.

257. "John Burt," Pensapedia.

258. *New York Times,* March 5, 1994.

259. *Pensacola News Journal,* June 11 and 12, 2003; April 2 and May 13, 2004.

260. "John Burt," Prisoners of Christ, http://www.armyofgod.com/JohnBurt.html (accessed Nov. 27, 2013).

261. "The Neo-Confederate Movement," SPLC, http://www.splcenter.org/the-neo-confederate-movement; "League of the South," SPLC, http://www.splcenter.org/get-informed/intelligence-files/groups/league-of-the-south (both accessed Nov. 28, 2013).

262. "A League of Their Own," SPLC *Intelligence Report,* Summer 2000, Issue Number 99; "League of the South Considers 'Black Spring Break' in Biloxi a Call to Arms," SPLC *Intelligence Report,* Summer 2000, Issue Number 99.

263. "Sons of Confederate Veterans in Its Own Civil War," SPLC *Intelligence Report,* Spring 2002, Issue Number 105.

264. Ibid.

265. "Memorandum: February 13, 1994," Western North Carolina Citizens for an End to Institutional Bigotry, http://www.main.nc.us/wncceib/94whole.htm; Save Confederate History from the Sons of Confederate Veterans, http://www.savethescv.org/Actions%20Fail%20Words.htm (both accessed Nov. 28, 2013).

266. "Sons of Confederate Veterans in Its Own Civil War."

267. Ibid.

268. "Sons of Confederate Veterans Leader Ron Wilson Faces Controversy," SPLC *Intelligence Report,* Winter 2003, Issue Number 112; "Rocked by Porn Scandal, SCV Attempts to Oust Moderates," SPLC *Intelligence Report,* Spring 2004, Issue Number 113; "Sons of Confederate Veterans' Strife Continues,"

SPLC *Intelligence Report,* Fall 2004, Issue Number 115; "Sons of Confederate Veterans Heads in More Radical Direction."

269. "Despite Revelations, Heritage Groups Keep Convicted 'Aryan' Plotter in the Fold," SPLC *Intelligence Report,* Winter 2004, Issue Number 116; "The Year in Hate, 2004," SPLC *Intelligence Report,* Spring 2005, Issue Number 117; "The Velvet Glove," SPLC *Intelligence Report,* Winter 2013, Issue Number 152.

270. "Sons of Confederate Veterans Heads in More Radical Direction."

271. Ibid.; "A Resolution by the Jefferson Davis Camp 635 Sons of Confederate Veterans," April 14, 2006, http://www.scvcamp635.org/Resolution.htm (accessed Nov. 28, 2013).

272. "SCV Once Again Elects Radical National Leaders," SPLC *Intelligence Report,* Fall 2006, Issue Number 123; "Sons of Confederate Veterans Heads in More Radical Direction"; Mark Potok, "Once Again, Racism Rears Up in the Sons of Confederate Veterans," SPLC Hatewatch, Feb. 11, 2011.

273. Global Terrorism Database: http://www.start.umd.edu/gtd/search/Results.aspx?perpetrator=10005 (accessed Nov. 28, 2013); *Los Angeles Times,* March 30, 1996, and Jan. 15, 1997; Elohim City," ADL Archives.

274. Mark Hamm, *In Bad Company: America's Terrorist Underground* (Boston: Northeastern University Press, 2001), pp. 93, 288; "The Oklahoma Conspiracy," *The Independent* (London), May 11, 2001; *Los Angeles Times,* Jan. 15, 1997; "Elohim City," ADL Archives, http://archive.adl.org/learn/Ext_US/Elohim.asp?xpicked=3&item=13 (accessed Nov. 29, 2013).

275. Global Terrorism Database; *Los Angeles Times,* Jan. 15, 1997; "Aryan Republican Army," Metapedia, http://en.metapedia.org/wiki/Aryan_Republican_Army; Friedrich Seiltgen, "Aryan Republican Army Hits 22 U.S. Banks," The Counter Terrorist, http://online digitalpublishing.com/article/ARYAN_REPUBLICAN_ARMY_HITS_22_U.S._BANKS/883803/87543/article.html (both accessed Nov. 29, 2013).

276. Lou Michel and Dan Herbeck, *American Terrorist: Timothy McVeigh and the Oklahoma City Bombing* (New York: Harper, 2001), pp. 87–8; Mark Hamm, *Apocalypse in Oklahoma: Waco and Ruby Ridge Revenged* (Boston: Northeastern University Press, 1997), p. 173; "Terror on Trial: Who Was Timothy McVeigh?" CNN.com, http://www.cnn.com/2007/US/law/12/17/court.archive.mcveigh2; "The Aryan Republican Army, Elohim City, and the OKC Bombing," American Patriot Friends Network, http://www.apfn.org/apfn/ara_okc.htm (both accessed Nov. 29, 2013).

277. *Los Angeles Times,* Jan. 15, 1997; *New York Times,* May 14, 1995; *The Independent,* May 11, 2001.

278. *The Independent,* May 11, 2001.

279. Ibid.; Hamm, *In Bad Company,* p. 221; Declaration of Peter Kevin Langan, *Jesse C. Trentadue v. Federal Bureau of Investigation,* Case 2:04-cv-00772-DAK, Document 112-7, filed April 16, 2007, p. 3.

280. "The Aryan Republican Army, Elohim City, and the OKC Bombing"; "Elohim City," ADL Archives; Michel and Herbeck, *American Terrorist,* p. 215; "Memorandum: February 13, 1994," Western North Carolina Citizens for an End to Institutional Bigotry.

281. Sheryll Shariat, Sue Mallonee, and Shelli Stephens, *Oklahoma City Bombing Injuries* (Oklahoma City: Oklahoma Department of Health, 1998); FBI, "Terror Hits Home: The Oklahoma City Bombing," http://www.fbi.gov/about-us/history/famous-cases/oklahoma-city-bombing (accessed Nov. 29, 2013); Shawnee (OK) *News-Star,* Feb. 25, 2009; *Philadelphia Inquirer,* May 14, 1995.

282. *New York Times,* April 21 and May 20, 1995; Oct. 9, 1999; Jeff Elliott, "A Short History of April 19, 1995," The Albion Monitor, http://www.albionmonitor.com/0105b/mcveigh.html (accessed Nov. 29, 2013); Brandon Stickney, *All-American Monster: The Unauthorized Biography of Timothy McVeigh* (Amherst, NY: Prometheus, 1996), p. 234.

283. Global Terrorism Database; *Los Angeles Times,* Jan. 15, 1997; *Los Angeles Times,* March 30, 1996, and Jan. 15, 1997; *Philadelphia Inquirer,* July 31, 1996; Seiltgen, "Aryan Republican Army Hits 22 U.S. Banks."

284. Leonard Zeskind, "Backgrounder: Arizona Mail Bomber Dennis Mahon to Be Sentenced"; "The Aryan Republican Army, Elohim City, and the OKC Bombing"; "Dennis Mahon," ADL Archives.

285. "Elohim City," ADL Archives; "Update on Kirk Lyons, CAUSE, and Other White Supremacist/Militia Activity in Western North Carolina," Mountain Area Information Network; "The Aryan Republican Army, Elohim City, and the OKC Bombing"; Roger Charles and J. D. Cash, "Strassmeir Still Mystery Man in Oklahoma City Bombing," 911Truth.org, http://www.911truth.org/article.php?story=2007042382851207 (accessed Nov. 30, 2013).

286. *Los Angeles Times,* July 13, 1996, Jan. 15 and 31, 1997; *Philadelphia Inquirer,* Feb. 19 and May 21, 1997; Seiltgen, "Aryan Republican Army Hits 22 U.S. Banks"; "Update on Kirk Lyons, CAUSE, and Other White Supremacist/Militia Activity in Western North Carolina," Mountain Area Information Network.

287. *Washington Post,* June 3, 1997, May 28, 1998, and June 5, 1998; *New York Times,* June 12, 2001, and Aug. 10, 2004; *Los Angeles Times,* Jan. 21, 2006.

288. ADL, "'Retro' Calendar of Conspiracy: A Chronicle of Anti-Government Extremist Criminal Activity for the Year 1994"; "Don Black," SPLC; "Profile: Stormfront (.org)," History Commons, http://www.cooperativeresearch.org/entity.jsp?entity=storm front_org_1 (accessed Nov. 30, 2013).

289. "Q&A on Fayetteville Murders and Hate and the Military," ADL Archives.

290. *Chicago Tribune,* May 11, June 14 and July 19, 1995.

291. *National Church Arson Task Force: Second Year Report for the President* (Washington, DC: U.S. Government Printing Office, 1998), p. 1.

292. *Seattle Times,* Aug. 15, 1996; *New York Times,* Dec. 11, 1996; *Macedonia Baptist Church v. Christian Knights of the Ku Klux Klan,* Case No. 96-CP-14-217, Court of Common Pleas for the Third Judicial Circuit.

Chapter 11

1. CNN, Feb. 20, 1996; *Chicago Tribune,* June 9, 1996; *Los Angeles Times,* June 27, 1996; "Former Klan Leader James Roesch Says 'I Came to Christ,'" SPLC *Intelligence Report,* Winter 2008, Issue Number 132.

2. *San Francisco Chronicle,* Feb. 23 and 26, 1996.

3. *Seattle Times,* June 16, June 21, and Oct. 2, 1996.

4. ADL, "Calendar of Conspiracy, Volume 2, Number 2: A Chronology of Anti-Government Extremist Criminal Activity, April to June 1998." The Militia Watchdog, http://archive.adl.org/mwd/leo.html (accessed Dec. 2, 2013).

5. Ibid.

6. Spokane *Spokesman-Review,* Jan. 20, 2001; Portland *Oregonian,* Jan. 21, 2001; "In Montana, a New Challenge to Butler," SPLC *Intelligence Report,* Spring 2001, Issue Number 101; Montana Human Rights Network, "Church of True Israel's 'The Gathering,'" July 13, 2004, p. 2.

7. *Savannah Morning News,* Oct. 19, 2011; "1996 Presidential General Election Results," U.S. Election Atlas, http://uselectionatlas.org/RESULTS/national.php?year=1996&minper=0&f=0&off=0&elect=0 (accessed Dec. 2, 2013).

8. "Pat Buchanan's Skeleton Closet," Real People for Real Change, http://realchange.org/buchanan.htm (accessed Dec. 2, 2013).

9. Ibid.; "Update on Kirk Lyons, CAUSE, and Other White Supremacist/Militia Activity in Western North Carolina," Mountain Area Information Network.

10. "Electoral History of David Duke," Wikipedia.

11. Adam Pitluk, "White Greetings," *Broward/Palm Beach New Times,* June 21, 2001.

12. "Terror from the Right: Plots, Conspiracies and Racist Rampages Since Oklahoma City," SPLC, http://www.splcenter.org/get-informed/publications/terror-from-the-right (accessed Dec. 2, 2013).

13. "Update on Recent Hate Activity in Western North Carolina," Mountain Area Information Network (Summer 1998), http://www.main.nc.us/wncceib/98whole.htm#Item%2011 (accessed Dec. 2, 2013).

14. Antisemitism and Xenophobia Today, http://www.axt.org.uk/antisem/archive/archive2/usa; "Brotherhood of Klans," SPLC, http://www.splcenter.org/get-informed/intelligence-files/groups/brotherhood-of-klans (both accessed Dec. 2, 2013).

15. *New York Times,* April 6, 1997; *Philadelphia Inquirer,* April 21, 1997.

16. Trends in Hate, http://www.trendsinhate.com/dateinhate.html (accessed Dec. 2, 2013).

17. "Shop of Horrors," SPLC *Intelligence Report,* Summer 2008, Issue Number 130; "Black Church Awarded KKK Shop," RT America (Jan. 3, 2012), http://rt.com/usa/church-shop-kennedy-rev-171 (accessed Dec. 2, 2013).

18. *Chicago Sun-Times,* Jan. 23, 1998; *The Times* (Munster, IN), Sept. 3, 1998.

19. Michael Cuffley, *Knights of the Ku Klux Klan, Realm of Missouri v. Joe Mickes et al.,* 208 F.3d 702 (8th Cir. 2000); *Los Angeles Times,* Mach 6, 2001.

20. *Orlando Sentinel,* Aug. 27, 1997, and March 17, 1998.

21. *Reading* (PA) *Eagle,* Sept. 27, 1997.

22. Trends in Hate, http://www.trendsinhate.com/dateinhate.html.

23. *Wilmington Morning Star,* Nov. 3, 1997.

24. *New York Times,* Nov. 22, 1997.

25. ADL, "Calendar of Conspiracy, Volume 1, Number 4: A Chronology of Anti-Government Extremist Criminal Activity, October to December 1997."

26. *Asheville Citizen-Times,* Dec. 23, 1997.

27. *Jouhari/Horton v. United Klans of America/Frankhouser,* Case No. 03-98-0692-8 & 03-98-0797-8, Administrative Complaint filed with the U.S. Department of Housing and Urban Development, Aug. 28, 1998; *Philadelphia Inquirer,* May 14, 2000.

28. "Update on Recent Hate Activity in Western North Carolina," Mountain Area Information Network (Summer 1998).

29. Chicago *Post-Tribune,* Feb. 1, 1998.

30. *St. Louis Post Dispatch,* Feb. 24, 1998; *Alton* (IL) *Telegraph,* April 19, 1998; ADL, "Calendar of Conspiracy," Volume 2, Numbers 1–4, January through December 1998.

31. "Kirk Lyons Steps Up as Leader of Neo-Confederate Movement"; "Update on Recent Hate Activity in Western North Carolina," Mountain Area Information Network (Summer 1998).

32. "Klan's Free Press," SPLC *Intelligence Report,* Spring 1998, Issue Number 90.

33. Deposition of Jonathan Mozzochi, *Irving v. Penguin Books et al.,* High Court of Justice, Queen's Bench Division, May 1998; *Pittsburgh Post-Gazette,* Jan. 22, 2000.

34. *Detroit Free Press,* April 9, 1998.

35. *Detroit Legal News,* June 2, 1998.

36. "Update on Recent Hate Activity in Western North Carolina," Mountain Area Information Network (Summer 1998).

37. "Barry Black," SPLC; "The Supreme Court: Allowing Cross Burning," Infoplease, http://www.infoplease.com/cig/supreme-court/allowing-cross-burning.html (accessed Dec. 3, 2013).

38. "3 Whites Indicted in Dragging Death of Black Man in Texas," CNN, July 6, 1998.

39. Trends in Hate, http://www.trendsinhate.com/dateinhate.html.

40. *Los Angeles Times,* June 17, 1998; *Amarillo Globe-News,* Oct. 11, 1998; "Church of the American Knights of the KKK," ADL, http://archive.adl.org/backgrounders/american_knights_kkk.asp (accessed Dec. 3, 2013).

41. Trends in Hate, http://www.trendsinhate.com/dateinhate.html.

42. Matthew Shepard and James Byrd, Jr. Hate Crimes Prevention Act, signed by President Barack Obama on Oct. 28, 2009.

43. ADL, "Calendar of Conspiracy, Volume 2, Number 3: A Chronology of Anti-Government Extremist Criminal Activity, July to September 1998."

44. Ibid., Volume 2, Number 3, and Volume 3, Numbers 3 and 4.

45. Trends in Hate, http://www.trendsinhate.com/dateinhate.html.

46. Ibid., ADL, "Calendar of Conspiracy," Volume 2, Number 4, and Volume 4, Number 1.

47. "Church of the American Knights of the KKK," SPLC.

48. *Austin American-Statesman,* April 14 and Sept. 15, 1999; ADL, "Calendar of Conspiracy, Volume 3, Numbers 1 and 3.

49. *Cincinnati Enquirer,* April 16–18 and July 31, 1999.

50. "LA District 1—Special Election," Our Campaigns, http://www.ourcampaigns.com/RaceDetail.html?RaceID=88588 (accessed Dec. 3, 2013).

51. ADL, "Calendar of Conspiracy,

Volume 3, Number 2"; J. Keith Akins, "The Ku Klux Klan: America's Forgotten Terrorists," *Law Enforcement Executive Forum* 5 (2006), p. 135, http://www.uhv.edu/asa/articles/kkkamericasforgottenterrorists.pdf (accessed Dec. 3, 2013).

52. ADL, "Calendar of Conspiracy, Volume 3, Number 3"; *Orlando Sentinel,* May 21, 1999.

53. Trends in Hate, http://www.trendsinhate.com/dateinhate.html.

54. ADL, "Calendar of Conspiracy, Volume 3, Number 4."

55. *George Sells IV and Heidi Thiels v. Jeff Berry,* Case No. 1:00-CV-30, U.S. District Court Northern District of Indiana (2000); "Klan Leader Sentenced to Seven Years in Prison," ADL Archives, http://archive.adl.org/learn/news/Kleader_7.asp (accessed Dec. 5, 2013).

56. *Pittsburgh Post-Gazette,* Dec. 17, 1999.

57. "The World of 'Patriots,'" SPLC *Intelligence Report,* Spring 1999, Issue Number 94.

58. Morris Dees and James Corcoran, "Still 'A Recipe for Disaster,'" *USA Weekend Magazine,* April 12–14, 1996, pp. 4–5.

59. *Greensboro News & Record,* June 26, 1995.

60. "Memorandum: November 1995," Western North Carolina Citizens for an End to Institutional Bigotry, http://www.main.nc.us/wncceib/94whole.htm (accessed Dec. 3, 2013).

61. Nicholas Kennedy, "Klan Power Wanes; Hate, Bigotry Edge Toward the Militias," *National Catholic Reporter,* Oct. 25, 1996.

62. Tim Bullard, "The Beast and the S.C. Civilian Militia," http://www.timbullard.com/s.c.militia.htm (accessed Dec. 5, 2013).

63. "Militia of Montana," ADL Archives, http://archive.adl.org/learn/ext_us/mom.html?xpicked=3&item=mom (accessed Dec. 5, 2013).

64. "Dennis Mahon," ADL Archives.

65. Konfederate Klavaliers Arkansas Volunteer Militia Kavalry, http://www.geocities.ws/klavaliers/cavaliers.html (accessed Dec. 5, 2013).

66. *Montgomery Advertiser,* March 2, 1999.

67. Jackson (MS) *Clarion-Ledger,* Dec. 12, 1997; Jan. 2 and 17, 1998.

68. Ibid., Feb. 6 and 10, 1998; May 29, 1998.

69. Ibid., March 12, 1998.

70. Ibid., May 29, June 10 and June 11, 1998.

71. Ibid., July 22, 1998.

72. Ibid., Aug. 2, 1998.

73. Ibid., Aug. 19, 20 and 22, 1998; *New York Times,* Aug. 21, 1998, and Nov. 6, 2006; *Milwaukee Journal-Sentinel,* Sept. 21, 1998; Associated Press, June 15, 1999.

74. "Factual Information About Rev. Teàrlach Barra Eoin Ròs Dunsford Mac a' Phearsoin."

75. *National Post* (Ontario), July 15, 2002.

76. "Brotherhood of Klans," SPLC.

77. Chris Waters, "Canadian Empire," United Klans of America, http://theuka.us/CANADIAN_EMPIRE.html (accessed Dec. 5, 2013).

78. *La Estrella* (Panama City), Nov. 12, 2008; *National Post* (Ontario), November 13, 2008; CanWest News Services, May 25, 2009; Okke Ornstein, "Emerald Passport MLM Scheme Deploys Former Ku Klux Klan Grand Wizard to Panama," Banana Republic, http://www.bananamarepublic.com/2008/10/27/emerald-passport-mlm-scheme-deploys-former-ku-klux-klan-grand-wizard-to-panama (accessed Dec. 6, 2013).

79. "The European White Knights of the Ku Klux Klan Are Back!" Stormfront (Nov. 27, 2007), http://www.stormfront.org/forum/t440496 (Dec. 5, 2013).

80. "UNSK-KKK European Division," Stormfront (Aug. 26, 2009), http://www.stormfront.org/forum/t633888 (accessed Dec. 5, 2013).

81. "Wacko in Wales," *Sky Magazine,* March 1994; "The Klan Overseas," SPLC *Intelligence Report,* Winter 1998, Issue Number 89; BBC News, Feb. 14, 2002, and Oct. 31, 2013; *Sunday Times* (London), March 21, 1999; *The Independent* (London), April 18, 1999; "Don Black," SPLC; *Daily Mirror* (London), Oct. 19, 2011; *South Wales Evening Post,* Aug. 6, 2013.

82. Florian Gathmann, "Racist 'Scandal': German Police Kept Jobs Despite KKK Involvement." *Der Spiegel,* Aug. 2, 2012; Frederik Obermaier and Tanjev Schultz, "The Neo-Nazi Double Agent Who Started a KKK Chapter in Germany," *Suddeutsche Zeitung,* Nov. 2, 2013; Sven Heymanns, "German Ku Klux Klan Founded by State's Intelligence Agency," World Socialist Web Site, http://www.wsws.org/en/articles/2012/11/bade-n01.html (accessed Dec. 5, 2013).

83. "Ku Klux Klan in Europe (Serbia)," YouTube, http://www.youtube.com/watch?v=9woGAarr_Ug, (uploaded Jan. 11, 2007; accessed Dec. 5, 2013).

84. *The Sofia Echo* (Bulgaria), Sept. 29, 2009.

85. BBC News, June 2, 1999; *New Zealand Herald,* June 5, 1999.

86. *China Daily,* Nov. 11, 2004; Australia Broadcasting Company News, Aug. 11, 2006; *The Australian,* May 14, 2010; *Sydney Morning Herald,* Nov. 11, 2013.

87. *The Australian,* Feb. .5, 2007; *Sydney Morning Herald,* July 10, 2009.

88. Akins, "The Ku Klux Klan: America's Forgotten Terrorists," p. 134.

89. ADL, "Calendar of Conspiracy, Volume 4, Number 1"; *Orlando Sentinel*, Jan. 27, 2000.

90. ADL, "Calendar of Conspiracy, Volume 4, Number 2."

91. "Confederates in Black," Intelligence Report, Summer 2000: Issue 99; Southern Heritage 411, http://www.southernheritage411.com (accessed Dec. 6, 2013).

91. Trends in Hate, http://www.trendsinhate.com/dateinhate.html.

92. "US Domestic Terrorism: Ku Klux Klan," History Commons, http://www.historycommons.org/timeline.jsp?timeline=us_domestic_terrorism_tmln&haitian_elite_2021_organizations=us_domestic_terrorism_tmln_ku_klux_klan (accessed Dec. 6, 2013); *Chicago Sun-Times*, June 6, 2001.

93. Center for New Community, *Party Crashers: White Nationalists and Election 2000* (Chicago: CNC, 2000), pp. 8–15.

94. *Chicago Tribune*, Aug. 12, 2000; "Patrick Buchanan's Reform Party Begins to Unravel," SPLC *Intelligence Report*, Fall 2002, Issue Number 107; Charles Johnson, "Pat Buchanan and the American Friends of the BNP," Little Green Footballs, http://littlegreenfootballs.com/article/33916_Pat_Buchanan_and_the_American_Friends_of_the_BNP; "2000 Presidential General Election Results," US Election Atlas, http://uselectionatlas.org/RESULTS/national.php?year=2000 (both accessed Dec. 6, 2013).

95. *The Times Record* (Fort Smith, AR), Sept. 14, 2000; "Arkansas," The Green Papers: Off-Year Election 2001, http://www.thegreenpapers.com/G01/AR.html (accessed Dec. 6, 2013).

96. "Church of the National Knights of the Ku Klux Klan," SPLC.

97. Trends in Hate, http://www.trendsinhate.com/dateinhate.html.

98. "Klan Leader Sentenced in Harassment Case," ADL Archives, http://archive.adl.org/learn/news/klan_sent.asp; "Klan Presence Leads Indiana Community to Adopt 'Hate Activity' Law," ADL Archives, http://archive.adl.org/learn/news/hate_activity_law.asp (both accessed Dec. 6, 2013).

99. *Belleville* (IL) *News-Democrat*, Sept. 30, 2001.

100. "Investigation Leads to Klan Arrests in Louisiana," ADL Archives, http://archive.adl.org/learn/news/Klan_arrest.asp (accessed Dec. 6, 2013).

101. Mark Gaddo, "The Birmingham Church Bombing: Bombingham," Crime Library, http://www.trutv.com/library/crime/terrorists_spies/terrorists/birmingham_church/index.html (accessed Dec. 6, 2013).

102. "Birmingham Church Bomber Guilty, Gets Four Life Terms," CNN, May 1, 2001.

103. *New York Times*, May 23, 2002; *Washington Post*, Nov. 19, 2004.

104. U.S. Department of Justice press release, Feb. 28, 2003; *New York Times*, June 17, 2004.

105. "Kidnapping Suspect Arrested at Klan Base in Indiana," ADL Archives, http://archive.adl.org/learn/news/klan_indiana.asp (accessed Dec. 7, 2013); "Church of the National Knights of the Ku Klux Klan," SPLC.

106. Akins, "The Ku Klux Klan: America's Forgotten Terrorists," p. 127; "Church of the National Knights of the Ku Klux Klan," SPLC; "North Carolina Klan Leader Arrested for Alleged Bomb Plot," ADL Archives, http://archive.adl.org/learn/news/Leader_arrested_klan.asp; "Four with Klan Ties Face Murder Charges," ADL Archives, http://archive.adl.org/learn/news/nc_murder_kkk.asp; Casey Sanchez, "Accused Klan Boss Found Incompetent," SPLC Hatewatch, http://www.splcenter.org/blog/2007/12/14/accused-klan-boss-found-incompetent; Bill Morlin, "Klan Leader Who Plotted to Murder NC Sheriff Gets 15 Years," SPLC Hatewatch, http://www.splcenter.org/blog/2013/02/07/klan-leader-who-plotted-to-murder-nc-sheriff-gets-15-years (all accessed Dec. 7, 2013).

107. Trends in Hate, http://www.trendsinhate.com/dateinhate.html; *Orlando Sentinel*, Nov. 17, 2002; "Drug Raid Louisiana Nabs Klan Members," ADL Archives, http://archive.adl.org/learn/news/drug_louisiana (accessed Dec. 7, 2013).

108. Associated Press, July 24 and September 20, 2002.

109. Federal Bureau of Investigation, "Terrorism 2002–2005," http://www.fbi.gov/stats-services/publications/terrorism-2002-2005/terror02_05 (accessed Dec. 7, 2013).

110. *Boston Globe*, June 25, 2009; *Arizona Republic*, May 22, 2012; Trends in Hate, http://www.trendsinhate.com/dateinhate.html.

111. Trends in Hate, http://www.trendsinhate.com/dateinhate.html.

112. "KKK Initiation Ceremony Goes Astray," SPLC *Intelligence Report*, Spring 2004, Issue Number 113.

113. Trends in Hate, http://www.trendsinhate.com/dateinhate.html.

114. "Ku Klux Klan—Criminal Activity and Violence," ADL Archives, http://archive.adl.org/learn/ext_us/kkk/crime.asp?xpicked=4&item=kkk (accessed Dec. 7, 2013).

115. "Freedom Summer," Barry Bradford, http://barrybradford.com/mississippi-burning (accessed Dec. 7, 2013).

116. *Los Angeles Times*, Jan. 7 and 8; March 5 and 11; June 17, 21, 22 and 24, 2005; Associated Press, Nov. 5, 2013.

117. *Jackson* (MS) *Free Press*, Jan. 31, 2007; "Miss. Officials Agree to Settlement in '64 Slayings," National Public Radio, June 21, 2010; *United States v. James Ford Seale*, No. 09-166 (2009); Mark Potok, "Civil-Rights Era Klan Murderer Dies in Prison," SPLC Hatewatch, http://www.splcenter.org/blog/2011/08/03/civil-rights-era-klan-murderer-dies-in-prison (accessed Dec. 7, 2013).

118. Trends in Hate, http://www.trendsinhate.com/dateinhate.html.

119. "Klan Leader's Son Arrested in Near-Fatal Attack on Father," SPLC *Intelligence Report*, Fall 2006, Issue Number 123; *Indianapolis Star*, July 23, 2007; "Klan Organizer Could Be Headed for U.S. Army," SPLC *Intelligence Report*, Spring 2007, Issue Number 125.

120. Trends in Hate, http://www.trendsinhate.com/dateinhate.html; *Jordan Gruver v. Imperial Klans of America*, Civil Action No. 07-CI-00082, Commonwealth of Kentucky, 46th Judicial District, Division 1, Meade Circuit Court (2007).

121. *The Herald-Mail* (Hagerstown, MD), Feb. 9 and July 13, 2007.

122. CBS News, May 7, 2010; "Klan Murder Shines Light on Bogalusa, La.," SPLC *Intelligence Report*, Summer 2009, Issue Number 134; Larry Keller, "'Sons of Dixie' Leader Indicted for Klan Initiation Murder," SPLC Hatewatch, http://www.splcenter.org/blog/2009/02/18/sons-of-dixie-leader-indicted-for-klan-initiation-murder (accessed Dec. 7, 2013).

123. "March 1995: White Supremacist Launches Stormfront, Related Web Site," History Commons, http://www.cooperativeresearch.org/context.jsp?item=a0395hatesite#a0395hatesite (accessed Dec. 7, 2013).

124. "Hate on the Internet: The Anti-Defamation League Perspective."

125. "Profile: Adrian Edward Marlow," History Commons, http://www.historycommons.org/entity.jsp?entity=adrian_edward_marlow_1 (accessed Dec. 7, 2013).

126. Jew Watch, http://www.jewwatch.com (accessed Dec. 7, 2013).

127. "EURO," SPLC, http://www.splcenter.org/get-informed/intelligence-files/groups/euro (accessed Dec. 7, 2013).

128. "Hate on the Internet: The Anti-Defamation League Perspective."

129. Welcome to the Ku Klux Klan, http://www.kkk.com (accessed Dec. 8, 2013).

130. White Camelia Knights of the Ku Klux Klan, http://www.wckkkk.org/index.html (accessed Dec. 8, 2013).

131. Loyal White Knights of the Ku Klux Klan, http://kkkknights.com/main_page.html (accessed Dec. 8, 2013).

132. Imperial Klans of America, http://www.kkkk.net (accessed Dec. 8, 2013).

133. Knight Riders Knights of the Ku Klux Klan, http://knightriderskkkk.org/ (accessed Dec. 8, 2013).

134. "Hate Groups Multiply Online," NBC Nightly News, March 2, 2005.

135. "Anonymous Hacking Collective Declares 'Operation Blitzkrieg' Against Neo-Nazi Websites," SPLC *Intelligence Report,* Summer 2012, Issue Number 146.

136. "Hate Websites in the U.S.," SPLC *Intelligence Report,* Spring 2011, Issue 141.

137. WhitePrideTV.com, http://www.thomasrobb.com (accessed Dec. 8, 2013).

138. "The New Orleans Protocol," Stormfront, http://www.stormfront.org/forum/t135634.

139. Ibid.

140. Vanguard News Network, http://www.vanguardnewsnetwork.com (accessed Dec. 8, 2013).

141. Alex Linder, "Between the Lines: 'New Orleans Protocol,'" Vanguard News Network, http://www.vanguardnewsnetwork.com/v1/2004b/60604btllinder.htm (accessed Dec. 8, 2013).

142. "LA—District 1," Our Campaigns, http://www.ourcampaigns.com/RaceDetail.html?RaceID=4156 (accessed Dec. 8, 2013).

143. "Ku Klux Klan—Recent Developments," ADL Archives, http://archive.adl.org/learn/ext_us/kkk/expansion.asp?learn_cat=extremism&learn_subcat=extremism_in_america&xpicked=4&item=kkk (accessed Dec. 8, 2013).

144. "Ku Klux Klan—Active Groups (by state)," ADL Archives, http://archive.adl.org/learn/ext_us/kkk/active_group_2006.asp?LEARN_Cat=Extremism&LEARN_SubCat=Extremism_in_America&xpicked=4&item=kkk (accessed Dec. 8, 2013).

145. "Hate Groups Active in the Year 2006," SPLC *Intelligence Report,* Spring 2007, Issue 125.

146. "Arkansas Klan Group Loses Legal Battle with North Carolina Newspaper," ADL, http://www.adl.org/combating-hate/domestic-extremism-terrorism/c/arkansas-klan-group-loses-legal-battle.html (accessed Dec. 8, 2013).

147. "Glenn Miller," Metapedia, http://en.metapedia.org/wiki/Glenn_Miller (accessed December 8, 2013).

148. David Peisner, "Why White Supremacists Support Barack Obama," *Esquire,* http://www.esquire.com/the-side/feature/racists-support-obama-061308 (accessed Dec. 8, 2013); *Tampa Bay Times,* Sept. 22, 2008.

149. *Tampa Bay Times,* Sept. 22, 2008; *The Telegraph* (London), Nov. 6, 2008.

150. "Don Black," SPLC.

151. *New York Times,* Dec. 11, 2008; Larry Keller, "GOP Boots Former Klan Leader's Son," SPLC Hatewatch, http://www.splcenter.org/blog/2008/12/04/gop-boots-former-klan-leader%E2%80%99s-son (accessed Dec. 8, 2013).

152. *Miami Herald,* July 22, 2008; "Woman with Ties to White Supremacists Represents School for Blacks and Hispanics," Fox News, July 30, 2008; "Billionaire Won't Fire Assistant for KKK Link," Page Six, http://pagesix.com/2010/10/09/billionaire-wont-fire-assisant-for-kkk-link (accessed Dec. 8, 2013).

153. "White Supremacists Strategize Around Inauguration Day," ADL Archives, http://archive.adl.org/nr/exeres/2546231f-35dc-40b2-8c09-770114f24440,8c8c250f-da79-405f-b716-d4409cab5396,frameless.html (accessed Dec. 8, 2013).

154. "The National Socialist Movement," ADL Archives.

155. Andrew Smith, "Psychology Department to Issue Statement on Professor's Controversial Literature," *Daily 49er,* Feb. 7. 2008; Tiffany Rider, "Academic Senate Disassociates Itself from Professor MacDonald," *Daily 49er,* Oct. 6, 2008; "American Freedom Party," SPLC, http://www.splcenter.org/get-informed/intelligence-files/groups/american-freedom-party (accessed Dec. 8, 2013).

156. Anti-Defamation League, *Extremism in Florida: The Dark Side of the Sunshine State,* 3d ed. (New York: ADL, 2011), pp. 15–17.

157. *Orlando Sentinel,* Jan. 8, 2010.

158. Mark Potok, "What If They Gave a Klan Rally and Nobody Came?" SPLC Hatewatch, http://www.splcenter.org/blog/2010/04/05/what-if-they-gave-a-klan-rally-and-nobody-came (accessed Dec. 8, 2013).

159. "Tom Metzger," SPLC; Miriam Raftery, "White Supremacist Tom Metzger Runs for Congress—Again," *East County Magazine* (San Diego, CA), March 30, 2010; Tom Metzger, U.S. Congress, Indiana 3rd District, http://www.resist.com/tommetzgerrunsforcongress.html (accessed Dec. 8, 2013).

160. "BANISHED!!!!" and replies, Stormfront, www.stormfront.org/forum/t713767 (accessed Dec. 8, 2013).

161. FBI press release (July 14, 2011), http://www.fbi.gov/atlanta/press-releases/2011/former-klansman-who-traveled-to-georgia-for-sex-with-two-underage-girls-sentenced-to-20-years-in-prison (accessed Dec. 8, 2013).

162. Trends in Hate, http://www.trendsinhate.com/dateinhate.html.

163. "The National Socialist Movement," ADL Archives.

164. *Orlando Sentinel,* Dec. 23, 2010.

165. "Anti-Racist Turncoat Johnny Lee Clary Banned from Two High Schools in Alice Springs, Australia Because He Is Allegedly Anti-Islamic and Homophobic," White Reference, http://whitereference.blogspot.com/2011/03/anti-racist-turncoat-johnny-lee-clary.html (accessed Dec. 8, 2013).

166. Ryan Lenz, "It's a Mad, Mad, Mad World: Klan Takes on Westboro Gay-Bashers," SPLC Hatewatch, http://www.splcenter.org/blog/2011/05/31/its-a-mad-mad-mad-world-klan-takes-on-westboro-gay-bashers (accessed Dec. 8, 2013).

167. Bill Morlin, "Racist Leader Billy Roper Shutters White Revolution, Joins Klan," SPLC Hatewatch, http://www.splcenter.org/blog/2011/09/08/bill-roper-shutters-white-revolution-joins-klan (accessed Dec. 8, 2013).

168. *The Militant,* Vol. 76, No. 11, March 19, 2012.

169. "Presidency 2012," Ron Gunzburger's Politics 1, http://www.politics1.com/p2012.htm (accessed Dec. 8, 2013).

170. "2012 National Faith and Freedom Conference," Knights Party, http://www.knightspartyveteransleague.com/?p=163; Hamilton Nolan, "My Kasual Kountry Weekend with the Knights of the Ku Klux Klan," Gawker, http://gawker.com/5898493/my-kasual-kountry-weekend-with-the-knights-of-the-ku-klux-klan (both accessed Dec. 8, 2013).

171. *Huffington Post,* Oct. 15, 2012.

172. "True Story: Cadre of Clowns Disrupts North Carolina Nazi and KKK Gathering," The Blaze, http://www.theblaze.com/stories/2012/11/12/true-story-cadre-of-clowns-disrupts-north-carolina-nazi-and-kkk-gathering (accessed Dec. 8, 2013).

173. Annie-Rose Strasser, "Virginia KKK Uses Obama's Presidency as a Recruiting Tool," Think Progress, http://thinkprogress.org/justice/2013/01/09/1422471/virginia-kkk-obama-recruiting (accessed Dec. 9, 2013).

174. *Huffington Post,* Feb. 7, 2013; *Memphis Flyer,* March 30, 2013; Associated Press, Sept. 16, 2013; "White Supremacists to Stage Protest Over Memphis Parks," ADL Blog, http://blog.adl.org/tags/ku-klux-klan; Don Terry, "On Eve of Memphis Klan Rally, Officials Prepare for 'KKK Mayhem,'" SPLC Hatewatch, http://www.splcenter.org/blog/2013/03/29/on-eve-of-memphis-klan-rally-officials-prepare-for-kkk-mayhem (both accessed Dec. 9, 2013).

175. Don Terry, "Strange Bedfellows Snuggle Under White Sheets," SPLC Hatewatch, http://www.splcenter.org/blog/2013/03/01/strange-bedfellows-snuggle-under-white-sheets (accessed Dec. 9, 2013).

176. WTEV, Channel 47 (Jacksonville, FL), March 22, 2013.

177. *International Business Times,* June 19, 2013; *Daily Mail* (London), June 19, 2013; *The Sun* (London), June 21, 2013.

178. *Arkansas Times,* June 21, 2013;

UALR Public Radio (Little Rock, AR), Aug. 24, 2013.

179. Federal Bureau of Investigation press release, Oct. 24, 2013.

180. *Casper* (WY) *Star-Tribune,* Sept. 2, 2013.

181. WJXT TV, Channel 4 (Jacksonville, FL), July 10, 2013; Associated Press, Nov. 4, 2008; *Huffington Post,* Sept. 9, 2013; *Business Insider,* Nov. 10, 2013.

182. KSL TV, Channel 5 (Salt Lake City), Nov. 5, 2013.

183. Panama City *New Herald,* Nov. 7, 2013.

184. David Edwards, "NC KKK Mistakenly Attempts Recruiting Drive in Black Florida Neighborhood," The Raw Story, http://www.rawstory.com/rs/2013/11/13/nc-kkk-mistakenly-attempts-recruiting-drive-in-black-florida-neighborhood (accessed Dec. 9, 2013); *Hispanically Speaking News* (Chicago), Nov. 23, 2013.

185. *The Republic* (Columbus, IN), Nov. 29, 2013.

186. WBIW Radio (Bedford, IN), Dec. 11, 2013.

187. *Washington Examiner,* Dec. 19, 2013.

188. *Augusta Chronicle,* Dec. 23, 2013.

189. Laura Bauer, Dave Helling and Brian Burnes, "Man with History of Anti-Semitism Jailed in Fatal Shooting of Three at Johnson County Jewish Centers," *Kansas City Star,* April 13, 2014.

190. Saeed Ahmed, Ed Lavandara and Catherine E. Shoichet, "Alleged Kansas Jewish Center Gunman Charged with Murder," CNN News, April 15, 2014.

191. Ibid.

192. Matt Pearce, "Missouri Mayor, Friend to Jewish Center Shooting Suspect, Resigns," *Los Angeles Times,* April 22, 2014.

193. Rheana Murray, "Former KKK Leader Says Jewish Center Shooting Suspect Went 'Insane,'" ABC News, April 15, 2014.

194. "Louis Beam," ADL Archives.

195. "Edward Fields," ADL Archives; *Houston Chronicle,* April 29, 2013.

196. *USA Today,* Dec. 13, 2002; Fox News, March 12, 2003.

197. Trends in Hate, http://www.trendsinhate.com/dateinhate.html; *The Telegraph* (London), May 13, 2009.

198. *The Telegraph* (London), May 13, 2009.

199. *Austrian Times,* Dec. 1, 2011.

200. *Huffington Post,* Nov. 29, 2011.

201. *Chicago Tribune,* Dec. 5, 2013.

202. "KKK Leader Dies at Age 69," Stormfront, http://www.stormfront.org/forum/t11246 (accessed Dec. 9, 2013).

203. *New York Times,* March 20, 2003; Robert E. Scoggin Papers, J. Murrey Atkins Library, University of North Carolina.

204. *New York Times,* April 23, 2005.

205. "David Lane," ADL Archives.

206. *New York Times,* Feb. 17, 2009.

207. *Reading* (PA) *Eagle,* May 16, 2009.

208. *Akron Beacon Journal,* Jan. 29, 2011.

209. Bill Morlin, "Jeff Berry, Former Klan Leader, Dies at 64," SPLC Hatewatch, http://www.splcenter.org/blog/2013/06/07/jeff-berry-former-klan-leader-dies-at-64 (accessed Dec. 9, 2013).

210. Casey Sanchez, "Former Klan Leader James Roesch Says 'I Came to Christ,'" SPLC *Intelligence Report,* Winter 2008, Issue Number 132.

211. Sonia Scherr, "Dubious Declarations Department: Long-Time Neo-Nazi Boss Officially Judged 'Reformed,'" SPLC Hatewatch, http://www.splcenter.org/blog/2009/05/07/dubious-declarations-department-long-time-neo-nazi-boss-officially-judged-reformed (accessed Dec. 9, 2013).

212. Trends in Hate, http://www.trendsinhate.com/dateinhate.html; "Klan Leader Ron Edwards Arrested by FBI in Drug Bust," ADL Blog, http://www.adl.org/combating-hate/domestic-extremism-terrorism/c/klan-leader-ron-edwards-arrested-drug-bust.html (accessed Dec. 9, 2013).

213. "National Knights of the KKK Honor Grand Wizard," SPLC *Intelligence Repo*rt, Winter 2010, Issue Number 140; *Elkhart* (IN) *Truth,* April 16, 2012.

214. Clary, "The Truth About Thom Robb."

215. "About National Director Pastor Thomas Robb," The Knights Party.

216. All information in this subsection: SPLC Hate Map, http://www.splcenter.org/get-informed/hate-map (accessed Dec. 10, 2013).

217. "Ku Klux Klan," SPLC, http://www.splcenter.org/get-informed/intelligence-files/ideology/ku-klux-klan (accessed Dec. 10, 2013).

218. William Joseph Simmons, *The Ku Klux Klan: Yesterday, Today and Forever* (Atlanta: Knights of the Ku Klux Klan, n.d.).

Selected Bibliography

Books

Alexander, Charles. *The Ku Klux Klan in the Southwest*. Norman: University of Oklahoma Press, 1965.

Anti-Defamation League. *Extremism on the Right: A Handbook*. New York: ADL, 1983.

_____. *Hate Groups in America: A Record of Bigotry and Violence*. New York: ADL, 1988.

_____. *The KKK and the Neo-Nazis: A 1984 Status Report*. New York: ADL, 1984.

_____. *Ku Klux Klan Rebounds*. New York: ADL, 2007.

Baker, Kelly. *Gospel According to the Klan: The KKK's Appeal to Protestant America, 1915–1930*. Lawrence: University Press of Kansas, 2011.

Ball, Howard. *Murder in Mississippi: United States v. Price and the Struggle for Civil Rights*. Lawrence: University Press of Kansas, 2004.

Barkun, Michael. *Religion and the Racist Right: The Origins of the Christian Identity Movement*. Chapel Hill: University of North Carolina Press, 1994.

Bartley, Numan. *The Rise of Massive Resistance: Race and Politics in the South During the 1950s*. Baton Rouge: Louisiana State University Press, 1997.

Blee, Kathleen. *Women of the Klan: Racism and Gender in the 1920s*. Berkeley: University of California Press, 1991.

Bridges, Tyler. *The Rise of David Duke*. Oxford: University Press of Mississippi, 1994.

Bullard, Sara. *The Ku Klux Klan: A History of Racism and Violence,* 4th ed. Collingdale, PA: Diane, 1996.

Cagin, Seth, and Philip Dray. *We Are Not Afraid: The Story of Goodman, Schwerner, and Chaney, and the Civil Rights Campaign for Mississippi*. New York: Scribner, 1988.

Carter, Dan. *The Politics of Rage: George Wallace, the Origins of the New Conservatism, and the Transformation of American Politics*. New York: Simon and Schuster, 1995.

Chalmers, David. *Backfire: How the Ku Klux Klan Helped the Civil Rights Movement*. Lanham, MD: Rowman and Littlefield, 2005.

_____. *Hooded Americanism: The History of the Ku Klux Klan*, 3d ed. Durham, NC: Duke University Press, 1981.

Cook, James. *The Segregationists*. New York: Appleton-Century-Crofts, 1962.

Cunningham, David. *Klansville, U.S.A.: The Rise and Fall of the Civil Rights-Era Ku Klux Klan*. New York: Oxford University Press, 2013.

_____. *There's Something Happening Here: The New Left, the Klan, and FBI Counterintelligence*. Berkeley: University of California Press, 2004.

Davis, Susan. *Authentic History, Ku Klux Klan, 1865–1877*. New York: The Author, 1924.

Eagles, Charles. *Outside Agitator: Jon Daniels and the Civil Rights Movement in Alabama*. Tuscaloosa: University of Alabama Press, 2000.

Flynn, Kevin, and Gary Gerhardt. *The Silent Brotherhood*. New York: Signet, 1995.

Forster, Arnold, and Benjamin Epstein. *Report on the Ku Klux Klan*. New York: Anti-Defamation League, 1966.

Fox, Craig. *Everyday Klansfolk: White Protestant Life and the KKK in 1920s Michigan*. East Lansing: Michigan State University Press, 2011.

Fry, Gladys-Marie. *Night Riders in Black Folk History*. Knoxville: University of Tennessee Press, 1975.

Gillette, Paul, and Eugene Tillinger. *Inside Ku Klux Klan*. New York: Pyramid, 1965.

Goldberg, Robert. *Hooded Empire: The Ku Klux Klan in Colorado*. Champaign: University of Illinois Press, 1982.

Greene, Melissa. *The Temple Bombing*. Boston: Addison-Wesley, 1996.

Haas, Ben. *KKK*. Evanston, IL: Regency, 1963.

Horn, Stanley. *Invisible Empire: The Story of the Ku Klux Klan, 1866–1871*. New York: Houghton Mifflin, 1939.

Horowitz, David. *Inside the Klavern: The Secret History of a Ku Klux Klan of the 1920s*. Carbondale: Southern Illinois University Press, 1999.

Huie, William. *Three Lives for Mississippi*. New York: Signet, 1968.

Hurst, Jack. *Nathan Bedford Forrest: A Biography*. New York: Random House, 1993.

Jackson, Kenneth. *The Ku Klux Klan in the City, 1915–1930*. New York: Oxford University Press, 1967.

Jenkins, William. *Steel Valley Klan: The Ku Klux Klan in Ohio's Mahoning Valley*. Kent: Kent State University Press, 1990.

Kelly, Patrick. *Hatred in Georgia, 1989: A Chronology and Analysis of Hate Activity*. Atlanta: Neighbors Network, 1990.

_____. *Hatred in Georgia, 1990: A Chronology and Analysis of Hate Activity*. Atlanta: Neighbors Network, 1991.

_____. *Hatred in Georgia, 1991: A Chronology and Analysis of Hate Activity*. Atlanta: Neighbors Network, 1992.

_____. *Hatred in Georgia, 1992: A Chronology and Analysis of Hate Activity*. Atlanta: Neighbors Network, 1993.

_____. *Hatred in Georgia, 1993: A Chronology and Analysis of Hate Activity*. Atlanta: Neighbors Network, 1994.

Kennedy, Stetson. *After Appomattox: How the South Won the War*. Gainesville: University Press of Florida, 1995.

_____. *The Klan Unmasked*. Gainesville: University Press of Florida, 1990.

_____. *Southern Exposure*. Garden City, NY: Doubleday, 1946.

Lay, Shawn. *Hooded Knights on the Niagara: The Ku Klux Klan in Buffalo, New York*. New York: New York University Press, 1995.

_____, ed. *The Invisible Empire in the West: Toward a New Historical Appraisal of the Ku Klux Klan of the 1920s*. Champaign: University of Illinois Press, 1992.

_____. *War, Revolution, and the Ku Klux Klan: A Study of Intolerance in a Border City*. El Paso: Texas Western Press, 1985.

Levitas, Daniel. *The Terrorist Next Door: The Militia Movement and the Radical Right*. New York: St. Martin's, 2002.

Luntz, Benjamin. *Forgotten Turmoil: The Southeastern Kentucky Ku Klux Klan*. Bloomington, IN: Xlibris, 2006.

Lutz, Chris. *They Don't All Wear Sheets: A Chronology of Racist and Far Right Violence—1980–1986*. Atlanta: Center for Democratic Renewal, 1987.

MacClean, Harry. *The Past Is Never Dead: The Trial of James Ford Seale and Mississippi's Struggle for Redemption*. New York: BasicCitivas, 2009.

MacLean, Nancy. *Behind the Mask of Chivalry: The Making of the Second Ku Klux Klan*. New York: Oxford University Press, 1994.

Martinez, J. Michael. *Carpetbaggers, Cavalry, and the Ku Klux Klan: Exposing the Invisible Empire During Reconstruction*. Lanham, MD: Rowman and Littlefield, 2007.

Massengill, Reed. *Portrait of a Racist: The Real Life of Byron De La Beckwith*. New York: St. Martin's, 1997.

May, Gary. *The Informant: The FBI, the Ku Klux Klan, and the Murder of Viola Liuzzo*. New Haven, CT: Yale University Press, 2005.

McIlhany, William II. *Klandestine: The Untold Story of Delmar Dennis and His Role in the FBI's War Against the Ku Klux Klan*. New Rochelle, NY: Arlington House, 1975.

McMillen, Neil. *The Citizens' Council: Organized Resistance to the Second Reconstruction, 1954–64*. Champaign: University of Illinois Press, 1971.

McVeigh, Rory. *The Rise of the Ku Klux Klan: Right-Wing Movements and National Politics*. Minneapolis: University of Minnesota Press, 2009.

McWhorter, Diane. *Carry Me Home: Birmingham, Alabama: The Climactic Battle of the Civil Rights Revolution*. New York: Simon and Schuster, 2001.

Mendelsohn, Jack. *The Martyrs: Sixteen Who Gave Their Lives for Racial Justice*. New York: Harper & Row, 1966.

Moore, Leonard. *Citizen Klansmen: The Ku Klux Klan in Indiana, 1921–1928*. Chapel Hill: University of North Carolina Press, 1991.

Neil, Maudeen. *Fiery Crosses in the Green Mountains: The Story of the Ku Klux Klan in Vermont*. Randolph Center, VT: Greenhills Books, 1989.

Nelson, Jack. *Terror in the Night: The Klan's Campaign Against the Jews*. New York: Simon and Schuster, 1993.

Newton, Michael. *The FBI and the KKK: A Critical History*. Jefferson, NC: McFarland, 2005.

_____. *The Invisible Empire: The Ku Klux Klan in Florida*. Gainesville: University Press of Florida, 2001.

_____. *The Ku Klux Klan: History, Organization, Language, Influence and Activities of America's Most Notorious Secret Society*. Jefferson, NC: McFarland, 2006.

_____. *The Ku Klux Klan in Mississippi: A History*. Jefferson, NC: McFarland, 2010.

_____. *Ku Klux Terror: Birmingham, Alabama, from 1866-Present*. Atglen, PA: Schiffer, 2013.

Nunnelly, William. *Bull Connor*. Tuscaloosa: University of Alabama Press, 1990.

Parker, Thomas, ed. *Violence in the U.S. Volume 1: 1956– 67*. New York: Facts on File, 1974.

Pegram, Thomas. *One Hundred Percent American: The Rebirth and Decline of the Ku Klux Klan in the 1920s*. Lanham, MD: Ivan R. Dee, 2011.

Pitsula, James. *Keeping Canada British: The Ku Klux Klan in 1920s Saskatchewan*. Vancouver, BC: University of British Columbia Press, 2013.

Quarles, Chester. *The Ku Klux Klan and Related American Racialist and Antisemitic Organizations*. Jefferson, NC: McFarland, 2008.

Rice, Arnold. *The Ku Klux Klan In American Politics*. Washington, DC: Public Affairs Press, 1962.

Ridgeway, James. *Blood in the Face: The Ku Klux Klan, Aryan Nations, Nazi Skinheads, and the Rise of a New White Culture*. New York: Thunder's Mouth, 1995.

Rosenthal, A. M., and Arthur Gelb. *One More Victim: The Life and Death of an American-Jewish Nazi*. New York: New American Library, 1967.

Rowe, Gary. *My Undercover Years with the Ku Klux Klan*. New York: Bantam, 1976.

Rubin, Jay. *The Ku Klux Klan in Binghamton, New York, 1923–1928*. Binghamton, NY: Broome County Historical Society, 1973.

Ruiz, Jim. *The Black Hood of the Ku Klux Klan*. San Francisco: Austin and Winfield, 1997.

Schmaltz, William. *Hate: George Lincoln Rockwell and the American Nazi Party*. Washington, DC: Brassey's, 1999.

Simonelli, Frederick. *American Fuehrer: George Lincoln Rockwell and the American Nazi Party*. Champaign: University of Illinois Press, 1999.

Sims, Patsy. *The Klan*. New York: Stein and Day, 1978.

Soule, Sarah, and Nella Van Dyke. "Black Church Arson

in the United States, 1989–1996." In *Hate and Bias Crime*. New York: Routledge, 2003.

Southern Poverty Law Center. *Hate Violence and White Supremacy: A Decade Review, 1980–1990*. Montgomery, AL: SPLC, 1989.

Stanton, Bill. *Klanwatch: Bringing the Ku Klux Klan to Justice*. New York: Grove Weidenfeld, 1991.

Stanton, Mary. *Freedom Walk: Mississippi or Bust*. Jackson: University Press of Mississippi, 2003.

_____. *From Selma to Sorrow: The Life and Death of Viola Liuzzo*. Athens: University of Georgia Press, 1998.

Stern, Kenneth. *A Force Upon the Plain: The American Militia Movement and the Politics of Hate*. Norman: University of Oklahoma Press, 1997.

Thompson, Brad. *Under The Hood: Unmasking the Modern Ku Klux Klan*. North Manchester, IN: DeWitt, 1998.

Trelease, Allen. *White Terror: The Ku Klux Klan Conspiracy and Southern Reconstruction*. Baton Rouge: Louisiana State University Press, 1971.

Tucker, Richard. *The Dragon and the Cross: The Rise and Fall of the Ku Klux Klan in Middle America*. North Haven, CT: Archon, 1991.

Tucker, Todd. *Notre Dame vs. the Klan: How the Fighting Irish Defeated the Ku Klux Klan*. Chicago: Loyola, 2004.

Wade, Wyn. *The Fiery Cross: The Ku Klux Klan in America*. New York: Simon and Schuster, 1987.

Webb, Clive. *Rabble Rousers: The American Far Right in the Civil Rights Era*. Athens: University of Georgia Press, 2010.

West, Jerry. *The Reconstruction Ku Klux Klan in York County, South Carolina, 1865–1877*. Jefferson, NC: McFarland, 2010.

Wexler, Stuart, and Larry Hancock. *The Awful Grace of God: Religious Terrorism, White Supremacy, and the Unsolved Murder of Martin Luther King, Jr*. Berkeley, CA: Counterpoint, 2012.

Whitehead, Don. *Attack on Terror: The FBI Against the Ku Klux Klan in Mississippi*. New York: Funk and Wagnalls, 1970.

Williams, Lou. *The Great South Carolina Ku Klux Klan Trials, 1871–1872*. Athens: University of Georgia Press, 2004.

Articles

Anti-Defamation League. "The Ku Klux Klan Tries a Comeback." *Facts* 25 (Nov. 1979): 1–16.

_____. "The Ku Klux Klans: 1978." *Facts* 24 (March 1978): 1–9.

_____. "Neo-Nazi Skinheads: A 1990 Status Report." *Terrorism* 13 (1990): 243–275.

Atkins, J. Keith. "The Ku Klux Klan: America's Forgotten Terrorists." *Law Enforcement Executive Forum* 5 (2006): 127–144.

Burghardt, Tom. "Neo-Nazis Salute Anti-Abortion Extremists." *Covert Action Quarterly* 52 (Spring 1995): 26–33.

Burris, Val, Emery Smith, and Ann Strahm. "White Supremacist Networks on the Internet." *Sociological Focus* 33 (May 2000): 215–235.

Castle, Tammy, and Meagan Chevalier. "The Women of Stormfront: An Examination of White Nationalist Discussion Threads on the Internet." *Internet Journal of Criminology* (2011): 1–14.

Drabble, John. "The FBI, COINTELPRO-WHITE HATE, and the Decline of Ku Klux Klan Organizations in Alabama, 1964–1971." *Alabama Review* 61 (January 2008): 297–328.

_____. "The FBI, COINTELPRO-WHITE HATE, and the Decline of Ku Klux Klan Organizations in Mississippi, 1964–1971." *Journal of Mississippi History* 66 (Winter 2004): 353–401.

Dudley, J. Wayne. "'Hate' Organizations of the 1940s: The Columbians, Inc." *Phylon* 42 (1981): 262–74.

Flowers, Richmond. "Southern Plain Talk About the Ku Klux Klan." *Look* (May 3, 1966): 36–44.

Gerstenfeld, Phyllis, Diana Grant, and Chau-Pu Chiang. "Hate Online: A Content Analysis of Extremist Internet Sites." *Analyses of Social Issues and Public Policy*, 3 (2003): 29–44.

Hall, Andy. "The Ku Klux Klan in Southern Illinois in 1875." *Journal of the Illinois State Historical Society* 46 (Winter 1953): 363–372.

Holmes, William. "Moonshiners and Whitecaps in Alabama, 1893," *Alabama Review* 34 (1981): 31–49.

_____. "Moonshining and Collective Violence: Georgia, 1889–1895," *Journal of American History* 67 (1980): 589–611.

_____. "Whitecapping: Agrarian Violence in Mississippi, 1902–1906." *The Journal of Southern History*. 35 (1969):165–185.

_____. "Whitecapping: Anti-Semitism in the Populist Era." *American Jewish Historical Quarterly*. 63 (1974): 244–261.

_____. "Whitecapping in Georgia: Carroll and Houston Counties, 1893." *Georgia Historical Quarterly* 64 (1980): 388–403.

Knebel, Fletcher, and Clark Mollenhoff. "Eight Klans Bring New Terror to the South," *Look* (April 30, 1957): 59–63, 68–9.

Patrick, Robert, Jr. "A Nail in the Coffin of Racism: The Story of the Columbians." *Georgia Historical Quarterly* 85 (Summer 2001): 245–266.

Pegram, Thomas. "Hoodwinked: The Anti-Saloon League and the Ku Klux Klan in 1920s Prohibition Enforcement." *Journal of the Gilded Age and Progressive Era* 7 (January 2008): 89–119.

Rangel, Nicholas Jr. "Ambiguously Articulating 'Americanism': The Rhetoric of Hiram Wesley Evans and the Klan of the 1920s." *American Communication Journal* 11 (Summer 2009):

Sherrill, Robert. "A Look Inside the Invisible Empire." *New South* 23 (Spring 1968): 4–30.

Snell, William. "The Revised Ku Klux Klan in East Tennessee." *Border States: Journal of the Kentucky- Tennessee American Studies Association* 7 (1989): 1–4.

Suall, Irwin, and David Lowe. "The Hate Movement Today: A Chronicle of Violence and Disarray." *Terrorism* 10 (1987): 345–364.

Weisenburger, Steven, "The Columbians, Inc.: A Chapter of Racial Hatred from the Post–World War II South." *Journal of Southern History* 69 (2003): 821–860.

Woodward, Karen. "Mob Violence and the Ku Klux Klan Act: State of the Law after *Park v. City of Atlanta.*" *Stetson Law Review* 28 (1999): 699–721.

Zerzan, John. "Rank-and-File Radicalism Within the Ku Klux Klan of the 1920s." *Anarchy* 37 (Summer 1993): 1–12.

Dissertations and Theses

Brister, Paul. "Ku Klux Rising: Toward an Understanding of Right Wing Terrorist Campaigns." Naval Post Graduate School, Monterey, CA, 2011.

Duffee, Eldridge. "The National States Rights Party." University of Maryland at Baltimore, 1968.

Fair, Richard. "'The Good Angel of Practical Fraternity': The Ku Klux Klan in McLennan County, 1915-1924." Baylor University, 2009.

Hague, Seth. "'Niggers Ain't Gonna Run This Town': Militancy, Conflict and the Sustenance of Hegemony in Bogalusa, Louisiana." Loyola University New Orleans, 1997.

Hill, Lance. "The Deacons for Defense and Justice: Armed Self-Defense and the Civil Rights Movement." Tulane University, 1997.

Hernando, Matthew. "The Bald Knobbers of Southwest Missouri, 1885–1889: A Study of Vigilante Justice in the Ozarks." Louisiana State University, 2011.

Kerbaway, Kelli. "Knights in White Satin: Women of the Ku Klux Klan." Marshall University, 2007.

Kirschenbaum, Robert. "Klan and Commonwealth: The Ku Klux Klan and Politics in Kentucky 1921-1928." University of Kentucky, 2005.

Law, Jack. "The Fall of the Ku Klux Klan in the Postbellum South." San Diego State University, 2011.

Lee, Gordon. "The Ku Klux Klan in Wisconsin in the 1920's." University of Wisconsin–La Crosse, 1968.

Magel, Trevor. "The Political Effect of the Ku Klux Klan in North Dakota." University of Nebraska, 2011.

Mikkelson, Vincent. "Coming from Battle to Face a War: The Lynching of Black Soldiers in the World War I Era." Florida State University, 2007.

Proctor, Bradley. "The Reconstruction of White Supremacy: The Ku Klux Klan in Piedmont North Carolina, 1868 to 1872." University of North Carolina–Chapel Hill, 2009.

Shotwell, John. "Crystallizing Public Hatred: Ku Klux Klan Public Relations in the Early 1920s." University of Wisconsin, 1974.

Smith, Mika. "Hooded Crusaders: The Ku Klux Klan in the Panhandle and South Plains, 1921–1925." Texas Tech University, 2008.

Turcheneske, John Jr. "The Ku Klux Klan in Northwestern Wisconsin." Wisconsin State University–River Falls, 1971.

Weaver, Norman. "The Knights of the Ku Klux Klan in Wisconsin, Indiana, Ohio and Michigan." University of Wisconsin–Madison, 1954.

White, Joseph. "The Ku Klux Klan in Indiana in the 1920's as Viewed by the *Indiana Catholic* and *Record.*" Butler University, 1974.

Zampogna, Ashley. "America May Not Perish: The Italian-American Fight Against the Ku Klux Klan in the Mahoning Valley." Youngstown State University, 2008.

Official Sources

Federal Bureau of Investigation Files. "American Nazi Party."

_____. "Aryan Nation."

_____. "Black Legion."

_____. "Christian Identity Movement."

_____. "COINTELPRO."

_____. "The Covenant, The Sword, The Arm of the Lord."

_____. "Emmett Till."

_____. "Freedom Riders."

_____. "The Ku Klux Klan."

_____. "Mack Charles Parker."

_____. "Medgar Evers."

_____. "MIBURN Case."

_____. "National States Rights Party."

_____. "Original Knights of the KKK."

_____. "Sixteenth Street Church Bombing."

_____. "Viola Liuzzo."

_____. "White Supremacist Groups."

_____. "White Aryan Resistance."

Illinois Legislative Investigating Commission. *Ku Klux Klan: A Report to the Illinois General Assembly.* Chicago: ILIC, 1976.

U.S. Congress. *Report of the Select Committee to Inquire into the State of Affairs in the Late Insurrectionary States.* 13 vols. Washington, DC: U.S. Government Printing Office, 1872.

U.S. House of Representatives, Committee on Rules. *The Ku Klux Klan.* Washington, DC: U.S. Government Printing Office, 1921.

U.S. House of Representatives, Committee on Un-American Activities. *The Present-Day Ku Klux Klan Movement.* 6 vols. Washington, DC: U.S. Government Printing Office, 1967.

U.S. Senate. *Report of the Select Committee to Inquire into the Mississippi Election of 1875.* 2 vols. Washington, DC: U.S. Government Printing Office, 1876.

Internet Sources

Anti-Klan

Anti-Defamation League, http://www.adl.org.

Southern Poverty Law Center, http://www.splcenter.org.

Pro-Klan

Aryan Nations World Headquarters, http://www.aryan-nation.org.

Church of the National Knights of the Ku Klux Klan, https://sites.google.com/site/cnkrealmofky/home.

Imperial Klans of America, http://www.kkkk.net.

Knight Riders Knights of the Ku Klux Klan, http://knightriderskkkk.org.

Knights Party, USA, http://www.kkk.com.

Loyal White Knights of the Ku Klux Klan, http://kkkknights.com.

Original Knights of America, Knights of the Ku Klux Klan, http://originalknightsofamerica.webs.com.

Stormfront, http://www.stormfront.org/forum.

United Northern and Southern Knights of the Ku Klux Klan, http://www.unskkkk.com.

United White Knights of the Ku Klux Klan, http://www.uwkkkk.com.

Index